19th International Conference on Spoken Language Translation (IWSLT 2022)

Dublin, Ireland
26 – 27 May 2022

ISBN: 978-1-7138-6743-2

Printed from e-media with permission by:

Curran Associates, Inc.
57 Morehouse Lane
Red Hook, NY 12571

Some format issues inherent in the e-media version may also appear in this print version.

Printed with permission by Curran Associates, Inc. (2023)

For permission requests, please contact the Association for Computational Linguistics at the address below.

Association for Computational Linguistics
209 N. Eighth Street
Stroudsburg, Pennsylvania 18360

Phone: 1-570-476-8006
Fax: 1-570-476-0860

acl@aclweb.org

Additional copies of this publication are available from:

Curran Associates, Inc.
57 Morehouse Lane
Red Hook, NY 12571 USA
Phone: 845-758-0400
Fax: 845-758-2633
Email: curran@proceedings.com
Web: www.proceedings.com

IWSLT 2022

The 19th International Conference on Spoken Language Translation

Proceedings of the Conference

May 26-27, 2022

The IWSLT organizers gratefully acknowledge the support from the following sponsors and donors:

Diamond

Platinum

Bronze

Introduction

The International Conference on Spoken Language Translation (IWSLT) is the premiere annual scientific conference for the study, development and evaluation of spoken language translation technology. Launched in 2004 and spun out from the C-STAR speech translation consortium before it (1992-2003), IWSLT is the main venue for scientific exchange on all topics related to speech-to-text translation, speech-to-speech translation, simultaneous and consecutive translation, speech dubbing, cross-lingual communication including all multimodal, emotional, paralinguistic, and stylistic aspects and their applications in the field. The conference organizes evaluations around challenge areas, and presents scientific papers and system descriptions.

This year, IWSLT features eight shared tasks: (i) Simultaneous speech translation, (ii) Offline speech translation, (iii) Speech to speech translation, (iv) Low-resource speech translation, (v) Multilingual speech translation, (vi) Dialect speech translation. (vii) Formality control for spoken language translation, (viii) Isometric spoken language translation. These topics represent open problems toward effective cross-lingual communication and we expect the community effort and discussion will greatly advance the state of the field. Each shared task was coordinated by one or more chairs. The resulting evaluation campaigns attracted a total of 27 teams, from academia, research centers and industry. System submissions resulted in system papers that will be presented at the conference. Following our call for papers, this year 44 submissions were received. In a blind review process, 9 research papers were selected out of 18 for oral presentation (50%) in addition to 25 system papers.

The program committee is excited about the quality of the accepted papers and expects lively discussion and exchange at the conference. The conference chairs and organizers would like to express their gratitude to everyone who contributed and supported IWSLT. In particular, we wish to thank our Diamond sponsors and donors Apple, AWS, Meta and Zoom, our Platinum sponsor Microsoft, and our Bronze sponsor AppTek. We thank the shared tasks chairs, organizers, and participants, the program chair and committee members, as well as all the authors that went the extra mile to submit system and research papers to IWSLT, and make this year's conference a most vibrant event. We also wish to express our sincere gratitude to ACL for hosting our conference and for arranging the logistics and infrastructure that allow us to hold IWSLT 2022, for the first time, as a hybrid conference.

Welcome to IWSLT 2022 wherever you are joining us in person, in Dublin, or remotely!

Marcello Federico and Alex Waibel, Conference Chairs

Organizing Committee

Conference Chairs

Marcello Federico, AWS AI Labs, USA
Alex Waibel, CMU, USA

Program Chair

Marta Costa-jussà, Meta AI, France

Evaluation Chairs

Sebastian Stüker, KIT, Germany
Jan Niehues, KIT, Germany

Website and Publication Chair

Elizabeth Salesky, JHU, USA

Program Committee

Program Committee

Duygu Ataman, University of Zurich, Switzerland
Nguyen Bach, Alibaba, USA
Laurent Besacier, IMAG, France
Anna Currey, AWS AI Labs, USA
Mattia Di Gangi, AppTek, Germany
Georgiana Dinu, AWS AI Labs, Germany
Akiko Eriguchi, Microsoft, USA
Carlos Escolano, Universitat Politècnica de Catalunya, Spain
Markus Freitag, Google, USA
Gerard I. Gallego, Universitat Politècnica de Catalunya, Spain
Cuong Hoang, AWS AI Labs, USA
Matthias Huck, LMU, Germany
Hirofumi Inaguma, Kyoto University, Japan
Takatomo Kano, Nara Institute of Science and Technology, Japan
Yves Lepage, U. Waseda, Japan
Yuchen Liu, Princeton, USA
Xutai Ma, Johns Hopkins University, USA
Evgeny Matusov, AppTek, Germany
Surafel Melaku Lakew, Amazon AI, USA
Maria Nadejde, AWS AI Labs, USA
Matteo Negri, FBK, Italy
Juan Pino, Meta AI, USA
Raghavendra Pappagari, AWS AI Labs, USA
Julian Salazar, Amazon AWS AI, USA
Elizabeth Salesky, Johns Hopkins University, USA
Matthias Sperber, Apple, USA
Sebastian Stüker, Karlsruhe Institute of Technology, Germany
Katsuhito Sudoh, NAIST, Japan
Yun Tang, Meta AI, USA
Brian Thompson, AWS AI Labs, USA
Ioannis Tsiamas, Universitat Politècnica de Catalunya, Spain
Marco Turchi, FBK, Italy
David Vilar, Google, Germany
Changhan Wang, Meta AI, USA
Chengyi Wang, Nankai University, China
Krzystof Wolk, Polish-Japanese Academy of Information Technology, Poland

Invited Speakers

Frederic Chaume, Universitat Jaume I

Keynote Talk: Synchronization in translation for dubbing: implications for its automation

Frederic Chaume
Universitat Jaume I

Abstract: Synchronization (or lip-sync, also spelled lip-synch) is one of the key factors in audiovisual translation, especially in the context of dubbing. Although it is often considered as the distinguishing feature of dubbing, it is only one of several important aspects such as the 'natural' reproduction of a pre-fabricated oral discourse or the translation problems posed by the interaction between image and word. If we take a look at the research on lip-sync, it is regarded as an urgent, vital issue, as can be seen from the wide range of publications on the subject. Beyond doubt synchronization has a direct impact on the translation process and product, and as such, puts all the translator's creative skills to the test. Dubbing is a well-known example of the invisibility of translation, an artistic and technical exercise that intentionally replaces the original dialogue track with a new track on which target language (TL) dialogue exchanges are recorded. In contrast to voice-over for example, the emphasis in dubbing lies in matching the translation to the silent mouths of the original actors. The result is that viewers watch and hear foreign actors speaking in the viewers' own language, a paradox which has been naturally accepted in all dubbing countries. This talk will deal with the definition and scope of synchronization in the audiovisual translation field, will explain the three main synchronization types, will tackle issues related to different language pairs combinations and will present the last efforts carried out by some start-ups and research groups to automate this technical and artistic process. The talk will be illustrated with clips from films and TV series dubbed into six different languages.

Bio: Frederic Chaume is a Full Professor of Audiovisual Translation at Universitat Jaume I (Spain), where he teaches audiovisual translation theory and translation and adaptation for dubbing; and Honorary Professor at University College London (UK), where he teaches translation and adaptation for voice-over and dubbing, Universidad Ricardo Palma (Perú) and Universidad Peruana de Ciencias Aplicadas (Perú). He is author of eight books and has also coedited two books and three special journal issues (Textus, Perspectives, Prosopopeya). He is the director of the TRAMA book series (Publicacions de la Universitat Jaume I), the first collection of monographs on audiovisual translation and media localization. Prof. Chaume has published over 100 articles, book chapters and encyclopedic entries on audiovisual translation and has given numerous keynote lectures on this topic in international translation studies conferences and in several European and American universities. He also teaches regularly in some of them (University College London-UK, Universidad de Granada-Spain, Università di Torino-Italy, among others). He has supervised or co-supervised 20 PhD theses on the topic of audiovisual translation and some of them have received different Spanish and European awards. He is also in close contact with the industry, serves as a consultant for Netflix and has signed several research agreements with different stakeholders of the media localization sector. He coordinates the research group TRAMA (www.trama.uji.es) and is the recipient of the Berlanga Award (2010), the Xènia Martínez Award (2016) and the Jan Ivarsson's Award (2020) for his constant and enthusiastic support to media localization as well as his constant university training in this field.

Table of Contents

Scientific Papers:

Evaluation Campaign:

SubER: A Metric for Automatic Evaluation of Subtitle Quality

Patrick Wilken
AppTek
Aachen, Germany
pwilken@apptek.com

Panayota Georgakopoulou
Athena Consultancy
Athens, Greece
yota@athenaconsultancy.eu

Evgeny Matusov
AppTek
Aachen, Germany
ematusov@apptek.com

Abstract

This paper addresses the problem of evaluating the quality of automatically generated subtitles, which includes not only the quality of the machine-transcribed or translated speech, but also the quality of line segmentation and subtitle timing. We propose SubER - a single novel metric based on edit distance with shifts that takes all of these subtitle properties into account. We compare it to existing metrics for evaluating transcription, translation, and subtitle quality. A careful human evaluation in a post-editing scenario shows that the new metric has a high correlation with the post-editing effort and direct human assessment scores, outperforming baseline metrics considering only the subtitle text, such as WER and BLEU, and existing methods to integrate segmentation and timing features.

1 Introduction

The use of automatically created subtitles has become popular due to improved speech recognition (ASR) and machine translation (MT) quality in recent years. Most notably, they are used on the web to make content available to a broad audience in a cost-efficient and scalable way. They also gain attraction in the media industry, where they can be an aid to professional subtitlers and lead to increased productivity.

In this work, we address the problem of measuring the quality of such automatic subtitling systems. We argue that existing metrics which compare the plain text output of an ASR or MT system to a reference text are not sufficient to reflect the particularities of the subtitling task. We consider two use cases: 1) running speech recognition on the audio track of a video to create subtitles in the original language; 2) translating existing subtitle files with an MT system. For the first case, the word error rate (WER) of the ASR system is a natural choice for quality control. For MT there exist a wider range of automatic metrics such as BLEU (Papineni et al., 2002), TER (Snover et al., 2006), chrF (Popović, 2015) and, more recently, learned metrics like BertScore (Zhang et al., 2019) and COMET (Rei et al., 2020).

These existing metrics are suited to measure the quality of ASR and MT in terms of recognized or translated content only. However, subtitles are defined by more than just their textual content: they include timing information, as well as formatting with possible line breaks within a sentence in syntactically and semantically proper positions. Figure 1 shows examples of subtitle files in the common SubRip text (SRT) format. Evidently, it differs from plain text, in particular:

- The text is segmented into blocks. These blocks are distinct from sentences. A sentence can span several blocks, a block can contain multiple sentences.
- A block may be further split into lines.
- Start and end times define when text is displayed.

All of these additional characteristics are crucial for the viewers' comprehension of the content. Professional subtitlers check and possibly improve them as part of the machine-assisted process of subtitle creation.

To assess the quality of automatically created subtitle files, it is beneficial to have a *single* metric that evaluates the ASR/MT quality and the quality of the characteristics listed above.

The main contributions of this work are:

1. A novel segmentation- and timing-aware quality metric designed for the task of automatic subtitling.
2. A human evaluation that analyzes how well the proposed metric correlates with human judgements of subtitle quality, measured in

Proceedings of the 19th International Conference on Spoken Language Translation (IWSLT 2022), pages 1 - 10
May 26-27, 2022 ©2022 Association for Computational Linguistics

694 00:50:45,500 -> 00:50:47,666 For the brandy and champagne you bought me. 695 00:50:47,750 -> 00:50:51,375 As I remember, it was the booze that put you to sleep a little prematurely. 696 00:50:52,208 -> 00:50:54,291 Ladies and gentlemen, 697 00:50:54,916 -> 00:50:57,291 the dance is about to begin.	634 00:50:44,960 -> 00:50:47,680 For the champagne and brandy you bought me. 635 00:50:47,760 -> 00:50:51,200 As I recall, the booze put you to sleep a little prematurely. 636 00:50:52,200 -> 00:50:57,120 Ladies and gentlemen, the dance is about to begin.

Figure 1: Two examples of subtitles in SRT format for the same video excerpt. Note the different line and block segmentation. Also note that subtitles on the right have been condensed for improved readability.

post-editing effort as well as direct assessment scores.

3. The publication of a scoring tool to calculate the proposed metric as well as many baseline metrics, directly operating on subtitle files: `https://github.com/apptek/SubER`

2 Subtitle Quality Assessment in the Media Industry

Related to this work are subtitling quality metrics used in the media industry. The most widely used ones to date are NER (Romero-Fresco and Pérez, 2015) and NTR (Romero-Fresco and Pöchhacker, 2017) for live subtitle quality, the former addressing intralingual subtitles or captions and the latter interlingual ones.

Offline interlingual subtitles have traditionally been assessed on the basis of internal quality guidelines and error typologies produced by media localization companies. To address this gap, the FAR model (Pedersen, 2017) was developed and there have also been attempts to implement a version of MQM[1].

None of the above metrics, however, are automatic ones. They require manual evaluation by an expert to categorize errors and assign appropriate penalties depending on their severity. This makes their use costly and time-consuming. In this work we therefore address automatic quality assessment of subtitle files by comparing them to a professionally created reference.

[1]Multidimensional Quality Metrics (MQM) Definition http://www.qt21.eu/mqm-definition/definition-2015-12-30.html

3 Automatic Metrics for Subtitling

3.1 Baseline Approaches

When subtitling in the original language of a video, the baseline quality measurement is to calculate word error rate (WER) against a reference transcription. Traditionally, WER is computed on lower-cased words and without punctuation. We show results for a cased and punctuated variant as well, as those are important aspects of subtitle quality. Because of the efficiency of the Levenshtein algorithm, WER calculation can be done on the whole file without splitting it into segments.

For translation, automatic metrics are usually computed on sentence level. Karakanta et al. (2020a) and other related work assumes hypothesis-reference sentence pairs to be given for subtitle scoring. However, in the most general case we only have access to the reference subtitle file and the hypothesis subtitle file to be scored. They do not contain any explicit sentence boundary information. To calculate traditional MT metrics (BLEU, TER and chrF), we first define reference segments and then align the hypothesis subtitle text to these reference segments by minimizing the edit distance ("Levenshtein alignment") (Matusov et al., 2005). Two choices of reference segments are reasonable: 1) subtitle blocks; 2) sentences, split according to simple rules based on sentence-final punctuation, possibly spanning across subtitle blocks. Only for the case of translation from a subtitle template, which preserves subtitle timings, there is a third option, namely to directly use the parallel subtitle blocks as units without any alignment step. This makes the metric sensitive to how translated sentences are distributed among several subtitles, which is a problem a subtitle translation system has to solve.

To evaluate subtitle segmentation quality in isolation, Alvarez et al. (2017); Karakanta et al. (2020b,c) calculate precision and recall of predicted breaks. Such an analysis is only possible when the subtitle text to be segmented is fixed and the only degree of freedom is the position of breaks. We however consider the general case, where subtitles that differ in text, segmentation and timing are compared and evaluated.

3.2 Line Break Tokens

A simple method to extend the baseline metrics to take line and subtitle breaks into account is to insert special tokens at the corresponding positions into the subtitle text (Karakanta et al., 2020a; Matusov et al., 2019). Figure 2 shows an example. The automatic metrics treat these tokens as any other word, e.g. BLEU includes them in n-grams, WER and TER count edit operations for them. Therefore, subtitles with a segmentation not matching the reference will get lower scores.

3.3 Timing-Based Segment Alignment

The time alignment method proposed in Cherry et al. (2021) to calculate t-BLEU is an alternative to Levenshtein hypothesis-to-reference alignment that offers the potential advantage of punishing mistimed words. It uses interpolation of the hypothesis subtitle timings to word-level. Mistimed words may get assigned to a segment without a corresponding reference word, or will even be dropped from the hypothesis if they do not fall into any reference segment.

In this work we consider translation from a template file, thus time alignment is equivalent to using subtitle blocks as unit. However, for the transcription task, where subtitle timings of hypothesis and reference are different, we analyze a variant of WER that operates on "t-BLEU segments", i.e. allows for word matches only if hypothesis and reference word are aligned in time (according to interpolated hypothesis word timings). We refer to this variant as t-WER.

3.4 New Metric: Subtitle Edit Rate (SubER)

None of the above-mentioned metrics considers *all* of the relevant information present in a subtitle file, namely subtitle text, line segmentation and timing. We therefore propose a new metric called subtitle edit rate (SubER) that attempts to cover all these aspects, and on top avoids segmentation of the subtitle files into aligned hypothesis-reference pairs as a pre-processing step.

We choose TER (Snover et al., 2006) as the basis of SubER because of its interpretability, especially in the case of post-editing. It corresponds to the number of edit operations, namely substitutions, deletions, insertions and shifts of words that are required to turn the hypothesis text into the reference. Also, it allows for easy integration of segmentation and timing information by extending it with break edit operations and time-alignment constraints.

We define the SubER score to be the minimal possible value of (read "#" as "number of"):

$$\text{SubER} = \frac{\#\text{ word edits} + \#\text{ break edits} + \#\text{ shifts}}{\#\text{ reference words} + \#\text{ reference breaks}}$$

where

- a hypothesis word is only regarded as correct (**no edit**) if it is part of a subtitle that overlaps in time with the subtitle containing the matching reference word (otherwise edits are required, e.g. deletion + insertion).
- **word edits** are insertions, deletions and substitutions of words, substitutions being only allowed if the hypothesis and reference word are from subtitles that overlap in time.
- **break edits** are insertions, deletions and substitutions of breaks, treated as additional tokens (`<eol>` and `<eob>`) inserted at the positions of the breaks. Substitutions are only allowed between end-of-line and end-of-block, not between a word and a break, and the same time-overlap condition as for word substitution applies.
- **shifts** are movements of one or more adjacent hypothesis tokens to a position of a matching phrase in the reference. Only allowed if all the shifted words come from a hypothesis subtitle that overlaps in time with the subtitle of the matching reference word. The shifted phrase may consist of any combination of words and break tokens.

We only consider subtitle timings present in the subtitle files, as opposed to interpolating timings of words as done by Cherry et al. (2021). This avoids hypothesis words "falling off the edges" of reference subtitles, e.g. in case the hypothesis subtitle

```
For the champagne <eol> and brandy you bought me. <eob>
As I recall, the booze put you <eol> to sleep a little prematurely. <eob>
Ladies and gentlemen, <eol> the dance is about to begin. <eob>
```

Figure 2: Example for usage of end-of-line (<eol>) and end-of-block tokens (<eob>) to represent subtitle formatting. Corresponds to right subtitle from Figure 1. Symbols are adopted from Karakanta et al. (2020b).

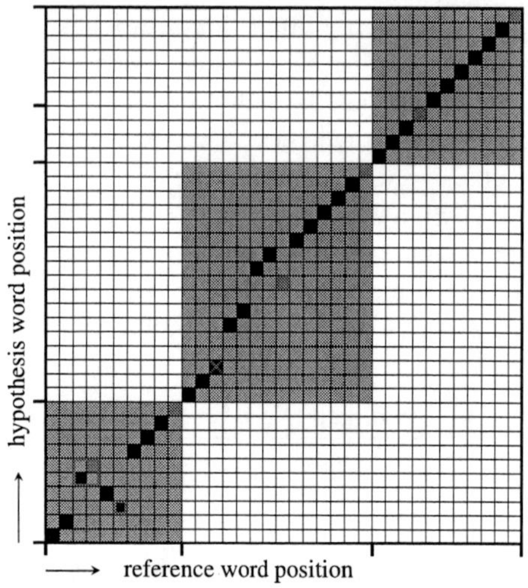

Figure 3: Visualization of SubER applied to the subtitles from Figure 1 (hypothesis left, reference right). Ticks on the axes indicate subtitle block boundaries. Grey areas show regions of time-overlapping reference and hypothesis subtitles. Word matches, substitutions and shifts are allowed only within those areas. Black squares represent word alignments, blue squares represent break token alignments. Red borders mark shifted phrases, red crosses indicate substitutions. 35 reference words (including breaks), 3 insertions, 2 substitutions, 3 shifts lead to a SubER score of $(3+2+3)/35 = 22.86\%$.

starts a fraction of a second early. It also prevents alignment errors originating from the assumption that all words have the same duration.

The time-overlap condition can be thought of as constraining the search space for Levenshtein-distance calculation. Figure 3 visualizes this for the subtitles from Figure 1. In the white areas no word matches are allowed, this can be exploited for an efficient implementation. The last two hypothesis subtitles overlap with the last reference subtitle and therefore form a single time-aligned region. The shifted 2-word phrase in the bottom left region is "champagne <eol>", showcasing that words and breaks can be shifted in a single operation. In the center region we see the substitution of "recall" with "remember", the inserted (i.e. unaligned) hypothesis words "it", "was" and "that", and a shift of the line break to a different position. The break substitution in the upper right region corresponds to the fact that the last block of the right subtitles in Figure 1 is split into two, i.e. end-of-line is replaced by end-of-block.

3.4.1 Implementation Details

We modify the TER implementation of SacreBLEU (Post, 2018) to implement SubER. We adopt the approximation of greedily searching for the best shift until no further reduction of the edit distance can be achieved (Snover et al., 2006). Break tokens (<eol> and <eob>) are inserted into the input text. String comparisons between hypothesis and reference words are replaced by a function additionally checking the time-overlap condition. To make SubER calculation feasible for large subtitle files we split hypothesis and reference into parts at time positions where both agree that no subtitle is displayed. The number of edit operations is then added up for all parts. By definition this does not affect the metric score, in contrast to e.g. segmenting into sentence vs. subtitle blocks when calculating BLEU (Section 3.1).

4 Human Evaluation

To analyze the expressiveness of SubER we conduct a human post-editing experiment on both subtitles automatically generated from audio, as well as automatic translations of subtitle text files. For each of the two post-editing tasks we employ three professional subtitlers with multiple years of experience in the subtitling industry. We evaluate how well automatic metric scores correlate with their post-editing effort and their MT quality judgements.

There exists previous work measuring the productivity gains from post-editing automatic subtitles under the aspect of MT quality (Etchegoyhen et al., 2014; Bywood et al., 2017; Koponen et al., 2020) and segmentation quality (Álvarez et al., 2016; Alvarez et al., 2017; Matusov et al., 2019), but to the best of our knowledge we conduct the first study with the goal of evaluating an automatic quality metric for subtitling.

4.1 Data

We perform our experiment using one episode from each of the following shows:

- *Master of None:* a comedy-drama series
- *Midnight Mass:* a supernatural horror series
- *Peaky Blinders:* an early 20th century British gangster drama

Each of the three videos has a duration of approximately 55 minutes. They are originally in English, for translation we choose Spanish as the target language. We use pre-existing English subtitles as template files for human translation, and also as the reference when scoring automatic transcriptions. Pre-existing Spanish subtitles, which follow the English template, are used as reference for MT output.

To gather data points for which we can compare post-editing effort with automatic scores, we manually split the videos into segments of roughly 1 minute, each containing 15 subtitle blocks and 103 words on average. We keep the first 15 minutes of each video as one large segment where we measure baseline speed of the subtitlers. Excluding these, we end up with 35, 38 and 37 segments for the videos, respectively, amounting to a total of 110 source-target reference subtitle pairs.

4.2 Automatic Subtitling Systems

For human post-editing, we create automatic English and Spanish subtitle files. We use several different subtitling systems to obtain evaluation data with a wider variety. The systems differ in ASR/MT, punctuation and segmentation quality.

We create a single automatic English and Spanish subtitle file for each video, each containing segments coming from different automatic subtitling systems. The subtitlers did not know about any of the details on how these files were created to avoid any bias.

4.2.1 Transcription Systems

To create automatic English subtitles from the audio track of the video we use three different systems:

1. A hybrid ASR system, the output of which is punctuated and cased by a bi-directional LSTM model and then split into lines and subtitles using a beam search decoder that combines scores of a neural segmentation model and hard subtitling constraints, based on the algorithm proposed by Matusov et al. (2019);
2. same as 1., but without using a neural model for subtitle segmentation;
3. an online provider offering automatic transcription in SRT format.

We transcribe an equal number of video segments with each of the three systems and combine them into a single subtitle file which is delivered to the subtitlers for post-editing. The first segment of 15 minutes is not transcribed automatically. Instead, the subtitlers are asked to transcribe it from scratch to measure their baseline productivity.

4.2.2 Translation Systems

To create Spanish subtitles we translate the pre-existing English subtitles with 5 different systems:

1. A Transformer-based MT system, the output of which is split into lines and subtitles using a neural segmentation model and hard subtitling constraints;
2. same as 1., but without using a neural model for subtitle segmentation;
3. same as 1., but with additional inputs for length control and genre, similarly to the systems proposed in (Schioppa et al., 2021; Matusov et al., 2020);
4. an LSTM-based MT system with lower quality than 1., but also using the neural segmentation model;
5. an online provider offering subtitle translation in SRT format.

Also here, we distribute the video segments among the systems such that each system contributes a roughly equal portion of the assembled MT subtitle file delivered to the translators. We extract full sentences from the source subtitle file based on punctuation before translation. The first 15 minute segment of each video is translated directly from the source template without access to MT output to measure baseline productivity of the translators.

4.3 Methodology

4.3.1 Productivity Gain Measurement

For both transcription and translation, we ask the subtitlers to measure the time t_n (in minutes) spent to post-edit each of the 110 video segments. As a measure of post-editing productivity P_n we compute the number of subtitles S_n created per minute of work for the n-th segment:

$$P_n = \frac{S_n}{t_n} \quad (1)$$

To make these values comparable between subtitlers we normalize them using the subtitler's baseline speed P_{base}. It is computed by averaging the productivity in the first 15-minute segment P_1, where the subtitlers work from scratch, over all three videos. Finally, we average the normalized productivities across the three subtitlers $h = 1, 2, 3$ per task to get an average post-editing productivity gain for segment n:

$$\hat{P}_n = \frac{1}{3}\sum_{h=1}^{3} \frac{P_{n,h}}{P_{\text{base},h}} \quad (2)$$

To evaluate the expressiveness of a given metric we compute the Spearman's rank correlation coefficient r_s between the per-segment metric scores and $\hat{P}_n$ for all segments of all three videos. We choose Spearman's correlation in favour of Pearson's correlation because subtitle quality varies a lot for different video segments and different systems, and we don't expect the metrics to behave linearly in this range.

4.3.2 Direct Assessment

For the translation task we additionally gather direct assessment scores for each segment. For this we ask the translators to give two scores (referred to as U_n and Q_n, respectively) according to the following descriptions:

1. "Rate the overall **usefulness** of the automatically translated subtitles in this segment for post-editing purposes on a scale from 0 (completely useless) to 100 (perfect, not a single change needed)."
2. "Rate the overall **quality** of the automatically translated subtitles in this segment as perceived *by a viewer* on a scale from 0 (completely incomprehensible) to 100 (perfect, completely fluent and accurate). The score should reflect how well the automatic translation conveys the semantics of the original subtitles, and should also reflect how well the translated subtitles are formatted."

These scores are standardized into z-scores by subtracting the average and dividing by the standard deviation of scores per translator. Finally, we average the z-scores across the three translators to get expected usefulness and quality assessment scores for each segment, which we will refer to as $\hat{U}_n$ and $\hat{Q}_n$, respectively.

4.4 Results

4.4.1 Post-Editing of English Transcription

The baseline productivities P_{base} of the three subtitlers A, B and C when transcribing the first 15 minutes of each video from scratch are 3.4, 2.8 and 2.7 subtitles per minute of work, respectively. Post-editing changes their productivities to 3.9, 2.6 and 3.1 subtitles per minute on average for the other segments, meaning subtitlers A and C work faster when post-editing automatic subtitles, while subtitler B does not benefit from them.

Table 1 shows the analysis of the correlation between automatic metric scores and productivity gains, calculated for each of the 110 one-minute video segments. Word error rate (WER) can predict the averaged productivity gain $\hat{P}_n$ with a Spearman's correlation of -0.676. This confirms the natural assumption that the more words the ASR system recognized correctly in a given segment, the less time is necessary for post-editing. Subtitler A's post-editing gains are more predictable than those of the other two subtitlers. This indicates that the subtitlers have different workflows and do not make use of the automatic subtitles with the same consistency.

Row 2 shows that making WER case-sensitive and keeping punctuation marks as part of the words does not improve correlation consistently. Although we believe that casing and punctuation errors harm subtitle quality, these errors might not have a significant impact on post-editing time because correcting them requires changing single characters only. Row 3 shows that extending the original WER definition by simply inserting end-of-line and end-of-block tokens into the text does not lead to improvements either. This can be explained by the fact that the original WER algorithm allows for substitution of break symbols with words. Such substitutions have no meaningful interpretation. Also, it does not support shifts of break symbols, which leads to breaks at wrong positions being punished more than completely missing ones.

Our proposed metric SubER achieves the overall best correlation of -0.692. We attribute this in part to a proper way of handling segmentation information: without it, as shown in the last row

Metric	Subtitler A	Subtitler B	Subtitler C	Combined
WER	-0.731	-0.494	-0.499	-0.676
+ case/punct	-0.671	**-0.512**	-0.509	-0.650
+ break tokens	-0.725	-0.494	-0.512	-0.678
t-WER	-0.661	-0.440	-0.476	-0.625
TER-br	-0.573	-0.489	-0.434	-0.562
SubER (ours)	**-0.746**	-0.506	**-0.517**	**-0.692**
+ case/punct	-0.670	-0.507	-0.500	-0.645
- break tokens	-0.741	-0.495	-0.502	-0.682

Table 1: Spearman's correlation r_s between automatic metric scores and post-editing productivity gains P_n on all 110 video segments for the **English transcription task**. The last column shows correlation to the productivity gain averaged across subtitlers $\hat{P}_n$.

of Table 1, the correlation is lower. Unfortunately, for the same reasons as for the case of WER, we have to apply SubER to lower-cased text - as it is the default setting for the TER metric - to avoid a drop in correlation.

Correlations for t-WER (see Section 3.3) suggest that a word-level time-alignment using interpolation may result in misalignments which are punished too harsh in comparison to which mistimings are still tolerated by the post-editors. This supports our design choice of using subtitle-level timings for SubER.

Finally, we include TER-br from Karakanta et al. (2020a) in the results. It is a variant of TER + break tokens where each real word is replaced by a mask token. Given that the metric has no access to the actual words it achieves surprisingly high correlations. This shows that the subtitle formatting defined by the number of subtitle blocks, number of lines and number of words per line is in itself an important feature affecting the post-editing effort.

4.4.2 Post-Editing of Spanish Translation

Baseline productivities P_{base} of the translators D, E and F are 1.9, 1.8 and 1.1 subtitles per minute, respectively. On average, their productivity changes to 1.6, 2.0 and 1.1 when post-editing, meaning only subtitler B gains consistently. Subtitler A is more productive on one of the videos, but slows down significantly for the other two.

Table 2 shows performances of the different MT metrics. In addition to post-edit effort, we show how well the metrics agree with human judgments of the usefulness and quality (see Section 4.3.2) for each of the 110 one-minute video segments.

Overall, the correlation of productivity gains is much lower than for the transcription task. This can be explained by the fact that a translator has more freedom than a transcriber. The translator's word choices are influenced by clues outside the scope of the translated text, like the style of language and references to other parts of the plot. Sometimes even research is required (e.g. bible verses for *Midnight Mass*). Despite this, the subjectively perceived usefulness $\hat{U}_n$ of the automatic subtitles for post-editing can be predicted from automatic scores with a Spearman's correlation of up to -0.591. The quality judgement $\hat{Q}_n$ shows even higher correlations of up to 0.659.

We compare the baseline MT metrics BLEU and TER when applied to the subtitle block-level vs. the sentence-level. We note that BLEU on subtitle-level is identical to t-BLEU (Cherry et al., 2021) for the considered case of template translation, where timestamps in hypothesis and reference are identical. Overall, BLEU and TER perform similarly. For both, evaluation on subtitle-level outperforms evaluation on sentence-level. This is because the sentence-pairs extracted from the subtitle files preserve no formatting information, while using subtitle blocks as units is sensitive to how words of a sentence are distributed among subtitles after translation, especially in case of word re-ordering.

Extending BLEU and TER with break tokens to take subtitle segmentation into account shows only minor improvements for the subtitle-level, but significantly improves correlations for the sentence-level. This could be attributed to the extended context after end-of-block tokens that is not available for scoring on subtitle-level. Especially the way "BLEU + break tokens" punishes n-grams that are disrupted by an erroneous line break seems to lead to good results.

Our proposed metric SubER consistently outperforms all considered baseline metrics except for sentence-level BLEU with break tokens, which has a higher correlation for $\hat{Q}_n$ and for the scores given by subtitler F. For this subtitler we also observe

Metric	Subtitler D			Subtitler E			Subtitler F			Combined		
	P_n	U_n	Q_n	P_n	U_n	Q_n	P_n	U_n	Q_n	$\hat{P}_n$	$\hat{U}_n$	$\hat{Q}_n$
Subtitle-level												
BLEU	0.03	0.34	0.52	0.22	0.21	0.39	0.07	0.58	0.49	0.172	0.541	0.595
+ break tokens	0.04	0.35	0.53	0.22	0.24	0.43	0.12	0.58	0.46	0.210	0.554	0.595
TER	0.03	-0.35	-0.54	-0.22	-0.23	-0.41	-0.11	-0.63	-0.51	-0.182	-0.554	-0.618
+ break tokens	0.00	-0.36	-0.54	-0.23	-0.24	-0.41	-0.10	-0.61	-0.50	-0.200	-0.558	-0.606
Sentence-level												
BLEU	-0.03	0.31	0.51	0.21	0.13	0.33	0.04	0.60	0.51	0.126	0.494	0.573
+ break tokens	0.02	0.35	0.55	0.25	0.22	0.43	0.16	0.63	**0.55**	0.240	0.583	**0.659**
TER	0.07	-0.32	-0.52	-0.22	-0.14	-0.34	-0.07	-0.59	-0.48	-0.133	-0.484	-0.559
+ break tokens	0.00	-0.36	-0.55	-0.25	-0.19	-0.38	-0.13	-0.58	-0.45	-0.218	-0.515	-0.574
chrF	-0.09	0.26	0.52	0.21	0.10	0.28	0.04	0.64	0.51	0.104	0.483	0.556
TER-br	0.03	-0.32	-0.42	-0.11	-0.07	-0.24	-0.13	-0.43	-0.40	-0.137	-0.345	-0.426
SubER (ours)	-0.06	**-0.38**	**-0.57**	**-0.27**	**-0.28**	**-0.47**	-0.16	-0.61	-0.52	**-0.274**	**-0.591**	-0.651
+ case/punct	0.00	-0.36	-0.56	-0.25	-0.23	-0.42	-0.15	-0.61	-0.49	-0.237	-0.554	-0.612
- break tokens	0.02	-0.34	-0.54	-0.24	-0.25	-0.44	-0.11	**-0.65**	**-0.55**	-0.197	-0.572	-0.645

Table 2: Spearman's correlation r_s between automatic metric scores and P_n, U_n and Q_n on all 110 video segments for the **English→Spanish translation task**. P_n are segment-wise productivity gains from post-editing measured in subtitles per minute of work. U_n and Q_n are segment-wise usefulness and quality scores, respectively, which the subtitlers assigned to the automatically generated subtitle segments.

that calculating SubER without break tokens improves results. In fact, subtitler F stated that moving around text is not a taxing procedure for him as he is very proficient with keyboard commands. For the other subtitlers, break tokens as part of the metric are shown to have a clear positive effect.

4.4.3 System-level Results

For both transcription and translation we have a pair of systems which differ only in subtitle segmentation (systems 1 and 2). We expect the system using a neural segmentation model to perform better overall. By definition, WER cannot distinguish between the transcription systems, scores for both are 40.6, 14.2 and 29.5 (%) for the three videos *Master of None*, *Midnight Mass* and *Peaky Blinders*, respectively. (High WER on *Master of None* is caused by colloquial and mumbling speech.) SubER scores for system 1 are 46.4, 20.3 and 33.1, for system 2 they are 47.3, 22.1 and 34.7. This means, for all videos SubER scores are able to reflect the better segmentation quality of system 1.

The same is true for translation: sentence-level BLEU scores are the same for systems 1 and 2, namely 18.9, 26.7 and 37.9 for the three videos. SubER scores for the system with neural segmentation are 65.1, 56.5 and 41.8, whereas the system without it gets worse scores of 67.4, 60.5 and 46.9.

5 Release of Code

We release the code to calculate the SubER metric as part of an open-source subtitle evaluation toolkit[2] to encourage its use in the research community as well as the media industry and to further promote research of automatic subtitling systems.

In addition to SubER, the toolkit implements all baseline metrics used in Table 1 and 2, as well as t-BLEU (Cherry et al., 2021). This includes implementations of hypothesis to reference alignment via the Levenshtein algorithm (Section 3.1) or via interpolated word timings (Section 3.3). We use the JiWER[3] Python package for word error rate calculations and SacreBLEU (Post, 2018) to compute BLEU, TER and chrF values.

All metrics can be calculated directly from SRT input files. Support for other subtitle file formats will be added on demand.

6 Conclusion

In this work, we proposed SubER – a novel metric for evaluating quality of automatically generated intralingual and interlingual subtitles. The metric is based on edit distance with shifts, but considers not only the automatically transcribed or translated text, but also subtitle timing and line segmentation information. It can be used to compare an automatically generated subtitle file to a human-generated one even if the two files contain a different number of subtitles with different timings.

A thorough evaluation by professional subtitlers confirmed that SubER correlates well with their transcription post-editing effort and direct assessment scores of translations. In most cases, SubER

[2] `https://github.com/apptek/SubER`
[3] `https://github.com/jitsi/jiwer`

shows highest correlation as compared to metrics that evaluate either the quality of the text alone, or use different approaches to integrate subtitle timing and segmentation information.

The source code for SubER will be publicly released for the benefit of speech recognition and speech translation research communities, as well as the media and entertainment industry.

References

Aitor Álvarez, Marina Balenciaga, Arantza del Pozo, Haritz Arzelus, Anna Matamala, and Carlos-D. Martínez-Hinarejos. 2016. Impact of automatic segmentation on the quality, productivity and self-reported post-editing effort of intralingual subtitles. In *Proceedings of the Tenth International Conference on Language Resources and Evaluation (LREC'16)*, pages 3049–3053, Portorož, Slovenia. European Language Resources Association (ELRA).

Aitor Alvarez, Carlos-D Martínez-Hinarejos, Haritz Arzelus, Marina Balenciaga, and Arantza del Pozo. 2017. Improving the automatic segmentation of subtitles through conditional random field. *Speech Communication*, 88:83–95.

Lindsay Bywood, Panayota Georgakopoulou, and Thierry Etchegoyhen. 2017. Embracing the threat: machine translation as a solution for subtitling. *Perspectives*, 25(3):492–508.

Colin Cherry, Naveen Arivazhagan, Dirk Padfield, and Maxim Krikun. 2021. Subtitle translation as markup translation. *Proc. Interspeech 2021*, pages 2237–2241.

Thierry Etchegoyhen, Lindsay Bywood, Mark Fishel, Panayota Georgakopoulou, Jie Jiang, Gerard van Loenhout, Arantza del Pozo, Mirjam Sepesy Maučec, Anja Turner, and Martin Volk. 2014. Machine translation for subtitling: A large-scale evaluation. In *Proceedings of the Ninth International Conference on Language Resources and Evaluation (LREC'14)*, pages 46–53, Reykjavik, Iceland. European Language Resources Association (ELRA).

Alina Karakanta, Matteo Negri, and Marco Turchi. 2020a. Is 42 the answer to everything in subtitling-oriented speech translation? In *Proceedings of the 17th International Conference on Spoken Language Translation*, pages 209–219, Online. Association for Computational Linguistics.

Alina Karakanta, Matteo Negri, and Marco Turchi. 2020b. MuST-cinema: a speech-to-subtitles corpus. In *Proceedings of the 12th Language Resources and Evaluation Conference*, pages 3727–3734, Marseille, France. European Language Resources Association.

Alina Karakanta, Matteo Negri, and Marco Turchi. 2020c. Point break: Surfing heterogeneous data for subtitle segmentation. In *CLiC-it*.

Maarit Koponen, Umut Sulubacak, Kaisa Vitikainen, and Jörg Tiedemann. 2020. MT for subtitling: User evaluation of post-editing productivity. In *Proceedings of the 22nd Annual Conference of the European Association for Machine Translation*, pages 115–124, Lisboa, Portugal. European Association for Machine Translation.

Evgeny Matusov, Gregor Leusch, Oliver Bender, and Hermann Ney. 2005. Evaluating machine translation output with automatic sentence segmentation. In *Proceedings of the Second International Workshop on Spoken Language Translation*, Pittsburgh, Pennsylvania, USA.

Evgeny Matusov, Patrick Wilken, and Yota Georgakopoulou. 2019. Customizing neural machine translation for subtitling. In *Proceedings of the Fourth Conference on Machine Translation (Volume 1: Research Papers)*, pages 82–93, Florence, Italy. Association for Computational Linguistics.

Evgeny Matusov, Patrick Wilken, and Christian Herold. 2020. Flexible customization of a single neural machine translation system with multi-dimensional metadata inputs. In *Proceedings of the 14th Conference of the Association for Machine Translation in the Americas (Volume 2: User Track)*, pages 204–216, Virtual. Association for Machine Translation in the Americas.

Kishore Papineni, Salim Roukos, Todd Ward, and Wei-Jing Zhu. 2002. Bleu: a method for automatic evaluation of machine translation. In *Proceedings of the 40th Annual Meeting of the Association for Computational Linguistics*, pages 311–318, Philadelphia, Pennsylvania, USA. Association for Computational Linguistics.

J. Pedersen. 2017. The FAR model: assessing quality in interlingual subtitling. In *Journal of Specialized Translation*, volume 18, pages 210–229.

Maja Popović. 2015. chrF: character n-gram F-score for automatic MT evaluation. In *Proceedings of the Tenth Workshop on Statistical Machine Translation*, pages 392–395, Lisbon, Portugal. Association for Computational Linguistics.

Matt Post. 2018. A call for clarity in reporting BLEU scores. In *Proceedings of the Third Conference on Machine Translation: Research Papers*, pages 186–191, Brussels, Belgium. Association for Computational Linguistics.

Ricardo Rei, Craig Stewart, Ana C Farinha, and Alon Lavie. 2020. COMET: A neural framework for MT evaluation. In *Proceedings of the 2020 Conference on Empirical Methods in Natural Language Processing (EMNLP)*, pages 2685–2702, Online. Association for Computational Linguistics.

P. Romero-Fresco and F. Pöchhacker. 2017. Quality assessment in interlingual live subtitling: The NTR model. In *Linguistica Antverpiensia, New Series:*

Themes in Translation Studies, volume 16, pages 149–167.

P. Romero-Fresco and J.M. Pérez. 2015. Accuracy rate in live subtitling: The NER model. In *Audiovisual Translation in a Global Context. Palgrave Studies in Translating and Interpreting*. R.B., Cintas J.D. (eds), Palgrave Macmillan, London.

Andrea Schioppa, David Vilar, Artem Sokolov, and Katja Filippova. 2021. Controlling machine translation for multiple attributes with additive interventions. In *Proceedings of the 2021 Conference on Empirical Methods in Natural Language Processing*, pages 6676–6696, Online and Punta Cana, Dominican Republic. Association for Computational Linguistics.

Matthew Snover, Bonnie Dorr, Rich Schwartz, Linnea Micciulla, and John Makhoul. 2006. A study of translation edit rate with targeted human annotation. In *Proceedings of the 7th Conference of the Association for Machine Translation in the Americas: Technical Papers*, pages 223–231, Cambridge, Massachusetts, USA. Association for Machine Translation in the Americas.

Tianyi Zhang, Varsha Kishore, Felix Wu, Kilian Q Weinberger, and Yoav Artzi. 2019. BERTScore: Evaluating text generation with BERT. In *International Conference on Learning Representations*.

Improving Arabic Diacritization by Learning to Diacritize and Translate

Brian Thompson*
AWS AI Labs
brianjt@amazon.com

Ali Alshehri
Apple
a_alshehri@apple.com

Abstract

We propose a novel multitask learning method for diacritization which trains a model to both diacritize and translate. Our method addresses data sparsity by exploiting large, readily available bitext corpora. Furthermore, translation requires implicit linguistic and semantic knowledge, which is helpful for resolving ambiguities in diacritization. We apply our method to the Penn Arabic Treebank and report a new state-of-the-art word error rate of 4.79%. We also conduct manual and automatic analysis to better understand our method and highlight some of the remaining challenges in diacritization. Our method has applications in text-to-speech, speech-to-speech translation, and other NLP tasks.

هيا لنذهب → هَيَّا لِنَذْهَبْ

[hjaː lnðhb] [hajːaː linaðhab]

Figure 1: Arabic diacritization is the task of adding diacritics (markings above and below characters, shown in red) to Arabic text. Diacritics clarify how a word is pronounced, including short vowels and elongation, and disambiguate word meaning. Here, we show the diacritization of هيا لنذهب (let's go). The IPA pronunciations below each word demonstrate that the diacritics are crucial for pronouncing each word: the undiacritized form maps to an incorrect pronunciation, while the diacritized form maps to the correct pronunciation (the contributions the diacritics make to the pronunciation are also shown in red).

1 Introduction

Arabic is typically written without short vowels and other pronunciation indication markers,[1] collectively referred to as diacritics. A longstanding task in Natural Language Processing (NLP) is to take undiacritized text and add the diacritics, referred to as diacritization (see Figure 1). Diacritics indicate both how to pronounce the word and resolve ambiguities in meaning between different words with the same (undiacritized) written form.

Diacritic prediction is the dominant source of errors in Arabic grapheme to phoneme conversion (Ali et al., 2020), a crucial component in many text-to-speech and speech-to-speech translation systems.

Diacritization also has applications in Automatic Speech Recognition (ASR) (Vergyri and Kirchhoff, 2004; Ananthakrishnan et al., 2005; Biadsy et al., 2009), Machine Translation (MT) (Diab et al., 2007) morphological analysis (Habash et al., 2016), lexical recognition tests (Hamed and Zesch, 2018; Hamed, 2019), and homograph resolution (Alqahtani et al., 2019a).

We focus on Modern Standard Arabic (MSA), a standardized dialect of Arabic used in most academic, legal, and news publications, and an obvious choice for Text-to-Speech (TTS) systems. MSA is the 5th most spoken[2] language in the world with about 274M speakers (Eberhard et al., 2021).

1.1 Challenge #1: Data Sparsity

Arabic is a Morphologically Rich Language (MRL), where significant information concerning syntactic units and relations is expressed at word-level. For example, a word like فأسقيناكموه is roughly translated to: 'and we gave it to you to drink'. In this example, linguistic units that are typically expressed by individual words in English such as coordinating conjunctions and personal pronouns are expressed within the word form in Arabic. This fact results in Arabic having a large vocabulary (by way of example, the number of unique, undiacritized words in the Arabic bible from Christodouloupoulos and Steedman (2015)

* Work done while at Apple.

[1] Notable exceptions include the Quran and many children's books.

[2] "Speaker" is a bit of a misnomer: Most Arabic speakers can understand MSA but would not typically produce it.

Proceedings of the 19th International Conference on Spoken Language Translation (IWSLT 2022), pages 11 - 21
May 26-27, 2022 ©2022 Association for Computational Linguistics

is about 4.38x larger than the number of unique, lower-cased words in the English equivalent.) Finally, high-quality diacritized datasets tend to be quite small: The Penn Arabic Treebank (PATB) training subset used in this work is only 15,789 lines, and data available in other dialects can be substantially smaller. These factors result in Arabic being quite data sparse, with diacritics models typically needing to handle a large number of unseen words.

1.2 Challenge #2: Ambiguity

Many of the morphological variants in Arabic are differentiated by only diacritics. This results in un-diacritized Arabic having a huge number of homographs which must be resolved when adding diacritics. Furthermore, as mentioned above, Arabic is a MRL, where information such as gender (male, female), number (singular, dual, plural), case (nominative, accusative, genitive), aspect (perfect, imperfect), voice (active, passive) and mood (indicative, imperative, subjunctive) is expressed on the word-level, sometime with as little as one diacritic. These factors result in undiacritized Arabic being highly ambiguous; Debili et al. (2002) reported an average of 11.6 possible diacritizations for every non-diacritized word in Arabic. For example, the form كتب could be diacritized as كَتَبَ 'he wrote', كُتِبَ 'it was written', كُتِّبَ 'it was written repeatedly', كُتُبٌ 'books' (nominative case), or كُتُبٍ 'books' (genitive case).

1.3 Overview of Proposed Method

We propose a novel Multitask Learning (MTL) (Caruana, 1997) based approach to improve the semantic and linguistic knowledge of a diacritization model. Specifically, we propose augmenting diacritics training data with bitext to train a model to both diacritize Arabic and translate into and out of Arabic.

Our approach addresses data sparsity by substantially increasing the amount of training data seen by the model. Our approach also enables the use of large, readily available MT datasets, which are available not only in Arabic but in many other languages with diacritics as well.[3] In our experiments on the PATB, adding bitext increases training data from 502k to 138M Arabic words, and decreases the Out of Vocabulary (OOV) rate from 7.33% to 1.14%.

Our approach also addresses ambiguity, since the task of translation requires (implicit) semantic and linguistic knowledge. Training on bitext injects semantic and linguistic knowledge into the model which is helpful for resolving ambiguities in diacritization (see Table 1).

These factors contribute to our method achieving a new State-of-the-Art (SOTA) Word Error Rate (WER) of 4.79% on the PATB, vs 7.49% for an equivalent baseline without MTL.

1.4 Main Contributions of This Work

The main contributions of this work are:

- We present a novel MTL approach for diacritization, which does not require a morphological analyzer or specialized annotations (and thus is likely extensible to other languages, dialects and domains).
- We achieve a new SOTA WER of 4.79% on the PATB test set.
- We perform extensive automatic analysis of our method to see how it performs on various conditions including different parts of speech, genders, word frequencies, and sentence lengths.
- We perform detailed manual error analysis of our method, illustrating both issues in the PATB dataset as well as the remaining challenges in Arabic diacritization.

2 Related Work

2.1 Diacritization

Many works have explored using neural networks for Arabic diacritization (Zalmout and Habash, 2017, 2019; Alqahtani and Diab, 2019; Alqahtani et al., 2019b).

Alqahtani et al. (2020) and Zalmout and Habash (2020) both explore MTL regimes in which a model learns to predict Arabic diacritics simultaneously with other features in the PATB. Alqahtani et al. (2020) uses additional features of syntactic diacritization, word segmentation, and POS tagging, while Zalmout and Habash (2020) use additional features of lemmas, aspect, case, gender, person, POS, number, mood, state, voice, enclitics, and proclitics. By also report further improvements by adding an external morphological analyzer. These papers illustrate the potential of MTL, but they re-

[3]In contrast, prior MTL work in diacritization has used hand-curated features such as Part of Speech (POS), gender, and case (see §2.1), severely limiting both the size of available data and the applicability to other languages, which may not have such resources.

#	Arabic Sentence	English Sentence	Diacritized	Pronunciation	Translation
0	علم السعودية أخضر وأبيض اللون	The flag of Saudi Arabia is green and white	عَلَمُ	[ʕalamu]	flag
1	أحب علم الفلك	I love space science	عِلمَ	[ʕilma]	science
2	علم ناصر أحمد السباحة	Nasser taught Ahmad how to swim	عَلَّمَ	[ʕal:ama]	taught

Table 1: Adding bitext to our training data improves the semantic and linguistic knowledge of our diacritization model. For example, in order to correctly translate علم out of Arabic, the model must learn to implicitly perform homographic resolution to determine if the word is being used to mean "flag," "science," "taught," or other meanings. This knowledge is helpful for diacritization since diacritized forms are intrinsically linked with word meaning. The model can also implicitly learn, for example, that علم in example #2 is being used as a causative past tense verb. This can help the model diacritize this use of علم correctly (عَلَّمَ), even if عَلَّمَ does not appear in the diacritization training data, since عَلَّمَ follows a common diacritization pattern for causative past tense verbs.

quire additional hand-curated features. This limits both the datasets they can use (neither are able to take advantage of large outside datasets) and the languages they could be applied to.

2.1.1 Contextual Embeddings

Náplava et al. (2021) show that contextual embeddings can result in substantial improvements in diacritization error rates in several languages, but unfortunately they do not report results on Arabic.

Qin et al. (2021) start with a strong baseline built on ZEN 2.0 (Song et al., 2021), an n-gram aware BERT variant. Their BERT-based baseline outperforms prior work on PATB. They then claim even stronger results on PATB with two methods that incorporate multitask training with a second, auxiliary decoder trained to predict the diacritics produced by the Farasa morphological analyzer (Abdelali et al., 2016). We argue that their experimental setup is fundamentally flawed, since Farasa was trained on the PATB test set[4] and can leak information about the test set to the model.[5] They also report results on the Tashkeela training/test data (Zerrouki and Balla, 2017; Fadel et al., 2019), which does not have a potential testset contamination problem, and find that their method underperforms a straightforward bidirectional LSTM,[6] which supports the hypothesis that their strong PATB results are due to training on a derivative of the test set.

2.2 Character-Level and Multilingual MT

Multilingual MT (Dong et al., 2015) has been shown to dramatically improve low-resource translation, including enabling transfer from higher resource language pairs to lower-resource language pairs (Zoph et al., 2016; Nguyen and Chiang, 2017; Neubig and Hu, 2018). In our case, we set up learning to encourage transfer from undiacritized Arabic to much lower-resourced diacritized Arabic.

Most MT systems operate at the subword (Sennrich et al., 2016; Kudo and Richardson, 2018); however, such approaches would result in diacritized and undiacritized versions of the same word having little to no overlap in subwords. We instead train a character-level encoder-decoder model (Lee et al., 2017; Cherry et al., 2018), to maximize the number of shared representations between diacritized and undiacritized words. Character-level diacritics models have also been shown to outperform subword-level models (Alqahtani and Diab, 2019).

3 Method

We train a single Transformer-based (Vaswani et al., 2017) encoder-decoder model to both translate and diacritize, with the hypothesis that the translation task is complementary to diacritization. To maximize the number of shared representations between diacritized and undiacritized words, we train our model at the character-level. Following

[4]Farasa was trained on PATB parts 1, 2 and 3 *in their entirety*, and then tested on a separate collection of hand curated news articles (Abdelali et al., 2016).

[5]To understand how leakage from the test set can occur, consider the word النجمة (the star; female). النجمة appears three times in the training data, once without diacritics (likely an error) and twice as النَّجْمَةِ . However, it appears 9 times in the test set, each time diacritized as النَّجْمَة . Farasa is trained on both the training and test data, so from it's perspective, النَّجْمَة is by far the most likely diacritization of النجمة . Thus when the model sees النجمة in training, Farasa can artificially bias the model toward producing the diacritized form in the test set, despite that form never appearing in the training data.

[6]Qin et al. (2021) claim to achieve state-of-the-art performance on both datasets, but this is not supported by their results (see their Table 2, noting that bold does *not* denote the best performing system).

work in multilingual MT, we prepend a tag to each output sentence to tell the model whether the output is undiacritized Arabic, diacritized Arabic, English, French, or Spanish during training. At inference time we force decode the tag to request that the model produce diacritized Arabic.

3.1 Decoding

In Arabic, simple rules dictate where diacritics can be placed. During decoding, we enforce these rules by keeping track of which input characters the decoder has produced (i.e. copied from input to output) and constrain the decoder as follows: If the previous output is a non-diacritic Arabic character, we restrict the decoder to produce any diacritic or the next input character. If the previous output is a shadda, we restrict the decoder to produce a non-shadda diacritic or the next input character. Otherwise, the model is forced to produce the next input character. Without these restrictions, we found that the model would occasionally produce minor paraphrastic variations of the input.[7]

3.2 Long Sentence Handling

The computational complexity of Transformer layers is proportional to sequence length squared (Vaswani et al., 2017), so we do not want to train or evaluate on an arbitrarily long sequences of characters. Instead, we limit the maximum input and output sequence to 600. To diacritize a sentence with more than 300 input characters, we take overlapping windows of 300 characters with a step size of 100 characters. We predict diacritics independently for each window, and reconstruct the original sentence using the first 200 characters from the first window, the input characters of the last window excluding the first 100 characters, and the middle 100 characters from any windows in between. This ensures that we only use output with at least 100 characters of context. For the bitext data, we simply discard sentence pairs with greater than 600 input or output characters.

4 Experiments

We train a character-level transformer encoder-decoder model on both diacritics data and the bitext. Our primary model performs diacritization, translation from Arabic (Ar) to English (En), French (Fr), and Spanish (Es), and translation from English, French, and Spanish to Arabic. However, we also perform ablations for analysis purposes, leaving out (1) the Ar→{En,Fr,Es} data, (2) the {En,Fr,Es}→Ar data, and (3) all of the bitext data. Each model uses a single encoder and decoder for all tasks.

Name	Form	Sound [IPA]
Fatha	◌َ	/a/
Fathatan	◌ً	/an/
Kasra	◌ِ	/i/
Kasratan	◌ٍ	/in/
Damma	◌ُ	/u/
Dammatan	◌ٌ	/un/
Dagger Alif	◌ٰ	/a:/
Maddah	◌ٓ	/ʕa:/
Shadda	◌ّ	Elongation (:)
Sukun	◌ْ	None

Table 2: Diacritics considered in this work.

	Ar-En	Ar-Es	Ar-Fr	Diacs
Global Voices	0.9	0.9	0.5	-
CCAligned	-	21.9	21.7	-
News Commentary	5.0	5.0	4.3	-
United Nations	20.7	19.9	19.5	-
WikiMatrix	15.0	1.7	1.6	-
PATB	-	-	-	0.5
Total	40.8	48.4	47.1	0.5

Table 3: Size (millions of Arabic words) of training datasets used in this work. Note that total bitext is about 275x larger than diacritics data.

4.1 Diacritics Data

We chose to use PATB part 1 v4.1 (LDC2010T13), part 2 v3.1 (LDC2011T09) and part 3 v3.2 (LDC2010T08), following the train/dev/test splits proposed by Diab et al. (2013). The PATB was chosen because in addition to diacritics, it contains many carefully annotated features which we use to analyze the performance of our models (see §6). We perform unicode NFKD normalization on the text in order to (1) split Unicode characters which contain both a non-diacritic and diacritic (e.g. the Unicode character for alif with maddah above (U+0622) is split into alif (U+0627) and maddah (U+0653)) and (2) normalize the order of characters (e.g. alif + high hamza + fatha and alif + fatha + high hamza both render as أَ and are normalized to alif + high hamza + fatha). The diacritics considered in this work are shown in Table 2.

[7]The tendency of a multilingual MT model to paraphrase the input has been noted (and exploited) in Tiedemann and Scherrer (2019) and Thompson and Post (2020b).

Training Data	OOV Rate (Undiacritized)
PATB	7.33%
PATB + Bitext	1.14%

Table 4: OOV rates (rate of seeing a word at inference time that was not seen in training), for the encoder, which sees words without diacritics.

4.2 MT Data

We use Ar↔{En,Fr,Es} data from Wikimatrix (Schwenk et al., 2019), Global Voices,[8] United Nations (Ziemski et al., 2016), and NewsCommentary,[9] and Ar↔{Fr,Es} data from CCAligned (El-Kishky et al., 2020), after joining on English urls. We filter out noisy sentence pairs (Khayrallah and Koehn, 2018) using the scripts[10] provided by Thompson and Post (2020a), using more aggressive thresholds of min_laser_score=1.06, max_3gram_overlap=0.1 for the CCAligned data and using values from Thompson and Post (2020a) otherwise. We limit each dataset to 1M lines per language pair, so that no one data type dominates training. Data size are shown in Table 3. We upsample PATB by 20x when combining it with the bitext, since it is much smaller than the bitext.

We filter out the (very infrequent) diacritics from the MT data to ensure that any benefits observed are due to MTL and not simply the result of including more diacritized data in training.[11]

The impact that adding bitext has on the OOV rate is shown in Table 4.

4.3 Models & Training

We train character-level Transformer models in fairseq (Ott et al., 2019). Metaparameters are tuned on the development set. The (non-MTL) baseline has 6 encoder and decoder layers, encoder and decoder embedding dimensions of 1024, encoder and decoder feed-forward network embedding dimensions of 8192, and 16 heads. All embeddings are shared. The model is trained with learning rate of 0.0004, label smoothing of 0.1, dropout of 0.4 with no attention or activation dropout, 40k characters per batch, for 50 epochs. All MTL models have 6 encoder and decoder layers, encoder and decoder embedding dimensions of 1280, encoder and decoder feed-forward network embedding dimensions of 12288, and 20 heads. All embeddings are shared. The model is trained with learning rate of 0.0004, label smoothing of 0.1, dropout of 0.2 with no attention and activation dropout each set to 0.1, 40k characters per batch, for 20 epochs. We select the best performing model for each run using WER on the development set.

5 Results

The word error rates for our method (main model, both ablation models, and baseline) are shown in Table 5, along with error rates reported by prior work. Our main model achieves 4.71% WER on the development set, a relative improvement of 22.8% over the previous best development set result from Zalmout and Habash (2020), who trained a multitask model on PATB features and incorporated a morphological analyzer. On the test set, it achieves 4.79% WER, a relative improvement of 18.8% over the best previously reported test set result from Qin et al. (2021), who trained a BERT-based model.

Our ablation models also outperform all prior work, with the model trained on Ar→{En,Es,Fr} (denoted Ar→∗) bitext outperforming the model trained on {En,Es,Fr}→Ar (denoted ∗→Ar) bitext, but neither perform as well as the main model trained on both Ar→∗ and ∗→Ar. (See §6 for more detailed comparisons between the models trained in this work.)

Finally, our baseline model, consisting of a character-based Transformer with no augmentation or word embeddings, slightly outperforms prior models from Alqahtani et al. (2019b) and Alqahtani and Diab (2019), that also do not use MTL, morphological analyzers, or contextual embeddings.

6 Automatic Analysis

6.1 Case Endings

We compute the Diacritic Error Rate (DER) for all models trained in this work for several different settings: all characters (including whitespace, punctuation, and non-Arabic characters), Arabic characters, Arabic case endings, and Arabic characters excluding case endings: see Table 6. We use POS tags to determine which words have case end-

[8] casmacat.eu/corpus/global-voices.html

[9] data.statmt.org/news-commentary/

[10] github.com/thompsonb/prism_bitext_filter

[11] In practice, there may be some benefit to retaining diacritics in the MT data, but this was not explored in this work.

	Multitask	Morphological Analyzer	Word Embeddings	Dev WER ↓	Test WER ↓
Alqahtani et al. (2019b)	No	No	No		8.20%
Alqahtani and Diab (2019)	No	No	No		7.60%
Alqahtani et al. (2020)	PATB Features	No	fastText		7.51%
Zalmout and Habash (2019)	PATB Features	Train & Test	fastText	7.30%	7.50%
Zalmout and Habash (2020)	PATB Features	Train & Test	fastText	6.10%	
Qin et al. (2021)†	No	No	Zen 2.0	6.49%	5.90%‡
This word (baseline)	No	No	No	7.46%	7.49%
This work (ablation)	Translate $*\rightarrow$Ar	No	No	5.60%	5.83%
This work (ablation)	Translate Ar$\rightarrow *$	No	No	5.24%	5.32%
This work	Translate $*\rightarrow$Ar & Ar$\rightarrow *$	No	No	**4.71%**	**4.79%**

Table 5: Development and Test WER (lower is better) for our main system, ablation systems, and baseline, compared to recent work. Our main system outperforms all prior work, as do both ablation systems. †:We exclude the experiments of Qin et al. (2021) which use Farasa in training, as Farasa was trained on the test set (see §2.1.1). ‡:Mean of 5 runs with different random seeds.

	Baseline	Multitask Learning $*\rightarrow$Ar	Ar$\rightarrow *$	Both
All	2.34%	1.85%	1.73%	**1.52%**
Arabic	2.97%	2.35%	2.21%	**1.94%**
Arabic CE	6.90%	4.71%	4.18%	**3.61%**
Arabic non-CE	2.48%	2.06%	1.96%	**1.73%**

Table 6: Diacritic error rate for all characters (including whitespace and non-Arabic characters), Arabic characters only, Arabic case endings (CE), and Arabic characters excluding case endings (non-CE). We use POS tags to determine which words contain case endings.

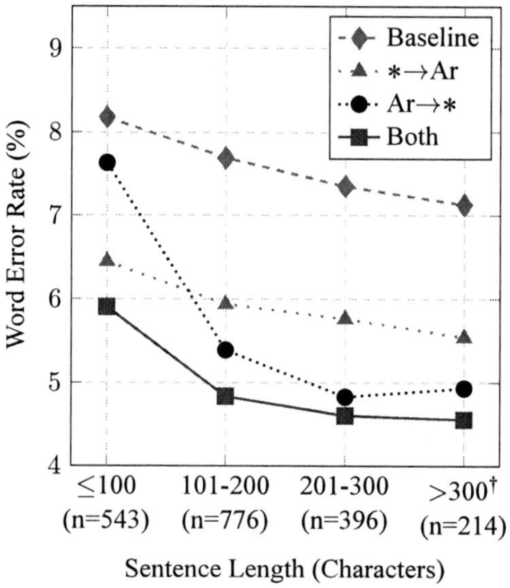

Figure 2: Word error rate vs (undiacritized) character length. †:Sentences over 300 characters are processed in overlapping windows of 300 characters (see §3.2).

ings when computing DER.[12] Comparing our main model to the baseline, we see that MTL training improves case endings more than non-case endings: case ending DER is improved by a 47.7% (3.61% vs 6.90%) vs 30.2% (1.72% vs 2.48%) for non case ending characters. Furthermore, comparing the ablation models, the performance difference between them is more pronounced on case endings, where the $*\rightarrow$Ar model is 12.7% worse than the Ar$\rightarrow *$ model, while the difference is only 5.1% for non case endings.

6.2 WER vs Sentence Length

We show WER as a function of sentence length (in undiacritized characters) in Figure 2. We note that while both the $*\rightarrow$Ar and the Ar$\rightarrow *$ models tend to improve with sentence length, the improvement is much more pronounced for the Ar$\rightarrow *$ model. In other words, the Ar$\rightarrow *$ model is benefiting much more from increased context than the $*\rightarrow$Ar model.

In conjunction with the DER results in §6.1, this indicates that training the model to translate out of Arabic is more helpful at injecting semantic and linguistic knowledge into the model to address ambiguity. The fact that the two translation directions are complementary suggests that training the model to translate into Arabic is addressing data sparsity issues in the model's decoder, despite the mismatch between the bitext being undiacritized and the model needing to produce diacritized output.

[12]Several prior works have reported DER of just the last character as a stand-in for case-ending DER. However, this analysis is muddied by the fact that not all words in Arabic have case endings; in the PATB test set, for example, the POS tags indicate that only about 46.8% of words have them.

	Male		Female		Bias
	#	WER	#	WER	
Pronoun	835	6.23%	641	8.11%	30.3%
Verb	3579	5.34%	2083	6.39%	19.6%
Suffix	901†	5.22%	10222	5.71%	9.5%

Table 7: WER for male and female pronouns, verbs, and nouns/adjectives with gendered suffixes, along with their counts in the test set. †:We include only suffixes which are explicitly marked in the PATB for gender, which tend to be female (see §6.3).

6.3 Gender Bias

Gender bias has been noted in many aspects of NLP (Sun et al., 2019) but we are not aware of any prior work looking at gender bias in diacritization. We use the PATB POS tags to isolate three types of gendered words: pronouns, verbs, and suffixes. "Suffixes" refer to nouns and adjectives that have a gendered suffix. Unsurprisingly, we find that the model is better at diacritizing male words than female words in all three cases (see Table 7), with words in the male categories being diacritized correctly 9.5% to 30.3% more often than their female equivalents. We suspect that this bias is due at least in part to representation within the data: Male pronouns and verbs are 30% and 72% more common than their female counterparts. Counts of suffixes are complicated by the fact that that PATB only marks certain nouns and adjectives for gender (including those with taa marbuta, which tend to be female). By manual inspection, the remainder appear to be male, but we were unable to confirm this in the PATB annotation guidelines so we included only those explicitly marked for gender.

6.4 WER vs POS

The PATB includes detailed POS tagging. We exploit this feature to examine how our model performs on different parts of speech: see Table 8. Note that the PATB has one *or more* POS tags per word, with about 2.19 tags per word on average in the test set. We do not attempt to split words into their respective parts, as we find cases where this is not straightforward. Instead, such words are counted multiple times. As an example, الأَوَّلُون (the first) is both a determiner and cardinal adjective, and contributes to the WER of both.

For parts of speech with at least 500 occurrences in the test set, the worst performing POS for the MTL model by far is proper nouns (count=5969) at 14.09% WER. This is followed by imperfect verbs (count=2598) at 7.89% WER, possessive pronouns (count=1609) at 6.60%, and adjectives (excluding cardinal and comparative) (count=6106) at 6.49%.

Comparative adjectives, which are relatively infrequent (count=264) also have a high WER of 9.95%, but the worst POS considered by far is the extremely infrequent (count=18) imperative verbs, with a WER of 72.22%. Imperative verbs illustrate the importance of domain; news data contains very few imperatives, and imperative verbs are often distinguished from from imperfect or perfect verbs by diacritics alone. For example, استمر على الطريق can be diacritized إِستَمِر عَلَى الطَّرِيقِ (Continue on the road) or إِستَمَرَّ عَلَى الطَّرِيقِ (He continued on the road). This results in the model choosing the much more common perfect or imperfect forms in the majority of cases that should be imperative.

6.5 WER vs Word Frequency

MTL improves learning across all word frequencies: see Table 9. The biggest improvements are seen for words seen once and 2-4 times in training, with relative improvements of 43.5% and 45.4%, respectively.

7 Manual Analysis

To better understand the performance of our MTL model, we manually annotate all differences between our model prediction and the gold test set for a randomly selected 20% of the 1246 sentences in the test set that contain at least one disagreement.

We find that approximately 66% of the disagreements between the gold test set and the model are the result of model errors, which we denote as "true errors". The majority of these errors are due to case markings being either incorrect (38.6% of all true errors) or missing (16.5% of all true errors), while the rest of the word is correct.

However, we find that in approximately 32% of disagreements the model output is, in fact, correct. We denote such cases as "false errors." About half (50.3%) of the false errors were due to the test set missing diacritics and another 31.2% of all false errors were due to errors in the test set diacritics. 10.7% of the false errors were the result of valid variations which did not change the meaning of the sentence in any way (e.g. يُكْشِفْ vs يَكْشِفْ and الدُّوَلِي vs الدَّوْلِي). Another 4.4% of false errors were the result of valid variations that changed the meaning of the sentence while still resulting in a plausible meaning. A very small number of words (3.4%

	Count	Baseline WER	MTL WER	Rel. imprv.	Examples
Noun: Proper	5969	18.24%	**14.09%**	22.8%	مَريَم (Mary); أحمَد (Ahmed)
Noun: Numeric	1609	3.29%	**2.11%**	35.8%	عَشَرَة (ten); أَربَعَة (four)
Noun: Quantity	451	10.42%	**5.32%**	48.9%	أَيَّة (any; fem); بَعض (some)
Noun: Other	22795	8.43%	**5.03%**	40.3%	يَوم (day); دُوَيلَة (small country)
Pronoun: Possessive	1681	11.42%	**6.60%**	42.2%	كِتابِيَ (my book); كِتابُكُن(your book; fem)
Pronoun: Demonstrative	601	**0.00%**	0.17%	-	هٰذا (this; male singular); هاتان (these, fem dual)
Pronoun: Other	1154	1.04%	**0.52%**	50.0%	شاهَدَتنِي (she saw me); أَنتَ (you; male singular)
Verb: Inflected, Perfect	3273	9.53%	**4.89%**	48.7%	ذَهَبَ (he went); قُبِلَ (it was accepted)
Verb: Inflected, Imperfect	2598	13.55%	**7.89%**	41.8%	يَذهَبُ (he goes); تُقبَلُ (it is accepted)
Verb: Inflected, Imperative	18	83.33%	**72.22%**	13.3%	اِذهَب (go; male); قِفِي (stop; fem)
Adverb	260	**0.00%**	0.38%	-	مَتَى (when); حِينَذاك (then)
Adjective: Cardinal	348	7.18%	**4.31%**	40.0%	القَرن (19th century); الأَوَّلُون (the first)
Adjective: Comparative	264	16.67%	**9.85%**	40.9%	أَحرَصُ (more cautious); الأَحسَن (the best)
Adjective: Other	6106	10.87%	**6.49%**	40.4%	تارِخِيٌّ (historic); يَهُودِيٌّ (Jewish)
Determiner	15337	8.72%	**5.85%**	32.9%	التُونِسِي (the Tunisian); اليَومُ (the day)

Table 8: WER for our baseline and our main MTL model, for various parts of speech, and their associated count in the test set. Note: many words have more than one POS and contribute to 2+ categories (see §6.4).

# Occur in PATB-train	Baseline	Multitask Learning $*\to$Ar	Ar$\to*$	Both
0	30.93%	26.30%	23.20%	**21.92%**
1	17.63%	12.46%	10.33%	**9.95%**
2-4	11.94%	8.32%	7.56%	**6.51%**
5-16	8.78%	6.83%	6.50%	**5.67%**
17-64	7.80%	5.81%	5.50%	**4.86%**
65-256	6.33%	4.97%	4.55%	**3.76%**
257-1024	4.34%	3.28%	3.16%	**2.94%**
>1024	0.30%	**0.20%**	0.29%	0.22%

Table 9: WER vs number of times a word occurs in PATB-train (ignoring diacritics), for all four models trained in this work.

of false errors) had trivial diacritic variations that do not change meaning or pronunciation (e.g. one having a sakun while the other had no diacritic, or one having a fatha before an alif while the other did not).

Finally, about 2% of the disagreements are cases where the input to the model is not a real word, making the correct output undefined.

8 Conclusion

We demonstrate that training a diacritics model to both diacritize and translate substantially outperforms a model trained on the diacritization task alone. Adding translation data substantially increases the amount of training data seen by the model, addressing data sparsity issues in diacritization. The translation task also injects semantic and linguistic knowledge into the model, helping the model resolve ambiguities in diacritization.

Our method achieves a new state-of-the-art word error rate of 4.79% on the Penn Arabic Treebank datasets, using the standard data splits of Diab et al. (2013).

Finally, we present extensive manual and automatic analysis which provides insight into our method and highlights several challenges that still remain in Arabic diacritization, including proper nouns, female word forms, and case endings.

References

Ahmed Abdelali, Kareem Darwish, Nadir Durrani, and Hamdy Mubarak. 2016. Farasa: A fast and furious segmenter for Arabic. In *Proceedings of the 2016 Conference of the North American Chapter of the Association for Computational Linguistics: Demonstrations*, pages 11–16, San Diego, California. Association for Computational Linguistics.

Ikbel Hadj Ali, Zied Mnasri, and Zied Lachiri. 2020. Dnn-based grapheme-to-phoneme conversion for arabic text-to-speech synthesis. *International Journal of Speech Technology*, 23(3):569–584.

Sawsan Alqahtani, Hanan Aldarmaki, and Mona Diab. 2019a. Homograph disambiguation through selective diacritic restoration. In *Proceedings of the Fourth Arabic Natural Language Processing Workshop*, pages 49–59, Florence, Italy. Association for Computational Linguistics.

Sawsan Alqahtani and Mona Diab. 2019. Investigating input and output units in diacritic restoration. In

2019 18th IEEE International Conference On Machine Learning And Applications (ICMLA), pages 811–817.

Sawsan Alqahtani, Ajay Mishra, and Mona Diab. 2019b. Efficient convolutional neural networks for diacritic restoration. In *Proceedings of the 2019 Conference on Empirical Methods in Natural Language Processing and the 9th International Joint Conference on Natural Language Processing (EMNLP-IJCNLP)*, pages 1442–1448, Hong Kong, China. Association for Computational Linguistics.

Sawsan Alqahtani, Ajay Mishra, and Mona Diab. 2020. A multitask learning approach for diacritic restoration. In *Proceedings of the 58th Annual Meeting of the Association for Computational Linguistics*, pages 8238–8247, Online. Association for Computational Linguistics.

Sankaranarayanan Ananthakrishnan, Shrikanth Narayanan, and Srinivas Bangalore. 2005. Automatic diacritization of arabic transcripts for automatic speech recognition. In *Proceedings of the 4th International Conference on Natural Language Processing*, pages 47–54.

Fadi Biadsy, Nizar Habash, and Julia Hirschberg. 2009. Improving the Arabic pronunciation dictionary for phone and word recognition with linguistically-based pronunciation rules. In *Proceedings of Human Language Technologies: The 2009 Annual Conference of the North American Chapter of the Association for Computational Linguistics*, pages 397–405, Boulder, Colorado. Association for Computational Linguistics.

Rich Caruana. 1997. Multitask learning. *Machine learning*, 28(1):41–75.

Colin Cherry, George Foster, Ankur Bapna, Orhan Firat, and Wolfgang Macherey. 2018. Revisiting character-based neural machine translation with capacity and compression. In *Proceedings of the 2018 Conference on Empirical Methods in Natural Language Processing*, pages 4295–4305, Brussels, Belgium. Association for Computational Linguistics.

Christos Christodouloupoulos and Mark Steedman. 2015. A massively parallel corpus: the bible in 100 languages. *Language resources and evaluation*, 49(2):375–395.

Fathi Debili, Hadhémi Achour, and Emna Souissi. 2002. La langue arabe et l'ordinateur: de l'étiquetage grammatical à la voyellation automatique. *Correspondances*, 71:10–28.

Mona Diab, Mahmoud Ghoneim, and Nizar Habash. 2007. Arabic diacritization in the context of statistical machine translation. In *Proceedings of MT-Summit*. Citeseer.

Mona Diab, Nizar Habash, Owen Rambow, and Ryan Roth. 2013. Ldc arabic treebanks and associated corpora: Data divisions manual. *arXiv preprint arXiv:1309.5652*.

Daxiang Dong, Hua Wu, Wei He, Dianhai Yu, and Haifeng Wang. 2015. Multi-task learning for multiple language translation. In *Proceedings of the 53rd Annual Meeting of the Association for Computational Linguistics and the 7th International Joint Conference on Natural Language Processing (Volume 1: Long Papers)*, pages 1723–1732, Beijing, China. Association for Computational Linguistics.

David M. Eberhard, Gary F. Simons, and Charles D. Fennig, editors. 2021. *Ethnologue: Languages of the World*, 24th edition. SIL International.

Ahmed El-Kishky, Vishrav Chaudhary, Francisco Guzmán, and Philipp Koehn. 2020. CCAligned: A massive collection of cross-lingual web-document pairs. In *Proceedings of the 2020 Conference on Empirical Methods in Natural Language Processing (EMNLP 2020)*.

Ali Fadel, Ibraheem Tuffaha, Mahmoud Al-Ayyoub, et al. 2019. Arabic text diacritization using deep neural networks. In *2019 2nd international conference on computer applications & information security (ICCAIS)*, pages 1–7. IEEE.

Nizar Habash, Anas Shahrour, and Muhamed Al-Khalil. 2016. Exploiting Arabic diacritization for high quality automatic annotation. In *Proceedings of the Tenth International Conference on Language Resources and Evaluation (LREC'16)*, pages 4298–4304, Portorož, Slovenia. European Language Resources Association (ELRA).

Osama Hamed. 2019. Automatic diacritization as prerequisite towards the automatic generation of Arabic lexical recognition tests. In *Proceedings of the 3rd International Conference on Natural Language and Speech Processing*, pages 100–106, Trento, Italy. Association for Computational Linguistics.

Osama Hamed and Torsten Zesch. 2018. The role of diacritics in increasing the difficulty of Arabic lexical recognition tests. In *Proceedings of the 7th workshop on NLP for Computer Assisted Language Learning*, pages 23–31, Stockholm, Sweden. LiU Electronic Press.

Huda Khayrallah and Philipp Koehn. 2018. On the impact of various types of noise on neural machine translation. In *Proceedings of the 2nd Workshop on Neural Machine Translation and Generation*, pages 74–83, Melbourne, Australia. Association for Computational Linguistics.

Taku Kudo and John Richardson. 2018. SentencePiece: A simple and language independent subword tokenizer and detokenizer for neural text processing. In *Proceedings of the 2018 Conference on Empirical Methods in Natural Language Processing: System Demonstrations*, pages 66–71, Brussels, Belgium. Association for Computational Linguistics.

Jason Lee, Kyunghyun Cho, and Thomas Hofmann. 2017. Fully character-level neural machine translation without explicit segmentation. *Transactions* of the Association for Computational Linguistics, 5:365–378.

Jakub Náplava, Milan Straka, and Jana Straková. 2021. Diacritics Restoration using BERT with Analysis on Czech language. *The Prague Bulletin of Mathematical Linguistics*, 116:27–42.

Graham Neubig and Junjie Hu. 2018. Rapid adaptation of neural machine translation to new languages. In *Proceedings of the 2018 Conference on Empirical Methods in Natural Language Processing*, pages 875–880, Brussels, Belgium. Association for Computational Linguistics.

Toan Q. Nguyen and David Chiang. 2017. Transfer learning across low-resource, related languages for neural machine translation. In *Proceedings of the Eighth International Joint Conference on Natural Language Processing (Volume 2: Short Papers)*, pages 296–301, Taipei, Taiwan. Asian Federation of Natural Language Processing.

Myle Ott, Sergey Edunov, Alexei Baevski, Angela Fan, Sam Gross, Nathan Ng, David Grangier, and Michael Auli. 2019. fairseq: A fast, extensible toolkit for sequence modeling. In *Proceedings of the 2019 Conference of the North American Chapter of the Association for Computational Linguistics (Demonstrations)*, pages 48–53, Minneapolis, Minnesota. Association for Computational Linguistics.

Han Qin, Guimin Chen, Yuanhe Tian, and Yan Song. 2021. Improving Arabic diacritization with regularized decoding and adversarial training. In *Proceedings of the 59th Annual Meeting of the Association for Computational Linguistics and the 11th International Joint Conference on Natural Language Processing (Volume 2: Short Papers)*, pages 534–542, Online. Association for Computational Linguistics.

Holger Schwenk, Vishrav Chaudhary, Shuo Sun, Hongyu Gong, and Francisco Guzmán. 2019. Wikimatrix: Mining 135m parallel sentences in 1620 language pairs from wikipedia. *CoRR*, abs/1907.05791.

Rico Sennrich, Barry Haddow, and Alexandra Birch. 2016. Neural machine translation of rare words with subword units. In *Proceedings of the 54th Annual Meeting of the Association for Computational Linguistics (Volume 1: Long Papers)*, pages 1715–1725, Berlin, Germany. Association for Computational Linguistics.

Yan Song, Tong Zhang, Yonggang Wang, and Kai-Fu Lee. 2021. Zen 2.0: Continue training and adaption for n-gram enhanced text encoders. *arXiv preprint arXiv:2105.01279*.

Tony Sun, Andrew Gaut, Shirlyn Tang, Yuxin Huang, Mai ElSherief, Jieyu Zhao, Diba Mirza, Elizabeth Belding, Kai-Wei Chang, and William Yang Wang. 2019. Mitigating gender bias in natural language processing: Literature review. In *Proceedings of the 57th Annual Meeting of the Association for Computational Linguistics*, pages 1630–1640, Florence, Italy. Association for Computational Linguistics.

Brian Thompson and Matt Post. 2020a. Automatic machine translation evaluation in many languages via zero-shot paraphrasing. In *Proceedings of the 2020 Conference on Empirical Methods in Natural Language Processing (EMNLP)*, pages 90–121, Online. Association for Computational Linguistics.

Brian Thompson and Matt Post. 2020b. Paraphrase generation as zero-shot multilingual translation: Disentangling semantic similarity from lexical and syntactic diversity. In *Proceedings of the Fifth Conference on Machine Translation*, pages 561–570, Online. Association for Computational Linguistics.

Jörg Tiedemann and Yves Scherrer. 2019. Measuring semantic abstraction of multilingual NMT with paraphrase recognition and generation tasks. In *Proceedings of the 3rd Workshop on Evaluating Vector Space Representations for NLP*, pages 35–42, Minneapolis, USA. Association for Computational Linguistics.

Ashish Vaswani, Noam Shazeer, Niki Parmar, Jakob Uszkoreit, Llion Jones, Aidan N Gomez, Ł ukasz Kaiser, and Illia Polosukhin. 2017. Attention is all you need. In I. Guyon, U. V. Luxburg, S. Bengio, H. Wallach, R. Fergus, S. Vishwanathan, and R. Garnett, editors, *Advances in Neural Information Processing Systems 30*, pages 5998–6008. Curran Associates, Inc.

Dimitra Vergyri and Katrin Kirchhoff. 2004. Automatic diacritization of Arabic for acoustic modeling in speech recognition. In *Proceedings of the Workshop on Computational Approaches to Arabic Script-based Languages*, pages 66–73, Geneva, Switzerland. COLING.

Nasser Zalmout and Nizar Habash. 2017. Don't throw those morphological analyzers away just yet: Neural morphological disambiguation for Arabic. In *Proceedings of the 2017 Conference on Empirical Methods in Natural Language Processing*, pages 704–713, Copenhagen, Denmark. Association for Computational Linguistics.

Nasser Zalmout and Nizar Habash. 2019. Adversarial multitask learning for joint multi-feature and multi-dialect morphological modeling. In *Proceedings of the 57th Annual Meeting of the Association for Computational Linguistics*, pages 1775–1786, Florence, Italy. Association for Computational Linguistics.

Nasser Zalmout and Nizar Habash. 2020. Joint diacritization, lemmatization, normalization, and fine-grained morphological tagging. In *Proceedings of the 58th Annual Meeting of the Association for Computational Linguistics*, pages 8297–8307, Online. Association for Computational Linguistics.

Taha Zerrouki and Amar Balla. 2017. Tashkeela: Novel corpus of arabic vocalized texts, data for auto-diacritization systems. *Data in brief*, 11:147.

Michał Ziemski, Marcin Junczys-Dowmunt, and Bruno Pouliquen. 2016. The United Nations parallel corpus v1.0. In *Proceedings of the Tenth International Conference on Language Resources and Evaluation (LREC'16)*, pages 3530–3534, Portorož, Slovenia. European Language Resources Association (ELRA).

Barret Zoph, Deniz Yuret, Jonathan May, and Kevin Knight. 2016. Transfer learning for low-resource neural machine translation. In *Proceedings of the 2016 Conference on Empirical Methods in Natural Language Processing*, pages 1568–1575, Austin, Texas. Association for Computational Linguistics.

Simultaneous Neural Machine Translation with Prefix Alignment

Yasumasa Kano and **Katsuhito Sudoh** and **Satoshi Nakamura**
Nara Institute of Science and Technology, Japan
kano.yasumasa.kw4@is.naist.jp

Abstract

Simultaneous translation is a task that requires starting translation before the speaker has finished speaking, so we face a trade-off between latency and accuracy. In this work, we focus on prefix-to-prefix translation and propose a method to extract alignment between bilingual prefix pairs. We use the alignment to segment a streaming input and fine-tune a translation model. The proposed method demonstrated higher BLEU than those of baselines in low latency ranges in our experiments on the IWSLT simultaneous translation benchmark.

1 Introduction

Simultaneous machine translation (SimulMT) is a task to start outputting translation before observing the whole input sentence. SimulMT is more difficult than the translation with the whole input sentence because it cannot use the latter part of the sentence as context. SimulMT has to decide whether to wait for more input or to output partial translation using the input so far, in real-time. The translation quality should become better if we can use longer inputs and *vice versa*. We have to handle such a trade-off between the quality and latency of the translation by decision *policies* to choose the next action between *read* (waiting for the next input segment) and *write* (outputting a translation segment) for a given input-output history (Gu et al., 2017). Neural Machine Translation (NMT) models used for SimulMT can be roughly categorized into *policy-dependent* and *policy-independent*.

A policy-dependent model is trained with the constraints given by the policy, in order to translate an input prefix into an output prefix. Ma et al. (2019) proposed a simple method with a fixed policy called *wait-k*, where the NMT first takes k read actions followed by alternating write and read actions until the end of the translation output. Arivazhagan et al. (2019) proposed a joint training framework for flexible policies and the corresponding NMT model using a latency-augmented loss function and Monotonic Infinite Lookback (MILk) attention.

In contrast, a policy-independent model is a standard NMT model to translate the whole input into the whole output and used for SimulMT along with a given policy in the inference. We can share one NMT model for different policies, so the quality-latency trade-off can be controlled easily. Dalvi et al. (2018) achieved some latency reduction with a small loss in BLEU by the use of a fixed policy called *STATIC-RW*. Ma et al. (2019) also applied their *wait-k* policy using a sentence-based NMT model, called *test-time wait-k*. Zhang et al. (2020) proposed a flexible policy to predict segment boundaries in an input. Once a boundary is found, the segment is translated using a sentence-based NMT model. The model based on their segmentation demonstrated better results in quality-latency trade-off than those using wait-k and MILk in Chinese-to-English SimulMT. Kano et al. (2021) proposed another flexible policy using simple rules with syntactic constituent label prediction and showed better performance than MU-based SimulMT in English-to-Japanese.

One problem in the use of a policy-independent model in SimulMT is the difference between training and inference conditions; the NMT model is trained in the sentence level but is used to translate the prefix of a sentence in inference. This causes unexpectedly long translation and hurts the quality of SimulMT (Kano et al., 2021). To mitigate the problem, we propose a method for data augmentation to fine-tune a policy-independent NMT model to the problem of prefix-to-prefix translation, called *Bilingual Prefix Alignment*. We use a pre-trained sentence-based NMT model to align source language prefix and target language prefix of sentences in the training corpus and collect prefix translation pairs. The proposed method demonstrated higher

Proceedings of the 19th International Conference on Spoken Language Translation (IWSLT 2022), pages 22 - 31
May 26-27, 2022 ©2022 Association for Computational Linguistics

BLEU than baselines in low latency ranges, in our SimulMT experiments using IWSLT English-to-Japanese and English-to-German datasets.

2 Related Work

The problem of SimulMT has been tackled for a decade. In early attempts using statistical machine translation, decision policies were combined with the beam search decoding (Sankaran et al., 2010; Bangalore et al., 2012). Fujita et al. (2013) used phrase reordering probabilities used in phrase-based statistical machine translation for their decision policy. In later years, feature-based learned policies were proposed. Oda et al. (2014) proposed a feature-based policy optimization to maximize BLEU. Syntactic features also successfully used for the policies (Rangarajan Sridhar et al., 2013; Oda et al., 2015).

Recently, most SimulMT studies are based on NMT, and such methods can output more fluent translation than before. Among NMT-based SimulMT studies, one major approach is to train an NMT model optimized for given or jointly-learned policies. Wait-k (Ma et al., 2019) is a very simple fixed policy that waits for *k* input tokens first. Zheng et al. (2020) proposed an ensemble of different wait-*k*-based models for adaptive SimulMT. To make the policies more flexible, latency-augmented loss functions are used to jointly optimize accuracy and latency in the training of the SimulMT model (Raffel et al., 2017; Arivazhagan et al., 2019; Ma et al., 2020b).

Another approach employs such policies only in inference, using a standard sentence-based NMT model. Fixed policies can be applied to this approach easily (Dalvi et al., 2018; Ma et al., 2019). Cho and Esipova (2016) proposed greedy decoding with policies conditioned by the decoder's prediction, called *Wait-If-Worse* and *Wait-If-Diff*. Kano et al. (2021) proposed a rule-based policy using incremental prediction of the syntactic constituents. To learn segmentation policies from the bilingual corpus, reinforcement learning-based methods were proposed (Grissom II et al., 2014; Satija and Pineau, 2016; Gu et al., 2017; Alinejad et al., 2018). It is a straightforward way to optimize latency and accuracy jointly, but its training process is relatively complex and sometimes unstable. Instead of the joint learning of a segmentation policy and policy-dependent model, Zheng et al. (2019) proposed a method to find oracle read and write actions using a pre-trained NMT model. Zhang et al. (2020) also used a pre-trained NMT model to find segments called Meaningful Units (MUs).

This work is motivated by Dalvi et al. (2018) and Zhang et al. (2020) and extends them with Bilingual Prefix Alignment using a pre-trained NMT model. Our method finds appropriate segment boundaries based on the similarity between reference and translation hypothesis for given prefix segments in a different way from Zhang et al. (2020). We also fine-tune the pre-trained NMT model using the bilingual prefix pairs, which is a more sophisticated way than Dalvi et al. (2018)[1].

3 Simultaneous Machine Translation

A sentence-level NMT is formulated as follows, letting $\boldsymbol{x} = x_1, x_2, ..., x_n$ be an input sentence and $\boldsymbol{y} = y_1, y_2, ..., y_m$ be its translation:

$$p(\boldsymbol{y}|\boldsymbol{x}) = \prod_{t=1}^{m} P(y_t|\boldsymbol{x}, \boldsymbol{y}_{<t}). \tag{1}$$

SimulMT takes a prefix of the input for its incremental decoding, formulated as follows:

$$p(\boldsymbol{y}|\boldsymbol{x}) = \prod_{t=1}^{m} P(y_t|\boldsymbol{x}_{\leq g(t)}, \boldsymbol{y}_{<t}), \tag{2}$$

where $g(t)$ is a monotonic non-decreasing function that represents the number of input tokens read by the t-th step so that $\boldsymbol{x}_{\leq g(t)}$ means an input prefix given so far, and $\boldsymbol{y}_{<t}$ is a prefix translation by the previous step. This means that we can obtain a pair of a input prefix and the corresponding prefix translation $(\boldsymbol{x}_{\leq g(t)}, \boldsymbol{y}_{\leq t})$ at t-th step.

In this work, we use chunk-based incremental decoding (Kano et al., 2021), in which we translate an input prefix from the beginning. It is similar to an approach called *re-translation* (Niehues et al., 2016; Arivazhagan et al., 2020), but we force the decoder to follow already translated output prefixes in the same way as the teacher forcing in NMT training.

4 Proposed Method

Figure 1 shows the whole translation process of the proposed method at the inference step. We propose Prefix Alignment for training a segmentation policy and fine-tuning a sentence-level NMT model for the policy-dependent SimulMT. Suppose we have a

[1]Note that the authors reported they obtained no performance improvement by the fine-tuning.

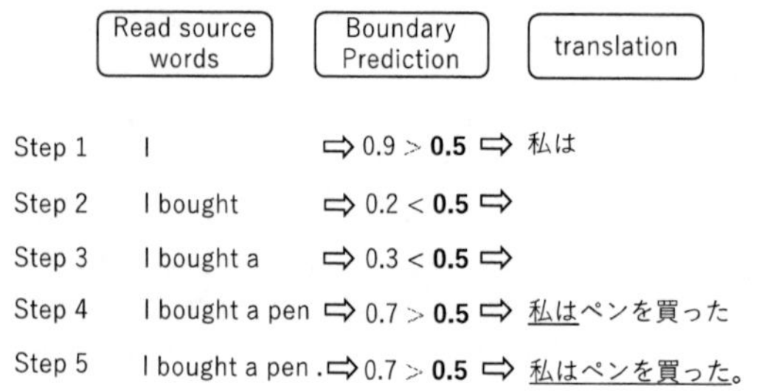

Figure 1: The translation process of the proposed method from English to Japanese. The threshold of boundary probability is 0.5 in this case. The underlined part is the forced output prefix.

pre-trained NMT model and a bilingual corpus for fine-tuning the model for SimulMT. The proposed method consists of the following steps:

1. Collect prefix translation pairs using the pre-trained model
2. Find reference prefixes corresponding to the prefix translation pairs
3. Train a boundary prediction model
4. Fine-tune the NMT model

Their details are described in the following subsections.

4.1 Collecting Prefix Translation Pairs

In this step, we collect *prefix translation pairs* from the bilingual corpus using the pre-trained NMT model. For every source language sentence in the bilingual corpus, we extract prefix translation pairs using NMT results of the source language sentence, by the following procedure. First, we translate the source language sentence $\boldsymbol{x}$ into the target language sentence $\boldsymbol{y}$ using the NMT model. Then, we translate a prefix of $\boldsymbol{x}$ with one word[2], $\boldsymbol{x}_{|w|\leq 1}$, into a target language prefix $\bar{\boldsymbol{y}}^{(1)}$. Here, if the *longest common prefix* $\bar{\boldsymbol{y}}^{(1)}_{lcp}$ between $\boldsymbol{y}$ and $\bar{\boldsymbol{y}}^{(1)}$ is not empty, we extract the pair $(\boldsymbol{x}_{|w|\leq 1}, \bar{\boldsymbol{y}}^{(1)}_{lcp})$ as a prefix translation pair. We iterate this prefix translation pair extraction with enlarging the prefix length one by one; we translate the i-word prefix $\boldsymbol{x}_{|w|\leq i}$ into $\bar{\boldsymbol{y}}^{(i)}$ and check $\bar{\boldsymbol{y}}^{(i)}_{lcp}$. In the iteration, we may obtain the same longest common prefix with different source language prefixes. We just extract the first appearance and ignore the rest with longer source language prefixes in such cases. Furthermore, once we extract a prefix translation pair $(\boldsymbol{x}_{|w|\leq i}, \bar{\boldsymbol{y}}^{(i)}_{lcp})$, we use the target language prefix $\bar{\boldsymbol{y}}^{(i)}_{lcp}$ as a forced output prefix and applied it to update the sentence-level translation $\boldsymbol{y}$ and to generate prefix translation $\bar{\boldsymbol{y}}^{(j)}$ for $j > i$. This is because the translation for longer prefixes or the whole sentence may change by a beam search when a forced output prefix is given.

Our prefix extraction strategy is different from that by Zhang et al. (2020), in which the whole prefix translation $\bar{\boldsymbol{y}}^{(i)}$ should be a prefix of the sentence-level translation $\boldsymbol{y}$, not taking the longest common prefix as in this work.

Figure 2 shows an example. The first prefix translation ends with a punctuation mark, so Meaningful Unit (Zhang et al., 2020) cannot extract the first prefix as the pair because the mark does not match with the end of prefix of full-sentence translation. In contrast, the proposed method can extract the matched target prefix by ignoring the latter part of the prefix translation. Therefore, the proposed method identifies more boundaries than Meaningful Unit.

Another difference from Meaningful Unit relates to the extraction strategy above. Since the original pre-trained NMT model often generates unnecessary tokens like punctuation marks at prefix boundaries, we fine-tune the pre-trained model using the extracted prefix pairs to avoid such problems.

4.2 Prefix Alignment with References

Since the prefix translations obtained through the process above are NMT results and different from their references in general, we also extract corresponding reference prefixes from the bilingual corpus. We use BERTScore (Zhang* et al., 2020) to find the correspondence between an NMT-based prefix and a reference prefix, varying the length of the reference prefix. We choose the reference prefix that has the largest BERTScore F-measure as the corresponding one to a given NMT-based prefix. Using this correspondence, we can align a source language prefix and its reference counterpart to make bilingual prefix alignment.

4.3 Training a Boundary Predictor

We train a boundary predictor for the chunk-based SimulMT using the extracted source language pre-

[2]Here, we use the word-based prefix length even though we use subwords. Thus, $\boldsymbol{x}_{|w|\leq 1}$ may consists of one or more subwords.

Source Prefix	Source prefix Translation	Full-sentence translation	Extracted Target Prefix	Boundary
I	私は。	私はペン買った。	私は	1
I bought	私は買った。	私はペンを買った。		0
I bought a	私は買った。	私はペンを買った。		0
I bought a pen	私はペンを買った	私はペンを買った。	私はペンを買った	1
I bought a pen .	私はペンを買った。	私はペンを買った。	私はペンを買った。	1

Figure 2: Extract Prefix Alignment

fixes. It is a binary classifier, and its training data consist of pairs of a source language sentence prefix and the boundary label. The label is set to 1 for the prefixes in the extracted prefix translation pairs and 0 for the other possible prefixes of the corresponding source sentence, as shown in Figure 2.

4.4 Fine-Tuning a SimulMT Model

We fine-tune the pre-trained NMT model using the extracted bilingual prefix pairs for our SimulMT model. The model is used to translate an input incrementally in the chunk-based manner as presented in Section 3.

5 Experimental Setup

We conducted experiments on English-to-German (En-De) and English-to-Japanese (En-Ja) simultaneous translation to compare the proposed method with the baselines in the quality-latency trade-off.

5.1 Dataset and Preprocessing

In En-De translation, we used WMT 2014 training set (4.5 M sentence pairs) for pre-training and IWSLT 2017 training set (206 K sentence pairs) for fine-tuning. We used IWSLT dev2010, tst2010, tst2011 and tst2012 (5,589 sentence pairs in total) for the development dataset. We used 1,080 sentence pairs from IWSLT tst2015 for the evaluation.

In En-Ja translation, we used WMT 2020 (17.9 M sentence pairs) for pre-training and IWSLT 2017 (223 K sentence pairs) for fine-tuning dataset. We used IWSLT dev2010, tst2011, tst2012, and tst2013 (5,312 sentence pairs in total) for development dataset. We used 1,442 sentence pairs from IWSLT dev2021 for the evaluation.

Prefix translation pairs are collected only from the IWSLT dataset. We tokenized Japanese sentences using MeCab (Kudo, 2005). English and German sentences were tokenized using `tokenizer.perl` in Moses (Koehn et al., 2007). We prepared a shared subword vocabulary with 16 K entries based on Byte Pair Encoding (BPE) (Sennrich et al., 2016) for each language pair.

5.2 Model Settings

We mainly compared the following four methods in the experiments:

Prefix Alignment The proposed method has a hyperparameter to adjust latency, the threshold of boundary probability output by the boundary predictor. We used 0.5 as the default value for the binary classification and tried the following values for further investigation: [0.1, 0.15,..., 0.95], [0.99, 0.991, 0.992,..., 0.999], and [0.9991, 0.9992,..., 0.9999]. We also compared a one look-ahead boundary predictor that took one future word as the input at the cost of the delay in one word (`PA-1`), in addition to a standard (no look-ahead) boundary predictor (`PA-0`).

Meaningful Unit We used the same boundary probability thresholds as in PA. We implemented the refined version of MU-based method to translate with low latency following (Zhang et al., 2020), but did not apply the removal of monotonic translation examples following Kano et al. (2021). We also compared one look-ahead (`MU-1`) and no look-ahead (`MU-0`) boundary predictors.

Incremental Constitutent Label Prediction (`ICLP`) Following Kano et al. (2021), we used a one look-ahead label predictor. We segmented the input sequence based on their rules with the predicted labels `VP` and `S`. The minimum segment length adjusts latency. The range is [1, 2, 3, ..., 29].

`Wait-k` We tried [2, 4, 6, ..., 30] for the hyperparameter *k*.

NMT Settings We trained a standard NMT model (`full-sentence`) using WMT and

IWSLT training dataset. This model was used for MU, PA and ICLP as the pre-trained NMT model.

All the NMT models were based on Transformer-base (Vaswani et al., 2017) implemented with fairseq (Ott et al., 2019). Their hyperparameter settings basically followed the official baseline for IWSLT 2021[3], for both pre-training and fine-tuning. The models were saved on checkpoints in every 5,000 updates for pre-training and every 200 updates for fine-tuning. We applied early stopping with the patience for four checkpoints, based on the loss on the development set. We set the learning rate to 0.0007, minibatch size to 4,096 with the parameter update frequency of 4. We applied a chunk-based beam search for the methods other than wait-k, in which the low-scored hypotheses out of the specified beam size were eliminated at the end of the chunk. We used greedy-decoding for wait-k, due to the nature of its model.

Boundary Predictor The boundary predictors for the chunk-based methods were implemented similarly using BERT (Devlin et al., 2019) with a pre-trained model `bert-base-uncased` and the corresponding subword tokenizer from Huggingface transformers (Wolf et al., 2020). We set the learning rate to 5e-5 and the batch size to 512 instances. The models were saved at every epoch, and we applied early stopping with patience for three epochs based on the loss on the development set.

5.3 Evaluation Metrics

We used BLEU (Papineni et al., 2002) and Average Lagging (AL) (Ma et al., 2019) for our quality and latency evaluation metrics. They were calculated using SimulEval (Ma et al., 2020a) and drawn in scatterplots to show the quality-latency trade-off.

6 Results

6.1 English-to-German

Figure 3 shows the BLEU and AL results in English-to-German simultaneous translation. The proposed method (PA-0 and PA-1) showed best performance among the compared methods. On the other hand, the other chunk-based SimulMT (MU-0, MU-1, and ICLP) did not outperform Wait-k. We can also see the look-ahead boundary prediction did not improve BLEU both for PA and MU but increased AL.

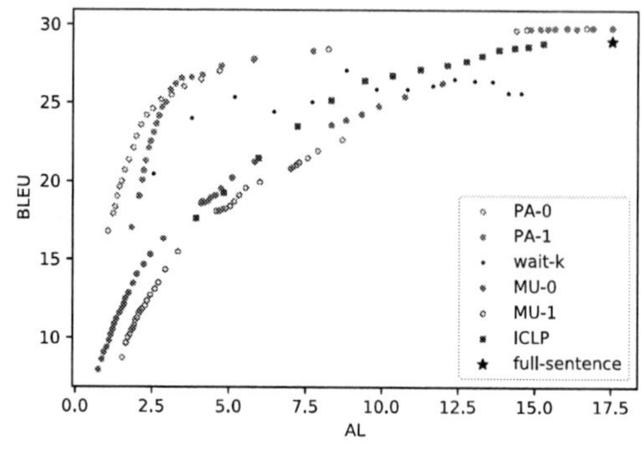

Figure 3: BLEU and Average Lagging (En-De)

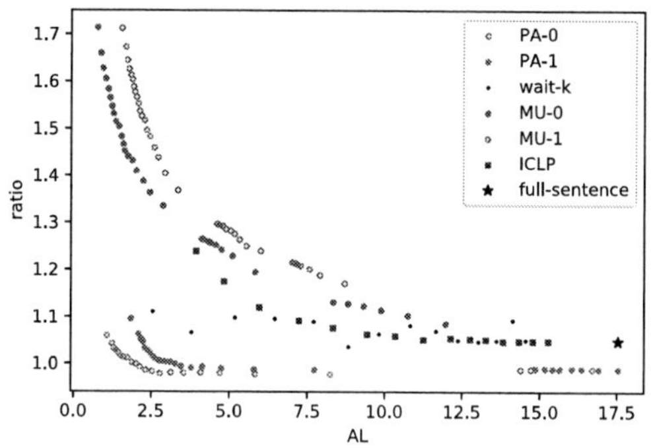

Figure 4: Length ratio and Average Lagging (En-De)

Figure 4 shows the results in the length ratio between a translation result and its reference. The proposed method demonstrated better results in the translation length than the other methods. The other chunk-based SimulMT methods generated much longer translation results than the references and resulted in a large drop in BLEU due to the brevity penalty.

6.2 English-to-Japanese

Figure 5 shows the BLEU and AL results in English-to-Japanese simultaneous translation. This shows a large difference from the results in English-to-German; the proposed method outperformed the baselines in very small latency ranges around AL of 2, but showed worse BLEU in the large latency ranges.

Figure 6 shows the results in the length ratio. The proposed method generated shorter transla-

[3] https://github.com/pytorch/fairseq/blob/master/examples/simultaneous_translation/docs/enja-waitk.md, https://github.com/pytorch/fairseq/issues/346

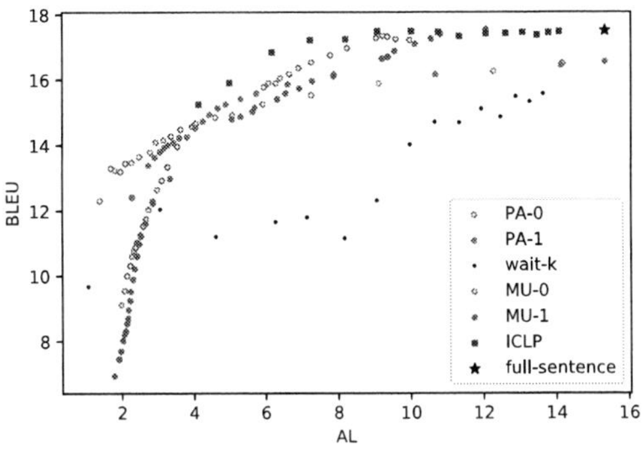

Figure 5: BLEU and Average Lagging (En-Ja)

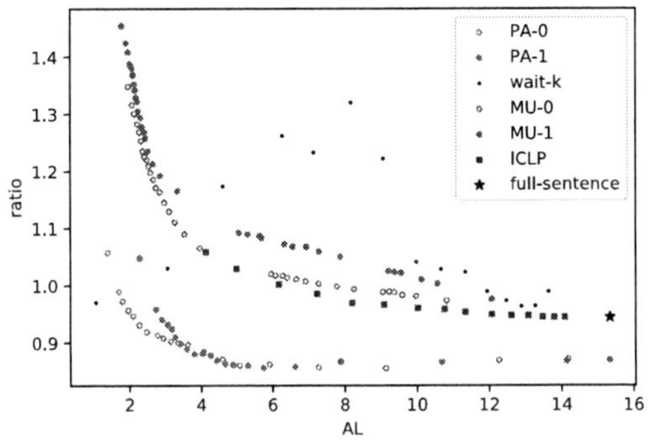

Figure 6: Length ratio and Average Lagging (En-Ja)

tion results especially with the large latency ranges, even though the other methods resulted in a better length ratio of around 1.0. The difference between the two language directions would come from the length issue; the full-sentence NMT resulted in the length ratio slightly larger than 1.0 in English-to-German and around 0.9 in English-to-Japanese. The proposed method encouraged to shorten the translation length in general so that it did not contribute to the BLEU improvement in English-to-Japanese.

7 Analysis

7.1 Effect of PA-based NMT fine-tuning

For the detailed analyses, we investigated the performance of the chunk-based SimulMT without the fine-tuning using the bilingual prefix pairs. Here, only the boundary predictor was used to segment the input for the chunk-based SimulMT. Figures 7, 8, 9, and 10 show the results by the proposed method with the pre-trained NMT model (`PAoff-0` and `PAoff-1`). They clearly show

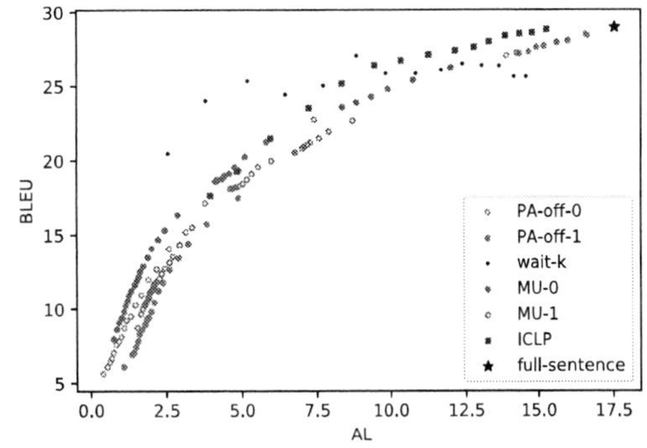

Figure 7: BLEU and Average Lagging (En-De) without PA-based NMT fine-tuning

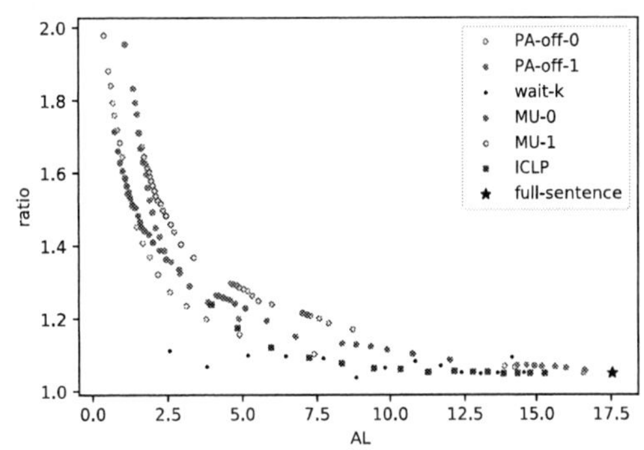

Figure 8: Length ratio and Average Lagging (En-De) without PA-based NMT fine-tuning

the proposed method does not work well without fine-tuning the NMT model; it resulted in a longer translation length so BLEU decreased due to the brevity penalty. These results suggest the segmentation policy in the chunk-based SimulMT should match the prefix translation models because a full-sentence translation model often generates a too-long translation result for a short prefix input.

7.2 Length Distribution in training dataset

	En-De	En-Ja
# Source prefixes	1,874,909	1,059,865
# Words in sentences	4,228,604	4,593,194

Table 1: Statistics of the training data

We investigated the length issue on the training data. Table 1 shows statistics of the IWSLT training set, in the number of source language prefixes extracted for the fine-tuning of the SimulMT models

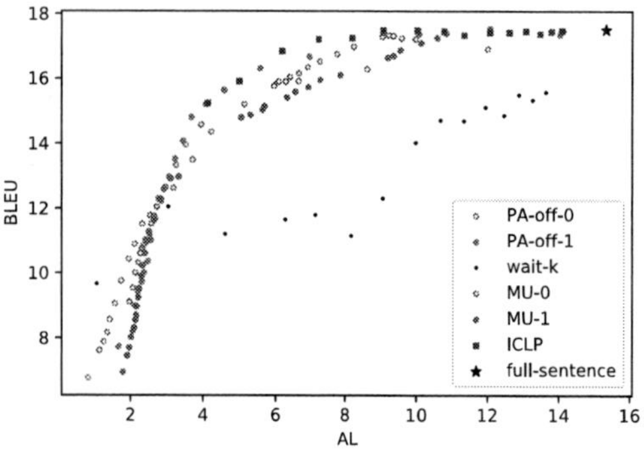

Figure 9: BLEU and Average Lagging (En-Ja) without PA-based NMT fine-tuning

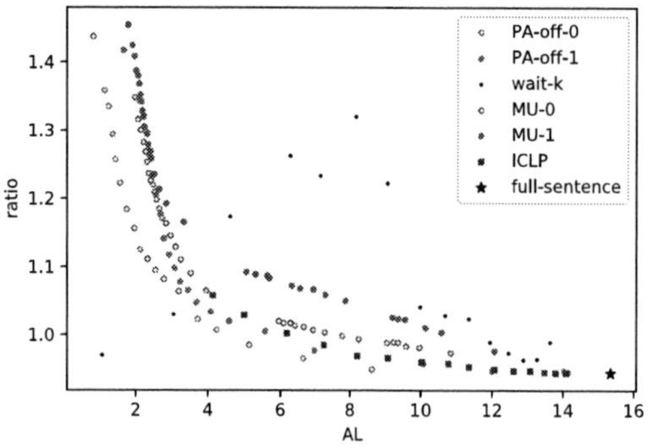

Figure 10: Length ratio and Average Lagging (En-Ja) without PA-based NMT fine-tuning

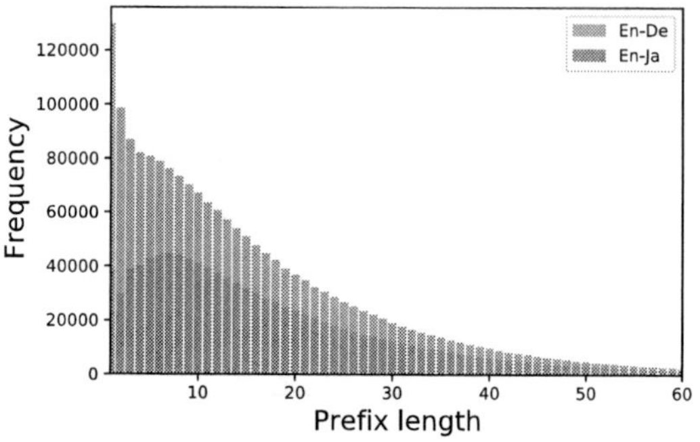

Figure 11: Source prefix length distribution in the IWSLT training data

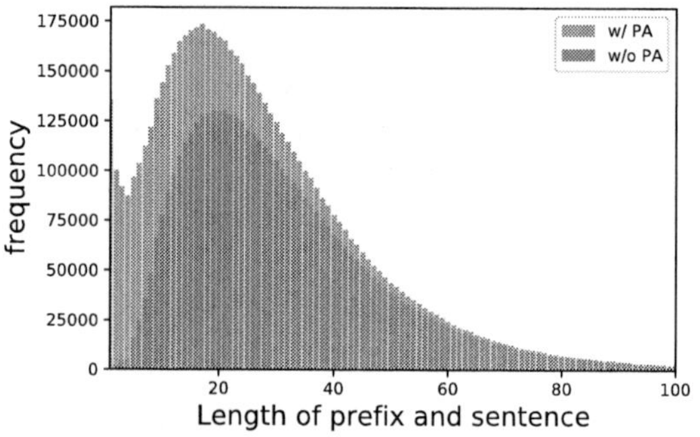

Figure 12: Source sentence length distribution in the training data (En-De)

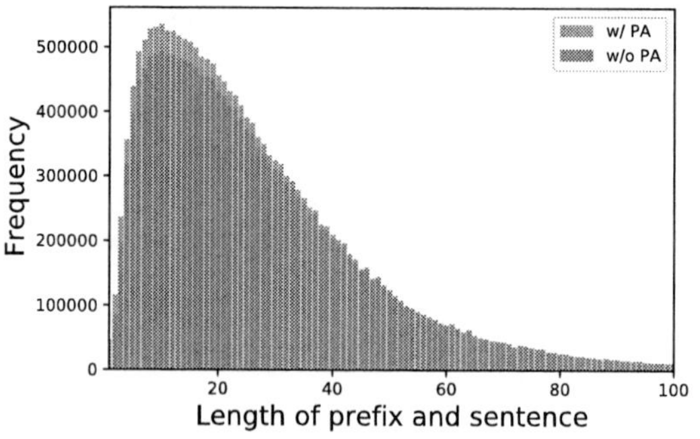

Figure 13: Source sentence length distribution in the training data (En-Ja)

and the number of words in the whole sentences.

Even though the number of words is almost similar, the number of prefixes is largely different; that in En-De is almost two times larger than that in En-Ja. This is because of the large word order difference between English and Japanese, compared to that between English and German. The word order difference should cause poor prefix matches in the prefix translation pair extraction, so just a few short prefix pairs are found. Figure 11 shows the source prefix length distribution in the IWSLT training data. The peak of the En-Ja distribution is to the right of that of En-De distribution because of this word order difference. The number of the En-De shortest prefixes is more than three times larger than that of En-Ja ones. This large number of short prefixes contributed to the improvement of En-De SimulMT.

Figures 12 and 13 show the change of length distribution of the training data; blue bars represent the original distribution on the whole training data (WMT and IWSLT), and red bars represent that on the training data augmented by the additional prefix pairs. The change in English-to-German was much larger than that in English-to-Japanese, because of the large difference in the number of bilingual prefix pairs. These findings suggest the proposed method had a larger effect in English-to-German than English-to-Japanese.

8 Conclusion

We proposed a method to train the neural SimulMT model by extracting bilingual prefix pairs by Prefix Alignment. The proposed method outperformed the baselines in quality-latency trade-off in English-to-German simultaneous translation but showed mixed results in English-to-Japanese. We investigated the results in detail and found the difference in the translation length made a large effect on the results, caused by the performance of the sentence-level NMT model and the word order difference.

In future work, we extend the method to work for language pairs with the large word order differences such as English-Japanese, in the wide range of AL. The proposed method to extract source prefixes can be adapted to speech input. We applied this method to Speech-to-text simultaneous machine translation system submitted to the IWSLT 2022 Evaluation Campaign (Anastasopoulos et al., 2022; Fukuda et al., 2022).

Acknowledgements

Part of this work was supported by JSPS KAKENHI Grant Numbers JP21H05054 and JP21H03500.

References

Ashkan Alinejad, Maryam Siahbani, and Anoop Sarkar. 2018. Prediction improves simultaneous neural machine translation. In *Proceedings of the 2018 Conference on Empirical Methods in Natural Language Processing*, pages 3022–3027, Brussels, Belgium. Association for Computational Linguistics.

Antonios Anastasopoulos, Luisa Bentivogli, Marcely Z. Boito, Ondřej Bojar, Roldano Cattoni, Anna Currey, Georgiana Dinu, Kevin Duh, Maha Elbayad, Marcello Federico, Christian Federmann, Hongyu Gong, Roman Grundkiewicz, Barry Haddow, Benjamin Hsu, Dávid Javorský, Věra Kloudová, Surafel M. Lakew, Xutai Ma, Prashant Mathur, Paul McNamee, Kenton Murray, Maria Nădejde, Satoshi Nakamura, Matteo Negri, Jan Niehues, Xing Niu, Juan Pino, Elizabeth Salesky, Jiatong Shi, Sebastian Stüker, Katsuhito Sudoh, Marco Turchi, Yogesh Virkar, Alex Waibel, Changhan Wang, and Shinji Watanabe. 2022. FINDINGS OF THE IWSLT 2022 EVALUATION CAMPAIGN. In *Proceedings of the 19th International Conference on Spoken Language Translation (IWSLT 2022)*, Dublin, Ireland. Association for Computational Linguistics.

Naveen Arivazhagan, Colin Cherry, Wolfgang Macherey, Chung-Cheng Chiu, Semih Yavuz, Ruoming Pang, Wei Li, and Colin Raffel. 2019. Monotonic infinite lookback attention for simultaneous machine translation. In *Proceedings of the 57th Annual Meeting of the Association for Computational Linguistics*, pages 1313–1323, Florence, Italy. Association for Computational Linguistics.

Naveen Arivazhagan, Colin Cherry, I Te, Wolfgang Macherey, Pallavi Baljekar, and George Foster. 2020. Re-Translation Strategies for Long Form, Simultaneous, Spoken Language Translation. In *ICASSP 2020 - 2020 IEEE International Conference on Acoustics, Speech and Signal Processing (ICASSP)*, pages 7919–7923.

Srinivas Bangalore, Vivek Kumar Rangarajan Sridhar, Prakash Kolan, Ladan Golipour, and Aura Jimenez. 2012. Real-time incremental speech-to-speech translation of dialogs. In *Proceedings of the 2012 Conference of the North American Chapter of the Association for Computational Linguistics: Human Language Technologies*, pages 437–445, Montréal, Canada. Association for Computational Linguistics.

Kyunghyun Cho and Masha Esipova. 2016. Can neural machine translation do simultaneous translation? *arXiv preprint arXiv:1606.02012*.

Fahim Dalvi, Nadir Durrani, Hassan Sajjad, and Stephan Vogel. 2018. Incremental decoding and training methods for simultaneous translation in neural machine translation. In *Proceedings of the 2018 Conference of the North American Chapter of the Association for Computational Linguistics: Human Language Technologies, Volume 2 (Short Papers)*, pages 493–499, New Orleans, Louisiana. Association for Computational Linguistics.

Jacob Devlin, Ming-Wei Chang, Kenton Lee, and Kristina Toutanova. 2019. BERT: Pre-training of deep bidirectional transformers for language understanding. In *Proceedings of the 2019 Conference of the North American Chapter of the Association for Computational Linguistics: Human Language Technologies, Volume 1 (Long and Short Papers)*, pages 4171–4186, Minneapolis, Minnesota. Association for Computational Linguistics.

Tomoki Fujita, Graham Neubig, Sakriani Sakti, Tomoki Toda, and Satoshi Nakamura. 2013. Simple, Lexicalized Choice of Translation Timing for Simultaneous Speech Translation. In *Proc. Interspeech 2013*, pages 3487–3491.

Ryo Fukuda, Yuka Ko, Yasumasa Kano, Kosuke Doi, Hirotaka Tokuyama, Sakriani Sakti, Katsuhito Sudoh, and Satoshi Nakamura. 2022. NAIST Simultaneous Speech-to-Text Translation System for IWSLT 2022. In *Proceedings of the 19th International Conference on Spoken Language Translation (IWSLT 2022)*, Dublin, Ireland. Association for Computational Linguistics.

Alvin Grissom II, He He, Jordan Boyd-Graber, John Morgan, and Hal Daumé III. 2014. Don't until the final verb wait: Reinforcement learning for simultaneous machine translation. In *Proceedings of the 2014 Conference on Empirical Methods in Natural Language Processing (EMNLP)*, pages 1342–1352, Doha, Qatar. Association for Computational Linguistics.

Jiatao Gu, Graham Neubig, Kyunghyun Cho, and Victor O.K. Li. 2017. Learning to translate in real-time with neural machine translation. In *Proceedings of the 15th Conference of the European Chapter of the Association for Computational Linguistics: Volume 1, Long Papers*, pages 1053–1062, Valencia, Spain. Association for Computational Linguistics.

Yasumasa Kano, Katsuhito Sudoh, and Satoshi Nakamura. 2021. Simultaneous neural machine translation with constituent label prediction. In *Proceedings of the Sixth Conference on Machine Translation*, pages 1124–1134, Online. Association for Computational Linguistics.

Philipp Koehn, Hieu Hoang, Alexandra Birch, Chris Callison-Burch, Marcello Federico, Nicola Bertoldi, Brooke Cowan, Wade Shen, Christine Moran, Richard Zens, Chris Dyer, Ondřej Bojar, Alexandra Constantin, and Evan Herbst. 2007. Moses: Open source toolkit for statistical machine translation. In *Proceedings of the 45th Annual Meeting of the Association for Computational Linguistics Companion Volume Proceedings of the Demo and Poster Sessions*, pages 177–180, Prague, Czech Republic. Association for Computational Linguistics.

Taku Kudo. 2005. Mecab : Yet another part-of-speech and morphological analyzer. `http://mecab.sourceforge.net/`.

Mingbo Ma, Liang Huang, Hao Xiong, Renjie Zheng, Kaibo Liu, Baigong Zheng, Chuanqiang Zhang, Zhongjun He, Hairong Liu, Xing Li, Hua Wu, and Haifeng Wang. 2019. STACL: Simultaneous translation with implicit anticipation and controllable latency using prefix-to-prefix framework. In *Proceedings of the 57th Annual Meeting of the Association for Computational Linguistics*, pages 3025–3036, Florence, Italy. Association for Computational Linguistics.

Xutai Ma, Mohammad Javad Dousti, Changhan Wang, Jiatao Gu, and Juan Pino. 2020a. SIMULEVAL: An evaluation toolkit for simultaneous translation. In *Proceedings of the 2020 Conference on Empirical Methods in Natural Language Processing: System Demonstrations*, pages 144–150, Online. Association for Computational Linguistics.

Xutai Ma, Juan Miguel Pino, James Cross, Liezl Puzon, and Jiatao Gu. 2020b. Monotonic Multihead Attention. In *International Conference on Learning Representations*.

Jan Niehues, Thai Son Nguyen, Eunah Cho, Thanh-Le Ha, Kevin Kilgour, Markus Müller, Matthias Sperber, Sebastian Stüker, and Alex Waibel. 2016. Dynamic Transcription for Low-Latency Speech Translation. In *Interspeech 2016*, pages 2513–2517.

Yusuke Oda, Graham Neubig, Sakriani Sakti, Tomoki Toda, and Satoshi Nakamura. 2014. Optimizing segmentation strategies for simultaneous speech translation. In *Proceedings of the 52nd Annual Meeting of the Association for Computational Linguistics (Volume 2: Short Papers)*, pages 551–556, Baltimore, Maryland. Association for Computational Linguistics.

Yusuke Oda, Graham Neubig, Sakriani Sakti, Tomoki Toda, and Satoshi Nakamura. 2015. Syntax-based simultaneous translation through prediction of unseen syntactic constituents. In *Proceedings of the 53rd Annual Meeting of the Association for Computational Linguistics and the 7th International Joint Conference on Natural Language Processing (Volume 1: Long Papers)*, pages 198–207, Beijing, China. Association for Computational Linguistics.

Myle Ott, Sergey Edunov, Alexei Baevski, Angela Fan, Sam Gross, Nathan Ng, David Grangier, and Michael Auli. 2019. fairseq: A fast, extensible toolkit for sequence modeling. In *Proceedings of the 2019 Conference of the North American Chapter of the Association for Computational Linguistics (Demonstrations)*, pages 48–53, Minneapolis, Minnesota. Association for Computational Linguistics.

Kishore Papineni, Salim Roukos, Todd Ward, and Wei-Jing Zhu. 2002. Bleu: a method for automatic evaluation of machine translation. In *Proceedings of the 40th Annual Meeting of the Association for Computational Linguistics*, pages 311–318, Philadelphia, Pennsylvania, USA. Association for Computational Linguistics.

Colin Raffel, Minh-Thang Luong, Peter J. Liu, Ron J. Weiss, and Douglas Eck. 2017. Online and Linear-Time Attention by Enforcing Monotonic Alignments. In *Proceedings of the 34th International Conference on Machine Learning, ICML 2017, Sydney, NSW, Australia, 6-11 August 2017*, volume 70 of *JMLR Workshop and Conference Proceedings*, pages 2837–2846. JMLR.org.

Vivek Kumar Rangarajan Sridhar, John Chen, Srinivas Bangalore, Andrej Ljolje, and Rathinavelu Chengalvarayan. 2013. Segmentation strategies for streaming speech translation. In *Proceedings of the 2013 Conference of the North American Chapter of the Association for Computational Linguistics: Human Lan-*

guage Technologies, pages 230–238, Atlanta, Georgia. Association for Computational Linguistics.

Baskaran Sankaran, Ajeet Grewal, and Anoop Sarkar. 2010. Incremental decoding for phrase-based statistical machine translation. In *Proceedings of the Joint Fifth Workshop on Statistical Machine Translation and MetricsMATR*, pages 216–223, Uppsala, Sweden. Association for Computational Linguistics.

Harsh Satija and Joelle Pineau. 2016. Simultaneous machine translation using deep reinforcement learning. In *Workshops of International Conference on Machine Learning*, page 110–119.

Rico Sennrich, Barry Haddow, and Alexandra Birch. 2016. Neural machine translation of rare words with subword units. In *Proceedings of the 54th Annual Meeting of the Association for Computational Linguistics (Volume 1: Long Papers)*, pages 1715–1725, Berlin, Germany. Association for Computational Linguistics.

Ashish Vaswani, Noam Shazeer, Niki Parmar, Jakob Uszkoreit, Llion Jones, Aidan N Gomez, Ł ukasz Kaiser, and Illia Polosukhin. 2017. Attention is All you Need. In *Advances in Neural Information Processing Systems*, volume 30. Curran Associates, Inc.

Thomas Wolf, Lysandre Debut, Victor Sanh, Julien Chaumond, Clement Delangue, Anthony Moi, Pierric Cistac, Tim Rault, Remi Louf, Morgan Funtowicz, Joe Davison, Sam Shleifer, Patrick von Platen, Clara Ma, Yacine Jernite, Julien Plu, Canwen Xu, Teven Le Scao, Sylvain Gugger, Mariama Drame, Quentin Lhoest, and Alexander Rush. 2020. Transformers: State-of-the-art natural language processing. In *Proceedings of the 2020 Conference on Empirical Methods in Natural Language Processing: System Demonstrations*, pages 38–45, Online. Association for Computational Linguistics.

Ruiqing Zhang, Chuanqiang Zhang, Zhongjun He, Hua Wu, and Haifeng Wang. 2020. Learning adaptive segmentation policy for simultaneous translation. In *Proceedings of the 2020 Conference on Empirical Methods in Natural Language Processing (EMNLP)*, pages 2280–2289, Online. Association for Computational Linguistics.

Tianyi Zhang*, Varsha Kishore*, Felix Wu*, Kilian Q. Weinberger, and Yoav Artzi. 2020. BERTScore: Evaluating Text Generation with BERT. In *International Conference on Learning Representations*.

Baigong Zheng, Kaibo Liu, Renjie Zheng, Mingbo Ma, Hairong Liu, and Liang Huang. 2020. Simultaneous translation policies: From fixed to adaptive. In *Proceedings of the 58th Annual Meeting of the Association for Computational Linguistics*, pages 2847–2853, Online. Association for Computational Linguistics.

Baigong Zheng, Renjie Zheng, Mingbo Ma, and Liang Huang. 2019. Simpler and faster learning of adaptive policies for simultaneous translation. In *Proceedings of the 2019 Conference on Empirical Methods in Natural Language Processing and the 9th International Joint Conference on Natural Language Processing (EMNLP-IJCNLP)*, pages 1349–1354, Hong Kong, China. Association for Computational Linguistics.

Locality-Sensitive Hashing for Long Context Neural Machine Translation

Frithjof Petrick **Jan Rosendahl** **Christian Herold** **Hermann Ney**
Human Language Technology and Pattern Recognition Group
Computer Science Department
RWTH Aachen University
D-52056 Aachen, Germany
surname@i6.informatik.rwth-aachen.de

Abstract

After its introduction, the Transformer architecture (Vaswani et al., 2017) quickly became the gold standard for the task of neural machine translation. A major advantage of the Transformer compared to previous architectures is the faster training speed achieved by complete parallelization across timesteps due to the use of attention over recurrent layers. However, this also leads to one of the biggest problems of the Transformer, namely the quadratic time and memory complexity with respect to the input length. In this work we adapt the locality-sensitive hashing approach of Kitaev et al. (2020) to self-attention in the Transformer, we extended it to cross-attention and apply this memory efficient framework to sentence- and document-level machine translation. Our experiments show that the LSH attention scheme for sentence-level comes at the cost of slightly reduced translation quality. For document-level NMT we are able to include much bigger context sizes than what is possible with the baseline Transformer. However, more context does neither improve translation quality nor improve scores on targeted test suites.

1 Introduction

After its introduction in 2017, the Transformer architecture (Vaswani et al., 2017) quickly became the gold standard for the task of neural machine translation (NMT) (Ott et al., 2018). Furthermore, variants of the Transformer have since been used very successfully for a variety of other tasks such as language modeling (LM) (Irie et al., 2019), natural language understanding (NLU) (Devlin et al., 2019; Liu et al., 2019), speech translation (ST) (Vila et al., 2018), automatic speech recognition (ASR) (Zeyer et al., 2019; Mohamed et al., 2019) and image processing (Parmar et al., 2018).

A major advantage of the Transformer compared to previous architectures is the faster training speed achieved by complete parallelization across timesteps. However, this also leads to one of the biggest problems of the Transformer, namely the quadratic time and memory complexity of attention layers with respect to the sequence length. For sentence-level NMT this is not a big issue as most of the time the length of sequences is relatively short and can be handled efficently, even if subword segmentation is applied (Sennrich et al., 2016; Kudo, 2018). However, this drastically changes when moving towards character-level (Gupta et al., 2019) or document-level (Tiedemann and Scherrer, 2017) NMT. Especially for the latter, speed and memory issues are one of the biggest roadblocks towards 'true' document level systems (Junczys-Dowmunt, 2019). This leads to the situation where most works make do with including just a few sentences as a form of 'local' context information (Tiedemann and Scherrer, 2017; Jean et al., 2017; Bawden et al., 2018) or heavily compressing the document information (Tu et al., 2018; Kuang et al., 2018; Morishita et al., 2021).

More recently research focus has been shifting towards more efficient attention calculation for longer input sentences in several LM and NLU tasks (Tay et al., 2020). Among these works is the approach by Kitaev et al. (2020), in which the authors propose to make the attention matrix sparse by pre-selecting the relevant positions. They report good results on the LM objective while at the same time drastically reducing computational complexity. In this work we take the approach of Kitaev et al. (2020) as a starting point to improve the efficiency of (document-level) NMT systems.

Our contribution is three-fold:

- We adapt the locality-sensitive hashing (LSH) approach of Kitaev et al. (2020) to self-attention in the Transformer NMT framework.[1]

[1]The source code is available at https://github.com/rwth-i6/returnn-experiments/tree/master/2022-lsh-attention.

Proceedings of the 19th International Conference on Spoken Language Translation (IWSLT 2022), pages 32 - 42
May 26-27, 2022 ©2022 Association for Computational Linguistics

- We expand the concept of LSH to encoder-decoder cross-attention and provide insights on how this concept affects the behavior of the system.
- We use this more memory-efficient NMT framework to conduct experiments on document-level NMT with more context information as would be possible with the baseline architecture.

2 Related Work

The problem of quadratic time and memory complexity of the attention framework has received increasing attention since the success of the Transformer architecture (Vaswani et al., 2017).

For ASR, ST and image processing the complexity can be reduced with relative ease by reducing the size of the time dimension with convolutional (Gulati et al., 2020) or pooling layers (Zeyer et al., 2019). Furthermore, it is possible to restrict the attention to a few neighboring positions (Parmar et al., 2018). However, this is not optimal for text input, as neighboring input words do not necessarily have the same strong correlation as neighboring audio frames or image pixels.

Existing work on improving the text processing complexity of the Transformer mainly focuses on the case where all attention inputs come from the same embedding space, e.g. language modeling: Dai et al. (2019) and Rae et al. (2019) utilize a segment-level recurrence mechanism similar to what has been used in recurrent architectures. Wang et al. (2020) project the time dimension of key and value down to a smaller, fixed-size dimension while leaving the queries untouched. Directly altering the attention computation, Child et al. (2019), Sukhbaatar et al. (2019) and Qiu et al. (2020) limit the attention to a local neighborhood or a fixed stride while Zaheer et al. (2020) and Beltagy et al. (2020) combine multiple sparse attention masks. In a more flexible approach, matching positions can be pre-selected using a locality-sensitive hashing function (Kitaev et al., 2020) or clustering (Roy et al., 2021). In the present work, we pick one of the most efficient and best performing approaches up to date, namely the approach by Kitaev et al. (2020) and apply it to the task of machine translation. We confirm that the concepts can work for the self-attention in NMT systems and expand the framework for the case of cross-attention.

Most work related to document-level NMT limit the inter sentence context to few neighboring sentences. The simplest approach which we also follow in the present work, is to concatenate consecutive sentences using a special sentence separator token (Tiedemann and Scherrer, 2017). There exist more sophisticated approaches which utilize separate encoders for the context information (Jean et al., 2017; Bawden et al., 2018) but later work seems to suggest that these approaches do not significantly outperform the simpler concatenation approach (Huo et al., 2020; Lopes et al., 2020).

In the realm of NMT, not so much work exists regarding improving the efficiency of the system and the work that exists mainly focuses on document-level NMT. Morishita et al. (2021) propose to compress the context into a single vector which then can be attended to as an additional token embedding. Tu et al. (2018) and Kuang et al. (2018) utilize a cache that holds context information. Zhang et al. (2020) and Bao et al. (2021) mask out the attention energies between tokens from different sentences, showing that the full context is not necessary to achieve good translation performance. Raganato et al. (2020) and You et al. (2020) replace most attention heads with fixed patterns but only for sentence-level NMT and only for self-attention as they report a severe degradation when doing the same for the cross-attention.

There exist several different ways to implement LSH (Paulevé et al., 2010). The LSH scheme used by Kitaev et al. (2020) and consecutively in this work was proposed by Andoni et al. (2015). LSH has also been successfully applied to efficiently calculate pairwise embedding similarity for information retrieval (Ture et al., 2011; Zhao et al., 2015). Shi and Knight (2017) use LSH to pre-select embeddings in the softmax operation of an NMT system to speed up the decoding process.

3 Locality-sensitive Hashing Attention

At the core of the Transformer architecture is the attention mechanism that compares a sequence of queries $q_1, \dots q_I$ to a sequence of key-value pairs $(k_1, v_1), \dots (k_J, v_J)$ via a soft-lookup $\alpha(j|i) = \alpha(q_i, j, k_1^J)$ and maps them to context vectors

$$c_i := \sum_{j=1}^{J} \alpha(j\,|\,i) v_j.$$

To compute the full sequence of context vectors, $\mathcal{O}(IJ)$ operations are required. In the special case

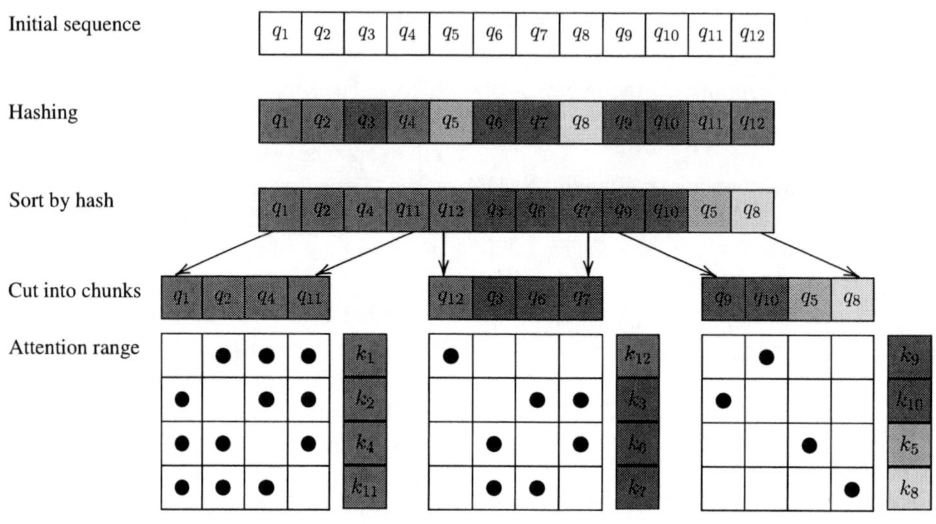

Figure 1: Locality-sensitive hashing for self-attention as presented in Kitaev et al. (2020) with bidirectional context. For self-attention with key and queries shared it holds that $q_i = k_i$. Colors indicate the hash class of the query/key. Note that no position can attend to itself if other attention points are available.

of self-attention, i.e. $I = J$ and $q_i = k_i \; \forall i$, the amount of operations grows quadratically with the sequence length I. Since this can be problematic for long sequences, Kitaev et al. (2020) proposed to use locality-sensitive hashing (LSH) attention.

In the following, we first describe the concept of LSH for self-attention, here we omit the left-to-right masking originally used (Kitaev et al., 2020) and describe the concept for bidirectional self-attention instead. Afterwards, we describe our extension of LSH to cross-attention.

In LSH the context vector for query position i is computed via

$$c_i^{(\text{lsh})} := \sum_{j \in P_i} \hat{\alpha}(j \,|\, i) v_j$$

where a locality-sensitive hashing function h is used to determine

$$P_i := \{j \in \{1, \ldots, J\} \setminus \{i\} \,|\, h(j) = h(i)\}$$

and $\hat{\alpha}$ is normalized over P_i instead of $\{1, \ldots, J\}$.

The hashing function h maps to a small number of classes $\{1, \ldots, n_{\text{hash}}\}$ and is locality-sensitive, i.e. if two vectors are close-by they are likely to get assigned the same hash value. Kitaev et al. (2020) consider the case of self-attention and approximate the set P_i to keep computation efficient. First the original sequence of keys is sorted by their hash value as primary criterion and original sequence order as secondary criterion. The resulting sequence is cut into chunks C_i of fixed size and

$$\hat{P}_i := \{j \in C_i \setminus \{i\} \,|\, h(j) = h(i)\}$$

is used as an approximation to P_i. However, if $\hat{P}_i = \emptyset$ the fallback $\hat{P}_i := \{i\}$ is used. This process is illustrated in Figure 1.

Kitaev et al. (2020) consider only the case of a) self-attention and b) shared query and key transformation matrices within each head. This focus on self-attention leads to several simplifications, in particular that the chunks of the key and query sequence are identical. In order to extend the concept of LSH to cross-attention (i.e. queries and keys are distinct) we need to solve several problems.

How to find an adequate key chunk for each query chunk? Hashing and chunking is done for both the key and the query sequences, resulting in two different chunk sequences. We propose to calculate an alignment from the query chunks to the key chunks. For each query chunk C we find an aligned key chunk $K(C)$ that contains queries with similar hash classes. To do this, the range of hash classes $(h_{\text{min}}, h_{\text{max}})$ of the query chunk C is determined. Next, we enumerate all key chunks $K_1, \ldots, K_n$ and search for the first key chunk K_{j_1} that contains an entry hashed to h_{min} and the last key chunk K_{j_2} that corresponds to h_{max}. Then the middle chunk $K_{\lceil \frac{j_2+j_1}{2} \rceil}$ is selected, resulting in

$$\hat{P}_i := \{j \in K(C_i) \,|\, h(j) = h(i)\}.$$

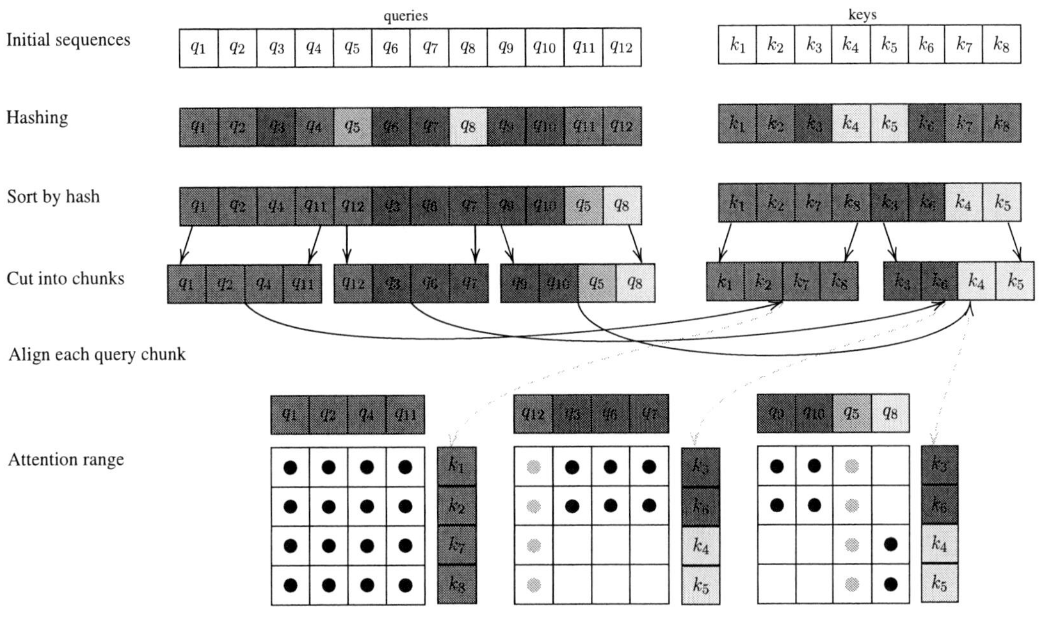

Figure 2: Locality-sensitive hashing for cross-attention. Colors indicate the hash class of the query/key. Greyed out dots in the attention range matrices indicate that attention weights are fixed to $\frac{1}{\ell_{\text{chunk}}} = \frac{1}{4}$, since no possible attention point corresponds to the current hash class.

What happens if a query belongs to a hash class that is not represented in the aligned key chunk? Since no keys are found that are close to the current query q_i, we use the average value of the aligned query chunk. That is, we set $\hat{P}_i := K(C_i)$ and obtain

$$c_i^{(\text{lsh})} := \frac{1}{|K(C_i)|} \sum_{j \in K(C_i)} v_j.$$

Throughout our experiments both key and query chunks are of equal size ℓ_{chunk}. The LSH cross-attention is shown in Figure 2.

To reduce the impact of the chunking we compute attention not only within the aligned chunk but also one chunk to the left and right, similar to Kitaev et al. (2020). This is applied both in self- and cross-attention. For unidirectional attention components, only the left context is considered.

Multi-round LSH Attention

Kitaev et al. (2020) show that multi-round hashing can help to improve the performance of LSH attention systems. For multi-round hashing different hash functions h^r are used to determine the corresponding (chunked) hash classes $\hat{P}_i^r$ and the context vector is calculated over the union

$$c_i^{(\text{lsh})} := \sum_{j \in \bigcup_r \hat{P}_i^r} \hat{\alpha}(j \,|\, i) v_j.$$

with $\hat{\alpha}(j \,|\, i)$ normalized over $\bigcup_r \hat{P}_i^r$. Multi-round hashing can be applied to both self- and cross-attention. For details on an efficient implementation we refer to Kitaev et al. (2020).

4 Experimental Setup

We evaluate our extensions to the attention by training Transformer (Vaswani et al., 2017) models with varying attention mechanisms on four MT tasks: The WMT 2016 news translation Romanian to English data with 612k parallel sentences (Europarl v8 & SE Times), the WMT 2019 English to German data with 329k parallel sentences (News Commentary v14), as well as the IWSLT 2017 English to German and English to Italian data consisting of 232k and 206k parallel sentences (TED talks). The data is pre-processed by applying 20k SPM merge operations (15k for both IWSLT tasks) (Kudo, 2018). The average sentence length for both WMT tasks is 30 subwords and 24 subwords for the IWSLT tasks.

The WMT EN→DE and the IWSLT EN→DE and EN→IT sentences are grouped by document. For document-level systems we utilize this information in a pre-processing step by simply concatenating the k preceding sentences on source and target side to each sentence pair like Tiedemann and Scherrer (2017) do, but experiment with larger

Attention method	Ro→En WMT		En→De WMT		En→De IWSLT		En→It IWSLT	
	BLEU	TER	BLEU	TER	BLEU	TER	BLEU	TER
Full attention (baseline)	34.2	53.3	32.1	56.7	23.3	68.4	32.8	53.6
LSH self-attention	33.5	54.3	30.5	58.6	22.9	68.6	31.6	54.7
LSH self- & cross-attention	33.3	54.3	29.3	60.0	22.3	69.4	31.9	54.7

Table 1: Translation performance when training models with LSH attention on different sentence-level tasks. We vary where to apply LSH attention: nowhere (baseline), encoder and decoder self-attention, or three-fold. All systems use $n_{\text{hash}} = 4$, $\ell_{\text{chunk}} = 6$ and four hash rounds. BLEU and TER are given in percentage.

context sizes $k \in \{0, 3, 9, 12\}$. In particular $k = 0$ yields a sentence-level system without any document context. In between the concatenated sentences we add a special separator token. We do not utilize right side context to ensure source and target have roughly the same length.

The general system architecture follows the 'base' configuration of Vaswani et al. (2017) with 6 encoder/decoder layers of feature dimension $d_{\text{model}} = 512$, 8 attention heads and key/value dimension $d_k = 64$. We share the source/target embeddings as well as the transposed projections and employ training dropout of 30 % (20 % for Ro→En). All models are implemented in RETURNN (Zeyer et al., 2018).

We use the Adam optimizer (Kingma and Ba, 2015) with initial learning rate of 10^{-3}. After training the systems for 200 checkpoints (1/4 of all data for WMT Ro→En, 1/2 for WMT En→De and the full data for both IWSLT tasks), we select the best checkpoint based on the dev perplexity on which we report BLEU using SacreBLEU (Post, 2018) and TER using TERCom (Snover et al., 2006) on an unseen test set. As systems with larger document-context see more frames in each epoch, we already stop training after 100 checkpoints for $k \geq 9$. We find that the converged document-level systems are able to predict the correct number of target sentences with almost perfect accuracy. We extract the last predicted sentence for each sample and then calculate BLEU and TER on the sentence-level data.

When deploying LSH in the cross-attention, we found it crucial for training stability to first shuffle the key and query sequences as secondary criterion before sorting by hash classes. This helps during training in cases where the amount of queries/keys with the same hash class exceeds the window size.

5 Experimental Results

5.1 Sentence-level

We first evaluate the impact of our LSH attention approximation on different sentence-level tasks by replacing the self- and/or cross-attention components of the baseline with LSH attention. For LSH we use $n_{\text{hash}} = 4$ hash classes, chunks of size $\ell_{\text{chunk}} = 6$ and four hash rounds. This way the LSH attention could cover sentences of length $n_{\text{hash}} \cdot \ell_{\text{chunk}} = 4 \cdot 6 = 24$ entirely by partitioning it into n_{hash} hash classes of size ℓ_{chunk} (neglecting the forward/backward window and the multiple hash rounds), roughly matching the average sentence length. The results are shown in Table 1. We use LSH both while training and during inference.

Across all tasks the LSH-approximated attention performs worse than full attention. All systems but the WMT En→De system perform at most 1 % BLEU worse then the baseline when using three-fold LSH. For WMT En→De however, the performance degradation is much higher (2.8 % BLEU), suggesting that LSH does not work equally well across different tasks and language pairs.

In general, approximating the cross-attention is more damaging than LSH in the self-attention. In an extended analysis we find that the decoder self-attention seems least delicate and can be replaced by LSH attention with almost no decrease in translation capability.

5.2 Document-level

As the sequences in the sentence-level setting are relatively short, employing LSH does not save any memory but instead has a large computational overhead in comparison to the full dot-attention implemented with a few simple matrix multiplications. With increasing document-level context however, the quadratic memory usage of the full attention becomes a limiting factor which is overcome by

Attention method	Context	EN→DE WMT BLEU	EN→DE WMT TER	EN→DE IWSLT BLEU	EN→DE IWSLT TER	EN→IT IWSLT BLEU	EN→IT IWSLT TER	ContraPro Accuracy	Peak Mem. [GB]
Full att. (baseline)	0	32.1	56.7	23.3	68.4	32.8	53.6	42.4	5.5
	3	31.9	57.1	23.6	67.5	31.9	54.7	69.2	7.8
	9	30.8	58.6	OOM		OOM		OOM	9.6
	12	OOM		OOM		OOM		OOM	OOM
LSH self-attention	0	30.2	58.9	22.6	68.8	32.5	53.6	38.4	5.1
	3	30.8	58.5	23.0	68.3	32.5	53.8	50.1	5.7
	9	30.5	58.5	23.2	68.1	32.2	53.6	50.4	6.8
	12	29.8	59.2	23.6	67.6	31.8	53.9	46.3	7.0
LSH self- & cross-att.	0	29.0	60.2	22.5	68.7	31.5	54.7	40.3	9.6
	3	29.4	60.1	22.7	68.4	31.7	55.2	59.8	9.3
	9	27.3	64.8	22.1	69.9	31.4	54.5	51.7	9.0
	12	25.8	62.7	19.8	69.3	29.6	57.6	51.8	9.4

Table 2: Training LSH attention systems with different document-level context sizes. Besides BLEU and TER on the test set, we report the accuracy of the IWSLT EN→DE system on the ContraPro task (Müller et al., 2018). These three metrics are given in percentage. All systems use the same batch size during training, we exemplarily report the memory usage of the WMT EN→DE system. 'OOM' indicates that a system requires too much memory and cannot be trained.

using LSH attention.

We conduct a series of experiments with varying document-level context sizes, concatenating up to 13 sentences at once. For each context size, we train models with a) full attention everywhere, b) LSH in the encoder- and decoder-self-attention, and c) LSH in all three attention components.

In all LSH components we fix the LSH chunk size to $\ell_{\text{chunk}} = 10$, meaning each query can only attend to a constant number regardless of how many context sentences the system utilizes. We set the number of hash classes equal to the number of concatenated sentences (i.e. $k + 1$, but rounded to an even number which is required by Kitaev et al. (2020)'s hash function). The systems trained with LSH only in the self-attention use single rounded hashing as this is more memory-efficient. For the three-fold LSH systems we use four hash rounds.

Table 2 shows the results in BLEU and TER as well as the peak memory consumption on a GTX 1080 which fits about 10 GB. All systems are trained with a batch size of 3133 subwords. Additionally, we report the accuracy on the EN→DE contrastive pronoun resolution test set ContraPro (Müller et al., 2018). To resolve the pronouns properly context of up to three sentences is necessary.

With increasing context size, the full attention systems drastically use more memory as the computation of the full attention matrix scales quadratically in the sequence length. The memory usage of the LSH attention on the contrary only scales linearly in the sequence length and therefore is constant w.r.t. a fixed batch size. When the context size is too large, all full attention systems crash during training as a single training batch no longer fits into the 10 GB GPU memory. Replacing the self-attention with LSH is not only in absolute numbers more memory-efficient than the baseline but also scales much more softly in the document-level context size, making it possible to easily train a system with 12 sentences context where all full attention systems crash. Also, replacing the cross-attention with LSH finally means that the memory consumption remains constant w.r.t. the document-level context size, as it scales fully linearly in the number of tokens. Note however that because we use multi-round hashing here, it requires more memory than full attention when used on short sequences.

In terms of translation quality, we see similar results as in Table 1 when comparing the three different system architectures in the sentence-level setting: Employing LSH in the self-attention decreases BLEU by 0.3–0.9 % BLEU. Three-fold LSH performs 0.8 and 1.3 % BLEU worse than the baseline for the IWSLT EN→DE and EN→IT tasks respectively, but 3.1 % BLEU worse on WMT

Hash classes	Class size range	LSH inference		Full inference		Full attention
		BLEU	TER	BLEU	TER	covered by LSH
1 (baseline)		35.7	51.4	35.7	51.4	100.0
2	49.7 – 50.3	35.6	51.6	35.4	51.6	64.5
4	24.1 – 25.7	35.2	51.9	35.1	51.9	42.4
8	11.0 – 13.4	34.6	52.2	34.6	52.2	29.5

Table 3: WMT RO→EN sentence-level systems trained with single-round LSH cross-attention and full self-attention. We set the chunk size large enough to always cover the entire sequence and vary the number of hash classes. For each system, we aggregate the hash class distribution of all queries/keys on the dev set and report the size of the smallest and largest class in percentage. We report BLEU and TER on the dev set a) using LSH and b) using full attention not restricted to the same hash class. Further we average the sum of all attention weights of the full attention inference that would have been covered by LSH attention and report it in percent.

EN→DE as also observed before.

While increasing the document-level context slightly worsens BLEU and TER for the full attention systems, the accuracy on the ContraPro test set increases significantly from 42.4 % to 69.2 % when including the three previous sentences as this task requires knowledge of the last few sentences.

Both the system with LSH in self-attention only and the three-fold LSH system perform equally well as the sentence-level systems even for high context sizes. Only for very large sizes ($k = 12$), performance starts to decrease.

6 Extended Analysis

6.1 Hash Quality

To evaluate the impact of approximating the full attention LSH we train systems with varying number of hash classes n_{hash} in the cross attention. As described in Section 3, queries may only attend to keys of the same hash class. The results for this are shown in Table 3. We explain the different columns in the following paragraphs.

In a first step we want to answer the question whether LSH attention actually makes use of different hash classes. Otherwise, if one hash class is over- or underrepresented, the chunk size used by the system will not be large enough to actually attend to all relevant keys. To verify this, we extract the distribution of all key and query vectors the system generated on the development set and count the sizes of all hash classes. We find that indeed the hash classes are approximately equally distributed, i.e. all have a size close to $\frac{1}{n_{\text{hash}}}$.

Increasing the number of hash classes decreases the number of keys each query can attend to. This also decreases translation performance in terms of BLEU and TER, but only minorly: The system using 8 hash classes, i.e. only attending to one eighth of all keys per query, only performs 1.1 % BLEU worse than the baseline when also using LSH during inference.

The previous results all also use LSH during inference. Alternatively, we also experiment with full attention during inference after training the system with LSH. In this case, performance is almost equal to the LSH-restricted attention, even when using many hash classes. For each sentence pair, we extract the attention weights using full attention and sum over the key positions the LSH system attends to. This is the share of full attention covered by the LSH approximation, which however in the LSH system is renormalized to have a sum of 1 for each query. The average of this over all dev sentences and attention heads is shown in the last column of Table 3. Even though with increasing number of hash classes the share of covered attention decreases drastically, both LSH inference and full inference perform equally well in terms of BLEU and TER. This indicates that LSH is able to focus on the most important positions.

6.2 Effective Window Size

The number of keys each query can attend to depends on a) the LSH chunk size, b) the number of attention heads used in parallel, and c) the number of hash rounds used in each attention head. Fixing the product of these three factors, which combination leads to the best translation performance?

As shown in Table 4, a larger chunk size or more attention heads do not improve performance. Using two hash rounds increases performance by 0.5 % BLEU. Different hash rounds allow the system to partition the key sequences w.r.t. different

Chunk size	Heads	Rounds	BLEU	TER
6	8	1	35.0	52.1
12	8	1	34.7	52.2
6	16	1	35.0	52.1
6	8	2	35.5	51.7
6	8	4	35.4	51.6

Table 4: WMT RO→EN sentence-level systems trained with LSH encoder self-attention, varying three parameters determining the how many keys each query may attend to. All systems with $\ell_{\text{chunk}} = 6$ use $n_{\text{hash}} = 4$ ($n_{\text{hash}} = 8$ for $\ell_{\text{chunk}} = 12$). We report BLEU and TER on the dev set in percentage.

aspects described by different hash functions. This effect is limited however, as four hash rounds perform equally well as just two.

6.3 Training Time and Memory

While LSH is more memory-efficient than full attention, it requires more operations to compute due to its increased complexity. For example, training for one checkpoint for the sentence-level WMT EN→DE system (Table 2) takes 49 min when using full-attention, 69 min when using single-round LSH in the self-attention, and 120 min when using three-fold LSH with four hash rounds. In particular, the time complexity of LSH scales linearly in the amount of hash rounds.

To still be able to train the full attention systems with large document-level context, a simple option is to reduce the batch size at the cost of a longer training time. With $k = 12$ sentences context, if we reduce the batch size to 2500 subwords, we can run the full attention system at a speed of 165 min / checkpoint. For this however note that we need to remove a few very long sequences no longer fitting into a single batch. In comparison, the self-attention system with a tuned batch size takes about the same time, 163 min / checkpoint.

7 Conclusion

We present a method to make the Transformer NMT architecture more memory-efficient when handling long input sequences. This is achieved by pre-selecting the most relevant candidates in self-attention and cross-attention using an LSH scheme that has been successfully applied for language modeling in previous work. We modify the existing LSH scheme to work in the NMT framework and conduct experiments on both sentence-level and document-level NMT tasks.

Our experiments show that the LSH attention scheme can be used for sentence-level NMT, although the approximation comes at the cost of slightly reduced translation quality. For document-level NMT we are able to include much bigger context sizes than what is possible with the baseline Transformer. However, more context does neither improve translation quality nor improve scores on targeted test suites.

In the future, we plan to use this approach for speech translation where long input sequences are a more pressing issue.

Acknowledgements

This project has received funding from the European Research Council (ERC) under the European Union's Horizon 2020 research and innovation programme (grant agreement No 694537, project "SEQCLAS"). The work reflects only the authors' views and the European Research Council Executive Agency (ERCEA) is not responsible for any use that may be made of the information it contains.

References

Alexandr Andoni, Piotr Indyk, Thijs Laarhoven, Ilya Razenshteyn, and Ludwig Schmidt. 2015. Practical and optimal lsh for angular distance. *Advances in neural information processing systems*, 28.

Guangsheng Bao, Yue Zhang, Zhiyang Teng, Boxing Chen, and Weihua Luo. 2021. G-transformer for document-level machine translation. In *Proceedings of the 59th Annual Meeting of the Association for Computational Linguistics and the 11th International Joint Conference on Natural Language Processing (Volume 1: Long Papers)*, pages 3442–3455.

Rachel Bawden, Rico Sennrich, Alexandra Birch, and Barry Haddow. 2018. Evaluating discourse phenomena in neural machine translation. In *Proceedings of the 2018 Conference of the North American Chapter of the Association for Computational Linguistics: Human Language Technologies, NAACL-HLT 2018, New Orleans, Louisiana, USA, June 1-6, 2018, Volume 1 (Long Papers)*, pages 1304–1313. Association for Computational Linguistics.

Iz Beltagy, Matthew E. Peters, and Arman Cohan. 2020. Longformer: The long-document transformer. *CoRR*, abs/2004.05150.

Rewon Child, Scott Gray, Alec Radford, and Ilya Sutskever. 2019. Generating long sequences with sparse transformers. *CoRR*, abs/1904.10509.

Zihang Dai, Zhilin Yang, Yiming Yang, Jaime G Carbonell, Quoc Le, and Ruslan Salakhutdinov. 2019. Transformer-xl: Attentive language models beyond a fixed-length context. In *Proceedings of the 57th Annual Meeting of the Association for Computational Linguistics*, pages 2978–2988.

Jacob Devlin, Ming-Wei Chang, Kenton Lee, and Kristina Toutanova. 2019. Bert: Pre-training of deep bidirectional transformers for language understanding. In *Proceedings of the 2019 Conference of the North American Chapter of the Association for Computational Linguistics: Human Language Technologies, Volume 1 (Long and Short Papers)*, pages 4171–4186.

Anmol Gulati, James Qin, Chung-Cheng Chiu, Niki Parmar, Yu Zhang, Jiahui Yu, Wei Han, Shibo Wang, Zhengdong Zhang, Yonghui Wu, et al. 2020. Conformer: Convolution-augmented transformer for speech recognition. *Proc. Interspeech 2020*, pages 5036–5040.

Rohit Gupta, Laurent Besacier, Marc Dymetman, and Matthias Gallé. 2019. Character-based NMT with transformer. *CoRR*, abs/1911.04997.

Jingjing Huo, Christian Herold, Yingbo Gao, Leonard Dahlmann, Shahram Khadivi, and Hermann Ney. 2020. Diving deep into context-aware neural machine translation. In *Proceedings of the Fifth Conference on Machine Translation*, pages 604–616.

Kazuki Irie, Albert Zeyer, Ralf Schlüter, and Hermann Ney. 2019. Language modeling with deep transformers. *Proc. Interspeech 2019*, pages 3905–3909.

Sébastien Jean, Stanislas Lauly, Orhan Firat, and Kyunghyun Cho. 2017. Does neural machine translation benefit from larger context? *CoRR*, abs/1704.05135.

Marcin Junczys-Dowmunt. 2019. Microsoft translator at wmt 2019: Towards large-scale document-level neural machine translation. In *Proceedings of the Fourth Conference on Machine Translation (Volume 2: Shared Task Papers, Day 1)*, pages 225–233.

Diederik P. Kingma and Jimmy Ba. 2015. Adam: A method for stochastic optimization. In *3rd International Conference on Learning Representations, ICLR 2015, San Diego, CA, USA, May 7-9, 2015, Conference Track Proceedings*.

Nikita Kitaev, Lukasz Kaiser, and Anselm Levskaya. 2020. Reformer: The efficient transformer. In *8th International Conference on Learning Representations, ICLR 2020, Addis Ababa, Ethiopia, April 26-30, 2020*. OpenReview.net.

Shaohui Kuang, Deyi Xiong, Weihua Luo, and Guodong Zhou. 2018. Modeling coherence for neural machine translation with dynamic and topic caches. In *Proceedings of the 27th International Conference on Computational Linguistics*, pages 596–606.

Taku Kudo. 2018. Subword regularization: Improving neural network translation models with multiple subword candidates. In *Proceedings of the 56th Annual Meeting of the Association for Computational Linguistics, ACL 2018, Melbourne, Australia, July 15-20, 2018, Volume 1: Long Papers*, pages 66–75. Association for Computational Linguistics.

Yinhan Liu, Myle Ott, Naman Goyal, Jingfei Du, Mandar Joshi, Danqi Chen, Omer Levy, Mike Lewis, Luke Zettlemoyer, and Veselin Stoyanov. 2019. Roberta: A robustly optimized BERT pretraining approach. *CoRR*, abs/1907.11692.

António Lopes, M Amin Farajian, Rachel Bawden, Michael Zhang, and André FT Martins. 2020. Document-level neural mt: A systematic comparison. In *Proceedings of the 22nd Annual Conference of the European Association for Machine Translation*, pages 225–234.

Abdelrahman Mohamed, Dmytro Okhonko, and Luke Zettlemoyer. 2019. Transformers with convolutional context for ASR. *CoRR*, abs/1904.11660.

Makoto Morishita, Jun Suzuki, Tomoharu Iwata, and Masaaki Nagata. 2021. Context-aware neural machine translation with mini-batch embedding. In *Proceedings of the 16th conference of the European chapter of the association for computational linguistics: main volume*, pages 2513–2521.

Mathias Müller, Annette Rios, Elena Voita, and Rico Sennrich. 2018. A large-scale test set for the evaluation of context-aware pronoun translation in neural machine translation. In *Proceedings of the Third Conference on Machine Translation: Research Papers, WMT 2018, Belgium, Brussels, October 31 - November 1, 2018*, pages 61–72. Association for Computational Linguistics.

Myle Ott, Sergey Edunov, David Grangier, and Michael Auli. 2018. Scaling neural machine translation. In *Proceedings of the Third Conference on Machine Translation: Research Papers*, pages 1–9, Brussels, Belgium. Association for Computational Linguistics.

Niki Parmar, Ashish Vaswani, Jakob Uszkoreit, Lukasz Kaiser, Noam Shazeer, Alexander Ku, and Dustin Tran. 2018. Image transformer. In *International Conference on Machine Learning*, pages 4055–4064. PMLR.

Loïc Paulevé, Hervé Jégou, and Laurent Amsaleg. 2010. Locality sensitive hashing: A comparison of hash function types and querying mechanisms. *Pattern recognition letters*, 31(11):1348–1358.

Matt Post. 2018. A call for clarity in reporting BLEU scores. In *Proceedings of the Third Conference on Machine Translation: Research Papers, WMT 2018, Belgium, Brussels, October 31 - November 1, 2018*, pages 186–191. Association for Computational Linguistics.

Jiezhong Qiu, Hao Ma, Omer Levy, Wen-tau Yih, Sinong Wang, and Jie Tang. 2020. Blockwise self-attention for long document understanding. In *Findings of the Association for Computational Linguistics: EMNLP 2020*, pages 2555–2565.

Jack W Rae, Anna Potapenko, Siddhant M Jayakumar, Chloe Hillier, and Timothy P Lillicrap. 2019. Compressive transformers for long-range sequence modelling. In *International Conference on Learning Representations*.

Alessandro Raganato, Yves Scherrer, and Jörg Tiedemann. 2020. Fixed encoder self-attention patterns in transformer-based machine translation. In *Findings of the Association for Computational Linguistics: EMNLP 2020*, pages 556–568.

Aurko Roy, Mohammad Saffar, Ashish Vaswani, and David Grangier. 2021. Efficient content-based sparse attention with routing transformers. *Transactions of the Association for Computational Linguistics*, 9:53–68.

Rico Sennrich, Barry Haddow, and Alexandra Birch. 2016. Neural machine translation of rare words with subword units. In *Proceedings of the 54th Annual Meeting of the Association for Computational Linguistics (Volume 1: Long Papers)*, pages 1715–1725, Berlin, Germany. Association for Computational Linguistics.

Xing Shi and Kevin Knight. 2017. Speeding up neural machine translation decoding by shrinking run-time vocabulary. In *Proceedings of the 55th Annual Meeting of the Association for Computational Linguistics (Volume 2: Short Papers)*, pages 574–579.

Matthew G. Snover, Bonnie J. Dorr, Richard M. Schwartz, Linnea Micciulla, and John Makhoul. 2006. A study of translation edit rate with targeted human annotation. In *Proceedings of the 7th Conference of the Association for Machine Translation in the Americas: Technical Papers, AMTA 2006, Cambridge, Massachusetts, USA, August 8-12, 2006*, pages 223–231. Association for Machine Translation in the Americas.

Sainbayar Sukhbaatar, Édouard Grave, Piotr Bojanowski, and Armand Joulin. 2019. Adaptive attention span in transformers. In *Proceedings of the 57th Annual Meeting of the Association for Computational Linguistics*, pages 331–335.

Yi Tay, Mostafa Dehghani, Dara Bahri, and Donald Metzler. 2020. Efficient transformers: A survey. *CoRR*, abs/2009.06732.

Jörg Tiedemann and Yves Scherrer. 2017. Neural machine translation with extended context. *DiscoMT 2017*, page 82.

Zhaopeng Tu, Yang Liu, Shuming Shi, and Tong Zhang. 2018. Learning to remember translation history with a continuous cache. *Transactions of the Association for Computational Linguistics*, 6:407–420.

Ferhan Ture, Tamer Elsayed, and Jimmy Lin. 2011. No free lunch: Brute force vs. locality-sensitive hashing for cross-lingual pairwise similarity. In *Proceedings of the 34th International ACM SIGIR Conference on Research and Development in Information Retrieval*, SIGIR '11, page 943–952, New York, NY, USA. Association for Computing Machinery.

Ashish Vaswani, Noam Shazeer, Niki Parmar, Jakob Uszkoreit, Llion Jones, Aidan N Gomez, Łukasz Kaiser, and Illia Polosukhin. 2017. Attention is all you need. *Advances in neural information processing systems*, 30.

Laura Cross Vila, Carlos Escolano, José AR Fonollosa, and Marta R Costa-Jussa. 2018. End-to-end speech translation with the transformer. In *IberSPEECH*, pages 60–63.

Sinong Wang, Belinda Z. Li, Madian Khabsa, Han Fang, and Hao Ma. 2020. Linformer: Self-attention with linear complexity. *CoRR*, abs/2006.04768.

Weiqiu You, Simeng Sun, and Mohit Iyyer. 2020. Hard-coded gaussian attention for neural machine translation. In *Proceedings of the 58th Annual Meeting of the Association for Computational Linguistics*, pages 7689–7700.

Manzil Zaheer, Guru Guruganesh, Kumar Avinava Dubey, Joshua Ainslie, Chris Alberti, Santiago Ontanon, Philip Pham, Anirudh Ravula, Qifan Wang, Li Yang, and Amr Ahmed. 2020. Big bird: Transformers for longer sequences. In *Advances in Neural Information Processing Systems*, volume 33, pages 17283–17297. Curran Associates, Inc.

Albert Zeyer, Tamer Alkhouli, and Hermann Ney. 2018. RETURNN as a generic flexible neural toolkit with application to translation and speech recognition. In *Proceedings of ACL 2018, Melbourne, Australia, July 15-20, 2018, System Demonstrations*, pages 128–133. Association for Computational Linguistics.

Albert Zeyer, Parnia Bahar, Kazuki Irie, Ralf Schlüter, and Hermann Ney. 2019. A comparison of transformer and lstm encoder decoder models for asr. In *2019 IEEE Automatic Speech Recognition and Understanding Workshop (ASRU)*, pages 8–15. IEEE.

Pei Zhang, Boxing Chen, Niyu Ge, and Kai Fan. 2020. Long-short term masking transformer: A simple but effective baseline for document-level neural machine translation. In *Proceedings of the 2020 Conference on Empirical Methods in Natural Language Processing (EMNLP)*, pages 1081–1087.

Kai Zhao, Hany Hassan, and Michael Auli. 2015. Learning translation models from monolingual continuous representations. In *Proceedings of the 2015 Conference of the North American Chapter of the Association for Computational Linguistics: Human Language Technologies*, pages 1527–1536.

Anticipation-Free Training for Simultaneous Machine Translation

Chih-Chiang Chang, Shun-Po Chuang, Hung-yi Lee
National Taiwan University
{r09922057,f04942141,hungyilee}@ntu.edu.tw

Abstract

Simultaneous machine translation (SimulMT) speeds up the translation process by starting to translate before the source sentence is completely available. It is difficult due to limited context and word order difference between languages. Existing methods increase latency or introduce adaptive read-write policies for SimulMT models to handle local reordering and improve translation quality. However, the long-distance reordering would make the SimulMT models learn translation mistakenly. Specifically, the model may be forced to predict target tokens when the corresponding source tokens have not been read. This leads to aggressive anticipation during inference, resulting in the hallucination phenomenon. To mitigate this problem, we propose a new framework that decompose the translation process into the monotonic translation step and the reordering step, and we model the latter by the auxiliary sorting network (ASN). The ASN rearranges the hidden states to match the order in the target language, so that the SimulMT model could learn to translate more reasonably. The entire model is optimized end-to-end and does not rely on external aligners or data. During inference, ASN is removed to achieve streaming. Experiments show the proposed framework could outperform previous methods with less latency.

1 Introduction

Simultaneous machine translation (SimulMT) is an extension of neural machine translation (NMT), aiming to perform streaming translation by outputting the translation before the source input has ended. It is more applicable to real-world scenarios such as international conferences, where people could communicate fluently without delay.

However, SimulMT faces additional difficulties compared to full-sentence translation – such a model needs to translate with limited context, and the different word order between languages would make streaming models learn translation mistakenly. The problems can often be alleviated by increasing the context. Using more context allows the model to translate with more information, trading off speed for quality. But the word order could be very different among languages. Increasing the context could only solve the local reordering problem. If long-distance reordering exists in training data, the model would be forced to predict tokens in the target language when the corresponding source tokens have not been read. this is called *anticipation* (Ma et al., 2019). Ignoring the long-distance reordering may cause unnecessarily high latency, or encourage aggressive anticipation, resulting in the hallucination phenomenon (Müller et al., 2020).

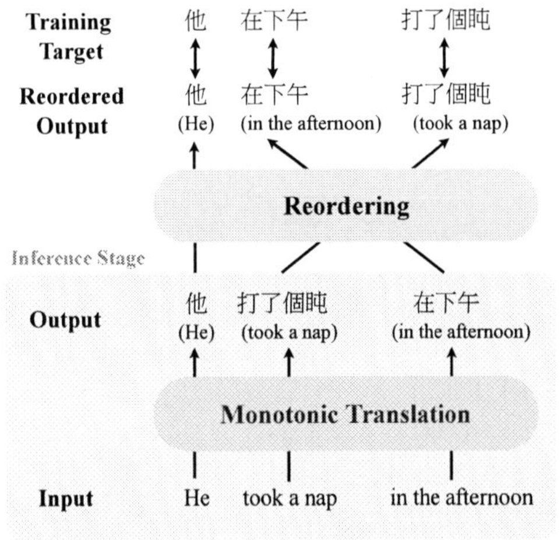

Figure 1: Illustration of the training process. The translated output is rearranged to match the order of training target, reducing anticipation. We use the gray part during inference.

It sheds light on the importance of matching the word order between the source and target languages. Existing methods aim to reduce anticipation by using syntax-based rules to rewrite the translation target (He et al., 2015). It requires additional language-specific prior knowledge and con-

Proceedings of the 19th International Conference on Spoken Language Translation (IWSLT 2022), pages 43 - 61
May 26-27, 2022 ©2022 Association for Computational Linguistics

stituent parse trees. Other approaches pre-train a full-sentence model, then incrementally feed the source sentence to it to generate monotonic translation target (pseudo reference) (Chen et al., 2021b; Zhang et al., 2020). However, the full-sentence model was not trained to translate incrementally, which creates a train-test mismatch, resulting in varying prediction quality. They require combining with the original data to be effective.

To this end, this work aims to address long-distance reordering by incorporating it directly into the training process, as Figure 1 shows. We decompose the typical translation process into the *monotonic translation* step and the *reordering* step. Inspired by the Gumbel-Sinkhorn network (Mena et al., 2018), we proposed an auxiliary sorting network (ASN) for the *reordering* step. During training, the ASN explicitly rearranges the hidden states to match the target language word order. The ASN will not be used during inference, so that the model could translate monotonically. The proposed method reduces anticipation, thus increases the lexical precision (He et al., 2015) of the model without compromising its speed. We apply the proposed framework to a simple model – a causal Transformer encoder trained with connectionist temporal classification (CTC) (Graves et al., 2006). The CTC loss can learn an adaptive policy (Chousa et al., 2019), which performs local reordering by predicting blank symbols until enough information is read, then write the information in the target order. Even so, it still suffers from high latency and under-translation due to long-distance reordering in training data. Our ASN handles these long-distance reordering, improving both the latency and the quality of the CTC model. We conduct experiments on CWMT English to Chinese and WMT15 German to English translation datasets. Our contributions are summarized below:

- We proposed a new framework for SimulMT. The ASN could apply on various causal models to handle long-distance reordering.
- Experiments showed that the proposed method could outperform the pseudo reference method. It indicated the proposed method could better handle the long-distance reordering.
- The proposed model is a causal encoder, which is parameter efficient and could outperform wait-k Transformer with less latency.

Our implementation is based on fairseq (Ott et al., 2019). The instructions to access our source code is provided in Appendix A.

2 Related Works

2.1 Simultaneous Translation

SimulMT is first achieved by applying fixed read-write policies on NMT models. Wait-if-worse and Wait-if-diff (Cho and Esipova, 2016) form decisions based on the next prediction's probability or its value. Static Read and Write (Dalvi et al., 2018) first read several tokens, then repeatedly read and write several tokens at a time. Wait-k (Ma et al., 2019) trains end-to-end models for SimulMT. Its policy is similar to Static Read and Write.

On the other hand, adaptive policies seek to learn the read-write decisions. Some works explored training agents with reinforcement learning (RL) (Gu et al., 2017; Luo et al., 2017). Others design expert policies and apply imitation learning (IL) (Zheng et al., 2019a,b). Monotonic attention (Raffel et al., 2017) integrates the read-write policy into the attention mechanism to jointly train with NMT. MoChA (Chiu and Raffel, 2018) enhances monotonic attention by adding soft attention over a small window. MILk (Arivazhagan et al., 2019) extends such window to the full encoder history. MMA (Ma et al., 2020c) extends MILk to multi-head attention. Connectionist temporal classification (CTC) were also explored for adaptive policy by treating the blank symbol as wait action (Chousa et al., 2019). Recently, making read-write decisions based on segments of meaningful unit (MU) (Zhang et al., 2020) improves the translation quality. Besides, an adaptive policy can also be derived from an ensemble of fixed-policy models (Zheng et al., 2020).

When performing simultaneous interpretation, humans avoid long-distance reordering whenever possible (Al-Khanji et al., 2000; He et al., 2016). Thus, some works seek to reduce the anticipation in data to ease the training of simultaneous models. These include syntax-based rewriting (He et al., 2015), or generating pseudo reference by test-time wait-k (Chen et al., 2021b) and prefix-attention (Zhang et al., 2020). We reduce anticipation from a different approach: instead of rewriting the target, we let the model match its hidden states to the target on its own. As shown in experiments, our method is comparable or superior to the pseudo reference method.

2.2 Gumbel-Sinkhorn Network

The Sinkhorn Normalization (Adams and Zemel, 2011) is an iterative procedure that converts a matrix into doubly stochastic form. It was initially proposed to perform gradient-based rank learning. Gumbel-Sinkhorn Network (Mena et al., 2018) combines the Sinkhorn Normalization with the Gumbel reparametrization trick (Kingma and Welling, 2014). It approximates sampling from a distribution of permutation matrices. Subsequently, Sinkhorn Transformer (Tay et al., 2020) applied this method to the Transformer (Vaswani et al., 2017) to model long-distance dependency in language models with better memory efficiency. This work applies the Gumbel-Sinkhorn Network to model the reordering between languages, in order to reduce anticipation in SimulMT.

3 Proposed Method

For a source sentence $\mathbf{x} = \langle x_1, x_2, ..., x_{|\mathbf{x}|} \rangle$ and a target sentence $\mathbf{y} = \langle y_1, y_2, ..., y_{|\mathbf{y}|} \rangle$, in order to perform SimulMT, the conditional probability of translation $p(\mathbf{y}|\mathbf{x})$ is modeled by the prefix-to-prefix framework (Ma et al., 2019). Formally,

$$p_g(\mathbf{y}|\mathbf{x}) = \prod_{t=1}^{|\mathbf{y}|} p(y_t|\mathbf{x}_{\leq g(t)}, \mathbf{y}_{<t}). \quad (1)$$

where $g(t)$ is a monotonic non-decreasing function. This way, the t-th token $\hat{\mathbf{y}}_t$ can be predicted with a limited context $\mathbf{x}_{\leq g(t)}$. However, if long-distance reordering exists in the training data, the model is forced to generate target tokens whose corresponding source tokens have not been revealed yet. This issue is known as anticipation.

3.1 Training Framework

To overcome this, we introduce a latent variable $\mathbf{Z}$: a permutation matrix capturing the reordering process from $\mathbf{x}$ to $\mathbf{y}$. Thus, the translation probability can be expressed as a marginalization over $\mathbf{Z}$:

$$p(\mathbf{y}|\mathbf{x}) = \sum_{\mathbf{Z}} \underbrace{p_g(\mathbf{y}|\mathbf{x}, \mathbf{Z})}_{\substack{\text{monotonic} \\ \text{translation}}} \underbrace{p(\mathbf{Z}|\mathbf{x})}_{\text{reordering}}. \quad (2)$$

During training, since $\mathbf{Z}$ captures reordering, the $p_g(\mathbf{y}|\mathbf{x}, \mathbf{Z})$ corresponds to monotonic translation, which can be correctly modeled by a prefix-to-prefix model without anticipation. During inference, we can translate monotonically by simply removing the effect of $\mathbf{Z}$:

$$\hat{\mathbf{y}} = \arg\max_{\mathbf{y}} p_g(\mathbf{y}|\mathbf{x}, \mathbf{Z} = \mathbf{I}). \quad (3)$$

where $\mathbf{I}$ is the identity matrix. However, equation 2 is intractable due to the factorial search space of permutations. One could select the most likely permutation using an external aligner (Ran et al., 2021), but such a method requires an external tool, and it could not be end-to-end optimized. Instead, we use the ASN to learn the permutation matrix $\mathbf{Z}$ associated with source-target reordering. By doing this, the entire model is optimized end-to-end.

Figure 2 shows the proposed framework applied on the CTC model. It is composed of a causal Transformer encoder, an ASN, and a length projection network. We describe each component in detail below.

3.2 Causal Encoder

The encoder maps the source sequence $\mathbf{x}$ to hidden states $\mathbf{H} = \langle h_1, h_2, ..., h_{|\mathbf{x}|} \rangle$. During training, the encoder uses a causal attention mask so that it can be streamed during inference. To enable the trade-off between quality and latency, we introduce a tunable delay in the causal attention mask of the first encoder layer. We define the delay in a similar sense to wait-k: For delay-k, the t-th hidden state h_t is computed after observing the $(t + k - 1)$-th source token.

We pre-train the encoder with CTC loss (Libovický and Helcl, 2018). Since the CTC is an adaptive policy already capable of local reordering, initializing from it encourages the ASN to only handle long-distance reordering. We study the effectiveness of this technique in Section 5.2.

3.3 Auxiliary Sorting Network (ASN)

The ASN samples a permutation matrix $\mathbf{Z}$, which would sort the encoder hidden states $\mathbf{H}$ into the target order. To do so, the ASN first computes intermediate variables $\mathbf{Q} = \langle q_1, q_2, ..., q_{|\mathbf{x}|} \rangle$ using a stack of M non-causal Transformer decoder layers. These layers use the target token embeddings as the context for cross attention. Providing this context guides the reordering process[1], inspired by the word alignment task (Zhang and van Genabith, 2021; Chen et al., 2021a). We randomly mask out

[1]Although ASN has decoder layers and takes target tokens as input, which are unavailable during inference, they are only used to assist training.

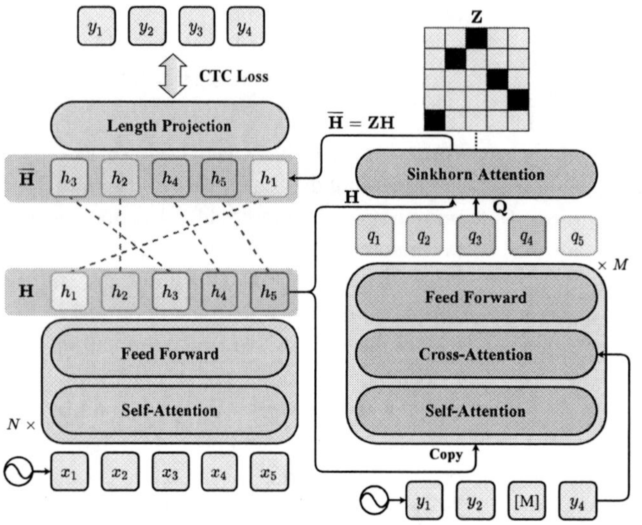

(a) The model consists of a causal encoder (lower left, blue), an ASN (right, orange), and a length projection network (upper left, blue). "[M]" is the masking embedding.

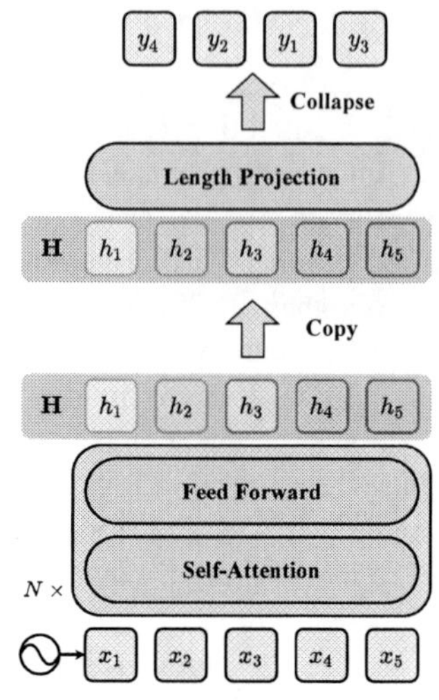

(b) During inference, only the encoder and length projection (blue) are used.

Figure 2: The architecture of the proposed model. Add & Norm layers are omitted for simplicity.

γ% of the context in ASN to avoid collapsing to a trivial solution.

Subsequently, the Sinkhorn Attention in ASN computes the attention scores between $\mathbf{Q}$ and $\mathbf{H}$ using the scaled dot-product attention:

$$\mathbf{A} = \frac{\mathbf{QH}^T}{\sqrt{d_h}}, \tag{4}$$

where d_h is the last dimension of $\mathbf{H}$. To convert the attention scores $\mathbf{A}$ to a permutation matrix $\mathbf{Z}$, ASN applies the Gumbel-Sinkhorn operator. Such operator approximates sampling from a distribution of permutation matrices (Mena et al., 2018). It is described by first adding the Gumbel noise (equation 5), then scaling by a positive temperature τ, and finally applying the l-iteration Sinkhorn normalization (denoted by $S^l(\cdot)$) (Adams and Zemel, 2011). We also add a scaling factor δ to adjust the Gumbel noise level (equation 6). The output would be doubly stochastic (Sinkhorn, 1964), which is a relaxation of permutation matrix. We leave the detailed description of the Gumbel-Sinkhorn operator in Appendix F.

$$\boldsymbol{\mathcal{E}} \in \mathbb{R}^{N\times N} \overset{i.i.d.}{\sim} Gumbel(0,1), \tag{5}$$

$$\mathbf{Z} = S^l\left(\left(\mathbf{A} + \delta\boldsymbol{\mathcal{E}}\right)/\tau\right), \tag{6}$$

Next, we use a matrix multiplication of $\mathbf{Z}$ and $\mathbf{H}$ to reorder $\mathbf{H}$, the result is denoted by $\overline{\mathbf{H}}$:

$$\overline{\mathbf{H}} = \mathbf{ZH} \tag{7}$$

Since $\mathbf{Z}$ approximates a permutation matrix, using matrix multiplication is equivalent to permuting the vectors in $\mathbf{H}$. This preserves the content of its individual vectors, and is essential to our method as we will show in Section 5.1.

3.4 Length Projection

To optimize the model with CTC loss function, we tackle the length mismatch between $\overline{\mathbf{H}}$ and $\mathbf{y}$ by projecting $\overline{\mathbf{H}}$ to a μ-times longer sequence via an affine transformation (Libovický and Helcl, 2018). The μ represents the upsample ratio. For ASN to learn reordering effectively, it is required that the projection network and the loss must not perform reordering. Our length projection is time-independent, and CTC is monotonic, both satisfy our requirement.

3.5 Inference Strategy

To enable streaming, we remove the ASN during inference[2] (Figure 2(b)). Specifically, when a new input token x_t arrives, the encoder computes the hidden state h_t, then we feed h_t directly to the length projection to predict the next token(s). The prediction is post-processed by the CTC collapse function in an online fashion. Namely, we only output a new token if 1) it is not the blank symbol and 2) it is different from the previous token.

[2]While this seemingly creates a train-test discrepancy, we address this in FAQ

4 Experiments

4.1 Datasets

We conduct experiments on English-Chinese and German-English datasets. For En-Zh, we use a subset[3] of CWMT (Chen and Zhang, 2019) parallel corpora as training data (7M pairs). We use NJU-newsdev2018 as the development set and report results on CWMT2008, CWMT2009, and CWMT2011. The CWMT test sets have up to 3 references. Thus we report the 3-reference BLEU score. For De-En, we use WMT15 (Callison-Burch et al., 2009) parallel corpora as training data (4.5M pairs). We use newstest2013 as the development set and report results on newstest2015.

We use SentencePiece (Kudo and Richardson, 2018) on each language separately to obtain its vocabulary of 32K subword units. We filter out sentence pairs that have empty sentences or exceed 1024 tokens in length.

4.2 Experimental Setup

All SimulMT models use causal encoders. During inference, the encoder states are computed incrementally after each read, similar to (Elbayad et al., 2020). The causal encoder models follow a similar training process to non-autoregressive translation (NAT) (Gu et al., 2018; Libovický and Helcl, 2018; Lee et al., 2018; Zhou et al., 2020). We adopt sequence level knowledge distillation (Seq-KD) (Kim and Rush, 2016) for all systems. The combination of Seq-KD and CTC loss has been shown to achieve state-of-the-art performance (Gu and Kong, 2021) and could deal with the reordering problem (Chuang et al., 2021). Specifically, we first train a full-sentence model as a teacher model on the original dataset, then we use beam search with beam width 5 to decode the Seq-KD set. We use the Seq-KD set in subsequent experiments. We list the Transformer and ASN hyperparameters separately in Appendix C and D.

We use Adam (Kingma and Ba, 2015) with an inverse square root schedule for the optimizer. The max learning rate is 5e-4 with 4000 warm-up steps. We use gradient accumulation to achieve an effective batch size of 128K tokens for the teacher model and 32K for others. We optimize the model with the 300K steps. Early stopping is applied when the validation BLEU does not improve within 25K steps. Label smoothing (Szegedy et al., 2016) with $\epsilon_{ls} = 0.1$ is applied on cross-entropy and CTC loss. For CTC, this reduces excessive blank symbol predictions (Kim et al., 2018). Random seeds are set in training scripts in our source code. For the hardware information and environment settings, see Appendix E.

For latency evaluation, we use SimulEval (Ma et al., 2020a) to compute Average Lagging (AL) (Ma et al., 2019) and Computation Aware Average Lagging (AL-CA) (Ma et al., 2020b). AL is measured in words or characters, whereas AL-CA is measured in milliseconds. We describe these metrics in detail in Appendix G. For quality evaluation, we use BLEU (Papineni et al., 2002) calculated by SacreBLEU (Post, 2018). We conduct statistical significance test for BLEU using paired bootstrap resampling (Koehn, 2004). For multiple references, we use the first reference to run SimulEval[4] and use all available references to run SacreBLEU. The language-specific settings for SimulEval and SacreBLEU can respectively be found in Appendix H and I.

4.3 Baselines

We compare our method with two target rewrite methods which generate new datasets:

- **Pseudo reference** (Chen et al., 2021b): This approach first trains a full-sentence model and uses it to generate monotonic translation. The approach applies the test-time wait-k policy (Ma et al., 2019), and performs beam search with beam width 5 to generate pseudo references. The pseudo reference set is the combination of original dataset and the pseudo references. We made a few changes 1) instead of the full-sentence model, we use the wait-9 model[5]. 2) instead of creating a new dataset for each k, we only use $k = 9$ since it has the best quality.
- **Reorder**: We use the word alignments to reorder the target sequence. We use *awesome-align* (Dou and Neubig, 2021) to obtain word alignments on the Seq-KD set, and we sort the target tokens based on their corresponding source tokens. Target tokens that did not align to a source token are placed at the position after their preceding target token.

[3]We use casia2015, casict2011, casict2015, neu2017.

[4]we use SimulEval for latency metrics only. Only one reference is required to run it.

[5]our wait-9 model has higher training set BLEU score than applying test-time wait-k on full-sentence model.

We train two types of models on either the Seq-KD set, the pseudo reference set or the reorder set:

- **wait-k**: an encoder-decoder model. It uses a fixed policy that first reads k tokens, then repeatedly reads and writes a single token.
- **CTC**: a causal encoder trained with CTC loss. The policy is adaptive, i.e., it outputs blank symbols until enough content is read, outputs the translated tokens, then repeats.

4.4 Quantitative Results

Figure 3 shows the latency-quality trade-off on the CWMT dataset, each node on a line represents a different value of k. Due to space limit, the significant test results are reported in Appendix J.

First of all, although the vanilla CTC model has high latency in terms of AL, they are comparable to or faster than the wait-k model according to AL-CA. This is due to the reduced parameter size. Besides, CTC models outperform wait-k in low latency settings. The pseudo reference method improves the quality of wait-k and CTC models, and it slightly improves the latency of the CTC model. In contrast, the reorder method harms the performance of both models. Meanwhile, our method significantly improves both the quality and latency of the CTC model across all latency settings, outperforming the pseudo reference method and the reorder method. In particular, our $k = 1, 3$ models outperform wait-1 by around 13-15 BLEUs with a faster speed in terms of AL-CA. This shows that our models are more efficient than wait-k models under low latency regimes.

Figure 4 shows the latency-quality trade-off on the WMT15 De-En dataset. The vanilla CTC model is much more competitive in De-En. It outperforms vanilla wait-k in low latency settings in BLEU and AL-CA, and its AL is much less than those in En-Zh. Our method improves the quality of the CTC model, comparable to the pseudo reference method. However, our method does not require combining with the original dataset to improve the performance.

To understand why our method is more effective on CWMT, we calculate the k-Anticipation Rate (k-AR) (Chen et al., 2021b) on the evaluation sets of both datasets. For the definition of k-AR, see Appendix G. Intuitively, k-AR describes the amount of anticipation (or reordering) in the corpus whose range is longer than k source tokens. We report k-AR across $1 \leq k \leq 9$ in Figure 5. En-Zh has much higher k-AR in general, and it decreases slower as k increases. When $k = 9$, over 20% of anticipations remain in En-Zh, while almost none remains in De-En. We conclude that En-Zh has much more reordering, and over 20% of them are longer than 9 words. The abundance of long-distance reordering gives our method an advantage, which explains the big improvement observed on CWMT. On the other hand, De-En reordering is less common and mostly local, so ASN has limited effect. Indeed, we found that ASN predicts matrices close to the identity matrix on De-En, whereas, on En-Zh, it predicts non-identity matrices throughout training.

4.5 Qualitative Results

We show some examples from the CWMT test set. We compare the predictions from wait-k, CTC, and CTC+ASN models in Figure 6. In the first example, wait-k predicts the sentence *"demonstrative is one of the major languages in the world's languages,"* which is clearly hallucination. CTC failed to translate *"8000"* and *"assets,"* which shows that CTC may under-translate and ignore source information. In the second example, wait-k hallucinates the sentence *"this is the world's best contest, but to a earthquake without earthquake, it's the opening remarks."* CTC under-translates *"silver said in a telephone interview."* Our method generally provides translation that preserves the content. Although our model prediction is a bit less fluent than wait-k, they are generally comprehensible. See Appendix N for more examples.

We study the output of the ASN to verify that reordering information is being learned. Figure 7 shows an example of the permutation matrix $\mathbf{Z}$ predicted by the ASN. The horizontal axis is labeled with the source tokens. The vertical axis is the output positions, each are labeled with 2 target tokens (due to the length projection). In the example, the English phrase *"for all green hands"* come late in the source sentence, but their corresponding Chinese tokens appear early in target, which causes anticipation. Our ASN permutes the hidden states of this phrase to early positions, so anticipation no longer happens, and provides the correct training signal for the model. We provide additional examples in Appendix M.

5 Ablation Study

We perform ablation studies on the CWMT dataset.

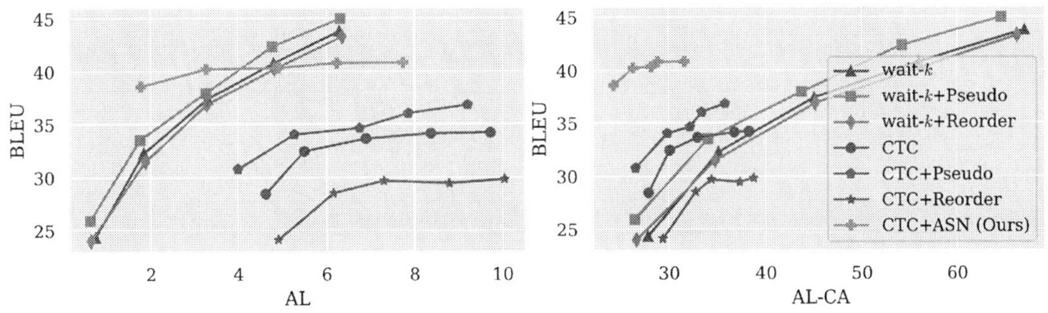

Figure 3: Latency-quality trade off on the CWMT En-Zh dataset. Each line represents a system, and the 5 nodes from left to right corresponds to $k = 1, 3, 5, 7, 9$. The figures share the legend.

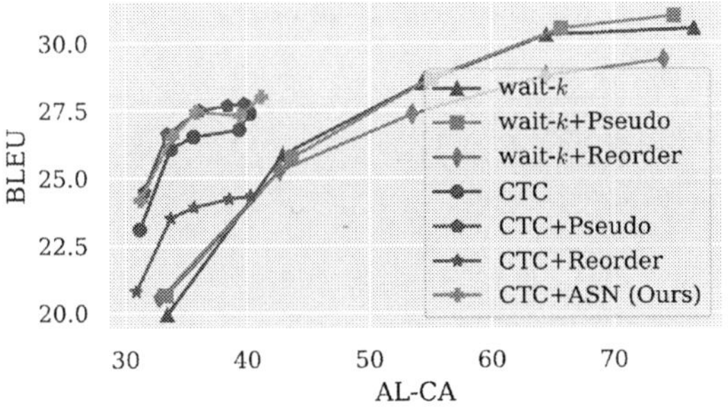

Figure 4: Latency-quality trade off on the WMT15 De-En dataset.

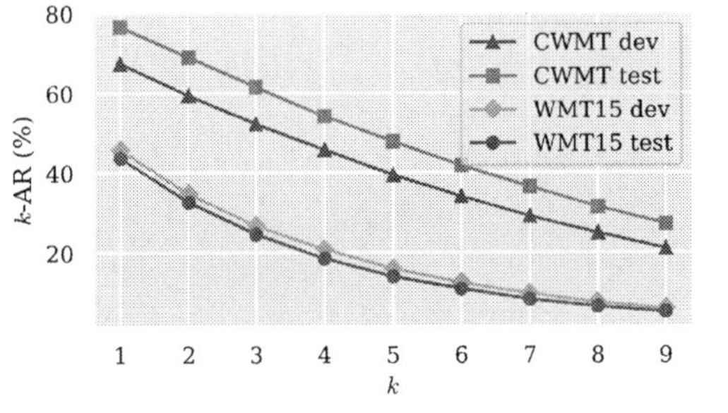

Figure 5: The k-anticipation rate computed on CWMT En-Zh and WMT15 De-En development and test sets.

5.1 Gumbel-Sinkhorn Network

We show that the Gumbel-Sinkhorn Network is crucial to our method. We train CTC+ASN models with $k = 3$ under the following settings:[6]

- **No temperature**: Set the temperature τ to 1.
- **No noise**: Set the Gumbel noise factor δ to 0.
- **Gumbel softmax**: Replace Sinkhorn normalization with softmax.
- **Default**: The Gumbel-Sinkhorn Network.

[6]we do not use weight initialization in this subsection.

Table 1 shows the result of these settings. Without low temperature, the ASN output $\mathbf{Z}$ is not sparse, which means the content of individual vectors in $\mathbf{H}$ is not preserved after applying ASN. Because ASN is removed during inference, this creates a train-test mismatch for the projection network, which is detrimental to the prediction quality ((a) v.s. (d)). Removing the noise ignores the sampling process, which hurts the robustness of the model ((b) v.s. (d)). Using softmax instead of Sinkhorn normalization makes $\mathbf{Z}$ not doubly stochastic, which means $\overline{\mathbf{H}}$ might not cover every vector in $\mathbf{H}$. Those not covered are not optimized for generation during training. However, during inference, all vectors in $\mathbf{H}$ are passed to length projection to generate tokens. This mismatch is also harmful to the result ((c) v.s. (d)).

Settings	BLEU(↑)
(a) No temperature	28.39
(b) No noise	27.88
(c) Gumbel softmax	36.54
(d) Default	**38.92**

Table 1: Test set BLEU scores of different settings.

5.2 Weight Initialization

We investigate the effectiveness of initializing encoder parameters from the CTC baseline model. Specifically, we train the CTC+ASN model from scratch to compare it with the weight initialized setting. As Figure 8 reveals, the weight initialization significantly improves the translation quality while slightly increasing the latency.

This improvement comes from what was already learned by the CTC baseline model. The CTC baseline model learns to perform reordering, i.e., it

Input	the adic is one of the world's richest sovereign funds, with an estimated $800bn of assets under management.
wait-*k*	指示语 是 语言 世界的 主要 语言 之一，它 被 许多 最富有的 投资者 估计为 800亿 美元 资产。 demonstrative is language world's major language one of, it by many richest investor estimated 80billion USD asset.
CTC	迪奇 是 是 世界上 最富有的 主权 基金 之一，估计 亿 美元 的 管理 迪奇 is is world's richest sovereign funds one of, estimated 0.1 billion USD 's management
CTC+ASN	ad陀 是 是 世界上 最富有的 主权 基金 之一，估计 为 000亿 美元 的 资产 正在 管理 中 ad陀 is is world's richest sovereign funds one of , estimated is 00billion USD 's asset under management (under)
Input	it's the opening up of cracks before an earthquake, silver said in a telephone interview.
wait-*k*	"这 是 世界上 最好的 比赛，但 对于 一个 没有 地震的 地震 中 银 来说，这 是 开场白。 this is world's best contest, but for a without earthquake earthquake in silver (for) , this is opening remarks.
CTC	"这 是 地震 前 裂缝 裂缝 开放 this is earthquake before crack crack opening up
CTC+ASN	"这 是 开放的 裂缝 地震 前，" 西尔弗 说 :" 在 在 一次 电话 采访 中 this is open crack earthquake before silver said in in a telephone interview (in)

Figure 6: Examples from CWMT En→Zh. Text in red are hallucinations unrelated to source. We use $k = 3$ models.

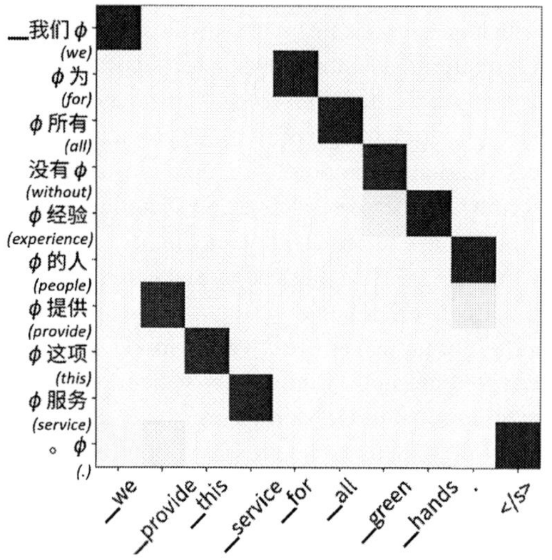

Figure 7: The **Z** predicted by ASN. The horizontal axis is the source tokens. The vertical axis is the output positions, each corresponds to 2 target tokens.

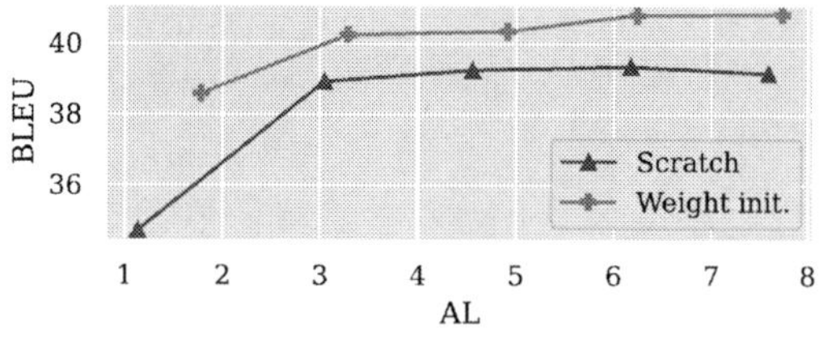

Figure 8: Latency and quality comparison between the model trained from scratch and one with weight initialization.

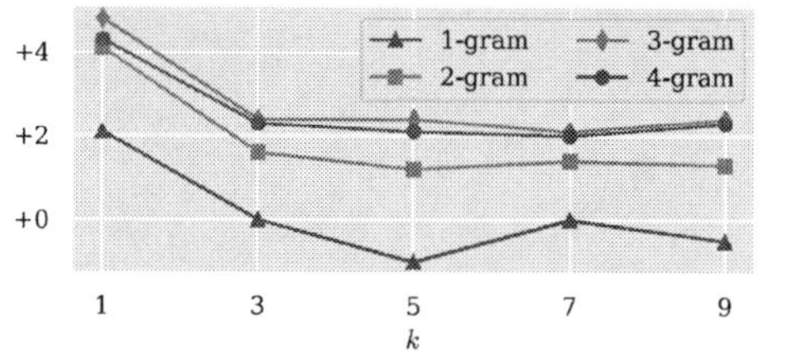

Figure 9: The n-gram precision improvement of weight initialization compared to Scratch across different delays (k).

outputs blank symbols when reading the information, then outputs the content in the target language order. Such information might span several source tokens, so the AL of the CTC baseline model is high (Figure 3). In our weight initialized setting, ASN handles the long-distance reordering that CTC was struggling with, while the local reordering already learned by CTC is preserved. In contrast, when trained from scratch, ASN would learn most of the reordering, so the encoder would not learn to perform local reordering. We hypothesize that if the model performs local reordering during inference, its latency might increase, but the higher order n-grams precision can improve, which benefits its quality. Indeed, Figure 9 indicates that the weight initialization mostly improves the 2,3,4-gram precision of the BLEU score.

6 Conclusion

We proposed a framework to alleviate the impact of long-distance reordering on simultaneous translation. We apply our method to the CTC model and show that it improves the translation quality and latency, especially English to Chinese translation. We verified that the ASN indeed learns the correct alignment between source and target. Besides, we showed that a single encoder can perform simultaneous translation with competitive quality in low latency settings and enjoys the speed advantage over wait-k Transformer.

References

Ryan Prescott Adams and Richard S Zemel. 2011. Ranking via sinkhorn propagation. *arXiv preprint arXiv:1106.1925*.

Raja Al-Khanji, Said El-Shiyab, and Riyadh Hussein. 2000. On the use of compensatory strategies in simultaneous interpretation. *Meta: Journal des traducteurs/Meta: Translators' Journal*, 45(3):548–557.

Naveen Arivazhagan, Colin Cherry, Wolfgang Macherey, Chung-Cheng Chiu, Semih Yavuz, Ruoming Pang, Wei Li, and Colin Raffel. 2019. Monotonic infinite lookback attention for simultaneous machine translation. In *Proceedings of the 57th Annual Meeting of the Association for Computational Linguistics*, pages 1313–1323, Florence, Italy. Association for Computational Linguistics.

Lukas Biewald. 2020. Experiment tracking with weights and biases. Software available from wandb.com.

Chris Callison-Burch, Philipp Koehn, Christof Monz, and Josh Schroeder. 2009. Findings of the 2009 Workshop on Statistical Machine Translation. In *Proceedings of the Fourth Workshop on Statistical Machine Translation*, pages 1–28, Athens, Greece. Association for Computational Linguistics.

Chi Chen, Maosong Sun, and Yang Liu. 2021a. Mask-align: Self-supervised neural word alignment. In *Proceedings of the 59th Annual Meeting of the Association for Computational Linguistics and the 11th International Joint Conference on Natural Language Processing (Volume 1: Long Papers)*, pages 4781–4791, Online. Association for Computational Linguistics.

Jiajun Chen and Jiajun Zhang. 2019. *Machine Translation: 14th China Workshop, CWMT 2018, Wuyishan, China, October 25-26, 2018, Proceedings*, volume 954. Springer.

Junkun Chen, Renjie Zheng, Atsuhito Kita, Mingbo Ma, and Liang Huang. 2021b. Improving simultaneous translation by incorporating pseudo-references with fewer reorderings. In *Proceedings of the 2021 Conference on Empirical Methods in Natural Language Processing*, pages 5857–5864, Online and Punta Cana, Dominican Republic. Association for Computational Linguistics.

Chung-Cheng Chiu and Colin Raffel. 2018. Monotonic chunkwise attention. In *6th International Conference on Learning Representations, ICLR 2018, Vancouver, BC, Canada, April 30 - May 3, 2018, Conference Track Proceedings*. OpenReview.net.

Kyunghyun Cho and Masha Esipova. 2016. Can neural machine translation do simultaneous translation? *ArXiv preprint*, abs/1606.02012.

Katsuki Chousa, Katsuhito Sudoh, and Satoshi Nakamura. 2019. Simultaneous neural machine translation using connectionist temporal classification.

Shun-Po Chuang, Yung-Sung Chuang, Chih-Chiang Chang, and Hung-yi Lee. 2021. Investigating the reordering capability in CTC-based non-autoregressive end-to-end speech translation. In *Findings of the Association for Computational Linguistics: ACL-IJCNLP 2021*, pages 1068–1077, Online. Association for Computational Linguistics.

Fahim Dalvi, Nadir Durrani, Hassan Sajjad, and Stephan Vogel. 2018. Incremental decoding and training methods for simultaneous translation in neural machine translation. In *Proceedings of the 2018 Conference of the North American Chapter of the Association for Computational Linguistics: Human Language Technologies, Volume 2 (Short Papers)*, pages 493–499, New Orleans, Louisiana. Association for Computational Linguistics.

Zi-Yi Dou and Graham Neubig. 2021. Word alignment by fine-tuning embeddings on parallel corpora. In *Proceedings of the 16th Conference of the European Chapter of the Association for Computational Linguistics: Main Volume*, pages 2112–2128, Online. Association for Computational Linguistics.

Maha Elbayad, Laurent Besacier, and Jakob Verbeek. 2020. Efficient wait-k models for simultaneous machine translation. In *Interspeech 2020, 21st Annual Conference of the International Speech Communication Association, Virtual Event, Shanghai, China, 25-29 October 2020*, pages 1461–1465. ISCA.

Alex Graves, Santiago Fernández, Faustino J. Gomez, and Jürgen Schmidhuber. 2006. Connectionist temporal classification: labelling unsegmented sequence data with recurrent neural networks. In *Machine Learning, Proceedings of the Twenty-Third International Conference (ICML 2006), Pittsburgh, Pennsylvania, USA, June 25-29, 2006*, volume 148 of *ACM International Conference Proceeding Series*, pages 369–376. ACM.

Jiatao Gu, James Bradbury, Caiming Xiong, Victor O. K. Li, and Richard Socher. 2018. Non-autoregressive neural machine translation. In *6th International Conference on Learning Representations, ICLR 2018, Vancouver, BC, Canada, April 30 - May 3, 2018, Conference Track Proceedings*. OpenReview.net.

Jiatao Gu and Xiang Kong. 2021. Fully non-autoregressive neural machine translation: Tricks of the trade. In *Findings of the Association for Computational Linguistics: ACL-IJCNLP 2021*, pages 120–133, Online. Association for Computational Linguistics.

Jiatao Gu, Graham Neubig, Kyunghyun Cho, and Victor O.K. Li. 2017. Learning to translate in real-time with neural machine translation. In *Proceedings of the 15th Conference of the European Chapter of the Association for Computational Linguistics: Volume 1, Long Papers*, pages 1053–1062, Valencia, Spain. Association for Computational Linguistics.

He He, Jordan Boyd-Graber, and Hal Daumé III. 2016. Interpretese vs. translationese: The uniqueness of human strategies in simultaneous interpretation. In *Proceedings of the 2016 Conference of the North American Chapter of the Association for Computational Linguistics: Human Language Technologies*, pages 971–976, San Diego, California. Association for Computational Linguistics.

He He, Alvin Grissom II, John Morgan, Jordan Boyd-Graber, and Hal Daumé III. 2015. Syntax-based rewriting for simultaneous machine translation. In *Proceedings of the 2015 Conference on Empirical Methods in Natural Language Processing*, pages 55–64, Lisbon, Portugal. Association for Computational Linguistics.

Suyoun Kim, Michael L. Seltzer, Jinyu Li, and Rui Zhao. 2018. Improved training for online end-to-end speech recognition systems. In *Interspeech 2018, 19th Annual Conference of the International Speech Communication Association, Hyderabad, India, 2-6 September 2018*, pages 2913–2917. ISCA.

Yoon Kim and Alexander M. Rush. 2016. Sequence-level knowledge distillation. In *Proceedings of the 2016 Conference on Empirical Methods in Natural Language Processing*, pages 1317–1327, Austin, Texas. Association for Computational Linguistics.

Diederik P. Kingma and Jimmy Ba. 2015. Adam: A method for stochastic optimization. In *3rd International Conference on Learning Representations, ICLR 2015, San Diego, CA, USA, May 7-9, 2015, Conference Track Proceedings*.

Diederik P. Kingma and Max Welling. 2014. Auto-encoding variational bayes. In *2nd International Conference on Learning Representations, ICLR 2014, Banff, AB, Canada, April 14-16, 2014, Conference Track Proceedings*.

Philipp Koehn. 2004. Statistical significance tests for machine translation evaluation. In *Proceedings of the 2004 Conference on Empirical Methods in Natural Language Processing*, pages 388–395, Barcelona, Spain. Association for Computational Linguistics.

Taku Kudo and John Richardson. 2018. SentencePiece: A simple and language independent subword tokenizer and detokenizer for neural text processing. In *Proceedings of the 2018 Conference on Empirical Methods in Natural Language Processing: System Demonstrations*, pages 66–71, Brussels, Belgium. Association for Computational Linguistics.

Jason Lee, Elman Mansimov, and Kyunghyun Cho. 2018. Deterministic non-autoregressive neural sequence modeling by iterative refinement. In *Proceedings of the 2018 Conference on Empirical Methods in Natural Language Processing*, pages 1173–1182, Brussels, Belgium. Association for Computational Linguistics.

Jindřich Libovický and Jindřich Helcl. 2018. End-to-end non-autoregressive neural machine translation with connectionist temporal classification. In *Proceedings of the 2018 Conference on Empirical Methods in Natural Language Processing*, pages 3016–3021, Brussels, Belgium. Association for Computational Linguistics.

Yuping Luo, Chung-Cheng Chiu, Navdeep Jaitly, and Ilya Sutskever. 2017. Learning online alignments with continuous rewards policy gradient. In *2017 IEEE International Conference on Acoustics, Speech and Signal Processing, ICASSP 2017, New Orleans, LA, USA, March 5-9, 2017*, pages 2801–2805. IEEE.

Mingbo Ma, Liang Huang, Hao Xiong, Renjie Zheng, Kaibo Liu, Baigong Zheng, Chuanqiang Zhang, Zhongjun He, Hairong Liu, Xing Li, Hua Wu, and Haifeng Wang. 2019. STACL: Simultaneous translation with implicit anticipation and controllable latency using prefix-to-prefix framework. In *Proceedings of the 57th Annual Meeting of the Association for Computational Linguistics*, pages 3025–3036, Florence, Italy. Association for Computational Linguistics.

Xutai Ma, Mohammad Javad Dousti, Changhan Wang, Jiatao Gu, and Juan Pino. 2020a. SIMULEVAL: An evaluation toolkit for simultaneous translation. In *Proceedings of the 2020 Conference on Empirical Methods in Natural Language Processing: System Demonstrations*, pages 144–150, Online. Association for Computational Linguistics.

Xutai Ma, Juan Pino, and Philipp Koehn. 2020b. SimulMT to SimulST: Adapting simultaneous text translation to end-to-end simultaneous speech translation. In *Proceedings of the 1st Conference of the Asia-Pacific Chapter of the Association for Computational Linguistics and the 10th International Joint Conference on Natural Language Processing*, pages 582–587, Suzhou, China. Association for Computational Linguistics.

Xutai Ma, Juan Miguel Pino, James Cross, Liezl Puzon, and Jiatao Gu. 2020c. Monotonic multihead attention. In *8th International Conference on Learning Representations, ICLR 2020, Addis Ababa, Ethiopia, April 26-30, 2020*. OpenReview.net.

Gonzalo E. Mena, David Belanger, Scott W. Linderman, and Jasper Snoek. 2018. Learning latent permutations with gumbel-sinkhorn networks. In *6th International Conference on Learning Representations, ICLR 2018, Vancouver, BC, Canada, April 30 - May 3, 2018, Conference Track Proceedings*. OpenReview.net.

Mathias Müller, Annette Rios, and Rico Sennrich. 2020. Domain robustness in neural machine translation. In *Proceedings of the 14th Conference of the Association for Machine Translation in the Americas (Volume 1: Research Track)*, pages 151–164, Virtual. Association for Machine Translation in the Americas.

Myle Ott, Sergey Edunov, Alexei Baevski, Angela Fan, Sam Gross, Nathan Ng, David Grangier, and Michael

Auli. 2019. fairseq: A fast, extensible toolkit for sequence modeling. In *Proceedings of the 2019 Conference of the North American Chapter of the Association for Computational Linguistics (Demonstrations)*, pages 48–53, Minneapolis, Minnesota. Association for Computational Linguistics.

Kishore Papineni, Salim Roukos, Todd Ward, and Wei-Jing Zhu. 2002. Bleu: a method for automatic evaluation of machine translation. In *Proceedings of the 40th Annual Meeting of the Association for Computational Linguistics*, pages 311–318, Philadelphia, Pennsylvania, USA. Association for Computational Linguistics.

Maja Popović. 2015. chrF: character n-gram F-score for automatic MT evaluation. In *Proceedings of the Tenth Workshop on Statistical Machine Translation*, pages 392–395, Lisbon, Portugal. Association for Computational Linguistics.

Maja Popović. 2016. chrF deconstructed: beta parameters and n-gram weights. In *Proceedings of the First Conference on Machine Translation: Volume 2, Shared Task Papers*, pages 499–504, Berlin, Germany. Association for Computational Linguistics.

Matt Post. 2018. A call for clarity in reporting BLEU scores. In *Proceedings of the Third Conference on Machine Translation: Research Papers*, pages 186–191, Brussels, Belgium. Association for Computational Linguistics.

Colin Raffel, Minh-Thang Luong, Peter J. Liu, Ron J. Weiss, and Douglas Eck. 2017. Online and linear-time attention by enforcing monotonic alignments. In *Proceedings of the 34th International Conference on Machine Learning, ICML 2017, Sydney, NSW, Australia, 6-11 August 2017*, volume 70 of *Proceedings of Machine Learning Research*, pages 2837–2846. PMLR.

Qiu Ran, Yankai Lin, Peng Li, and Jie Zhou. 2021. Guiding non-autoregressive neural machine translation decoding with reordering information. *Proceedings of the AAAI Conference on Artificial Intelligence*, 35(15):13727–13735.

Richard Sinkhorn. 1964. A relationship between arbitrary positive matrices and doubly stochastic matrices. *The annals of mathematical statistics*, 35(2):876–879.

Christian Szegedy, Vincent Vanhoucke, Sergey Ioffe, Jonathon Shlens, and Zbigniew Wojna. 2016. Rethinking the inception architecture for computer vision. In *2016 IEEE Conference on Computer Vision and Pattern Recognition, CVPR 2016, Las Vegas, NV, USA, June 27-30, 2016*, pages 2818–2826. IEEE Computer Society.

Yi Tay, Dara Bahri, Liu Yang, Donald Metzler, and Da-Cheng Juan. 2020. Sparse sinkhorn attention. In *Proceedings of the 37th International Conference on Machine Learning, ICML 2020, 13-18 July 2020, Virtual Event*, volume 119 of *Proceedings of Machine Learning Research*, pages 9438–9447. PMLR.

Ashish Vaswani, Noam Shazeer, Niki Parmar, Jakob Uszkoreit, Llion Jones, Aidan N. Gomez, Lukasz Kaiser, and Illia Polosukhin. 2017. Attention is all you need. In *Advances in Neural Information Processing Systems 30: Annual Conference on Neural Information Processing Systems 2017, December 4-9, 2017, Long Beach, CA, USA*, pages 5998–6008.

Jingyi Zhang and Josef van Genabith. 2021. A bidirectional transformer based alignment model for unsupervised word alignment. In *Proceedings of the 59th Annual Meeting of the Association for Computational Linguistics and the 11th International Joint Conference on Natural Language Processing (Volume 1: Long Papers)*, pages 283–292, Online. Association for Computational Linguistics.

Ruiqing Zhang, Chuanqiang Zhang, Zhongjun He, Hua Wu, and Haifeng Wang. 2020. Learning adaptive segmentation policy for simultaneous translation. In *Proceedings of the 2020 Conference on Empirical Methods in Natural Language Processing (EMNLP)*, pages 2280–2289, Online. Association for Computational Linguistics.

Baigong Zheng, Kaibo Liu, Renjie Zheng, Mingbo Ma, Hairong Liu, and Liang Huang. 2020. Simultaneous translation policies: From fixed to adaptive. In *Proceedings of the 58th Annual Meeting of the Association for Computational Linguistics*, pages 2847–2853, Online. Association for Computational Linguistics.

Baigong Zheng, Renjie Zheng, Mingbo Ma, and Liang Huang. 2019a. Simpler and faster learning of adaptive policies for simultaneous translation. In *Proceedings of the 2019 Conference on Empirical Methods in Natural Language Processing and the 9th International Joint Conference on Natural Language Processing (EMNLP-IJCNLP)*, pages 1349–1354, Hong Kong, China. Association for Computational Linguistics.

Baigong Zheng, Renjie Zheng, Mingbo Ma, and Liang Huang. 2019b. Simultaneous translation with flexible policy via restricted imitation learning. In *Proceedings of the 57th Annual Meeting of the Association for Computational Linguistics*, pages 5816–5822, Florence, Italy. Association for Computational Linguistics.

Chunting Zhou, Jiatao Gu, and Graham Neubig. 2020. Understanding knowledge distillation in non-autoregressive machine translation. In *8th International Conference on Learning Representations, ICLR 2020, Addis Ababa, Ethiopia, April 26-30, 2020*. OpenReview.net.

A Source Code

Our source code is available at `https://github.com/George0828Zhang/sinkhorn-simultrans`. Please follow the instructions in `README.md` to reproduce the results.

B Datasets

We use the CWMT English to Chinese and WMT15 German to English datasets for experiments. They can be downloaded in the following links: 1) CWMT `http://nlp.nju.edu.cn/cwmt-wmt/)` 2) WMT15 `http://www.statmt.org/wmt15/translation-task.html`. The WMT15 De-En is a widely used corpus for simultaneous machine translation, in the news domain. Another popular dataset is the NIST En-Zh corpus, however, NIST is not publicly available, thus we use CWMT corpus instead. CWMT is also in the news domain.

Both datasets are publicly available. We didn't find any license information for both. We adhered to the terms of use for both. We didn't find any information on names or uniquely identified individual people or offensive content and the steps taken to protect or anonymize them.

C Transformer Hyperparameters

Our architecture related hyperparameters are listed in Table 2. We follow the *base* configuration of Transformer for encoder-decoder models. For models without decoder, we follow the same configuration for its encoder. The total parameter count for Transformer is 76.9M. For encoder-only models without ASN, it is 52.2M. The ASN has 12.6M parameters.

Hyperparameter	(A)	(B)
encoder layers	6	6
decoder layers	6	0
embed dim	512	512
feed forward dim	2048	2048
num heads	8	8
dropout	0.1	0.1

Table 2: Transformer architecture related hyperparameters for each model. (A) full-sentence and wait-k model (B) CTC encoder model.

D ASN Hyperparameters

We perform a Bayesian hyperparameter optimization on both datasets using the sweep utility provided by Weights & Biases (Biewald, 2020). Table 3 shows the search range and the selected values. We found a well performing set in the 7th run for CWMT and 1st run for WMT15. It is possible that different k might prefer different hyperparameters. However, we use the same set to fairly compare to wait-k, and to reduce the cost. All subsequent results are obtained using this set of values if not specified.

Hyperparameter	CWMT	WMT15	Range
layers M	3	3	1, 3
iterations l	16	16	4, 8, 16
temperature τ	0.25	0.13	[0.05, 0.3]
noise factor δ	0.3	0.45	[0.1, 0.3]
upsample ratio μ	2	2	2, 3
mask ratio γ	0.5	0.5	[0., 0.7]

Table 3: ASN related hyperparameters and the search range. We use Bayesian hyperparameter optimization, so the combinations are not exhaustively searched.

E Hardware and Environment

For training, each run are conducted on a container with a single Tesla V100-SXM2-32GB GPU, 4 CPU cores and 90GB memory. The operating system is `Linux-3.10.0-1127.el7.x86_64-x86_64-with-glibc2.10`. The version of Python is 3.8.10, and version of PyTorch is 1.9.0. We use a specific version of fairseq (Ott et al., 2019) toolkit, the instructions are provided in `README.md` of our source code. All run uses mixed precision (i.e. fp16) training implemented by fairseq. All training took 10-15 hours to converge (early stopped).

For inference, the evaluation are conducted on another machine with 12 CPU cores (although we restrict the evaluation to only use 2 threads), 32GB memory and no GPU is used. The operating system is `Linux-5.11.0-25-generic-x86_64-with-glibc2.10`.

F Gumbel-Sinkhorn Operator

The Sinkhorn normalization (Adams and Zemel, 2011) iteratively performs row-wise and column-wise normalization on a matrix, converting it to a doubly stochastic matrix. Formally, for a N dimensional square matrix $X \in \mathbb{R}^{N \times N}$, the Sinkhorn normalization $S(X)$ is defined as:

$$S^0(X) = \exp(X), \tag{8}$$

$$S^l(X) = \mathcal{T}_c\left(\mathcal{T}_r\left(S^{l-1}(X)\right)\right), \tag{9}$$

$$S(X) = \lim_{l \to \infty} S^l(X). \tag{10}$$

where $\mathcal{T}_r$ and $\mathcal{T}_c$ are row-wise and column-wise normalization operators on a matrix, defined below:

$$\mathcal{T}_r(X) = X \oslash (X \mathbf{1}_N \mathbf{1}_N^\top), \tag{11}$$

$$\mathcal{T}_c(X) = X \oslash (\mathbf{1}_N \mathbf{1}_N^\top X). \tag{12}$$

The $\oslash$ denotes the element-wise division, and $\mathbf{1}_N$ denotes a column vector full of ones. As the number of iterations l grows, $S^l(X)$ will eventually converge to a doubly stochastic matrix (equation 10) (Sinkhorn, 1964). In practice, we often consider the truncated version, where l is finite.

On the other hand, the Gumbel-Sinkhorn operator adds the Gumbel reparametrization trick (Kingma and Welling, 2014) to the Sinkhorn normalization, in order to approximate the sampling process. It can be used to estimate marginal probability via sampling. Formally, suppose that a noise matrix ε is sampled from independent and identically distributed (i.i.d.) Gumbel distributions:

$$\boldsymbol{\mathcal{E}} \in \mathbb{R}^{N \times N} \overset{i.i.d.}{\sim} Gumbel(0, 1). \tag{13}$$

The Gumbel-Sinkhorn operator is described by first adding the Gumbel noise $\boldsymbol{\mathcal{E}}$, then scaling by a positive temperature τ, and finally applying the Sinkhorn normalization:

$$S((X + \boldsymbol{\mathcal{E}})/\tau). \tag{14}$$

By taking the limit $\tau \to 0^+$, the output converges to a permutation matrix. The Gumbel-Sinkhorn operator approximates sampling from a distribution of permutation matrices. Thus, the equation 2 can be estimated through sampling:

$$p(\mathbf{y}|\mathbf{x}) = \mathbb{E}_{\mathbf{Z} \sim p(\mathbf{Z}|\mathbf{x})}\left[p_g(\mathbf{y}|\mathbf{x}, \mathbf{Z})\right]. \tag{15}$$

In practice, we sample from $p(\mathbf{Z}|\mathbf{x}, \mathbf{y})$ instead, as it is easier to perform word alignment ($p(\mathbf{Z}|\mathbf{x}, \mathbf{y})$) than directly predicting order ($p(\mathbf{Z}|\mathbf{x})$).

G Details on Evaluation Metrics

G.1 Average Lagging (AL)

The AL measures the degree the user is out of sync with the speaker (Ma et al., 2019). It measures the system's lagging behind an oracle wait-0 policy. For a read-write policy $g(\cdot)$, define the cut-off step $\tau_g(|\mathbf{x}|)$ as the decoding step when source sentence finishes:

$$\tau_g(|\mathbf{x}|) = \min\{t| \quad g(t) = |\mathbf{x}|\}$$

Then the AL for an example $\mathbf{x}, \mathbf{y}$ is defined as:

$$\mathrm{AL}_g(\mathbf{x}, \mathbf{y}) = \frac{1}{\tau_g(|\mathbf{x}|)} \sum_{t=1}^{\tau_g(|\mathbf{x}|)} g(t) - \frac{t-1}{|\mathbf{y}|/|\mathbf{x}|}$$

The second term in the summation represents the ideal latency of an oracle wait-0 policy in terms of target words (or characters for Chinese). The AL averaged across the test set is reported.

G.2 Computation Aware Average Lagging (AL-CA)

Originally proposed for simultaneous speech-to-text translation (Ma et al., 2020b), the AL-CA is similar to AL, but takes the actual computation time into account, and is measured in milliseconds.

$$\begin{aligned}&\mathrm{AL}_g^{CA}(\mathbf{x}, \mathbf{y}) \\ &= \frac{1}{\tau_g(|\mathbf{x}|)} \sum_{i=1}^{\tau_g(|\mathbf{x}|)} d_{CA}(y_i) - \frac{(i-1) \cdot T_s}{|\mathbf{y}|/|\mathbf{x}|}\end{aligned} \tag{16}$$

The $d_{CA}(y_i)$ is the the time that elapses from the beginning of the process to the prediction of y_i, **which considers computation**. T_s represents the actual duration of each source feature. The second term in the summation represents the ideal latency of an oracle wait-0 policy in terms of milliseconds, **without considering computation**. In speech-to-text translation, T_s corresponds to the duration of each speech feature. However, since our source feature is text, the "actual duration" for a word is unavailable, so we set $T_s = 1$.

The motivation behind using AL-CA here is to show the speed advantage of CTC models. When calculating AL-CA, we account for variance by running the evaluation 3 times and report the average.

G.3 Character n-gram F-score (chrF)

The general formula for the chrF score is given by:

$$\text{chrF}\beta = (1+\beta^2)\frac{\text{chrP} \cdot \text{chrR}}{\beta^2 \cdot \text{chrP} + \text{chrR}}. \tag{17}$$

where

- chrP: percentage of character n-grams in the hypothesis which have a counterpart in the reference.
- chrR: percentage of character n-grams in the reference which are also present in the hypothesis.
- β: a parameter which assigns β times more importance to recall than to precision.

The maximum n-gram length N is optimal when $N = 6$ (Popović, 2015), and the optimal β is shown to be $\beta = 2$ (Popović, 2016).

The motivation behind using chrF2 is that 1) as machine translation researchers, we are encouraged to report multiple automatic evaluation metrics. 2) BLEU is purely precision-based, while chrF2 is F-score based, which takes recall into account. 3) chrF2 is shown to correlate better with human rankings than the BLEU score.

G.4 k-Anticipation Rate (k-AR)

For each sentence pair, we first use *awesome-align* (Dou and Neubig, 2021) to extract word alignments, then for each aligned target word y_j, it is considered a k-anticipation if it is aligned to a source word x_i that is k words behind, in other words, if $i - k + 1 > j$. See Figure 10 for an example of 2-anticipation. The k-AR is calculated as the percentage of k-anticipation among all aligned word pairs.

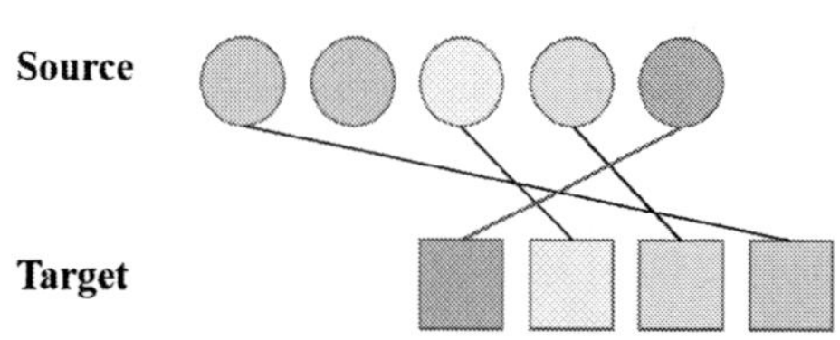

Figure 10: An example of 2-anticipation. The links are alignments, and the red link is an instance of anticipation.

H SimulEval Configuration

Table 4 show the language specific options for latency evaluation on SimulEval, which affect the AL calculation.

Options	En	Zh
–eval-latency-unit	word	char
–no-space	false	true

Table 4: Configuration for SimulEval under different target languages.

I SacreBLEU Signatures

Table 5 shows the signatures of SacreBLEU evaluation.

Lang	Metric	Signature
Zh	BLEU	nrefs:var|bs:1000|seed:12345 |case:lc|eff:no|tok:zh |smooth:exp|version:2.0.0
Zh	chrF2	nrefs:var|bs:1000|seed:12345 |case:lc|eff:yes|nc:6 |nw:0 |space:no|version:2.0.0
En	BLEU	nrefs:1|bs:1000|seed:12345 |case:lc|eff:no|tok:13a |smooth:exp|version:2.0.0
En	chrF2	nrefs:1|bs:1000|seed:12345 |case:lc|eff:yes|nc:6 |nw:0 |space:no|version:2.0.0

Table 5: The SacreBLEU signatures for each target language and each metric.

J Detailed Statistics of Quality Metrics

Table 7 shows the detailed distributional statistics of the quality metrics evaluated on the CWMT and WMT15 datasets. All settings are trained once, but we use statistical significant test using bootstrap resampling.

K Latency-quality results with chrF

Figure 11 show the quality-latency trade off with chrF on the CWMT En-zh dataset. Figure 12 show the quality-latency trade off with chrF on the WMT15 De-En dataset. These results have similar trends with BLEU score.

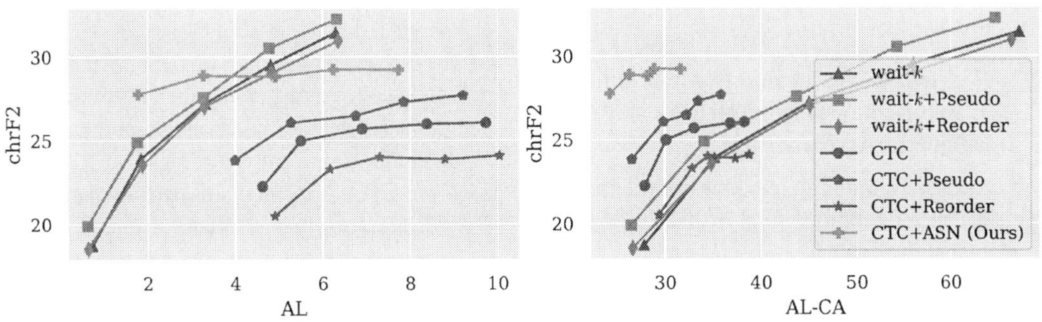

Figure 11: Latency-quality trade off with chrF score on the CWMT En-Zh dataset. Each line represents a system, and the 5 nodes corresponds to $k = 1, 3, 5, 7, 9$, from left to right. The figures share the same legend.

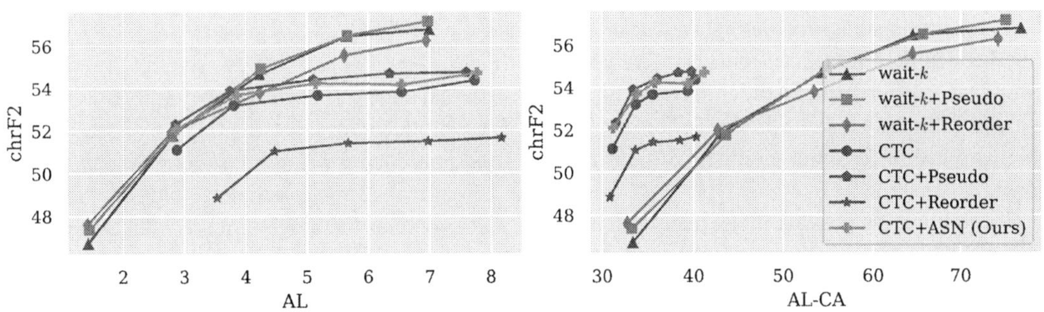

Figure 12: Latency-quality trade off with chrF score on the WMT15 De-En dataset. Each line represents a system, and the 5 nodes corresponds to $k = 1, 3, 5, 7, 9$, from left to right. The figures share the same legend.

L Performance with Oracle Reordering

We study our encoder models' performance when the oracle reordering is provided. To achieve this, we re-use the ASN during inference, and fed the (first) reference translation as the context to ASN to estimate $\mathbf{Z}$. The results compared to default setting is shown in Table 6. This result serves as a upperbound for the performance of CTC-based encoder models.

M More on ASN Output

We describe how the target tokens are placed on the vertical axis of the ASN output illustration. Since the length projection upsamples $\overline{\mathbf{H}}$ to 2 times longer, each position of $\overline{\mathbf{H}}$ corresponds to two target tokens (including repetition and blank symbols introduced by CTC). To find the optimal position for each target tokens and blank symbols, we use the Viterbi alignment (an implementation is publicly available at `https://github.com/rosinality/imputer-pytorch`) to align the model's logits and the actual target tokens.

Figure 13 shows more examples of the approximated permutation matrix predicted by the ASN.

k	Method	BLEU	1/2/3/4-gram	BP
1	Default	38.58	76.7 / 51.0 / 32.5 / 20.6	0.96
	+ Oracle	41.59	76.0 / 52.7 / 35.9 / 23.9	0.96
3	Default	40.24	79.5 / 53.7 / 34.8 / 22.6	0.94
	+ Oracle	41.75	77.5 / 53.7 / 36.5 / 24.4	0.95
5	Default	40.34	78.8 / 53.5 / 35.0 / 22.7	0.94
	+ Oracle	41.70	76.0 / 52.4 / 35.5 / 23.6	0.98
7	Default	40.81	80.0 / 54.2 / 35.2 / 22.9	0.94
	+ Oracle	43.37	78.8 / 55.2 / 37.9 / 25.8	0.96
9	Default	40.83	79.5 / 54.1 / 35.4 / 23.1	0.94
	+ Oracle	41.77	76.3 / 52.7 / 35.5 / 23.6	0.98

Table 6: The BLEU score on the CWMT dataset, including n-gram precision and brevity penalty (BP), of the CTC+ASN system for each k with and without oracle order.

The sentence pairs are from CWMT En-Zh test set.

N More CWMT Examples

Figure 14 shows more examples from CWMT test set and the predictions of wait-k, CTC and CTC+ASN models.

O FAQ

Q1 The trained ASN cannot be used during inference, how to guarantee the model can still perform reordering?

We categorize reordering into local reordering and long-distance reordering. Our goal is for the ASN to primarily deal with long-distance reordering. In Section 5.2, we observed that employing the weight initialization improves the 2,3,4-gram precision (but not the unigram), and slightly increases the latency. This suggest that CTC+ASN model can indeed perform local reordering during inference.

As for long-distance reordering, we stress that in simultaneous interpretation, humans actively avoid long-distance reordering in order to reduce latency, which is also the goal of SimulMT. This provides the justification for removing the ASN during inference. (equation 3)

We additionally provide the performance when **Z** is available during inference in Appendix L.

Q2 Using ASN during training may cause the model to rely on Z, which may cause train-test discrepancy during inference?

In terms of the mismatch of hidden representation, because Gumbel-Sinkhorn gaurantees that **Z** is doubly stochastic (and almost permutation, depending on τ), the representation before and after ASN would only differ by a permutation. This is also discussed in Section 5.1 where removing Sinkhorn nomalization indeed negatively impact the performance.

As for the mismatch of the order of the representation, we note that the length projection network is merely a position-wise affine transformation, which means it is independent of time, so the mismatch of order between training and testing would not negatively impact the prediction made by the length projection network.

Q3 Proposed method underperform wait-k in high latency.

Simultaneous translation aims to translate in a short time, hence our work focuses on improving the translation quality under low latency setting. The higher latency model is less acceptable in practice. For instance, a $k = 9$ model decodes a single word after seeing 9 words. We included the results for experimental completeness purpose.

For the reason why proposed method underperform wait-k model: Based on the observation in Appendix L, 43.37 is the best performance of CTC+ASN method. It is inferior to the wait-9 model's 43.80. We suspect that it is caused by the inherent difference between non-autoregressive (NAR) model and auto-regressive (AR) model. However, CTC+ASN method's performance is relatively consistent when the latency decreases, while wait-k's performance decreases drastically. Therefore, to fit the simultaneous translation setting, our proposed method is more suitable than wait-k.

Q4 Explanation for why ASN could outperform Reorder and Pseudo reference baselines?

For the Reorder baseline, we suspect that since the external aligner is fixed and not jointly optimized, it may produce incorrect alignments, or miss correct ones, producing wrongful training targets.

As for the Pseudo reference baseline, there are two problems that might limit its effectiveness. For one, the pseudo reference is produced from a full-sentence model while using a wait-k decoding strategy, which is a train-test discrepancy. For another, in order to compensate for the first issue, the original translation is included as a second target for each example. This leads to the infamous multi-modality problem for non-autoregressive models, which might be harmful to our CTC-based encoder.

Q5 What are the limitations of the proposed method?

First of all, for SimulMT to be applicable to a conference setting, we assume a streaming ASR is available. However, we did not account for ASR errors in our SimulMT models.

Second, as discussed in Section 4.4, our method is only effective if the language pair includes sufficient long-distance reordering. For instance, when translation from English to Spanish, we there's hardly any reason to employ our method.

Finally, as discussed in Q3, our method is less advantageous when the latency budget is high.

Q6 What are the risks of the proposed method?

One risk is that our method may favor low-latency over high precision, which means that erroneous translation may occur, which might twist the meaning of source sentence. However, latency and quality is inherently a trade-off, and erroneous translation could be mitigated by refinement or post-editing techniques.

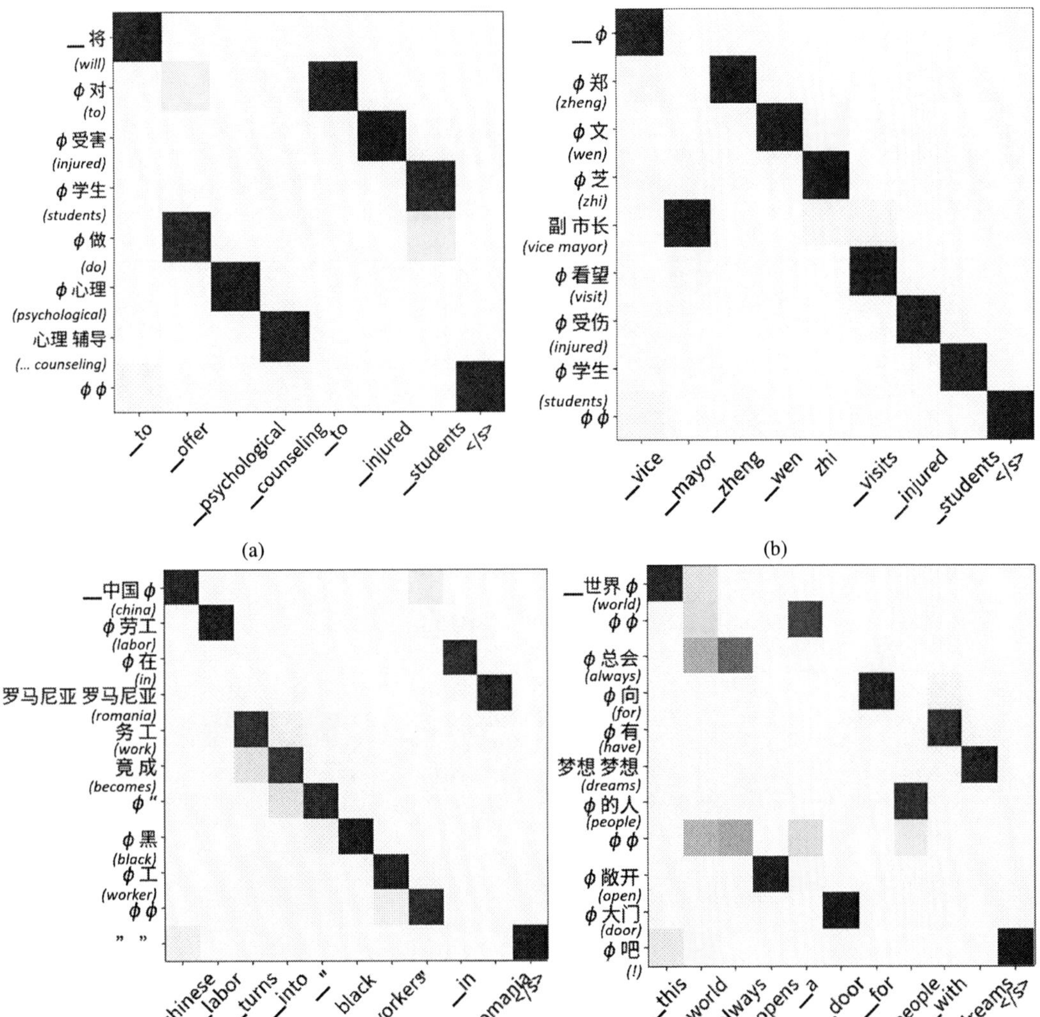

Figure 13: More approximated permutation matrices predicted by ASN.

		CWMT En→Zh				WMT15 De→En			
Delay	**Method**	**BLEU**	**μ±95%CI**	**chrF2**	**μ±95%CI**	**BLEU**	**μ±95%CI**	**chrF2**	**μ±95%CI**
offline	Transformer	45.85	45.85±0.60	32.46	32.46±0.45	31.67	31.70±0.77	57.65	57.67±0.61
	wait-k	24.31	24.29±0.62	18.69	18.67±0.43	19.91	19.91±0.68	46.68	46.70±0.69
	wait-k+Pseudo	*25.93	25.91±0.66	*19.89	19.87±0.46	*20.63	20.63±0.68	*47.34	47.35±0.68
	wait-k+Reorder	23.98	23.96±0.59	18.50	18.49±0.39	*20.54	20.55±0.65	*47.59	47.61±0.68
$k=1$	CTC	28.44	28.42±0.56	22.24	22.24±0.35	23.08	23.09±0.69	51.11	51.13±0.56
	CTC+Pseudo	†30.77	30.75±0.61	†23.81	23.81±0.38	†**24.48**	24.49±0.69	†**52.31**	52.32±0.56
	CTC+Reorder	†24.09	24.08±0.58	†20.49	20.48±0.36	†20.77	20.78±0.65	†48.84	48.85±0.56
	CTC+ASN	†**38.58**	38.57±0.45	†**27.74**	27.73±0.32	†24.17	24.19±0.70	†52.08	52.10±0.54
	wait-k	32.27	32.25±0.65	23.90	23.90±0.43	25.85	25.87±0.78	51.79	51.81±0.67
	wait-k+Pseudo	*33.53	33.52±0.64	*24.88	24.87±0.44	25.74	25.76±0.77	51.76	51.78±0.66
	wait-k+Reorder	*31.47	31.46±0.66	*23.54	23.54±0.45	*25.26	25.28±0.73	51.97	51.99±0.65
$k=3$	CTC	32.45	32.44±0.61	24.97	24.96±0.39	26.07	26.09±0.69	53.19	53.21±0.58
	CTC+Pseudo	†34.03	34.03±0.61	†26.05	26.05±0.39	†**26.61**	26.63±0.68	†**53.89**	53.91±0.55
	CTC+Reorder	†28.52	28.50±0.62	†23.28	23.28±0.40	†23.50	23.52±0.71	†51.04	51.06±0.55
	CTC+ASN	†**40.24**	40.23±0.51	†**28.88**	28.87±0.34	†26.53	26.55±0.73	†53.68	53.70±0.57
	wait-k	37.40	37.39±0.65	27.19	27.19±0.44	**28.52**	28.54±0.82	**54.66**	54.68±0.64
	wait-k+Pseudo	*37.96	37.95±0.67	*27.56	27.56±0.46	**28.68**	28.71±0.78	**54.92**	54.95±0.60
	wait-k+Reorder	*36.86	36.84±0.65	27.00	26.99±0.44	*27.35	27.38±0.75	*53.78	53.81±0.63
$k=5$	CTC	33.64	33.63±0.62	25.67	25.66±0.39	26.51	26.53±0.77	53.66	53.68±0.58
	CTC+Pseudo	†34.65	34.64±0.61	†26.45	26.45±0.40	†27.48	27.49±0.76	†**54.41**	54.43±0.60
	CTC+Reorder	†29.68	29.68±0.61	†23.99	23.98±0.38	†23.90	23.91±0.72	†51.41	51.44±0.57
	CTC+ASN	†**40.34**	40.33±0.50	†**28.81**	28.81±0.36	†27.43	27.45±0.75	†54.24	54.27±0.57
	wait-k	40.78	40.76±0.67	29.50	29.50±0.48	**30.28**	30.32±0.80	**56.44**	56.47±0.62
	wait-k+Pseudo	***42.34**	42.34±0.62	***30.50**	30.50±0.45	**30.53**	30.56±0.82	**56.47**	56.49±0.64
	wait-k+Reorder	*40.23	40.23±0.61	*29.03	29.03±0.45	*28.77	28.79±0.75	*55.55	55.58±0.57
$k=7$	CTC	34.14	34.12±0.58	25.96	25.95±0.40	26.77	26.78±0.72	53.82	53.84±0.62
	CTC+Pseudo	†36.04	36.04±0.63	†27.27	27.27±0.41	†27.66	27.67±0.75	†54.70	54.72±0.58
	CTC+Reorder	†29.45	29.44±0.64	†23.86	23.85±0.40	†24.21	24.23±0.70	†51.50	51.53±0.57
	CTC+ASN	†40.81	40.80±0.49	†29.22	29.21±0.35	†27.30	27.32±0.74	†54.18	54.21±0.57
	wait-k	43.80	43.79±0.63	31.42	31.42±0.45	30.52	30.55±0.77	56.77	56.79±0.61
	wait-k+Pseudo	***44.99**	44.98±0.57	***32.23**	32.23±0.45	***30.99**	31.02±0.79	***57.14**	57.16±0.62
	wait-k+Reorder	*43.27	43.27±0.62	*30.92	30.92±0.44	*29.37	29.39±0.80	*56.25	56.27±0.58
$k=9$	CTC	34.20	34.18±0.60	26.03	26.02±0.41	27.37	27.38±0.74	54.37	54.39±0.59
	CTC+Pseudo	†36.83	36.83±0.64	†27.67	27.66±0.41	†27.72	27.74±0.75	†54.75	54.77±0.58
	CTC+Reorder	†29.81	29.79±0.65	†24.07	24.06±0.40	†24.32	24.33±0.71	†51.66	51.68±0.58
	CTC+ASN	†40.83	40.82±0.51	†29.21	29.20±0.35	†28.00	28.02±0.78	†54.71	54.74±0.60

Table 7: Detailed quality metrics statistics on both datasets. Significance tests are conducted with paired bootstrap resampling. "*" suggests **significantly different (better or worst)** from the wait-k baseline with p-value < 0.05. "†" suggests significantly different from the CTC baseline. **Bold** text suggests the best value in the same k. If multiple values are in bold, it means that these values are not significantly different according to paired bootstrap resampling.

Input	it took a huge leap of faith to travel to india.
wait-*k*	花了 很大的 劲 才 把 这条鱼 带到 印度 去. took huge strength have this fish brought to india
CTC	旅行 巨大的 信心 飞跃 travel huge faith leap
CTC+ASN	花了 巨大的 飞跃 信心 旅行 去 印度 took huge leap faith travel to india
Input	this is the first of a five-part travelogue recounting that journey.
wait-*k*	这 是 第一次, 一个 五星级 酒店、一个 豪华的 酒店, 一个 豪华的 酒店。 this is the first time a five star hotel, a luxurious hotel, a luxurious hotel.
CTC	这 是 五 这次 旅行的 this is five this time journey's
CTC+ASN	这 是 这 是 的 第一个 五部分 旅游记 中, 述 这次 旅行中的 this is this is 's first five-part travelogue in describe this time in the journey
Input	one man had his foot stitched up with nothing to kill the pain but his son's embrace.
wait-*k*	有一个人 脚 被缝好了, 什么也杀不了 疼痛, 只有 他的 儿子 的 脚 被拥抱着。 someone foot is stitched up, nothing can kill pain, only his his son 's foot is embraced.
CTC	一个 男人 把 脚 缝,, 但 他儿子 one man had foot stitch but his son
CTC+ASN	有一个人 把 脚 缝, 无 任何 杀死 疼痛 除了, 儿子的 拥抱 someone had foot stitch no anything kill pain except, son's embrace
Input	in recent months, a number of iconic buildings on manhattan's skyline have been the target of middle eastern investors.
wait-*k*	近几个月来, 一些 标志性 建筑 在 曼哈顿的 地平线上 被建造成 一座大型的 中东 投资者的 目标。 in recent months, some iconic buildings on manhattan's horizon is built into a large scale middle eastern investors' target.
CTC	近几个月来, 一些 曼哈顿 地平线上 一些 标志性 建筑 中东 投资者的 目标 in recent months, some manhattan horizon some iconic buildings middle eastern investors' target.
CTC+ASN	近几个月来, 一些 标志性 建筑 在 曼哈顿的 天际线 一直是 的 目标 中东 投资者的 目标 in recent months, some iconic buildings on manhattan's skyline has been 's target middle eastern investors' target.
Input	it would be boring for the other teams because they would be racing only for second place.
wait-*k*	"如果 人们 不 注意 的话, 对 其他 球队 来说, 这 太无聊了。" if people don't pay attention (if...), for other teams (for...) this too boring.
CTC	"其他 球队 来说 无聊, 因为 他们 只 为 第二名 other team (for...) boring, because they only for second place
CTC+ASN	"将 太无聊 来说 其他 球队的, 因为 他们 只 为 第二名 比赛 would be too boring (for...) other team's, because they only for second place racing
Input	then he looks at me and says, 'jens, read my lips: stay together.'
wait-*k*	利5 又 看我 、说 、 约拿、念 给 我的 嘴、 要 在一起。 again look at me says Jonah read to my mouth must be together.
CTC	,他 看着 我, 说,、 念 我的 嘴唇, 住 , he look at me, says, read my lips, stay
CTC+ASN	"那么, 他 看了看 我, 说 '斯、听 我 我的 嘴唇、同住 then, he looks at me says s listen me my lips live together

Figure 14: More examples from CWMT En→Zh. Text in red are hallucinations unrelated to source. We use $k = 3$ models.

Who Are We Talking About?
Handling Person Names in Speech Translation

Marco Gaido[1,2], Matteo Negri[1] and Marco Turchi[1]
[1]Fondazione Bruno Kessler
[2]University of Trento
Trento, Italy
{mgaido,negri,turchi}@fbk.eu

Abstract

Recent work has shown that systems for speech translation (ST) – similarly to automatic speech recognition (ASR) – poorly handle person names. This shortcoming does not only lead to errors that can seriously distort the meaning of the input, but also hinders the adoption of such systems in application scenarios (like computer-assisted interpreting) where the translation of named entities, like person names, is crucial. In this paper, we first analyse the outputs of ASR/ST systems to identify the reasons of failures in person name transcription/translation. Besides the frequency in the training data, we pinpoint the nationality of the referred person as a key factor. We then mitigate the problem by creating multilingual models, and further improve our ST systems by forcing them to jointly generate transcripts and translations, prioritising the former over the latter. Overall, our solutions result in a relative improvement in token-level person name accuracy by 47.8% on average for three language pairs (en→es,fr,it).

1 Introduction

Automatic speech translation (ST) is the task of generating the textual translation of utterances. Research on ST (Anastasopoulos et al., 2021; Bentivogli et al., 2021) has so far focused on comparing the *cascade* (a pipeline of an automatic speech recognition – ASR – and a machine translation – MT – model) and *direct* paradigms (Bérard et al., 2016; Weiss et al., 2017), or on improving either of them in terms of overall quality. Quality is usually measured with automatic metrics such as BLEU (Papineni et al., 2002) and TER (Snover et al., 2006), possibly corroborated by manual analyses.

These metrics – as well as neural-based ones like COMET (Rei et al., 2020) – are relatively insensitive to errors on named entities (NEs) and numbers (Amrhein and Sennrich, 2022), which instead are of paramount importance for human readers (Xie et al., 2022). As such, the blind pursue of higher scores can lead to systems biased toward the metrics and not targeted on real users.

In addition, there are cases in which users are interested only in NEs. For instance, interpreters easily craft more fluent and intelligible translations than machines (Fantinuoli and Prandi, 2021), but during simultaneous sessions suffer from a high cognitive workload (Prandi, 2018; Desmet et al., 2018), to which NEs and specific terminology significantly contribute (Jones, 1998; Gile, 2009; Prandi, 2018; Desmet et al., 2018). Indeed, these elements *i)* are hard to remember (Liu et al., 2004), *ii)* can be unknown to interpreters and difficult to recognize (Griffin and Bock, 1998), and *iii)* differently from other types of words, usually have one or few correct translations. For this reason, modern computer-assisted interpreting (CAI – Fantinuoli 2017) tools aim at automatically recognizing, displaying, and *translating* NEs and terms. However, current solutions rely on predefined dictionaries to identify and translate the elements of interest (Fantinuoli et al., 2022), preventing them to both generalize and disambiguate homophones/homonyms. This would be instead possible using ST system, but they need to reliably recognize and translate NEs and terms, without generating wrong suggestions that are even harmful (Stewart et al., 2018).

In contrast with these needs, Gaido et al. (2021) recently showed on their newly created benchmark – NEuRoparl-ST – that both ASR models (and thus cascade ST systems) and direct ST systems perform poorly on person names, with transcription/translation accuracy of ~40%. Hence, as a first step toward ST systems more targeted for human needs, and in particular toward the long-term goal of integrating ST models in assistant tools for live interpreting, this work focuses on *i)* identifying the factors that lead to the wrong transcription and translation of person names, and *ii)* proposing dedicated solutions to mitigate the problem.

Proceedings of the 19th International Conference on Spoken Language Translation (IWSLT 2022), pages 62 - 73
May 26-27, 2022 ©2022 Association for Computational Linguistics

To achieve these objectives, our first contribution (§3.1) is the annotation[1] of each person name occurring in NEuRoparl-ST with information about their nationality and the nationality of the speaker (as a proxy of the native language) – e.g. if a German person says "*Macron is the French president*", the speaker nationality is German, while the referent nationality is French. Drawing on this additional information, our second contribution (§3.2-3.3) is the analysis of the concurring factors involved in the correct recognition of person names. Besides their frequency, we identify as key discriminating factor the presence in the training data of speech uttered in the referent's native language (e.g. French in the above example). This finding, together with an observed accuracy gap between person name transcription (ASR) and translation (ST), leads to our third contribution (§4): a multilingual ST system that jointly transcribes and translates the input audio, giving higher importance to the transcription task in favour of a more accurate translation of names. Our model shows relative gains in person name translation by 48% on average on three language pairs (en→es,fr,it), producing useful translations for interpreters in 66% of the cases.

2 Related Work

When the source modality is text, person names can often be "copied", i.e. replicated unchanged, into the output. This task has been shown to be well accomplished by both statistical and neural translation systems (Koehn and Knowles, 2017). On the contrary, when the source modality is speech (as in ASR and ST), systems struggle due to the impossibility to copy the audio source. The recognition of person names from speech is a complex task that has mostly been studied in the context of recognizing a name from a pre-defined list, such as phone contacts (Raghavan and Allan, 2005; Suchato et al., 2011; Bruguier et al., 2016). The scenario of an open or undefined set of possible names is instead under-explored. Few studies (Ghannay et al., 2018; Caubrière et al., 2020) focus on comparing end-to-end and cascade approaches in the transcription and recognition of NEs from speech. They do not directly investigate person names though, as they do not disaggregate their results by NE category. Similarly, Porjazovski et al. (2021) explore NE recognition from speech in low-resource languages, and propose two end-to-end methods: one adds a tag after each word in the generated text to define whether it is a NE or not, and one uses a dedicated decoder. However, they do not provide specific insights on the system ability to correctly generate person names and limit their study to ASR, without investigating ST. Closer to our work, Gaido et al. (2021) highlight the difficulty of ASR/ST neural models to transcribe/translate NEs and terminology. Although they identify person names as the hardest NE category by far, they neither analyse the root causes nor propose mitigating solutions.

3 Factors Influencing Name Recognition

As shown in (Gaido et al., 2021), the translation of person names is difficult both for direct and cascade ST systems, which achieve similar accuracy scores (~40%). The low performance of cascade solutions is largely due to errors made by the ASR component, while the MT model usually achieves nearly perfect scores. For this reason, henceforth we will focus on identifying the main issues related to the transcription and translation of person names, respectively in ASR and *direct* ST.

We hypothesize that three main factors influence the ability of a system to transcribe/translate a person name: *i)* its frequency in the training data, as neural models are known to poorly handle rare words, *ii)* the nationality of the referent, as different languages may involve different phoneme-to-grapheme mappings and may contain different sounds, and *iii)* the nationality of the speaker, as non-native speakers typically have different accents and hence different pronunciations of the same name. To validate these hypotheses, we inspect the outputs of Transformer-based (Vaswani et al., 2017) ASR and ST models trained with the configuration defined in (Wang et al., 2020). For the sake of reproducibility, complete details on our experimental settings are provided in the Appendix.[2]

3.1 Data and Annotation

To enable fine-grained evaluations on the three factors we suppose to be influential, we enrich the NEuRoparl-ST benchmark by adding three (one for each factor) features to each token annotated as *PERSON*. These are: *i)* the token frequency in the target transcripts/translations of the training set, *ii)* the nationality of the referent, and *iii)* the

[1] Available at: `https://ict.fbk.eu/neuroparl-st/`.

[2] Code available at: `https://github.com/hlt-mt/FBK-fairseq`.

nationality of the speaker. The nationality of the referents was manually collected by the authors through online searches. The nationality of the speakers, instead, was automatically extracted from the personal data listed in LinkedEP (Hollink et al., 2017) using the country they represent in the European Parliament.[3] All our systems are trained on Europarl-ST (Iranzo-Sánchez et al., 2020) and MuST-C (Cattoni et al., 2021), and evaluated on this new extended version of NEuRoparl-ST.

3.2 The Role of Frequency

As a first step in our analysis, we automatically check how the three features added to each *PERSON* token correlate with the correct generation of the token itself. Our aim is to understand the importance of these factors and to identify interpretable reasons behind the correct or wrong handling of person names. To this end, we train a classification decision tree (Breiman et al., 1984). Classification trees recursively divide the dataset into two groups, choosing a feature and a threshold that minimize the entropy of the resulting groups with respect to the target label. As such, they do not assume a linear relationship between the input and the target (like multiple regression and random linear mixed effects do) and are a good fit for categorical features as most of ours are. Their structure makes them easy to interpret (Wu et al., 2008): the first decision (the root of the tree) is the most important criterion according to the learned model, while less discriminative features are pushed to the bottom.

We feed the classifier with 49 features, corresponding to: *i)* the frequency of the token in the training data, *ii)* the one-hot encoding of the speaker nationality, and *iii)* the one-hot encoding of the referent nationality.[4] We then train it to predict whether our ASR model is able to correctly transcribe the token in the output. To this end, we use the implementation of scikit-learn (Pedregosa et al., 2011), setting to 3 the maximum depth of the tree, and using Gini index as entropy measure.

Unsurprisingly, the root node decision is based on the frequency of the token in the training data, with 2.5 as split value. This means that person names occurring at least 3 times in the training data are likely to be correctly handled by the models. Although this threshold may vary across datasets of different size, it is an indication on the necessary number of occurrences of a person name, eventually useful for data augmentation techniques aimed at exposing the system to relevant instances at training time (e.g. names of famous people in the specific domain of a talk to be translated/interpreted). We validate that this finding also holds for ST systems by reporting in Table 1 the accuracy of person tokens for ASR and the three ST language directions, split according to the mentioned threshold of frequency in the training set. On average, names occurring at least 3 times in the training set are correctly generated in slightly more than 50% of the cases, a much larger value compared to those with less than 3 occurrences.

	All	Freq. >= 3	Freq. < 3
ASR	38.46	55.81	4.55
en-fr	28.69	45.45	0.00
en-es	35.29	53.57	19.05
en-it	29.70	46.77	2.56
Average	33.04	50.40	6.54

Table 1: Token-level accuracy of person names divided into two groups according to their frequency in the training set for ASR and ST (en→es/fr/it) systems.

The other nodes of the classification tree contain less interpretable criteria, which can be considered as spurious cues. For instance, at the second level of the tree, a splitting criterion is "*is the speaker from Denmark?*" because the only talk by a Danish speaker contains a mention to *Kolarska-Bobinska* that systems were not able to correctly generate.

We hence decided to perform further dedicated experiments to better understand the role of the the other two factors: referent and speaker nationality.

3.3 The Role of Referent Nationality

Humans often struggle to understand names belonging to languages that are different from their native one or from those they know. Moreover, upon manual inspection of the system outputs, we observed that some names were Englishized (e.g. *Youngsen* instead of *Jensen*). In light of this, we posit that a system trained to recognize English sounds and to learn English phoneme-to-grapheme mappings might be inadequate to handle non-English names.

We first validate this idea by computing the accuracy for names of people from the United Kingdom[5] ('UK" henceforth) and for names of people

[3] For each speech in Europarl-ST, the speaker is referenced by link to LinkedEP.

[4] Speakers and referents respectively belong to 17 and 31 different nations.

[5] We are aware that our annotation is potentially subject to noise, due to the possible presence of UK citizens with non-anglophone names. A thorough study on the best strategies

Referent	ASR	en-fr	en-es	en-it	Freq.
UK	52.38	59.09	63.16	41.18	46.21
non-UK	35.78	22.00	30.00	27.38	21.96
All	38.46	28.69	35.29	29.70	25.65

Table 2: Token-level accuracy of ASR and ST (en-fr, en-es, en-it) systems for UK/non-UK *referents*.

from the rest of the World ("non-UK"). Looking at Table 2, we notice that our assumption seems to hold for both ASR and ST. However, the scores correlate with the frequency (Freq.) of names in the training set[6] as, on average, UK referents have more than twice the occurrences (46.21) of non-UK referents (21.96). The higher scores for UK referents may hence depend on this second factor.

To disentangle the two factors and isolate the impact of referents' nationality, we create a training set with balanced average frequency for UK and non-UK people by filtering out a subset of the instances containing UK names from the original training set.[3] To ensure that our results are not due to a particular filtering method, we randomly choose the instances to remove and run the experiments on three different filtered training sets. The results for the three ST language pairs and ASR (see Table 3) confirm the presence of a large accuracy gap between UK and non-UK names (9.22 on average), meaning that the accuracy on non-UK names (23.62) is on average ~30% lower than the accuracy on UK names (32.84). As in this case we can rule out any bias in the results due to the frequency in the training set, we can state that the nationality of the referent is an important factor.

	ASR	en-fr	en-es	en-it	Avg.
UK	42.86	25.76	33.33	29.41	32.84
non-UK	29.05	22.67	23.33	19.44	23.62
ΔAccuracy	13.81	3.09	10.00	9.97	9.22

Table 3: Token-level accuracy of UK/non-UK *referents* averaged over three runs with balanced training sets.

3.4 The Role of Speaker Nationality

Another factor likely to influence the correct understanding of person names from speech is the speaker accent. To verify its impact, we follow a similar procedure to that of the previous section. First, we check whether the overall accuracy is higher for names uttered by UK speakers than for those uttered by non-UK speakers. Then, to ascertain whether the results depend on the proportion of UK/non-UK speakers, we randomly create three training sets featuring a balanced average frequency of speakers from the two groups.

Speaker	ASR	en-fr	en-es	en-it	Freq.
UK	41.03	32.43	36.84	29.41	34.55
non-UK	37.36	27.06	34.57	29.85	21.76
All	38.46	28.69	35.29	29.70	25.65

Table 4: Token-level accuracy of ASR and ST systems for names uttered by UK/non-UK *speakers*.

Table 4 shows the overall results split according to the two groups of speaker nationalities. In this case, the accuracy gap is minimal (the maximum gap is 5.37 for en-fr, while it is even negative for en-it), suggesting that the speaker accent has marginal influence, if any, on how ASR and ST systems handle person names.

The experiments on balanced training sets (see Table 5) confirm the above results, with an average accuracy difference of 2.78 for ASR and the three ST language directions. In light of this, we can conclude that, differently from the other two factors, speakers' nationality has negligible effects on ASR/ST performance on person names.

Speaker	ASR	en-fr	en-es	en-it	Avg.
UK	29.91	29.73	28.95	23.53	28.03
non-UK	33.33	22.75	25.51	19.40	25.25
ΔAccuracy	-3.42	6.98	3.43	4.13	2.78

Table 5: Token-level accuracy of person names uttered by UK/non-UK *speakers* averaged over three runs with balanced training sets.

4 Improving Person Name Translation

The previous section has uncovered that only two of the three considered factors actually have a tangible impact: the frequency in the training set, and the referent nationality. The first issue can be tackled either by collecting more data, or by generating synthetic instances (Alves et al., 2020; Zheng et al., 2021). Fine-tuning the model on additional material is usually a viable solution in the use case of assisting interpreters since, during their preparation phase, they have access to various sources of information (Díaz-Galaz et al., 2015), including recordings of previous related sessions. Focusing on the second issue, we hereby explore *i)* the cre-

to maximise the accuracy of UK/non-UK label assignment is a task *per se*, out of the scope of this work. By now, as a manual inspection of the names revealed no such cases in our data, we believe that the few possible wrong assignments do not undermine our experiments, nor the reported findings.

[6]Notice that the ASR and the ST training sets mostly contain the same data, so frequencies are similar in the four cases.

	Monolingual				Multilingual				
	ASR	en-fr	en-es	en-it	ASR	en-fr	en-es	en-it	
	WER (↓)	BLEU (↑)			WER (↓)	BLEU (↑)			
Europarl-ST	13.65	32.42	34.11	25.72	13.29	33.92	35.59	26.55	
MuST-C	11.17	32.81	27.18	22.81	11.86	33.34	27.72	23.02	
	Token-level Person Name Accuracy (↑)								**Avg. Δ**
Overall	38.46	28.69	35.29	29.70	46.15	38.52	44.54	36.63	+8.43
UK	52.38	59.09	63.16	41.18	66.67	59.09	63.16	52.94	+6.51
non-UK	35.78	22.00	30.00	27.38	42.20	34.00	41.00	33.33	+8.84

Table 6: Transcription/translation quality measured respectively with WER and SacreBLEU[7] (Post, 2018) and token-level person name accuracy, both overall and divided into UK/non-UK referents. *Avg.* Δ indicates the difference between multilingual and monolingual systems averaged over the ASR and the three ST directions.

ation of models that are more robust to a wider range of phonetic features and hence to names of different nationalities (§4.1), and *ii)* the design of solutions to close the gap between ASR and ST systems attested by previous work (Gaido et al., 2021) and confirmed by our preliminary results shown in Table 1 (§4.2).

4.1 Increasing Robustness to non-UK Referents

As illustrated in §3.3, one cause of failure of our ASR/ST models trained on English audio is the tendency to force every sound to an English-like word, distorting person names from other languages. Consequently, we posit that a multilingual system, trained to recognize and translate speech in different languages, might be more robust and, in turn, achieve better performance on non-English names.

We test this hypothesis by training multilingual ASR and ST models that are fed with audio in different languages, and respectively produce transcripts and translations (into French, Italian, or Spanish in our case). The ST training data (*→es/fr/it) consists of the en→es/fr/it sections of MuST-C and the {nl, de, en, es, fr, it, pl, pt, ro}→es/fr/it sections of Europarl-ST. Notice that, in this scenario, the English source audio constitutes more than 80% of the total training data, as MuST-C is considerably bigger than Europarl-ST and the English speeches in Europarl-ST are about 4 times those in the other languages.[8] For ASR, we use the audio-transcript pairs of the *-it training set defined above. Complete details on our experimental settings are provided in the Appendix.??

We analyze the effect of including additional languages both in terms of general quality (measured as WER for ASR, and BLEU for ST) and in terms of person name transcription/translation accuracy. Looking at the first two rows of Table 6, we notice that the improvements in terms of generic translation quality (BLEU) are higher on the Europarl-ST than on the MuST-C test set – most likely because the additional data belongs to the Europarl domain – while in terms of speech recognition (WER) there is a small improvement for Europarl-ST and a small loss for MuST-C. Turning to person names (third line of the table), the gains of the multilingual models (+8.43 accuracy on average) are higher and consistent between ASR and the ST language pairs.

By dividing the person names into the two categories discussed in §3.3 – UK and non-UK referents – the results become less consistent across language pairs. On ST into French and Spanish, the accuracy of UK names remains constant, while there are significant gains (respectively +12 and +11) for non-UK names. These improvements seem to support the intuition that models trained on more languages learn a wider range phoneme-to-grapheme mappings and so are able to better handle non-English names. However, the results for ASR and for ST into Italian seemingly contradict our hypothesis, as they show higher improvements for UK names (~11-14) than for non-UK names (~6-7).

We investigate this behavior by further dividing the non-UK group into two sub-categories: the names of referents whose native language is included in the training set ("in-train" henceforth), and those of referents whose native language is not included in the training set ("out-of-train"). For in-train non-UK names, the monolingual ASR accuracy is 33.33 and is outperformed by the multilingual counterpart by 16.66, i.e. by a margin higher than that for UK names (14.29). For the out-of-train names, instead, the gap between the monolingual ASR accuracy (36.71) and the multilingual ASR accuracy (39.24) is marginal (2.5). Similarly,

[7] `BLEU+c.mixed+#.1+s.exp+tok.13a+v.1.5.0`

[8] For instance, in *-fr the training set amounts to 671 hours of audio, 573 (i.e. 83%) having English audio.

Model	WER (↓)	BLEU (↑)			Person Accuracy					
	ASR	en-es	en-fr	en-it	ASR	en-es	en-fr	en-it	ST Avg.	ASR-ST
Base	13.29	35.86	33.99	26.80	46.15	44.54	38.52	36.63	39.90	6.25
Triangle	14.25	37.42	35.44	28.20	42.31	43.70	41.80	41.58	42.36	-0.05
λ_{ASR}=0.8, λ_{ST}=0.2	13.75	36.48	34.85	27.30	47.69	44.54	43.44	50.50	46.16	1.53

Table 7: WER (for ASR), SacreBLEU (for ST), and token-level person name accuracy computed on the NEuRoparl-ST test set. For triangle models, ASR scores are computed on the transcript output of the *-it model, as throughout the paper we evaluate ASR on the English transcript of the en-it section. *ST Avg.* is the the average accuracy on the 3 language pairs (en→es,fr,it) and *ASR-ST* is the difference between the ASR and the average ST accuracy.

for ST into Italian the in-train group accuracy improves by 8.70 (from 34.78 to 43.48), while the out-of-train group accuracy has a smaller gain of 4.92 (from 24.59 to 29.51). These results indicate that adding a language to the training data helps the correct handling of person names belonging to that language, even when translating/transcribing from another language. Further evidence is exposed in §5, where we analyse the errors made by our systems and how their distribution changes between a monolingual and a multilingual one.

4.2 Closing the Gap Between ASR and ST

The previous results – in line with those of Gaido et al. (2021) – reveal a gap between ASR and ST systems, although their task is similar when it comes to person names. Indeed, both ASR and ST have to recognize the names from the speech, and produce them as-is in the output. Contextually, Gaido et al. (2021) showed that neural MT models are good at "copying" from the source or, in other words, at estimating $p(Y|T)$ – where Y is the target sentence and T is the textual source sentence – when Y and T are the same string. Hence, we hypothesize that an ST model can close the performance gap with the ASR by conditioning the target prediction not only on the input audio, but also on the generated transcript. Formally, this means estimating $p(Y|X,T')$, where T' denotes a representation of the generated transcript, such as the embeddings used to predict them; and this estimation is what the triangle architecture (Anastasopoulos and Chiang, 2018) actually does.

The triangle model is composed of a single encoder, whose output is attended by two decoders that respectively generate the transcript (ASR decoder) and the translation (ST decoder). The ST decoder also attends to the output embeddings (i.e. the internal representation before the final linear layer mapping to the output vocabulary dimension and softmax) of the ASR decoder in all its layers. In particular, the output of the cross-attention on the encoder output and the cross-attention on the ASR decoder output are concatenated and fed to a linear layer. The model is optimized with a multi-loss objective function, defined as follows:

$$L(X) = -\sum_{x \in X} \Big(\lambda_{ASR} * \sum_{t \in T_x} log(p_\theta(t_i|x, t_{i-1,\dots,0})) \\ + \lambda_{ST} * \sum_{y \in Y_x} log(p_\theta(y_i|x, T, y_{i-1,\dots,0}))\Big)$$

where T is the target transcript, Y is the target translation, and x is the input utterance. λ_{ASR} and λ_{ST} are two hyperparameters aimed at controlling the relative importance of the two tasks. Previous works commonly set them to 0.5, giving equal importance to the two tasks (Anastasopoulos and Chiang, 2018; Sperber et al., 2020). To the best of our knowledge, ours is the first attempt to inspect performance variations in the setting of these two parameters, calibrating them towards the specific needs arising from our application scenario.

In Table 7, we compare the multilingual models introduced in §4.1 with triangle ST multilingual models trained on the same data (second row). Although the transcripts are less accurate (about +1 WER), the translations have higher quality (+1.4-1.6 BLEU on the three language pairs). Person names follow a similar trend: in the transcript the accuracy is lower (-3.84), while in ST it increases (on average +2.46). Interestingly, the accuracy gap between ASR and ST is closed by the triangle model (see the ASR-ST column), confirming our assumption that neural models are good at copying. However, due to the lower ASR accuracy (42.31), the ST accuracy (42.36) does not reach that of the base ASR model (46.15). The reason of this drop can be found in the different kind of information required by the ASR and ST tasks. Chuang et al. (2020) showed that the semantic content of the utterance is more important for ST, and that joint ASR/ST training leads the model to focus more on the semantic content of the utterance, yielding

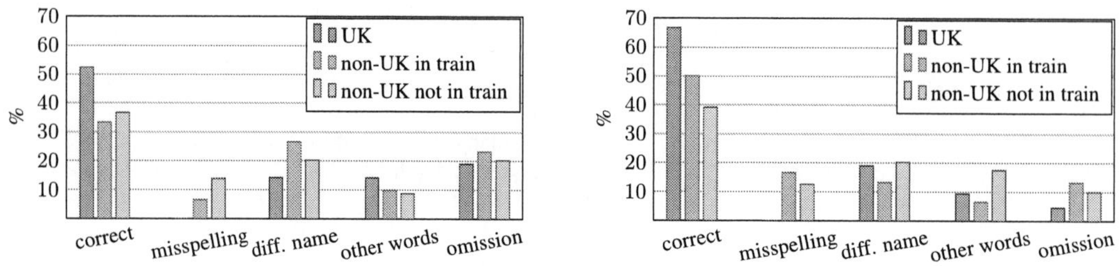

(a) Base ASR errors.

(b) Multilingual ASR errors.

Figure 1: Correct person names and the categories of errors of the baseline and multilingual ASR systems.

BLEU gains at the expense of higher WER. As person names are usually close in the semantic space (Das et al., 2017), the higher focus on semantic content may be detrimental to their correct handling and hence explain the lower person name accuracy.

In light of this observation, we experimented with changing the weights of the losses in the triangle training, assigning higher importance to the ASR loss (third row of Table 7). In this configuration, as expected, transcription quality increases (-0.5 WER) at the expense of translation quality, which decreases (-0.8 BLEU on average) but remains higher than that of the base model. The accuracy of person names follows the trend of transcription quality: the average accuracy on ST (46.16) increases by 3.8 points over the base triangle model (42.36), becoming almost identical to that of the base ASR model (46.15). All in all, our solution achieves the same person name accuracy of an ASR base model without sacrificing translation quality compared to a base ST system.

5 Error Analysis

While the goal is the correct rendering of person names, not all the errors have the same weight. For interpreters, for instance, minor misspellings of a name may not be problematic, an omission can be seen as a lack of help, but the generation of a wrong name is harmful, as potentially distracting and/or confusing. To delve into these aspects, we first carried out a manual analysis on the ASR outputs (§5.1) and then compared the findings with the same analysis on ST outputs (§5.2).

5.1 ASR Analysis

Two authors with at least C1 English knowledge and linguistic background annotated each error assigning it to a category.[9] The categories, chosen by analysing the system outputs, are: **misspelling** – when a person name contains minor errors leading to similar pronunciation (e.g. *Kozulin* instead of *Kazulin*); **replacement with a different name** – when a person name is replaced with a completely different one in terms of spelling and/or pronunciation (e.g. *Mr Muhammadi* instead of *Mr Allister*); **replacement with other words** – when a proper person name is replaced by a common noun, other parts of speech, and/or proper nouns that do not refer to people, such as geographical names (e.g. *English Tibetan core* instead of *Ingrid Betancourt*) **omission** – when a person name, or part of a sentence containing it, is ignored by the system.

The results of the annotations are summarized in the graphs in Figure 1. Looking at the baseline system (Figure 1a), we notice that omissions and replacements with a different name are the most common errors, closely followed by replacements with other words, although for non-UK names the number of misspellings is also significant. The multilingual system (Figure 1b) does not only show a higher percentage of correct names, but also a different distribution of errors, in particular for the names belonging to the languages added to the training set (non-UK in train). Indeed, the misspellings increase to the detriment of omissions and replacements with a different name and other words. Omissions also decrease for UK names and for names in languages not included in the training set (non-UK not in train). For UK names, the previously-missing names fall either into the correct names or into the replacements with a different name; for the non-UK not in train, instead, they are

[9]The inter-annotator agreement on label assignments was calculated using the *kappa coefficient* in Scott's π formulation (Scott, 1955; Artstein and Poesio, 2008), and resulted in 87.5%, which means "almost perfect" agreement in the standard interpretation (Landis and Koch, 1977).

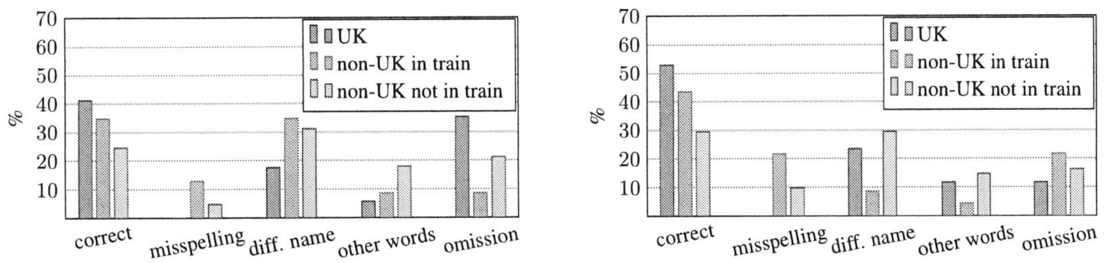

(a) Base en-it ST errors.

(b) Multilingual ST *-it errors.

Figure 2: Correct person names and the categories of errors of the baseline and multilingual ST-into-Italian systems.

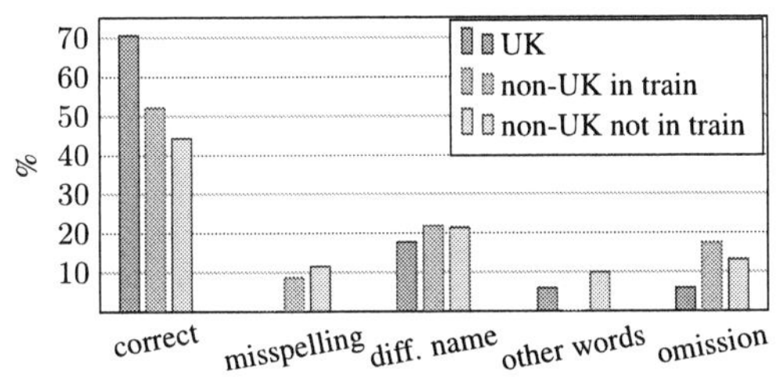

Figure 3: Correct person names and the different categories of errors of the ST-into-Italian triangle system with λ_{ASR}=0.8, λ_{ST}=0.2 expressed in percentages.

replaced by different names or other words.

Considering multilingual outputs, we observe that for the languages in the training set (including English), in 66% of the cases the system generates a name that could be helpful for an interpreter (either correct or with minor misspellings). Confusing/distracting outputs (i.e. replacements with a different person name) occur in about 15% of the cases. Future work should precisely assess whether these scores are sufficient to help interpreters in their job, or which level of accuracy is needed.

Moreover, we notice that the system is able to discern when a person name should be generated (either correct, misspelled, or replaced by a different name) in more than 80% of the cases. This indicates their overall good capability to recognize patterns and/or appropriate contexts in which a person name should occur.

5.2 ST Analysis

The same analysis was carried out for ST systems translating into Italian (see Figure 2) by two native speakers, co-authors of this paper. Although results are lower in general, when moving from the monolingual (Figure 2a) to the multilingual (Figure 2b) system we can see similar trends to ASR, with the number of omissions and replacements with a different name that decreases in favor of a higher number of correct names and misspellings. Looking at the analysis of the triangle model with λ_{ASR}=0.8, λ_{ST}=0.2 presented in §4.2 (Figure 3), we observe that misspellings, omissions, and replacements with other words diminish, while correct names increase. Moreover, both the accuracy (i.e. *correct* in the graphs) and the error distributions of this system are similar to those of the ASR multilingual model (Figure 1b). On one side, this brings to similar conclusions, i.e. ST models can support interpreters in $\sim$66% of the cases, and can discern when a person name is required in the translation in $\sim$80% of the cases. On the other, it confirms that the gap with the ASR system is closed, as observed in §4.2.

6 Conclusions

Humans and machines have different strengths and weaknesses. Nonetheless, we have shown that when it comes to person names in speech, they both struggle in handling names in languages they do not know and names that they are not used to hear. This finding seems to insinuate that humans cannot expect help from machines in this regard, but we demonstrated that there is hope, moving the first steps toward ST systems that can better handle person names. Indeed, since machines are faster learners than humans, we can train them on more data and more languages. Moreover, we can design dedicated architectural solutions aimed to add an inductive bias and to improve the ability to handle specific elements. Along this line of research, we have shown that a multilingual ST model, which jointly predicts the transcript and conditions the translation on it, has relative improvements in person name accuracy by 48% on average. We also acknowledge that much work is still needed in this area, with large margin of improvements available, especially to avoid the two most common type of errors pointed out by our analysis: omissions and replacements with different person names.

Acknowledgement

This work has been carried out as part of the project Smarter Interpreting (`https://kunveno.digital/`) financed by CDTI Neotec funds.

References

Diego Alves, Askars Salimbajevs, and Mārcis Pinnis. 2020. Data augmentation for pipeline-based speech translation. In *9th International Conference on Human Language Technologies - the Baltic Perspective (Baltic HLT 2020)*, Kaunas, Lithuania.

Chantal Amrhein and Rico Sennrich. 2022. Identifying weaknesses in machine translation metrics through minimum bayes risk decoding: A case study for comet. *ArXiv*, abs/2202.05148.

Antonios Anastasopoulos, Ondřej Bojar, Jacob Bremerman, Roldano Cattoni, Maha Elbayad, Marcello Federico, Xutai Ma, Satoshi Nakamura, Matteo Negri, Jan Niehues, Juan Pino, Elizabeth Salesky, Sebastian Stüker, Katsuhito Sudoh, Marco Turchi, Alexander Waibel, Changhan Wang, and Matthew Wiesner. 2021. FINDINGS OF THE IWSLT 2021 EVALUATION CAMPAIGN. In *Proceedings of the 18th International Conference on Spoken Language Translation (IWSLT 2021)*, pages 1–29, Bangkok, Thailand (online). Association for Computational Linguistics.

Antonios Anastasopoulos and David Chiang. 2018. Tied Multitask Learning for Neural Speech Translation. In *Proceedings of the 2018 Conference of the North American Chapter of the Association for Computational Linguistics: Human Language Technologies, Volume 1 (Long Papers)*, pages 82–91, New Orleans, Louisiana.

Ron Artstein and Massimo Poesio. 2008. Inter-coder agreement for computational linguistics. *Computational Linguistics*, 34(4):555–596.

Luisa Bentivogli, Mauro Cettolo, Marco Gaido, Alina Karakanta, Alberto Martinelli, Matteo Negri, and Marco Turchi. 2021. Cascade versus Direct Speech Translation: Do the Differences Still Make a Difference? In *Proceedings of the 59th Annual Meeting of the Association for Computational Linguistics and the 11th International Joint Conference on Natural Language Processing (Volume 1: Long Papers)*, pages 2873–2887, Online. Association for Computational Linguistics.

Leo Breiman, Jerome H. Friedman, Richard A. Olshen, and Charles J. Stone. 1984. *Classification and regression trees*. Routledge.

Antoine Bruguier, Fuchun Peng, and Françoise Beaufays. 2016. Learning Personalized Pronunciations for Contact Name Recognition. In *Interspeech 2016*, pages 3096–3100.

Alexandre Bérard, Olivier Pietquin, Christophe Servan, and Laurent Besacier. 2016. Listen and Translate: A Proof of Concept for End-to-End Speech-to-Text Translation. In *NIPS Workshop on end-to-end learning for speech and audio processing*, Barcelona, Spain.

Roldano Cattoni, Mattia Antonino Di Gangi, Luisa Bentivogli, Matteo Negri, and Marco Turchi. 2021. MuST-C: A multilingual corpus for end-to-end speech translation. *Computer Speech & Language*, 66:101155.

Antoine Caubrière, Sophie Rosset, Yannick Estève, Antoine Laurent, and Emmanuel Morin. 2020. Where are we in Named Entity Recognition from Speech? In *Proceedings of the 12th Language Resources and Evaluation Conference*, pages 4514–4520, Marseille, France. European Language Resources Association.

Shun-Po Chuang, Tzu-Wei Sung, Alexander H. Liu, and Hung-yi Lee. 2020. Worse WER, but Better BLEU? Leveraging Word Embedding as Intermediate in Multitask End-to-End Speech Translation. In *Proceedings of the 58th Annual Meeting of the Association for Computational Linguistics*, pages 5998–6003, Online. Association for Computational Linguistics.

Arjun Das, Debasis Ganguly, and Utpal Garain. 2017. Named Entity Recognition with Word Embeddings and Wikipedia Categories for a Low-Resource Language. *ACM Trans. Asian Low-Resour. Lang. Inf. Process.*, 16(3).

Bart Desmet, Mieke Vandierendonck, and Bart Defrancq. 2018. Simultaneous interpretation of numbers and the impact of technological support. In Claudio Fantinuoli, editor, *Interpreting and technology*, Translation and Multilingual Natural Language Processing, pages 13–27. Language Science Press.

Mattia A. Di Gangi, Marco Gaido, Matteo Negri, and Marco Turchi. 2020. On Target Segmentation for Direct Speech Translation. In *Proceedings of the 14th Conference of the Association for Machine Translation in the Americas (AMTA 2020)*, pages 137–150, Virtual.

Stephanie Díaz-Galaz, Presentacion Padilla, and María Teresa Bajo. 2015. The role of advance preparation in simultaneous interpreting: A comparison of professional interpreters and interpreting students. *Interpreting*, 17(1):1–25.

Claudio Fantinuoli. 2017. *Chapter 7: Computer-assisted Interpreting: Challenges and Future Perspectives*, pages 153–174. Brill, Leiden, The Netherlands.

Claudio Fantinuoli, Giulia Marchesini, David Landan, and Lukas Horak. 2022. Kudo interpreter assist: Automated real-time support for remote interpretation. In *Proceedings of Translator and Computer 43 Conference*.

Claudio Fantinuoli and Bianca Prandi. 2021. Towards the evaluation of automatic simultaneous speech translation from a communicative perspective. In *Proceedings of the 18th International Conference on Spoken Language Translation (IWSLT 2021)*, pages 245–254, Bangkok, Thailand (online). Association for Computational Linguistics.

Marco Gaido, Susana Rodríguez, Matteo Negri, Luisa Bentivogli, and Marco Turchi. 2021. Is "moby dick" a Whale or a Bird? Named Entities and Terminology in Speech Translation.

Sahar Ghannay, Antoine Caubrière, Yannick Estève, Antoine Laurent, and Emmanuel Morin. 2018. End-to-end named entity extraction from speech.

Daniel Gile. 2009. *Basic Concepts and Models for Interpreter and Translator Training: Revised edition*. John Benjamins.

Zenzi M. Griffin and Kathryn Bock. 1998. Constraint, Word Frequency, and the Relationship between Lexical Processing Levels in Spoken Word Production. *Journal of Memory and Language*, 38(3):313–338.

Laura Hollink, Astrid van Aggelen, Henri Beunders, Martijn Kleppe, Max Kemman, and Jacco van Ossenbruggen. 2017. Talk of Europe - The debates of the European Parliament as Linked Open Data.

Javier Iranzo-Sánchez, Joan Albert Silvestre-Cerdà, Javier Jorge, Nahuel Roselló, Adrià Giménez, Albert Sanchis, Jorge Civera, and Alfons Juan. 2020. Europarl-ST: A Multilingual Corpus for Speech Translation of Parliamentary Debates. In *ICASSP 2020 - 2020 IEEE International Conference on Acoustics, Speech and Signal Processing (ICASSP)*, pages 8229–8233.

Roderick Jones. 1998. Conference interpreting explained. *Interpreting*, 3(2):201–203.

Diederik P. Kingma and Jimmy Ba. 2015. Adam: A Method for Stochastic Optimization. In *3rd International Conference on Learning Representations, ICLR 2015, San Diego, CA, USA, May 7-9, 2015, Conference Track Proceedings*.

Philipp Koehn and Rebecca Knowles. 2017. Six Challenges for Neural Machine Translation. In *Proceedings of the First Workshop on Neural Machine Translation*, pages 28–39, Vancouver. Association for Computational Linguistics.

Taku Kudo and John Richardson. 2018. SentencePiece: A simple and language independent subword tokenizer and detokenizer for Neural Text Processing. In *Proceedings of the 2018 Conference on Empirical Methods in Natural Language Processing: System Demonstrations*, pages 66–71, Brussels, Belgium. Association for Computational Linguistics.

J. Richard Landis and Gary G. Koch. 1977. The measurement of observer agreement for categorical data. *Biometrics*, 33(1).

Minhua Liu, Diane L. Schallert, and Patrick J. Carroll. 2004. Working memory and expertise in simultaneous interpreting. *Interpreting*, 6(1):19–42.

Kishore Papineni, Salim Roukos, Todd Ward, and Wei-Jing Zhu. 2002. BLEU: a Method for Automatic Evaluation of Machine Translation. In *Proceedings of the 40th Annual Meeting of the Association for Computational Linguistics*, pages 311–318, Philadelphia, Pennsylvania. Association for Computational Linguistics.

Daniel S. Park, William Chan, Yu Zhang, Chung-Cheng Chiu, Barret Zoph, Ekin D. Cubuk, and Quoc V. Le. 2019. SpecAugment: A Simple Data Augmentation Method for Automatic Speech Recognition. In *Proceedings of Interspeech 2019*, pages 2613–2617, Graz, Austria.

Fabian Pedregosa, Gaël Varoquaux, Alexandre Gramfort, Vincent Michel, Bertrand Thirion, Olivier Grisel, Mathieu Blondel, Peter Prettenhofer, Ron Weiss, Vincent Dubourg, Jake Vanderplas, Alexandre Passos, David Cournapeau, Matthieu Brucher, Matthieu Perrot, and Édouard Duchesnay. 2011. Scikit-learn: Machine learning in python. *Journal of Machine Learning Research*, 12(85):2825–2830.

Dejan Porjazovski, Juho Leinonen, and Mikko Kurimo. 2021. Attention-Based End-to-End Named Entity Recognition from Speech. In *Text, Speech, and Dialogue*, pages 469–480, Cham. Springer International Publishing.

Matt Post. 2018. A Call for Clarity in Reporting BLEU Scores. In *Proceedings of the Third Conference on Machine Translation: Research Papers*, pages 186–191, Belgium, Brussels. Association for Computational Linguistics.

Bianca Prandi. 2018. An exploratory study on CAI tools in simultaneous interpreting: Theoretical framework and stimulus validation.

Hema Raghavan and James Allan. 2005. Matching Inconsistently Spelled Names in Automatic Speech Recognizer Output for Information Retrieval. In *Proceedings of Human Language Technology Conference and Conference on Empirical Methods in Natural Language Processing*, pages 451–458, Vancouver, British Columbia, Canada. Association for Computational Linguistics.

Ricardo Rei, Craig Stewart, Ana C Farinha, and Alon Lavie. 2020. COMET: A neural framework for MT evaluation. In *Proceedings of the 2020 Conference on Empirical Methods in Natural Language Processing (EMNLP)*, pages 2685–2702, Online. Association for Computational Linguistics.

William A. Scott. 1955. Reliability of Content Analysis:The Case of Nominal Scale Coding. *Public Opinion Quarterly*, 19(3):321–325.

Rico Sennrich, Barry Haddow, and Alexandra Birch. 2016. Neural Machine Translation of Rare Words with Subword Units. In *Proceedings of the 54th Annual Meeting of the Association for Computational Linguistics (Volume 1: Long Papers)*, pages 1715–1725, Berlin, Germany. Association for Computational Linguistics.

Matthew Snover, Bonnie Dorr, Richard Schwartz, Linnea Micciulla, and John Makhoul. 2006. A Study of Translation Edit Rate with Targeted Human Annotation. In *Proceedings of the 7th Conference of the Association for Machine Translation in the Americas,*, pages 223–231, Cambridge. Association for Machine Translation in the Americas.

Matthias Sperber, Hendra Setiawan, Christian Gollan, Udhyakumar Nallasamy, and Matthias Paulik. 2020. Consistent Transcription and Translation of Speech. *Transactions of the Association for Computational Linguistics*, 8:695–709.

Craig Stewart, Nikolai Vogler, Junjie Hu, Jordan Boyd-Graber, and Graham Neubig. 2018. Automatic Estimation of Simultaneous Interpreter Performance. In *Proceedings of the 56th Annual Meeting of the Association for Computational Linguistics (Volume 2: Short Papers)*, pages 662–666, Melbourne, Australia. Association for Computational Linguistics.

Atiwong Suchato, Proadpran Punyabukkana, Patanan Ariyakornwijit, and Teerat Namchaisawatwong. 2011. Automatic speech recognition of Thai person names from dynamic name lists. In *The 8th Electrical Engineering/ Electronics, Computer, Telecommunications and Information Technology (ECTI) Association of Thailand - Conference 2011*, pages 962–966.

Christian Szegedy, Vincent Vanhoucke, Sergey Ioffe, Jon Shlens, and Zbigniew Wojna. 2016. Rethinking the Inception Architecture for Computer Vision. In *Proceedings of 2016 IEEE Conference on Computer Vision and Pattern Recognition (CVPR)*, pages 2818–2826, Las Vegas, Nevada, United States.

Ashish Vaswani, Noam Shazeer, Niki Parmar, Jakob Uszkoreit, Llion Jones, Aidan N. Gomez, Lukasz Kaiser, and Illia Polosukhin. 2017. Attention is All You Need. In *Proc. of Advances in Neural Information Processing Systems 30 (NIPS)*, pages 5998–6008, Long Beach, California.

Changhan Wang, Yun Tang, Xutai Ma, Anne Wu, Dmytro Okhonko, and Juan Pino. 2020. Fairseq S2T: Fast Speech-to-Text Modeling with Fairseq. In *Proceedings of the 1st Conference of the Asia-Pacific Chapter of the Association for Computational Linguistics and the 10th International Joint Conference on Natural Language Processing: System Demonstrations*, pages 33–39, Suzhou, China. Association for Computational Linguistics.

Ron J. Weiss, Jan Chorowski, Navdeep Jaitly, Yonghui Wu, and Zhifeng Chen. 2017. Sequence-to-Sequence Models Can Directly Translate Foreign Speech. In *Proceedings of Interspeech 2017*, pages 2625–2629, Stockholm, Sweden.

Xindong Wu, Vipin Kumar, J. Ross Quinlan, Joydeep Ghosh, Qiang Yang, Hiroshi Motoda, Geoffrey J. McLachlan, Angus Ng, Bing Liu, Philip S. Yu, Zhi-Hua Zhou, Michael Steinbach, David J. Hand, and Dan Steinberg. 2008. Top 10 algorithms in data mining. *Knowledge and Information Systems*, 14(1):1–37.

Shufang Xie, Yingce Xia, Lijun Wu, Yiqing Huang, Yang Fan, and Tao Qin. 2022. End-to-end entity-aware neural machine translation. *Machine Learning*.

Xianrui Zheng, Yulan Liu, Deniz Gunceler, and Daniel Willett. 2021. Using Synthetic Audio to Improve the Recognition of Out-of-Vocabulary Words in End-to-End Asr Systems. In *2021 IEEE International Conference on Acoustics, Speech and Signal Processing (ICASSP)*, pages 5674–5678.

A Experimental Settings

Our ASR and ST models share the same architecture. Two 1D convolutional layers with a Gated Linear Unit non-linearity between them shrink the input sequence over the temporal dimension, having 2 as stride. Then, after adding sinusoidal positional embeddings, the sequence is encoded by 12 Transformer encoder layers, whose output is attended by 6 Transformer decoder layers. We use 512 as Transformer embedding size, 2048 as intermediate dimension of the feed forward networks, and 8 heads. In the case of the triangle model, we keep the same settings and the configurations are the same for the two decoders. The number of parameters is ~74M for the base system and ~117M for the triangle model.

We filter out samples whose audio segment lasts more than 30s, extract 80 features from audio segments, normalize them at utterance level, and apply SpecAugment (Park et al., 2019). The target text is segmented into BPE (Sennrich et al., 2016) subwords using 8,000 merge rules (Di Gangi et al., 2020) with SentencePience (Kudo and Richardson, 2018).

Models are optimized with Adam (Kingma and Ba, 2015) to minimize the label smoothed cross entropy (Szegedy et al., 2016). The learning rate increases up to 1e-3 for 10,000 warm-up updates, then decreases with an inverse square-root scheduler. We train on 4 K80 GPUs with 12GB of RAM, using mini-batches containing 5,000 tokens, and accumulating the gradient for 16 mini-batches. We average 5 checkpoints around the best on the validation loss. All trainings last ~4 days for the multilingual systems, and ~3 days for the base system.

Joint Generation of Captions and Subtitles with Dual Decoding

Jitao Xu[†] **François Buet**[†] **Josep Crego**[‡] **Elise Bertin-Lemée**[‡] **François Yvon**[†]

[†]Université Paris-Saclay, CNRS, LISN, 91400, Orsay, France
[‡]SYSTRAN, 5 rue Feydeau, 75002 Paris, France
{firstname.lastname}@{[†]limsi.fr,[‡]systrangroup.com}

Abstract

As the amount of audio-visual content increases, the need to develop automatic captioning and subtitling solutions to match the expectations of a growing international audience appears as the only viable way to boost throughput and lower the related post-production costs. Automatic captioning and subtitling often need to be tightly intertwined to achieve an appropriate level of consistency and synchronization with each other and with the video signal. In this work, we assess a dual decoding scheme to achieve a strong coupling between these two tasks and show how adequacy and consistency are increased, with virtually no additional cost in terms of model size and training complexity.

1 Introduction

As the amount of online audio-visual content continues to grow, the need for captions and subtitles[1] in multiple languages also steadily increases, as it widens the potential audience of these contents.

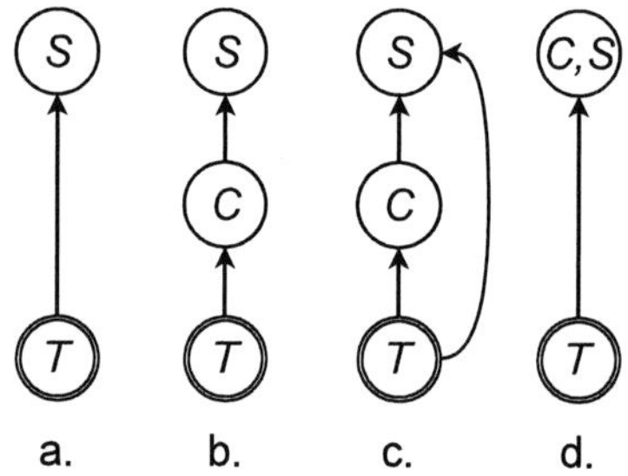

Figure 1: A graphical view of various captioning and subtitling strategies. T refers to transcripts. C and S respectively denote captions and subtitles.

Both activities are closely related: human subtitle translators often generate subtitles directly based on the original captions without viewing or listening to the original audio/video file. This strategy however runs the risk of amplifying, in the subtitle approximations, simplifications or errors present in the captioning. It may even happen that both texts need to be simultaneously displayed on screen: for instance, in countries with several official languages, or to help foreign language learners. This means that captions and subtitles need to be consistent not only with the video content, but also with each other. It also implies that they should be synchronized (Karakanta et al., 2021). Finally, even in scenarios where only subtitles would be needed, generating captions at the same time may still help to better check the correctness of subtitles.

Early approaches to automatic subtitling (e.g. Piperidis et al., 2004) also assumed a pipeline architecture (Figure 1 (b)), where subtitles are translated from captions derived from automatic speech transcripts. A recent alternative (Figure 1 (a)), which mitigates cascading errors, is to independently perform captioning and subtitling in an end-to-end manner (Liu et al., 2020; Karakanta et al., 2020a); the risk however is to generate inconsistencies (both in alignment and content) between the two textual streams. This approach might also be limited by the lack of appropriate training resources (Sperber and Paulik, 2020). Various ways to further strengthen the interactions between these tasks by sharing parameters or loss terms are evaluated by Sperber et al. (2020). Figure 1 (c) illustrates these approaches.

In this work, we explore an even tighter integration consisting of *simultaneously generating both captions and subtitles* from automatic speech recognition (ASR) transcripts *using one single dual decoding process* (Zhou et al., 2019; Wang et al., 2019; Le et al., 2020; He et al., 2021; Xu and Yvon, 2021), illustrated in Figure 1 (d). Generally speak-

[1]We use 'caption' to refer to a text written in the same language as the audio and 'subtitle' when translated into another language. Captions, which are often meant for viewers with hearing difficulties, and subtitles, which are produced for viewers with an imperfect command of the source language, may have slightly different traits, that we ignore here.

Proceedings of the 19th International Conference on Spoken Language Translation (IWSLT 2022), pages 74 - 82
May 26-27, 2022 ©2022 Association for Computational Linguistics

Transcript	**i 'm** combining specific types of signals **the** mimic how our body **response** to **in an injury** to help us regenerate
Caption	**I'm** combining specific types of signals **[eob] that** mimic how our body **responds** to **injury [eol]** to help us regenerate**. [eob]**
Subtitle	Je combine différents types de signaux [eob] qui imitent la réponse du corps [eol] aux blessures pour nous aider à guérir. [eob]

Table 1: Example of a triplet (transcript, caption, subtitle) from our tri-parallel data. Differences between transcript and caption are in bold.

ing, automatically turning ASR transcripts into full-fledged captions involves multiple changes, depending on the specification of the captioning task. In our case, this transformation comprises four main aspects: segmentation for display (via tag insertion), removal of certain features from spoken language (eg. fillers, repetitions or hesitations), ASR errors correction, and punctuation prediction. The transcript-to-subtitle task involves the same transformations, with an additional translation step to produce text in another language. Table 1 illustrates the various transformations that occur between input transcripts and the corresponding output segments.

As our experiments suggest, a tighter integration not only improves the quality and the consistency of captions and subtitles, but it also enables a better use of all available data, *with hardly any impact on model size or training complexity*. Our main contributions are the following: (i) we show that simultaneously generating captions and subtitles can improve performance in both languages, reporting significant improvements in BLEU score with respect to several baselines; (ii) we initialize dual decoder from a standard encoder-decoder model trained with large scale data, thereby mitigating the data scarcity problem; (iii) we explore a new parameter sharing scheme, where the two decoders share all their parameters, and achieve comparable performance at a much reduced model size in our experimental conditions; (iv) using 2-round decoding, we show how to alleviate the exposure bias problem observed in dual decoding, leading to a clear boost in performance.

2 Dual Decoding

2.1 Model

In a nutshell, dual decoding aims to generate two output sentences $\mathbf{e}^1$ and $\mathbf{e}^2$ for each input sentence $\mathbf{f}$. This means that instead of having two independent models (Eq. (1)), the generation of each target is influenced by the other output (Eq. (2)):

$$P(\mathbf{e}^1, \mathbf{e}^2|\mathbf{f}) = \prod_{t=1}^{T} P(\mathbf{e}^1_t|\mathbf{f}, \mathbf{e}^1_{<t}) P(\mathbf{e}^2_t|\mathbf{f}, \mathbf{e}^2_{<t}) \quad (1)$$

$$P(\mathbf{e}^1, \mathbf{e}^2|\mathbf{f}) = \prod_{t=1}^{T} P(\mathbf{e}^1_t|\mathbf{f}, \mathbf{e}^1_{<t}, \mathbf{e}^2_{<t}) \times P(\mathbf{e}^2_t|\mathbf{f}, \mathbf{e}^1_{<t}, \mathbf{e}^2_{<t}), \quad (2)$$

where $T = max(|\mathbf{e}^1|, |\mathbf{e}^2|)$.

In our experiments, ASR transcripts are considered as the source language while captions and subtitles are the two target languages (Wang et al., 2019; He et al., 2021; Xu and Yvon, 2021). The dual decoder model has also been proposed in several application scenarios other than multi-target translation such as bi-directional translation (Zhou et al., 2019; Zhang et al., 2020a; He et al., 2021), and also to simultaneously generate transcripts and translations from the audio source (Le et al., 2020).

To implement the interaction between the two decoders, we mostly follow Le et al. (2020) and Xu and Yvon (2021) who add a decoder cross-attention layer in each decoder block, so that the hidden states of previous layers of each decoder H^1_l and H^2_l can attend to each other. The decoder cross-attention layers take the form:[2]

$$H^1_{l+1} = \text{Attention}(H^1_l, H^2_l, H^2_l)$$
$$H^2_{l+1} = \text{Attention}(H^2_l, H^1_l, H^1_l)$$

Both decoders are thus fully synchronous since each requires the hidden states of the other to compute its own hidden states.

2.2 Sharing Decoders

One weakness of the dual decoder model is that it contains two separate decoders, yielding an increased number of parameters ($\times 1.6$ in our models w.r.t. standard translation models). Inspired by

[2]We define the Attention(Q, K, V) function as in (Vaswani et al., 2017) as a function of three arguments standing respectively for Query, Key and Value.

the idea of tying parameters in embedding matrices (Inan et al., 2017; Press and Wolf, 2017), we extend the dual decoder model by *sharing all the parameters matrices in the two decoders*: in this way, the total number of parameters remains close to that of a standard translation model ($\times 1.1$), since the only increase comes from the additional decoder cross-attention layer. When implementing inference with this multilingual shared decoder, we prefix each target sentence with a tag indicating the intended output (captioning or subtitling).

2.3 Training and Fine-tuning

The dual decoder model is trained using a joint loss combining the log-likelihood of the two targets:

$$L(\theta) = \sum_{D}(\sum_{t=1}^{|\mathbf{e}^1|} \log P(\mathbf{e}_t^1|\mathbf{e}_{<t}^1, \mathbf{e}_{<t}^2, \mathbf{f}; \theta) + \sum_{t=1}^{|\mathbf{e}^2|} \log P(\mathbf{e}_t^2|\mathbf{e}_{<t}^2, \mathbf{e}_{<t}^1, \mathbf{f}; \theta)),$$

where θ represents the set of parameters. Training this model requires triplets of instances associating one source with two targets. Such resources are difficult to find and the largest tri-parallel open source corpus we know of is the MuST-Cinema dataset (Karakanta et al., 2020b), which is clearly smaller than what exists to separately train automatic transcription or translation systems.

In order to leverage large scale parallel translation data for English-French, we adopt a fine-tuning strategy where we initially pre-train a standard (encoder-decoder) translation model using all available resources, which serves to initialize the parameters of our dual decoder model. As the dual decoder network employs two decoders with shared parameters, we use also the decoder of the pre-trained model to initialize this subnetwork. Fine-tuning is performed on a tri-parallel corpus. We discuss the effect of decoder initialization in Section 3.4.1. Finally, for all fine-tuned models, the decoder cross-attention layer which binds the two decoders together is always randomly initialized.

3 Experiments

3.1 Datasets and Resources

For our experiments, we use MuST-Cinema[3] (Karakanta et al., 2020b), a multilingual Speech-to-Subtitles corpus compiled from TED talks, in which subtitles contain additional segmentation tags indicating changes of screen ([eob]) or line ([eol]). Our experiments consider the translation from English (EN) into French (FR). Our tri-parallel data also includes a pre-existing unpunctuated ASR output generated by Karakanta et al. (2020a), which achieves a WER score of 39.2% on the MuST-Cinema test set speech transcripts (details in Appendix A). For pre-training, we use all available WMT14 EN-FR data. During fine-tuning, we follow the recommendations and procedures of Zhou et al. (2019); Wang et al. (2019); He et al. (2021); Xu and Yvon (2021), and use synthetic tri-parallel data, in which we alternatively replace one of the two target side references by hypotheses generated from the baseline system for the corresponding direction via forward-translation. For more details about synthetic tri-parallel data generation, we refer to (Zhou et al., 2019; Xu and Yvon, 2021). We tokenize all data with Moses scripts and use a shared source-target vocabulary of 32K Byte Pair Encoding units (Sennrich et al., 2016) learned with `subword-nmt`.[4]

3.2 Experimental Settings

We implement the dual decoder model based on the Transformer (Vaswani et al., 2017) model using `fairseq`[5] (Ott et al., 2019).[6] All models are trained until no improvement is found for 4 consecutive checkpoints on the development set, except for the EN→FR pre-trained translation model which is trained during 300k iterations (further details in Appendix B). We mainly measure performance with SacreBLEU (Post, 2018);[7] TER and BERTScores (Zhang et al., 2020b) are also reported in Appendix D. Segmentation tags in subtitles are taken into account and BLEU scores are computed over full sentences. In addition to BLEU score, measuring the consistency between captions and subtitles is also an important aspect. We reuse the structural and lexical consistency score proposed by Karakanta et al. (2021). *Structural consistency* measures the percentage of utterances having the same number of blocks in both languages, while *lexical scores* count the proportion of words in the two languages that are aligned in the same block

[3] `https://ict.fbk.eu/must-cinema/`

[4] `https://github.com/rsennrich/subword-nmt`

[5] `https://github.com/pytorch/fairseq`

[6] Our implementation is open-sourced at `https://github.com/jitao-xu/dual-decoding`

[7] BLEU+case.mixed+numrefs.1+smooth.exp+tok.13a+version.1.5.1

(refer to Appendix C for additional details).

We call the dual decoder model `dual`. Baseline translation models trained separately on each direction (T_{en}→C_{en}, T_{en}→S_{fr}) are denoted by `base`. To study the effectiveness of dual decoding, we mainly compare `dual` with a `pipeline` system. The latter uses the `base` model to produce captions which are then translated into subtitles using an independent system trained to translate from caption to subtitle (T_{en}→C_{en}→S_{fr}).

Like the `dual` model, `base` and `pipeline` systems also benefit from pre-training. For the former, we pre-train the direct transcript-to-subtitle translation model (T_{en}→S_{fr}); for `pipeline`, the caption-to-subtitle model (C_{en}→S_{fr}) is pre-trained, while the first step (T_{en}→C_{en}) remains as in the `base` system. Note that all fine-tuned systems start with the same model pre-trained using WMT EN-FR data.

3.3 Main Results

Model	BLEU			Consistency	
	EN	FR	Avg	Struct.	Lex.
`base`	55.7	23.9	39.8	55.3	70.7
`base` +FT	55.7	24.9	40.3	54.5	71.4
`pipeline`	55.7	23.6	39.7	95.7	96.0
`pipeline` +FT	55.7	24.2	40.0	98.4	98.3
`dual` +FT	**56.9**	25.6	**41.3**	65.1	79.1
`share` +FT	56.5	**25.8**	41.2	**66.7**	**80.0**

Table 2: BLEU scores for captions (EN) and subtitles (FR), with measures of structural and lexical consistency between the two hypotheses. These scores are in percentage (higher is better). The `base` and `pipeline` settings are trained from scratch with original data. `share` refers to tying all decoder parameters.

We only report in Table 2 the performance of the two baselines and fine-tuned (+FT) models, as our preliminary experiments showed that training the dual decoder model with only tri-parallel data was not optimal. The BLEU score of the *do nothing* baseline, which copies the source ASR transcripts to the output, is 28.0, which suggests that the captioning task actually involves much more transformations than simply inserting segmentation tags. We see that fine-tuning improves subtitles generated by `base` and `pipeline` systems by ~1 BLEU. Our `dual` decoder model, after fine-tuned using synthetic tri-parallel data, respectively outperforms `base`+FT by 0.7 BLEU, and `pipeline`+FT by 1.4 BLEU. Sharing all parameters of both decoders yields further increase of 0.2 BLEU, with about one third less parameters.

We also measure the structural and lexical consistency between captions and subtitles generated by our systems (see Table 2). As expected, `pipeline` settings always generate very consistent pairs of captions and subtitles, as subtitles are direct translations of the captions; all other methods generate both outputs from the ASR transcripts. `dual` models do not perform as well, but are still able to generate captions and subtitles with a much higher structural and lexical consistency between the two outputs than in the `base` systems. Xu and Yvon (2021) show that dual decoder models generate translations that are more consistent in content. We further show here that our `dual` models generates hypotheses which are also more consistent in structure. Examples output captions and subtitles are in Appendix E.

3.4 Analyses and Discussions

3.4.1 The Effect of Fine-tuning

As the pre-trained uni-directional translation model has never seen sentences in the source language on the target side, we first only use it to initialize the subtitling decoder, and use a random initialization for the captioning decoder. To study the effect of initialization, we conduct an ablation study by comparing three settings: initializing only the subtitling decoder, both decoders or the shared decoder (see Table 3). Initializing both decoders brings improvements in both directions, with a gain of 1.6 BLEU for captioning and 0.3 BLEU for subtitling. Moreover, sharing parameters between decoders further boost the subtitling performance by 0.2 BLEU. As it seems, the captioning decoder also benefits from a decoder pre-trained in another language.

Model	EN	FR	Avg
`dual` 1-decoder +FT	55.3	25.3	40.3
`dual` +FT	56.9	25.6	41.3
`share` +FT	56.5	25.8	41.2

Table 3: BLEU scores for multiple initializations.

3.4.2 Exposure Bias

Due to error accumulations in both decoders, the exposure bias problem seems more severe for dual decoder model than for regular translation models (Zhou et al., 2019; Zhang et al., 2020a; Xu and Yvon, 2021). These authors propose to use *pseudo tri-parallel data with synthetic references* to alleviate this problem. We analyze the influence of this exposure bias issue in our application scenario.

To this end, we compare fine-tuning the `dual` model with original vs artificial tri-parallel data. For simplicity, we only report in Table 4 the average BLEU scores of captioning and subtitling. Results show that fine-tuning with the original data (w.real) strongly degrades the automatic metrics for the generated text , resulting in performance that are worse than the baseline.

Model	Normal	2-round	Ref
`dual` +FT w.real	39.2	40.9	45.0
`share` +FT w.real	38.6	40.1	43.9
`dual` +FT	41.3	41.2	41.0
`share` +FT	41.2	40.9	40.5

Table 4: Performance of various decoding methods. All BLEU scores are averaged over the two outputs. *2-round* (resp. *Ref*) refers to decoding with model predictions (resp. references) as forced prefix in one direction.

In another set of experiments, we follow Xu and Yvon (2021) and perform asynchronous 2-round decoding. We first decode the `dual` models to obtain hypotheses in both languages e_1' and e_2'. During the second decoding round, we use the output English caption e_1' as a forced prefix when generating the French subtitles e_2''. The final English caption e_1'' is obtained similarly. Note that when generating the t-th token in e_2'', the decoder cross-attention module only attends to the t first tokens of e_1', even though the full of e_1' is actually known. The 2-round scores for e_1'' and e_2'' are in Table 4, and compared with the optimal situation where we use references instead of model predictions as forced prefix in the second round (in col. 'Ref').

Results in Table 4 suggest that dual decoder models fine-tuned with original data (w.real) are quite sensible to exposure bias, which can be mitigated with artificial tri-parallel data. Their performance can however be improved by $\sim$1.5 BLEU when using 2-round decoding, thereby almost closing the initial gap with models using synthetic data. The latter approach is overall slightly better and also more stable across decoding configurations.

4 Conclusion

In this paper, we have explored dual decoding to jointly generate captions and subtitles from ASR transcripts. Experimentally, we found that dual decoding improves translation quality for both captioning and subtitling, while delivering more consistent output pairs. Additionally, we showed that (a) model sharing on the decoder side is viable and effective, at least for related languages; (b) initializing with pre-trained models vastly improves performance; (c) 2-round decoding allowed us to mitigate the exposure bias problem in our model. In the future, we would like to experiment on more distant language pairs to validate our approach in a more general scenario.

5 Acknowledgement

The authors wish to thank Alina Karakanta for providing the ASR transcripts and the evaluation script for the consistency measures. We would also like to thank the anonymous reviewers for their valuable suggestions. This work was granted access to the HPC resources of IDRIS under the allocation 2021-[AD011011580R1] made by GENCI. The first author is partly funded by SYSTRAN and by a grant Transwrite from Région Ile-de-France. This work has also been funded by the BPI-France investment programme "Grands défis du numérique", as part of the ROSETTA-2 project (Subtitling RObot and Adapted Translation).

References

Piotr Bojanowski, Edouard Grave, Armand Joulin, and Tomas Mikolov. 2017. Enriching word vectors with subword information. *Transactions of the Association for Computational Linguistics*, 5:135–146.

Eunah Cho, Jan Niehues, and Alex Waibel. 2012. Segmentation and punctuation prediction in speech language translation using a monolingual translation system. In *Proceedings of the 9th International Workshop on Spoken Language Translation: Papers*, pages 252–259, Hong Kong, Table of contents.

Chris Dyer, Victor Chahuneau, and Noah A. Smith. 2013. A simple, fast, and effective reparameterization of IBM model 2. In *Proceedings of the 2013 Conference of the North American Chapter of the Association for Computational Linguistics: Human Language Technologies*, pages 644–648, Atlanta, Georgia. Association for Computational Linguistics.

Kyle Gorman. 2016. Pynini: A Python library for weighted finite-state grammar compilation. In *Proceedings of the SIGFSM Workshop on Statistical NLP and Weighted Automata*, pages 75–80, Berlin, Germany. Association for Computational Linguistics.

Hao He, Qian Wang, Zhipeng Yu, Yang Zhao, Jiajun Zhang, and Chengqing Zong. 2021. Synchronous interactive decoding for multilingual neural machine translation. In *Proceedings of the AAAI Conference on Artificial Intelligence*, volume 35, pages 12981–12988.

Hakan Inan, Khashayar Khosravi, and Richard Socher. 2017. Tying word vectors and word classifiers: A loss framework for language modeling. In *5th International Conference on Learning Representations, ICLR 2017, Toulon, France, April 24-26, 2017, Conference Track Proceedings*. OpenReview.net.

Alina Karakanta, Marco Gaido, Matteo Negri, and Marco Turchi. 2021. Between flexibility and consistency: Joint generation of captions and subtitles. In *Proceedings of the 18th International Conference on Spoken Language Translation (IWSLT 2021)*, pages 215–225, Bangkok, Thailand (online). Association for Computational Linguistics.

Alina Karakanta, Matteo Negri, and Marco Turchi. 2020a. Is 42 the answer to everything in subtitling-oriented speech translation? In *Proceedings of the 17th International Conference on Spoken Language Translation*, pages 209–219, Online. Association for Computational Linguistics.

Alina Karakanta, Matteo Negri, and Marco Turchi. 2020b. MuST-cinema: a speech-to-subtitles corpus. In *Proceedings of the 12th Language Resources and Evaluation Conference*, pages 3727–3734, Marseille, France. European Language Resources Association.

Hang Le, Juan Pino, Changhan Wang, Jiatao Gu, Didier Schwab, and Laurent Besacier. 2020. Dual-decoder transformer for joint automatic speech recognition and multilingual speech translation. In *Proceedings of the 28th International Conference on Computational Linguistics*, pages 3520–3533, Barcelona, Spain (Online). International Committee on Computational Linguistics.

Danni Liu, Jan Niehues, and Gerasimos Spanakis. 2020. Adapting end-to-end speech recognition for readable subtitles. In *Proceedings of the 17th International Conference on Spoken Language Translation*, pages 247–256, Online.

Mehryar Mohri. 2002. Semiring frameworks and algorithms for shortest-distance problems. *J. Autom. Lang. Comb.*, 7(3):321–350.

Myle Ott, Sergey Edunov, Alexei Baevski, Angela Fan, Sam Gross, Nathan Ng, David Grangier, and Michael Auli. 2019. fairseq: A fast, extensible toolkit for sequence modeling. In *Proceedings of the 2019 Conference of the North American Chapter of the Association for Computational Linguistics (Demonstrations)*, pages 48–53, Minneapolis, Minnesota. Association for Computational Linguistics.

Vassil Panayotov, Guoguo Chen, Daniel Povey, and Sanjeev Khudanpur. 2015. Librispeech: An ASR corpus based on public domain audio books. In *2015 IEEE International Conference on Acoustics, Speech and Signal Processing, ICASSP 2015, South Brisbane, Queensland, Australia, April 19-24, 2015*, pages 5206–5210. IEEE.

Stelios Piperidis, Iason Demiros, Prokopis Prokopidis, Peter Vanroose, Anja Hoethker, Walter Daelemans, Elsa Sklavounou, Manos Konstantinou, and Yannis Karavidas. 2004. Multimodal, multilingual resources in the subtitling process. In *Proceedings of LREC*.

Matt Post. 2018. A call for clarity in reporting BLEU scores. In *Proceedings of the Third Conference on Machine Translation: Research Papers*, pages 186–191, Brussels, Belgium. Association for Computational Linguistics.

Daniel Povey, Arnab Ghoshal, Gilles Boulianne, Lukas Burget, Ondrej Glembek, Nagendra Goel, Mirko Hannemann, Petr Motlicek, Yanmin Qian, Petr Schwarz, et al. 2011. The kaldi speech recognition toolkit. In *IEEE 2011 workshop on automatic speech recognition and understanding*, CONF. IEEE Signal Processing Society.

Ofir Press and Lior Wolf. 2017. Using the output embedding to improve language models. In *Proceedings of the 15th Conference of the European Chapter of the Association for Computational Linguistics: Volume 2, Short Papers*, pages 157–163, Valencia, Spain. Association for Computational Linguistics.

Rico Sennrich, Barry Haddow, and Alexandra Birch. 2016. Neural machine translation of rare words with subword units. In *Proceedings of the 54th Annual Meeting of the Association for Computational Linguistics (Volume 1: Long Papers)*, pages 1715–1725, Berlin, Germany. Association for Computational Linguistics.

Matthias Sperber and Matthias Paulik. 2020. Speech translation and the end-to-end promise: Taking stock of where we are. In *Proceedings of the 58th Annual Meeting of the Association for Computational Linguistics*, pages 7409–7421, Online. Association for Computational Linguistics.

Matthias Sperber, Hendra Setiawan, Christian Gollan, Udhyakumar Nallasamy, and Matthias Paulik. 2020. Consistent transcription and translation of speech. *Transactions of the Association for Computational Linguistics*, 8:695–709.

Ashish Vaswani, Noam Shazeer, Niki Parmar, Jakob Uszkoreit, Llion Jones, Aidan N Gomez, Ł ukasz Kaiser, and Illia Polosukhin. 2017. Attention is all you need. In I. Guyon, U. V. Luxburg, S. Bengio, H. Wallach, R. Fergus, S. Vishwanathan, and R. Garnett, editors, *Advances in Neural Information Processing Systems 30*, pages 5998–6008. Curran Associates, Inc.

Yining Wang, Jiajun Zhang, Long Zhou, Yuchen Liu, and Chengqing Zong. 2019. Synchronously generating two languages with interactive decoding. In

Proceedings of the 2019 Conference on Empirical Methods in Natural Language Processing and the 9th International Joint Conference on Natural Language Processing (EMNLP-IJCNLP), pages 3350–3355, Hong Kong, China. Association for Computational Linguistics.

Jitao Xu and François Yvon. 2021. One source, two targets: Challenges and rewards of dual decoding. In *Proceedings of the 2021 Conference on Empirical Methods in Natural Language Processing*, pages 8533–8546, Online and Punta Cana, Dominican Republic. Association for Computational Linguistics.

Jiajun Zhang, Long Zhou, Yang Zhao, and Chengqing Zong. 2020a. Synchronous bidirectional inference for neural sequence generation. *Artificial Intelligence*, 281:103234.

Tianyi Zhang, Varsha Kishore, Felix Wu, Kilian Q. Weinberger, and Yoav Artzi. 2020b. BERTScore: Evaluating Text Generation with BERT. In *International Conference on Learning Representations*.

Long Zhou, Jiajun Zhang, and Chengqing Zong. 2019. Synchronous bidirectional neural machine translation. *Transactions of the Association for Computational Linguistics*, 7:91–105.

A Data Processing Details

For the English to French language pair, MuST-Cinema[8] (Karakanta et al., 2020b) contains 275k sentences for training and 1079 and 544 lines for development and testing, respectively. The ASR system used by Karakanta et al. (2020a) to produce transcripts was based on the KALDI toolkit (Povey et al., 2011), and had been trained on the clean portion of LibriSpeech (Panayotov et al., 2015) (~460h) and a subset of MuST-Cinema (~450h). In order to emulate a real production scenario, we segment these transcripts as if they were from an ASR system performing segmentation based on prosody. As this kind of system tends to produce longer sequences compared to typical written text (Cho et al., 2012), we randomly concatenate the English captions into longer sequences, to which we align the ASR transcripts using the conventional edit distance, thus adding a subsegmentation aspect to the translation task. Edit distance computations are based on a Weighted Finite-State Transducer (WSFT), implemented with Pynini (Gorman, 2016), which represents editing operations (match, insertion, deletion, replacement) at the character level, with weights depending on the characters and the previous operation context. After composing the edit WFST with the transcript string and the caption string, the optimal operation sequence is computed using a shortest-distance algorithm (Mohri, 2002). The number of sentences to be concatenated is sampled normally, with an average around of 2. This process results in 133k, 499 and 255 lines for training, development and testing, respectively.

For pre-training, we use all available WMT14 EN-FR data,[9] in which we discard sentence pairs with invalid language label as computed by `fasttext` language identification model[10] (Bojanowski et al., 2017). This pre-training data contains 33.9M sentence pairs.

B Experimental Details

We build our dual decoder model with a hidden size of 512 and a feedforward size of 2048. We optimize with Adam, set up with a maximum learning rate of 0.0007 and an inverse square root decay schedule, as well as 4000 warmup steps. For fine-tuning, we use Adam with a fixed learning rate of 8e−5. For all models, we share lexical embeddings between the encoder and the input and output decoder matrices. All models are trained with mixed precision and a batch size of 8192 tokens on 4 V100 GPUs.

The two models in the `base` setting are trained separately using transcript→caption and transcript→subtitle data. The second model of the `pipeline` setting is trained using caption→subtitle data. When performing fine-tuning, we first pre-train an EN→FR translation model `pre-train` using WMT EN-FR data. For `base`+FT setting, the transcript→subtitle model is fine-tuned from `pre-train`, while the transcript→caption is the same as `base` since languages on both source and target sides are English. For `pipeline`+FT, the caption→subtitle model is fine-tuned from `pre-train`. For `dual`+FT, the encoder and the two decoders are fine-tuned from the same `pre-train` model. The decoder cross-attention layers cannot be fine-tuned and are randomly initialized. Due to computation limits, we are not able to conduct multiple runs for our models. However, all results are obtained by using the parameters averaged over the last 5 checkpoints.

[8]License: CC BY-NC-ND 4.0

[9]`https://statmt.org/wmt14`

[10]`https://dl.fbaipublicfiles.com/fasttext/supervised-models/lid.176.bin`

C Consistency Score

Consider the following example from (Karakanta et al., 2021):

0:00:50,820, 00:00:53,820
To put the assumptions very clearly:
Enonçons clairement nos hypothèses : le capitalisme,

00:00:53,820, 00:00:57,820
capitalism, after 150 years, has become acceptable,
après 150 ans, est devenu acceptable, au même titre

00:00:58,820, 00:01:00,820
and so has democracy.
que la democratie.

As defined by Karakanta et al. (2021), for the stuctural consistency, both captions (EN) and subtitles (FR) have the same number of 3 blocks. For lexical consistency, there are 6 tokens of the subtitles which are not aligned to captions in the same block: *"le capitalisme ," , "au même titre"*. The $Lex_{C \to S}$ is calculated as the percentage of aligned words normalized by number of words in the caption. Therefore, $Lex_{C \to S} = \frac{20}{22} = 90.9\%$; the computation is identical in the other direction, yielding $Lex_{S \to C} = \frac{17}{23} = 73.9\%$, the average lexical consistency of this segment is thus $Lex_{pair} = \frac{Lex_{C \to S} + Lex_{S \to C}}{2} = 82.4\%$.

When computing the *lexical consistency* between captions and subtitles, we use the WMT14 EN-FR data to train an alignment model using `fast_align`[11] (Dyer et al., 2013) in both directions and use it to predict word alignments for model outputs.

D Additional Metric

Table 5 reports TER and BERTScores[12] (Zhang et al., 2020b). Note that for BERTScores, we remove segmentation tokens ([eob] and [eol]) from hypotheses and references, as special tokens are out-of-vocabulary for pre-trained BERT models.

E Examples

Some examples of dual decoding improving the quality of both captioning and subtitling compared to the pipeline system are in Table 6.

[11] `https://github.com/clab/fast_align`
[12] `https://github.com/Tiiiger/bert_score`

Model	TER ↓ EN	FR	Avg	BERTScore-F1 ↑ EN	FR	Avg	BLEU ↑ EN	FR	Avg	Consistency ↑ Struct.	Lex.
`base`	0.264	0.662	0.463	0.7346	0.3961	0.5654	55.7	23.9	39.8	55.3	70.7
`base` +FT	0.264	0.654	0.459	0.7346	0.4026	0.5686	55.7	24.9	40.3	54.5	71.4
`pipeline`	0.264	0.650	0.457	0.7346	0.3912	0.5629	55.7	23.6	39.7	95.7	96.0
`pipeline` +FT	0.264	0.652	0.458	0.7346	0.3924	0.5635	55.7	24.2	40.0	98.4	98.3
`dual` +FT	**0.256**	**0.640**	**0.448**	0.7378	**0.4074**	0.5726	**56.9**	25.6	**41.3**	65.1	79.1
`share` +FT	0.259	**0.640**	0.450	**0.7396**	0.4066	**0.5731**	56.5	**25.8**	41.2	**66.7**	**80.0**

Table 5: TER, BERTScore and BLEU scores for captions (EN) and subtitles (FR), with measures of structural and lexical consistency between the two hypotheses. The `base` and `pipeline` settings are trained from scratch with original data. `share` refers to tying all decoder parameters. Signature of BERTScore (EN): microsoft/deberta-xlarge-mnli_L40_no-idf_version=0.3.11(hug_trans=4.10.3)-rescaled_fast-tokenizer. Signature of BERTScore (FR): bert-base-multilingual-cased_L9_no-idf_version=0.3.11(hug_trans=4.10.3)-rescaled_fast-tokenizer.

Source	take time to write down your values your objectives and your key results do it today
EN `pipeline` +FT	Take time to write down [eol] your values, your objectives, [eob] and your key results do it today. [eob]
EN `share` +FT	Take time to write down your values, **[eol]** your objectives, [eob] and your key results do it today. [eob]
EN ref	Take time to write down your values, [eob] your objectives and your key results. [eob] Do it today. [eob]
FR `pipeline` +FT	Prenez le temps d'écrire vos valeurs, [eol] vos objectifs, [eob] et vos principaux résultats [eol] le font aujourd'hui. [eob]
FR `share` +FT	Prenez le temps d'écrire vos valeurs, **[eob]** vos objectifs et **vos résultats clés. [eob] Faites-le** aujourd'hui. [eob]
FR ref	Prenez le temps d'écrire vos valeurs, [eob] vos objectifs et vos résultats clés. [eob] Faites-le aujourd'hui. [eob]
Source	and as it turns out what are you willing to give up is exactly the right question to ask
EN `pipeline` +FT	And as it turns out, what are you willing [eol] to give up is exactly [eob] the right question to ask? [eob]
EN `share` +FT	And as it turns out, what are you willing [eol] to give up **[eob]** is exactly the right question to ask? [eob]
EN ref	And as it turns out, [eob] "What are you willing to give up?" [eob] is exactly the right question to ask. [eob]
FR `pipeline` +FT	Et il s'avère que ce que vous voulez abandonner [eol] est exactement [eob] la bonne question à poser ? [eob]
FR `share` +FT	Et il s'avère que ce que vous voulez abandonner **[eob]** est exactement la bonne question à poser. [eob]
FR ref	Et il s'avère que [eob] « Qu'êtes-vous prêts à abandonner ? » [eob] est exactement la question à poser. [eob]

Table 6: Examples of dual decoding improving both captioning and subtitling. Major improvements are marked in bold.

MirrorAlign: A Super Lightweight Unsupervised Word Alignment Model via Cross-Lingual Contrastive Learning

Di Wu
Peking University, China
inbath@163.com

Liang Ding
The University of Sydney, Australia
liangding.liam@gmail.com

Shuo Yang
iFlytek Research, China
shuoyang7@iflytek.com

Mingyang Li
Independent Researcher, China
liamlmy@163.com

Abstract

Word alignment is essential for the downstream cross-lingual language understanding and generation tasks. Recently, the performance of the neural word alignment models (Garg et al., 2019; Ding et al., 2019; Zenkel et al., 2020) has exceeded that of statistical models. However, they heavily rely on sophisticated translation models. In this study, we propose a super lightweight unsupervised word alignment model named *MirrorAlign*, in which a bidirectional symmetric attention trained with a contrastive learning objective is introduced, and an agreement loss is employed to bind the attention maps, such that the alignments follow mirror-like symmetry hypothesis. Experimental results on several public benchmarks demonstrate that our model achieves competitive, if not better, performance compared to the state of the art in word alignment while significantly reducing the training and decoding time on average. Further ablation analysis and case studies show the superiority of our proposed MirrorAlign. Notably, we recognize our model as a pioneer attempt to unify bilingual word embedding and word alignments. Encouragingly, our approach achieves *16.4× speedup* against GIZA++, and *50× parameter compression* compared with the Transformer-based alignment methods. We release our code to facilitate the community[1].

1 Introduction

Word alignment, aiming to find the word-level correspondence between a pair of parallel sentences, is a core component of the statistical machine translation (Brown et al., 1993, SMT). It also has benefited several downstream tasks, *e.g.*, computer-aided translation (Dagan et al., 1993), semantic role labeling (Kozhevnikov and Titov, 2013), cross-lingual dataset creation (Yarowsky et al., 2001), cross-lingual modeling (Ding et al., 2020a), and cross-lingual text generation (Zan et al., 2022).

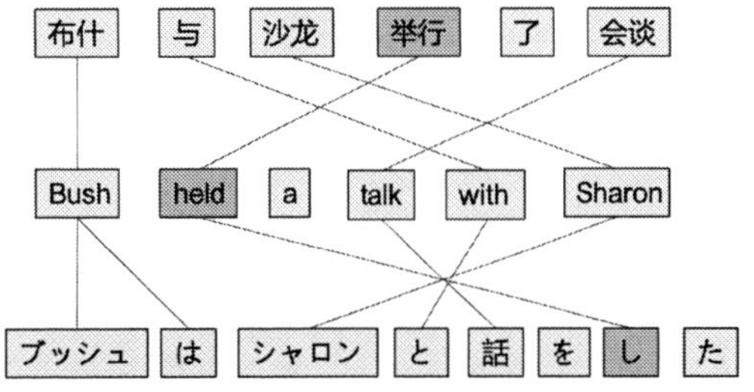

Figure 1: Two examples of word alignment. The upper and bottom cases are the Chinese and Japanese references, respectively.

Recently, in the era of neural machine translation (Bahdanau et al., 2015; Vaswani et al., 2017, NMT), the attention mechanism plays the role of the alignment model in translation system. Unfortunately, Koehn and Knowles (2017) show that attention mechanism may in fact dramatically diverge with word alignment. The works of Ghader and Monz (2017); Li et al. (2019) also confirm this finding.

Although there are some studies attempt to mitigate this problem, most of them are rely on a sophisticated translation architecture (Garg et al., 2019; Zenkel et al., 2020). These methods are trained with a translation objective, which computes the probability of each target token conditioned on source tokens and previous target tokens. This will bring tremendous parameters and noisy alignments. Most recent work avoids the noisy alignment of translation models but employed too much expensive human-annotated alignments (Stengel-Eskin et al., 2019). Given these disadvantages, simple statistical alignment tools, *e.g.,* FastAlign (Dyer et al., 2013) and GIZA++ (Och and Ney, 2003)[2], are still the most representative solutions due to their efficiency and unsupervised fashion. We argue that the word alignment task, intuitively, is much simpler than translation, and thus should be performed before translation rather than inducing

[1] https://github.com/moore3930/MirrorAlign

[2] GIZA++ employs the IBM Model 4 as default setting.

Proceedings of the 19th International Conference on Spoken Language Translation (IWSLT 2022), pages 83 - 91
May 26-27, 2022 ©2022 Association for Computational Linguistics

alignment matrix with heavy neural machine translation models. For example, the IBM word alignment model, *e.g.*, FastAlign, is the prerequisite of SMT. *However, related research about lightweight neural word alignment without NMT is currently very scarce.*

Inspired by cross-lingual word embeddings (Luong et al., 2015b, CLWEs), we propose to implement a super lightweight unsupervised word alignment model in Section 3, named MirrorAlign, which encourages the embedding distance between aligned words to be closer. We also provide the theoretical justification from mutual information perspective for our proposed contrastive learning objective in Section 3.4, demonstrating the reasonableness of our method. Figure 1 shows an English sentence, and its corresponding Chinese and Japanese sentences, and their word alignments. The links indicate the correspondence between English⇔Chinese and English⇔Japanese words. If the Chinese word "举行" can be aligned to English word "held", the reverse mapping should also hold. Specifically, a bidirectional attention mechanism with contrastive estimation is proposed to capture the alignment between parallel sentences. In addition, we employ an agreement loss to constrain the attention maps such that the alignments follow symmetry hypothesis (Liang et al., 2006).

Our contributions can be summarized as follows:

- We propose a super lightweight unsupervised alignment model (MirrorAlign), even merely updating the embedding matrices, achieves better alignment quality on several public benchmark datasets compare to baseline models while preserving comparable training efficiency with FastAlign.

- To boost the performance of our model, we design a theoretically and empirically proved bidirectional symmetric attention with contrastive learning objective for word alignment task, in which we introduce extra objective to follow the mirror-like symmetry hypothesis.

- Further analysis show that the by-product of our model in training phase has the ability to learn bilingual word representations, which endows the possibility to unify these two tasks in the future.

2 Related Work

Word alignment studies can be divided into two classes:

Statistical Models Statistical alignment models directly build on the lexical translation models of (Brown et al., 1993), also known as IBM models. The most popular implementation of this statistical alignment model is FastAlign (Dyer et al., 2013) and GIZA++ (Och and Ney, 2000, 2003). For optimal performance, the training pipeline of GIZA++ relies on multiple iterations of IBM Model 1, Model 3, Model 4 and the HMM alignment model (Vogel et al., 1996). Initialized with parameters from previous models, each subsequent model adds more assumptions about word alignments. Model 2 introduces non-uniform distortion, and Model 3 introduces fertility. Model 4 and the HMM alignment model introduce relative distortion, where the likelihood of the position of each alignment link is conditioned on the position of the previous alignment link. FastAlign (Dyer et al., 2013), which is based on a reparametrization of IBM Model 2, is almost the existing fastest word aligner, while keeping the quality of alignment.

In contrast to GIZA++, our model achieves nearly 15× speedup during training, while achieving the comparable performance. Encouragingly, our model is at least 1.5× faster to train than FastAlign and consistently outperforms it.

Neural Models Most neural alignment approaches in the literature, such as Alkhouli et al. 2018, rely on alignments generated by statistical systems that are used as supervision for training the neural systems. These approaches tend to learn to copy the alignment errors from the supervising statistical models. Zenkel et al. (2019) use attention to extract alignments from a dedicated alignment layer of a neural model without using any output from a statistical aligner, but fail to match the quality of GIZA++. Garg et al. (2019) represents the current state of the art in word alignment, outperforming GIZA++ by training a single model that is able to both translate and align. This model is supervised with a guided alignment loss, and existing word alignments must be provided to the model during training. Garg et al. (2019) can produce alignments using an end-to-end neural training pipeline guided by attention activations, but this approach underperforms GIZA++. The performance of GIZA++ is only surpassed by training

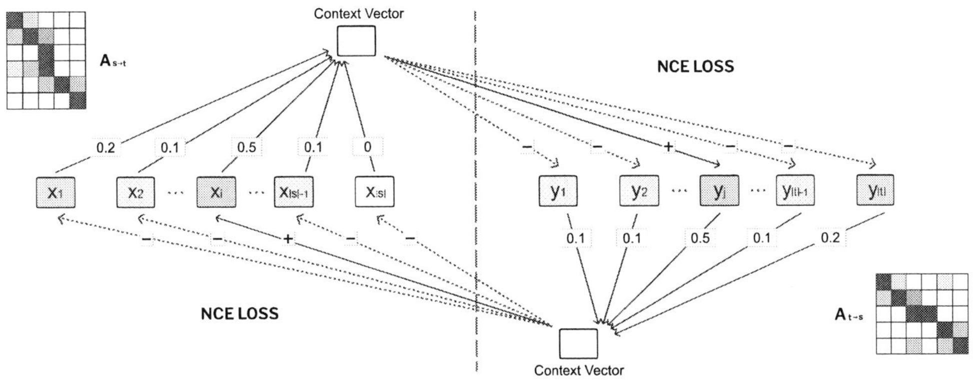

Figure 2: Illustration of MirrorAlign, where a pair of sentences are given as example. Each x_i and y_j are the representation of words in source and target part respectively. Given y_j, we can calculate context vector in source part. The NCE training objective is encouraging the dot product of this context vector and y_j to be large. The process in the other direction is consistent. By stacking all of the soft weights, two attention maps $A_{s\to t}$ and $A_{t\to s}$ can be produced, which will be bound by an agreement loss to encourage symmetry.

the guided alignment loss using GIZA++ output. Stengel-Eskin et al. (2019) introduce a discriminative neural alignment model that uses a dot-product-based distance measure between learned source and target representation to predict if a given source-target pair should be aligned. Alignment decisions are conditioned on the neighboring decisions using convolution. The model is trained using gold alignments. Zenkel et al. (2020) uses guided alignment training, but with large number of modules and parameters, they can surpass the alignment quality of GIZA++.

They either use translation models for alignment task, which introduces a extremely huge number of parameters (compared to ours), making the training and deployment of the model cumbersome. Or they train the model with the alignment supervision, however, these alignment data is scarce in practice especially for low resource languages. These settings make above approaches less versatile.

Instead, our approach is fully unsupervised at word level, that is, it does not require gold alignments generated by human annotators during training. Moreover, our model achieves comparable performance and is at least 50 times smaller than theirs, i.e., #Parameters: 4M (ours) vs. 200M (above).

3 Our Approach

Our model trains in an unsupervised fashion, where the word level alignments are not provided. Therefore, we need to leverage sentence-level supervision of the parallel corpus. To achieve this, we introduce negative sampling strategy with contrastive learning to fully exploit the corpus. Besides, inspired by the concept of cross-lingual word embedding, we design the model under the following assumption: *If a target token can be aligned to a source token, then the dot product of their embedding vectors should be large.* Figure 2 shows the schema of our approach **MirrorAlign**.

3.1 Sentence Representation

For a given source-target sentence pair $(\mathbf{s}, \mathbf{t})$, $s_i, t_j \in \mathbb{R}^d$ represent the i-th and j-th word embeddings for the source and target sentences, respectively. Luong et al. (2015a); Ding et al. (2020b) illustrate that modelling the neighbour words within the local window helps to understand the current words. Inspired by this, we perform a extremely simple but effective mean pooling operation with the representations of its surrounding words to capture the contextualized information. Padding operation is used to ensure the sequence length. As a result, the final representation of each word can be calculated by element-wisely adding the mean pooling embedding and its original embedding:

$$x_i = \text{MEANPOOL}([s_i]^{win}) + s_i, \quad (1)$$

where win is the pooling window size. We can therefore derive the sentence level representations $(x_1, x_2, ..., x_{|s|}), (y_1, y_2, ..., y_{|t|})$ for $\mathbf{s}$ and $\mathbf{t}$. In addition to modeling words, modeling structured information (such as syntactic information) may be helpful to enhance the sentence representation (Li et al., 2017; Marcheggiani and Titov, 2017; Ding and Tao, 2019), thus improving the word alignment. We leave this exploration for future work.

3.2 Bidirectional Symmetric Attention

Bidirectional symmetric attention is the basic component of our proposed model. The aim of this module is to generate the source-to-target (*aka.* s2t) and target-to-source (*aka.* t2s) soft attention maps. The details of the attention mechanism: given a source side word representation x_i as query $q_i \in \mathbb{R}^d$ and pack all the target tokens together into a matrix $V_t \in \mathbb{R}^{|t| \times d}$. The attention context can be calculated as:

$$\text{ATTENTION}\,(q_i, V_t, V_t) = (a_t^i \cdot V_t)^\intercal, \quad (2)$$

where the vector $a_t^i \in \mathbb{R}^{1 \times |t|}$ represents the attention probabilities for q_i in source sentence over all the target tokens, in which each element signifies the relevance to the query, and can be derived from:

$$a_t^i = \text{SOFTMAX}\,(V_t \cdot q_i)^\intercal\,. \quad (3)$$

For simplicity, we denote the attention context of q_i in the target side as $att_t(q_i)$. s2t attention map $A_{s,t} \in \mathbb{R}^{|s| \times |t|}$ is constructed by stacking the probability vectors a_t^i corresponding to all the source tokens.

Reversely, we can obtain t2s attention map $A_{t,s}$ in a symmetric way. Then, these two attention matrices $A_{s,t}$ and $A_{t,s}$ will be used to decode alignment links. Take s2t for example, given a target token, the source token with the highest attention weight is viewed as the aligned word.

3.3 Agreement Mechanism

Intuitively, the two attention matrices $A_{s,t}$ and $A_{t,s}^T$ should be very close. However, the attention mechanism suffers from symmetry error in different direction (Koehn and Knowles, 2017).

To bridge this discrepancy, we introduce agreement mechanism (Liang et al., 2006), acting like a mirror that precisely reflects the matching degree between $A_{s,t}$ and $A_{t,s}$, which is also empirically confirmed in machine translation (Levinboim et al., 2015). In particular, we use an agreement loss to bind above two matrices:

$$\mathcal{L}oss_{disagree} = \sum_i \sum_j (A_{i,j}^{s,t} - A_{j,i}^{t,s})^2. \quad (4)$$

In Section 4.6, we empirically show this agreement can be complementary to the bidirectional symmetric constraint, demonstrating the effectiveness of this component.

3.4 Training Objective and Theoretical Justification

Suppose that $(q_i, att_t(q_i))$ is a pair of s2t word representation and corresponding attention context sampled from the joint distribution $p_t(q, att_t(q))$ (hereinafter we call it a positive pair), the primary objective of the s2t training is to maximize the alignment degree between the elements within a positive pair. Thus, we first define an alignment function by using the sigmoid inner product as:

$$\text{ALIGN}(q, att_t(q)) = \sigma(\langle q, att_t(q)\rangle), \quad (5)$$

where $\sigma(\cdot)$ denotes the sigmoid function and $\langle \cdot, \cdot \rangle$ is the inner product operation. However, merely optimizing the alignment of positive pairs ignores important positive-negative relation knowledge (Mikolov et al., 2013).

To make the training process more informative, we reform the overall objective in the contrastive learning manner (Oord et al., 2018; Saunshi et al., 2019) with Noise Contrastive Estimation (NCE) loss (Mikolov et al., 2013), which has been widely used in many NLP tasks (Xiong et al., 2021; Gao et al., 2021; Wang et al., 2022). Specifically, we first sample k negative word representations q_j[3] from the margin $p_t(q)$. Then, we can formulate the overall NCE objective as following:

$$\mathcal{L}oss_{s\to t}^i = - \mathop{\mathbb{E}}_{\{att_t(q_i), q_i, q_j\}} \left[\log \frac{\text{ALIGN}(q_i, att_t(q_i))}{\text{ALIGN}(q_i, att_t(q_i)) + \sum_{j=1}^{k} \text{ALIGN}(q_j, att_t(q_i))}\right] \quad (6)$$

It is evident that the objective in Eq. (6) explicitly encourages the alignment of positive pair $(q_i, att_t(q_i))$ while simultaneously separates the negative pairs $(q_j, att_t(q_i))$.

Moreover, a direct consequence of minimizing Eq. (6) is that the optimal estimation of the alignment between the representation and attention context is proportional to the ratio of joint distribution and the product of margins $\frac{p_t(q, att_t(q))}{p_t(q) \cdot p_t(att_t(q))}$ which

[3]In the contrastive learning setting, q_j and $att_t(q_i)$ can be sampled from different sentences. If q_j and $att_t(q_i)$ are from the same sentence, $i \neq j$; otherwise, j can be a random index within the sentence length. For simplicity, in this paper, we use q_j where $i \neq j$ to denote the negative samples, although with a little bit ambiguity.

Method	EN-FR	FR-EN	sym	RO-EN	EN-RO	sym	DE-EN	EN-DE	sym
NNSA	22.2	24.2	15.7	47.0	45.5	40.3	36.9	36.3	29.5
FastAlign	16.4	15.9	10.5	33.8	35.5	32.1	28.4	32.0	27.0
MirrorAlign	**15.3**	**15.6**	**9.2**	34.3	**35.2**	**31.6**	31.1	**28.0**	**24.8**

Table 1: AER of each method in different direction. "sym" means grow-diag symmetrization.

Model	EN-FR	RO-EN	DE-EN
Naive Attention	31.4	39.8	50.9
NNSA	15.7	40.3	-
FastAlign	10.5	32.1	27.0
MirrorAlign	**9.2**	**31.6**	**24.8**
(Zenkel et al., 2020)	8.4	24.1	17.9
(Garg et al., 2019)	7.7	26.0	20.2
GIZA++	5.5	26.5	18.7

Table 2: Alignment performance (with grow-diagonal heuristic) of each model.

is the point-wise mutual information, and we can further have the following proposition with repect to the mutual information:

Proposition 1. *The mutual information between the word representation q and its corresponding attention context $att_t(q)$ is lower-bounded by the negative $\mathcal{L}oss^i_{s\to t}$ in Eq. (6) as:*

$$I(q, att_t(q)) \geq \log(k) - \mathcal{L}oss^i_{s\to t}, \quad (7)$$

where k is the number of the negative samples.

The detailed proof can be found in (Oord et al., 2018). Proposition 1 indicates that the lower bound of the mutual information $I(q, att_t(q))$ can be maximized by achieving the optimal NCE loss, which provides theoretical guarantee for our proposed method.

Our training schema over parallel sentences is mainly inspired by the bilingual skip-gram model (Luong et al., 2015b) and invertibility modeling (Levinboim et al., 2015). Therefore, the ultimate training objective should consider both forward ($s \to t$) and backward ($t \to s$) direction, combined with the mirror agreement loss. Technically, the final training objective is:

$$\mathcal{L}oss = \sum_i^{|t|} \mathcal{L}oss^i_{s\to t} + \sum_j^{|s|} \mathcal{L}oss^j_{t\to s} + \alpha \cdot \mathcal{L}oss_{disagree}, \quad (8)$$

where $\mathcal{L}oss_{s\to t}$ and $\mathcal{L}oss_{t\to s}$ are symmetrical and α is a loss weight to balance the likelihood and disagreement loss.

4 Experiments

4.1 Datasets and Evaluation Metrics

We perform our method on three widely used datasets: English-French (**EN-FR**), Romanian-English (**RO-EN**) and German-English (**DE-EN**). Training and test data for **EN-FR** and **RO-EN** are from NAACL 2003 share tasks (Mihalcea and Pedersen, 2003). For **RO-EN**, we add Europarl v8 corpus, increasing the amount of training data from 49K to 0.4M. For **DE-EN**, we use the Europarl v7 corpus as training data and test on the gold alignments. All above data are lowercased and tokenized by Moses. The evaluation metrics are Precision, Recall, F-score (F1) and Alignment Error Rate (AER).

4.2 Baseline Methods

Besides two strong statistical alignment models, i.e. FastAlign and GIZA++, we also compare our approach with neural alignment models where they induce alignments either from the attention weights or through feature importance measures.

FastAlign One of the most popular statistical method which log-linearly reparameterize the IBM model 2 proposed by (Dyer et al., 2013).

GIZA++ A statistical generative model (Och and Ney, 2003), in which parameters are estimated using the Expectation-Maximization (EM) algorithm, allowing it to automatically extract bilingual lexicon from parallel corpus.

NNSA A unsupervised neural alignment model proposed by (Legrand et al., 2016), which applies an aggregation operation borrowed from the computer vision to design sentence-level matching loss. In addition to the raw word indices, following three extra features are introduced: distance to the diagonal, part-of-speech and unigram character position. To make a fair comparison, we report the result of raw feature in NNSA.

Naive Attention Averaging all attention matrices in the Transformer architecture, and selecting the source unit with the maximal attention value for

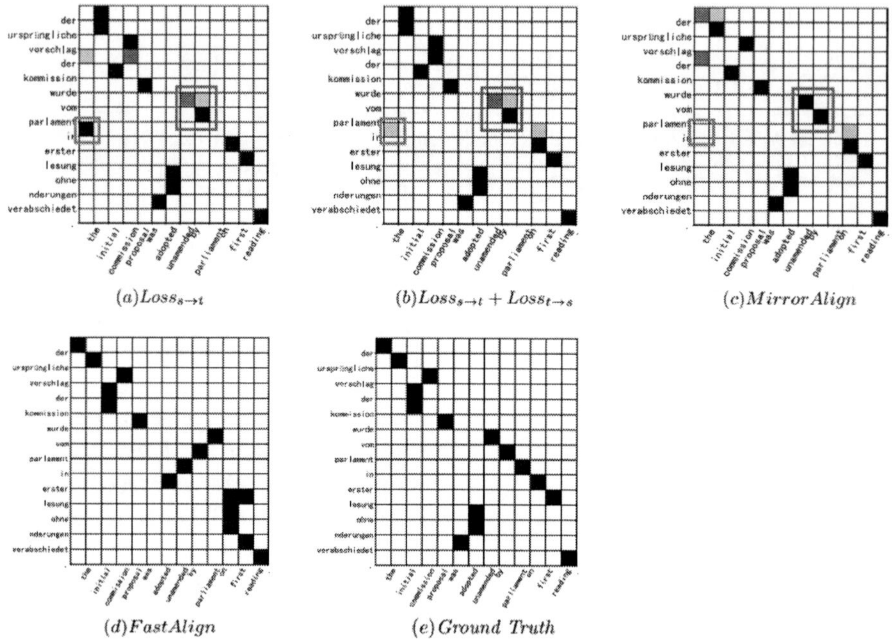

Figure 3: An visualized alignment example. (a-c) illustrate the effects when gradually adding the symmetric component, (d) shows the result of FastAlign, and (e) is the ground truth. The more emphasis is placed on the symmetry of the model, the better the alignment results model achieved. Meanwhile, as depicted, the results of the attention map become more and more diagonally concentrated.

each target unit as alignments. We borrow the results reported in (Zenkel et al., 2019) to highlight the weakness of such naive version, where significant improvement are achieved after introducing an extra alignment layer.

Others Garg et al. (2019) and Zenkel et al. (2020) represent the current developments in word alignment, which both outperform GIZA++. However, They both implement the alignment model based on a sophisticated translation model. Further more, the former uses the output of GIZA++ as supervision, and the latter introduces a pre-trained state-of-the-art neural translation model. It is unfair to compare our results directly with them. We report them in Table 2 as references.

4.3 Setup

For our method (MirrorAlign), all the source and target embeddings are initialized by Xavier method (Glorot and Bengio, 2010). The embedding size d and pooling window size are set to 256 and 3, respectively. The hyper-parameters α is tested by grid search from 0.0 to 1.0 at 0.1 intervals. For FastAlign, we train it from scratch by the open-source pipeline[4]. Also, we report the results of NNSA and machine translation based model (Section 4.2). All experiments of MirrorAlign are run on 1 `Nvidia P40` GPU. The CPU model is Intel(R) Xeon(R) CPU E5-2620 v3 @ 2.40GHz. Both FastAlign and MirrorAlign take nearly half a hour to train one million samples.

4.4 Main Results

Table 2 summarizes the AER of our method over several language pairs. Our model outperforms all other baseline models. Comparing to FastAlign, we achieve 1.3, 0.5 and 2.2 AER improvements on **EN-FR**, **RO-EN**, **DE-EN** respectively.

Notably, our model exceeds the naive attention model in a big margin in terms of AER (ranging from 8.2 to 26.1) over all language pairs. We attribute the poor performance of the straightforward attention model (translation model) to its contextualized word representation. For instance, when translating a verb, contextual information will be paid attention to determine the form (*e.g.*, tense) of the word, that may interfere the word alignment.

Experiment results in different alignment directions can be found in Table 1. The grow-diag sym-

[4]https://github.com/lilt/alignment-scripts

Setup	P	R	F1	AER
$\mathcal{L}oss_{s\to t}$	74.9	86.0	80.4	20.9
$\mathcal{L}oss_{t\to s}$	71.9	85.3	77.3	23.3
$\mathcal{L}oss_{s\leftrightarrow t}$	81.5	**90.1**	86.1	14.1
MirrorAlign	**91.8**	89.1	**90.8**	**9.2**

Table 3: Ablation results on EN-FR dataset.

metrization benifits all the models.

4.5 Speed Comparison

Take the experiment on EN-FR dataset as an example, MirrorAlign converges to the best performance after running 3 epochs and taking 14 minutes totally, where FastAlign and GIZA++ cost 21 and 230 minutes, respectively, to achieve the best results. Notably, the time consumption will rise dozens of times in neural translation fashion.

4.6 Ablation Study

To further explore the effects of several components (*i.e.*, bidirectional symmetric attention, agreement loss) in our MirrorAlign, we conduct an ablation study. Table 3 shows the results on **EN-FR** dataset. When the model is trained using only $\mathcal{L}oss_{s\to t}$ or $\mathcal{L}oss_{t\to s}$ as loss functions, the AER of them are quite high (20.9 and 23.3). As expected, combined loss function improves the alignment quality significantly (14.1 AER). It is noteworthy that with the rectification of agreement mechanism, the final combination achieves the best result (9.2 AER), indicating that the agreement mechanism is the most important component in MirrorAlign.

To better present the improvements brought by adding each component, we visualize the alignment case in Figure 3. As we can see, each component is complementary to others, that is, the attention map becomes more diagonally concentrated after adding the bidirectional symmetric attention and the agreement constraint.

5 Analysis

Alignment Case Study Figure 4 shows an alignment example. Our model correctly aligns "*do not believe*" in English to "*glauben nicht*" in German. Our model, based on word representation, makes better use of semantics to accomplish alignment such that inverted phrase like "*glauben nicht*" can be well handled. Instead, FastAlign, relied on the positional assumption[5], fails here.

china		distinctive	
EN	**DE**	**EN**	**DE**
china	chinas	distinctive	unverwechselbaren
chinese	china	distinct	besonderheiten
china's	chinesische	peculiar	markante
republic	chinesischer	differences	charakteristische
china'	chinesischem	diverse	einzelnen
cat		**love**	
EN	**DE**	**EN**	**DE**
cat	hundefelle	love	liebe
dog	katzenfell	affection	liebt
toys	hundefellen	loved	liebe
cats	kuchen	loves	lieben
dogs	schlafen	passion	lieb

Table 4: Top 5 nearest English (**EN**) and German (**DE**) words for each of the following words: *china*, *distinctive*, *cat*, and *love*.

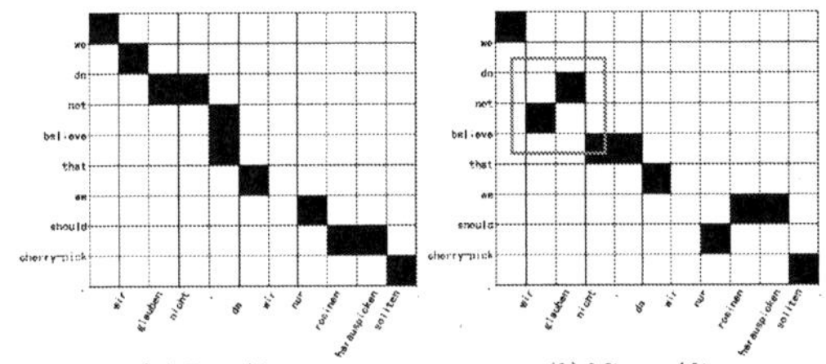

(a) *FastAlign* (b) *MirrorAlign*

Figure 4: Example of the DE-EN alignment. (a) is the result of FastAlign, and (b) shows result of our model, which is closer to the gold alignment. The horizontal axis shows German sentence "*wir glauben nicht , da wir nur rosinen herauspicken sollten .*", and the vertical axis shows English sentence "*we do not believe that we should cherry-pick .*".

Word Embedding Clustering To further investigate the effectiveness of our model, we also analyze the word embeddings learned by our model. In particular, following (Collobert et al., 2011), we show some words together with its nearest neighbors using the Euclidean distance between their embeddings. Table 4 shows some examples to demonstrates that our learned representations possess a clearly clustering structure bilingually and monolingually. We attribute the better alignment results to the ability of our model that could learn bilingual word representation.

6 Conclusion and Future Work

In this paper, we presented a super lightweight neural alignment model, named MirrorAlign, that has achieved better alignment performance compared to FastAlign and other existing neural alignment models while preserving training efficiency. We

[5]A feature h of position is introduced in FastAlign to encourage alignments to occur around the diagonal. $h(i,j,m,n) = -\left|\frac{i}{m} - \frac{j}{n}\right|$, i and j are source and target indices and m and n are the length of sentences pair.

empirically and theoretically show its effectiveness over several language pairs. In the future, we would further explore the relationship between CLWEs and word alignments. A promising attempt is using our model as a bridge to unify cross-lingual embeddings and word alignment tasks.

References

Tamer Alkhouli, Gabriel Bretschner, and Hermann Ney. 2018. On the alignment problem in multi-head attention-based neural machine translation. In *WMT*.

Dzmitry Bahdanau, KyungHyun Cho, and Yoshua Bengio. 2015. Neural machine translation by jointly learning to align and translate. In *ICLR*.

Peter F Brown, Vincent J Della Pietra, Stephen A Della Pietra, and Robert L Mercer. 1993. The mathematics of statistical machine translation: Parameter estimation. *Computational linguistics*.

Ronan Collobert, Jason Weston, Léon Bottou, Michael Karlen, Koray Kavukcuoglu, and Pavel Kuksa. 2011. Natural language processing (almost) from scratch. *Journal of machine learning research*.

Ido Dagan, Kenneth Church, and Willian Gale. 1993. Robust bilingual word alignment for machine aided translation. In *Very Large Corpora: Academic and Industrial Perspectives*.

Liang Ding and Dacheng Tao. 2019. Recurrent graph syntax encoder for neural machine translation. *arXiv*.

Liang Ding, Longyue Wang, and Dacheng Tao. 2020a. Self-attention with cross-lingual position representation. In *ACL*.

Liang Ding, Longyue Wang, Di Wu, Dacheng Tao, and Zhaopeng Tu. 2020b. Context-aware cross-attention for non-autoregressive translation. In *COLING*.

Shuoyang Ding, Hainan Xu, and Philipp Koehn. 2019. Saliency-driven word alignment interpretation for neural machine translation. In *WMT*.

Chris Dyer, Victor Chahuneau, and Noah A Smith. 2013. A simple, fast, and effective reparameterization of ibm model 2. In *NAACL*.

Tianyu Gao, Xingcheng Yao, and Danqi Chen. 2021. Simcse: Simple contrastive learning of sentence embeddings. In *EMNLP*.

Sarthak Garg, Stephan Peitz, Udhyakumar Nallasamy, and Matthias Paulik. 2019. Jointly learning to align and translate with transformer models. In *EMNLP*.

Hamidreza Ghader and Christof Monz. 2017. What does attention in neural machine translation pay attention to? In *IJCNLP*.

Xavier Glorot and Yoshua Bengio. 2010. Understanding the difficulty of training deep feedforward neural networks. In *ICML*.

Philipp Koehn and Rebecca Knowles. 2017. Six challenges for neural machine translation. In *WNMT*.

Mikhail Kozhevnikov and Ivan Titov. 2013. Cross-lingual transfer of semantic role labeling models. In *ACL*.

Joël Legrand, Michael Auli, and Ronan Collobert. 2016. Neural network-based word alignment through score aggregation. In *WMT*.

Tomer Levinboim, Ashish Vaswani, and David Chiang. 2015. Model invertibility regularization: Sequence alignment with or without parallel data. In *NAACL*.

Junhui Li, Deyi Xiong, Zhaopeng Tu, Muhua Zhu, Min Zhang, and Guodong Zhou. 2017. Modeling source syntax for neural machine translation. In *ACL*.

Xintong Li, Guanlin Li, Lemao Liu, Max Meng, and Shuming Shi. 2019. On the word alignment from neural machine translation. In *ACL*.

Percy Liang, Ben Taskar, and Dan Klein. 2006. Alignment by agreement. In *NAACL*.

Minh-Thang Luong, Hieu Pham, and Christopher D Manning. 2015a. Effective approaches to attention-based neural machine translation. In *EMNLP*.

Thang Luong, Hieu Pham, and Christopher D Manning. 2015b. Bilingual word representations with monolingual quality in mind. In *NAACL Workshop*.

Diego Marcheggiani and Ivan Titov. 2017. Encoding sentences with graph convolutional networks for semantic role labeling. In *EMNLP*.

Rada Mihalcea and Ted Pedersen. 2003. An evaluation exercise for word alignment. In *NAACL*.

Tomas Mikolov, Ilya Sutskever, Kai Chen, Greg S Corrado, and Jeff Dean. 2013. Distributed representations of words and phrases and their compositionality. In *NeurIPS*.

Franz Josef Och and Hermann Ney. 2000. Improved statistical alignment models. In *ACL*.

Franz Josef Och and Hermann Ney. 2003. A systematic comparison of various statistical alignment models. *Computational linguistics*.

Aaron van den Oord, Yazhe Li, and Oriol Vinyals. 2018. Representation learning with contrastive predictive coding. *arXiv*.

Nikunj Saunshi, Orestis Plevrakis, Sanjeev Arora, Mikhail Khodak, and Hrishikesh Khandeparkar. 2019. A theoretical analysis of contrastive unsupervised representation learning. In *ICML*.

Elias Stengel-Eskin, Tzu-Ray Su, Matt Post, and Benjamin Van Durme. 2019. A discriminative neural model for cross-lingual word alignment. In *EMNLP*.

Ashish Vaswani, Noam Shazeer, Niki Parmar, Jakob Uszkoreit, Llion Jones, Aidan N Gomez, Lukasz Kaiser, and Illia Polosukhin. 2017. Attention is all you need. In *NeurIPS*.

Stephan Vogel, Hermann Ney, and Christoph Tillmann. 1996. HMM-based word alignment in statistical translation. In *COLING*.

Bing Wang, Liang Ding, Qihuang Zhong, Ximing Li, and Dacheng Tao. 2022. A contrastive cross-channel data augmentation framework for aspect-based sentiment analysis. In *ArXiv*.

Lee Xiong, Chenyan Xiong, Ye Li, Kwok-Fung Tang, Jialin Liu, Paul Bennett, Junaid Ahmed, and Arnold Overwijk. 2021. Approximate nearest neighbor negative contrastive learning for dense text retrieval. In *ICLR*.

David Yarowsky, Grace Ngai, and Richard Wicentowski. 2001. Inducing multilingual text analysis tools via robust projection across aligned corpora. In *HLT*.

Changtong Zan, Liang Ding, Li Shen, Yu Cao, Weifeng Liu, and Dacheng Tao. 2022. Bridging cross-lingual gaps during leveraging the multilingual sequence-to-sequence pretraining for text generation. In *ArXiv*.

Thomas Zenkel, Joern Wuebker, and John DeNero. 2019. Adding interpretable attention to neural translation models improves word alignment. In *arXiv*.

Thomas Zenkel, Joern Wuebker, and John DeNero. 2020. End-to-end neural word alignment outperforms GIZA++. In *ACL*.

On the Impact of Noises in Crowd-Sourced Data for Speech Translation

Siqi Ouyang[1], **Rong Ye**[2], **Lei Li**[1]
[1]University of California, Santa Barbara, CA, USA
siqiouyang@ucsb.edu, leili@cs.ucsb.edu
[2]ByteDance AI Lab, Shanghai, China
yerong@bytedance.com

Abstract

Training speech translation (ST) models requires large and high-quality datasets. MuST-C is one of the most widely used ST benchmark datasets. It contains around 400 hours of speech-transcript-translation data for each of the eight translation directions. This dataset passes several quality-control filters during creation. However, we find that MuST-C still suffers from three major quality issues: audio-text misalignment, inaccurate translation, and unnecessary speaker's name. What are the impacts of these data quality issues for model development and evaluation? In this paper, we propose an automatic method to fix or filter the above quality issues, using English-German (En-De) translation as an example. Our experiments show that ST models perform better on clean test sets, and the rank of proposed models remains consistent across different test sets. Besides, simply removing misaligned data points from the training set does not lead to a better ST model.

1 Introduction

Speech-to-text translation (ST) aims to translate a speech of a certain language into a text translation of another language. Recent advances of end-to-end ST models have been largely boosted by the release of large high-quality parallel datasets (Kocabiyikoglu et al., 2018; Di Gangi et al., 2019; Wang et al., 2021). A clean test set is essential to evaluate the effectiveness of proposed models, and a sizeable well-aligned training set is important to train powerful ST models (Wang et al., 2020).

Currently, the most widely-used ST benchmark dataset is MuST-C (Di Gangi et al., 2019). It consists of around 400 hours of speech-transcript-translation data from English into eight languages (German, Spanish, French, Italian, Dutch, Portuguese, Romanian, and Russian). MuST-C was built upon English TED Talks, which are often transcribed and translated by voluntary human annotators. A bilingual sentence-level text corpus is firstly constructed based on sentence segmentation and Gargantua alignment tool (Braune and Fraser, 2010). Then, the transcription is aligned to the corresponding audio tracks using Gentle forced aligner[1] built on Kaldi ASR toolkit (Povey et al., 2011). During alignment, entire talks are discarded if greater than 15% of words cannot be recognized, and sentences are removed if none of the words was aligned.

Though MuST-C passed through several quality-control filters, this dataset is still not perfect. Through manual checking, we find three major quality issues in the dataset – inaccurate translation, audio-text misalignment, and unnecessary speaker's name. Along with the three issues identified, more importantly, we are interested in the following questions: Do they affect the robustness of end-to-end speech translation models trained on this corpus? Can we trust the results from existing works using this data?

In order to answer the above questions, we propose an automatic method to filter or fix the aforementioned errors in both the training and test sets. And based on the original and the fixed datasets, we evaluate many popular ST systems including codebases such as ESPnet (Inaguma et al., 2020) and published models such as XSTNet (Ye et al., 2021). Our experiments have shown that the performance of models we test is actually better than we thought, and their rank remains consistent across test sets. Besides, simply removing those data points with audio-text misalignment from the training set cannot significantly improve ST models.

2 Quality Issues in MuST-C Corpus

In this section, we identify three issues that harm the quality of MuST-C dataset. We choose the En-De direction as an example since it is the most

[1]https://github.com/lowerquality/gentle

Proceedings of the 19th International Conference on Spoken Language Translation (IWSLT 2022), pages 92 - 97
May 26-27, 2022

Audio Id	Transcripts	Translations
ted_319_84	That's what we were looking forward to. That is where we're going — this union, this convergence of the atomic and the digital.	Danach sehnen wir uns. Das ist wo wir hingehen - Diese Einheit, die Konvergenz des Atomaren und des Digitalen.
ted_319_85	this convergence of the atomic and the digital. And so one of the consequences of that, I believe, is that where we have this sort of spectrum of media right now — TV, film, video — that basically becomes one media platform.	die Konvergenz des Atomaren und des Digitalen. Eine Konsequenz davon ist, glaube ich, dass wir dieses aktuelle Spektrum an Medien - TV, Film, Video - zu einer Medienplatzform wird.
ted_319_86	film, video — that basically becomes one media platform. And while there's many differences in some senses, they will share more and more in common with each other.	Film, Video - zu einer Medienplatzform wird. Es wird viele Unterschiede im gewissen Sinn geben, sie werden aber mehr und mehr miteinander gemeinsam haben.

Table 1: **Examples of misalignment between audio and text.** Extra words that are not in the given transcript but included in the audio are highlighted in red, and missing words that are included in the transcript but not in the audio are highlighted in blue.

widely used direction for demonstrating the performance of ST models.

Audio-Text Misalignment We randomly sample 1000 utterances from the training set of MuST-C En-De dataset and manually verify whether the audio and text are misaligned. We find 69 cases of misalignment out of 1000 given samples. Most of the time, the audio include extra words from the previous or subsequent sentence of its corresponding transcript and translation and omit some of the words of the correct text. This misalignment, once occurs, affects not only one utterance but also utterances around it.

Table 1 shows a typical case where misalignment happens in consecutive utterances. Each audio contains words of its preceding utterance and omits the last few words of its correct text counterpart. Since MuST-C was built by first constructing bilingual text corpus and then aligning English transcripts with audio tracks, audio-translation misalignments usually occur once audio tracks and transcripts are misaligned. In our sample, 68 out of 69 cases follow this observation. Note that this kind of error can be automatically detected and possibly fixed by a well-trained forced aligner.

Inaccurate Translation We uniformly sample 200 audio-transcript-translation triples from tst-COMMON set and ask human translators proficient in both English and German to label which German translations are not accurate based on given audio files and transcripts.

Table 2 demonstrates typical errors that human translators find. In the first case, the English word "unless" is missing in its German translation, which completely changes the meaning of sentence. In the second case, the German word "Vollmachtszertifikat" means "power of attorney" rather than "certificate authority". In the third case, "the most peaceful" is translated to "very peaceful". In the last case, German translation adds an extra sentence "Bei dem vorigen Beispiel ging es darum, Einzelheiten zu finden" in the beginning that is not expressed in the audio and transcript.

Some of the errors might be caused by human annotators who volunteered to translate the subtitles for the TED Talk (e.g., case 1,2 and 3), and others might be caused by transcript-translation alignment tools used in dataset creation (e.g., case 4). However, it is hard to quantify the number of translation errors, and we will see its empirical impact in the next section.

Unnecessary Speaker's Name Since MuST-C dataset is built on top of subtitles of TED talks, sometimes the subtitle will include additional information like the speaker's name in a multi-speaker scenario. This additional information cannot be recognized given the single audio segment. However, the impact is negligible since names are usually relatively short (less than 20 characters) compared to the entire utterance (more than 100 characters), and it does not frequently happen (around 7% in our sample). We merely showcase here the existence of such a problem.

To summarize, we have identified three quality issues, misalignment, inaccurate translation, and unnecessary extra information in the MuST-C dataset. In the next section, we will empirically quantify the impact of these issues in training and testing scenarios.

3 Examining the Impact of Quality Issues

In this section we examine the impact of discovered quality issues on both training and test set of MuST-

#Case	Transcripts	Inaccurate Translations
I	Woman: 80's revival meets skater-punk, unless it's laundry day.	Frau: 80er Revival trifft auf Skaterpunk, ~~es sei denn,~~ außer am Waschtag.
II	DigiNotar is a certificate authority from the Netherlands – or actually, it was.	DigiNotar ist ein Vollmachtszertifikat aus den Niederlanden – bzw. war es das.
III	Steve Pinker has showed us that, in fact, we're living during the most peaceful time ever in human history.	Steve Pinker hat uns gezeigt, dass wir derzeit in einer sehr friedlichen Zeit der Menschengeschichte leben.
VI	But what if you want to see brush strokes?	Bei dem vorigen Beispiel ging es darum, Einzelheiten zu finden, aber was, wenn man die Pinselstriche sehen will?

Table 2: **Examples of inaccurate translations found by human translators.** Errors are highlighted in red. The strikethrough corresponds to words that are missed in the inaccurate translation.

C En-De dataset. We first fix errors for training and test sets. Then we train models on both original and clean training sets and evaluate their empirical performances on test sets with and without errors.

3.1 Detecting and Fixing Errors

We apply different techniques to fix training and test sets due to the size difference and different quality requirements. It is unrealistic to fix erroneous translations for the training set since it requires enormous human effort. Thus, we develop an automatic tool to detect the misalignment and remove them to obtain a clean training set.

Specifically, we first expand the given audio track by one second in both ends and leverage a pre-trained automatic speech recognition (ASR) model (Baevski et al., 2020)[2] to conduct forced alignment between the expanded audio and transcript. If the given alignment exceeds the time range of the original audio by 0.15 seconds, we treat it as a misalignment. However, this alone cannot deal with the case that audio completely covers the transcript but also has extra content. Thus, we use the same model to conduct ASR task to extract the transcript. If the edit distance between the extracted transcript and the transcript given beforehand is larger than 0.7 times length of the given transcript, we also treat it as a misalignment. We choose the hyper-parameters based on 1000 random samples of the dataset to achieve a high recall and an acceptable precision (95% and 82% measured on these samples), since we want the dataset to be as clean as possible. By removing these misaligned cases, we obtain a clean training set with 19.4k utterances compared to the original 22.9k utterances in the MuST-C training set.

For the test set, we uniformly sample 200 data points (about 10% of tst-COMMON) and manually fix the aforementioned errors one by one. This provides us four versions of test sets:

- **tst-200**: the sampled 200 data points without modification.
- **tst-200-fix-misalignment**: tst-200 with misalignment fixed.
- **tst-200-fix-translation**: tst-200 with translation errors fixed.
- **tst-200-fix-all**: tst-200 with both errors fixed.

Note that we align the audio tracks and the text translations by adjusting the audio time ranges rather than the translations since misaligned audio tracks correspond to incomplete sentences. The code will be released at `https://github.com/owaski/MuST-C-clean`.

3.2 Examining the Impact

Experiment Setup We adopt a baseline model architecture W2V2-Transformer as in Ye et al. (2021) which concatenates a pretrained Wav2vec2 audio encoder[3] and a Transformer (Vaswani et al., 2017) with six encoder and decoder layers respectively. We also adopt the same training procedure as Ye et al. (2021) except that we also pre-train the Transformer on WMT14 En-De MT dataset. Training arguments can be referred in the Appendix. We have also collected several representative open-sourced models, including codebases (ESPnet (Inaguma et al., 2020), Fairseq ST (Ott et al., 2019), NeurST (Zhao et al., 2021)) and published models (JT-S-MT (Tang et al., 2021), Chimera (Han et al., 2021), XSTNet (Ye et al., 2021) and Speechformer (Papi et al., 2021)), to robustify our experiments. The models are tested on the aforementioned four versions of test sets. We report case-sensitive deto-

[2] `https://huggingface.co/facebook/wav2vec2-large-960h`

[3] We adopt the wav2vec 2.0 base model, which passes raw waveform through 7 convolution layers and 12 Transformer encoder layers. It can be accessed here `https://dl.fbaipublicfiles.com/fairseq/wav2vec/wav2vec_small.pt`

Models	tst-200	tst-200-fix-all	tst-COMMON
w/o external MT data			
ESPnet ST	21.7	23.8	22.9
Fairseq ST	22.4	24.3	22.7
NeurST	21.0	24.0	22.8
Speechformer	24.4	27.1	23.6
XSTNet base	25.5	27.4	25.5
w/ external MT data			
Baseline	25.1	27.3	24.6
JT-S-MT	26.0	28.4	26.8
XSTNet expand	28.1	30.8	27.1
Chimera	28.2	31.1	27.1

Table 3: Empirical performance of models evaluated on different test sets. tst-200 is an uniformly sampled 200-data-point subset of tst-COMMON. tst-200-fix-all is another version of tst-200 with all quality issues fixed.

kenized BLEU scores using sacreBLEU[4].[5]

Impact on Model Evaluation We are interested in whether the original test set is enough to serve as the metric for offline speech translation. Therefore, we examine if the rank of existing models will be different after fixing the errors. Results are shown in Table 3.

The BLEU score increase after switching to the clean test set is consistent across all models, indicating that the performance of these models is better than we previously thought. More importantly, the rank of models evaluated on tst-200 is also consistent with that evaluated on tst-200-fix-all. This demonstrates that the original test set, though noisy, can still assess models' performance.

We also conduct a case study to qualitatively examine the effect after fixing each of the errors. We run Chimera on both misaligned and aligned inputs to evaluate the effectiveness of fixing misalignment. Table 4 shows two cases. As highlighted in blue, the translations generated by Chimera are more accurate given aligned inputs.

We also compare the BLEU score difference brought by fixing inaccurate references in Table 5. In both cases, the BLEU scores increase by a large margin, indicating the model performs actually better than we originally thought.

Impact on Model Training We examine the impact of discovered quality issues on the training set by training baseline models on the original and clean versions of the training set and evaluate them on four versions of test set. The BLEU scores are shown in Table 6.

When tested on tst-200, the baseline model trained using the original training set performs better than the one trained using a clean counterpart. This phenomenon can be attributed to the larger dataset size and similarity between original training set and tst-200. Both scores increase after fixing misalignment and translation. Interestingly, fixing misalignment does not bring higher score increase for the model trained on clean data. After fixing all the errors, both models behave equally well. Based on these results, we conclude that simply removing the misaligned cases in the training set does not positively impact the model.

4 Related Works

The quality control of ST datasets is an essential but hard to solve task for dataset creators. MuST-C (Di Gangi et al., 2019) was built upon TED Talks, which naturally comes with the question of inaccurate audio segmentation and audio-text alignment. Other datasets like CoVoST 2 (Kocabiyikoglu et al., 2018; Wang et al., 2021), which was built by reading given sentences, do not possess this kind of problems. Besides, MuST-C used Gentle to conduct the forced alignment and there are other newly developed forced aligners we can use such as the one we developed in this paper and Montreal Forced Aligner (McAuliffe et al., 2017) which both take advantage of deep Transformer model and large audio datasets.

5 Conclusion

In this paper, we first identify three types of error in MuST-C En-De dataset: inaccurate translation, audio-text misalignment, and unnecessary

[4]`https://github.com/mjpost/sacrebleu`

[5]BLEU signature: nrefs:1|bs:1000|seed:12345|case:mixed|eff:no|tok:13a|smooth:exp|version:2.0.0

#Case	Transcript	Reference	Translation w/ Misalignment	Translation w/o Misalignment
I	Who are they actually supposed to be informing?	Wen wollen Sie eigentlich damit informieren?	Angenommen, wer sind sie eigentlich?	CA: Wer sollen sie eigentlich informieren?
II	And so if we think about that, we have an interesting situation in hands.	Und deshalb, falls wir darüber nachdenken haben wir eine interessante Situation vor uns.	Wenn wir also darüber nachdenken, haben wir eine interessante Situation.	Wenn wir also darüber nachdenken, haben wir eine interessante Situation in unseren Händen.

Table 4: Examples of translation with misaligned and without misaligned audio tracks. Improvements brought by aligned inputs are underlined in blue.

#Case	Transcript	Inaccurate Reference	Fixed Reference	Translation	BLEU
I	Steve Pinker has showed us that, in fact, we're living during the most peaceful time ever in human history.	Steve Pinker hat uns gezeigt, dass wir derzeit in einer sehr friedlichen Zeit der Menschengeschichte leben.	Steve Pinker hat uns gezeigt, dass wir in der Tat in der friedlichsten Zeit der Menschheitsgeschichte leben.	Steve Pinker zeigte uns, dass wir in der Tat in einer der friedlichsten Zeiten der Menschheitsgeschichte leben.	13.1 → 50.7
II	This idea of fireflies in a jar, for some reason, was always really exciting to me.	Glühwürmchen in einem Glas fand ich immer ganz aufregend.	Die Vorstellung von Glühwürmchen in einem Glas fand ich aus irgendeinem Grund immer ganz aufregend.	Die Idee von Glühwürmchen und einem Kiefer war aus irgendeinem Grund immer sehr aufregend für mich.	1.6 → 19.3

Table 5: Examples of BLEU score difference brought by fixing inaccurate translations.

Test-set \ Train-set	Original	Clean
tst-200	25.06	24.38
tst-200-fix-misalignment	25.38	24.63
tst-200-fix-translation	26.86	26.99
tst-200-fix-all	27.34	27.32
tst-COMMON	24.60	24.03

Table 6: BLEU scores of baseline model trained on raw/clean datasets and evaluated on different test sets.

speaker's name. We then examine the impact of these errors by training models on both original and clean datasets and evaluate them on test sets before and after fixing these errors. Empirical results demonstrate that the existing noisy test set can still serve as the metric for evaluating speech translation models. However, the model's performance is actually better than we previously thought. As for training, a clean training set does not significantly benefit the model's performance.

References

Alexei Baevski, Yuhao Zhou, Abdelrahman Mohamed, and Michael Auli. 2020. wav2vec 2.0: A framework for self-supervised learning of speech representations. *Advances in Neural Information Processing Systems*, 33:12449–12460.

Fabienne Braune and Alexander Fraser. 2010. Improved unsupervised sentence alignment for symmetrical and asymmetrical parallel corpora. In *Coling 2010: Posters*, pages 81–89, Beijing, China. Coling 2010 Organizing Committee.

Mattia A. Di Gangi, Roldano Cattoni, Luisa Bentivogli,

Matteo Negri, and Marco Turchi. 2019. MuST-C: a Multilingual Speech Translation Corpus. In *Proceedings of the 2019 Conference of the North American Chapter of the Association for Computational Linguistics: Human Language Technologies, Volume 1 (Long and Short Papers)*, pages 2012–2017, Minneapolis, Minnesota. Association for Computational Linguistics.

Chi Han, Mingxuan Wang, Heng Ji, and Lei Li. 2021. Learning shared semantic space for speech-to-text translation. In *Findings of the Association for Computational Linguistics: ACL-IJCNLP 2021*, pages 2214–2225, Online. Association for Computational Linguistics.

Hirofumi Inaguma, Shun Kiyono, Kevin Duh, Shigeki Karita, Nelson Yalta, Tomoki Hayashi, and Shinji Watanabe. 2020. ESPnet-ST: All-in-one speech translation toolkit. In *Proceedings of the 58th Annual Meeting of the Association for Computational Linguistics: System Demonstrations*, pages 302–311, Online. Association for Computational Linguistics.

Ali Can Kocabiyikoglu, Laurent Besacier, and Olivier Kraif. 2018. Augmenting librispeech with French translations: A multimodal corpus for direct speech translation evaluation. In *Proceedings of the Eleventh International Conference on Language Resources and Evaluation (LREC 2018)*, Miyazaki, Japan. European Language Resources Association (ELRA).

Michael McAuliffe, Michaela Socolof, Sarah Mihuc, Michael Wagner, and Morgan Sonderegger. 2017. Montreal Forced Aligner: Trainable Text-Speech Alignment Using Kaldi. In *Proc. Interspeech 2017*, pages 498–502.

Myle Ott, Sergey Edunov, Alexei Baevski, Angela Fan, Sam Gross, Nathan Ng, David Grangier, and Michael Auli. 2019. fairseq: A fast, extensible toolkit for sequence modeling. In *Proceedings of the 2019 Conference of the North American Chapter of the Association for Computational Linguistics (Demonstrations)*, pages 48–53, Minneapolis, Minnesota. Association for Computational Linguistics.

Sara Papi, Marco Gaido, Matteo Negri, and Marco Turchi. 2021. Speechformer: Reducing information loss in direct speech translation. In *Proceedings of the 2021 Conference on Empirical Methods in Natural Language Processing*, pages 1698–1706, Online and Punta Cana, Dominican Republic. Association for Computational Linguistics.

Daniel Povey, Arnab Ghoshal, Gilles Boulianne, Lukas Burget, Ondrej Glembek, Nagendra Goel, Mirko Hannemann, Petr Motlicek, Yanmin Qian, Petr Schwarz, Jan Silovsky, Georg Stemmer, and Karel Vesely. 2011. The kaldi speech recognition toolkit. In *IEEE 2011 Workshop on Automatic Speech Recognition and Understanding*. IEEE Signal Processing Society. IEEE Catalog No.: CFP11SRW-USB.

Yun Tang, Juan Pino, Xian Li, Changhan Wang, and Dmitriy Genzel. 2021. Improving speech translation by understanding and learning from the auxiliary text translation task. In *Proceedings of the 59th Annual Meeting of the Association for Computational Linguistics and the 11th International Joint Conference on Natural Language Processing (Volume 1: Long Papers)*, pages 4252–4261, Online. Association for Computational Linguistics.

Ashish Vaswani, Noam Shazeer, Niki Parmar, Jakob Uszkoreit, Llion Jones, Aidan N Gomez, Łukasz Kaiser, and Illia Polosukhin. 2017. Attention is all you need. *Advances in neural information processing systems*, 30.

Changhan Wang, Anne Wu, Jiatao Gu, and Juan Pino. 2021. CoVoST 2 and Massively Multilingual Speech Translation. In *Proc. Interspeech 2021*, pages 2247–2251.

Chengyi Wang, Yu Wu, Shujie Liu, Ming Zhou, and Zhenglu Yang. 2020. Curriculum pre-training for end-to-end speech translation. In *Proceedings of the 58th Annual Meeting of the Association for Computational Linguistics*, pages 3728–3738, Online. Association for Computational Linguistics.

Rong Ye, Mingxuan Wang, and Lei Li. 2021. End-to-End Speech Translation via Cross-Modal Progressive Training. In *Proc. Interspeech 2021*, pages 2267–2271.

Chengqi Zhao, Mingxuan Wang, Qianqian Dong, Rong Ye, and Lei Li. 2021. NeurST: Neural speech translation toolkit. In *the 59th Annual Meeting of the Association for Computational Linguistics (ACL): System Demonstrations*.

A Appendix

A.1 Training Arguments of W2V2-Transformer

We first pre-train Transformer on WMT14 En-De MT dataset using Adam optimizer with $\beta_1 = 0.9, \beta_2 = 0.98$ and learning rate 5e-4. The effective batch size is 32,768 tokens. We firsly warmup the learning rate by 4k steps and then apply an inverse square root schedule algorithm to it. The norm of gradient is clipped to 10. We set label smoothing to 0.1. The model is trained for up to 500k steps, and we select the one with the highest BLEU score on the validation set.

Then W2V2-Transformer is fine-tuned on MuST-C En-De dataset. The learning rate is 2e-4 and we warmup the it by 25k steps. The effective batch size is 16M frames. Other hyperparameters are the same as MT pre-training.

FINDINGS OF THE IWSLT 2022 EVALUATION CAMPAIGN

Antonios Anastasopoulos George Mason U.
Loïc Barrault Le Mans University
Luisa Bentivogli FBK
Marcely Zanon Boito U. Avignon
Ondřej Bojar Charles U.
Roldano Cattoni FBK
Anna Currey AWS
Georgiana Dinu AWS
Kevin Duh JHU
Maha Elbayad Meta
Clara Emmanuel Apple
Yannick Estève Avignon University
Marcello Federico AWS
Christian Federmann Microsoft
Souhir Gahbiche Airbus
Hongyu Gong Meta
Roman Grundkiewicz Microsoft
Barry Haddow U. of Edinburgh
Benjamin Hsu AWS
Dávid Javorský Charles U.
Věra Kloudová Charles U.
Surafel M. Lakew AWS
Xutai Ma JHU/Meta
Prashant Mathur AWS
Paul McNamee JHU
Kenton Murray JHU
Maria Nădejde AWS
Satoshi Nakamura NAIST
Matteo Negri FBK
Jan Niehues KIT
Xing Niu AWS
John Ortega Le Mans University
Juan Pino Meta
Elizabeth Salesky JHU
Jiatong Shi CMU
Matthias Sperber Apple
Sebastian Stüker Zoom
Katsuhito Sudoh NAIST
Marco Turchi FBK
Yogesh Virkar AWS
Alex Waibel CMU/KIT
Changhan Wang Meta
Shinji Watanabe CMU

Abstract

The evaluation campaign of the 19th International Conference on Spoken Language Translation featured eight shared tasks: (i) Simultaneous speech translation, (ii) Offline speech translation, (iii) Speech to speech translation, (iv) Low-resource speech translation, (v) Multilingual speech translation, (vi) Dialect speech translation, (vii) Formality control for speech translation, (viii) Isometric speech translation. A total of 27 teams participated in at least one of the shared tasks. This paper details, for each shared task, the purpose of the task, the data that were released, the evaluation metrics that were applied, the submissions that were received and the results that were achieved.

1 Introduction

The International Conference on Spoken Language Translation (IWSLT) is the premier annual scientific conference for all aspects of spoken language translation. IWSLT is organized by the Special Interest Group on Spoken Language Translation, which is supported by ACL, ISCA and ELRA. Like in all previous editions (Akiba et al., 2004; Eck and Hori, 2005; Paul, 2006; Fordyce, 2007; Paul, 2008, 2009; Paul et al., 2010; Federico et al., 2011, 2012; Cettolo et al., 2013, 2014, 2015, 2016, 2017; Niehues et al., 2018, 2019; Ansari et al., 2020; Anastasopoulos et al., 2021), this year's conference was preceded by an evaluation campaign featuring shared tasks addressing scientific challenges in spoken language translation.

This paper reports on the 2022 IWSLT Evaluation Campaign, which offered eight shared tasks:

- **Simultaneous speech translation**, addressing low latency speech translation either streamed by a speech recognition (ASR) system or directly from the audio source. The translation directions for both conditions are: English to German, English to Japanese, and English to Mandarin Chinese.

- **Offline speech translation**, proposing speech

Proceedings of the 19th International Conference on Spoken Language Translation (IWSLT 2022), pages 98 - 157
May 26-27, 2022

Team	Organization
AISP-SJTU	Shanghai Jiao Tong University, China (Zhu et al., 2022)
ALEXA AI	Amazon Alexa AI, USA (Shanbhogue et al., 2022)
APPTEK	AppTek, Germany (Wilken and Matusov, 2022)
APV	Amazon Prime Video, USA (Zhang et al., 2022a)
CMU	Carnegie Mellon University, USA (Yan et al., 2022)
CUNI-KIT	Charles University, Czech Republic, and KIT, Germany (Polák et al., 2022)
FBK	Fondazione Bruno Kessler, Italy (Gaido et al., 2022)
GMU	George Mason University, USA
HW-TSC	Huawei Translation Services Center, China (Li et al.; Wang et al.; Guo et al.; Li et al.)
JHU	Johns Hopkins University, USA (Yang et al., 2022)
KIT	Karlsruhe Institute of Technology, Germany (Pham et al., 2022; Polák et al., 2022)
MLLP-VRAIN	Universitat Politècnica de València, Spain (Iranzo-Sánchez et al., 2022)
NA	Neural.AI, China
NAIST	Nara Institute of Science and Technology, Japan (Fukuda et al., 2022)
NIUTRANS	NiuTrans, China (Zhang et al., 2022c)
NUV	Navrachana University, India (Bhatnagar et al., 2022)
NEMO	NVIDIA NeMo, USA(Hrinchuk et al., 2022)
ON-TRAC	ON-TRAC Consortium, France (Boito et al., 2022b)
UOS	University of Sheffield, UK (Vincent et al., 2022)
TALTECH	Tallinn University of Technology, Estonia
UMD	University of Maryland, USA (Rippeth et al., 2022)
UPC	Universitat Politècnica de Catalunya, Spain (Tsiamas et al., 2022a)
USTC-NELSLIP	University of Science and Technology of China (Zhang et al., 2022b)
XIAOMI	Xiaomi AI Lab, China (Guo et al., 2022a)
YI	Yi, China (Zhang and Ao, 2022)

Table 1: List of Participants

translation of talks from English to German, English to Japanese, and English to Mandarin Chinese, using either cascade architectures or end-to-end models able to directly translate source speech into target text;

- **Speech to speech translation**, investigating for the first time automatic translation of human speech in English into synthetic speech in German, either with cascaded or direct neural models.

- **Low-resource speech translation**, focusing on resource-scarce settings for translating input speech in Tamasheq into French text, and input speech in Tunisian Arabic into English text.

- **Multilingual speech translation**, analyzing the performance of multi-lingual versus bilingual translation models for the Offline speech translation tasks (discussed in the Offline task section);

- **Dialect speech translation**, addressing speech translation from Tunisian into English under three training data conditions: (i) only with limited dialect-specific training data (provided by the organizers); (ii) with also larger amount of related-language data (Modern Standard Arabic); (iii) with any kind of publicly available data.

- **Formality control for SLT**, addressing the formality level (formal vs. informal) in spoken language translation from English into German, Spanish, Hindi, Japanese, Italian and Russian. The task focuses in particular on zero-shot learning in multilingual models, given that for the last two directions no formality-annotated training data is provided.

- **Isometric SLT**, addressing the generation of translations similar in length to the source, from English into French, German and Spanish.

The shared tasks attracted 27 participants (see Table 1) from both academic and industrial organizations. The following sections report on each shared task in detail, in particular: the goal and automatic metrics adopted for the task, the data used for training and testing data, the received submissions and the summary of results. Detailed results for some of the shared tasks are reported in a corresponding appendix.

2 Simultaneous Speech Translation

Simultaneous translation is the task of generating translations incrementally given partial text or speech input only. Such capability enables multilingual live communication and access to multilingual multimedia content in real time. The goal of this challenge, organized for the third consecutive year, is to examine systems that translate text or audio in a source language into text in a target language from the perspective of both translation quality and latency.

2.1 Challenge

Participants were given two parallel tracks to enter and encouraged to enter all tracks:

- text-to-text: translating the output of a streaming ASR system in real time from English to German, English to Japanese, and English to Mandarin Chinese.
- speech-to-text: translating speech into text in real time from English to German, English to Japanese, and English to Mandarin Chinese.

For the speech-to-text track, participants were encouraged to submit systems either based on cascaded or end-to-end approaches. Participants were required to upload their system as a Docker image so that it could be evaluated by the organizers in a controlled environment. We also provided example implementations and baseline systems for English-German speech-to-text translation, English-Japanese speech-to-text translation and English-Japanese text-to-text translation.

2.2 Data and Metrics

The training and development data conditions were identical as in the Offline Speech Translation track. More details are available in §3.2.

Systems were evaluated with respect to quality and latency. Quality was evaluated with the standard BLEU metric (Papineni et al., 2002) and, as a first trial this year, also manually. Latency was evaluated with metrics developed for simultaneous machine translation, including average proportion (AP), average lagging (AL) and differentiable average lagging (DAL, Cherry and Foster 2019), and later extended to the task of simultaneous speech translation (Ma et al., 2020b).

The evaluation was run with the SIMULEVAL toolkit (Ma et al., 2020a). For the latency measurement of all systems, we contrasted computation-aware and non computation-aware latency metrics. Computation-aware latency was also computed for text-to-text systems by taking into account the timestamps obtained from the ASR transcript generated by a streaming ASR model. The latency was calculated at the word level for English-German systems and at the character level for English-Japanese and English-Mandarin systems. BLEU was computed via sacrebleu (Post, 2018) (as integrated into SIMULEVAL) with default options for English-German, with the "zh" option for English-Mandarin and with the MeCab tokenizer for English-Japanese.

The systems were ranked by the translation quality (measured by BLEU) in different latency regimes, low, medium and high. Each regime was determined by a maximum latency threshold measured by AL on the Must-C tst-COMMON set. The thresholds were set to 1000, 2000 and 4000 for English-German, 2500, 4000 and 5000 for English-Japanese and 2000, 3000 and 4000 for English-Japanese, and were calibrated by the baseline system. Participants were asked to submit at least one system per latency regime and were encouraged to submit multiple systems for each regime in order to provide more data points for latency-quality trade-off analyses. The organizers confirmed the latency regime by rerunning the systems on the tst-COMMON set.

The systems were run on the test set segmented in three ways: the first segmentation, called gold, leverages the transcript to force align and segment the audio; the second and third segmentations, called Segmentation 1 and Segmentation 2, use a voice activity detection tool to segment the input audio without relying on the transcript.

2.3 Novelties for the Third Edition

Text-to-text track moving closer to the speech-to-text track This year, we used the output of a streaming ASR system as input instead of the gold transcript. As a result, both text-to-text and speech-to-text systems can be ranked together for a given language pair.

Language pairs We added Mandarin Chinese as a target language, resulting in three pairs: English-German, English-Japanese and English-Mandarin.

Human Evaluation and Human Interpretation Benchmark We added an experimental manual evaluation for the English-to-German speech-to-text track as well as a human interpretation benchmark (Section 2.6.1). Independently, English-to-Japanese speech-to-text track outputs were also manually scored, using the MQM setup, see Section 2.6.2.

Segmentation We reverted to the setting of the first edition where we only used segmented input in order to reduce the number of conditions and also because we noticed that existing latency metrics were not well adapted to long unsegmented input. However, recent improvements to the latency metrics (Iranzo-Sánchez et al., 2021) could allow to work with unsegmented input in the future.

2.4 Submissions

The simultaneous task received submissions from 7 teams, the highest number to date. 5 teams entered the English-German speech-to-text track, 3 teams entered the English-Mandarin speech-to-text track and 3 teams entered the English-Japanese speech-to-text track. For text-to-text, there were 3 teams for English-Mandarin, 1 team for English-German and 1 team for English-Japanese. Given that the majority of submissions were on the speech-to-text track, we are considering consolidating the task into speech-to-text only in future editions.

XIAOMI (Guo et al., 2022a) entered the text-to-text track for English-Mandarin. Their model is transformer-based and leverages R-Drop and a deep architecture. Data augmentation methods include tagged backtranslation, knowledge distillation and iterative backtranslation. Simultaneous models use the multi-path wait-k algorithm. Finally, two error correction models are introduced in order to make the systems more robust to ASR errors.

MLLP-VRAIN (Iranzo-Sánchez et al., 2022) entered the speech-to-text track for English-German. They adopt a cascaded approach, with a chunking-based DNN-HMM ASR model, followed by a multi-path wait-k transformer-based MT model. Speculative beam search is employed at inference time.

HW-TSC (Wang et al., 2022) entered all tracks, i.e. speech-to-text and text-to-text for English-German, English-Japanese and English-Mandarin. Moreover, the authors contrasted cascaded and end-to-end methods for the speech-to-text track.

CUNI-KIT (Polák et al., 2022) entered the speech-to-text track for English-German, English-Japanese and English-Mandarin. They propose a method for converting an offline model to a simultaneous model without adding modifications to the original model. The offline model is an end-to-end multilingual speech-to-text model that leverages a pretrained wav2vec 2.0 encoder and a pretrained mBART decoder. The input is broken down into chunks and decoding is run for each new chunk. Once a stable hypothesis is identified, that hypothesis is displayed. Various stable hypothesis detection methods are investigated.

AISP-SJTU (Zhu et al., 2022) entered the speech-to-text and text-to-text tracks for English-Mandarin. Their model is based on an ASR + MT cascade. They propose dynamic-CAAT, an improvement over CAAT (Liu et al., 2021) that uses multiple right context window sizes during training. The proposed method is compared to wait-k and multi-path wait-k. Data augmentation methods include knowledge distillation, tagged back-translation and marking data with lowercased and non punctuated input with a special token.

FBK (Gaido et al., 2022) entered the speech-to-text track for English-German with an end-to-end model. The authors' main goal is to reduce computation requirements in order to democratize the task to more academic participants. First, they show how to avoid ASR encoder pretraining by using a conformer architecture and a CTC loss on top of an intermediate layer in the encoder. In addition, they use the same model for the offline task as for the simultaneous task. The auxiliary CTC loss is used to predict word boundaries and informs a wait-k policy. The latency is also controlled by the speech segment size. Finally, two data filtering methods based on negative log likelihood of an initial model and length ratio are investigated in order to make training more efficient.

NAIST (Fukuda et al., 2022) entered the speech-to-text track for English-German and English-Japanese. The proposed model applies decoding each time a new input speech segment is detected and to constrain the decoder on previously output predictions. An offline model is trained first and then finetuned on prefix pairs. The prefix pairs are extracted by translating prefixes and checking that the generated target is a prefix of the translation of the entire input. Prefixes with length imbalance are filtered out. An input segment boundary predictor is trained as a classifier by considering all prefixes and giving a positive labels to those prefixes that were extracted previously.

2.5 Results

Results are summarized in Figure 1, Figure 2 and Figure 3. We also present the text-to-text results on English-Mandarin [1] in Figure 4. More details are available in the appendix. The results include both text-to-text systems and speech-to-text systems. When participants submitted both a text-to-text system and a speech-to-text system, we retain the best system. The only participant with only a text-to-text system is XIAOMI and we can see that the system is at a disadvantage due to the noise introduced by the provided streaming ASR model. The ranking are consistent across the medium and high latency regime. However, for the low latency regime, we note a degradation from the FBK system and we observe that the NAIST system is robust to lower latency.

2.6 Human Evaluation

We conducted a human evaluation for English-to-German and English-to-Japanese independently.

2.6.1 English-to-German

For English-to-German, the human evaluation was inspired by Javorský et al. (2022). This evaluation examined (1) the best system from each latency regime selected by BLEU score, and (2) transcription of human interpretation by a professional English-German interpreter (certified conference interpreter and sworn translator and interpreter for the Czech and English languages) in February 2022. The interpreting was carried out remotely and transcribed by students of German for Intercultural Communication at the Institute of Translation Studies, Charles University, Faculty of Arts.[2]

The English-to-German task used two parts of the test set: (1) the Common part is used as the blind test set in the automatic evaluation and also in the Offline speech translation task, and (2) the Non-Native part comes from IWSLT 2019 Non-Native Translation Task.

Details of the human evaluation are provided in Section A.1.1 of the Appendix and results are shown in Table 18.

The Common part of the test set is kept confidential for future use. For the Non-Native part, we release system outputs as well as manual judgements on the corresponding IWSLT page.[3]

2.6.2 English-to-Japanese

For English-to-Japanese, we used *JTF Translation Quality Evaluation Guidelines* (JTF, 2018) based on Multidimensional Quality Metrics (MQM). We chose four systems for the evaluation and asked a professional translator to evaluate the translations for one talk in the blind test set. We followed the error weighting by a previous study (Freitag et al., 2021a) to calculate error scores. Details of the human evaluation are provided in A.1.2 in Appendix.

The results are shown in Table 16, and we can find the error scores positively correlate with BLEU.

2.7 Future Editions

Possible changes to future editions include:

- changing the latency metric in order to support long unsegmented input.
- extending the task to support speech output.
- removing the text-to-text track in order to consolidate tracks.

3 Offline Speech Translation

Offline speech translation, defined in various forms over the years, is one of the speech tasks with the longest tradition at the IWSLT campaign. This year,[4] it focused on the translation of English audio data extracted from TED talks[5] into text in one of the three target languages comprising the 2022 sub-tasks, i.e. German, Japanese, and Mandarin Chinese.

[1] Only this language pair has more than one text-to-text systems submitted.

[2] http://utrl.ff.cuni.cz/en

[3] https://iwslt.org/2022/simultaneous

[4] http://iwslt.org/2022/offline

[5] http://www.ted.com

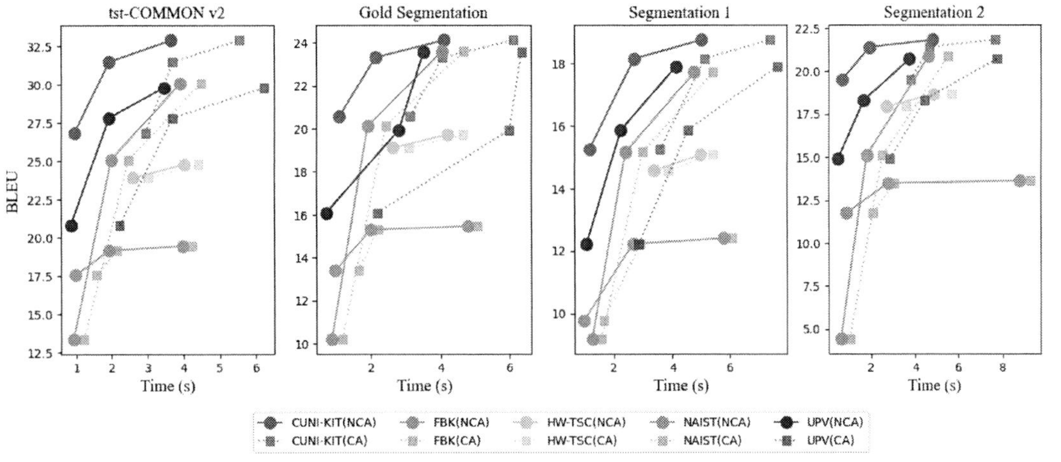

Figure 1: Latency-quality tradeoff curves for English-German.

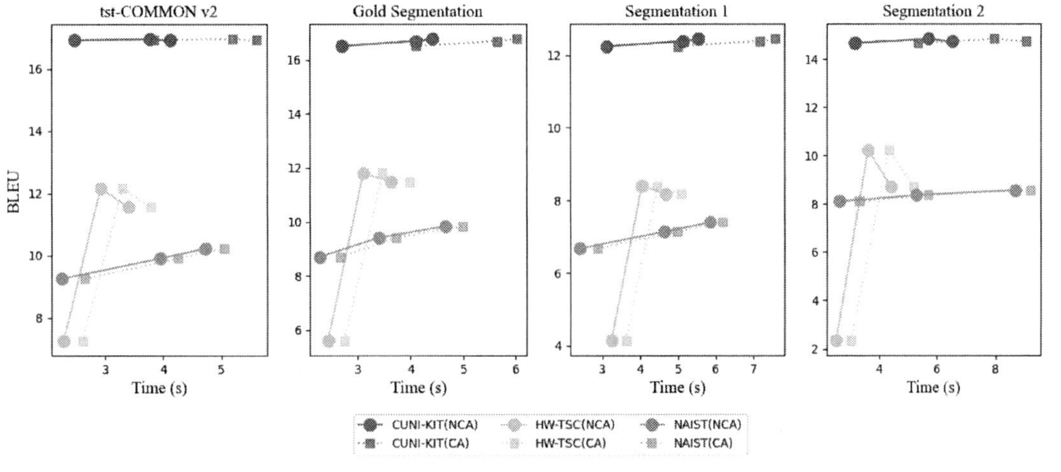

Figure 2: Latency-quality tradeoff curves for English-Japanese.

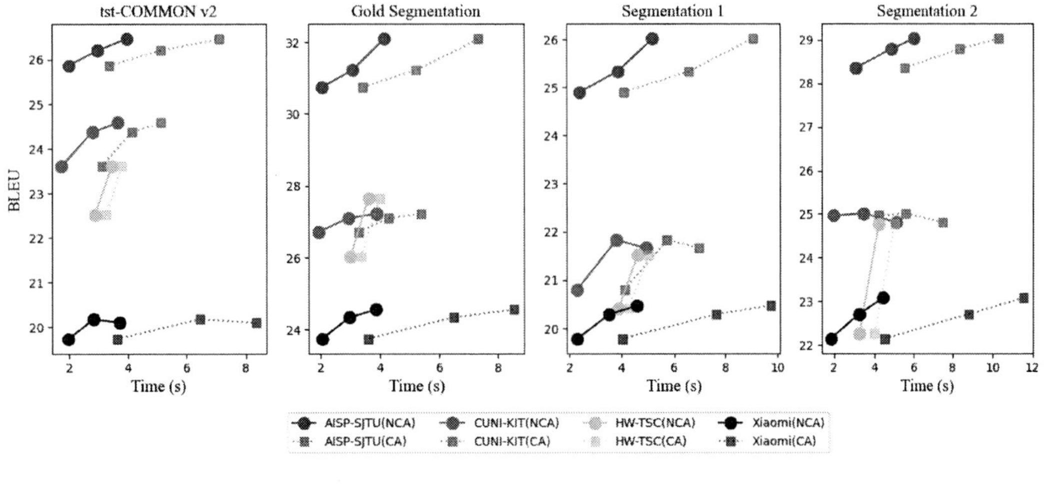

Figure 3: Latency-quality tradeoff curves for English-Mandarin.

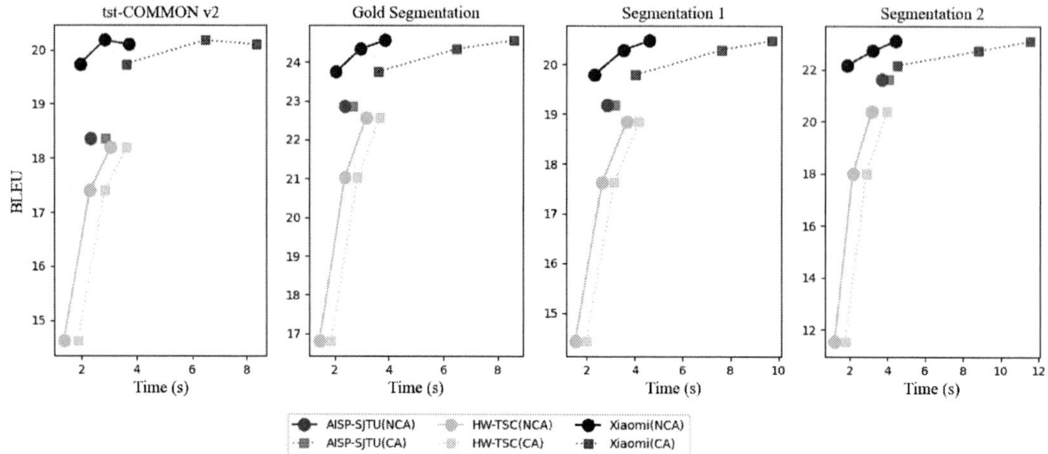

Figure 4: Latency-quality tradeoff curves for English-Mandarin (text-to-text track).

3.1 Challenge

In recent years, offline speech translation (ST) has seen a rapid evolution, characterized by the steady advancement of *direct* end-to-end models (building on a single neural network that directly translates the input audio into target language text) that were able to significantly reduce the performance gap with respect to the traditional *cascade* approach (integrating ASR and MT components in a pipelined architecture). In light of the IWSLT results of the last two years (Ansari et al., 2020; Anastasopoulos et al., 2021) and of the findings of recent work attesting that the gap between the two paradigms has substantially closed (Bentivogli et al., 2021), also this year a key element of the evaluation was to set up a shared framework for their comparison. For this reason, and to reliably measure progress with respect to the past rounds, the general evaluation setting was kept unchanged.

On the architecture side, participation was allowed both with cascade and end-to-end (also known as direct) systems. In the latter case, valid submissions had to be obtained by models that: *i)* do not exploit intermediate symbolic representations (e.g., source language transcription or hypotheses fusion in the target language), and *ii)* rely on parameters that are all jointly trained on the end-to-end task.

On the test set provision side, also this year participants could opt for processing either a precomputed automatic segmentation of the test set or a version of the same test data segmented with their own approach. This option was maintained not only to ease participation (by removing one of the obstacles in audio processing) but also to gain further insights into the importance of properly segmenting the input speech. As shown by the results of recent IWSLT campaigns, effective preprocessing to reduce the mismatch between the provided training material (often "clean" corpora split into sentence-like segments) and the supplied unsegmented test data is in fact a common trait of top-performing systems.

Concerning the types of submission, also this year two conditions were offered to participants: constrained, in which only a pre-defined list of resources is allowed, and unconstrained.

Multiple submissions were allowed, but participants had to explicitly indicate their "primary" (one at most) and "contrastive" runs, together with the corresponding type of system (cascade/end-to-end), training data condition (constrained/unconstrained), and test set segmentation (own/given).

Novelties of the 2022 offline ST task. Within this consolidated overall setting, the organization of this year's task took into consideration new emerging challenges, namely: *i)* the availability of new data covering more language directions, *ii)* the development of new and gigantic pre-trained models, and *iii)* the need for more accurate evaluations. Accordingly, three main differences with respect to previous editions characterize this year's edition:

- To measure systems performance in **different language settings**, two new target languages have been added, extending the number of offline ST sub-tasks to three: English-German (the traditional one), English-Chinese, and English-Japanese.

- To understand the effect of exploiting popular **pre-trained models** in state-of-the-art ST systems, participants were given the possibility to exploit some of them in addition to the allowed training resources for the constrained condition.
- To shed light on the reliability of system ranking based on automatic metrics, and to align our task with other evaluation campaigns (e.g. WMT[6]), the outputs of all the submitted primary systems have been manually evaluated by professional translators. On this basis, a new ranking based on **direct human assessments** was also produced.

3.2 Data and Metrics

Training and development data. Also this year, participants had the possibility to train their systems using several resources available for ST, ASR and MT.

To extend the language directions covered by the offline task, new data was selected from the English-Chinese and English Japanese sections of the MuST-C V2 corpus[7]. For both languages, they include training, dev, and test (Test Common), in the same structure of the MuST-C V2 English-German section (Cattoni et al., 2021) used last year.

Besides the two new language directions of MuST-C V2, also this year the allowed training corpora include:

- MuST-C V1 (Di Gangi et al., 2019);
- CoVoST (Wang et al., 2020a);
- WIT[3] (Cettolo et al., 2012) ;
- Speech-Translation TED corpus[8];
- How2 (Sanabria et al., 2018)[9];
- LibriVoxDeEn (Beilharz and Sun, 2019)[10];
- Europarl-ST (Iranzo-Sánchez et al., 2020);
- TED LIUM v2 (Rousseau et al., 2014) and v3 (Hernandez et al., 2018);
- WMT 2019[11] and 2020[12];
- OpenSubtitles 2018 (Lison et al., 2018);
- Augmented LibriSpeech (Kocabiyikoglu et al., 2018)[13]
- Mozilla Common Voice[14] ;
- LibriSpeech ASR corpus (Panayotov et al., 2015);
- VoxPopuli[15] (Wang et al., 2021).

The only addition over last year is the VoxPopuli dataset.

Similarly to the training data, participants were also provided with a list of pre-trained models that can be used in the constrained condition. The list includes:

- Wav2vec 2.0[16] (Baevski et al., 2020a);
- Hubert[17];
- MBART[18] (Liu et al., 2020);
- MBART50[19] (Tang et al., 2020);
- M2M100[20] (Fan et al., 2021);
- Delta LM[21] (Ma et al., 2021);
- T5[22] (Raffel et al., 2020).

[6] http://www.statmt.org/wmt22/
[7] http://ict.fbk.eu/must-c/
[8] http://i13pc106.ira.uka.de/~mmueller/iwslt-corpus.zip
[9] only English - Portuguese
[10] only German - English
[11] http://www.statmt.org/wmt19/
[12] http://www.statmt.org/wmt20/
[13] only English - French
[14] http://voice.mozilla.org/en/datasets – English version en_1488h_2019-12-10
[15] https://github.com/facebookresearch/voxpopuli
[16] https://github.com/pytorch/fairseq/blob/main/examples/wav2vec/README.md
[17] https://github.com/pytorch/fairseq/tree/main/examples/hubert
[18] https://github.com/pytorch/fairseq/blob/main/examples/mbart/README.md
[19] https://github.com/pytorch/fairseq/tree/main/examples/multilingual#mbart50-models
[20] https://github.com/pytorch/fairseq/tree/main/examples/m2m_100
[21] https://github.com/microsoft/unilm/tree/master/deltalm
[22] https://github.com/google-research/text-to-text-transfer-transformer

The development data allowed under the constrained condition consist of the dev set from IWSLT 2010, as well as the test sets used for the 2010, 2013, 2014, 2015, 2018, 2019, and 2020 IWSLT campaigns. Using other training/development resources was allowed but, in this case, participants were asked to mark their submission as unconstrained.

Test data. For each language direction, namely En-De, En-Zh and En-Ja, a new test set was created. The new test sets were built from 17 TED talks for En-De, 16 for En-Zh and 13 for En-Ja. None of these talks is included in the current public release of MuST-C. Similar to last year, participants were presented with the option of processing either an unsegmented version (to be split with their preferred segmentation method) or an automatically segmented version of the audio data. For the segmented version, the resulting number of segments is 2,059 (corresponding to about 3h34m of translated speech from 17 talks) for En-De, 1,874 (3h17m) for En-Zh and 1,758 (2h38m) for En-Ja. The details of the three test sets are reported in Table 2.

Lang	Talks	Sentences	Duration
En-De	17	2,059	3h34m
En-Zh	16	1,874	3h17m
En-Ja	13	1,768	2h38m

Table 2: Statistics of the official test sets for the offline speech translation task (*tst2022*).

To measure technology progress with respect to last year's round, participants were asked to process also the undisclosed 2021 En-De test set that, in the segmented version, consists of 2,037 segments (corresponding to about 4.1 hours of translated speech from 17 talks).

Metrics. The systems' performance was evaluated with respect to their capability to produce translations similar to the target-language references. This similarity is measured using the BLEU metric, computed with SacreBLEU (Post, 2018) with default settings.

Similar to the 2021 edition, we consider two different types of target-language references, namely:

- The original TED translations. Since these references come in the form of subtitles, they are subject to compression and omissions to adhere to the TED subtitling guidelines.[23] This makes them less literal compared to standard, unconstrained translations;
- Unconstrained translations. These references were created from scratch[24] by adhering to the usual translation guidelines. They are hence exact translations (i.e. literal and with proper punctuation).

Lang Pair	Lang	Sentences	Words
En-De	En	2,059	39,814
	De - Orig	2,059	32,361
	De - Uncon.	2,059	36,655
En-Zh	En	1,874	36,736
	Zh - Orig	1,874	63,876*
	Zh - Uncon.	1,874	64,767*
En-Ja	En	1,768	30,326
	Ja - Orig	1,768	62,778*
	Ja - Uncon.	1,768	74,637*

Table 3: Statistics of the official test set for the offline speech translation task (*tst2022*). * statistics are reported in terms of characters for Chinese and Japanese.

As shown in Table 3, the different approaches to generate the human translations led to significantly different references. For En-De, while the unconstrained translation has a similar length (counted in words) compared to the corresponding source sentence, the original is ~15% shorter in order to fulfil the additional constraints for subtitling. For En-Ja and En-Zh, it is difficult to make a proper comparison with the source data as the Japanese and Chinese data are counted in characters while the English one is counted in words. However, it is evident that the unconstrained translations have more characters than the original ones following a similar trend seen for En-De.

Besides considering separate scores for the two types of references, results were also computed by considering both of them in a multi-reference setting. Similar to last year, the submitted runs were ranked based on case-sensitive BLEU calculated on the test set by using automatic re-segmentation

[23] `http://www.ted.com/participate/translate/subtitling-tips`

[24] We would like to thank Meta for providing us with this new set of references.

of the hypotheses based on the reference translations by mwerSegmenter.[25]

3.3 Submissions

Overall, 10 different teams submitted at total of 29 primary submissions. For the English-to-German task 8 teams submitted 10 runs, for English-to-Chinese 9 teams 11 runs and for the English-to-Japanese task 6 teams participated with 8 primary runs. For all the language pairs two teams submitted a primary cascaded and a primary end-to-end system. Overall, most teams participated in all 3 language directions, partly with individual systems and partly with multi-lingual systems.

We encouraged the submission of end-to-end as well as cascaded systems. Several participants experimented with both types of architectures and in two instances primary end-to-end and cascaded systems were submitted. In total, we had 4 cascaded and 6 end-to-end submissions for the English-to-German tasks, 5 cascaded and 6 end-to-end for English-to-Chinese and 3 cascaded and 5 end-to-end submissions for English-to-Japanese.

One additional change in this year's evaluation campaign was that the use of a list of pre-trained models. Most of the teams investigated this research direction and integrated pre-trained models into their final submission. Both, the integration of pre-trained speech models as well as text models were successfully investigated. In addition, several teams focused on audio segmentation approaches.

- HW-TSC (Li et al., 2022a) submission is built in the cascaded form, including three types of ASR models and one type of translation model. Before performing the speech translation, the LIUM SpkDiarization tool (Rouvier et al., 2013), provided to the participants, was used to cut off the test set wav files into segments. For the ASR part, they use conformer, U2T-transformer and U2-conformer, and all of them are trained on a combination of the MUST-C, COVOST, LibriSpeech, TedLIUM datasets. The system is adapted to the TED domain using domain tags. For the translation model, they trained a Transformer-large on the WMT21-news dataset, and fine-tuned it on the MUST-C and IWSLT datasets. The output of the different ASR models has been re-ranked and the best combination selected as primary submission.

- FBK (Gaido et al., 2022) focused in their submission on reducing model training costs without sacrificing translation quality. They submitted an end-to-end speech translation system model using the conformer-architecture without pre-trained models. The model is trained on specifically filtered and resegmented parts of the corpus. The final submission is an ensemble of several models.

- USTC-NELSLIP (Zhang et al., 2022b) submitted primary end-to-end and cascaded systems for all three language directions which ensemble several individual models. In the cascaded condition, the ASR models combined transformer and conformer architectures and the MT models are trained on synthetic data to be robust against ASR errors. The end-to-end models also combine conformer and transformer encoders and are partly initialized from ASR systems.

- ALEXA AI (Shanbhogue et al., 2022) submitted an end-to-end speech translation system that leverages pretrained models and cross modality transfer learning for all three language directions. They used encoders for text as well as speech and initialized the models using pretrained speech and text models. The work mainly focused on improving knowledge transfer. In addition, a special focus was put on segmentation strategies.

- NIUTRANS (Zhang et al., 2022c) submission to the English-Chinese track is an end-to-end speech translation system composed of different pre-trained acoustic models and machine translation models. The models were combined by two kinds of adapters and the final submission is an ensemble of three individual speech translation models.

- UPC (Tsiamas et al., 2022a) submission is an end-to-end speech translation model which combines pre-trained speech encoder and text decoder for all the three language directions of the task. As a speech encoder wav2vec 2.0 and HuBERT are used, both already fine-tuned on English ASR data. As a text decoder

[25] http://www-i6.informatik.rwth-aachen.de/web/Software/mwerSegmenter.tar.gz

an mBART50 fine-tuned on multilingual MT (one-to-many) is used. These two modules are coupled with a length adaptor block and in the end-to-end training, additional adapters are trained. For the final submission several initial models are combined.

- KIT (Pham et al., 2022) submitted an end-to-end system using pre-trained audio and text models to all the three language directions. The systems were trained on the initial training data as well as on additional synthetic data. Furthermore, sentence segmentation strategies were investigated. The final submission is an ensemble of several models.

- YI (Zhang and Ao, 2022)) submitted primary end-to-end and cascaded systems for all three language directions using large-scale pre-trained models. Starting from pre-trained speech and language models, the authors investigated a multi-stage pre-training and the use of a task dependent fine-tuning for ASR, MT and speech translation. In addition, various efforts to perform data preparation was carried out. Finally, an ensemble of several models was submitted as the primary submission.

- NEURAL.AI submitted a cascaded speech translation system to the English-to-Chinese speech translation task. The ASR system consists of a conformer encoder and a transformer decoder. The MT system is a fined-tuned deltalm-base.

3.4 Results

This year, the submissions to the IWSLT Offline translation task were not only evaluated using automatic metrics, but also a human evaluation was carried out. All results are shown in detail in the appendix.

3.4.1 Automatic Evaluation

The results for each of the language pairs are shown in the tables in section A.5. For English-to-German we show the results for this year's test set (Table 19) as well as for last year's test set (Table 20). This enables us to also show the progress compared to last year. For the two new language pairs, English-to-Chinese (Table 21) and English-to-Japanese (Table 22), we present the numbers of this year's test set.

First, all the submissions are distributed in a range from 4 to 7 BLEU points. The only exception is Chinese, where one system performed significantly worse than the others. This large BLEU score range is significantly different than last year's ranking where all the submissions were close to each other. The overall 2022 ranking for the English-German task is quite similar to the ranking obtained for the test set 2021.

Progress The comparison between this year's submissions and last year's submission on test set 2021 in the English-to-German task allows us to measure the progress since last year. As shown in Table 20, 7 out of 9 systems performed better than the best system last year. This year's best system is 4 BLEU points better than last year's system. So, we are seeing a clear improvement in translation quality. One possible reason for the improvement is the additional allowed resources (the Vox-Populi dataset and the pre-trained models). However, also teams not using the additional resources (FBK) outperformed last year's system.

End-to-end vs. cascade As in previous years, we received cascaded and end-to-end submissions. While in the last years, end-to-end systems were able to close the gap to cascaded systems, we do not see this trend since last year. In this year, for all conditions, a cascaded system performed best. Furthermore, when looking at the participants who submitted both, a primary end-to-end and a primary cascaded system, in 6 out of 8 times, the cascaded system performed better than the end-to-end system. Whether this is partly due to the integration of pre-trained models has to be evaluated in further experiments.

Pre-trained models It is difficult to measure the impact of pre-trained models since there is no participant submitting both, a translation system with and without pre-trained models. However, there are some indications of the usefulness of pre-trained models. First, nearly all participants submitted systems with pre-trained models. Typically, these are audio encoders like wav2vec or Hubert for the encoder and text models like mBart for the decoder. Secondly, all winning systems are using this technology. And finally, we see large gains in translation quality compared to last year, where this technique was not allowed. Consequently, these models seem to be an interesting knowledge source. However, it should be noted that the models are rather large and therefore can also be a limiting factor for teams to participate in the evaluation campaign.

Multi-lingual models For the first time, since several years, this year's edition of the offline task included several language directions. Interestingly, this did not lead to a partition of participants into different language pairs, but most participants submitted translations for all three language pairs. While the best performing systems were individually optimized for each language, we also see multilingual models submitted to the tasks. Especially, the integration of pre-trained models, which are typically multi-lingual, made it easier to build translation systems for all three conditions. While the ranking between the languages is not the same, it is still very similar. This indicates that a good system in one language direction typically will also result in good performance in the other directions. While the amount of training resources is at least comparable, this is interesting since the languages are rather different.

3.4.2 Human Evaluation

We conducted a human evaluation of primary submissions based on a random selection of 1,350 segments from the test set of each language pair. Human graders were asked for a direct assessment, expressed through scores between 0 and 100. To minimize the impact of errors in the automatic segmentation, graders were also shown system output for the previous and the following sentence and asked not to let segmentation issues influence their scores. We used Appraise to compute system scores, statistical significance, and rankings. Details of the human evaluation are provided in Section A.2.

As for the results (Tables 23, 24, 25), the ranking of systems matches that of the automatic evaluation when accounting for statistical significance for English to German and English to Chinese, but not for English to Japanese. The scores indicate clear differences between systems (that usually persist across language pairs), but also significant overlap in the translation quality of different systems.

3.4.3 Final remarks

By inspecting this year's results, we can make three final observations.

The first is about the relation between the cascade and end-to-end technology. According to the automatic metrics, and in contrast to last year's campaign, cascade systems achieve the best performance in all the language directions. However, human evaluation does not validate automatic results for En-De and En-Jp, where the best cascade and end-to-end systems are in the same cluster and not statistically different. This outcome further confirms the findings of Bentivogli et al. (2021) for En-De but extends them to one new language pair out of the two addressed (En-Jp and En-Zh). For this reason, more investigation about the two technologies is still needed and will be further carried out in the next editions of this task.

The other observation is about the introduction of human evaluation in our task. While largely confirming the rankings obtained with automatic metrics, it provides the most reliable picture of the real differences between the systems, showing that they are not so evident as they were detected by automatic metrics. Given the importance of human evaluation to accurately assess state-of-the-art technologies, we plan to rely on it also in the next edition of the task.

The last observation is about the noticeable jump in performance on the progress test set compared to last year's systems. All the current systems have been able to outperform the best 2021 system, with gains reaching up to 6 BLEU score points when using multiple references. While it is difficult to ascribe this improvement to a single factor, it is worth to note that the main change in this year's task setting is the availability of pretrained models. We suggest that these models can have an important role in the final translation quality, and we plan to further investigate their usefulness in the next edition.

4 Speech to Speech Translation

Speech-to-speech translation is the task of translating audio input in a language into audio output in a target language. In the offline setting, systems are able to take into account an entire input audio segment in order to translate, similar to a consecutive interpreter. This is in contrast to streaming or simultaneous settings where systems are only exposed to partial input as in simultaneous interpretation. The goal of this task is to foster the development of automatic methods for offline speech-to-speech translation.

4.1 Challenge

Participants built speech-to-speech translation systems from English into German using any possible method, for example with a cascade system (speech recognition + machine translation + speech synthesis or end-to-end speech-to-text translation + speech synthesis) or an end-to-end or direct system.

4.2 Data and Metrics

Data. This task allowed the same training and testing data from the Offline task on English-German speech-to-text translation to more directly compare Offline S2T and S2ST systems. More details are available in §3.2. We note that while the evaluation data between the two tasks was the same, it was not directly parallel, as different sentence-level segmentation was used. For this task, gold sentence segmentation was used. This means that scores are not directly comparable between the two tasks, though we do evaluate a direct comparison for a subset of submissions.

In addition to the Offline task data, the following training data was allowed to help build German TTS and English-German speech-to-speech models:

- **Synthesized MuST-C**: Target speech for the German target text of MuST-C V2 (Cattoni et al., 2021) which was synthesized for this task using a VITS model (Kim et al., 2021) trained on the German portion of CSS10.
- **CSS10**: A single-speaker German TTS dataset (Park and Mulc, 2019)
- **Pretrained German TTS model**: A pretrained German VITS (Kim et al., 2021) TTS model to facilitate cascaded models and dual submission with the Offline task.

We note that several datasets allowed for the Offline task including Common Voice (Ardila et al., 2020) and LibriVoxDeEn (Beilharz and Sun, 2019) also contain multi-speaker German speech and text data, enabling their use for this task as well.

Metrics. While we evaluate with both automatic and human evaluation scores, systems were ranked according to the human evaluation.

Automatic metrics. To automatically evaluate translation quality, the speech output was automatically transcribed with an ASR system (Conneau et al., 2021),[26] and then BLEU (Papineni et al., 2002) was computed between the generated transcript and the human-produced text reference. Previous work (Salesky et al., 2021) has shown evaluating synthesized speech with ASR and chrF can be more robust than ASR and BLEU, so we additionally score with chrF (Popović, 2015). All scores were computed using SacreBLEU (Post, 2018).

Human evaluation. Output speech translations were evaluated with respect to translation quality and speech quality.

- **Translation quality:** Bilingual annotators were presented with the source audio and the target audio, and gave scores on the translation quality between 1 and 5. There were 3 annotators per sample and we retained the median score.
- **Output speech quality:** In addition to translation quality (capturing meaning), the quality of the speech output was also human-evaluated along three dimensions: naturalness (voice and pronunciation), clarity of speech (understandability), and sound quality (noise and other artifacts). These axes are more fine-grained than the traditional overall MOS score.

The detailed guidelines for output speech quality were as follows:

- **Naturalness:** Recordings that sound human-like, with natural-sounding pauses, stress, and intonation, should be given a high score. Recordings that sound robotic, flat, or otherwise unnatural should be given a low score.
- **Clarity of speech:** Recordings with clear speech and no mumbling and unclear phrases should be given a high score. Recordings with a large amount of mumbling and unclear phrases should be given a low score.
- **Sound quality:** Recordings with clean audio and no noise and static in the background should be given a high score. Recordings with a large amount of noise and static in the background should be given a low score.

[26] wav2vec2-large-xlsr-53-german

4.3 Submissions

We received submissions from four teams, one of which was withdrawn due to submission errors. We also compare two submissions to the Offline task which were retranslated with the gold segmentation and synthesized using the TTS model provided by the organizers.

MLLP-VRAIN (Iranzo-Sánchez et al., 2022) submitted a cascaded system of separate ASR, MT, and TTS models. They use the same ASR and MT models developed for the Simultaneous ST task, with a less restrictive pruning setup to allow a wider search space for the ASR model and without the multi-path wait-k policy used there for MT. They include a speaker-adaptive module in their TTS system to produce a high quality voice that mimics voice characteristics of the source speaker. Their TTS model is a typical two-stage approach, combining a Conformer-based model (Gulati et al., 2020) to produce spectrograms with a multi-band UnivNet (Jang et al., 2021) model to then produce speech waveforms. They include a speaker encoder, a modified ResNet-34 residual network architecture (He et al., 2016) from (Chung et al., 2018) more widely used for speaker recognition tasks and trained on the TED-LIUM v3 dataset (Hernandez et al., 2018), which is combined with the Conformer output to produce more faithful voices.

HW-TSC (Guo et al., 2022b) submitted a cascaded system of separate ASR, MT, and TTS models. The ASR model ensembles Conformer (Gulati et al., 2020) and S2T-Transformer models (Synnaeve et al., 2020), and is cleaned with the U2 model. The MT model is pretrained on news corpora and finetuned to MuST-C and IWSLT data, with context-aware MT reranking inspired by Yu et al. (2020). They use the provided pretrained VITS TTS model. They use domain tags for each training data source to improve performance. They submitted one primary and three contrastive systems, which ablate individual components. Contrastive1 includes the ASR ensemble but removes reranking for both ASR and MT. Constrastive2 uses the Conformer ASR model only without reranking. Contrastive3 uses the S2T-Transformer ASR model only without reranking.

UPC (Tsiamas et al., 2022a) submitted a cascaded system, extending their direct speech-to-text model submitted to the Offline task with the provided German VITS TTS model for S2ST. Their final speech-to-text model combined initialization using HuBERT models, LayerNorm and Attention finetuning (LNA), and knowledge distillation from mBART. For both tasks, they used SHAS segmentation during training (Tsiamas et al., 2022b) for consistent improvements. Data filtering and augmentation were also key aspects of their submission.

A direct S2ST model built upon the VITS synthesis model was submitted but withdrawn due to errors.

4.4 Results

Results as scored by automatic metrics are shown in Table 26 and human evaluation results are shown in Table 27 and Table 28 in the Appendix.

Overall results. From the automatic metric perspective, MLLP-VRAIN obtains the highest ASR-BLEU score, followed by HW-TSC and UPC. Note that there is a disagreement between BLEU and chrF ranking for MLLP-VRAIN and HW-TSC. For human evaluation along the speech quality perspective, MLLP-VRAIN obtains a higher quality system compared to the other systems. This is expected as HW-TSC, UPC and the reference system all use the default provided TTS system. It is interesting to note that for these 3 systems, all scores are close to each other on speech quality even though the output content is different. We thus hypothesize that speech quality is orthogonal to translation quality. Finally, for human evaluation along the translation quality perspective, HW-TSC obtained the highest score, followed by MLLP-VRAIN and UPC. Note that this ranking is consistent with the ASR-chrF but not with ASR-BLEU. Surprisingly, the reference system obtains the lowest score. We hypothesize that this may be due to misalignments in the test set between the source audio and the source transcript (rather than between the source transcript and the target translation since the target translations were generated by human translator given the source text transcripts). In addition, we found variance between raters, which could account for this. We will go through a review process for those instances prior to releasing the human judgments.

S2ST Approaches. This year, all systems except the withdrawn submission were cascaded systems, with two systems adopting an ASR + MT +

TTS approach and one system adopting an end-to-end S2T + TTS approach. This does not allow us to draw meaningful conclusions on various approaches to the task and we will encourage more direct and/or end-to-end submissions in future editions.

Automatic scoring. To compute automatic metrics, we apply several steps, which may affect quality assessment. The final row of Table 26 shows chrF and BLEU computed on normalized text translations and references; normalizing system output and references reduces scores slightly, by 0.8 BLEU and 0.3 chrF. The larger potential for degradation comes from the synthesis (TTS) and transcription (ASR) roundtrip, which we can directly evaluate the effects of using the reference translations and cascaded systems. Synthesizing the gold reference translation and transcribing with the wav2vec2-large-xlsr-53-german ASR model gives a BLEU score of 68.46 and chrF of 88.78 – degradation of 31.5 BLEU and 11.2 chrF. This confirms errors are introduced by imperfect TTS and ASR models when scoring S2ST systems in this way, and also shows the greater impact of slight variations introduced by TTS and ASR on word-level BLEU than on chrF, which does not necessarily reflect differences in human evaluation (see results in Section B.3). When synthesizing and transcribing machine translation output, there is also degradation in metric scores compared to directly evaluating the text output, but it is considerably smaller. For example, the FBK Offline submission + TTS scores are reduced by 6 BLEU and 4.6 chrF. We see comparing the FBK, KIT, and UPC submissions here, which were all also submitted to the Offline task as speech-to-text systems and then the translations synthesized with the same TTS model, that though there are degradations in performance from synthesis, the relative performance of these models is partly maintained. While the submissions from KIT and FBK both outperform UPC, the relative performance between KIT and FBK reverses according to BLEU – but not according to chrF. This suggests that a finer granularity translation metric may better reflect translation quality after synthesis.

4.5 Conclusion

This is the first time that speech output is introduced in one of the IWSLT shared tasks. The speech-to-speech task serves as a pilot for this kind of task and we plan to run future editions of this task. Possible future extensions include extending the task to the simultaneous setting and running human evaluations dedicated to additional aspects of the speech output (e.g. preservation of some non-lexical aspects of the input).

5 Low-Resource Speech Translation

This shared task focuses on the problem of developing speech transcription and translation tools for under-resourced languages. For the vast majority of the world's languages there exist little speech-translation parallel data at the scale needed to train speech translation models. Instead, in a real-world situation one might have access to limited, disparate resources (e.g. word-level translations, speech recognition, small parallel text data, monolingual text, raw audio, etc).

Building on last year's task that focused on two varieties of Swahili (Anastasopoulos et al., 2021), the shared task invited participants to build speech translation systems for translating out of two predominantly oral languages, Tamasheq and Tunisian Arabic, and into the linguae francae of the respective regions (English and French). The use of any pre-trained machine translation, speech recognition, speech synthesis, or speech translation model was allowed, as did unconstrained submissions potentially using data other than the ones the organizers provided.

5.1 Data and Metrics

Two datasets were shared for this year's low-resource speech translation track: the Tamasheq-French translation corpus (Boito et al., 2022a), and the Tunisian Arabic-English dataset from the Dialect Translation track (unconstrained condition). In this section we will focus on the Tamasheq corpus, leaving the results for Tunisian Arabic to be presented in Section 6.

The Tamasheq-French translation corpus[27] contains 17 h of speech in the Tamasheq language, which corresponds to 5,829 utterances translated to French. Additional audio data was also made available through the *Niger-Mali audio collection*: 224 h in Tamasheq and 417 h in geographically close languages (French from Niger, Fulfulde, Hausa, and Zarma).[28] For all this data, the

[27]https://github.com/mzboito/IWSLT2022_Tamasheq_data

[28]https://demo-lia.univ-avignon.fr/studios-tamani-kalangou/

speech style is radio broadcasting, and the dataset presents no transcription.

For this track, the main evaluation metric was lower-cased BLEU4 computed over the produced French translation.[29] We also shared with participants results for chrF++. Both are computed on `SacreBLEU` (Post, 2018).[30]

5.2 Submissions

For the Tamasheq language, we received submissions from three teams: ON-TRAC, TalTech and GMU. We now detail their speech translations models.

ON-TRAC: Boito et al. (2022b) submitted primary and contrastive end-to-end ST systems. Their primary submission focuses on the leveraging of intermediate representations produced by a pre-trained wav2vec 2.0 (Baevski et al., 2020b) base model trained on 234 h of Tamasheq audio. Their end-to-end ST system comprises: a partial wav2vec 2.0 module (in which the last 6 encoder layers were removed), a linear layer for down-projecting the output of the wav2vec 2.0 encoder, and a Transformer decoder with 3 heads, 4 layers and dimensionality of 256. Their contrastive model does not consider SSL features: it uses as input 512-dimensional mel filterbank features. This model leverages *approximate* transcriptions in Tamasheq produced by a French phonemic ASR model. These are used to train an end-to-end ST conformer model that jointly optimizes ASR, MT and ST losses. The model is made of 12 conformer layers of dimensionality 1024, and three transformer decoder layers of dimensionality 2048.

TalTech: Their system is an encoder-decoder ST model with a pretrained XLS-R (Babu et al., 2021) as encoder, and a mBART-50 (Tang et al., 2020) as decoder. For the encoder, they used all the 24 layers of the XLS-R 300M model implemented in `fairseq` (Ott et al., 2019), fine-tuning it on the provided unlabeled raw audio files in Tamasheq (224 h) for 5 epochs. For the decoder, they used the last 12 decoding layers available in the mBART-50 pretrained model.[31] The cross attention layers in the decoder were pointed to the XLS-R's hidden state output to mimic the original cross attention mechanism for text-to-text translation.

GMU: Their model uses the `fairseq S2T` extension (Wang et al., 2020b), using the transformer architecture. They first fine-tune the pre-trained XLS-R 300M encoder on French and Arabic ASR, using portions of the Multilingual TEDx dataset, and then train the whole model on the speech translation task using all provided data.

5.3 Results

All results are presented in Table 4. We observe that the dataset is very challenging: the best achieved BLEU is only 5.7 (ON-TRAC). This challenging setting inspired the teams to leverage pre-trained models: all submissions apply pre-trained initialization for reducing the *cold start* in direct ST in low-resource settings.

Detailing these, ON-TRAC submissions included the training of a wav2vec 2.0 model on target data, and the training of a phonetic French ASR. TalTech used massive multilingual off-the-shelf pre-trained models, and GMU pre-trained their speech encoder on French and Arabic. This illustrates the current trend for ST systems of incorporating pre-trained models. It is nonetheless noticeable that, even with the incorporation of powerful representation extractors (wav2vec 2.0, XLS-R, mBART-50), the achieved results are rather low.

This year's best submission (primary, ON-TRAC) leveraged a Tamasheq wav2vec 2.0 model trained on 234 h. In their post-evaluation results, they included a comparison with different larger wav2vec 2.0 models: XLSR-53 (Conneau et al., 2020), LeBenchmark-7K (Evain et al., 2021), and a multilingual wav2vec 2.0 trained on the Niger-Mali audio collection. Their results hint that smaller pre-trained models focused on the target data seemed to perform better in these low-resource settings. This might be due to the existing domain mismatch between pre-training data (from the off-the-shelf models) and the target data.[32]

The second best submission (contrastive, ON-TRAC) illustrates how even approximate transcriptions can attenuate the challenge of the direct ST task. The authors trained a phonetic French ASR model, and used the produced transcriptions

[29] SacreBLEU BLEU4 signature for the low-resource track: `nrefs:1|case:mixed|eff:no|tok:13a|smooth:exp|version:2.0.0`

[30] SacreBLEU chrF++ signature for the low-resource track: `nrefs:1|case:mixed|eff:yes|nc:6|nw:0|space:no|version:2.0.0`

[31] `https://huggingface.co/facebook/mbart-large-50-many-to-many-mmt`

[32] It was previously observed that the wav2vec 2.0 performance degrades when applied to audio data of different speech styles (Conneau et al., 2020).

Team	System	Pre-trained Models	BLEU	chrF++
ON-TRAC	primary	wav2vec 2.0 (Tamasheq)	5.7	31.4
	contrastive	ASR (French)	5.0	26.7
TalTech	primary	XLS-R, mBART-50	2.7	24.3
GMU	primary	XLS-R (Arabic, French)	0.5	16.9

Table 4: Summary of results for the Tamasheq-french corpus for the low-resource shared task.

as additional supervision for joint ASR, MT and ST optimization. This solution is very attractive for low-resource settings, as off-the-shelf ASR models – and annotated data to train new ones – are largely available for high-resourced languages.

Finally, we find that TalTech submission illustrates how the application of off-the-box pre-trained multilingual models can be challenging. A similar point can be made about the GMU submission, which despite multilingual finetuning failed to produce meaningful outputs for this challenging task.

In summary, this year's submissions focused on the application of large pre-trained models for end-to-end ST in low-resource settings. They illustrated how low-resource ST remains extremely challenging, even when leveraging powerful speech feature extractors (wav2vec 2.0), and massive multilingual decoders (mBART-50). In such settings, we find that the training of self-supervised models on target data, and the production of artificial supervision (approximate phonemic transcriptions) were the most effective approaches for translating 17 h of Tamasheq audio into French text.

6 Dialect Speech Translation

In some communities, two dialects of the same language are used by speakers under different settings. For example, in the Arabic-speaking world, Modern Standard Arabic (MSA) is used as spoken and written language for formal communications (e.g., news broadcasts, official speeches, religion), whereas informal communication is carried out in local dialects such as Egyptian, Moroccan, and Tunisian. This diglossia phenomenon poses unique challenges to speech translation. Often only the "high" dialect for formal communication has sufficient training data for building strong ASR and MT systems; the "low" dialect for informal communication may not even be commonly written. With this shared task (new for 2022), we hope to bring attention the unique challenges of dialects in diglossic scenarios.

6.1 Challenge

The goal of this shared task is to advance dialectal speech translation in diglossic communities. Specifically, we focus on Tunisian-to-English speech translation (ST), with additional ASR and MT resources in Modern Standard Arabic.

The ultimate goal of this shared task is to explore how transfer learning between "high" and "low" dialects can enable speech translation in diglossic communities. Diglossia is a common phenomenon in the world. Besides Arabic vs. its dialects, other examples include Mandarin Chinese vs. Cantonese/Shanghainese/Taiwanese/etc., Bahasa Indonesia vs. Javanese/Sundanese/Balinese/etc., Standard German vs. Swiss German, and Katharevousa vs. Demotic Greek. With this shared task, we imagine that techniques from multilingual speech translation and low-resource speech translation will be relevant, and hope that new techniques that specifically exploit the characteristics of diglossia can be explored.

6.2 Data and Metrics

Participants were provided with the following datasets:

- (a) 160 hours of Tunisian conversational speech (8kHz), with manual transcripts
- (b) 200k lines of manual translations of the above Tunisian transcripts into English, making a three-way parallel data (i.e. aligned audio, transcript, translation) that supports end-to-end speech translation models
- (c) 1200 hours of Modern Standard Arabic (MSA) broadcast news with transcripts for ASR, available from MGB-2 (Specifically, MGB-2 contains an estimated 70% MSA, with the rest being a mix of Egyptian, Gulf, Levantine, and North African dialectal Arabic. All of the MGB-2 train data is allowed.)

- Approximately 42,000k lines of bitext in MSA-English for MT from OPUS (specifically: Opensubtitles, UN, QED, TED, GlobalVoices, News-Commentary).

Datasets (a) and (b) are new resources developed by the LDC, and have been manually segmented at the utterance level. This three-way parallel data (Tunisian speech, Tunisian text, English text) enables participants to build end-to-end or cascaded systems that take Tunisian speech as input and generate English text as final output. The main evaluation metric is lower-cased BLEU on the final English translation[33].

Participants can build systems for evaluation in any of these conditions:

- **Basic condition:** train on datasets (a) and (b) only. This uses only Tunisian-English resources; the smaller dataset and simpler setup makes this ideal for participants starting out in speech translation research.
- **Dialect adaptation condition:** train on datasets (a), (b), (c), (d). The challenge is to exploit the large MSA datasets for transfer learning while accounting for lexical, morphological, and syntactic differences between dialects. This condition may be an interesting way to explore how multilingual models work in multi-dialectal conditions.
- **Unconstrained condition:** participants may use public or private resources for English and more Arabic dialects besides Tunisian (e.g., CommonVoice, TEDx, NIST OpenMT, MADAR, GALE). Multilingual models beyond Arabic and English are allowed. This condition is cross-listed with the low-resource shared task.

The data and conditions available to participants are summarized in Table 5. From the LDC-provided dataset LDC2022E01, we create official train/dev/test1 splits for the basic condition[34] and encourage participants to compare results on "test1." The official blind evaluation set LDC2022E02 is referred to as "test2"; it is collected in the same way as LDC2022E01 and utterance segmentation is given.

[33] SacreBLEU signature for dialect speech translation task: nrefs:1|case:lc|eff:no|tok:13a|smooth:exp|version:2.0.0

[34] For datasplit and preprocessing details: https://github.com/kevinduh/iwslt22-dialect

6.3 Submissions

We received submissions from three teams (CMU, JHU, ON-TRAC). Each team explored very different architectures and adaptation techniques. We recommend referring to the system descriptions for details; below is just a brief summary of their contributions:

CMU (Yan et al., 2022) focuses on the Multi-Decoder architecture (Dalmia et al., 2021) implemented in ESPnet, which is an end-to-end ST model that decomposes into ASR and MT subnets while maintaining differentiability. Intuitively, hidden states found by beam search from the ASR decoder are fed as input to the ST encoder. New enhancements on this architecture using hierarcharchical speech encoder and joint CTC/Attention ST decoding are introduced, with gains in BLEU.

Additionally, different approaches to integrating end-to-end and cascaded systems are examined in detailed; for example, one approach uses one system to generate N-best candidates, and the other system to help compute minimum Bayes risk. This resulted in the strongest system for this year's shared task.

In terms of dialect adaptation, the CMU team explored (a) using a Tunisian ASR model select similar MGB2 data by cross-entropy, and (b) using MSA-EN MT trained on OPUS to synthetically augment MGB2 with translations.

JHU (Yang et al., 2022) uses a cascaded architecture, where the ASR component is a conformer-based hybrid attention/CTC model implemented in ESPnet and the MT component is a Transformer model implemented in fairseq. ASR pre-training using wave2vec 2 (XLSR-53) is explored for the unconstrained condition. There is also an emphasis on text normalization to reduce variation in the Tunisian transcripts, which resulted in considerable BLEU gains.

In terms of dialect adaptation, the JHU team investigated a novel data augmentation technique for the MT component: First, a EN→MSA MT model is trained on OPUS and applied to decode LDC2022E01 train set (treating English as source input), synthesizing a paired MSA-Tunisian bitext. With this, a MSA→Tunisian MT model is trained and applied on OPUS, synthesizing a large Tunisian-English bitext. This can be then used in a fine-tuning setup with the original LDC2022E01

Dataset	Speech (#hours)	Text (#lines) Tunisian	MSA	English	Use
LDC2022E01 train	160	200k	-	200k	Basic condition
LDC2022E01 dev	3	3833	-	3833	Basic condition
LDC2022E01 test1	3	4204	-	4204	Unofficial evaluation
LDC2022E02 test2	3	4288	-	4288	Official evaluation for 2022
MGB2	1100	-	1.1M	-	Dialect adaptation; mostly MSA
OPUS	-	-	42M	42M	Dialect adaptation condition
Any other data	-	-	-	-	Unconstrained condition

Table 5: Datasets for Dialect Shared Task.

data.

ON-TRAC (Boito et al., 2022b) compares both end-to-end and cascaded systems. The end-to-end ST system is a conformer model trained with speed pertubation and SpecAugment, implemented in ESPnet. The cascaded system consists of an ASR component implemented in Speech-Brain, and MT component implemented in fairseq (either biLSTM or convolutional model). Specifically, the ASR component is composed of a wav2vec 2 module, followed by a dense hidden layer and a softmax output of 34 character vocabulary. The use of character outputs in the ASR component is unique to ON-TRAC; other teams employ sub-word units (1000 units for CMU, 400-1000 units for JHU).

In terms of dialect adaptation, the ON-TRAC team explored fine-tuning on the ASR component: first, the ASR model is trained on the MGB2 data; then the model is fine-tuned on the LDC2022E01 data, with the wav2vec portion fixed and the final two layers randomly initialized.

6.4 Results

6.4.1 Automatic evaluation

We are interested in two main scientific questions:

1. For speech translation of primarily spoken dialects, is it beneficial to incorporate data from related dialects with larger written resources? If so, what is the best way to incorporate these resources in training?

2. Does the inherent imbalance and heterogeneity of resources in different dialects favor end-to-end or cascaded architectures? Specifically, there are separate MSA datasets (MGB2, OPUS) that correspond to ASR and MT sub-tasks, but no single MSA dataset that corresponds to an end-to-end speech translation task like the Tunisian-English LDC2022E01 dataset.

Table 29 in the Appendix presents the full results on test2 and test1 sets. Table 6 here presents a summary of select systems in terms of the architecture and training data employed. First, we observe that mixing in MSA/English data tends to improve results over the basic condition of using only the Tunisian/English data. For example, CMU's E2 system obtains 20.8 BLEU, a 0.4 improvement over the E1 system; these are both multi-decoder ensembles, the difference being the training data used. Similarly, JHU's dialect adapt primary system outperforms its basic condition counterpart by 1.8 BLEU. While dialect adaptation is promising, some of the system description papers observe a plateauing effect with additional data, so more work may be needed.

Second, the comparison between end-to-end architectures (directing generating English text from Tunisian speech) vs. cascaded ASR+MT architectures (two stage Tunisian speech to text, followed Tunisian text to English text) is more complex. On one hand, the ON-TRAC system description reports stronger results from its cascaded architecture which exploits wav2vec and additional MGB2 data in its ASR component; on the other hand, the current best-performing model on this task is CMU's E2 system (20.8 BLEU on test2), which mixes both end-to-end and cascaded systems in a Minimum Bayes Risk (MBR) framework. We are not able to make a clear verdict regarding the best architecture for this task, but believe the distinction between end-to-end and cascade architecture may become more blurred in the future.

In summary, we conclude that (1) dialectal adaptation is a promising direction that deserves more research, and (2) the decision between end-to-end vs. cascaded architectures most likely will depend on complicated factors, and both should be pursued during development.

6.4.2 Human evaluation

For the text-based human evaluation in this task, we employed the Direct Assessment (DA) with document context and extended with Scalar Quality Metric (SQM). The overview of the DA+SQM is provided in Section A.4. In this section we only highlight adaptations specific to the task and discuss the results. Since the test set consisted of a few long conversations, human evaluation was run on a subset of it: we sampled 92 excerpts including 10 consecutive segments and used them as document context. We also adapted annotator guidelines for this task asking for judging correct meaning preservation more than grammatical inconsistencies that may appear in informal conversations, as presented on Figure 5.

We have collected 13,860 assessment scores for this task, after excluding quality control items (Table 7). The official results of the human evaluation are presented in Table 31. Systems from each participating teams are significantly different from other teams, but none of the systems was able to provide translation quality competing with the human reference. From the post-annotation survey, some translation issues noticed by annotators were mostly related to incorrect translation of terminology terms and colloquial phrases as well as grammatical and fluency inconsistencies. A few annotators mentioned that in some cases the context of 10 consecutive segments was insufficient and having an access to the original video or audio would help them with the assessment decisions. We will take this feedback into account in next editions of the human evaluation.

7 Formality Control for SLT

Machine translation (MT) models typically return one single translation for each input segment. Specific problems can arise for spoken language translation from English into languages that have multiple levels of formality expressed through honorifics or "grammatical register." For example, the sentence 'Are you sure?' can have two possible correct translations in German: 'Sind Sie sicher?' for the formal register and 'Bist du sicher?' for the informal one. Leaving the model to choose between different valid translation options can lead to translations with inconsistent tone that are perceived as inappropriate by users depending on their demographics and cultural backgrounds, in particular for certain use cases (e.g. customer service, business, gaming chat). Most prior research addressing this problem has been tailored to individual languages and proposed custom models trained on data with consistent formality (Viswanathan et al., 2019), or through side constraints to control politeness or formality (Sennrich et al., 2016; Niu et al., 2018; Feely et al., 2019; Schioppa et al., 2021a).

7.1 Challenge

The goal of this task was to advance research on controlling formality for spoken language translation across multiple diverse target languages and domains.[35] How formality distinctions are expressed grammatically and lexically can vary widely by language. In many Indo-European languages (e.g., German, Hindi, Italian, Russian, and Spanish), the formal and informal registers are distinguished by the second person pronouns and/or corresponding verb agreement. In Japanese, distinctions that express polite, respectful, and humble speech can be more extensive, including morphological markings on the main verb, as well as on some nouns and adjectives; specific lexical choices; and longer sentences. For this task we considered two formality levels: formal and informal. For Japanese, where more than two formality levels are possible, informal was mapped to *kudaketa* and formal to *teineigo*. We give examples of these phenomena in Table 8.

The task focused on text-to-text translation of spoken language with a special theme of zero-shot learning in multilingual models. The task covered supervised and zero-shot settings, both with constrained and unconstrained training data requirements. For the supervised setting, participants were provided with a formality-annotated dataset for training and development for four language pairs: English→German, Spanish, Hindi, Japanese. For the zero-shot task, which covered English→Italian, Russian, only targeted test data was provided after system submission period.

As this was the first shared task organized on formality control, one objective was to establish a standard benchmark including: formality-

[35] https://iwslt.org/2022/formality/

Team / Condition / System	Architecture	Training Data	BLEU	Δ
CMU / basic / E1	Mix	TA/EN	20.4	-
CMU / dialect adapt / E2	Mix	TA/EN + MSA/EN	20.8	0.4
JHU / basic / primary	Cascaded	TA/EN	17.1	-
JHU / dialect adapt / primary	Cascaded	TA/EN + MSA/EN	18.9	1.8
ON-TRAC / basic /primary	End-to-End	TA/EN	12.4	-
ON-TRAC / unconstrained / post-eval	Cascaded	TA/EN + MSA/EN	14.4	2.0

Table 6: Summary of select systems for Dialect Shared Task (BLEU on test2). We highlight the BLEU improvements (Δ) obtained when training with additional MSA/English data compared with just the Tunisian/English (TA/EN) in the basic condition.

Language pair	Sys.	Ass.	Ass./Sys.
Tunisian→English	7	13,860	1,980

Table 7: Amount of human assessments collected in the text-based evaluation for the Dialect Speech Translation Task run in Appraise. Counts after removing documents with quality control items.

Source	*Could you* provide *your* first name please?
Informal	**Könntest du** bitte **deinen** Vornamen angeben?
Formal	**Könnten Sie** bitte **Ihren** Vornamen angeben?
Source	OK, then please *follow* me to your table.
Informal	ではテーブルまで私について来て。
Formal	ではテーブルまで私について来てください。
Respectful	ではテーブルまで私についていらしてください。

Table 8: Contrastive translations for EN-DE and EN-JA with different formality. Phrases in bold were annotated by professional translators as marking formality. Example reproduced from Nădejde et al. (2022).

annotated train and test sets, an evaluation metric, pre-trained baseline models and human evaluation guidelines. To encourage further research in this area and improve the task definition, we will release all these resources (including system outputs and human evaluation annotations) under a shared repository.[36]

7.2 Data and Metrics

7.2.1 Formality-annotated data

For this task, the organizers provided formality-annotated parallel data comprising of source segments paired with two contrastive reference translations, one for each formality level (informal and formal). The dataset (CoCoA-MT), released by Nădejde et al. (2022), includes phrase-level annotations of formality markers in the target segments in order to facilitate evaluation and analysis (shown in **bold** in Table 8). Formality distinctions are expressed by the use of grammatical register or honorific language. The training set provided to participants comprises segments sourced from two domains: Topical-Chat (Gopalakrishnan et al., 2019) and Telephony. For the test set, organizers additionally included segments sourced from a third held-out domain: Call-Center.

Table 9 reports the number of source segments used for training and evaluation and the overlap between the references (informal vs. formal) as measured by BLEU. The lowest overlap is for Japanese and the highest overlap is for Hindi, indicating that the task of controlling formality is more challenging for Japanese than for Hindi.

Setting	Target	#train	#test	overlap
Supervised	DE	400	600	75.1
	ES	400	600	79.0
	HI	400	600	81.1
	JA	1,000	600	74.6
Zero-shot	IT	0	600	78.8
	RU	0	600	-

Table 9: Number of segments in the training and test data, and overlap between the references in the test set as measured by BLEU (informal vs. formal). Table adapted from Nădejde et al. (2022).

7.2.2 Task definition

Participants were allowed to submit systems under the constrained and unconstrained data settings. To train their systems, participants were allowed to use the formality-labeled dataset provided by the organizers as well as the additional resources described below.

Constrained task: Textual MuST-C v1.2 data (Di Gangi et al., 2019) (for EN-DE, EN-ES, EN-IT, EN-RU), data released for the WMT

[36] https://github.com/amazon-research/contrastive-controlled-mt/tree/main/IWSLT2022/

news translation tasks (WMT21[37] for EN-JA; WMT14[38] for EN-HI), multilingual data from the same dataset (e.g. using EN-FR MuST-C data for training EN-ES models). Participants were not allowed to use external auxiliary tools (e.g., morphological analysers) or pre-trained models (e.g., BERT).

Unconstrained task: Pre-trained models (e.g., mBERT, mBART), additional annotations from morphological analysers, data released by the WMT news translation tasks (WMT21 for EN-DE, EN-RU; WMT13[39] for EN-ES; News Commentary v16[40] and Europarl[41] for EN-IT) and ParaCrawl v9.[42] For EN-HI, EN-JA, participants were allowed to use any other publicly available textual datasets such as WikiMatrix[43] and JParaCrawl.[44]

In both settings, no additional manually created formality-labeled data was allowed. For the unconstrained setting, obtaining additional annotations automatically was allowed as long as the code and data would be publicly released.

Evaluation sets Systems were evaluated for overall quality on MuST-C v1.2 test sets (tst-COMMON) (Di Gangi et al., 2019) for EN→DE, ES, IT, RU. For EN→HI, JA, systems were evaluated on WMT newstest2014 and 2020, respectively. Formality control accuracy was evaluated on the CoCoA-MT formality-annotated test set.

Automatic metrics Overall quality was measured by `sacreBLEU` (Post, 2018) and COMET (Rei et al., 2020). Formality control accuracy was measured using the referenced-based corpus-level metric released with the CoCoA-MT dataset. The metric relies on the contrastive reference translations to automatically assign, with high precision, formality labels (formal vs. informal) to each hypothesis. The segment-level labels are then aggregated to compute the corpus level *Matched-Acccuracy* (M-ACC). For further details on and evaluation of the M-ACC automatic metric, we refer the reader to the corresponding CoCoA-MT paper (Nădejde et al., 2022).

7.3 Submissions

We received submissions from three teams. We briefly summarize their methodologies below and refer the reader to their system description papers for details.

ALEXA AI (Shanbhogue et al., 2022) focused on using data augmentation to generate additional formality data and on using post-editing strategies to convert outputs from a generic NMT system into the desired formality level. They participated in the unconstrained supervised setting for EN→HI, JA. The authors made use of the limited amount of formality data released for the shared task to fine-tune mBART to classify segments as formal or informal. The formality classifier was then used to augment the available training data with additional formal/informal examples which they used to fine-tune a generic NMT system. The final system output from this fine-tuned model was then post-edited using a variety of strategies that the authors examine.

For EN→HI, the post-editing strategy was a rule-based approach which turned informal pronouns to formal pronouns. For EN→JA, the authors focused on a rule-based method for conjugating verbs. Finally, the authors addressed expansion of their methods to something language-agnostic and examined a seq2seq model used to transform formal outputs into informal outputs (they assumed that the output from the fine-tuned model was formal already and the seq2seq model was only used to generate informal translations). Generally, the authors found that the rule-based approaches worked better than the seq2seq post-editing model.

UOS (Vincent et al., 2022) focused on using data augmentation to generate additional formality data and on re-ranking translations from a generic NMT system for a given formality level. They trained systems for all four settings: {constrained, unconstrained} × {supervised, zero-shot}. For the supervised settings, they submitted models for EN→DE, ES. For the zero-shot settings, they submitted models for EN→IT, RU.

In order to augment the formality data, the authors fine-tuned a language model which they

[37]`https://www.statmt.org/wmt21/translation-task.html`
[38]`https://www.statmt.org/wmt14/translation-task.html`
[39]`https://www.statmt.org/wmt13/translation-task.html`
[40]`https://data.statmt.org/news-commentary/v16/`
[41]`https://www.statmt.org/europarl/`
[42]`https://paracrawl.eu/`
[43]`https://opus.nlpl.eu/WikiMatrix.ph`
[44]`http://www.kecl.ntt.co.jp/icl/lirg/jparacrawl/`

used to rank sentences from the available parallel corpora (depending on the constrained or unconstrained setting) by their similarity with the released formal and informal data. Most similar sentences were extracted using a relative position difference algorithm. For the zero-shot case, they noted that a smaller subset of sentences were considered formal (or informal) across the supervised sets for EN→DE, ES. They considered these segments to be strongly formal/informal and used this to find pairs in the zero-shot languages.

They fine-tuned their generic NMT system using the augmented and released formality data. At inference time, they used a large beam width k for beam search and generated k-best hypotheses. The resulting set of hypotheses were re-ranked using a relative frequency model trained on the released formality data (or, for the zero-shot case, using the similar sentences extracted earlier).

UMD (Rippeth et al., 2022) proposed training a single multilingual model that can cover all target languages and formality levels, and experimented with both mBART and mT5 as this model. They also worked with different fine-tuning strategies using both the gold labeled data from the shared task and formality-labeled data extracted from the unlabeled parallel data through rule-based methods or through automatic classification. As fine-tuning strategies they compared using pre-trained models with adapted vector-valued interventions proposed by Schioppa et al. (2021a) against bilingual models optimized towards one formality level (formal or informal) by fine-tuning all model parameters. For automatically labeling data, the authors also relied on fine-tuning a pre-trained multilingual model (XLM-R) for binary classification.

7.4 Results

7.4.1 Automatic Evaluation

In Table 10 and Table 11, we report the formality control accuracy scores (M-ACC) defined in §7.2 for the unconstrained and constrained tracks respectively.[45] For the supervised language arcs (i.e. EN→DE, ES, HI, JA) and unconstrained setting, submitted systems were successfully able to control formality. Average scores across formality

Language Pair	System	F	I
EN→DE	UMD	99.4	96.5
	UoS	100.0	100.0
EN→ES	UMD	99.5	93.2
	UoS	98.1	100.0
EN→HI	ALEXA AI	99.6	99.8
	UMD	99.4	98.7
EN→JA	ALEXA AI	88.8	98.8
	UMD	86.3	97.5
EN→IT	UMD	32.8	97.9
	UoS	51.2	98.6
EN→RU	UMD	100.0	1.10
	UoS	99.5	85.8

Table 10: Formality control accuracy (M-ACC) reported for Formal (F) and Informal (I) for the *unconstrained* task. Note that EN→IT, RU are zero-shot settings.

Language Pair	System	F	I
EN→DE	UoS	100.0	88.6
EN→ES	UoS	87.4	98.0
EN→IT	UoS	29.5	92.9
EN→RU	UoS	98.1	15.4

Table 11: Formality control accuracy (M-ACC) reported for Formal (F) and Informal (I) for the *constrained* task. There was only one system submission by UoS for this track. Note that EN→IT, RU are zero-shot settings.

settings range from 99.4 for EN→HI to 92.9 for EN→JA. EN→JA was the language pair with the largest gap between formal and informal accuracy, with both submitted systems doing an average of 11.0 points better on informal translations than formal translations. Finally, we observed that the ALEXA AI and UoS teams generally performed better on the supervised unconstrained task than UMD, possibly due to the former's use of high-quality parallel training data as opposed to the latter's use of multilingual pre-trained models.

For the supervised and constrained setting, we had one submission from UoS for EN→DE, ES. On average over both formality settings, their systems achieved an accuracy of 94.3 on EN→DE and 92.7 on EN→ES. For EN→DE, performance was significantly better for formal translations vs. informal translations, while the reverse was true for EN→ES.

In the zero-shot (EN→IT, RU) unconstrained setting, results were more mixed. For the two sub-

[45] Here, we focus on results for formality accuracy. We additionally report overall machine translation quality on generic test sets in Table 32 in the appendix along with baseline (uncontrolled) model performance on the formality test-set.

Language Pair	System	F	I
EN→JA	ALEXA AI	89.3	92.5
	UMD	82.8	82.7
EN→IT	UMD	13.7	78.3
	UoS	6.0	81.0
EN→RU	UMD	77.2	0.7
	UoS	85.0	71.3

Table 12: Human evaluation of the system level formality accuracy (Formal (F) and Informal (I)) for models in the *unconstrained* setting. Note that EN→IT, RU are zero-shot settings.

Language Pair	System	F	I
EN→IT	UoS	6.0	81.0
EN→RU	UoS	85.0	71.3

Table 13: Human evaluation of the system level formality accuracy (Formal (F) and Informal (I)) for models in the *constrained* setting. Note that EN→IT, RU are zero-shot settings.

missions (from the UMD and UoS teams), there was a clear bias toward one formality level: both systems were better at generating informal Italian and formal Russian translations. This likely reflects the inherent bias toward one formality level in the training set. For the zero-shot constrained setting, only the UoS team submitted a system, and results on the two formality levels were similar, with one formality level outperforming the other. In going from the unconstrained to the constrained setting, the UoS system lost an average of 25 points in accuracy for the zero-shot setting, while only losing 6 points in the fully supervised setting.

7.4.2 Human Evaluation

To complement the automatic evaluations, we conducted human evaluations of formality accuracy for a subset of the language pairs and settings. We selected EN→JA for the unconstrained supervised task, since Japanese has more complex morphological differences between formal and informal translations than the other target languages. We selected both EN→IT, RU for the zero-shot tasks (both constrained and unconstrained).

For each system, we selected a random sample of 300 source segments and collected the formal and informal outputs of the source segments. Annotators were asked to evaluate the outputs and assess whether the translation was formal, informal, neutral, or other.[46] We summarize the results of the human evaluations here, and give full results in Table 34 in the appendix. System-level accuracy was computed as the number of translations matching their desired formality level divided by the total number of outputs for a given formality level. Inter-annotator agreement as measured by the Krippendorff's α coefficient (Hayes and Krippendorff, 2007) was high, with an average α of 0.89.

Results from the human evaluation of EN→JA for the unconstrained supervised setting were in line with those obtained by the automatic metric: the submitted systems were able to control the formality of the output translations with reasonably high accuracy (90.9 for UMD and 82.8 for ALEXA AI on average across formality levels).

Human evaluation results also corroborated the automatic evaluations for zero-shot formality transfer. The results underscore how challenging the task of zero-shot formality transfer is, with submitted systems generally performing significantly better on one formality level than the other: informal for EN→IT and formal for EN→RU. A notable exception is the UoS EN→RU unconstrained system, which achieves a reasonable accuracy for both formal (85.0) and informal (71.3) registers (again mirroring the findings of the automatic evaluation). Additionally, human evaluators labeled more systems as "neutral" or "other" (i.e., neither formal nor informal) in the zero-shot settings than in the supervised settings.

8 Isometric SLT

Isometric translation is the task of generating translations similar in length to the source input (Lakew et al., 2021b). As a new research area in machine translation, this is the first time isometric translation is proposed as a shared task.[47] We considered 3 translations directions (English - German, English-French and English-Spanish) and 2 training conditions: constrained and unconstrained.

8.1 Challenge

Isometric MT targets issues that emerge when MT is applied to downstream applications such as dubbing, subtitling, and translation of documents. In

[46] We refer the reader to Appendix A.5 for detailed evaluation guidelines and label definitions.

[47] https://iwslt.org/2022/isometric

particular, dubbing requires that the duration of the target speech to be the same of the source in order to achieve isochrony (Lakew et al., 2021b); subtitle translation requires the output to fit blocks of pre-defined length (Matusov et al., 2019); and, finally, document translation requires sometimes to control the translation length in order to preserve the original layout.

We define isometric translations as translations whose length (in characters) is within ±10% of the length of the source (Lakew et al., 2021a). Subjective evaluations of automatically dubbed videos show that isometric translations generated better dubs than translations without any length control (Lakew et al., 2021a).

A few works have focused on controlling the output length of neural MT. Lakew et al. (2019) proposed to split the parallel training data based on target to source length ratio and prepend control tokens. Lakew et al. (2019) and Niehues (2020) incorporated length-encoding mechanisms that adapts positional-encoding (Vaswani et al., 2017) to control the length of the output sequence. Post-hoc approaches have been proposed by Saboo and Baumann (2019) and (Lakew et al., 2021a), where MT system generates an N-best list and then each hypothesis is re-ranked based on its length and score. More recently, Schioppa et al. (2021b) proposed to combine embedding representing attributes (such as length and politeness) with the encoder representation, to control for multiple attributes at generation time; whereas Lakew et al. (2021b) applied self-training to let the model incrementally learn how to generate isometric translations from its own output.

In this shared task, we proposed isometric MT of spoken language transcripts from En → De, Fr, Es. These three directions exhibit different target-to-source length ratios in character count. The length-ratios on the MuST-C training set is 1.12 for En→De, 1.11 for En→Fr, and 1.04 for En→Es.

Shared task participants were invited to work under constrained or unconstrained training regimes and to to submit systems for one or multiple translation directions. When submitting their system outputs, participants were asked to score their performance using a script available for the evaluation period.[48] Participant were also asked to release their outputs under a MIT license to allow for a human evaluation and further analyses.

	En-De		En-Fr		En-Es	
Test set	LR	LC	LR	LC	LR	LC
MuST-C	1.2	33.2%	1.2	35.2%	1.0	53.2%
Blind	1.1	62.0%	1.1	70.5%	1.0	64.0%

Table 14: Target to source sample length ratio (LR), and length compliance (LC) within a ±10% range, with respect to the source in terms of characters counts, for the MuST-C (`tst-COMMON`) and blind test sets.

8.2 Data and Metrics

8.2.1 Task Definition

We proposed two types of training regimes:

Constrained task allows the participants to use language pair specific parallel data from the Ted Talks MuST-C v1.2 corpus (Di Gangi et al., 2019). This is an in-domain training data setting for evaluation using the MuST-C test set (tst-COMMON).

Unconstrained Task allows the participants to leverage WMT data, or any other parallel or monolingual data in addition to the MuST-C data which is available under Constrained task. Participants are also allowed to use any pre-trained models like mBART (Liu et al., 2020).[49]

8.2.2 Evaluation Sets

We evaluated isometric machine translation on two test sets:

- MuST-C (`tst-COMMON`): in-domain test ada that is publicly available for participants to optimize their models.
- Blind Test: a test set of 91 dialogues extracted from 3 YouTube videos.[50] Each dialogue is containing 5-17 utterances is segmented into sentences for a total of 200 sentences. During the evaluation period participants had only access to the source sentences (English).[51]

Target to source sample length ratio and length compliance (±10%) for these test sets are shown in Table 14. The blind dataset was manually post-edited for isometric translation condition i.e. the translators were asked to keep the length

[48] https://github.com/amazon-research/isometric-slt/blob/main/scripts/compute_isometric_slt_stat.sh

[49] https://www.statmt.org/wmt20/index.html

[50] https://github.com/amazon-research/isometric-slt/tree/main/dataset

[51] Dialogue level data and references will be released.

of the translation possibly within ±10% of the source length. As a result, it shows a lower length ratio and a higher length compliance than `tst-COMMON`. Length compliance of the blind set is however not 100% because translators did not find a way to generate translations for many source sentences (phrases) within the range.

8.2.3 Evaluation Metrics

Submissions were evaluated on two dimensions – translation quality and length compliance with respect to the source input.

Translation Quality metrics for isometric translation should be robust to length variations in the hypothesis. For this reason we assessed n-gram metrics such as BLEU (Papineni et al., 2002), and recently proposed semantic based metrics like COMET (Rei et al., 2020) and BERTSCore (Zhang et al., 2019). Our analysis shows that BERTScore is more robust to length variations in the hypothesis when compared with BLEU and COMET. The latter two tends to penalize short hypotheses even for cases where the semantics is preserved. As a result, we primarily use BERTScore to assess translation quality.

Length Compliance (LC) is formulated as the % of translations in the test set that meet the ±10% length criterion. That is, if the source length is 50 characters, a length compliant translation is between 45 to 55 characters. We calculate how many translations fall in this bracket and report the percentage over a test set. In this evaluation, LC is applied only for source samples with length above 10 characters.

8.3 Submissions

We have received four submission from AppTek, HW-TSC, APV, and NUV teams. Below we briefly present submitted systems, followed by the baseline approaches we considered for the evaluation.

AppTek (Wilken and Matusov, 2022) participated in the constrained task for En-De pair. They explored various length controlling approaches with data pre-processing, data augmentation, length tokens as indicators, and multi-pass decoding. For data augmentation, forward and backward translations are applied, together with sample length-targeted pre-processing. For modeling, they combine fine-grained length control token on the encoder/decoder (Lakew et al., 2019) and length encoding modifying positional encoding (Takase and Okazaki, 2019). As a post-hoc step after translation, the primary system applies a system combination (denoted as length ROVER) over multiple translations from 7 different length classes, ranging from "extra short" to "extra long".

HW-TSC (Li et al., 2022b) participated in the constrained and unconstrained tasks for En-De, and constrained tasks for En-Fr and En-Es. Their submission investigated bi-directional training, R-drop (Wu et al., 2021) (a variant of dropout), data augmentation in forward and backward translation setting, and model ensemble to improve translation quality. For length control they prepended length tokens to the encoder (Lakew et al., 2019), added length ratio based positional encoding (Takase and Okazaki, 2019), applied length aware beam (LAB) to generate N-best lists, and explored different re-ranking strategies. The primary system for HW-TSC was a combination of length token, decoding with LAB and re-ranking of different system outputs. It shows the highest LC score with, however, a tradeoff on translation quality w.r.t. BERTScore.

APV leverages human-in-the-loop mechanism to train an isometric translation model. Their approach builds on top of a multi-source transformer that takes a source and an hypothesis (Tebbifakhr et al., 2018) as input. The hypothesis comes from human post-editing effort for style variation such as matching translation length with the source input. Differently from previous work on interactive post-editing, their work proposes the isometric translation attribute as a new dimension in the human-in-the-loop translation modeling.

APV team participated in the unconstrained task for En-D and Fr-Es. Their result shows performance gains against the baseline model when utilizing the post-edited reference as addition model input. However, when adding the isometric criterion for the post-editing stage, translation quality degrades with a slight gain in LC.

NUV (Bhatnagar et al., 2022) participated in the unconstrained task for En-Fr. Their approach is to first translate and then paraphrase. Their MT system is a Marian-NMT system pre-trained on OPUS-MT data (Tiedemann et al., 2020) and fine-tuned on MuST-C training data with three to-

kens for "short", "normal" and "long" translations. Paraphrases are generated by a MT5 (Xue et al., 2020) model fine-tuned on the PAWS-X paraphrasing data set (Yang et al., 2019).
Baselines: based on the task definition two systems are considered as baselines:

- WEAKBASELINE is a standard neural MT model trained in the constrained data setting, without any isometric translation feature.
- STRONGBASELINE is trained in an unconstrained data setting and implements output length control as in Lakew et al. (2021a) by prepending a length token on the input, generating N-best hypotheses, and re-ranking them with a linear combination of model score and length ratio.

8.4 Evaluations

To assess the performance of isometric translation systems, we measure translation quality and length compliance via automatic and subjective metrics.

8.4.1 Automatic Evaluation

As discussed in Sec. 8.2 we leverage BERTScore and LC metrics to measure isometric translation performance. We take primary system run from each submission and the baseline systems for comparison. Scores are computed against the human post-edited reference of the the blind test set. The automatic evaluation results are given in Table 35.

Translation quality in terms of BERTScore shows that STRONGBASELINE is the best performing system for all directions and training conditions. APPTEK's constrained submission for En-De is the only system performing similarly to STRONGBASELINE. For length compliance, HW-TSC-Constrained shows the best result (LC>=96%) for all pairs. However, the high LC score comes at the cost of lower translation quality with BERTScore.

For the En-De direction, the system from APPTEK-Constrained shows the best trade-off between BERTScore and LC, followed by STRONGBASELINE and HW-TSC-Unconstrained. On En-Fr, NUV-Unconstrained has the best translation quality among all submitted systems in terms of BERTScore but with a significant trade-off on length compliance. On En-Es, APV-Unconstrained shows the highest translation quality but again with a significant trade-off on length compliance. Over all language pairs, STRONGBASELINE stands out when we look at trade-offs between translation quality and length compliance.

8.4.2 Human Evaluation of Machine Translation Quality

For the text-based human evaluation, we employed the Direct Assessment (DA) with document context and extended with Scalar Quality Metric (SQM). The overview of the DA+SQM is provided in Section A.4. In this section we only highlight modifications specific to the task and discuss the results. The original segmentation was preserved when generating annotation tasks for the human evaluation. In contrast to the Dialect Speech Translation Task, annotators were guided to assess both grammar and meaning of the translations, as presented on Figure 6. The total number of assessment scores collected in text-based human evaluation campaigns per language pair is listed in Table 15.

The official results of the human evaluation are presented in Table 36. Reference translations (TRANSLATOR-A) are significantly better than participating systems and baselines across all three language pairs. In En-De APPTEK-Constrained and the STRONGBASELINE are together in a separate cluster outperforming the rest of the systems. This is also reflected in the automatic metric, where the two systems standout with a higher BERTScore than the other systems. In En-Fr task, a single large cluster includes all systems and baselines. This mean none of the systems were significantly better than the other. In En-Es task, APV-Unconstrained outperformed HW-TSC-Constrained and show similar performance with the STRONGBASELINE.

In the post-annotation questionnaire, most frequently mentioned common issues found in the translation outputs by annotators were: *lack of coherence between segments and inter-sentential translation errors, terminology translation errors and grammatical inconsistencies*. Annotators noticed that one source of those issues was splitting source sentences into short utterances, which automatic systems treated and translated as full sentences.

Language pair	Sys.	Ass.	Ass./Sys.
English→German	7	12,996	1,857
English→French	6	11,286	1,881
English→Spanish	5	9,692	1,938

Table 15: Amount of human assessments collected in the text-based evaluation for the Isometric SLT Task run in Appraise. Counts after removing documents with quality control items.

8.5 Isometric SLT Use case

8.5.1 Automatic Dubbing

As noted in Sec. 8.1, Isometric SLT can be useful for Automatic dubbing that requires the dubbed synthetic speech in the target language to fit the duration of the original speech in the source language. In the previous section, DA+SQM evaluation mainly looked at the translation quality. In this section, using the dubbing architecture of (Federico et al., 2020b) we test the downstream dubbing quality of these translations. To adapt the translations for dubbing, we segment them so as to follow the *speech-pause* arrangement of the source audio using prosodic alignment (PA) (Virkar et al., 2021, 2022). Using the output from PA module, we produce the dubbed audio utilizing a commercial grade Text-to-Speech system with fine-grained duration control (Effendi et al., 2022). We then replace the original audio with the dubbed audio to produce the final dubbed video.

8.5.2 Human evaluation

We generate dubbed videos using all MT outputs and (segmented) post-edited references. To reduce cognitive load, each subject is asked to compare only two MT systems at a time. This results in a total of 31 evaluations across the three dubbing directions, i.e., En-De,Fr,Es. Subjects first watch the dubbed video produced using the reference translation and then rate dubbed videos from two MT outputs. We employed subjects native in the target language and asked them to grade each dubbed video on a scale of 0-10 (0 being the worst and 10 being the best). For each MT system, we compute % Wins, i.e., % subjects preference when comparing two MT systems. For example, if we have 100 clips and according to annotators system A performs better than system B on 60 clips and ties with system B for 10 clips, then %Wins is 60% for system A v/s 30% for system B. We do not use the absolute grading to avoid the bias of each subject towards dubbing content in general.

For our experiments, we selected 60 dialogues from the blind set, to create 15 video clips such that each clip contains 4 continuous dialogues. To achieve statistically significant results, we employed 15 to 20 subjects (depending on the directions) across all the evaluations.

Table 37 shows the results for % Wins for all 31 evaluations. Additionally, in Table 38, we show the ranking of MT systems based on their performance for the dubbing use case. To rank the systems, we use N_{Wins} that defines the number of evaluations for which a system was preferred over some other system. In general, similar to human assessment for MT quality, we found STRONGBASELINE to be the best system for all three languages and WEAKBASELINE to be the worst for French and Spanish.

Unlike MT human evaluation results, we found WEAKBASELINE to be worse compared to HW-TSC-Constrained even for English-German. In a similar manner, we find that compared to the rankings from MT evaluation, HW-TSCsystems are ranked either higher or on par to APV-Unconstrained and NUV-Constrained. To better understand these differences in the ranking, we computed the Smoothness metric (Federico et al., 2020a) that measures TTS speaking rate stability across contiguous sentences (or phrases) and also consider the LC metric. Note that degraded LC implies that we have either too high or too low speaking rates for the dubbed speech, i.e., LC directly impacts speech fluency (Federico et al., 2020a). Table 39 shows these metrics with systems in a similar order as their ranking. We find that WEAKBASELINE, APV-Unconstrained and NUV-Constrained generally have either a much lower Smoothness or a much lower LC compared to the other systems. This results in poor speaking rate control and impacts % Wins resulting in a different ranking from MT evaluation. The main takeaway is that MT evaluations do not show a complete picture for the downstream task of dubbing as we need not only high quality translations but also translations that permit good speaking rate control.

Acknowledgements

We would like to thank the IWSLT 2022 sponsors and donors Apple, AppTek, AWS, Meta, Microsoft, and Zoom for supporting the human evaluation of the shared tasks and student participants with computing credits. We would like to thank Mary Johnson, Tom Kocmi and Hitokazu Matsushita for their help with conducting parts of the human evaluation and providing useful comments. We are grateful to the many annotators who participated in the human evaluation and provided their feedback. We would like to thank Zhaoheng Ni, Jeff Hwang and the torchaudio team for providing a streaming ASR model for the simultaneous task. We would like to thank Justine Kao and Brian Bui for running the human evaluation for the speech-to-speech task. The creation of the reference interpretations was funded from the EU project H2020-ICT-2018-2-825460 (ELITR). Ondřej Bojar would like to acknowledge the grant 19-26934X (NEUREM3) of the Czech Science Foundation.

References

Farhad Akhbardeh, Arkady Arkhangorodsky, Magdalena Biesialska, Ondřej Bojar, Rajen Chatterjee, Vishrav Chaudhary, Marta R. Costa-jussa, Cristina España-Bonet, Angela Fan, Christian Federmann, Markus Freitag, Yvette Graham, Roman Grundkiewicz, Barry Haddow, Leonie Harter, Kenneth Heafield, Christopher Homan, Matthias Huck, Kwabena Amponsah-Kaakyire, Jungo Kasai, Daniel Khashabi, Kevin Knight, Tom Kocmi, Philipp Koehn, Nicholas Lourie, Christof Monz, Makoto Morishita, Masaaki Nagata, Ajay Nagesh, Toshiaki Nakazawa, Matteo Negri, Santanu Pal, Allahsera Auguste Tapo, Marco Turchi, Valentin Vydrin, and Marcos Zampieri. 2021. Findings of the 2021 conference on machine translation (WMT21). In *Proceedings of the Sixth Conference on Machine Translation*, pages 1–88, Online. Association for Computational Linguistics.

Yasuhiro Akiba, Marcello Federico, Noriko Kando, Hiromi Nakaiwa, Michael Paul, and Jun'ichi Tsujii. 2004. Overview of the IWSLT04 Evaluation Campaign. In *Proceedings of the International Workshop on Spoken Language Translation*, pages 1–12, Kyoto, Japan.

Antonios Anastasopoulos, Ondřej Bojar, Jacob Bremerman, Roldano Cattoni, Maha Elbayad, Marcello Federico, Xutai Ma, Satoshi Nakamura, Matteo Negri, Jan Niehues, Juan Pino, Elizabeth Salesky, Sebastian Stüker, Katsuhito Sudoh, Marco Turchi, Alexander Waibel, Changhan Wang, and Matthew Wiesner. 2021. FINDINGS OF THE IWSLT 2021 EVALUATION CAMPAIGN. In *Proceedings of the 18th International Conference on Spoken Language Translation (IWSLT 2021)*, pages 1–29, Bangkok, Thailand (online). Association for Computational Linguistics.

Ebrahim Ansari, Amittai Axelrod, Nguyen Bach, Ondrej Bojar, Roldano Cattoni, Fahim Dalvi, Nadir Durrani, Marcello Federico, Christian Federmann, Jiatao Gu, Fei Huang, Kevin Knight, Xutai Ma, Ajay Nagesh, Matteo Negri, Jan Niehues, Juan Pino, Elizabeth Salesky, Xing Shi, Sebastian Stüker, Marco Turchi, and Changhan Wang. 2020. Findings of the IWSLT 2020 Evaluation Campaign. In *Proceedings of the 17th International Conference on Spoken Language Translation (IWSLT 2020)*, Seattle, USA.

Rosana Ardila, Megan Branson, Kelly Davis, Michael Henretty, Michael Kohler, Josh Meyer, Reuben Morais, Lindsay Saunders, Francis M. Tyers, and Gregor Weber. 2020. Common voice: A massively-multilingual speech corpus. In *LREC*.

Arun Babu, Changhan Wang, Andros Tjandra, Kushal Lakhotia, Qiantong Xu, Naman Goyal, Kritika Singh, Patrick von Platen, Yatharth Saraf, Juan Pino, et al. 2021. XLS-R: Self-supervised cross-lingual speech representation learning at scale. *arXiv preprint arXiv:2111.09296*.

Alexei Baevski, Yuhao Zhou, Abdelrahman Mohamed, and Michael Auli. 2020a. wav2vec 2.0: A framework for self-supervised learning of speech representations. *Advances in Neural Information Processing Systems*, 33:12449–12460.

Alexei Baevski, Yuhao Zhou, Abdelrahman Mohamed, and Michael Auli. 2020b. wav2vec 2.0: A framework for self-supervised learning of speech representations. In *Advances in Neural Information Processing Systems*, volume 33, pages 12449–12460. Curran Associates, Inc.

BBC. 2019. BBC Subtitle Guidelines. BBC © 2018 Version 1.1.8.

Benjamin Beilharz and Xin Sun. 2019. LibriVoxDeEn - A Corpus for German-to-English Speech Translation and Speech Recognition.

Luisa Bentivogli, Mauro Cettolo, Marco Gaido, Alina Karakanta, Alberto Martinelli, and Marco Turchi Matteo Negri. 2021. Cascade versus Direct Speech Translation: Do the Differences Still Make a Difference? In *Proceedings of the 59th Annual Meeting of the Association for Computational Linguistics*, Bangkok, Thailand. Association for Computational Linguistics.

Aakash Bhatnagar, Nidhir Bhavsar, Muskaan Singh, and Petr Motlicek. 2022. Hierarchical Multi-task learning framework for Isometric-Speech Language Translation. In *Proceedings of the 19th International Conference on Spoken Language Translation (IWSLT)*.

Marcely Zanon Boito, Fethi Bougares, Florentin Barbier, Souhir Gahbiche, Loïc Barrault, Mickael Rouvier, and Yannick Estéve. 2022a. Speech resources in the tamasheq language. *Language Resources and Evaluation Conference (LREC)*.

Marcely Zanon Boito, John Ortega, Hugo Riguidel, Antoine Laurent, Loïc Barrault, Fethi Bougares, Firas Chaabani, Ha Nguyen, Florentin Barbier, Souhir Gahbiche, and Yannick Estève. 2022b. ON-TRAC Consortium Systems for the IWSLT 2022 Dialect and Low-resource Speech Translation Tasks. In *Proceedings of the 19th International Conference on Spoken Language Translation (IWSLT)*.

Roldano Cattoni, Mattia Antonino Di Gangi, Luisa Bentivogli, Matteo Negri, and Marco Turchi. 2021. Must-c: A multilingual corpus for end-to-end speech translation. *Computer Speech & Language*, 66:101155.

Mauro Cettolo, Marcello Federico, Luisa Bentivogli, Jan Niehues, Sebastian Stüker, K. Sudoh, K. Yoshino, and Christian Federmann. 2017. Overview of the IWSLT 2017 Evaluation Campaign. In *Proceedings of the 14th International Workshop on Spoken Language Translation (IWSLT 2017)*, pages 2–14, Tokyo, Japan.

Mauro Cettolo, Christian Girardi, and Marcello Federico. 2012. WIT^3: Web Inventory of Transcribed and Translated Talks. In *Proceedings of the Annual Conference of the European Association for Machine Translation (EAMT)*, Trento, Italy.

Mauro Cettolo, Jan Niehues, Sebastian Stüker, Luisa Bentivogli, Roldano Cattoni, and Marcello Federico. 2015. The IWSLT 2015 Evaluation Campaign. In *Proceedings of the 12th International Workshop on Spoken Language Translation (IWSLT 2015)*, Da Nang, Vietnam.

Mauro Cettolo, Jan Niehues, Sebastian Stüker, Luisa Bentivogli, and Marcello Federico. 2013. Report on the 10th IWSLT Evaluation Campaign. In *Proceedings of the Tenth International Workshop on Spoken Language Translation (IWSLT 2013)*, Heidelberg, Germany.

Mauro Cettolo, Jan Niehues, Sebastian Stüker, Luisa Bentivogli, and Marcello Federico. 2014. Report on the 11th IWSLT Evaluation Campaign, IWSLT 2014. In *Proceedings of the Eleventh International Workshop on Spoken Language Translation (IWSLT 2014)*, Lake Tahoe, USA.

Mauro Cettolo, Jan Niehues, Sebastian Stüker, Luisa Bentivogli, and Marcello Federico. 2016. The IWSLT 2016 Evaluation Campaign. In *Proceedings of the 13th International Workshop on Spoken Language Translation (IWSLT 2016)*, Seattle, USA.

Colin Cherry and George Foster. 2019. Thinking slow about latency evaluation for simultaneous machine translation. *arXiv preprint arXiv:1906.00048*.

Joon Son Chung, Arsha Nagrani, and Andrew Zisserman. 2018. VoxCeleb2: Deep Speaker Recognition. In *Interspeech*, pages 1086–1090.

Alexis Conneau, Alexei Baevski, Ronan Collobert, Abdelrahman Mohamed, and Michael Auli. 2021. Unsupervised Cross-Lingual Representation Learning for Speech Recognition. In *Proc. Interspeech 2021*, pages 2426–2430.

Alexis Conneau, Kartikay Khandelwal, Naman Goyal, Vishrav Chaudhary, Guillaume Wenzek, Francisco Guzmán, Edouard Grave, Myle Ott, Luke Zettlemoyer, and Veselin Stoyanov. 2020. Unsupervised cross-lingual representation learning at scale. In *Proceedings of the 58th Annual Meeting of the Association for Computational Linguistics*, pages 8440–8451, Online. Association for Computational Linguistics.

Siddharth Dalmia, Brian Yan, Vikas Raunak, Florian Metze, and Shinji Watanabe. 2021. Searchable hidden intermediates for end-to-end models of decomposable sequence tasks. In *Proceedings of the 2021 Conference of the North American Chapter of the Association for Computational Linguistics: Human Language Technologies*, pages 1882–1896, Online. Association for Computational Linguistics.

Mattia A. Di Gangi, Roldano Cattoni, Luisa Bentivogli, Matteo Negri, and Marco Turchi. 2019. MuST-C: a Multilingual Speech Translation Corpus. In *Proceedings of the 2019 Conference of the North American Chapter of the Association for Computational Linguistics: Human Language Technologies, Volume 1 (Long and Short Papers)*, pages 2012–2017, Minneapolis, Minnesota.

Matthias Eck and Chiori Hori. 2005. Overview of the IWSLT 2005 evaluation campaign. In *Proceedings of the International Workshop on Spoken Language Translation*, pages 1–22, Pittsburgh, PA.

Johanes Effendi, Yogesh Virkar, Roberto Barra-Chicote, and Marcello Federico. 2022. Duration modeling of neural tts for automatic dubbing. In *ICASSP 2022 - 2022 IEEE International Conference on Acoustics, Speech and Signal Processing (ICASSP)*, pages 8037–8041.

Solène Evain, Ha Nguyen, Hang Le, Marcely Zanon Boito, Salima Mdhaffar, Sina Alisamir, Ziyi Tong, Natalia Tomashenko, Marco Dinarelli, Titouan Parcollet, et al. 2021. Task agnostic and task specific self-supervised learning from speech with *LeBenchmark*. In *Thirty-fifth Conference on Neural Information Processing Systems Datasets and Benchmarks Track (Round 2)*.

Angela Fan, Shruti Bhosale, Holger Schwenk, Zhiyi Ma, Ahmed El-Kishky, Siddharth Goyal, Mandeep Baines, Onur Celebi, Guillaume Wenzek, Vishrav Chaudhary, et al. 2021. Beyond english-centric multilingual machine translation. *Journal of Machine Learning Research*, 22(107):1–48.

M. Federico, Y. Virkar, R. Enyedi, and R. Barra-Chicote. 2020a. Evaluating and optimizing prosodic alignment for automatic dubbing. In *Proceedings of Interspeech*, page 5.

Marcello Federico, Luisa Bentivogli, Michael Paul, and Sebastian Stüker. 2011. Overview of the IWSLT 2011 Evaluation Campaign. In *Proceedings of the International Workshop on Spoken Language Translation*, pages 11–27, San Francisco, USA.

Marcello Federico, Mauro Cettolo, Luisa Bentivogli, Michael Paul, and Sebastian Stüker. 2012. Overview of the IWSLT 2012 Evaluation Campaign. In *Proceedings of the International Workshop on Spoken Language Translation*, pages 11–27, Hong Kong, HK.

Marcello Federico, Robert Enyedi, Roberto Barra-Chicote, Ritwik Giri, Umut Isik, Arvindh Krishnaswamy, and Hassan Sawaf. 2020b. From Speech-to-Speech Translation to Automatic Dubbing. In *Proc. of IWSLT*, pages 257–264, Online. ACL.

Christian Federmann. 2018. Appraise evaluation framework for machine translation. In *Proceedings of the 27th International Conference on Computational Linguistics: System Demonstrations*, pages 86–88, Santa Fe, New Mexico. Association for Computational Linguistics.

Weston Feely, Eva Hasler, and Adrià de Gispert. 2019. Controlling Japanese honorifics in English-to-Japanese neural machine translation. In *Proceedings of the 6th Workshop on Asian Translation*, pages 45–53, Hong Kong, China. Association for Computational Linguistics.

Cameron Shaw Fordyce. 2007. Overview of the IWSLT 2007 evaluation campaign. In *Proceedings of the International Workshop on Spoken Language Translation*, pages 1–12, Trento, Italy.

Markus Freitag, George Foster, David Grangier, Viresh Ratnakar, Qijun Tan, and Wolfgang Macherey. 2021a. Experts, errors, and context: A large-scale study of human evaluation for machine translation. *Transactions of the Association for Computational Linguistics*, 9:1460–1474.

Markus Freitag, Ricardo Rei, Nitika Mathur, Chi-kiu Lo, Craig Stewart, George Foster, Alon Lavie, and Ondřej Bojar. 2021b. Results of the WMT21 metrics shared task: Evaluating metrics with expert-based human evaluations on TED and news domain. In *Proceedings of the Sixth Conference on Machine Translation*, pages 733–774, Online. Association for Computational Linguistics.

Ryo Fukuda, Yuka Ko, Yasumasa Kano, Kosuke Doi, Hirotaka Tokuyama, Sakriani Sakti, Katsuhito Sudoh, and Satoshi Nakamura. 2022. NAIST Simultaneous Speech-to-Text Translation System for IWSLT 2022. In *Proceedings of the 19th International Conference on Spoken Language Translation (IWSLT)*.

Marco Gaido, Sara Papi, Dennis Fucci, Giuseppe Fiameni, Matteo Negri, and Marco Turchi. 2022. Efficient yet Competitive Speech Translation: FBK@IWSLT2022. In *Proceedings of the 19th International Conference on Spoken Language Translation (IWSLT)*.

Karthik Gopalakrishnan, Behnam Hedayatnia, Qinlang Chen, Anna Gottardi, Sanjeev Kwatra, Anu Venkatesh, Raefer Gabriel, and Dilek Hakkani-Tür. 2019. Topical-Chat: Towards knowledge-grounded open-domain conversations. In *Proc. Interspeech 2019*, pages 1891–1895.

Yvette Graham, Timothy Baldwin, Alistair Moffat, and Justin Zobel. 2013. Continuous measurement scales in human evaluation of machine translation. In *Proceedings of the 7th Linguistic Annotation Workshop and Interoperability with Discourse*, pages 33–41, Sofia, Bulgaria. Association for Computational Linguistics.

Anmol Gulati, James Qin, Chung-Cheng Chiu, Niki Parmar, Yu Zhang, Jiahui Yu, Wei Han, Shibo Wang, Zhengdong Zhang, Yonghui Wu, and Ruoming Pang. 2020. Conformer: Convolution-augmented transformer for speech recognition. In *Proceedings of Interspeech 2020, 21st Annual Conference of the International Speech Communication Association*, pages 5036—-5040, Shanghai, China.

Bao Guo, Mengge Liu, Wen Zhang, Hexuan Chen, Chang Mu, Xiang Li, Jianwei Cui, Bin Wang, and Yuhang Guo. 2022a. The Xiaomi Text-to-Text Simultaneous Speech Translation System for IWSLT 2022. In *Proceedings of the 19th International Conference on Spoken Language Translation (IWSLT)*.

Jiaxin Guo, Yinglu Li, Minghan Wang, Xiaosong Qiao, Yuxia Wang, Hengchao Shang, Chang Su, Yimeng Chen, Min Zhang, Shimin Tao, Hao Yang, and Ying Qin. 2022b. The HW-TSC's Speech to Speech Translation System for IWSLT 2022 Evaluation. In *Proceedings of the 19th International Conference on Spoken Language Translation (IWSLT)*.

Andrew Hayes and Klaus Krippendorff. 2007. Answering the call for a standard reliability measure for coding data. *Communication Methods and Measures*, 1:77–89.

Kaiming He, Xiangyu Zhang, Shaoqing Ren, and Jian Sun. 2016. Deep residual learning for image recognition. In *2016 IEEE Conference on Computer Vision and Pattern Recognition (CVPR)*, pages 770–778.

François Hernandez, Vincent Nguyen, Sahar Ghannay, Natalia A. Tomashenko, and Yannick Estève. 2018. TED-LIUM 3: twice as much data and corpus repartition for experiments on speaker adaptation. *CoRR*, abs/1805.04699.

Oleksii Hrinchuk, Vahid Noroozi, Abhinav Khattar, Anton Peganov, Sandeep Subramanian, Somshubra Majumdar, and Oleksii Kuchaiev. 2022. NVIDIA NeMo Offline Speech Translation Systems for

IWSLT 2022. In *Proceedings of the 19th International Conference on Spoken Language Translation (IWSLT)*.

Javier Iranzo-Sánchez, Jorge Civera Saiz, and Alfons Juan. 2021. Stream-level latency evaluation for simultaneous machine translation. In *Findings of the Association for Computational Linguistics: EMNLP 2021*, pages 664–670, Punta Cana, Dominican Republic. Association for Computational Linguistics.

Javier Iranzo-Sánchez, Javier Jorge Cano, Alejandro Pérez-González de Martos, Adrián Giménez Pastor, Gonçal Garcés Díaz-Munío, Pau Baquero-Arnal, Joan Albert Silvestre-Cerdá, Jorge Civera Saiz, Albert Sanchis, and Alfons Juan. 2022. MLLP-VRAIN UPV systems for the IWSLT 2022 Simultaneous Speech Translation and Speech-to-Speech Translation tasks. In *Proceedings of the 19th International Conference on Spoken Language Translation (IWSLT)*.

Javier Iranzo-Sánchez, Joan Albert Silvestre-Cerdà, Javier Jorge, Nahuel Roselló, Adrià Giménez, Albert Sanchis, Jorge Civera, and Alfons Juan. 2020. Europarl-st: A multilingual corpus for speech translation of parliamentary debates. In *Proc. of 45th Intl. Conf. on Acoustics, Speech, and Signal Processing (ICASSP 2020)*, pages 8229–8233, Barcelona (Spain).

Won Jang, Dan Lim, Jaesam Yoon, Bongwan Kim, and Juntae Kim. 2021. UnivNet: A Neural Vocoder with Multi-Resolution Spectrogram Discriminators for High-Fidelity Waveform Generation. In *Interspeech*, pages 2207–2211.

Dávid Javorský, Dominik Macháček, and Ondřej Bojar. 2022. Comprehension of subtitles from re-translating simultaneous speech translation.

Japan Translation Federation JTF. 2018. JTF Translation Quality Evaluation Guidelines, 1st Edition (in Japanese).

Jaehyeon Kim, Jungil Kong, and Juhee Son. 2021. Conditional variational autoencoder with adversarial learning for end-to-end text-to-speech. In *ICML*.

Ali Can Kocabiyikoglu, Laurent Besacier, and Olivier Kraif. 2018. Augmenting Librispeech with French Translations: A Multimodal Corpus for Direct Speech Translation Evaluation. In *Proceedings of LREC 2018*, Miyazaki, Japan.

Philipp Koehn. 2004. Statistical significance tests for machine translation evaluation. In *Proceedings of the 2004 conference on empirical methods in natural language processing*, pages 388–395.

Surafel Lakew, Marcello Federico, Yue Wang, Cuong Hoang, Yogesh Virkar, Roberto Barra-Chicote, and Robert Enyedi. 2021a. Machine translation verbosity control for automatic dubbing. In *IEEE International Conference on Acoustics, Speech and Signal Processing (ICASSP)*.

Surafel M Lakew, Yogesh Virkar, Prashant Mathur, and Marcello Federico. 2021b. Isometric mt: Neural machine translation for automatic dubbing. *arXiv preprint arXiv:2112.08682*.

Surafel Melaku Lakew, Mattia Di Gangi, and Marcello Federico. 2019. Controlling the output length of neural machine translation. In *Proc. IWSLT*.

Yinglu Li, Minghan Wang, Jiaxin Guo, Xiaosong Qiao, Yuxia Wang, Daimeng Wei, Chang Su, Yimeng Chen, Min Zhang, Shimin Tao, Hao Yang, and Ying Qin. 2022a. The HW-TSC's Offline Speech Translation System for IWSLT 2022 Evaluation. In *Proceedings of the 19th International Conference on Spoken Language Translation (IWSLT)*.

Zongyao Li, JiaXin Guo, Daimeng Wei, Hengchao Shang, Minghan Wang, Ting Zhu, Zhanglin Wu, Zhengzhe Yu, Xiaoyu Chen, Lizhi Lei, Hao Yang, and Ying Qin. 2022b. HW-TSC's Participation in the IWSLT 2022 Isometric Spoken Language Translation. In *Proceedings of the 19th International Conference on Spoken Language Translation (IWSLT)*.

Pierre Lison, Jörg Tiedemann, and Milen Kouylekov. 2018. OpenSubtitles2018: Statistical rescoring of sentence alignments in large, noisy parallel corpora. In *Proceedings of the Eleventh International Conference on Language Resources and Evaluation (LREC 2018)*, Miyazaki, Japan. European Language Resources Association (ELRA).

Dan Liu, Mengge Du, Xiaoxi Li, Ya Li, and Enhong Chen. 2021. Cross attention augmented transducer networks for simultaneous translation. In *Proceedings of the 2021 Conference on Empirical Methods in Natural Language Processing*, pages 39–55, Online and Punta Cana, Dominican Republic. Association for Computational Linguistics.

Yinhan Liu, Jiatao Gu, Naman Goyal, Xian Li, Sergey Edunov, Marjan Ghazvininejad, Mike Lewis, and Luke Zettlemoyer. 2020. Multilingual denoising pre-training for neural machine translation. *Transactions of the Association for Computational Linguistics*, 8:726–742.

Shuming Ma, Li Dong, Shaohan Huang, Dongdong Zhang, Alexandre Muzio, Saksham Singhal, Hany Hassan Awadalla, Xia Song, and Furu Wei. 2021. DeltaLM: Encoder-decoder pre-training for language generation and translation by augmenting pretrained multilingual encoders. *arXiv*.

Xutai Ma, Mohammad Javad Dousti, Changhan Wang, Jiatao Gu, and Juan Pino. 2020a. SIMULEVAL: An evaluation toolkit for simultaneous translation. In *Proceedings of the 2020 Conference on Empirical Methods in Natural Language Processing: System Demonstrations*, pages 144–150, Online. Association for Computational Linguistics.

Xutai Ma, Juan Pino, and Philipp Koehn. 2020b. SimulMT to SimulST: Adapting simultaneous text translation to end-to-end simultaneous speech translation. In *Proceedings of the 1st Conference of the Asia-Pacific Chapter of the Association for Computational Linguistics and the 10th International Joint Conference on Natural Language Processing*, pages 582–587, Suzhou, China. Association for Computational Linguistics.

Dominik Macháček, Jonáš Kratochvíl, Tereza Vojtěchová, and Ondřej Bojar. 2019. A speech test set of practice business presentations with additional relevant texts. In *Statistical Language and Speech Processing*, pages 151–161, Cham, Switzerland. Springer Nature Switzerland AG.

Evgeny Matusov, Patrick Wilken, and Yota Georgakopoulou. 2019. Customizing neural machine translation for subtitling. In *Proceedings of the Fourth Conference on Machine Translation (Volume 1: Research Papers)*, pages 82–93, Florence, Italy. Association for Computational Linguistics.

J. Niehues, R. Cattoni, S. Stüker, M. Negri, M. Turchi, T. Ha, E. Salesky, R. Sanabria, L. Barrault, L. Specia, and M. Federico. 2019. The IWSLT 2019 Evaluation Campaign. In *Proceedings of the 16th International Workshop on Spoken Language Translation (IWSLT 2019)*, Hong Kong, China.

Jan Niehues. 2020. Machine translation with unsupervised length-constraints. In *Proceedings of the 14th Conference of the Association for Machine Translation in the Americas (AMTA 2020)*, pages 21–35.

Jan Niehues, Roldano Cattoni, Sebastian Stüker, Mauro Cettolo, Marco Turchi, and Marcello Federico. 2018. The IWSLT 2018 Evaluation Campaign. In *Proceedings of the 15th International Workshop on Spoken Language Translation (IWSLT 2018)*, pages 2–6, Bruges, Belgium.

Xing Niu, Sudha Rao, and Marine Carpuat. 2018. Multi-task neural models for translating between styles within and across languages. In *Proceedings of the 27th International Conference on Computational Linguistics*, pages 1008–1021, Santa Fe, New Mexico, USA. Association for Computational Linguistics.

Maria Nădejde, Anna Currey, Benjamin Hsu, Xing Niu, Marcello Federico, and Georgiana Dinu. 2022. CoCoA-MT: A dataset and benchmark for Contrastive Controlled MT with application to formality. In *Findings of the Association for Computational Linguistics: NAACL 2022*, Seattle, USA. Association for Computational Linguistics.

Myle Ott, Sergey Edunov, Alexei Baevski, Angela Fan, Sam Gross, Nathan Ng, David Grangier, and Michael Auli. 2019. fairseq: A fast, extensible toolkit for sequence modeling. In *Proceedings of NAACL-HLT 2019: Demonstrations*.

Vassil Panayotov, Guoguo Chen, Daniel Povey, and Sanjeev Khudanpur. 2015. Librispeech: An asr corpus based on public domain audio books. *2015 IEEE International Conference on Acoustics, Speech and Signal Processing (ICASSP)*, pages 5206–5210.

Kishore Papineni, Salim Roukos, Todd Ward, and Wei-Jing Zhu. 2002. Bleu: a method for automatic evaluation of machine translation. In *Proceedings of the 40th annual meeting on association for computational linguistics*. Association for Computational Linguistics.

Kyubyong Park and Thomas Mulc. 2019. Css10: A collection of single speaker speech datasets for 10 languages. *Interspeech*.

Michael Paul. 2006. Overview of the IWSLT 2006 Evaluation Campaign. In *Proceedings of the International Workshop on Spoken Language Translation*, pages 1–15, Kyoto, Japan.

Michael Paul. 2008. Overview of the IWSLT 2008 Evaluation Campaign. In *Proceedings of the International Workshop on Spoken Language Translation*, pages 1–17, Waikiki, Hawaii.

Michael Paul. 2009. Overview of the IWSLT 2009 Evaluation Campaign. In *Proceedings of the International Workshop on Spoken Language Translation*, pages 1–18, Tokyo, Japan.

Michael Paul, Marcello Federico, and Sebastian Stüker. 2010. Overview of the IWSLT 2010 Evaluation Campaign. In *Proceedings of the International Workshop on Spoken Language Translation*, pages 3–27, Paris, France.

Ngoc-Quan Pham, Tuan Nam Nguyen, Thai-Binh Nguyen, Danni Liu, Carlos Mullov, Jan Niehues, and Alexander Waibel. 2022. Efficient yet Competitive Speech Translation: FBK@IWSLT2022. In *Proceedings of the 19th International Conference on Spoken Language Translation (IWSLT)*.

Peter Polák, Ngoc-Quan Pham, Tuan Nam Nguyen, Danni Liu, Carlos Mullov, Jan Niehues, Ondřej Bojar, and Alexander Waibel. 2022. System for Simultaneous Speech Translation Task at IWSLT 2022. In *Proceedings of the 19th International Conference on Spoken Language Translation (IWSLT)*.

Maja Popović. 2015. chrF: character n-gram F-score for automatic MT evaluation. In *Proceedings of the Tenth Workshop on Statistical Machine Translation*, pages 392–395, Lisbon, Portugal. Association for Computational Linguistics.

Matt Post. 2018. A call for clarity in reporting BLEU scores. In *Proceedings of the Third Conference on Machine Translation: Research Papers*, pages 186–191, Belgium, Brussels. Association for Computational Linguistics.

Colin Raffel, Noam Shazeer, Adam Roberts, Katherine Lee, Sharan Narang, Michael Matena, Yanqi Zhou, Wei Li, and Peter J. Liu. 2020. Exploring the limits of transfer learning with a unified text-to-text transformer. *Journal of Machine Learning Research*, 21(140):1–67.

Ricardo Rei, Craig Stewart, Ana C Farinha, and Alon Lavie. 2020. Comet: A neural framework for mt evaluation. *arXiv preprint arXiv:2009.09025*.

Elijah Rippeth, Sweta Agrawal, and Marine Carpuat. 2022. Controlling Translation Formality Using Pretrained Multilingual Language Models. In *Proceedings of the 19th International Conference on Spoken Language Translation (IWSLT)*.

Anthony Rousseau, Paul Deléglise, and Yannick Esteve. 2014. Enhancing the ted-lium corpus with selected data for language modeling and more ted talks. In *LREC*.

M. Rouvier, G. Dupuy, P. Gay, E. Khoury, T. Merlin, and S. Meignier. 2013. An Open-source State-of-the-art Toolbox for Broadcast News Diarization. In *Proceedings of the Interspeech*.

Ashutosh Saboo and Timo Baumann. 2019. Integration of Dubbing Constraints into Machine Translation. In *Proc. of WMT*, pages 94–101, Florence, Italy. ACL.

Elizabeth Salesky, Julian Mäder, and Severin Klinger. 2021. Assessing evaluation metrics for speech-to-speech translation. In *ASRU*.

Ramon Sanabria, Ozan Caglayan, Shruti Palaskar, Desmond Elliott, Loïc Barrault, Lucia Specia, and Florian Metze. 2018. How2: a large-scale dataset for multimodal language understanding. In *Proceedings of the Workshop on Visually Grounded Interaction and Language (ViGIL)*. NeurIPS.

Andrea Schioppa, David Vilar, Artem Sokolov, and Katja Filippova. 2021a. Controlling machine translation for multiple attributes with additive interventions. In *Proceedings of the 2021 Conference on Empirical Methods in Natural Language Processing*, pages 6676–6696, Online and Punta Cana, Dominican Republic. Association for Computational Linguistics.

Andrea Schioppa, David Vilar, Artem Sokolov, and Katja Filippova. 2021b. Controlling machine translation for multiple attributes with additive interventions. In *Proceedings of the 2021 Conference on Empirical Methods in Natural Language Processing*, pages 6676–6696.

Rico Sennrich, Barry Haddow, and Alexandra Birch. 2016. Controlling politeness in neural machine translation via side constraints. In *Proceedings of the 2016 Conference of the North American Chapter of the Association for Computational Linguistics: Human Language Technologies*, pages 35–40, San Diego, California. Association for Computational Linguistics.

Akshaya Vishnu Kudlu Shanbhogue, Ran Xue, Ching-Yun Chang, and Sarah Campbell. 2022. Amazon Alexa AI's System for IWSLT 2022 Offline Speech Translation Shared Task. In *Proceedings of the 19th International Conference on Spoken Language Translation (IWSLT)*.

Gabriel Synnaeve, Qiantong Xu, Jacob Kahn, Edouard Grave, Tatiana Likhomanenko, Vineel Pratap, Anuroop Sriram, Vitaliy Liptchinsky, and Ronan Collobert. 2020. End-to-end asr: from supervised to semi-supervised learning with modern architectures. In *ICML*.

Sho Takase and Naoaki Okazaki. 2019. Positional Encoding to Control Output Sequence Length. *Proc. of NAACL*.

Yuqing Tang, Chau Tran, Xian Li, Peng-Jen Chen, Naman Goyal, Vishrav Chaudhary, Jiatao Gu, and Angela Fan. 2020. Multilingual translation with extensible multilingual pretraining and finetuning.

Amirhossein Tebbifakhr, Ruchit Agrawal, Matteo Negri, and Marco Turchi. 2018. Multi-source transformer with combined losses for automatic post editing. In *Proceedings of the Third Conference on Machine Translation: Shared Task Papers*, pages 846–852.

Jörg Tiedemann, Santhosh Thottingal, et al. 2020. Opus-mt–building open translation services for the world. In *Proceedings of the 22nd Annual Conference of the European Association for Machine Translation*. European Association for Machine Translation.

Ioannis Tsiamas, Gerard I. Gállego, Carlos Escolano, José A. R. Fonollosa, and Marta R. Costa-jussà. 2022a. Pretrained Speech Encoders and Efficient Fine-tuning Methods for Speech Translation: UPC at IWSLT 2022. In *Proceedings of the 19th International Conference on Spoken Language Translation (IWSLT)*.

Ioannis Tsiamas, Gerard I. Gállego, José A. R. Fonollosa, and Marta R. Costa-jussà. 2022b. Shas: Approaching optimal segmentation for end-to-end speech translation.

Ashish Vaswani, Noam Shazeer, Niki Parmar, Jakob Uszkoreit, Llion Jones, Aidan N Gomez, Łukasz Kaiser, and Illia Polosukhin. 2017. Attention is All You Need. In *Proceedings of NIPS 2017*.

Sebastian Vincent, Loïc Barrault, and Carolina Scarton. 2022. Controlling Formality in Low-Resource NMT with Domain Adaptation and Re-Ranking: SLT-CDT-UoS at IWSLT2022. In *Proceedings of the 19th International Conference on Spoken Language Translation (IWSLT)*.

Yogesh Virkar, Marcello Federico, Robert Enyedi, and Roberto Barra-Chicote. 2021. Improvements to Prosodic Alignment for Automatic Dubbing. In

ICASSP 2021 - 2021 IEEE International Conference on Acoustics, Speech and Signal Processing (ICASSP), pages 7543–7574. ISSN: 2379-190X.

Yogesh Virkar, Marcello Federico, Robert Enyedi, and Barra-Chicote Roberto. 2022. Prosodic alignment for off-screen automatic dubbing. *arXiv preprint arXiv:2204.02530*.

Aditi Viswanathan, Varden Wang, and Antonina Kononova. 2019. Controlling formality and style of machine translation output using AutoML. In *SIMBig*, volume 1070 of *Communications in Computer and Information Science*, pages 306–313. Springer.

Changhan Wang, Juan Pino, Anne Wu, and Jiatao Gu. 2020a. Covost: A diverse multilingual speech-to-text translation corpus. In *Proceedings of The 12th Language Resources and Evaluation Conference*, pages 4197–4203.

Changhan Wang, Morgane Riviere, Ann Lee, Anne Wu, Chaitanya Talnikar, Daniel Haziza, Mary Williamson, Juan Pino, and Emmanuel Dupoux. 2021. VoxPopuli: A large-scale multilingual speech corpus for representation learning, semi-supervised learning and interpretation. In *Proceedings of the 59th Annual Meeting of the Association for Computational Linguistics and the 11th International Joint Conference on Natural Language Processing (Volume 1: Long Papers)*, pages 993–1003, Online. Association for Computational Linguistics.

Changhan Wang, Yun Tang, Xutai Ma, Anne Wu, Dmytro Okhonko, and Juan Pino. 2020b. fairseq s2t: Fast speech-to-text modeling with fairseq. *arXiv preprint arXiv:2010.05171*.

Minghan Wang, Jiaxin GUO, Yinglu Li, Xiaosong Qiao, Yuxia Wang, Zongyao Li, Chang Su, Yimeng Chen, Min Zhang, Shimin Tao amd Hao Yang, and Ying Qin. 2022. The HW-TSC's Simultaneous Speech Translation System for IWSLT 2022 Evaluation. In *Proceedings of the 19th International Conference on Spoken Language Translation (IWSLT)*.

Patrick Wilken and Evgeny Matusov. 2022. AppTek's Submission to the IWSLT 2022 Isometric Spoken Language Translation Task. In *Proceedings of the 19th International Conference on Spoken Language Translation (IWSLT)*.

Lijun Wu, Juntao Li, Yue Wang, Qi Meng, Tao Qin, Wei Chen, Min Zhang, Tie-Yan Liu, et al. 2021. R-drop: regularized dropout for neural networks. *Advances in Neural Information Processing Systems*, 34.

Linting Xue, Noah Constant, Adam Roberts, Mihir Kale, Rami Al-Rfou, Aditya Siddhant, Aditya Barua, and Colin Raffel. 2020. mt5: A massively multilingual pre-trained text-to-text transformer. *arXiv preprint arXiv:2010.11934*.

Brian Yan, Patrick Fernandes, Siddharth Dalmia, Jiatong Shi, Yifan Peng, Dan Berrebbi, Xinyi Wang, Graham Neubig, and Shinji Watanabe. 2022. CMU's IWSLT 2022 Dialect Speech Translation System. In *Proceedings of the 19th International Conference on Spoken Language Translation (IWSLT)*.

Jinyi Yang, Amir Hussein, Matthew Wiesner, and Sanjeev Khudanpur. 2022. JHU IWSLT 2022 Dialect Speech Translation System Description. In *Proceedings of the 19th International Conference on Spoken Language Translation (IWSLT)*.

Yinfei Yang, Yuan Zhang, Chris Tar, and Jason Baldridge. 2019. Paws-x: A cross-lingual adversarial dataset for paraphrase identification. *arXiv preprint arXiv:1908.11828*.

Lei Yu, Laurent Sartran, Wojciech Stokowiec, Wang Ling, Lingpeng Kong, Phil Blunsom, and Chris Dyer. 2020. Better document-level machine translation with bayes' rule. *Transactions of the Association for Computational Linguistics*, 8(0):346–360.

Daniel Zhang, Jiang Yu, Pragati Verma, Ashwinkumar Ganesan, and Sarah Campbell. 2022a. Improving Machine Translation Formality Control with Weakly-Labelled Data Augmentation and Post Editing Strategies. In *Proceedings of the 19th International Conference on Spoken Language Translation (IWSLT)*.

Tianyi Zhang, Varsha Kishore, Felix Wu, Kilian Q Weinberger, and Yoav Artzi. 2019. Bertscore: Evaluating text generation with bert. *arXiv preprint arXiv:1904.09675*.

Weitai Zhang, Zhongyi Ye, Haitao Tang, Xiaoxi Li, Xinyuan Zhou, Jing Yang, Jianwei Cui, Dan Liu, Junhua Liu, and Lirong Dai. 2022b. The USTC-NELSLIP Offline Speech Translation Systems for IWSLT 2022. In *Proceedings of the 19th International Conference on Spoken Language Translation (IWSLT)*.

Yuhao Zhang, Canan Huang, Chen Xu, Xiaoqian Liu, Bei Li, Anxiang Ma, Tong Xiao, and Jingbo Zhu. 2022c. The NiuTrans's Submission to the IWSLT22 English-to-Chinese Offline Speech Translation Task. In *Proceedings of the 19th International Conference on Spoken Language Translation (IWSLT)*.

Ziqiang Zhang and Junyi Ao. 2022. The YiTrans Neural Speech Translation Systems for IWSLT 2022 Offline Shared Task. In *Proceedings of the 19th International Conference on Spoken Language Translation (IWSLT)*.

Qinpei Zhu, Renshou Wu, Guangfeng Liu, Xinyu Zhu, Xingyu Chen, Yang Zhou, Qingliang Miao, Rui Wang, and Kai Yu. 2022. The AISP-SJTU Simultaneous Translation System for IWSLT 2022. In *Proceedings of the 19th International Conference on Spoken Language Translation (IWSLT)*.

Appendix A. Human Evaluation

A Human Evaluation

Human evaluation was carried out for the following tasks: *(i)* Simultaneous Speech Translation, *(ii)* Offline speech translation, *(iii)* Speech to speech translation, *(iv)* Dialect speech translation, *(v)* Isometric SLT, and *(vi)* Formality control for SLT.

Different evaluation protocols were adopted, which are described in the following sections.

A.1 Simultaneous Speech Translation Task

Simultaneous Speech Translation Task ran two different types of manual evaluation: "continuous rating" for English-to-German and MQM for English-to-Japanese.

A.1.1 Human Evaluation for the English-to-German Simultaneous Task

Manual evaluation of English-to-German Simultaneous Task uses a variant of "continuous rating" as described by Javorský et al. (2022).

During the evaluation, bilingual annotators were presented with the source audio and subtitles. The subtitles were displayed in two lines below the audio following the guidelines for video subtitling (BBC, 2019). The annotators were asked to score the quality of the live-presented text output while listening to the input sound. Specifically, the instructions explicitly asked to focus on *content preservation*, or roughly the *adequacy*:

- We ask you to provide your assessment using so-called "continuous rating", which *continuously indicates the quality of the text output given the input utterance you hear* in the range from 1 (the worst) to 4 (the best) by clicking the corresponding buttons or pressing the corresponding keys.

- The rate of clicking/pressing depends on you. However, we suggest clicking *each 5-10 seconds* or when your assessment has changed. We encourage you to provide feedback *as often as possible* even if your assessment has *not changed.*

- The quality scale should reflect primarily the meaning preservation (i.e. evaluating primarily the "content" or very approximately the "adequacy") and the grammaticality and other qualitative aspects like punctuation (i.e. the "form" or extremely roughly the "fluency") should be the secondary criterion.

Context-Aware Judgements One important aspect of the evaluation is that the systems are run independently for each input segment while continuous rating is designed for following the whole speech. Our continuous rating can be thus seen a variant of document-level measure, although the context is (on purpose) available only from the history and not from the future.

When preparing the subtitles from system outputs, we concatenate all sentences into one continuous stream of words.

Time Shift for Better Simultaneity To ease the memory overload of the evaluators, we reduced the delay by shifting the subtitles ahead in time. The shift was done differently for the systems and for the interpretation:

- **Systems**: Each translated sentence was shifted such that its first word was emitted immediately as the source sentence audio began. If there were some words from previous sentence that have not been displayed yet, the emission of the words from the next sentence was delayed. These words were displayed right after all the last word of the previous sentence.

- **Interpreting**: Since we did not have the sentence alignment, we shifted the whole interpretation by a constant such that the last word was emitted with the end of the last uttered word in the source speech. This shift constant was chosen empirically.

Two Test Sets: Common and Non-Native There were two test sets used for the human evaluation: the common test set (consisting of the TED talks used in the Offline Speech Translation task and serving also in the automatic evaluation of Simultaneous Translation task); and a non-native test set. The non-native test set was already used in IWSLT Non-Native Translation Task in 2020 and it is described in Ansari et al. (2020) Appendix A.6. Specifically, we used the Antrecorp (Macháček et al., 2019; mock business presentations by high-school students) and the auditing presentations (SAO) parts.

We show the size of the corpus, as well as the amount of annotation collected in Table 17.

Processing of Collected Rankings Once the results are collected, they are processed as follows. We first inspect the timestamps on the ratings, and remove any that are more than 20 seconds greater than the length of the audio. Because of the natural delay (even with the time-shift) and because the collection process is subject to network and computational constraints, there can be ratings that are timestamped greater than the audio length. If the difference is however too high, we judge it to be an annotation error. We also remove any annotated audio where there is fewer than one rating per 20 seconds, since the annotators were instructed to annotate every 5-10 seconds.

Obtaining Final Scores To calculate a score for each system, we average the ratings across each annotated audio, then average across all the annotated audios pertaining to each system-latency combination. This type of averaging renders all input speeches equally important and it is not affected by the speech length.

The results are shown in Table 18. We observe that, overall, the systems do worse on the non-native audios than they do on the common portion of the test set, whereas the human interpreter performs similarly on both portions.

Indeed some of the high latency systems are rated slightly higher (on average) than the human interpreter on the common portion.

There is a clear effect of latency in almost all systems, with the low-latency subtitles generally rated poorer than the high-latency subtitles by our annotators. This effect is strong in some systems (e.g. FBK) but weaker in others (e.g. NAIST).

A.1.2 MQM-based Human Evaluation for English-to-Japanese Simultaneous Task

For the English-to-Japanese Simultaneous Translation Task, we conducted a human evaluation using a variant of Multidimensional Quality Metrics (MQM). MQM has been used in recent MT evaluation studies (Freitag et al., 2021a) and WMT Metrics shared task (Freitag et al., 2021b). For the evaluation of Japanese translations, we used *JTF Translation Quality Evaluation Guidelines* (JTF, 2018), distributed by Japan Translation Federation (JTF). The guidelines are based on MQM but include some modifications in consideration of the property of the Japanese language.

We hired a Japanese-native professional translator as the evaluator. The evaluator checked translation hypotheses along with their source speech transcripts and chose the corresponding error category and severity for each translation hypothesis using a spreadsheet. Here, we asked the evaluator to focus only on *Accuracy* and *Fluency* errors, because other types of errors in Terminology, Style, and Locale convention would not be so serious in the evaluation of simultaneous translation. Finally, we calculated the cumulative error score for each system based on the error weighting presented by (Freitag et al., 2021a), where *Critical* and *Major* errors are not distinguished.

A.2 Direct Assessment for Offline Speech Translation Task

For the Offline Speech Translation Task (Section 3) we conducted a human evaluation campaign featuring the source-based direct assessment (DA) (Graham et al., 2013; Cettolo et al., 2017; Akhbardeh et al., 2021). In this setting, assessments were performed on a continuous scale between 0 and 100.

Annotation Process We collected segment-level annotations based on the automatic segmentation of the test data. Because we did not want issues from the segmentation to influence scores negatively, we provided translators not only with the source sentence and system translation, but also with the system translation of the previous and following segments. Annotators were then instructed as follows:

"Sentence boundary errors are expected and should not be factored in when judging translation quality. This is when the translation appears to be missing or adding extra words but the source was segmented at a different place. To this end, we have included the translations for the previous and next sentences also. If the source and translation are only different because of sentence boundary issues, do not let this affect your scoring judgement." No video or audio context was provided. Segments were shuffled and randomly assigned to annotators to avoid bias related to the presentation order. Annotations were conducted by a trusted vendor, with professional translators fluent in the source language and native in the target language. For English to German, we additionally collected annotations for the references, which received a considerably higher score than the best submitted system as expected (90.8 vs. 88.9).

Computing rankings System rankings are produced from the average DA scores computed from the average human assessment scores without and with standardization according to each individual annotator's mean and standard deviation, similarly to Akhbardeh et al. (2021). Clusters are identified by grouping together those systems which significantly outperform all others in lower ranking clusters, according to Wilcoxon rank-sum test $p < 0.05$. In Tables 23, 24, and 25 – which show the rankings – clusters are indicated by horizontal lines. Rank ranges giving an indication of the respective system's translation quality within a cluster are based on the same head-to-head statistical significance tests.

Official rankings and details on the evaluation campaign for the Offline Speech Translation Task are presented in Section 3.

A.3 Speech to speech translation task

Output speech translations were evaluated with respect to translation quality and speech quality.

- **Translation quality:** Bilingual annotators were presented with the source audio and the target audio, and gave scores on the translation quality between 1 and 5.
- **Output speech quality:** In addition to translation quality (capturing meaning), the quality of the speech output was also human-evaluated along three dimensions: naturalness (voice and pronunciation), clarity of speech (understandability), and sound quality (noise and other artifacts). These axes are more fine-grained than the traditional overall MOS score.

The detailed guidelines for output speech quality were as follows:

- **Naturalness:** Recordings that sound human-like, with natural-sounding pauses, stress, and intonation, should be given a high score. Recordings that sound robotic, flat, or otherwise unnatural should be given a low score.
- **Clarity of speech:** Recordings with clear speech and no mumbling and unclear phrases should be given a high score. Recordings with a large amount of mumbling and unclear phrases should be given a low score.
- **Sound quality:** Recordings with clean audio and no noise and static in the background should be given a high score. Recordings with a large amount of noise and static in the background should be given a low score.

A.4 Direct Assessment with Scalar Quality Metric for the Dialect and Isometric Speech Translation Tasks

For the Dialect Speech Translation Task (Section 6) and Isometric SLT Task (Section 8) we piloted a human evaluation campaign featuring the source-based direct assessment (DA) (Graham et al., 2013; Cettolo et al., 2017; Akhbardeh et al., 2021) with document context extended with Scalar Quality Metric (SQM) (Freitag et al., 2021a). In this setting, assessments were performed on a continuous scale between 0 and 100 as in traditional DA but with 0-6 markings on the analogue slider and annotator guidelines based on those proposed by Freitag et al. (2021a). SQM helped standardizing scores across annotators.

Tool We used the Appraise evaluation framework[52] (Federmann, 2018) for collecting segment-level judgements within document context. No video or audio context was provided. Annotation guidelines were adapted specifically for each task as described in Sections 6 and 8. Screenshots of an example annotation for the Dialect and Isometric Speech Translation Tasks are presented on Figures 5 and 6.

Task generation A single task consisted of 100 segments from around 10 documents. Human references were included as additional system output to provide an estimate of human performance. Each individual annotator completed between 4 and 8 tasks. Whenever possible, we assigned tasks to annotators making sure that one annotator evaluates outputs from all systems on the same subset of the test set. This increased repetitiveness, but potentially improved consistency of assessments across systems.

Annotation and quality control All annotators were either professional translators or linguists fluent in the source language and native in the target language or linguists, and the majority of them had previous experience in the evaluation of translation outputs.[53] Although our annotators were professionals, we employed a standard quality filtering procedure. Around 10% of segments in each task were quality control items in the form of bad reference pairs distributed usually across one or two documents. Please refer to (Akhbardeh et al., 2021) for more details on the generation of bad references. Assessments of an annotator who has not demonstrated ability to reliably score degraded translations significantly lower than corresponding original system outputs using a paired significance test with $p < 0.05$ would be omitted from the evaluation. As expected, none of our annotators appeared unreliable.

We have collected 47,834 assessments. This number already excludes documents with quality control items, which provides almost 2,000 annotations per system, including references.

Computing rankings System rankings are produced from the average DA scores computed from the average human assessment scores without and with standardization according to each individual annotator's mean and standard deviation, similarly to Akhbardeh et al. (2021). We exclude entire documents with one or more quality control items from ranking computation. Clusters are identified by grouping those systems together which significantly outperform all others in lower ranking clusters, according to Wilcoxon rank-sum test $p < 0.05$. In Tables 31 and 36 – which show the rankings – clusters are indicated by horizontal lines. Rank ranges giving an indication of the respective system's translation quality within a cluster are based on the same head-to-head statistical significance tests.

Official rankings and details on the evaluation campaign for the Dialect Speech Translation Task and Isometric SLT Task are presented respectively in Sections 6 and 8.

A.5 Formality Control

In this section, we reproduce the instructions given to the translators for IT, JA and RU for the formality control shared task. Instructions for JA are similar but include some language-specific notes. For brevity, we also remove example translations show to the translators.

Overview We would like to annotate multiple system outputs. For each of the 300 sentence ids (sid) there are 4-6 system outputs - please shuffle the order of the systems when showing it to annotators. We would like two annotators per target language.

Guidelines You will be shown an English source sentence and a machine translation of the source sentence. Your task will be to label the translation based on the formality level. Note that labels that you generate will be on the sentence level (one label per sentence). For example, given the source sentence "It was nice chatting with you, have a great night!" and a translation "Es war schön, mit Ihnen zu plaudern, haben Sie eine tolle Nacht!", you would label the example based on the formality level of the translation as one of *Formal*, *Informal*, *Neutral*, *Other*.

[52] `https://github.com/AppraiseDev/Appraise`

[53] In the post annotation questionnaire, 57% of annotators indicated their experience as high (evaluating MT outputs regularly) and 32% as moderate (did it more than few times).

Special Cases to Consider

1. Only label formality level, and ignore other mistakes such as a wrong sense.
2. Only label based on the formality level of the translation. Note that we don't want to label whether the formality level is correct in translation, but rather which formality level is marked in the translation.
3. If at least one word in the source is not translated at all and some meaning is lost, then label the translation as Other.

Label Categories

1. **Formal** – The formality level is consistently Formal in the translation.
2. **Informal** – The formality level is consistently Informal in the translation.
3. **Neutral** – The translation is phrased in a way that does not explicitly express a formality level.
4. **Other** – Explain the reason in the Notes section.
   - The formality level is inconsistent such as using both formal and informal pronouns.
   - If at least one word in the source is not translated at all and should have been marked in the target language for formality and some meaning is lost.
   - If you feel strongly that the translation does not fit into any of the cases listed above, please label it as "other" and explain the reason in the Notes section.

Appendix B. Evaluation Results and Details

B.1. Simultaneous Speech Translation

Automatic Evaluation Results

· Summary of the results of the simultaneous speech translation for **English-German.**
· Results are reported on the blind test set and systems are grouped by latency regime (set on tst-COMMON v2)
· For each entry for latency metric, the upper one is non computation aware, while the lower one is computation aware.
· BLEU number in parenthesis indicate that the system does not satisfy the latency constraints.
· Raw system logs are also provided on the task web site.[54]

	Low Latency				**Medium Latency**				**High Latency**			
Team	BLEU	AL	AP	DAL	BLEU	AL	AP	DAL	BLEU	AL	AP	DAL
tst-COMMON v2												
CUNI-KIT	**26.82**	**0.96**	**0.77**	**2.07**	**31.47**	**1.93**	**0.86**	**2.96**	**32.87**	**3.66**	**0.96**	**4.45**
		2.94	**1.52**	**6.38**		**3.71**	**1.39**	**5.80**		**5.54**	**1.37**	**6.61**
FBK	13.38	0.94	0.58	1.31	25.08	1.99	0.80	2.36	30.07	3.92	0.95	4.15
		1.23	0.66	1.47		2.48	0.93	2.79		4.49	1.09	4.70
HW-TSC	(18.56)	1.96	0.79	2.41	23.90	2.61	0.87	3.07	24.78	4.02	0.96	4.31
		2.39	0.92	2.82		3.03	1.01	3.49		4.42	1.10	4.71
NAIST	17.54	0.99	0.68	1.50	19.15	1.93	0.82	3.63	19.45	3.98	0.94	5.17
		1.58	0.87	2.43		2.15	0.91	3.99		4.23	1.01	5.50
UPV	20.82	0.86	0.70	1.43	27.80	1.93	0.83	2.34	29.78	3.46	0.93	3.71
		2.23	1.18	3.71		3.70	1.43	5.06		6.23	1.71	7.53
Gold Segmentation												
CUNI-KIT	**20.56**	**1.09**	**0.76**	**2.25**	**23.31**	**2.13**	**0.85**	**3.24**	**24.11**	**4.10**	**0.96**	**4.92**
		3.13	**1.46**	**6.69**		**4.06**	**1.37**	**6.27**		**6.12**	**1.36**	**7.29**
FBK	10.23	0.87	0.54	1.28	20.12	1.91	0.78	2.37	23.59	4.05	0.95	4.36
		1.18	0.61	1.42		2.43	0.89	2.79		4.67	1.07	4.93
HW-TSC	(13.97)	1.91	0.77	2.47	19.10	2.62	0.86	3.18	19.73	4.20	0.95	4.57
		2.39	0.89	2.91		3.10	0.99	3.66		4.65	1.09	5.00
NAIST	13.40	0.97	0.67	1.55	15.29	1.98	0.82	3.96	15.47	4.80	0.96	5.79
		1.64	0.85	2.60		2.21	0.89	4.35		5.07	1.02	6.14
UPV	16.09	0.71	0.68	1.42	19.94	2.81	0.84	3.36	23.55	3.51	0.92	3.85
		2.18	1.13	3.78		6.00	1.58	7.76		6.35	1.63	7.82
Segmentation 1												
CUNI-KIT	**15.25**	**1.16**	**0.75**	**2.67**	**18.15**	**2.72**	**0.86**	**3.98**	**18.74**	**5.00**	**0.97**	**5.67**
		3.59	**1.47**	**7.23**		**5.12**	**1.36**	**6.99**		**7.38**	**1.37**	**8.16**
FBK	9.20	1.25	0.60	1.95	15.16	2.42	0.80	3.07	17.71	4.75	0.96	5.08
		1.58	0.66	2.14		3.00	0.91	3.58		5.41	1.07	5.71
HW-TSC	(10.66)	2.65	0.79	3.23	14.58	3.37	0.87	3.94	15.07	4.98	0.96	5.32
		3.10	0.88	3.59		3.86	0.99	4.36		5.40	1.08	5.71
NAIST	9.78	0.97	0.65	1.75	12.23	2.67	0.83	4.30	12.40	5.78	0.98	6.26
		1.66	0.82	2.66		2.91	0.89	4.67		6.08	1.03	6.59
UPV	12.23	1.06	0.68	1.86	15.86	2.26	0.80	2.87	17.89	4.12	0.93	4.51
		2.87	1.14	4.45		4.53	1.35	5.91		7.64	1.67	8.86
Segmentation 2												
CUNI-KIT	**19.51**	**0.73**	**0.66**	**2.71**	**21.41**	**1.95**	**0.74**	**4.10**	**21.82**	**4.81**	**0.88**	**7.06**
		3.79	**1.43**	**11.29**		**4.67**	**1.28**	**9.69**		**7.66**	**1.29**	**11.31**
FBK	4.45	0.68	0.34	1.17	15.12	1.82	0.61	2.65	20.89	4.62	0.85	5.50
		1.07	0.39	1.30		2.52	0.69	3.17		5.56	0.96	6.35
HW-TSC	(12.53)	1.92	0.63	2.81	17.92	2.71	0.75	3.77	18.66	4.86	0.86	5.84
		2.66	0.74	3.58		3.56	0.88	4.75		5.68	1.00	6.73
NAIST	11.77	0.93	0.60	1.92	13.49	2.76	0.84	7.75	13.64	8.76	0.97	10.62
		2.11	0.83	4.32		3.05	0.90	8.42		9.26	1.03	11.23
UPV	14.89	0.55	0.62	1.78	18.32	1.69	0.70	2.71	20.72	3.74	0.82	4.62
		2.85	1.03	5.84		4.43	1.17	7.29		7.75	1.48	11.16

[54] https://iwslt.org/2022/simultaneous

· Summary of the results of the simultaneous speech translation for **English-Japanese.**
· Results are reported on the blind test set and systems are grouped by latency regime (set on tst-COMMON v2)
· For each entry for latency metric, the upper one is non computation aware, while the lower one is computation aware.
· Raw system logs are also provided on the task web site.[55]

	Low Latency				**Medium Latency**				**High Latency**			
Team	BLEU	AL	AP	DAL	BLEU	AL	AP	DAL	BLEU	AL	AP	DAL
tst-COMMON v2												
CUNI-KIT	**16.92**	**2.46**	**0.90**	**3.22**	**16.94**	**3.77**	**0.97**	**4.29**	**16.91**	**4.13**	**0.98**	**4.53**
		3.84	**1.38**	**5.45**		**5.20**	**1.34**	**6.03**		**5.61**	**1.34**	**6.20**
HW-TSC	7.27	2.28	0.81	2.68	12.17	2.92	0.92	3.38	11.56	3.40	0.95	3.84
		2.61	0.92	2.91		3.30	1.06	3.71		3.79	1.09	4.16
NAIST	9.25	2.24	0.88	3.04	9.90	3.95	0.96	4.59	10.22	4.73	0.99	4.96
		2.65	1.03	3.50		4.26	1.07	4.94		5.05	1.09	5.30
Gold Segmentation												
CUNI-KIT	**16.50**	**2.71**	**0.90**	**3.35**	**16.68**	**4.10**	**0.97**	**4.57**	**16.75**	**4.42**	**0.98**	**4.80**
		4.10	**1.37**	**5.79**		**5.66**	**1.34**	**6.48**		**6.02**	**1.34**	**6.67**
HW-TSC	5.62	2.44	0.79	2.71	11.79	3.11	0.91	3.46	11.48	3.63	0.95	3.96
		2.75	0.89	2.92		3.48	1.04	3.80		4.00	1.08	4.30
NAIST	8.70	2.28	0.86	2.89	9.41	3.41	0.94	4.46	9.83	4.66	0.98	5.08
		2.68	0.99	3.40		3.73	1.04	4.87		4.98	1.06	5.44
Segmentation 1												
CUNI-KIT	**12.24**	**3.12**	**0.87**	**4.22**	**12.38**	**5.12**	**0.97**	**5.79**	**12.44**	**5.54**	**0.98**	**6.03**
		4.99	**1.34**	**7.14**		**7.17**	**1.33**	**8.10**		**7.58**	**1.33**	**8.22**
HW-TSC	4.15	3.25	0.79	3.75	8.40	4.05	0.91	4.55	8.18	4.68	0.95	5.14
		3.63	0.87	4.01		4.46	1.01	4.89		5.09	1.05	5.49
NAIST	6.67	2.40	0.81	3.35	7.13	4.64	0.93	5.56	7.39	5.86	0.98	6.23
		2.87	0.92	3.90		4.98	1.00	5.97		6.19	1.04	6.58
Segmentation 2												
CUNI-KIT	**14.65**	**3.19**	**0.77**	**4.54**	**14.82**	**5.71**	**0.90**	**7.37**	**14.71**	**6.55**	**0.93**	**8.11**
		5.34	**1.27**	**9.80**		**7.95**	**1.29**	**11.45**		**9.06**	**1.30**	**12.03**
HW-TSC	2.36	2.56	0.52	2.99	10.23	3.62	0.76	4.38	8.70	4.39	0.82	5.30
		3.05	0.58	3.26		4.33	0.87	5.01		5.17	0.94	5.96
NAIST	8.10	2.67	0.73	3.81	8.36	5.28	0.91	9.00	8.57	8.69	0.97	10.32
		3.32	0.85	4.82		5.71	0.99	9.72		9.20	1.03	10.94

[55] `https://iwslt.org/2022/simultaneous`

· Summary of the results of the simultaneous speech translation for **English-Mandarin.**
· Results are reported on the blind test set and systems are grouped by latency regime (set on tst-COMMON v2)
· For each entry for latency metric, the upper one is non computation aware, while the lower one is computation aware.
· BLEU number in parenthesis indicate that the system does not satisfy the latency constraints.
· Raw system logs are also provided on the task web site.[56]

	Low Latency				**Medium Latency**				**High Latency**			
Team	BLEU	AL	AP	DAL	BLEU	AL	AP	DAL	BLEU	AL	AP	DAL
tst-COMMON v2												
AISP-SJTU	**25.87**	**1.99**	**0.87**	**3.35**	**26.21**	**2.97**	**0.94**	**4.16**	**26.46**	**3.97**	**0.98**	**4.62**
		3.39	**1.81**	**6.53**		**5.14**	**1.97**	**7.80**		**7.12**	**2.05**	**8.42**
CUNI-KIT	23.61	1.75	0.85	2.56	24.37	2.79	0.93	3.49	24.58	3.67	0.97	4.22
		3.11	1.34	4.77		4.16	1.34	5.32		5.12	1.34	5.88
HW-TSC	(18.60)	2.18	0.84	2.66	22.51	2.88	0.92	3.33	23.60	3.46	0.95	3.81
		2.56	0.97	2.93		3.26	1.06	3.62		3.82	1.09	4.10
Xiaomi	19.74	1.97	0.83	2.64	20.18	2.84	0.90	3.62	20.10	3.73	0.95	4.18
		3.63	1.32	4.82		6.46	2.18	9.68		8.36	2.31	10.81
Gold Segmentation												
AISP-SJTU	**30.74**	**2.05**	**0.86**	**3.46**	**31.22**	**3.08**	**0.93**	**4.34**	**32.09**	**4.15**	**0.97**	**4.83**
		3.44	**1.56**	**6.72**		**5.22**	**1.72**	**8.06**		**7.34**	**1.81**	**8.75**
CUNI-KIT	26.71	1.92	0.83	2.65	27.09	2.93	0.92	3.62	27.22	3.90	0.97	4.44
		3.29	1.32	5.09		4.29	1.31	5.57		5.39	1.32	6.23
HW-TSC	(19.83)	2.25	0.82	2.68	26.02	3.00	0.91	3.43	27.65	3.62	0.95	3.97
		2.66	0.95	2.98		3.37	1.04	3.72		4.00	1.08	4.29
Xiaomi	23.75	2.04	0.82	2.62	24.34	2.97	0.90	3.71	24.56	3.87	0.95	4.29
		3.61	1.28	4.78		6.48	2.11	9.86		8.55	2.28	11.15
Segmentation 1												
AISP-SJTU	**24.90**	**2.39**	**0.83**	**4.12**	**25.33**	**3.87**	**0.93**	**5.30**	**26.01**	**5.18**	**0.97**	**5.93**
		4.11	**1.41**	**7.78**		**6.56**	**1.60**	**9.57**		**9.04**	**1.70**	**10.48**
CUNI-KIT	20.80	2.29	0.81	3.51	21.83	3.82	0.92	4.79	21.66	4.95	0.97	5.66
		4.13	1.27	6.30		5.73	1.30	7.16		6.96	1.31	7.81
HW-TSC	(16.09)	3.03	0.82	3.68	20.42	3.90	0.91	4.50	21.52	4.63	0.95	5.11
		3.47	0.91	3.99		4.31	1.00	4.80		5.04	1.05	5.43
Xiaomi	19.79	2.30	0.79	3.20	20.29	3.53	0.89	4.57	20.47	4.60	0.94	5.25
		4.03	1.19	5.43		7.62	1.97	11.32		9.72	2.09	12.54
Segmentation 2												
AISP-SJTU	**28.36**	**3.06**	**0.83**	**7.10**	**28.79**	**4.82**	**0.91**	**8.71**	**29.03**	**5.97**	**0.94**	**9.26**
		5.50	**1.50**	**14.52**		**8.33**	**1.64**	**16.96**		**10.29**	**1.70**	**17.68**
CUNI-KIT	24.96	1.97	0.70	3.41	25.01	3.46	0.80	5.19	24.81	5.11	0.88	7.01
		4.20	1.20	8.54		5.57	1.21	9.32		7.48	1.25	10.79
HW-TSC	(13.80)	2.26	0.59	3.00	22.27	3.24	0.74	4.21	24.77	4.21	0.82	5.21
		2.93	0.68	3.39		4.00	0.85	4.70		5.00	0.93	5.76
Xiaomi	22.15	1.85	0.69	3.04	22.71	3.23	0.77	4.84	23.08	4.43	0.83	5.63
		4.50	1.19	8.10		8.80	2.10	18.63		11.55	2.30	21.16

[56] `https://iwslt.org/2022/simultaneous`

· Summary of the results of the simultaneous speech translation for **text-to-text track, English-Mandarin**
· The input of the each system is the output from the provided streaming ASR model, and the latency is evaluated in seconds.
· Results are reported on the blind test set and systems are grouped by latency regime (set on tst-COMMON v2)
· For each entry for latency metric, the upper one is non computation aware, while the lower one is computation aware.
· Raw system logs are also provided on the task web site.[57]

	Low Latency				Medium Latency				High Latency			
Team	BLEU	AL	AP	DAL	BLEU	AL	AP	DAL	BLEU	AL	AP	DAL
tst-COMMON v2												
AISP-SJTU					18.36	2.35 2.89	0.88 1.05	4.04 4.83				
HW-TSC	14.63	1.38 1.88	0.73 0.86	2.01 2.43	17.40	2.31 2.85	0.86 1.00	2.90 3.37	18.19	3.08 3.65	0.92 1.07	3.57 4.08
Xiaomi	19.74	1.97 3.63	0.83 1.32	2.64 4.82	20.18	2.84 6.46	0.90 2.18	3.62 9.68	20.10	3.73 8.36	0.95 2.31	4.18 10.81
Gold Segmentation												
AISP-SJTU					22.85	2.38 2.67	0.87 0.96	4.17 4.56				
HW-TSC	16.82	1.44 1.86	0.71 0.81	1.96 2.29	21.03	2.37 2.85	0.85 0.97	2.89 3.29	22.56	3.18 3.68	0.91 1.03	3.61 4.05
Xiaomi	23.75	2.04 3.61	0.82 1.28	2.62 4.78	24.34	2.97 6.48	0.90 2.11	3.71 9.86	24.56	3.87 8.55	0.95 2.28	4.29 11.15
Segmentation 1												
AISP-SJTU					19.18	2.84 3.16	0.87 0.94	4.94 5.38				
HW-TSC	14.44	1.53 1.98	0.68 0.76	2.42 2.76	17.63	2.64 3.14	0.82 0.91	3.50 3.92	18.85	3.66 4.18	0.89 0.99	4.37 4.84
Xiaomi	19.79	2.30 4.03	0.79 1.19	3.20 5.43	20.29	3.53 7.62	0.89 1.97	4.57 11.32	20.47	4.60 9.72	0.94 2.09	5.25 12.54
Segmentation 2												
AISP-SJTU					21.61	3.71 4.08	0.88 0.94	8.70 9.35				
HW-TSC	11.56	1.20 1.77	0.50 0.57	2.05 2.42	18.00	2.17 2.88	0.68 0.76	3.25 3.76	20.37	3.17 3.99	0.77 0.86	4.33 4.96
Xiaomi	22.15	1.85 4.50	0.69 1.19	3.04 8.10	22.71	3.23 8.80	0.77 2.10	4.84 18.63	23.08	4.43 11.55	0.83 2.30	5.63 21.16

[57] `https://iwslt.org/2022/simultaneous`

Human Evaluation Results

English-Japanese	BLEU	Error score	#Critical	#Major	#Minor
CUNI-KIT (high)	19.43	219	0	31	64
CUNI-KIT (low)	18.29	225	0	31	70
HW-TSC (medium)	15.21	472	2	85	37
NAIST (medium)	11.49	628	12	109	23

Table 16: Human evaluation results on one talk in the English-to-Japanese Simultaneous speech-to-speech translation task. Error weights are 5 for Critical and Major errors and 1 for Minor errors.

	Common	Non-native
Number of distinct audios	17	43
Mean length of audio (secs)	886	209
Total of subtitled audios annotated	439	1159
Mean ratings per annotated audio	164.4	40.8

Table 17: Human evaluation for the English-to-German task on two test sets: the Common one used also in automatic scoring and Non-native one. We show the size of the evaluation corpus, and the number of ratings collected.

	Common			Non-native		
System	Low	Medium	High	Low	Medium	High
CUNI-KIT	**3.13**	3.26	**3.44**	**2.46**	**2.57**	**2.98**
UPV	2.96	**3.32**	3.40	2.07	2.55	2.72
FBK	2.23	3.02	**3.44**	1.76	2.20	2.36
HW-TSC	2.34	2.60	2.60	1.58	1.81	1.69
NAIST	2.28	2.31	2.44	1.77	1.64	1.60
Average±Std.dev.	2.59±0.38	2.90±0.39	3.06±0.45	1.93±0.31	2.15±0.38	2.27±0.55
Interpreting		2.99			3.22	

Table 18: Human evaluation results for English-to-German Simultaneous task. We calculate a mean score for each annotated audio file, then take the mean across all annotated audio files, for each system-latency combination. We highlight the best results in bold and report also the average across all submissions of a given latency band. The final row shows the results for human simultaneous interpreting (transcribed).

B.2. Offline Speech Translation

Automatic Evaluation Results

Speech Translation: TED English-German tst 2022

· Systems are ordered according to `BLEU_NewRef`: *BLEU* score computed on the NEW reference set (literal translations).
· *BLEU* scores are given as percent figures (%).

System	BLEU_NewRef	BLEU_TEDRef	BLEU_MultiRef
USTC-NELSLIP cascade	26.7	23.9	37.6
YI end2end	25.7	23.6	36.5
YI cascade	25.6	23.7	36.4
USTC-NELSLIP end2end	25.3	22.9	35.7
NEMO	24.7	22.3	34.8
HW-TSC	24.2	20.8	33.5
KIT	23.9	22.0	33.8
FBK	23.6	21.0	32.9
UPC	23.0	20.8	32.3
ALEXA AI	22.6	20.1	31.5

Table 19: Official results of the **automatic evaluation** for the Offline Speech Translation Task, English to German.

Speech Translation: TED English-German tst 2021

· Systems are ordered according to `BLEU_TEDRef`: *BLEU* score computed on the ORIGINAL reference set.
· *BLEU* scores are given as percent figures (%).
· End-to-end systems are indicated by gray background.

System	BLEU_NewRef	BLEU_TEDRef	BLEU_MultiRef
USTC-NELSLIP cascade	28.9	24.1	40.3
YI cascade	28.1	23.2	39.0
YI end2end	27.8	23.1	38.8
HW-TSC	27.5	21.2	36.9
USTC-NELSLIP end2end	27.2	23.0	38.4
FBK	25.5	21.3	35.6
KIT	24.7	22.4	36.2
last Year's best	24.6	20.3	34.0
UPC	24.5	20.9	34.8
ALEXA AI	24.4	20.6	34.5

Table 20: Progress test set results of the **automatic evaluation** for the Offline Speech Translation Task, English to Japanese.

Speech Translation: TED English-Chinese tst 2022

· Systems are ordered according to BLEU_TEDRef: *BLEU* score computed on the ORIGINAL reference set.
· *BLEU* scores are given as percent figures (%).
· End-to-end systems are indicated by gray background.

System	BLEU_NewRef	BLEU_TEDRef	BLEU_MultiRef
USTC-NELSLIP cascade	35.8	35.7	44.1
YI cascade	34.7	35.0	42.9
HW-TSC	34.6	33.4	42.1
YI end2end	34.1	34.6	42.3
USTC-NELSLIP end2end	33.8	34.1	41.9
NEMO	33.3	33.7	41.2
NIUTRANS	32.3	33.2	40.5
KIT	31.1	32.0	39.0
ALEXA AI	30.4	30.8	37.9
UPC	29.2	29.9	36.4
NEURAL.AI	22.8	23.0	28.2

Table 21: Official results of the **automatic evaluation** for the Offline Speech Translation Task, English to Chinese.

Speech Translation: TED English-Japanese tst 2022

· Systems are ordered according to BLEU_TEDRef: *BLEU* score computed on the ORIGINAL reference set.
· *BLEU* scores are given as percent figures (%).
· End-to-end systems are indicated by gray background.

System	BLEU_NewRef	BLEU_TEDRef	BLEU_MultiRef
HW-TSC	22.7	14.3	30.8
USTC-NELSLIP cascade	21.6	20.1	33.4
USTC-NELSLIP end2end	20.5	17.4	30.5
YI end2end	18.0	19.1	29.8
YI cascade	18.7	20.2	31.3
KIT	16.2	17.2	26.4
UPC	15.1	15.6	24.7
ALEXA AI	15.3	16.2	25.3

Table 22: Official results of the **automatic evaluation** for the Offline Speech Translation Task, English to Japanese.

Human Evaluation Results

Speech Translation: TED English-German tst 2022 (subset)

Rank	Ave.	Ave. z	System
1-3	88.9	0.142	USTC-NELSLIP cascade
1-4	87.4	0.075	USTC-NELSLIP end2end
1-4	87.6	0.063	YI cascade
4-9	86.5	0.008	KIT
4-9	86.1	-0.004	FBK
2-7	86.3	-0.011	YI end2end
4-9	85.6	-0.023	NEMO
5-9	85.4	-0.039	UPC
5-9	84.8	-0.076	HW-TSC
10	83.9	-0.133	ALEXA AI

Table 23: Official results of the **human evaluation** for the Offline Speech Translation Task, English to German. Systems ordered by the standardized DA z-score. Systems within clusters indicated by horizontal lines are considered tied. Scores collected using direct assessment with previous/next-sentence context.

Speech Translation: TED English-Chinese tst 2022 (subset)

1	85.6	0.184	USTC-NELSLIP cascade
2-5	84.2	0.121	YI end2end
2-7	84.0	0.097	YI cascade
2-7	83.5	0.086	USTC-NELSLIP end2end
3-8	83.1	0.061	NEMO
3-8	83.2	0.057	KIT
2-7	82.8	0.038	HW-TSC
6-9	82.4	0.023	NIUTRANS
8-10	81.6	-0.023	ALEXA AI
9-10	80.8	-0.055	UPC
11	71.2	-0.589	NEURAL.AI

Table 24: Official results of the **human evaluation** for the Offline Speech Translation Task, English to Chinese. Systems ordered by the standardized DA z-score. Systems within clusters indicated by horizontal lines are considered tied. Scores collected using direct assessment with previous/next-sentence context.

Speech Translation: TED English-Japanese tst 2022 (subset)

1-4	78.4	0.086	YI cascade
1-4	77.6	0.065	USTC-NELSLIP cascade
1-4	77.6	0.061	YI end2end
1-4	76.6	0.005	HW-TSC
5-6	76.3	-0.009	USTC-NELSLIP end2end
5-6	76.3	-0.013	KIT
7-8	74.7	-0.082	ALEXA AI
7-8	73.2	-0.113	UPC

Table 25: Official results of the **human evaluation** for the Offline Speech Translation Task, English to Japanese. Systems ordered by the standardized DA z-score. Systems within clusters indicated by horizontal lines are considered tied. Scores collected using direct assessment with previous/next-sentence context.

B.3. Speech to Speech Translation

Results for the speech to speech translation task, described in Section 4.

While both automatic metrics and human evaluation are provided, the task ranking was determined by human evaluation of translation quality (Table 28).

System	BLEU	chrF
MLLP-VRAIN	**19.70**	53.15
HW-TSC primary	19.58	**53.81**
HW-TSC contrastive3	19.35	53.75
HW-TSC contrastive1	19.22	53.65
HW-TSC contrastive2	18.90	53.00
UPC	16.38	50.20
Reference text (+TTS)	68.46	88.78
FBK Offline (+TTS)	17.37	51.21
KIT Offline (+TTS)	16.63	50.43
Reference text (+normalization)	100.00	100.00
FBK Offline (+normalization)	23.44	55.84
KIT Offline (+normalization)	23.51	55.18

Table 26: **S2ST: automatic metrics.** Speech output is first transcribed with ASR before scoring against reference text. Text is normalized for scoring (punctuation and case removed, whitespace standardized). The effects of synthesis + ASR transcription are shown by synthesizing the reference text and selected Offline task submissions and scoring after ASR.

System	nat.	clar.	sound.
MLLP-VRAIN	4.156 (0.037)	4.626 (0.028)	4.562 (0.028)
HW-TSC primary	3.135 (0.042)	3.835 (0.037)	3.867 (0.034)
UPC	3.118 (0.042)	3.786 (0.037)	3.862 (0.032)
Reference	3.116 (0.043)	3.678 (0.038)	3.799 (0.032)

Table 27: **S2ST: speech quality human evaluation.** System outputs were evaluated along 3 dimensions, which are more fine-grained than mean opinion score: speech naturalness (nat.), clarity of speech (clar.) and sound quality (sound.). Numbers in parenthesis indicate a 95% confidence interval.

System	Translation quality
HW-TSC primary	4.606 (0.034)
MLLP-VRAIN	4.439 (0.057)
UPC	4.374 (0.041)
Reference	4.369 (0.038)

Table 28: **S2ST: translation quality human evaluation.** The initial MLLP-VRAIN submission had a misalignment and was later fixed. As a result, the number of samples for MLLP-VRAIN is 1000 instead of 2059. Numbers in parenthesis indicate a 95% confidence interval.

B.4. Dialect Speech Translation

Automatic Evaluation Results

Tunisian Arabic→English

Team	Condition	System	test2					test1
			BLEU↑	BP	pr1	chrF2	TER↓	BLEU
CMU	dialect adapt	primary (E2)	20.8 ± 0.7	0.931	53.1	44.3	64.5	19.5
CMU	dialect adapt	contrastive	20.7 ± 0.7	0.929	53	44.1	64.6	19.3
CMU	basic	primary (E1)	20.4 ± 0.7	0.944	52.2	43.8	65.4	19.2
CMU	basic	contrastive	20.1 ± 0.7	0.936	52.2	43.5	65.3	19
CMU	dialect adapt	contrastive (D6)	19.8 ± 0.7	0.902	53.2	43.3	64.6	18.9
CMU	basic	contrastive (D3)	19.7 ± 0.7	0.916	52.4	43	65.5	18.7
CMU	dialect adapt	contrastive (D5)	19.5 ± 0.6	0.896	53.2	42.8	64.6	18.3
CMU	dialect adapt	contrastive (C6)	19.4 ± 0.6	0.937	50.7	43	67.1	17.9
CMU	basic	contrastive (D2)	19.1 ± 0.6	0.939	51.3	42.7	66.5	18.1
JHU	dialect adapt	primary	18.9 ± 0.7	0.99	48	42.1	70.2	17.8
JHU	unconstrain.	primary	18.7 ± 0.7	0.959	48.7	41.6	69.2	17.5
CMU	basic	contrastive (C3)	18.6 ± 0.6	0.942	49.4	41.8	68.3	17.5
JHU	basic	primary	17.1 ± 0.6	0.973	46.8	40.4	71.4	16.1
ON-TRAC	unconstrain.	post-evaluation	14.4 ± 0.6	1	42.7	36.5	76.7	-
ON-TRAC	unconstrain.	contrastive1	13.6 ± 0.6	1	41.7	35.7	78.3	-
ON-TRAC	basic	primary	12.4 ± 0.6	0.8	44.3	32.8	75.5	-
ON-TRAC	unconstrain.	contrastive2	11.3 ± 0.5	0.95	38.7	32.7	80.6	-
Baseline	basic	baseline E2E	11.1 ± 0.5	0.885	40	31.9	77.8	10.1

Table 29: Automatic evaluation results for the Dialect Speech Translation Task. Systems are ranked in order of the official metric: BLEU on test2 blind evaluation set. We also report chrF2, TER, as well as the brevity penalty (BP) and 1-gram precision (pr1) components of BLEU. We further use bootstrap resampling (1k samples) and report the 95% confidence interval for BLEU on test2 (Koehn, 2004). For details of each system, refer to the system name in the respective papers.

Tunisian Arabic ASR Automatic Evaluation Results

ASR System	WER↓		CER↓	
	Orig	Norm	Orig	Norm
JHU / basic / primary	70.5	43.8	30.5	22.5
JHU / dialect adapt / primary	70.1	42.9	30.4	22.3
JHU / unconstrained / primary	69.4	42.8	30.6	22.5
ON-TRAC / unconstrained / primary	68.2	45.1	28.4	21.5
ON-TRAC / unconstrained / post-eval	65.7	41.5	28.1	21.1

Table 30: Word Error Rate (WER) and Character Error Rate (CER) of the ASR component of submitted cascaded systems on test2. This is computed by comparing ASR hypotheses with the Tunisian manual transcripts. The original version (Orig) matches the minimal text pre-processing provided by the organizer's data preparation scripts, and results in relatively high WER. Transcription standards for primarily spoken dialects are challenging, so it may be beneficial as diagnosis to run some additional Arabic-specific normalization (Norm) for e.g. Alif, Ya, Ta-Marbuta on the hypotheses and transcripts before computing WER/CER. We are grateful to Ahmed Ali for assistance on this.

Human Evaluation Results

Tunisian Arabic→English

Rank	Ave.	Ave. z	Team / Condition / System
1	76.6	0.457	translator-A
2-3	66.5	0.119	CMU / dialect adapt / contrastive (D6)
2-3	66.5	0.114	CMU / dialect adapt / primary (E2)
4-5	62.7	-0.032	JHU / dialect adapt / primary
4-5	60.7	-0.093	JHU / basic condition / primary
6-7	56.1	-0.271	ON-TRAC / unconstrained / primary
6-7	55.3	-0.302	ON-TRAC / unconstrained / contrastive1

Table 31: Official results of the human evaluation for the Dialect Speech Translation Task. Systems ordered by the standardized DA z-score. Systems within clusters indicated by horizontal lines are considered tied. Scores collected using the document-level DA+SQM task in Appraise.

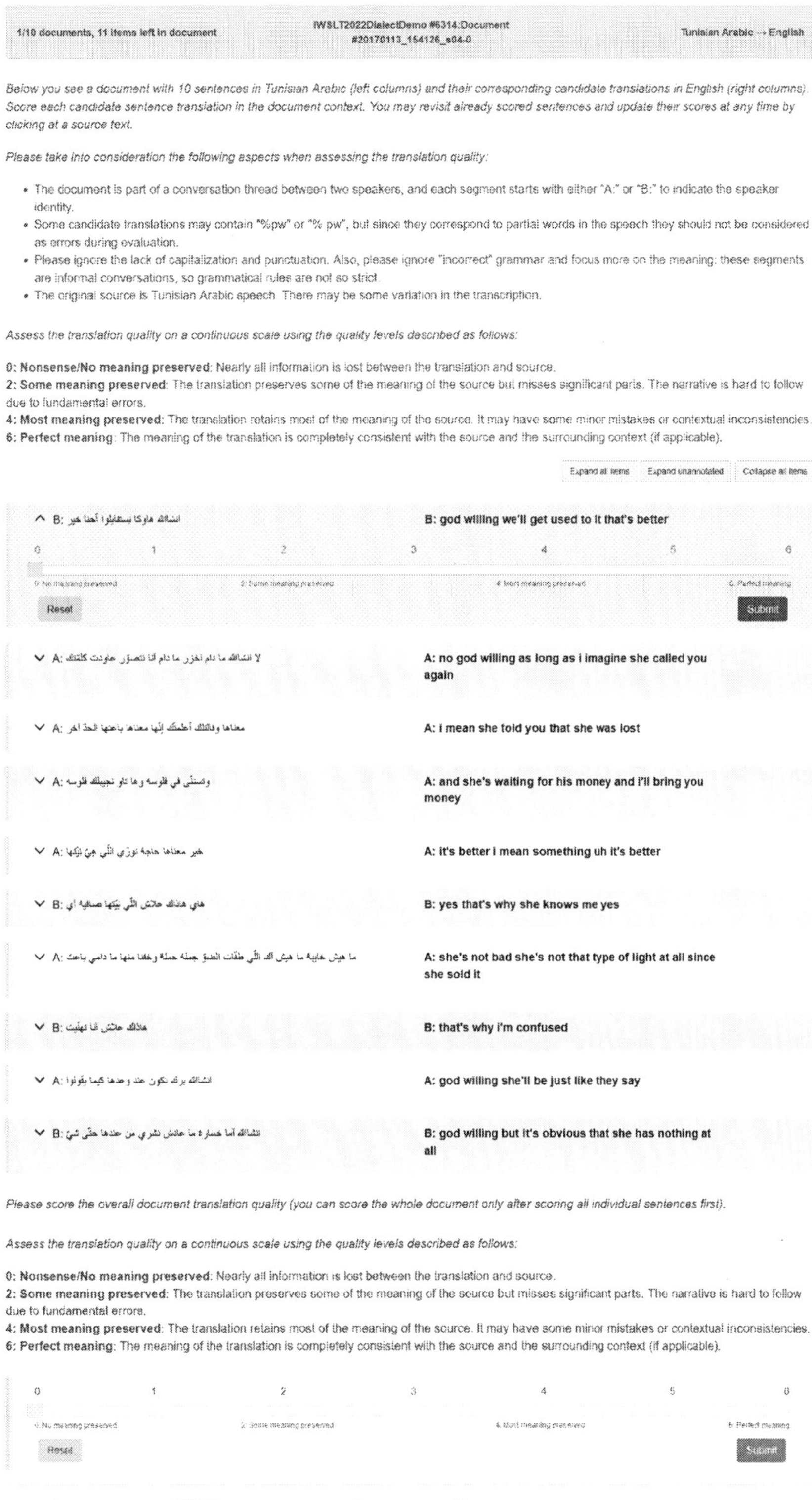

Figure 5: A screen shot of an example annotation task in Appraise featuring source-based document-level Direct Assessment with SQM for the Dialect Speech Translation Task.

B.5. Formality Control For Speech Translation

Automatic Evaluation Results

		EN→HI		EN→JA		EN→DE		EN→ES		EN→IT		EN→RU	
Setting	System	BLEU	COMET	BLEU	COMET	BLEU	COMET	BLEU	COMET	BLEU	COMET	BLEU	COMET
unconstrained	baseline	22.0	0.67	17.9	0.24	32.6	0.55	37.4	0.70	32.2	0.64	19.5	0.32
	ALEXA AI	38.9	0.874	19.4	0.378								
	UMD	12.1	0.192	11.6	-0.023	22.4	0.161	27.8	0.344	22.9	0.247	14.4	0.075
	UoS					32.5	0.497	37.0	0.635	33.1	0.562	21.5	0.357
constrained	UoS					31.5	0.448	36.5	0.608	33.1	0.553	21.4	0.329

Table 32: Automatic evaluation using sacrebleu and COMET on generic test sets. For EN→DE, ES, IT, RU participants were asked to evaluated their systems on MuST-C dataset. We have also included baseline models trained in the *unconstrained* setting for comparison. For EN→HI, JA participants were evaluated on WMT Newstest 2014 and 2020 respectively.

		Supervised								Zero-shot			
		EN→HI		EN→JA		EN→DE		EN→ES		EN→IT		EN→RU	
Setting	System	F	I	F	I	F	I	F	I	F	I	F	I
unconstrained	baseline (generic)	96.3	3.70	49.6	50.3	45.8	54.2	36.6	63.4	3.70	94.5	93.4	6.60
	ALEXA AI	99.6	99.8	88.8	98.8								
	UMD	99.4	98.7	86.3	97.5	99.4	96.5	99.5	93.2	32.8	97.9	100.0	1.10
	UoS					100.0	100.0	98.1	100.0	51.2	98.6	99.5	85.8
constrained	UoS					100.0	88.6	87.4	98.0	29.5	92.9	98.1	15.4

Table 33: Automatic evaluation of formality control accuracy (M-ACC) reported for Formal (F) and Informal (I). For comparison, we have included our baseline generic (uncontrolled) performance on the formality testset. For EN→IT, RU participants were given a zero-shot task and asked to train a formality controlled model without labelled training data in Italian or Russian.

Human Evaluation Results

Lang.	Setting	Sys.	Control	F	I	N	O	IAA
EN→JA	unconstrained	UMD	Formal	89.3	0.7	0.0	9.7	0.90
		UMD	Informal	2.0	92.5	0.0	5.5	
		ALEXA AI	Formal	82.8	1.3	0.0	15.5	
		ALEXA AI	Informal	3.0	82.7	0.0	14.3	
EN→IT	unconstrained	UMD	Formal	13.7	25.2	47.0	14.2	0.91
		UMD	Informal	1.0	78.3	11.5	9.2	
		UoS	Formal	6.0	7.2	81.3	5.5	
		UoS	Informal	0.3	81.0	13.2	5.5	
	constrained	UoS	Formal	0.2	10.2	87.7	2.0	
		UoS	Informal	0.2	36.3	58.3	5.2	
EN→RU	unconstrained	UMD	Formal	77.2	0.2	7.0	15.7	0.85
		UMD	Informal	74.3	0.7	7.8	17.2	
		UoS	Formal	85.0	0.3	6.0	8.7	
		UoS	Informal	10.3	71.3	3.2	15.2	
	constrained	UoS	Formal	85.3	2.0	5.7	7.0	
		UoS	Informal	65.0	12.7	6.3	16.0	

Table 34: Percentage of system outputs (with a given formality level (Control) and setting (Setting)) labeled by professional translators according to the formality level: formal (F), informal (I), neutral (N), other (O). IAA was computed using the Krippendorff's α coefficient.

B.6. Isometric Spoken Language Translation

Automatic MT Evaluation Results

En→De

System	BERTScore	LC	BLEU(detok)
STRONGBASELINE*	**77.44**	68.0	**21.6**
APPTEK-Constrained	77.32	86.5	18.7
HW-TSC-Unconstrained	75.79	96.5	20.2
APV-Unconstrained	73.68	39.0	16.5
WEAKBASELINE	74.86	43.0	15.5
HW-TSC-Constrained	74.07	**98.0**	17.9

En→Fr

System	BERTScore	LC	BLEU(detok)
STRONGBASELINE*	**81.75**	75.5	**36.2**
NUV-Unconstrained	79.96	47.5	27.1
APV-Unconstrained	77.77	45.0	32.9
HW-TSC-Constrained	76.11	**96.0**	31.5
WEAKBASELINE	77.18	37.0	25.2

En→Es

System	BERTScore	LC	BLEU(detok)
STRONGBASELINE*	**81.86**	80.5	**36**
APV-Unconstrained	80.87	49.5	35.3
HW-TSC-Constrained	78.57	**96.5**	29.9
WEAKBASELINE	78.32	51.0	27.7

Table 35: Automatic evaluation results for Isometric SLT task on the blind test set. Metrics are computed using the submissions primary system. System ranking follows the human evaluation ranking in Table 36. If BERTScore is a tie, system with the highest LC wins (*). BERTSCore and LC are the primary metrics for the task, detoknized-BLEU is provided only as a secondary reference. ***Bold** highlights the top score.*

MT Human Evaluation Results

En→De

Rank	Ave.	Ave. z	System
1	89.0	0.755	translator-A
2-3	72.6	0.189	STRONGBASELINE
2-3	69.9	0.123	APPTEK-Constrained
4-5	62.6	-0.153	HW-TSC-Unconstrained
4-6	62.1	-0.224	APV-Unconstrained
5-7	59.4	-0.298	WEAKBASELINE
6-7	56.3	-0.467	HW-TSC-Constrained

En→Fr

Rank	Ave.	Ave. z	System
1	80.8	0.624	translator-A
2-3	64.3	0.009	STRONGBASELINE
2-4	60.2	-0.152	NUV-constrained
3-6	58.0	-0.280	APV-Unconstrained
4-6	53.2	-0.348	HW-TSC-Constrained
4-6	53.6	-0.389	WEAKBASELINE

En→Es

Rank	Ave.	Ave. z	System
1	82.5	0.601	translator-A
2-3	70.3	0.020	STRONGBASELINE
2-3	69.9	-0.031	APV-Unconstrained
4-5	64.0	-0.283	HW-TSC-Constrained
4-5	59.8	-0.409	WEAKBASELINE

Table 36: Official results of the text-based human evaluation for the Isometric SLT Task. Systems ordered by the standardized DA z-score. Systems within clusters indicated by horizontal lines are considered tied. Scores collected using the document-level DA+SQM task in Appraise.

Automatic Dubbing Human Evaluation Results

En→De

Comparison	Wins (%)
WEAKBASELINE vs APPTEK-Constrained	32.9 vs 49.8*
WEAKBASELINE vs HW-TSC-Constrained	29.0 vs 49.4*
WEAKBASELINE vs HW-TSC-Unconstrained	41.1 vs 44.2
WEAKBASELINE vs APV-Unconstrained	37.9 vs 42.5
WEAKBASELINE vs STRONGBASELINE	29.0 vs 52.3*
APPTEK-Constrained vs HW-TSC-Constrained	42.4 vs 38.8
APPTEK-Constrained vs HW-TSC-Unconstrained	41.0 vs 38.0
APPTEK-Constrained vs APV-Unconstrained	43.9 vs 36.9
APPTEK-Constrained vs STRONGBASELINE	38.0 vs 39.6
HW-TSC-Constrained vs HW-TSC-Unconstrained	38.3 vs 36.0
HW-TSC-Constrained vs APV-Unconstrained	44.3 vs 37.7
HW-TSC-Constrained vs STRONGBASELINE	36.0 vs 42.7
HW-TSC-Unconstrained vs APV-Unconstrained	49.3 vs 32.7*
HW-TSC-Unconstrained vs STRONGBASELINE	37.2 vs 41.8
APV-Unconstrained vs STRONGBASELINE	31.3 vs 49.7*

En→Fr

Comparison	Wins (%)
WEAKBASELINE vs HW-TSC-Constrained	31.7 vs 51.7*
WEAKBASELINE vs NUV-Unconstrained	32.6 vs 50.9*
WEAKBASELINE vs APV-Unconstrained	25.7 vs 55.7*
WEAKBASELINE vs STRONGBASELINE	26.7 vs 57.0*
HW-TSC-Constrained vs NUV-Unconstrained	40.0 vs 40.0
HW-TSC-Constrained vs APV-Unconstrained	46.7 vs 34.7+
HW-TSC-Constrained vs STRONGBASELINE	31.9 vs 49.1*
NUV-Unconstrained vs APV-Unconstrained	35.6 vs 40.0
NUV-Unconstrained vs STRONGBASELINE	29.0 vs 48.6*
APV-Unconstrained vs STRONGBASELINE	34.3 vs 44.7

En→Es

Comparison	Wins (%)
WEAKBASELINE vs HW-TSC-Constrained	21.0 vs 51.0*
WEAKBASELINE vs APV-Unconstrained	30.3 vs 46.7*
WEAKBASELINE vs STRONGBASELINE	24.3 vs 53.7*
HW-TSC-Constrained vs APV-Unconstrained	37.7 vs 35.7
HW-TSC-Constrained vs STRONGBASELINE	34.3 vs 40.0
APV-Unconstrained vs STRONGBASELINE	30.3 vs 44.7*

Table 37: Automatic dubbing human evaluation results on pairwise comparisons of submitted systems for the Isometric SLT task. We report the Wins, i.e, the % of times one condition is preferred over the other with statistical significance levels $p < 0.01(^*)$ and $p < 0.05(^+)$.

En→De

Rank	N_{Wins}	System
1	5	STRONGBASELINE
2	4	APPTEK-Constrained
3	3	HW-TSC-Constrained
4	2	HW-TSC-Unconstrained
5	1	APV-Unconstrained
6	0	WEAKBASELINE

En→Fr

Rank	N_{Wins}	System
1	4	STRONGBASELINE
2	2	HW-TSC-Constrained
3	2	APV-Unconstrained
4	1	NUV-Constrained
5	0	WEAKBASELINE

En→Es

Rank	N_{Wins}	System
1	3	STRONGBASELINE
2	2	HW-TSC-Constrained
3	1	APV-Unconstrained
4	0	WEAKBASELINE

Table 38: Results of human evaluation of dubbed videos. Systems are ranked using N_{Wins}, i.e., the number of evaluations for which that systems was preferred over some other system.

En→De

Systems	Smoothness	LC
STRONGBASELINE	88.55	68
APPTEK-Constrained	86.22	86.5
HW-TSC-Constrained	88.45	98
HW-TSC-Unconstrained	88.92	96.5
APV-Unconstrained	82.53	39
WEAKBASELINE	84.22	43

En→Fr

Systems	Smoothness	LC
STRONGBASELINE	80.66	75.5
HW-TSC-Constrained	77.93	96
APV-Unconstrained	78.31	45
NUV-Constrained	75.52	47.5
WEAKBASELINE	66.84	37

En→Es

Systems	Smoothness	LC
STRONGBASELINE	92.01	80.5
HW-TSC-Constrained	92.65	96.5
APV-Unconstrained	92.02	49.5
WEAKBASELINE	85.21	51

Table 39: Results of automatic evaluation for subset of 60 dialogues used for dubbing evaluation using smoothness (Federico et al., 2020a) that measures the stability of speaking rate across contiguous phrases and length compliance (LC).

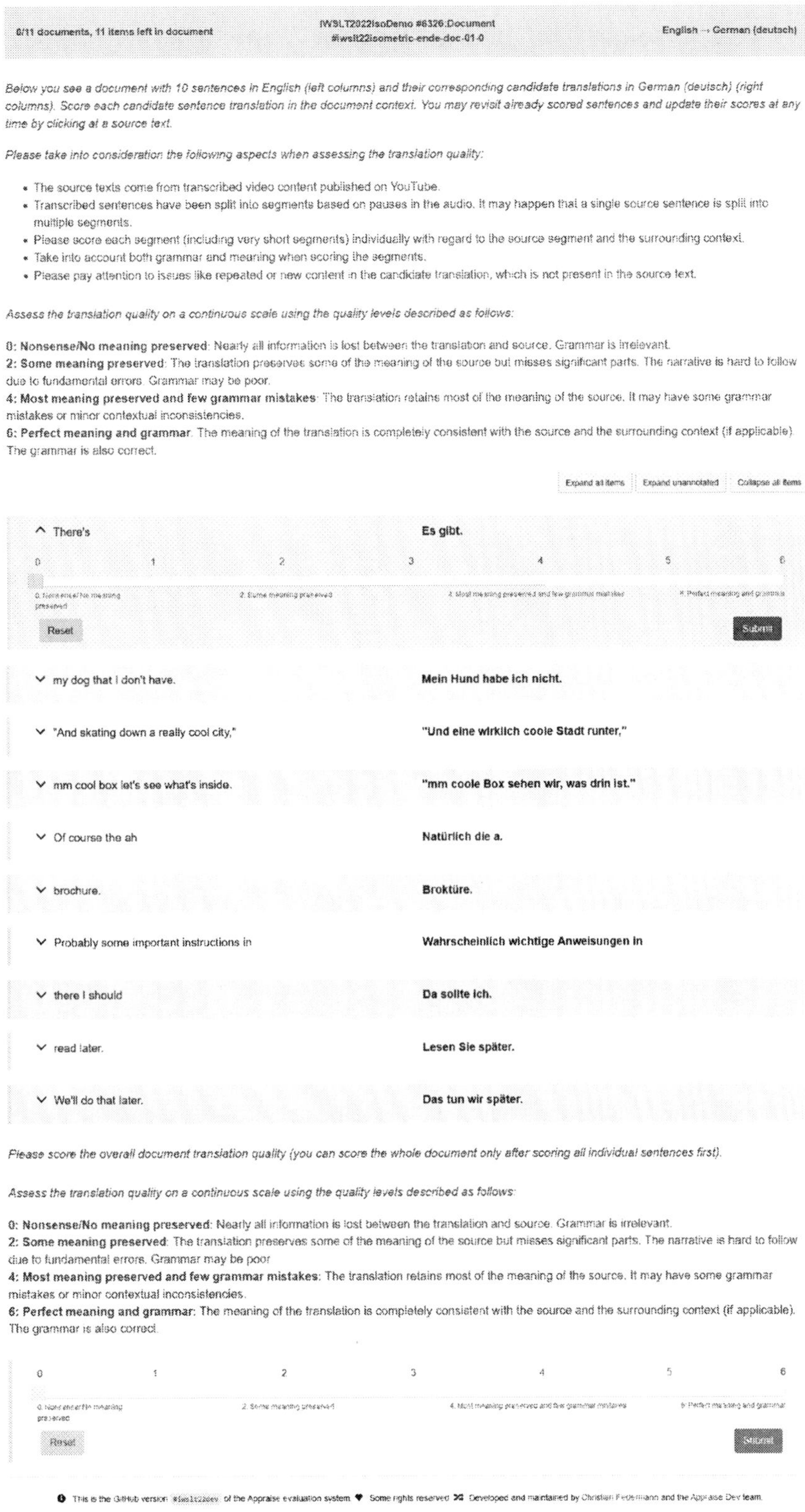

Figure 6: A screen shot of an example annotation task in Appraise featuring source-based document-level Direct Assessment with SQM for the Isometric SLT Task.

The YiTrans End-to-End Speech Translation System for IWSLT 2022 Offline Shared Task

Ziqiang Zhang[1]*, **Junyi Ao**[2,*]
[1]School of Information Science and Technology,
University of Science and Technology of China
[2]School of Data Science, The Chinese University of Hong Kong (Shenzhen)

Abstract

This paper describes the submission of our end-to-end YiTrans speech translation system for the IWSLT 2022 offline task, which translates from English audio to German, Chinese, and Japanese. The YiTrans system is built on large-scale pre-trained encoder-decoder models. More specifically, we first design a multi-stage pre-training strategy to build a multi-modality model with a large amount of labeled and unlabeled data. We then fine-tune the corresponding components of the model for the downstream speech translation tasks. Moreover, we make various efforts to improve performance, such as data filtering, data augmentation, speech segmentation, model ensemble, and so on. Experimental results show that our YiTrans system obtains a significant improvement than the strong baseline on three translation directions, and it achieves +5.2 BLEU improvements over last year's optimal end-to-end system on tst2021 English-German.

1 Introduction

In this paper, we describe our end-to-end speech translation system YiTrans which participates in the offline tracks of the IWSLT 2022 evaluation campaign. We evaluate our systems from English to German, Chinese and Japanese. We aim at exploring the pre-training methods for end-to-end systems, and bridging the quality gap with the cascaded approaches.

As self-supervised learning has been shown effective in speech-to-text tasks (Baevski et al., 2020; Hsu et al., 2021; Ao et al., 2021; Bapna et al., 2021), our teams are interested in building a multi-modality pre-trained model with self-supervised approaches by leveraging large amounts of speech and text data. Inspired by SpeechT5 (Ao et al., 2021), we design a multi-stage unified-modal training strategy for pre-training both the encoder and decoder. Our final end-to-end ST systems are built by fine-tuning the pre-trained models.

This paper also tries to improve the system performance by exploring various techniques for the related tasks. (1) To boost the performance with advanced speech segmentation (Anastasopoulos et al., 2021), we apply the pyannote toolkit (Bredin et al., 2020) and the merge algorithm from Inaguma et al. (2021) to segment the audio. Particularly, to overcome the long sentence problem in the dataset, we design a new segment algorithm. (2) Dataset is the key point for a ST system to perform well. Hence, we conduct refined data filtering and large-scale data augmentation (Jia et al., 2019). (3) We also employ progressive learning, back translation and multi-stage fine-tuning (Yang et al., 2021; Sennrich et al., 2015; Wang et al., 2020b) when fine-tuning our models. (4) Motivated by Tang et al. (2021a), we utilize joint ST and MT fine-tuning for our end-to-end ST models. (5) As comparison, we also build the cascaded systems for all three language pairs by fine-tuning ASR and MT models from pre-trained models.

The rest of this paper is organized as follows. In Section 2, we describe the data preparation, including the data pre-processing, data augmentation, and speech segmentation. Section 3 illustrates the unified-modal pre-training methods, and our systems for all three tasks. We share the experimental setting, results, and analyses in Section 4. Section 5 concludes the submission. We also present the official test results (Anastasopoulos et al., 2022) of our submitted system in Appendix A.

2 Data Preparation

2.1 Datasets

Our system is built under constraint conditions. The training data can be divided into five categories: unlabeled audio, monolingual text, ASR, MT, and

*Equal contribution.

Proceedings of the 19th International Conference on Spoken Language Translation (IWSLT 2022), pages 158 - 168
May 26-27, 2022 ©2022 Association for Computational Linguistics

ST corpora1.

Datasets	# Utterances	# Hours
Unlabeled Data		
VoxPopuli	1224.9k	28708
Labeled ASR Data		
MuST-C v1&v2	341.6k	616.9
ST-TED	171.1k	272.8
LibriSpeech	281.2k	961.1
CoVoST	288.4k	426.1
CommonVoice	1224.9k	1668.1
TEDLIUM v2&v3	361.2k	660.6
Europarl	34.3k	81.4
VoxPopuli ASR	177.0k	501.3
Labeled ST Data		
en-de		
MuST-C v2	249.8k	435.9
ST-TED	171.1k	272.8
CoVoST	288.4k	426.1
Europarl	32.6k	77.2
en-ja		
MuST-C v2	328.4k	534.5
CoVoST	288.4k	426.1
en-zh		
MuST-C v2	358.5k	586.8
CoVoST	288.4k	426.1

Table 1: English audio data statistics

Unlabeled Audio We utilize large-scale unlabeled and labeled audio for pre-training. As shown in Table 1, we pre-train our models by using around 28k hours of unlabeled audio data from VoxPopuli (Wang et al., 2021), and around 5.1k hours of labeled ASR data, which will be introduced later.

Monolingual Text Monolingual text is used either for pre-training or back-translation. We collect data for English as well as three target languages from WMT21 news translation task[1], including News Commentary[2], Europarl v10[3], News crawl[4], and Common Crawl[5]. As Common Crawl contains much noisier data, it is only used for **ja** and **zh** to expand the collected data size to 500M. The statistics are listed in Table 2.

[1]https://www.statmt.org/wmt21/translation-task.html
[2]http://data.statmt.org/news-commentary
[3]http://www.statmt.org/europarl/v10
[4]http://data.statmt.org/news-crawl
[5]http://data.statmt.org/ngrams

	en	de	ja	zh
Collected	341M	389M	500M	500M
Processed & filtered	50M	50M	50M	50M

Table 2: Monolingual text data statistics

ASR Corpus For training and evaluation of our ASR models, we use MuST-C v1 (Di Gangi et al., 2019), MuST-C v2 (Cattoni et al., 2021), ST-TED (Niehues et al., 2018), LibriSpeech (Panayotov et al., 2015), CoVoST 2 (Wang et al., 2020a), TED-LIUM v2 (Rousseau et al., 2012), TED-LIUM v3 (Hernandez et al., 2018), Europarl (Koehn, 2005), VoxPopuli ASR data, and Mozilla Common Voice (Ardila et al., 2019), which results in around 5188.3hr labled ASR data as shown in Table 1. For MuSTC-C and Europarl, we collected the data from all language pairs and removed the overlap audios according to the audio id.

Datasets	en-de	en-ja	en-zh
In-domain			
MuST-C v2	249.8k	328.4k	358.5k
TED	209.5k	223.1k	231.3k
Out-of-domain			
CoVoST	288.4k	288.4k	288.4k
Europarl	32.6k	-	-
OpenSubtitles2018	18.7M	1.9M	10.0M
WMT21	93.3M	16.6M	61.0M
Sum (processed)	82.0M	13.8M	51.5M
Sum (filtered)	16.1M	3.6M	7.6M

Table 3: MT data statistics

MT Corpus Machine translation (MT) corpora are used to translate the English transcription. For training and evaluation of our MT models, we use MuST-C v2 and TED corpus (Cettolo et al., 2012) as in-domain data. We also use CoVoST 2, Europarl, OpenSubtitles2018 (Lison and Tiedemann, 2016) as well as all available paired data provided by WMT21 as out-of-domain data. The statistics are listed in Table 3.

ST Corpus The ST corpus we used includes the MuST-C v2, ST-TED, CoVoST 2 and Europarl, as listed in Table 1. MuST-C v2 and ST-TED are treated as in-domain data. The ST corpus can be greatly expanded by large-scale data augmentation, which will be introduced in the following Section.

2.2 Text Processing & Filtering

For monolingual and out-of-domain MT data, we first process the text through the following steps:

(1) We clean up the data by removing sentences that have non-printing characters, http tags or words with length longer than 50 characters (words are separated by space, for **ja** and **zh** the threshold is 150). The processed text data is then deduplicated.

(2) We use fast-text [6] (Joulin et al., 2016) to filter out the sentences with invalid languages.

(3) For paired data, we use fast_align[7] (Dyer et al., 2013) to calculate the alignment quality, which is evaluated by the percentage of aligned words. We remove 20% of data with the lowest alignment quality.

(4) We then use XenC[8] (Rousseau, 2013) to perform domain filtering. It computes the distinction of two n-gram language models, which are in-domain and out-of-domain language models. The amount of selected data is 50M for monolingual text, and for paired text it depends on the XenC scores. The results are listed in Table 2 and 3.

2.3 Post processing

We only do post-processing for **en-ja** systems as an optional choice. It is because we noticed that for **en-ja** there is few punctuations in the target side of training data. To obtain translation results with rich punctuation, which are more natural in the real world, we train a punctuation model to post-process the translated results. The model is initialized from mBART50 (Tang et al., 2020) and trained to predict sentences with proper punctuation. The training data is collected from out-of-domain **en-ja** MT data. We select the sentences with rich punctuation in Japanese side.

2.4 Data Augmentation

The quality of end-to-end ST is often limited by a paucity of training data, since it is difficult to collect large parallel corpora of speech and translated transcript pairs In this paper, we attempt to build a large amount of synthetic data for ST and MT, separately. We will introduce the data augmentation method in Section 3 in detail.

2.5 Speech Segmentation

Algorithm 1 Segment audios based on pyannote toolkit

function SEGMENTAUDIO(x, P_{on}, P_{off}, T_{dur})
  $L \leftarrow VAD(x, P_{on}, P_{off})$ ▷ $\{a_1, ..., a_n\}$
  $L_{new} \leftarrow \{\}$
  for $a_i \in L$ **do**
    if $a_i.length > T_{dur}$ **then**
      if $P_{on} < 0.95$ or $P_{off} < 0.95$ **then**
        $L_{new} \leftarrow L_{new} \cup$ SEGMENTAUDIO(a_i, $P_{on} + \alpha_{on}$, $P_{off} + \alpha_{off}$, T_{dur})
      else
        $L_{new} \leftarrow L_{new} \cup$ EQUALSEGMENT(a_i)
      end if
    end if
  end for
  return L_{new}
end function

Similar to the previous evaluation, this year's evaluation data are segmented using an automatic tool, which does not ensure that segments are proper sentences nor that they are aligned with the translated text. In addition, there is an apparent mismatch for segmentation between using voice activity detection (VAD) and segmenting by punctuations, where the latter is usually used for segmenting the training data. These assign extra importance to develop methods for proper segmentation of the audio data, which was confirmed in the previous year's evaluation campaign, where all top submissions used their own segmentation algorithm (Anastasopoulos et al., 2021).

Therefore, we design a segmentation algorithm based on a VAD model provided by pyannote.audio[9] (Bredin et al., 2020), as illustrated in Algorithm 1. We find that long segments are difficult for the model to decode and need to be further segmented. More specifically, we firstly use the VAD model pre-trained on AMI dataset (Carletta, 2007) to segment the audio. Two hyperparameters, P_{on} and P_{off}, are set for the VAD model, which are the onset speaker activation threshold and offset speaker activation threshold, respectively. Then the segments longer than T_{dur} are further segmented by increasing P_{on} and P_{off} with α_{on} and α_{off} if P_{on} and P_{off} are smaller than 0.95. Otherwise, we segment the audio into several parts with the same length smaller than T_{dur}, as large activation thresholds may lead to incorrect segmentation. In our experiments, We use the default values of the pretrained model for P_{on} and P_{off}, which are 0.481

[6]https://github.com/facebookresearch/fastText
[7]https://github.com/clab/fast$_{align}$
[8]https://github.com/antho-rousseau/XenC

[9]https://huggingface.co/pyannote/voice-activity-detection

and 0.810. respectively. For segmenting long audios, we set the T_{dur} to 43.75 seconds, α_{on} to 0.1, and α_{off} to 0.028.

Moreover, some short segments are generated by the VAD model according to our observations, which may be incomplete sentences and harm the performance of our ST model. Merging the short segments helps the ST model utilize the context information. So we follow the algorithm in (Inaguma et al., 2021) to merge the short segments after the segmentation.

3 End-to-End YiTrans ST System

Recent studies, such as SpeechT5 (Ao et al., 2021) and SLAM (Bapna et al., 2021), have shown that joint pre-training of speech and text can boost the performance of spoken language processing tasks, such as speech translation. This section will mainly introduce the model architecture of our end-to-end YiTrans system, and the proposed methods to pre-train and fine-tune the models.

3.1 Model Architecture

Our evaluation system is based on an encoder-decoder model with state-of-the-art Transformer architecture. Figure 1 shows the framework of our end-to-end speech translation model, which consists of a speech encoder, text encoder, and text decoder. We employ the relative positional encoding (Shaw et al., 2018) for both the encoder and decoder network.

The speech encoder network contains a convolutional feature encoder and a Transformer encoder. The convolutional feature encoder is a convolutional network for extracting feature from waveform, which has seven 512-channel layers with kernel widths [10,3,3,3,3,2,2] and strides [5,2,2,2,2,2,2]. The Transformer encoder has 24 layers with model dimension 1024, inner dimension 4096 and 16 attention heads. The text encoder and decoder contain 12 layers and have a similar architecture to the Transformer encoder, except that the text decoder includes the cross-attention and the masked self attention. We optionally add an adaptor between the speech encoder and text encoder, which is three one-dimensional convolution layers with stride 2.

3.2 Multi-Stage Unified-Modal Pre-Training

To leverage large amounts of speech and text data, we firstly initialize the speech encoder with the HuBERT LARGE (Hsu et al., 2021) and the text encoder and decoder with the mBART50 (Tang et al., 2020). Then we design a multi-stage pre-training strategy to boost the performance of ASR and ST tasks.

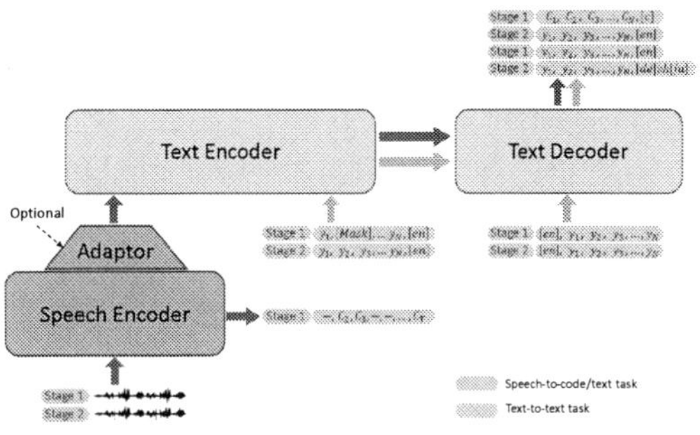

Figure 1: An illustration of the pre-training model.

In the first stage, we employ the speech to code pre-training method following Speech2C (Ao et al., 2022) to make full use of unlabeled speech data. More specifically, We set two pre-training tasks for the encoder-decoder pre-training using unlabeled speech data with pseudo codes, which are acoustic units learned from an offline clustering model. The encoder of Speech2C predicts the pseudo code via masked language modeling (MLM) in encoder output, like HuBERT model. In addition to MLM loss, the decoder of Speech2C learns to reconstruct pseudo codes auto-regressively, instead of generating real text transcription, both of which are discrete representations and have some semantic information corresponding to the speech signal. For the text data, the BART loss (Lewis et al., 2020) and cross entropy loss are used for the monolingual English data and MT data of three target languages, respectively. Note that the text data is only used for pre-training the text encoder and text decoder. For the second stage, we use the ASR data and the filtered MT data to continuously pre-train the model.

3.3 Joint Fine-Tuning

After pre-training, all the pre-trained modules (speech encoder, text encoder, text decoder and the optional adaptor) are used for directly fine-tunig a end-to-end ST model. We also make various efforts to improve the final perfermance.

Joint ST and MT Fine-Tuning We train the ST model along with an auxiliary text to text machine translation (MT) task. We utilize two methods from (Tang et al., 2021b) to enhance the performance of the primary ST task. First, a cross-attentive regularization is introduced for the encoders. It minimizes the L2 distance between two reconstructed encoder output sequences and encourages the encoder outputs from different modalities to be closer to each other. Second, online knowledge distillation learning is introduced for MTL in order to enhance knowledge transfer from the MT to the ST task.

Synthetic Data for ST To provide more parallel audio-translation pairs, we translate the English side of the ASR data with our MT model. Specifically, we translate all the transcriptions of labeled ASR data listed in Table 1 to three target languages. For **en-de**, we additionally generate a certain amount of (about 8000 hours) cascaded pseudo data from unlabeled VoxPopuli, by firstly generating pseudo transcriptions with ASR model and then translating them with MT model.

Multi-Stage Fine-Tuning Note that our ST data is from various domains, including synthetic data and out-of-domain data (e.g. CoVoST). To make out ST model better adapted to the TED domain, we adopt the multi-stage fine-tuning method according to data category: At the first stage, we fine-tune ST models with all ST data, including synthetic and true data; Then at the second stage, the ST models are continually fine-tuned with in-domain data, i.e. Must-C and ST-TED.

3.4 Cascaded Speech Translation

To compare with our end-to-end YiTrans system, we also build a cascaded system by fine-tuning ASR and MT models from pre-trained models, and these subsystems also has been used to construct synthetic data for ST.

3.4.1 Automatic Speech Recognition

We fine-tune our ASR model with the following strategies: (1) **Synthetic Data for ASR**. To make the transcriptions contain the punctuations, we train a punctuation model using the English text of the MuST-C dataset, and add punctuations to the transcriptions of the TEDLIUM and LibriSpeech dataset with this model. We also use a model trained on MuST-C dataset to synthesize data from the Voxpopuli corpus. (2) **Data Filtering**. We find that the ASR data contains some noise and the transcription of some utterances are wrong. Therefore, we also use a model trained on MuST-C dataset to calculate the WER of each sentence, which is used for filtering ASR data. (3) **In-Domain Fine-Tuning**. To let the model fit the TED domain, we train two models from the second stage of pre-training. For the first one, we directly fine-tune the model on the MuST-C dataset. For the second one, we train the model with the TED-style datasets, which include MuST-C, ST-TED, and TED-LIUM corpus. We also filter the utterances that the WER is larger than 50% for the second model.

3.4.2 Machine Translation

All of our MT models for the offline task are fine-tuned from the big pre-trained mBART50 model, with advanced techniques: (1) We inherit the idea of **Progressive Learning** (Li et al., 2020) to train the model from shallow to deep. Specifically, our MT model has 24 encoders and 12 decoder layers, where the top 12 encoder layers are randomly initialized and the rest layers are initialized from mBART50. (2) **Back Translation**. Following previous experience in WMT evaluation campaigns (Akhbardeh et al., 2021), we use the trained **{de,ja,zh}-en** MT models to generate the English side for the selected monolingual text from Table 2. The MT models are also fine-tuned form mBART50. All back-translated pairs and the true paired data are combined for training. (3) **Multi-Stage Fine-Tuning**. We also perform multi-stage fine-tuning for MT models, where the model is first fine-tuned with all (processed) MT data, then is fine-tuned with in-domain data for a few steps. There is also an optional stage between them, which is fine-tuning with in-domain filtered data (the last line in Table 3). (4) **ASR Output Adaptation**. To alleviate the mismatch between the ASR transcripts and the real text used for training MT models, we add the synthetic in-domain data at the in-domain fine-tuning stage. The synthetic data is generated by replacing the English site text with pseudo ASR labels.

4 Experiments & Results

4.1 Pre-Training Setup

All models are implemented in Fairseq [10] (Ott et al., 2019). We pre-train two models depending on the computational efficiency. The first has 24 speech encoder layers, 12 text encoder layers and 12 decoder layers (denoted as PT48). The second has 12 encoder layers, an adaptor, 12 text encoder layers and 12 decoder layers (denoted as PT36). The total

[10]https://github.com/pytorch/fairseq

number of parameters for the pre-trained model is about 927M and 803M, respectively. The vocabulary size is 250k, which is inherited from the mBART50 model.

For the first stage, we pre-train our model on 64 A100 GPUs with a batch size of 37.5s samples per GPU for speech and 1875 tokens per GPU for text and set the update frequency to 3 for 100k steps. We optimize the model with Adam (Kingma and Ba, 2014) and set the learning rate to 3e-5, which is warmed up for the first 8% of updates and linearly decayed for the following updates. For the second stage, we also use 64 A100 GPUs and train the model for 300k with a batch size of 30s samples per GPU for speech and 1500 tokens for text. The learning rate set to 3e-5 is warmed up for the first 10% steps, held as a constant for the following 40% steps, and is decayed linearly for the rest steps. We add a language ID symbol for four languages at the start of each sentence.

ID	Model	tst2019	tst2020
1	Hubert & mBART	30.72	31.58
2	+ in-domain FT	30.62	33.07
3	PT36 + joint FT	20.10 (*)	20.12 (*)
4	+ in-domain FT	30.01	32.65
5	PT48	30.56	33.26
6	+ in-domain FT	30.98	33.48
7	+ joint FT	30.65	33.16
8	+ in-domain FT	**31.02**	33.46
9	+ cascaded data	31.00	**33.52**
10	+ in-domain FT	30.91	33.42
11	Ensemble (10, 6)	31.46	34.03
12	Ensemble (10, 8, 6)	31.49	33.84
13	Ensemble (10, 9, 8, 6)	31.47	33.95
14	Ensemble (10, 9, 8, 6, 2)	**31.57**	33.96
15	Ensemble (10, 9, 8, 6, 4, 2)	31.40	**34.10**

Table 4: BLEU results of e2e **en-de** models.

	Model	tst-common
1	Hubert & mBART	18.13
2	+ in-domain FT	18.59
3	PT36 + joint FT	18.16
4	+ in-domain FT	18.86
5	PT48	17.67
6	+ in-domain FT	18.30
7	+ joint FT	18.71
8	+ in-domain FT	**19.13**
9	Ensemble (8, 6)	19.38
10	Ensemble (8, 6, 2)	19.48
11	Ensemble (8, 6, 4)	19.70
12	Ensemble (8, 6, 4, 2)	**19.81**

Table 5: BLEU results of e2e **en-ja** models.

4.2 End-to-End Speech Translation

Our e2e ST models are fine-tuned from various pre-trained models. When fine-tuning with all ST data, the learning rate is set to 5e-5 and then is decayed linearly to zero within 200k training steps. And when fine-tuning with in-domain data, the learning rate is set to 1e-5 for 30k steps. All ST models are fine-tuned on 8 A100 GPUs with a batch size of about 30s per GPU and update frequency of 4.

	Model	tst-common
1	Hubert & mBART	28.69
2	+ in-domain FT	28.71
3	PT36	28.62
4	+ in-domain FT	28.61
5	PT48	29.07
6	+ in-domain FT	**29.26**
7	+ joint FT	28.51
8	+ in-domain FT	29.14
9	Ensemble (8, 6)	29.38
10	Ensemble (8, 6, 4)	29.36
11	Ensemble (8, 6, 2)	29.48
12	Ensemble (8, 6, 4, 2)	**29.53**

Table 6: BLEU results of e2e **en-zh** models.

en-de We use *tst2019* and *tst2020* as validation sets. We do not use *tst-common* as we find that it has overlapped speech samples with ST-TED training data. All BLEU results are computed at paragraph level, as listed in Table 4. It is noticed that almost all of the models get improved when fine-tuned with in-domain data (in-domain FT). What's more, joint ST&MT fine-tuning (joint FT) and adding cascaded pseudo ST data also help the performance. While, Table 4 shows that PT36 fine-tuned models get some unexpectedly bad results without in-domain fine-tuning. After checking the results we found that sometimes the model could only be able to decode a small portion of a sample especially when the sample is long. Finally, our PT48 fine-tuned model achieves the best performance, and ensemble decoding (Liu et al., 2018) with different models continually brings improvement. Our final submitted system is the last line of Table 4.

en-ja We use *tst-common* as the validation set, which has sentence-level translations so that BLEUs are computed at the sentence level. The results are listed in Table 5, where the BLEUs are computed after tokenized by Mecab[11]. Cascaded pseudo ST data is not performed due to the time urgency. Similar phenomena could be observed in Ta-

[11] https://taku910.github.io/mecab/

Model	en-de tst-common	en-ja/zh tst-common	tst2019	tst2020
Fine-tune with TED-Style data	8.49	8.67	10.9	13.4
Fine-tune with MuST-C	8.55	8.70	10.9	13.6
ensemble	8.47	8.56	10.7	13.3

Table 7: WER results of ASR Systems.

ble 5, where in-domain fine-tuning, joint ST&MT fine-tuning as well as model ensemble benefit the translation performance. Again, our PT48 fine-tuned model achieves the best performance. Our submitted system are listed in the last line of Table 5.

en-zh The validation set is also *tst-common* and sentence level BLEUs with character tokenizer are reported in Table 6. We find that in-domain fine-tuning and joint ST&MT fine-tuning are not as effective here as that in **en-de** and **en-ja**. That might be due to the specific data property of **en-zh**, e.g. all ST data is not mismatched very much with in-domain data. Finally, PT48 fine-tuned models still achieve the best performance and model ensemble brings improvement. Our final submitted system are listed in the last line of Table 6. Note that the results in Table 6 are not post-processed, while in our submitted results of *tst2022*, we post-process the decoding results by correcting the punctuation to Chinese style.

4.3 Cascade Speech Translation

Automatic Speech Recognition For the ASR fine-tuning, we use the CTC and cross-entropy loss to train the model (Watanabe et al., 2017). The loss weights are are set to 0.5 for both of them. We fine-tune the model on 8 A100 GPUs with the update frequency 4 for 120k steps, and set the batch size to around 30s samples per GPU. The learning rate set to 3e-5 is scheduled with the same strategy as the stage 2 of pre-training.

As shown in Table 10, we investigate the impact of speech segmentation with the model fine-tuned on MuST-C dataset. The pyannote toolkit improve the performance significantly compared to the given segmentation. The merge algorithm from Inaguma et al. (2021) further decreases the WER. We adjust two parameters of merge algorithm, M_{dur} and M_{int}. M_{dur} means the maximum duration after merging, and M_{int} is the minimum interval of two segments that will be merged. The experiments show that when M_{dur} and M_{int} are set to 30s and 1s, respectively, the model achieves the best performance. We then apply our Algorithm 1 to further segment the utterance longer than 43.75s, and the final WERs are 10.9 for tst2019 set and 13.6 for tst2020 set. Table 7 shows the WER scores of two ASR systems. We ensemble these two models and use the results for the cascade system.

Machine Translation For all three language pairs, we fine-tune both base models (with 12 encoder layers) and deep models (with 24 encoder layers) as described in Section 3.4.2. All models are fine-tuned on 8 A100 or V100 GPUs with a batch size of 2048 tokens per GPU, the update frequency is 1. The learning rate is set to 1e-4 with 5k warming up steps, then it is linearly decayed to zero in total 200k steps. In case of using additional back-translated data, we set the total training step to 300k. For in-domain fine-tuning, we only change the learning rate to 1e-5 and the total training step to 30k.

The results of MT systems are shown in Table 8. All BLEUs are computed the same way as e2e ST systems. Similar to e2e ST results, in-domain fine-tuning (in-domain FT) benefits all MT models. Progressive learning with deeper models also outperforms their baselines for all languages (line 3 vs. line 1). While, data filtering is shown effective for **en-de** but slightly negative for **en-zh**, which might because we remain too little data for **en-zh** to train such big models. It is also noticed that **en-ja** gets un-normal improvement from filtered data (indicated by *), we speculate data filtering might allow us to collect too similar text to *tst-common* to make the model overfit. Finally, back translation is shown benefit to all languages (line 7), while for **en-de** it falls slightly behind the best results, probably because of the amount of paired data already sufficient.

Cascade Systems Cascade systems are built upon ASR and MT systems. Table 9 shows the cascade ST results when applying the MT model

	Method	Model size	MT en-de tst-common	MT en-ja tst-common	MT en-zh tst-common
1	Baseline	12-12	35.82	19.58	28.52
2	+ in-domain FT	12-12	37.01	20.21	30.10
3	Deep model	24-12	36.25	20.15	29.19
4	+ data filtering	24-12	37.38	24.52 (*)	29.22
5	+ in-domain FT	24-12	**38.27**	**24.91** (*)	29.94
6	Back-translation	24-12	37.29	18.62	28.65
7	+ in-domain FT	24-12	38.05	20.92	**30.43**

Table 8: BLEU results of MT systems. * indicates the results may be over-fitted on tst-common set.

ID	Method	Model size	en-de			en-ja	en-zh
			tst-common	tst2019	tst2020	tst-common	tst-common
1	Baseline	12-12	33.07	30.47	32.96	18.79	27.50
2	+ in-domain FT	12-12	34.17	31.12	33.71	19.40	28.76
3	Deep model	24-12	33.29	30.67	33.14	19.00	27.81
4	+ data filtering	24-12	34.65	31.34	33.85	22.77 (*)	27.99
5	+ in-domain FT	24-12	**35.42**	31.63	**34.29**	**23.45** (*)	28.65
6	Back-translation	24-12	34.54	31.10	33.57	17.61	27.44
7	+ in-domain FT	24-12	35.40	**31.72**	34.16	19.94	**29.12**

Table 9: BLEU results of cascaded systems. * indicates the results may be over-fitted on tst-common set.

VAD	M_{dur}(s)	M_{int}(s)	tst2019	tst2020
Given	-	-	26.2	27.3
pyannote	-	-	15.7	16.3
	20	1	11.2	14.5
	25	0.5	12.4	15.0
	25	1	11.0	14.4
	25	1.5	11.6	14.3
	30	0.5	12.4	14.9
	30	1	10.9	14.0
	30	1.5	11.1	14.3
	35	1	11.4	14.0
Algo 1	30	1	**10.9**	**13.6**

Table 10: Comparison of segmentation ways and merge algorithm for ASR in terms of WER score.

Ensembled Models	tst-common	tst2019	tst2020
en-de			
MT #5; ST #10	**36.44**	**31.90**	**34.60**
MT #5,#7; ST #10	36.31	31.89	34.60
MT #5,#7,#4; ST #10	36.16	31.90	34.45
en-ja			
*MT #5; ST #8	22.79	\	\
*MT #5,#4; ST #8	**23.26**	\	\
*MT #5,#4,#7; ST #8	22.97	\	\
MT #7; ST #8	20.02	\	\
MT #7,#2; ST #8	20.12	\	\
MT #7,#2,#3; ST #8	**20.45**	\	\
en-zh			
MT #7; ST #6	29.38	\	\
MT #7,#2; ST #6	**29.48**	\	\
MT #7,#2,#5; ST #6	29.32	\	\

Table 11: BLEU results of cascaded systems. * indicates the results may be over-fitted on tst-common set.

listed in Table 8 to our best ASR systems. It is shown that better MT models always lead to better ST results. To leverage the end-to-end ST models, we also explore the ensemble of MT and end-to-end ST models as shown in Table 11. For **en-ja**, since the BLEU results of MT model #4 and #5 may be over-fitted on tst-common set, we also choose another three models for the ensemble.

5 Conclusion

In this paper we describe our End-to-End YiTrans speech translation system for IWSLT 2022 offline task. We explore building ST systems from large-scale pre-trained models. Our proposed multi-stage pre-training strategy allows the model to learn multi-modality information from both labeled and unlabeled data, which further improves the performance of downstream end-to-end ST tasks. Our systems are also built on several popular methods such as data augmentation, joint fine-tuning, model ensemble, and so on. Massive experiments demonstrate the effectiveness of our system, and show that the end-to-end YiTrans achieves comparable performance with the strong cascade systems and outperforms the last year's best end-to-end system by 5.2 BLEU in term of English-German tst2021 set.

References

Farhad Akhbardeh, Arkady Arkhangorodsky, Magdalena Biesialska, Ondřej Bojar, Rajen Chatterjee, Vishrav Chaudhary, Marta R. Costa-jussa,

Cristina España-Bonet, Angela Fan, Christian Federmann, Markus Freitag, Yvette Graham, Roman Grundkiewicz, Barry Haddow, Leonie Harter, Kenneth Heafield, Christopher Homan, Matthias Huck, Kwabena Amponsah-Kaakyire, Jungo Kasai, Daniel Khashabi, Kevin Knight, Tom Kocmi, Philipp Koehn, Nicholas Lourie, Christof Monz, Makoto Morishita, Masaaki Nagata, Ajay Nagesh, Toshiaki Nakazawa, Matteo Negri, Santanu Pal, Allahsera Auguste Tapo, Marco Turchi, Valentin Vydrin, and Marcos Zampieri. 2021. Findings of the 2021 conference on machine translation (WMT21). In *Proceedings of the Sixth Conference on Machine Translation*, pages 1–88, Online. Association for Computational Linguistics.

Antonios Anastasopoulos, Luisa Bentivogli, Marcely Z. Boito, Ondřej Bojar, Roldano Cattoni, Anna Currey, Georgiana Dinu, Kevin Duh, Maha Elbayad, Marcello Federico, Christian Federmann, Hongyu Gong, Roman Grundkiewicz, Barry Haddow, Benjamin Hsu, Dávid Javorský, Věra Kloudová, Surafel M. Lakew, Xutai Ma, Prashant Mathur, Paul McNamee, Kenton Murray, Maria Nădejde, Satoshi Nakamura, Matteo Negri, Jan Niehues, Xing Niu, Juan Pino, Elizabeth Salesky, Jiatong Shi, Sebastian Stüker, Katsuhito Sudoh, Marco Turchi, Yogesh Virkar, Alex Waibel, Changhan Wang, and Shinji Watanabe. 2022. FINDINGS OF THE IWSLT 2022 EVALUATION CAMPAIGN. In *Proceedings of the 19th International Conference on Spoken Language Translation (IWSLT 2022)*, Dublin, Ireland. Association for Computational Linguistics.

Antonios Anastasopoulos, Ondřej Bojar, Jacob Bremerman, Roldano Cattoni, Maha Elbayad, Marcello Federico, Xutai Ma, Satoshi Nakamura, Matteo Negri, Jan Niehues, Juan Pino, Elizabeth Salesky, Sebastian Stüker, Katsuhito Sudoh, Marco Turchi, Alexander Waibel, Changhan Wang, and Matthew Wiesner. 2021. FINDINGS OF THE IWSLT 2021 EVALUATION CAMPAIGN. In *Proceedings of the 18th International Conference on Spoken Language Translation (IWSLT 2021)*, pages 1–29, Bangkok, Thailand (online). Association for Computational Linguistics.

Junyi Ao, Rui Wang, Long Zhou, Shujie Liu, Shuo Ren, Yu Wu, Tom Ko, Qing Li, Yu Zhang, Zhihua Wei, et al. 2021. Speecht5: Unified-modal encoder-decoder pre-training for spoken language processing. *arXiv preprint arXiv:2110.07205*.

Junyi Ao, Ziqiang Zhang, Long Zhou, Shujie Liu, Haizhou Li, Tom Ko, Lirong Dai, Jinyu Li, Yao Qian, and Furu Wei. 2022. Pre-training transformer decoder for end-to-end asr model with unpaired speech data. *arXiv preprint arXiv:2203.17113*.

Rosana Ardila, Megan Branson, Kelly Davis, Michael Henretty, Michael Kohler, Josh Meyer, Reuben Morais, Lindsay Saunders, Francis M Tyers, and Gregor Weber. 2019. Common voice: A massively-multilingual speech corpus. *arXiv preprint arXiv:1912.06670*.

Alexei Baevski, Yuhao Zhou, Abdelrahman Mohamed, and Michael Auli. 2020. wav2vec 2.0: A framework for self-supervised learning of speech representations. In *Proceedings of the 34th Conference on Neural Information Processing Systems*, volume 33, pages 12449–12460.

Ankur Bapna, Yu-an Chung, Nan Wu, Anmol Gulati, Ye Jia, Jonathan H Clark, Melvin Johnson, Jason Riesa, Alexis Conneau, and Yu Zhang. 2021. Slam: A unified encoder for speech and language modeling via speech-text joint pre-training. *arXiv preprint arXiv:2110.10329*.

Hervé Bredin, Ruiqing Yin, Juan Manuel Coria, Gregory Gelly, Pavel Korshunov, Marvin Lavechin, Diego Fustes, Hadrien Titeux, Wassim Bouaziz, and Marie-Philippe Gill. 2020. Pyannote.audio: Neural building blocks for speaker diarization. In *ICASSP 2020 - 2020 IEEE International Conference on Acoustics, Speech and Signal Processing (ICASSP)*, pages 7124–7128.

Jean Carletta. 2007. Unleashing the killer corpus: experiences in creating the multi-everything ami meeting corpus. *Language Resources and Evaluation*, 41:181–190.

Roldano Cattoni, Mattia Antonino Di Gangi, Luisa Bentivogli, Matteo Negri, and Marco Turchi. 2021. Must-c: A multilingual corpus for end-to-end speech translation. *Computer Speech Language*, 66:101155.

Mauro Cettolo, Christian Girardi, and Marcello Federico. 2012. Wit3: Web inventory of transcribed and translated talks. In *Conference of european association for machine translation*, pages 261–268.

Mattia A. Di Gangi, Roldano Cattoni, Luisa Bentivogli, Matteo Negri, and Marco Turchi. 2019. MuST-C: a Multilingual Speech Translation Corpus. In *Proceedings of the 2019 Conference of the North American Chapter of the Association for Computational Linguistics: Human Language Technologies, Volume 1 (Long and Short Papers)*, pages 2012–2017.

Chris Dyer, Victor Chahuneau, and Noah A Smith. 2013. A simple, fast, and effective reparameterization of ibm model 2. In *Proceedings of the 2013 Conference of the North American Chapter of the Association for Computational Linguistics: Human Language Technologies*, pages 644–648.

François Hernandez, Vincent Nguyen, Sahar Ghannay, Natalia Tomashenko, and Yannick Esteve. 2018. Tedlium 3: twice as much data and corpus repartition for experiments on speaker adaptation. In *International conference on speech and computer*, pages 198–208. Springer.

Wei-Ning Hsu, Benjamin Bolte, Yao-Hung Hubert Tsai, Kushal Lakhotia, Ruslan Salakhutdinov, and Abdelrahman Mohamed. 2021. Hubert: Self-supervised speech representation learning by masked prediction of hidden units. *IEEE/ACM Transactions on Audio, Speech, and Language Processing*, 29:3451–3460.

Hirofumi Inaguma, Brian Yan, Siddharth Dalmia, Pengcheng Guo, Jiatong Shi, Kevin Duh, and Shinji Watanabe. 2021. ESPnet-ST IWSLT 2021 offline speech translation system. In *Proceedings of the 18th International Conference on Spoken Language Translation (IWSLT 2021)*, pages 100–109, Bangkok, Thailand (online). Association for Computational Linguistics.

Ye Jia, Melvin Johnson, Wolfgang Macherey, Ron J Weiss, Yuan Cao, Chung-Cheng Chiu, Naveen Ari, Stella Laurenzo, and Yonghui Wu. 2019. Leveraging weakly supervised data to improve end-to-end speech-to-text translation. In *ICASSP 2019-2019 IEEE International Conference on Acoustics, Speech and Signal Processing (ICASSP)*, pages 7180–7184. IEEE.

Armand Joulin, Edouard Grave, Piotr Bojanowski, Matthijs Douze, Hérve Jégou, and Tomas Mikolov. 2016. Fasttext.zip: Compressing text classification models. *arXiv preprint arXiv:1612.03651*.

Diederik P Kingma and Jimmy Ba. 2014. Adam: A method for stochastic optimization. *arXiv preprint arXiv:1412.6980*.

Philipp Koehn. 2005. Europarl: A parallel corpus for statistical machine translation. In *Proceedings of machine translation summit x: papers*, pages 79–86.

Mike Lewis, Yinhan Liu, Naman Goyal, Marjan Ghazvininejad, Abdelrahman Mohamed, Omer Levy, Veselin Stoyanov, and Luke Zettlemoyer. 2020. BART: Denoising sequence-to-sequence pre-training for natural language generation, translation, and comprehension. In *Proceedings of the 58th Annual Meeting of the Association for Computational Linguistics*, pages 7871–7880, Online. Association for Computational Linguistics.

Bei Li, Ziyang Wang, Hui Liu, Yufan Jiang, Quan Du, Tong Xiao, Huizhen Wang, and Jingbo Zhu. 2020. Shallow-to-deep training for neural machine translation. In *Proceedings of the 2020 Conference on Empirical Methods in Natural Language Processing (EMNLP)*, pages 995–1005, Online. Association for Computational Linguistics.

Pierre Lison and Jörg Tiedemann. 2016. Opensubtitles2016: Extracting large parallel corpora from movie and tv subtitles.

Yuchen Liu, Long Zhou, Yining Wang, Yang Zhao, Jiajun Zhang, and Chengqing Zong. 2018. A comparable study on model averaging, ensembling and reranking in nmt. In *CCF International Conference on Natural Language Processing and Chinese Computing*, pages 299–308. Springer.

Jan Niehues, Rolando Cattoni, Sebastian Stüker, Mauro Cettolo, Marco Turchi, and Marcello Federico. 2018. The IWSLT 2018 evaluation campaign. In *Proceedings of the 15th International Conference on Spoken Language Translation*, pages 2–6, Brussels. International Conference on Spoken Language Translation.

Myle Ott, Sergey Edunov, Alexei Baevski, Angela Fan, Sam Gross, Nathan Ng, David Grangier, and Michael Auli. 2019. fairseq: A fast, extensible toolkit for sequence modeling. In *Proceedings of the 2019 Conference of the North American Chapter of the Association for Computational Linguistics (Demonstrations)*, pages 48–53.

Vassil Panayotov, Guoguo Chen, Daniel Povey, and Sanjeev Khudanpur. 2015. Librispeech: An asr corpus based on public domain audio books. In *2015 IEEE International Conference on Acoustics, Speech and Signal Processing (ICASSP)*, pages 5206–5210.

Anthony Rousseau. 2013. Xenc: An open-source tool for data selection in natural language processing. *The Prague Bulletin of Mathematical Linguistics*, 100(1):73.

Anthony Rousseau, Paul Deléglise, and Yannick Estève. 2012. TED-LIUM: an automatic speech recognition dedicated corpus. In *Proceedings of the Eighth International Conference on Language Resources and Evaluation (LREC'12)*, pages 125–129, Istanbul, Turkey. European Language Resources Association (ELRA).

Rico Sennrich, Barry Haddow, and Alexandra Birch. 2015. Improving neural machine translation models with monolingual data. *arXiv preprint arXiv:1511.06709*.

Peter Shaw, Jakob Uszkoreit, and Ashish Vaswani. 2018. Self-attention with relative position representations. In *Proceedings of the 2018 Conference of the North American Chapter of the Association for Computational Linguistics: Human Language Technologies, Volume 2 (Short Papers)*, pages 464–468.

Yun Tang, Hongyu Gong, Xian Li, Changhan Wang, Juan Pino, Holger Schwenk, and Naman Goyal. 2021a. FST: the FAIR speech translation system for the IWSLT21 multilingual shared task. In *Proceedings of the 18th International Conference on Spoken Language Translation (IWSLT 2021)*, pages 131–137, Bangkok, Thailand (online). Association for Computational Linguistics.

Yun Tang, Juan Pino, Xian Li, Changhan Wang, and Dmitriy Genzel. 2021b. Improving speech translation by understanding and learning from the auxiliary text translation task. *arXiv preprint arXiv:2107.05782*.

Yuqing Tang, Chau Tran, Xian Li, Peng-Jen Chen, Naman Goyal, Vishrav Chaudhary, Jiatao Gu, and Angela Fan. 2020. Multilingual translation with extensible multilingual pretraining and finetuning.

Changhan Wang, Morgane Riviere, Ann Lee, Anne Wu, Chaitanya Talnikar, Daniel Haziza, Mary Williamson, Juan Pino, and Emmanuel Dupoux. 2021. VoxPopuli: A large-scale multilingual speech corpus for representation learning, semi-supervised learning and interpretation. In *Proceedings of the 59th Annual*

Meeting of the Association for Computational Linguistics and the 11th International Joint Conference on Natural Language Processing (Volume 1: Long Papers), pages 993–1003, Online. Association for Computational Linguistics.

Changhan Wang, Anne Wu, and Juan Pino. 2020a. Covost 2: A massively multilingual speech-to-text translation corpus.

Qian Wang, Yuchen Liu, Cong Ma, Yu Lu, Yining Wang, Long Zhou, Yang Zhao, Jiajun Zhang, and Chengqing Zong. 2020b. CASIA's system for IWSLT 2020 open domain translation. In *Proceedings of the 17th International Conference on Spoken Language Translation*, pages 130–139, Online. Association for Computational Linguistics.

Shinji Watanabe, Takaaki Hori, Suyoun Kim, John R. Hershey, and Tomoki Hayashi. 2017. Hybrid ctc/attention architecture for end-to-end speech recognition. *IEEE Journal of Selected Topics in Signal Processing*, 11(8):1240–1253.

Jian Yang, Shuming Ma, Haoyang Huang, Dongdong Zhang, Li Dong, Shaohan Huang, Alexandre Muzio, Saksham Singhal, Hany Hassan Awadalla, Xia Song, et al. 2021. Multilingual machine translation systems from microsoft for wmt21 shared task. *arXiv preprint arXiv:2111.02086*.

A Appendix

We present the official test results for our submitted systems. For **en-de**, our end-to-end system achieves comparable performance with the cascade system, even the cascaded system is the ensemble of end-to-end and cascaded models. We also outperforms the best result of the last year by a great margin, especially for end-to-end systems. For **en-zh**, the gap between end-to-end and cascaded systems is also small (less than 1 point). While for **en-ja** cascaded systems performs better than end-to-end systems, probably because the end-to-end and cascaded models are complementary and resulting in a better ensemble. Meanwhile, it is noticed that adding punctuation for **en-ja** results is beneficial for *ref2* while harmful for *ref1*.

Model	BLEU ref2	BLEU ref1	BLEU both
Cascaded	25.6	23.7	36.4
E2E YiTrans	25.7	23.6	36.5

Table 12: Official results of our submitted **en-de** ST systems on tst2022.

Model	BLEU ref2	BLEU ref1	BLEU both
Cascaded			
IWSLT21 rank-1	24.6	20.3	34.0
The submission	28.1	23.2	39.0
End-to-end			
IWSLT21 rank-1	22.6	18.3	31.0
Our YiTrans	27.8	23.1	38.8

Table 13: Official results of our submitted **en-de** ST systems on tst2021.

Model	BLEU ref2	BLEU ref1	BLEU both
Cascaded	34.7	35.0	42.9
E2E YiTrans	34.1	34.6	42.3

Table 14: Official results of our submitted **en-zh** ST systems on tst2022.

Model	BLEU ref2	BLEU ref1	BLEU both
Cascaded	18.7	20.2	31.3
+ punc	22.8	14.7	30.0
E2E YiTrans	18.0	19.1	29.8
+ punc	21.8	13.7	28.2

Table 15: Official results of our submitted **en-ja** ST systems on tst2022.

Amazon Alexa AI's System for IWSLT 2022 Offline Speech Translation Shared Task

Akshaya Vishnu Kudlu Shanbhogue* **Ran Xue*** **Ching-Yun Chang** **Sarah Campbell**
Amazon Alexa AI
{ashanbho, ranxue, cychang, srh}@amazon.com

Abstract

This paper describes Amazon Alexa AI's submission to the IWSLT 2022 Offline Speech Translation Task. Our system is an end-to-end speech translation model that leverages pretrained models and cross modality transfer learning. We detail two improvements to the knowledge transfer schema. First, we implemented a new loss function that reduces knowledge gap between audio and text modalities in translation task effectively. Second, we investigate multiple finetuning strategies including sampling loss, language grouping and domain adaption. These strategies aims to bridge the gaps between speech and text translation tasks. We also implement a multi-stage segmentation and merging strategy that yields improvements on the unsegmented development datasets. Results show that the proposed loss function consistently improves BLEU scores on the development datasets for both English-German and multilingual models. Additionally, certain language pairs see BLEU score improvements with specific finetuning strategies.

1 Introduction

Multilingual Spoken Language Translation (SLT) enables translation of audio into text in multiple languages. Traditionally, SLT is solved by cascading automatic speech recognition (ASR) models, which convert audio to transcribed text, with text-to-text translation models. End-to-end (E2E) models, such as FAIR Speech Translation System (Tang et al., 2021a), allow a single model to translate from speech to text. Recent advances in E2E models show comparable results with cascaded architectures (Anastasopoulos et al., 2021; Ansari et al., 2020).

Our baseline end-to-end speech translation system leverages large-scale pretrained models on different data modalities following the approach proposed by Tang et al. (2021a). We adopt dynamic dual skew divergence (DDSD) loss function (Li et al., 2021b) to replace cross entropy (CE) for effective knowledge transfer from pretrained text-to-text (T2T) translation model to speech-to-text (S2T) translation model through joint task training. We observe that DDSD consistently outperforms CE across all language directions.

Our multilingual model supports translation of English (en) audio to German (de), Japanese (ja) and Chinese (zh). We find that finetuning this model based on language groups can improve the performance of the model. Additionally, we find that finetuning models by considering alternate translations can lead to subtle improvements in the overall performance of the models. While working with unsegmented data, we show that using a custom audio segmentation strategy can improve the translation performance by around +2.0 BLEU points. On IWSLT 2022 blind test sets, our system achieves 22.6, 15.3, and 30.4 BLEU score for en→de, en→ja, and en→zh respectively. On the progression test set, our E2E speech translation system performs on par with IWSLT 2021 winning cascaded system (Anastasopoulos et al., 2021).

2 Base Model

We adopt the end-to-end speech translation system proposed by Tang et al. (2021a), which takes both text and speech as input for translation task. The model's encoder consists of a text encoder and a speech encoder for each input data modality, respectively. The text encoder is a 12 layer transformer architecture initialized from the pretrained mBART encoder (Tang et al., 2020). The speech encoder is a 24 layer transformer architecture in which we initialize the speech feature extractor and first 12 layers from pretrained Wav2Vec 2.0 model (Xu et al., 2020). The remaining 12 layers of the speech encoder share weights with the text encoder.

*Akshaya Vishnu Kudlu Shanbhogue and Ran Xue have equal contribution to this work.

Proceedings of the 19th International Conference on Spoken Language Translation (IWSLT 2022), pages 169 - 176
May 26-27, 2022 ©2022 Association for Computational Linguistics

Between the speech encoder and text encoder, an adaptor (Li et al., 2021a) of 3 1-D convolution layers with a stride of two are inserted to compress the speech encoder output by a factor of eight. The model's decoder is initialized from mBART decoder and is shared by two data modalities. We alter the original model architecture to decoupled the mBART output layer and embedding layer instead of using a shared projection layer.

2.1 Pretrained models

We use two state-of-the-art pretrained models — Wav2Vec 2.0 and mBART — for speech and text data, respectively. Both models were trained independently with self-supervised tasks and then finetuned with the corresponding ASR and MT tasks using labeled data.

Wav2Vec 2.0 Wav2Vec 2.0 is a powerful transformer based framework pretrained on self-supervised tasks with large amount of unlabeled speech data (Baevski et al., 2020). There are three main modules in Wav2Vec 2.0 model. The feature encoder is a convolution neural network, which takes wave-form audio as inputs and converts them into a sequence of continuous feature vectors. Then the quantization module learns the latent discrete speech features from the continuous embeddings by sampling from Gumbel softmax distribution (Jang et al., 2017) using two codebooks of size 320. Finally, a transformer based context encoder extracts high quality contextual speech representations from the features. By finetuning on speech data with transcriptions, Wav2Vec 2.0 achieves outstanding performance on ASR task.

In this work, we adopt the Wav2Vec large model finetuned for ASR task ("wav2vec-vox-960h-pl") (Xu et al., 2020). The context encoder in the model has 24 transformer layers with 16 attention heads, and the hidden dimension is 1024. The model was pretrained on Librispeech and LibriVox audio corpus and then finetuned on 960 hours of transcribed Librispeech data (Panayotov et al., 2015), Libri-light data (Kahn et al., 2020a), and pseudo-labeled audio data (Kahn et al., 2020b).

mBART mBART is a sequence-to-sequence encoder-decoder architecture pretrained on large-scale multilingual unlabeled text corpus (Liu et al., 2020). During pretraining, mBART is trained as a denoising auto-encoder which reconstructs the corrupted input text to its original form. The pretrained mBART was fintuned with paralleled machine translation data and achieved significant performance gains on multilingual machine translation (MT) task. For this work, we used the mBART-large-50-one-to-many model, which consists of a 12-layer transformer encoder and a 12-layer transformer decoder. The model was pretrained on 50 languages and finetuned to translate English to the other 49 languages (Tang et al., 2020).

2.2 Multimodal training objectives

During training, both S2T translation and T2T translation tasks are performed using an online knowledge distillation process that mitigates the speech-text modality gap with the following loss function:

$$l = l_{st} + l_{t\_guide} + l_{mt} + l_{cross\_attn} \quad (1)$$

where l_{st} and l_{mt} are cross entropy loss between ground truth and hypothesis from speech and text inputs respectively, l_{t_guide} is the cross entropy loss between hypothesis from speech and text, and l_{cross_attn} is the cross attention regularization from two input data modalities (Tang et al., 2021b).

2.2.1 Dynamic Dual Skew Divergence

To improve the text-guided learning in joint task training, we replace the cross-entropy based text guide loss from eq. 1 with a loss based on Kullback-Leibler divergence that considers S2T translation errors from (1) generating an unlikely hypothesis and (2) not generating a plausible hypothesis when compared with the T2T translation. In previous studies, similar approaches have shown promising results when applied to machine translation task (Li et al., 2021b) and measuring text generation performance (Pillutla et al., 2021).

Kullback-Leibler Divergence Kullback-Leibler (KL) divergence measures the divergence of probability distributions $S(x)$ from $T(x)$:

$$D(T||S) = \sum T(x) \log \frac{T(x)}{S(x)} \quad (2)$$

We denote $T(x)$ as the translation hypothesis probability distribution from the text input and $S(x)$ as the probability distribution from the speech input. $D(T(x)||S(x))$ is an asymmetric distance metric that measures the deviation of S2T distribution with the T2T distribution (type II error). If we switch the sides of $T(x)$ and $S(x)$, minimizing $D(S(x)||T(x))$ emphasizes errors caused by hypotheses generated from the S2T task that are not

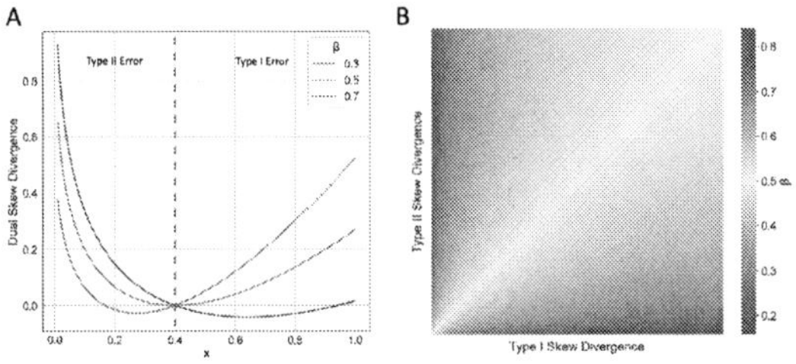

Figure 1: A) Depending on the dominant error types, higher or lower value of β tilts the dual skew divergence curve and providing a steeper slope of the loss curve for current training state. X axis represents S2T output, T2T output is set to 0.4 in this example. B) Value of β dynamically changes based on the values of type I and type II skew divergence

likely to be generated from the T2T task (type I error).

Dual Skew Divergence The definition of KL divergence holds when the observed distribution (e.g. $S(x)$ in the case of $D(T||S)$) is non-zero. However, during training, the probabilities of some tokens can go towards zero due to the large vocabulary size of mBART. To mitigate this issue, in dual divergence, we replace the KL divergence with the skew divergence:

$$D_s(T||S) = D(T||\alpha T + (1 - \alpha)S) \quad (3)$$

where α is a hyperparameter. In this study, we set α to 0.01 for all experiments.

To mitigate the modality gap between speech and text inputs, we consider both types of errors with dual skew KL divergence in training:

$$D_{ds}(T, S) = \beta D_s(S||T) + (1-\beta)D_s(T||S) \quad (4)$$

where β is a weight to balance the two types of errors. When using dual skew divergence as a loss function during training, the value of β affects convergence depending on the dominant error type at the current step. When S2T task undergenerates the probability distribution output by T2T task (higher type II error), a lower value of β motivates faster learning with higher magnitude of gradient. While type I error dominates, a higher value of β is favored by training instead (Figure 1A).

Dynamic Weight As the dominant error type could change during training, we dynamically tune the value of β in eq. 4 based on the values of two dual skew divergence components at each training step. We first normalize the skew divergence to achieve a value bounded between 0 and 1.

$$M(S||T, \beta) = \frac{\log(1 + \beta D_s(S||T))}{(1 + \log(1 + \beta D_s(S||T)))} \quad (5)$$

And then we solve for the value of β that maximizes the product of two measures derived with above equation:

$$\beta = \arg\max \Big((M(S||T, \beta) * M(T||S, 1-\beta)\Big) \quad (6)$$

This logic ensures that β is constantly updated based on type I and type II skew divergence to achieve the preferred dual skew divergence for the current training step (Figure 1B).

3 Finetuning Approaches

To avoid overfitting and moderate generalization, we finetune the base model with a proposed sampling loss algorithm. In addition, we experiment with the effect of finetuning on languages with similar linguistic typology or vocabulary to see if there is negative transferring with the multilingual setting. Finally, we test the consequence of using in-domain data.

The motivation for sampling loss comes from a hypothesis that the ground truth translations may lack diversity. We can make the translation model more robust and increase end-phrase diversity by training with alternate translations to supplement the ground truth translations. To achieve this, we clone the T2T components from the trained base model and use beam search as a mechanism to generate the alternate translations to guide the S2T components. During the beam search, the target probabilities of all the nodes visited are considered during loss computation as illustrated in Figure 2. We reuse the dynamic dual skew divergence loss to train the student model, and this is the only loss applied during our sampling loss finetuning. We recognize that other sampling strategies could also generate alternative translations.

A similar approach is explored in mixed cross entropy loss(Li and Lu, 2021). While mixed cross entropy loss achieves the same effect as sampling loss, sampling loss considers the complete target distribution as ground truth while training the student model.

```
Ground Truth: Today is a wonderful day.

Top 3 beams:
Today is a good  day.
This  is a good  day.
Today is a great day.

At timestep 5, DDSD uses target distribution
P(y | X, Today is a wonderful)

At timestep 5, Sampling Loss uses target distributions
P(y | X, Today is a good)
P(y | X, This  is a good)
P(y | X, Today is a great)
```

Figure 2: Sampling loss example with beam width=3. All target distributions are considered for loss computation.

3.1 Sampling Loss

3.2 Language Grouping

Several studies (Prasanna, 2018; Sachan and Neubig, 2018; Tan et al., 2019; Fan et al., 2021) have suggested that multilingual MT models benefit from training models with languages sharing similar linguistic features. In this work, we experiment with two grouping strategies. One is based on linguistic typology where German and Chinese are considered as subject–verb–object (SVO) languages[1] while Japanese is a subject–object–verb (SOV) language. The other is based on vocabulary sharing. Japanese kanji was derived from Chinese characters, and most of the time the meaning are the same or very similar. For this reason, we consider Japanese and Chinese as a shared-vocabulary group.

3.3 Domain Adaption

Finetuning is a popular approach for domain adaption in MT to boost model performance (Freitag and Al-Onaizan, 2016; Luong and Manning, 2015). As the IWSLT 2022 task uses TED talks as the test data, we evaluate the effect of finetuning our base model using the MuST-C V2 (Di Gangi et al., 2019) dataset, a multilingual speech translation corpus comprising English audio recordings from TED talks.

4 Experimental Setup

In this section, we first describe the datasets and hyperparameters settings used in our model training experiments, followed by a brief introduction of our audio segmentation approach that improves our model performance on unsegmented datasets.

[1]There is a small part of German is SOV.

4.1 Data

We train our models using MuST-C V2 (Di Gangi et al., 2019), CoVoST v2 (Wang et al., 2020) and Europarl-ST V1.1 train-clean dataset (Iranzo-Sánchez et al., 2020). The entire corpus contains paired audio-text samples for Speech Translation, including transcriptions of the source audios. MuST-C supports en-to-14 languages, including en→de, en→ja and en→zh. CoVoST supports en-to-15 languages, again including en→de, en→ja and en→zh. However, as Europarl-ST provides translation data between six European languages, only en→de is supported. Table 1 presents statistics on the datasets. We discard short audio clips of less than 50ms and long audio clips of greater than 30s. We hold out 1% of the data as the development set. Additionally, we evaluate our models using the unsegmented test set released for IWSLT 2019 and IWSLT 2020.

4.2 Training Details

We use the fairseq[2] library to train our models. For the base model using the cross-entropy as the text-guided loss, we set the loss weights of l_{st}, l_{t_guide}, l_{mt}, and l_{cross_attn} as 0.2, 0.8, 1.0, and 0.02, respectively. When training using the DDSD text-guided loss, we reduce l_{mt} to 0.2. For the fine-tuning experiments, the beam size is set to 1 for the sampling loss algorithm. We set dropout to 0.3. We use the Adam optimizer (Kingma and Ba, 2017) and inverse square root scheduler with an initial learning rate of 1e-8. We set the warm-up phase to 5000 steps and the training batch size to a maximum of three for both the base and finetuned models. The model parameters are updated every four batches; the maximum number of iterations is set to 120,000 for the base models, while we train the finetuned models until convergence with the early stopping strategy when the loss on the validation set increases for three consecutive evaluations. Each model is trained on eight NVIDIA V100 GPUs for around 24 to 48 hours.

4.3 Speech Segmentation

Previous years' IWSLT results show that the segmentation approach has significant impact on the performance of end-to-end speech translation (Ansari et al., 2020; Anastasopoulos et al., 2021). We use the WebRTCVAD[3] toolkit to split the unseg-

[2]https://github.com/pytorch/fairseq
[3]https://pypi.org/project/webrtcvad

	MuST-C			CoVoST			Europarl-ST
	en → de	en → ja	en → zh	en → de	en → ja	en → zh	en → de
Samples (in thousands)	238.0	314.0	343.9	289.0	289.0	289.0	31.3
Average audio length (s)	6.3	5.8	5.8	5.4	5.4	5.4	8.5
Average source text length (tokens)	27.2	25.5	25.5	17.8	17.8	17.8	31.4
Average target text length (tokens)	27.9	24.2	22.9	18.3	19.2	15.7	36.5

Table 1: Dataset statistics

Stage	Length threshold (s)	WebRTCVAD		
		A	FD(ms)	ST
1	0	1	10	0.9
2	21	3	30	0.9
3	30	3	10	0.5
4	21	-	-	-

Table 2: Parameter used at each stage of speech segmentation. We pick 21 seconds and 30 seconds as length thresholds as they represent the 99.5% percentile and max of the audio length of our training data. (A: aggressiveness, FD: frame duration, ST: silence threshold)

	Seg. Stage	BLEU	#Seg.	Seg. Length (P25/P50/P75)
IWSLT 2019	S1	23.21	2384	2.29/4.12/7.90
	S2	23.27	2881	2.32/4.06/7.43
	S3	23.27	2909	2.31/4.05/7.41
	S4	**25.00**	963	14.96/17.80/19.58
IWSLT 2020	S1	23.61	2071	2.40/4.21/7.74
	S2	24.42	2408	2.38/4.19/7.22
	S3	24.38	2464	2.37/4.16/7.22
	S4	**26.58**	811	15.07/17.78/19.68

Table 3: Speech translation performance on unsegmented development sets at each segmentation stage. All results are based on the DDSD_{de} model.

mented audio data with a multi-stage segmentation and merging strategy. In each of the first three stages, we split audios that are longer than a corresponding threshold with gradually increased aggressiveness. In the last stage, we merge the short audios from left to right until the merged audio reaches a certain length Table 2. This strategy generates audio segments that are neither too long to be processed by the end-to-end speech translation model nor too short to convey enough contextual information. Throughout this paper we refer to this as our 'own' segmentation.

5 Results and Analyses

In this section, we present our experimental results and analyses. All the reported results are obtained from a single run using one of the following model settings:

- **CE**: This is our baseline model which uses cross-entropy as the text-guided loss .
- **DDSD**: This model uses the DDSD described in Section 2.2.1 as the text-guided loss.
- **DDSD+DDSD**: This is a finetuned model where both of the base and finetuning training are using the DDSD as the text-guided loss.
- **DDSD+SL**: This is a finetuned model where the text-guided loss of the base and the finetuning training are the DDSD and the sampling loss algorithm explained in Section 3.1, respectively.

The corpora and target languages used in a model training are denoted in superscript and subscript, respectively. If no superscript or subscript appears, all the available corresponding corpora or target languages have been used. For example, DDSD_{de} means a bilingual en→de model trained using all the corpora mentioned in Section 4.1.

As for the evaluation datasets, if our model can directly handle the size of a given audio clip, such as the audio in the MuST-C dataset, we directly use the provided data. Otherwise, we use the algorithm described in Section 5.1 to split audio clips into smaller chunks.

5.1 Effect of Speech Segmentation

We tune the speech segmentation algorithm described in Section 5.1 using the IWSLT 2019 and IWSLT 2020 development sets. Table 3 summarizes the performance of the DDSD_{de} model at each segmentation stage. Since few segments have audio lengths longer than 30 seconds, Stage 3 only results in a minimal change to the number of segments and the audio length distribution. After merging short audio clips in Stage 4, the model performance improves by +1.73 and +2.20 BLEU points for the IWSLT 2019 set and IWSLT 2020 set respectively. We hypothesize that this improvement is the result of the model's ability to access more contextual information, and therefore generate better translations. For the rest of the experiments, we report

Model	IWSLT 2019* en → de	IWSLT 2020* en → de	Must-C COMMON en → de	en → ja	en → zh
CE_{de}	23.98	26.02	29.71	-	-
$DDSD_{de}$	**25.00 (+1.02)**	**26.58 (+0.56)**	**30.59 (+0.88)**	-	-
CE	23.25	24.44	28.46	16.27	25.41
DDSD	**24.20 (+0.95)**	**25.67 (+1.23)**	**30.25 (+1.79)**	**16.77 (+0.5)**	**26.69 (+1.28)**

Table 4: Comparison of results using cross-entropy (CE) and the DDSD text-guided loss. Numbers in parentheses show the BLEU difference between models using DDSD and CR losses. * indicates own segmentation.

finetuning Approach	Model	IWSLT 2019* en → de	IWSLT 2020* en → de	Must-C COMMON en → de	en → ja	en → zh
Sampling Loss	$DDSD_{de}$+SL_{de}	**+0.13**	**+0.33**	-0.43	-	-
	DDSD+SL	**+0.07**	**+0.02**	-0.07	**+0.13**	**+0.03**
Language Grouping: Linguistic Typology	DDSD+$DDSD_{de,zh}$	-0.15	-0.03	**+0.13**	-	**+0.02**
	DDSD+$DDSD_{ja}$	-	-	-	**+0.3**	-
Language Grouping: Vocabulary Sharing	DDSD+$DDSD_{ja,zh}$	-	-	-	**+0.44**	-0.10
	DDSD+$DDSD_{de}$	**+0.22**	**+0.17**	**+0.3**	-	-
Sampling Loss + Vocabulary Sharing	DDSD+$DDSD_{ja,zh}$+$SL_{ja,zh}$	-	-	-	**+0.48**	**+0.02**
	DDSD+$DDSD_{de}$+SL_{de}	-0.03	**+0.34**	**+0.36**	-	-
Domain Adaption	DDSD+$DDSD^{Must\text{-}C}$	**+0.08**	**+0.25**	+0.00	**+0.27**	-0.03

Table 5: Relative results of using different finetuning approaches compared with their base model, where numbers in bold mean the finetuned model has a higher BLEU score compared with its base model. * indicates own segmentation

results using segments generated at Stage 4 for the IWSLT 2019 and IWSLT 2020 development sets.

5.2 Effect of the DDSD

We train en→de translation models as well as one-to-many multilingual models using the cross-entropy loss or the DDSD loss as the text-guided loss, with the evaluation results presented in Table 4. From our experiments, en→de models always outperforms the multilingual models. However, the DDSD loss effectively reduces the quality gap between the bilingual and multilingual models from an average of -1.19 BLEU to -0.68 BLEU. Models with DDSD loss consistently outperform those with cross-entropy text-guided loss on all the tested language arcs for both en→de and multilingual models. The BLEU score improvement is in the range of +0.5 to +1.8, where the smallest +0.5 BLEU improvement is observed for the multilingual model's en→ja arc.

5.3 Effect of finetuning

We study three types of finetuning modifications: using the sampling loss, finetuning with language-based groupings and domain adaptation. Since DDSD has consistently improved BLEU metric values, all of our finetuning experiments use models initialized from those trained with the DDSD text-guided loss in the previous section. Table 5 summarizes the change in BLEU score of the proposed approaches comparing to the respective base model trained with DDSD text-guided loss.

Sampling Loss We experiment with the proposed sampling loss algorithm from Section 3.1 and report the results at the first two rows of Table 5. We observe mixed results when comparing $DDSD_{de}$ and DDSD models in Table 4. One explanation is that the base model has been trained with enough data diversity, and therefore the sampling loss has limited influence.

Language Grouping For the linguistic-typology-based finetuning, the finetuned DDSD+$DDSD_{de,zh}$ model (SVO languages) behaves almost the same as the base DDSD model. On the other hand, the vocabulary-sharing-based finetuned model, DDSD+$DDSD_{ja,\ zh}$, achieves a moderate +0.44 BLEU improvement on the en→ja arc while having a small degradation of -0.10 BLEU on the en→zh arc. These results suggest that the en→zh arc which is included in both of the language groups is not affected by either of the language grouping strategies. However, it is worthy to note that the result of en→ja finetuning (+0.3 BLEU) falls behind the en→ja+zh multilingual finetuning (+0.48 BLEU). We also consider finetuning the vocabulary-sharing-based models using the sampling loss where we don't observe consistent improvements in this set of results.

Model	Test set	Language	Segmentation	BLEU ref2	BLEU ref1	BLEU both
$DDSD_{de}$+SL_{de}	IWSLT 2022	en→de	own	22.6	20.1	31.5
	IWSLT 2021	en→de	own	24.4	20.6	34.5
			given	21.9	17.9	30.1
DDSD+$DDSD_{ja,zh}$+$SL_{ja,zh}$	IWSLT 2022	en→ja	own	15.3	16.2	25.3
		en→zh	own	30.4	30.8	37.9

Table 6: Performance of the submitted systems on IWSLT 2022 test sets and progression test set.

Domain Adaption We finetune the base model only using the Must-C dataset and report the results in the last row of the Table 5. Apart from increases of +0.27 and +0.25 BLEU score on the en→ja Must-C testset and en→de IWSLT 2020 testset respectively, there is little-to-no effect on the other testsets. One possible explanation is that the base model has been trained using a fair amount of the representative data, and therefore, the model cannot benefit from further finetuning on the Must-C dataset.

5.4 Submission

Based on the results obtained from the IWSLT development datasets and Must-C COMMON test sets, we submitted $DDSD_{de}$+SL_{de} and DDSD+$DDSD_{ja,zh}$+$SL_{ja,zh}$ as our primary systems for en→de and en→ja+zh with our own segmentation.

We present the results on the IWSLT 2022 and IWSLT 2021 test sets in Table 6. Our systems achieved 22.6, 15.3, and 30.4 BLEU scores on the IWSLT 2022 en→de, en→ja and en→zh blind test sets, respectively. On the en→de progression test set (IWSLT 2021), our system scored 24.4 with our own segmentation and 21.9 with the provided segmentation. Note that the IWSLT 2021 best BLEU scores on same test sets were 24.6 and 21.8 for own segmentation and provided segmentation, respectively, and both results were from cascaded systems (Anastasopoulos et al., 2021).

6 Conclusion

In this paper, we adapt and improve the existing dual skew divergence loss by dynamically balancing the model's quality and diversity via the DDSD text-guided loss. The DDSD text-guided loss outperforms the baseline cross-entropy loss on all the experimented language arcs. We observe that for CE and DDSD loss, one-to-one models always outperform one-to-many multilingual models, however DDSD reduces the performance gap between them. We also consider three different finetuning approaches: sampling loss, language grouping, and domain adaption. Overall, mixed results are observed and none of the finetuning strategies stand out from the others. In addition, the results of the segmentation experiments indicate that the translation quality can be boosted by presenting audios that are longer than the majority of the training data since more context can be taken into consideration. Our submitted end-to-end speech translation system achieves on par performance with the best cascaded system from IWSLT 2021.

References

Antonios Anastasopoulos, Ondřej Bojar, Jacob Bremerman, Roldano Cattoni, Maha Elbayad, Marcello Federico, Xutai Ma, Satoshi Nakamura, Matteo Negri, Jan Niehues, Juan Pino, Elizabeth Salesky, Sebastian Stüker, Katsuhito Sudoh, Marco Turchi, Alexander Waibel, Changhan Wang, and Matthew Wiesner. 2021. FINDINGS OF THE IWSLT 2021 EVALUATION CAMPAIGN. In *Proceedings of the 18th International Conference on Spoken Language Translation (IWSLT 2021)*, pages 1–29, Bangkok, Thailand (online). Association for Computational Linguistics.

Ebrahim Ansari, Amittai Axelrod, Nguyen Bach, Ondřej Bojar, Roldano Cattoni, Fahim Dalvi, Nadir Durrani, Marcello Federico, Christian Federmann, Jiatao Gu, Fei Huang, Kevin Knight, Xutai Ma, Ajay Nagesh, Matteo Negri, Jan Niehues, Juan Pino, Elizabeth Salesky, Xing Shi, Sebastian Stüker, Marco Turchi, Alexander Waibel, and Changhan Wang. 2020. FINDINGS OF THE IWSLT 2020 EVALUATION CAMPAIGN. In *Proceedings of the 17th International Conference on Spoken Language Translation*, pages 1–34, Online. Association for Computational Linguistics.

Alexei Baevski, Henry Zhou, Abdelrahman Mohamed, and Michael Auli. 2020. wav2vec 2.0: A framework for self-supervised learning of speech representations.

Mattia A. Di Gangi, Roldano Cattoni, Luisa Bentivogli, Matteo Negri, and Marco Turchi. 2019. MuST-C: a Multilingual Speech Translation Corpus. In *Proceedings of the 2019 Conference of the North American Chapter of the Association for Computational Linguistics: Human Language Technologies, Volume 1 (Long and Short Papers)*, pages 2012–2017,

Minneapolis, Minnesota. Association for Computational Linguistics.

Angela Fan, Shruti Bhosale, Holger Schwenk, Zhiyi Ma, Ahmed El-Kishky, Siddharth Goyal, Mandeep Baines, Onur Celebi, Guillaume Wenzek, Vishrav Chaudhary, et al. 2021. Beyond english-centric multilingual machine translation. *Journal of Machine Learning Research*, 22(107):1–48.

Markus Freitag and Yaser Al-Onaizan. 2016. Fast domain adaptation for neural machine translation.

J. Iranzo-Sánchez, J. A. Silvestre-Cerdà, J. Jorge, N. Roselló, A. Giménez, A. Sanchis, J. Civera, and A. Juan. 2020. Europarl-st: A multilingual corpus for speech translation of parliamentary debates. In *ICASSP 2020 - 2020 IEEE International Conference on Acoustics, Speech and Signal Processing (ICASSP)*, pages 8229–8233.

Eric Jang, Shixiang Gu, and Ben Poole. 2017. Categorical reparameterization with gumbel-softmax.

J. Kahn, M. Riviere, W. Zheng, E. Kharitonov, Q. Xu, P.E. Mazare, J. Karadayi, V. Liptchinsky, R. Collobert, C. Fuegen, T. Likhomanenko, G. Synnaeve, A. Joulin, A. Mohamed, and E. Dupoux. 2020a. Libri-light: A benchmark for asr with limited or no supervision.

Jacob Kahn, Ann Lee, and Awni Hannun. 2020b. Self-training for end-to-end speech recognition. *ICASSP 2020 - 2020 IEEE International Conference on Acoustics, Speech and Signal Processing (ICASSP)*.

Diederik P. Kingma and Jimmy Ba. 2017. Adam: A method for stochastic optimization.

Haoran Li and Wei Lu. 2021. Mixed cross entropy loss for neural machine translation. In *Proceedings of the 38th International Conference on Machine Learning, ICML 2021, 18-24 July 2021, Virtual Event*, volume 139 of *Proceedings of Machine Learning Research*, pages 6425–6436. PMLR.

Xian Li, Changhan Wang, Yun Tang, Chau Tran, Yuqing Tang, Juan Pino, Alexei Baevski, Alexis Conneau, and Michael Auli. 2021a. Multilingual speech translation with efficient finetuning of pretrained models.

Zuchao Li, Hai Zhao, Yingting Wu, Fengshun Xiao, and Shu Jiang. 2021b. Controllable dual skew divergence loss for neural machine translation.

Yinhan Liu, Jiatao Gu, Naman Goyal, Xian Li, Sergey Edunov, Marjan Ghazvininejad, Mike Lewis, and Luke Zettlemoyer. 2020. Multilingual denoising pre-training for neural machine translation.

Minh-Thang Luong and Christopher Manning. 2015. Stanford neural machine translation systems for spoken language domains. In *Proceedings of the 12th International Workshop on Spoken Language Translation: Evaluation Campaign*, pages 76–79, Da Nang, Vietnam.

Vassil Panayotov, Guoguo Chen, Daniel Povey, and Sanjeev Khudanpur. 2015. Librispeech: An asr corpus based on public domain audio books. *2015 IEEE International Conference on Acoustics, Speech and Signal Processing (ICASSP)*, pages 5206–5210.

Krishna Pillutla, Swabha Swayamdipta, Rowan Zellers, John Thickstun, Sean Welleck, Yejin Choi, and Zaid Harchaoui. 2021. Mauve: Measuring the gap between neural text and human text using divergence frontiers.

Raj Noel Dabre Prasanna. 2018. Exploiting multilingualism and transfer learning for low resource machine translation.

Devendra Singh Sachan and Graham Neubig. 2018. Parameter sharing methods for multilingual self-attentional translation models. *arXiv preprint arXiv:1809.00252*.

Xu Tan, Jiale Chen, Di He, Yingce Xia, Tao Qin, and Tie-Yan Liu. 2019. Multilingual neural machine translation with language clustering. *arXiv preprint arXiv:1908.09324*.

Yun Tang, Hongyu Gong, Xian Li, Changhan Wang, Juan Pino, Holger Schwenk, and Naman Goyal. 2021a. Fst: the fair speech translation system for the iwslt21 multilingual shared task.

Yun Tang, Juan Pino, Xian Li, Changhan Wang, and Dmitriy Genzel. 2021b. Improving speech translation by understanding and learning from the auxiliary text translation task.

Yuqing Tang, Chau Tran, Xian Li, Peng-Jen Chen, Naman Goyal, Vishrav Chaudhary, Jiatao Gu, and Angela Fan. 2020. Multilingual translation with extensible multilingual pretraining and finetuning.

Changhan Wang, Anne Wu, and Juan Pino. 2020. Covost 2: A massively multilingual speech-to-text translation corpus.

Qiantong Xu, Alexei Baevski, Tatiana Likhomanenko, Paden Tomasello, Alexis Conneau, Ronan Collobert, Gabriel Synnaeve, and Michael Auli. 2020. Self-training and pre-training are complementary for speech recognition.

Efficient yet Competitive Speech Translation: FBK@IWSLT2022

Marco Gaido[1,2] ✱, **Sara Papi**[1,2] ✱, **Dennis Fucci**[1,2], **Giuseppe Fiameni**[3],
Matteo Negri[1], **Marco Turchi**[1]
[1]Fondazione Bruno Kessler
[2]University of Trento
[3]NVIDIA AI Technology Center
{mgaido, spapi, dfucci, negri, turchi}@fbk.eu

Abstract

The primary goal of this FBK's systems submission to the IWSLT 2022 offline and simultaneous speech translation tasks is to reduce model training costs without sacrificing translation quality. As such, we first question the need of ASR pre-training, showing that it is not essential to achieve competitive results. Second, we focus on data filtering, showing that a simple method that looks at the ratio between source and target characters yields a quality improvement of 1 BLEU. Third, we compare different methods to reduce the detrimental effect of the audio segmentation mismatch between training data manually segmented at sentence level and inference data that is automatically segmented. Towards the same goal of training cost reduction, we participate in the simultaneous task with the same model trained for offline ST. The effectiveness of our lightweight training strategy is shown by the high score obtained on the MuST-C en-de corpus (26.7 BLEU) and is confirmed in high-resource data conditions by a 1.6 BLEU improvement on the IWSLT2020 test set over last year's winning system.

1 Introduction

The yearly IWSLT offline speech translation (ST) evaluation campaign aims at comparing the models produced by companies, universities, and research institutions on the task of automatically translating speech in one language into text in another language. Given a blind test set, participants' submissions are ranked according to the obtained SacreBLEU score (Post, 2018).

Over the years, the competition to achieve the highest score has driven to bigger and bigger models trained on large datasets: the 2021 winning model (Bahar et al., 2021b) has twice the number of encoder layers (12 vs 6), and a deeper (6 vs 4 layers) and larger (1024 vs 512 features) decoder compared to the 2019 winner (Potapczyk et al., 2019). In addition, most of the competitors have relied on knowledge transfer techniques (Ansari et al., 2020; Anastasopoulos et al., 2021b), such as the initialization of the ST model encoder with the encoder of an ASR system trained on large corpora (Bansal et al., 2019). All these practices have contributed to a remarkable increase in computational expenses and energy consumption that are antithetic with the recent rise of concerns on the social and environmental consequences of these costs (Strubell et al., 2019).

Among the harms inherent to the high computational cost of training ST systems, there is also the risk of restricting the participation in competitions like IWSLT to few big players from the industry sectors that can afford them. As part of a research institution, with this work we try to answer the question: *can we reduce the training cost of ST systems without sacrificing final translation quality?* Specifically, can we train a competitive direct ST model from scratch, without expensive pre-training (e.g. ASR pre-training or self-supervised learning on huge dataset – Baevski et al. 2020)?

To answer these questions, we perform a preliminary study on the English-German (en-de) section of MuST-C (Cattoni et al., 2021), one of the most widespread ST corpora and then we scale to the high-resource data condition allowed by the task organizers. On MuST-C, we show that with the aid of a Connectionist Temporal Classification (CTC) auxiliary loss (Graves et al., 2006) and compression (Gaido et al., 2021a) in the encoder, our Conformer-based (Gulati et al., 2020) model can outperform – to the best of our knowledge – the previous best reported value of 25.3 BLEU by Inaguma et al. (2021), even avoiding any additional pre-training or transfer learning. Moreover, with the addition of a simple data filtering method, we achieve the new state-of-the-art score of 26.7 BLEU for a direct ST model that does not exploit external (au-

✱ The authors contributed equally.

Proceedings of the 19th International Conference on Spoken Language Translation (IWSLT 2022), pages 177 - 189
May 26-27, 2022 ©2022 Association for Computational Linguistics

dio or textual) resources. Scaling to high-resource data conditions, we notice that the gap between an ASR pre-trained system and a system trained from scratch is closed only after a fine-tuning on in-domain data. Our submission to the offline task consists of an ensemble of three models that scores 32.2 BLEU on MuST-C v2 and 27.6 on IWSLT tst2020.

In the same vein of reducing the overall training computational costs, we participated also in the simultaneous task using our best offline model and without performing any additional training do adapt it to the simultaneous scenario (Papi et al., 2022). The simultaneous version of our offline-trained model is realized by applying the wait-k strategy (Ma et al., 2019) with adaptive word detection from the audio input (Ren et al., 2020) that determines the number of words in a speech segment using the greedy prediction of the CTC. Our SimulST model achieves competitive results on the MuST-C v2 test set compared to the last year systems, scoring 25 BLEU at medium latency ($< 2s$) and 30 BLEU at high latency ($< 4s$) while keeping low ($300 - 400ms$) the computation overhead and requiring no dedicated training.

2 Competitive ST without Pre-training

Before training systems on huge corpora, we conduct preliminary experiments on the MuST-C benchmark to find a promising setting aimed at reducing the high computational costs of ST. First, we validate on different architectures the finding of previous works (Gaido et al., 2021a; Papi et al., 2021b) that ST models trained with an additional CTC loss do not need an initialization of the encoder with that of an ASR model. To this aim, we add a CTC loss (Gaido et al., 2021a) whose targets are the lowercase transcripts without punctuation.[1] Second, we explore data selection mechanisms to increase model quality and reduce training time. We always use the same hyper-parameters used in our final trainings for all systems (see Section 6) unless otherwise specified.

2.1 Model Selection

As a first step, we compare different architectures proposed for ST: ST-adapted Transformer (Wang et al., 2020b), Conformer (Gulati et al., 2020), and Speechformer (Papi et al., 2021b). In addition, we also test a composite architecture made of a first stack of 8 Speechformer layers and a second stack of 4 Conformer layers. Hereinafter, we refer to this architecture as Speechformer Hybrid. As a side note, we also experimented with replacing the ReLU activation functions in the decoder of our Conformer model with the squared ReLU, in light of the recent findings on language models (So et al., 2021) showing accelerated model convergence, decreased training time, and improved performance. Unfortunately, these benefits were not observed in our experiments, as the introduction of the squared ReLU caused a small performance drop (-0.2 BLEU) and did not improve the convergence speed of the model. So, we do not consider this change in the rest of the paper.

In all the architectures, the encoder starts with two 1D convolutions. These layers compress the input sequence by a factor of 4 except for the Speechformer, where they do not perform any downsampling. Indeed, the Speechformer relies on a modified self-attention mechanism (ConvAttention) with reduced memory requirements and shrinks the length of the input sequence only on top of 8 ConvAttention layers by means of the CTC-compression (Gaido et al., 2021a) mechanism before feeding the sequence to 4 Transformer layers. However, in a randomly initialized state, the CTC compression may actually not reduce the input sequence (or only slightly), leading to OOM errors caused by the quadratic memory complexity with respect to the sequence length of the Transformer layers. For this reason Papi et al. (2021b) initialize their encoder layers up to the CTC-compression module with a pre-trained model. Since we aim at reducing the computational cost avoiding any pre-training, we introduce two methods that ensure a minimal compression factor of the input sequence after the CTC-compression:

- **Max Output Length**: if the sequence produced by the CTC compression is longer than a threshold (a hyper-parameter that we set to 1/4 of the maximum input sequence length[2]), we merge (averaging them) an equal number of consecutive vectors so that the final length of the sequence is inferior of the defined threshold. For instance, if the maximum

[1] We add the CTC loss in the 8th encoder layer since (Gaido et al., 2021a; Papi et al., 2021a) has demonstrated that it compares favourably with adding the CTC on top of the encoder outputs or in other layers (Bahar et al., 2019).

[2] This ensures that the resulting sequences are not longer than the maximum length obtained by the Transformer and Conformer architectures after the two 1D convolutions.

input sequence length is 4,000, we set the threshold to 1,000; in this case, if a sample results in a sequence of length 2,346 after the CTC compression, we merge the first 3 vectors, then the vectors from the 4th to the 6th, and so on. We use 3 because it is the minimum compression factor that satisfies the length requirement.[3]

- **Fixed compression**: for a given number of epochs n_E (a hyperparameter) the CTC compression is disabled and replaced by a fixed compression that averages 4 consecutive vectors. In this way, we directly control the length of the sequence after the compression, resembling the fixed compression performed by the initial 1D convolutional layers of Transformer and Conformer ST models.

We choose the n_E parameter of the fixed compression method among the values 6, 8, 10, and 12 according to the BLEU score[4] on the dev set. The best score was achieved with $n_E = 10$ (24.16 BLEU), which was lower than the score obtained by the Max Output Length method (24.26 BLEU). As such, in Table 1 (*w/o pretrain* column) we report the results of Speechformer and Speechformer Hybrid with the Max Output Length method.

The results show that the Speechformer-based models do need pre-training to reach their best scores while Conformer and Transformer models achieve comparable translation quality avoiding the pre-training. Specifically, the Conformer architecture with CTC compression obtains the best score without pre-training (25.5 BLEU) and has a negligible gap from the best result with pre-training (25.7 of Speechformer Hybrid). We can hence confirm the statement that ASR pre-training can be avoided at barely no translation quality cost, and hereinafter we use the Conformer with CTC compression without pre-training unless noted otherwise. It is worth mentioning that the introduction of the CTC compression in the Conformer encoder does not only increase translation quality; also, it reduces the RAM requirements and speeds up both the inference and training phases. Indeed, as the sequence length is significantly reduced in the last encoder layers and in the encoder-decoder attention, less computations are required and the mini-batch size – the number of samples processed in parallel – can be increased. Overall, this leads to save $\sim 35\%$ of the training and inference time.

Model	w pretrain	w/o pretrain
Transformer	23.6	23.6
Speechformer	24.5	24.3
Conformer	24.8	24.8
+ CTC compr.	25.6	**25.5**
Speechformer Hybrid	**25.7**	24.9

Table 1: SacreBLEU on the *tst-COMMON* set of MuST-C v1 en-de.

2.2 Data Filtering

Easy methods to improve the quality of ST systems – and deep neural networks in general – consist in providing them with *more* data or *better* data. The first approach comes at the cost of longer training time and higher computational requirements. This makes the second approach more appealing and in line with the overall goal and spirit of this work. We hence focus on the definition of an efficient filtering strategy that improves the quality of our training data (and consequently of our models) without additional computational costs.

We start from the observation that ST models estimate the probability of an output text given an input audio $p(Y|X)$, and a good ST model assigns a low probability to erroneous samples, which are outliers of the $p(Y|X)$ distribution. Although training a ST model only to filter the training data would be extremely computationally expensive, we decided to adopt this method as an upper bound for comparison with easier and feasible strategies. In particular, for each sample in the training set, we computed the negative log-likelihood[5] (NLL) with a strong ST model trained on all the data available for the competition (see Section 5) as a proxy of the probability of the sample. A high NLL means that a sample is unlikely, while a NLL close to 0 means that the sample has a very high probability. Based on this, we can filter all the samples above a threshold to remove the least probable ones. To set the threshold, we draw an histogram on all the training sets (see Figure 2 in the Appendix) that leads to the following considerations: *i)* each dataset has a different distribution, making it difficult to define a threshold valid for all of them, and *ii)* MuST-C has the highest NLL, meaning that it is more complex to fit for the model.

[3] A compression factor 2 would result in a sequence of length 1,173 – higher than the 1,000 threshold – while 3 produces a sequence of length 782.

[4] BLEU+case.mixed+smooth.exp+tok.13a+version.1.5.1

[5] The negative log-likelihood is defined as $-log(p(Y|X))$.

Through the approach described above, we selected the data of MuST-C - the dataset we used in these preliminary experiments - with a NLL greater than 4.0. Upon a manual inspection of a sample of these selected data (5-10% of the total), we noticed that two main categories were present: *i)* bad source/target text alignments[6] (e.g. two sentences in the target translation are paired with only one in the transcript or vice versa), and *ii)* free (non-literal) translations. Instead, no cases of bad audio-transcript alignments were found (this was only a non-exhaustive manual inspection though), meaning that this problem is likely less widespread and impactful than the textual alignment errors in the corpus.

These considerations motivated us to search for a feasible strategy that filter out the bad source/target text alignments. We first considered a simple method that discards samples with too high or low ratio between the target translation length (in characters) and the duration of the source audio.[7] The corresponding histogram on the training data can be found in Figure 3 in the Appendix. Looking at the plots, it emerges that this ratio is strongly dataset-dependent, likely due to the high variability in speaking rate for different domains and conditions, thus making it hard to set good thresholds. For this reason, also supported by the finding of the manual inspection on the good quality of audio-text alignments discussed above, we turn to examine the ratio between the target translation length and the *source transcript length*.[8] Figure 4 in the Appendix shows its histogram: in this case, the behavior is consistent on all datasets, making it easy to determine good values for the minimum and maximum ratio to admit (we set them to 0.8 and 1.6).

In Table 2 we report the results of our filtering method and we compare it with the upper bound of the NLL-based filtering strategy as well as with previous works both under the same data condition and with additional external data. First, we can notice that our simple method based on the target/source character ratio leads to a 1.2 BLEU gain, and has a very small gap (0.2 BLEU) with respect to the upper bound exploiting a strong ST model for filtering. Second, our score (26.7 BLEU) is significantly higher than those reported by previous direct ST works in the same data condition and is on par or even outperforms those of models trained with the addition of external resources. Finally, we compare the results of our model with those of the best cascade models reported in the same data conditions (Bahar et al., 2021a): the tightly-integrated cascade is close to our model (-0.2 BLEU), but ours also benefits from the data filtering technique we just discussed.

Model	BLEU
Cascade (Bahar et al., 2021a)	25.9
Tight Integrated Cascade (Bahar et al., 2021a)	26.5
Without external data	
SATE (Xu et al., 2021)	25.2
BiKD (Inaguma et al., 2021)	25.3
With external data	
JT-ST (Tang et al., 2021)	26.8
Chimera (Han et al., 2021)	26.3
This work	
Conformer + CTC compr.	25.5
+ char-ratio filter.	26.7
+ NLL-based filter.	26.9

Table 2: SacreBLEU on the *tst-COMMON* set of MuST-C v1 en-de. Chimera uses additional speech and WMT14 (Bojar et al., 2014), while JT-ST uses only WMT14 as external resource.

To sum up, we managed to define a training recipe that enables reaching state-of-the-art ST results on MuST-C en-de (26.7 BLEU) with a single training step and involves: *i)* the Conformer architecture, *ii)* an auxiliary CTC loss and CTC-compression in the 8th encoder layer, and *iii)* a simple yet effective filtering strategy based on the ratio between source and target number of characters. In the following section, we discuss the application of this procedure in high-resource data conditions.

3 Audio Segmentation Strategy

ST models are usually trained and evaluated in the ideal and unrealistic condition of audio utterances split at sentence level. As such, when fed with an unsegmented audio stream, they suffer from the mismatch between the training and inference data, which often results in significant performance drops. Accordingly, our last year submission (Papi et al., 2021a) focused on reducing the impact of this distributional shift, both by increasing the robustness of the model with a fine-tuning on a random re-segmentation of the MuST-C training set (Gaido et al., 2020a), and by means of a hybrid method for

[6] In the MuST-C corpus, the alignments between transcripts and translations of the training set are automatically produced, hence misalignments and textual differences can be present.

[7] In practice, we compute the number of characters divided by the number of $10ms$ audio frames.

[8] We used normalized transcript without punctuation, so the length of the target translation is on average 1.2X that of the source transcript.

audio segmentation (Gaido et al., 2021c), which considers both the audio content and the desired length of the resulting speech segments. The experiments showed that the two approaches accounted for complementary gains, both contributing to obtain our best scores.

Recently, Tsiamas et al. (2022) presented a novel Supervised Hybrid Audio Segmentation (SHAS) with excellent results in limiting the translation quality drop. SHAS adopts a probabilistic version of the Divide-and-Conquer algorithm by Potapczyk and Przybysz (2020) that progressively splits the audio at the frame with highest probability of being a splitting point until all segments are below a specified length. The probability of being a splitting point is estimated by a classifier fed with audio representations generated by wav2vec 2.0 (Baevski et al., 2020) and trained to approximate the manual segmentation of the existing corpora, i.e. to emit 1 for frames representing splitting points and 0 otherwise. Since this approach involves a prediction with neural models of considerable size, its superiority over the VAD-based ones comes with a significant computational cost and overhead. In addition, SHAS is not applicable to audio streams, as it requires the full audio to be available before start splitting. In the context of this competition, however, these limitations do not represent a significant issue.

Tsiamas et al. (2022) compare SHAS with previous segmentation methods only using models trained on well-formed sentence-utterance pairs. In this work, we validate their findings also on models fine-tuned on randomly segmented data to check: *i)* whether this fine-tuning brings benefits also with audio segmented with SHAS, and *ii)* whether the gap between SHAS and other segmentation is closed or not by the fine-tuning.

4 Simultaneous

In light of the recent work that questions the necessity of a dedicated training procedure for simultaneous model (Papi et al., 2022), we participate in the Simultaneous task with the same model used for the Offline task. Their finding is perfectly aligned with the spirit of this submission toward the reduction of training computational costs. We determine when to start generating the output translation adopting the wait-k strategy (Ma et al., 2019) that simply prescribes to wait for k words before starting to generate the translation, where k is a hyper-parameter controlled by the user that can be increased or decreased to directly control the latency of the system. The number of words in a given input speech is determined with an adaptive word detection strategy (Ren et al., 2020), because of its superiority over the fixed strategy (Ma et al., 2020b) in strong models trained in high-resource data conditions (Papi et al., 2022). Our adaptive word detection mechanism exploits the predicted output of CTC module in the encoder (Ren et al., 2020; Zeng et al., 2021) to count the number of words in the source speech.

The number of words to wait – k – is not the only hyper-parameter that controls the wait-k strategy. Another important factor is *how often* we check the number of uttered words that is the length of the *speech segment*. A short speech segment means that the system decides more frequently whether to wait for more input or to produce a part of output. This can reduce the latency, but it increases the number of forward passes through the encoder and hence the computational cost. In addition, a longer speech segment implies that the system takes decision with more context at disposal, possibly improving the quality. For this reason, we performed preliminary experiments exploring different speech segment dimensions (every $40ms$ ranging from $120ms$ to $720ms$) and we found $320ms$ and $640ms$ to be superior to other values. Accordingly, we report the results of our systems for these two speech segment durations varying the value of k to achieve different latency. In particular, we test our model with $k = \{1, 2, 3, 4, 5, 6, 7, 8, 9, 10, 11, 12, 13, 14\}$ in order to lie in the latency intervals prescribed by the Simultaneous Shared Task.[9] The latency intervals are determined by the Average Lagging (Ma et al., 2020b) – or AL – on MuST-C v2 tst-COMMON and are: *Low Latency* with $AL \leq 1000ms$, *Medium Latency* with $AL \leq 2000ms$, and *High Latency* with $AL \leq 4000ms$. We use a standard AL-BLEU graph to report the system performance, where in the x axis we find the AL values ranging from $700ms$ to $4000ms$ and in the y axis the corresponding BLEU values. Moreover, we also report the AL_{CA}, the computational aware version of the AL metric (Ma et al., 2020b) accounting also for the computational time spent by the model during inference, in an AL_{CA}-BLEU graph that will be used to additionally score the

[9] https://iwslt.org/2022/simultaneous

performance in the simultaneous task.

5 Data

As training set, we use the ASR and ST datasets allowed for the offline task,[10] which are the same allowed for the simultaneous one. The ASR data consist in *(speech, transcript)* pairs that, in our case, are in English. The ST data consist in *(speech, transcript, translation)* triplets from a source language (here English) to a target language (here German). The ASR data we used are: LibriSpeech (Panayotov et al., 2015), TEDLIUM version 3 (Hernandez et al., 2018), Voxpopuli (Wang et al., 2021), and Mozilla Common Voice.[11] The ST data we used are: MuST-C version 2 (Cattoni et al., 2021), CoVoST version 2 (Wang et al., 2020a), and Europarl-ST (Iranzo-Sánchez et al., 2020).

The ASR-native corpora were included in our ST training by applying Sequence Knowledge Distillation (Kim and Rush, 2016; Gaido et al., 2021b) – or SeqKD –, a popular data augmentation method used in the past IWSLT editions (Ansari et al., 2020; Anastasopoulos et al., 2021a) in which a teacher MT model is used to translate the source transcripts into the target language. To avoid additional computational costs, we choose as MT teacher the freely available pre-trained model by Tran et al. (2021) for WMT2021 that was trained on the corresponding WMT2021 dataset (Akhbardeh et al., 2021), allowed by the IWSLT2022 Offline Task. The SeqKD method was also applied to MuST-C v2 in order to augment the scarce ST available data. As such, our training set comprised the synthetic data built using SeqKD and the native ST data, both filtered with the method described in Section 2.2. The two types of data were distinguished by means of a tag pre-pended to the target text (Gaido et al., 2020b; Papi et al., 2021a).

6 Experimental Settings

All the models used for our participation were implemented on Fairseq-ST (Wang et al., 2020b).[12] All the architectures (Transformer, Speechformer, Speechformer Hybrid, and Conformer) consist in 12 encoder layers and 6 decoder layers, 512 features for the attention layers and 2,048 hidden units in the feed-forward layers. We used 0.1 dropout for the feed-forward layer and attention layer. For Conformer convolutional layers we also apply 0.1 dropout and we set the kernel size to 31 for the point- and depth-wise convolutions. We trained with the Adam optimizer (Kingma and Ba, 2015) ($\beta_1 = 0.9$, $\beta_2 = 0.98$). The learning rate was set to increase linearly from 0 to $2e-3$ for the first 25,000 warm-up steps and then to decay with an inverse square root policy. Differently, it was kept constant for model fine-tuning, with a value of $1e{-}3$. The vocabularies are built via SentencePiece models (Sennrich et al., 2016). In our preliminary experiments only on MuST-C, the number of merge operations was set to 8,000 (Di Gangi et al., 2020) for the German translations and 5,000 (Wang et al., 2020b) for the lowercase punctuation-free English transcripts. In the experiments on high-resource data condition, we doubled these values. We normalize the audio features before passing them to our models with Cepstral Mean and Variance Normalization. Specifically, in offline ST the mean and variance are estimated at utterance level, while for simultaneous ST inference the normalization is based on the global mean and variance estimated on the MuST-C version 2 training set.

Trainings were performed on 4 NVIDIA A100 GPUs with 40GB RAM. We set the maximum number of tokens to 40k per mini-batch and 2 as update frequency for the Conformer with CTC-compression. The other models were trained with 20k tokens per mini-batch and 4 as update frequency. We trained each model for 100,000 updates, corresponding to about 28 hours for the Conformer with CTC-compression. For offline generation, the maximum number of tokens was decreased to 25k, since we used a single K80 GPU with 12GB RAM and we applied the beam search strategy with `num_beams=5`. For simultaneous generation based on SimulEval (Ma et al., 2020a), we used a K80 GPU and greedy search.

7 Results

In this section, we report our experiments in high-resource data conditions and we discuss our submission to the Offline (section 7.1 and Simultaneous (section 7.2) tasks.

7.1 Offline

Fine-tuning on in-domain data. In addition to training our models in the high-resource data con-

[10] https://iwslt.org/2022/offline

[11] https://commonvoice.mozilla.org/en/datasets

[12] Code available at: https://github.com/hlt-mt/FBK-fairseq.

	Model	BLEU
I.	Conformer	30.6
II.	+ in-domain fn	31.6
III.	Conformer_pretrain	31.5
IV.	+ in-domain fn	**31.7**
V.	Ensemble (II, III)	32.0
VI.	Ensemble (III, IV)	31.7
VII.	Ensemble (II, IV)	**32.2**

Table 3: BLEU on MuST-C v2 tst-COMMON for Conformer with pretraining (*Conformer_pretrain*) and without it (*Conformer*). We also report the scores after fine-tuning on in-domain data (+ *in-domain fn*).

dition, we also investigate whether fine-tuning on in-domain data brings advantages or not. The results are reported in Table 3. As we can notice, the Conformer with pre-training outperforms its version trained from scratch by 0.9 BLEU. However, when both the systems are fine-tuned on the in-domain data (rows II and IV), this difference becomes negligible (0.1 BLEU) meaning that the pre-training phase can be skipped in favor of a single fine-tuning step. This might also suggest that the learning rate scheduler and the hyper-parameters we used – tuned on MuST-C corpus – may be sub-optimal when a large amount of data is available. For time reasons, we did not investigate this aspect, which we leave to future work. In addition, we compared several model ensembles: the Conformer with fine-tuning (II) and the pre-trained Conformer (III); the pre-trained Conformer (III) and the pre-trained Conformer with fine-tuning (IV); the Conformer with fine-tuning (II) and the pre-trained Conformer with fine-tuning (IV). Our results show that ensembling the pre-trained Conformer and its fine-tuned version (VI) does not bring benefits, while selecting the Conformer without pre-training fine-tuned on in-domain data and the Conformer with pre-training (V) leads to some improvements, which are enhanced when the two fine-tuned models are used (VII). We also tested ensembles with more than 2 models without obtaining any advantage in terms of translation quality.

Fine-tuning on re-segmented data. As introduced in Section 3, we tested two audio segmentation methods: the *Hybrid* segmentation (Gaido et al., 2021c), and the *SHAS* segmentation (Tsiamas et al., 2022). Also, we fine-tuned our ST models on automatically re-segmented data to reduce the mismatch between train and evaluation conditions. The results are shown in Table 4. First, we notice that the SHAS segmentation method improves over the Hybrid one, with gains from 0.7 to 3.4 BLEU. Secondly, we see that the fine-tuning on re-segmented data – useful with the Hybrid segmentation – becomes useless if using SHAS. In fact, the best overall results are obtained using SHAS on a model that is not fine-tuned on resegmented data (row 2), which scores 30.4 BLEU on the MuST-C v2 tst-COMMON and 26.8 BLEU on the IWSLT 2020 test set. As such, we can conclude that fine-tuning on resegmented data is not needed if the audio is segmented with SHAS.

Ensembles. Since in the experiments on in-domain fine-tuning the best overall score was obtained by an ensemble of models, we compared the best combination (Ensemble VII in Table 3) with other ensembles obtained by combining models fine-tuned on re-segmented data and models without this fine-tuning. As we can see from rows 7-10 of Table 4, the best scores are realized by adding a model fine-tuned on re-segmented data (6) to Ensemble VII, although the gap between all the ensembles is small on both test sets ($\leq$ 0.4 BLEU). This 3-models ensemble (10) obtained the best overall BLEU of 31.3 on MuST-C v2 tst-COMMON and 27.6 on IWSLT 2020 test set, outperforming by 1.6 BLEU the best result reported last year (Inaguma et al., 2021).

Offline Submissions. Given the results of the Ensemble (1, 2, 6), we chose its output as our *primary* submission for the Offline Shared task. On the basis of the small performance drop on both test sets (0.4 BLEU) and to verify the possibility of avoiding the fine-tuning on re-segmented data, we choose the Ensemble (1, 2) as *contrastive* submission. Lastly, we can notice that the single Conformer model without pre-training (1) falls behind the best Ensemble by only 1 BLEU for MuST-C v2 tst-COMMON and 1.2 BLEU for IWSLT 2020 test set. This suggests that users can be served with sound and competitive translations even with a single model obtained with less than 30 hours of total training time on 4 GPUs. To test this hypothesis, we sent the translations generated by the latter system as additional *contrastive* submission. We report in Table 5 the official results for the tst2022 and tst2021 sets. The scores confirm our findings that the gap between the best ensemble and the single model without pre-training is limited to less than 1 BLEU. Most significantly, this single model outperforms the best direct system reported last

	Model	Hybrid		SHAS	
		tst-COMMON	iwslt2020	tst-COMMON	iwslt2020
1.	Conformer + in-domain fn	27.4	23.8	30.3	26.4
2.	Conformer_pretrain + in-domain fn	28.1	24.4	**30.4**	**26.8**
	with fine-tuning on resegmented data				
3.	Conformer + resegm. fn	28.3	25.2	29.3	26.1
4.	Conformer + in-domain fn + resegm. fn	29.1	25.0	29.9	26.2
5.	Conformer_pretrain + resegm. fn	29.0	25.9	29.8	26.7
6.	Conformer_pretrain + in-domain fn + resegm. fn	29.0	25.7	29.7	**26.8**
	Ensembles				
7.	Ensemble (1, 2)	28.6	24.7	30.9	27.2
8.	Ensemble (4, 6)	29.7	26.0	30.5	27.2
9.	Ensemble (2, 6)	28.9	25.7	30.8	27.4
10.	Ensemble (1, 2, 6)	28.9	25.8	**31.3**	**27.6**

Table 4: BLEU scores of Hybrid and SHAS audio segmentation methods of the models with and without fine-tuning on re-segmented data (*resegm. fn*) on the MuST-C v2 tst-COMMON and the IWSLT2020 test set.

Model		tst2022			tst2021		
		ref2	ref1	both	ref2	ref1	both
Best direct IWSLT 2021	(Bahar et al., 2021b)	-	-	-	22.6	18.3	31.0
Best cascade IWSLT 2021	HW-TSC (Anastasopoulos et al., 2021b)	-	-	-	24.6	20.3	34.0
	This work						
primary	Ensemble (1, 2, 6)	**23.6**	**21.0**	**32.9**	**25.5**	**21.3**	**35.6**
contrastive1	Ensemble (1, 2)	23.4	20.6	32.5	25.4	20.9	35.2
contrastive2	Conformer + in-domain fn	22.8	20.1	31.6	24.5	20.2	33.9

Table 5: BLEU scores on the official blind tst2022 and tst2021 sets of our primary and contrastive submissions.

year (Bahar et al., 2021b) by 1.9 BLEU on the two single references and 2.9 BLEU on both references. Our primary submission increases these gains to 2.9-3.0 BLEU on the single references and 4.6 BLEU on both references, and beats the best cascade system from last year campaign (HW-TSC – Anastasopoulos et al. 2021b) by 0.9-1.0 BLEU on the single references and 1.6 BLEU on both references. All in all, we can conclude that this work has shown that a lightweight training procedure is possible without dramatically sacrificing the quality and competitiveness of the system. We believe that our results are promising for future works in this direction.

7.2 Simultaneous

For the SimulST task participation we use the best performing offline model, namely the Conformer with pre-training and fine-tuning on in-domain data, to which we apply the wait-k policy with adaptive word detection. The AL- and AL_{CA}-BLEU graphs are shown in Figure 1.

As we can see from the AL-BLEU graph, the systems with speech segment $320ms$ and $640ms$ have similar behaviour in terms of quality. The main difference between them is the minimum latency from which they start: the system with speech segment $320ms$ starts at an AL of about $800ms$ while the system with speech segment $640ms$ starts at about $900ms$. On average, if the k value increases, the AL increases by $300ms$ for both systems, with a wider latency interval at the beginning that progressively shrinks at high latency values. In spite of this, the system with speech segment $320ms$ achieves the highest BLEU slightly before the *Medium Latency* (25.1) and *High Latency* thresholds (30.1), making it the best candidate for submission. If we look at the AL_{CA}-BLEU graph, the results partially change because the system with speech segment $640ms$ has a lower computational burden, achieving up to 2 BLEU points improvement at low latency against the other system. Thus, looking at the computational aware metric, the best candidate is the system with speech segment $640ms$. We can conclude that $320ms$ is the best speech segment value for the AL ranking while $640ms$ is the best for the AL computational aware version. Since the organizers encourage multiple submissions, we participate with both the speech segment values.

8 Conclusions

We described the FBK participation in the IWSLT 2022 offline and simultaneous tasks (Anastasopoulos et al., 2022). Our focus was to build a system with the least number of training steps but capable of obtaining competitive results with state-of-

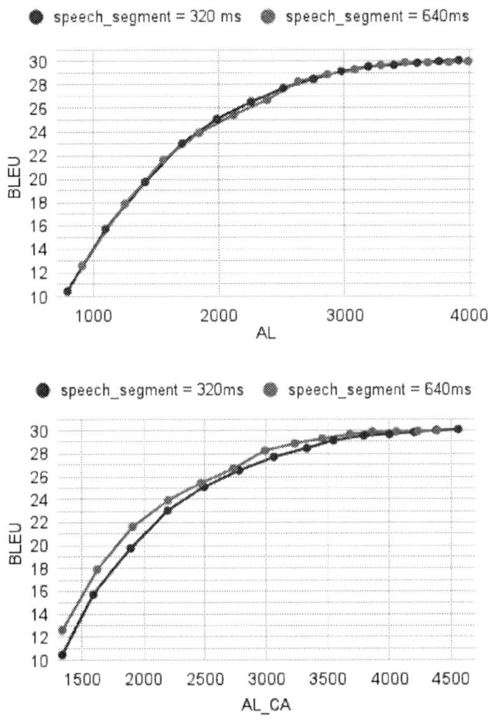

Figure 1: AL- and AL_{CA}-BLEU curves on MuST-C v2 tst-COMMON.

the-art models, which typically undergo complex and longer training procedures. To this aim, we *i)* showed that ASR pre-training of the encoder can be avoided without a significant impact on the final system performance, *ii)* proposed a simple yet effective data filtering technique to enhance translation quality while reducing the training time, and *iii)* compared different solutions to deal with automatic audio segmentation at inference time. Our results on the IWSLT2020 test set indicate that a single Conformer-based model without pre-training falls behind our best model ensemble by only 1.2 BLEU and outperforms the best score reported last year by 0.4 BLEU. The same trend occurs on the blind tst2021 and tst2022 sets, with a 0.8-1.1 BLEU gap from our best model ensemble, which in turn beats by $\sim$1 BLEU the best reported result last year. These promising results are also confirmed in the simultaneous scenario in which, using the offline-trained model without any adaptation for the simultaneous task, we reach good quality-latency balancing, especially in the more realistic computational aware evaluation setting.

9 Acknowledgements

This work has been supported by the ISCRA-B project *DireSTI* granted by CINECA, and by Amazon Web Services. The submission to the simultaneous track has been carried out as part of the project Smarter Interpreting (`https://kunveno.digital/`) financed by CDTI Neotec funds.

References

Farhad Akhbardeh, Arkady Arkhangorodsky, Magdalena Biesialska, Ondřej Bojar, Rajen Chatterjee, Vishrav Chaudhary, Marta R. Costa-jussa, Cristina España-Bonet, Angela Fan, Christian Federmann, Markus Freitag, Yvette Graham, Roman Grundkiewicz, Barry Haddow, Leonie Harter, Kenneth Heafield, Christopher Homan, Matthias Huck, Kwabena Amponsah-Kaakyire, Jungo Kasai, Daniel Khashabi, Kevin Knight, Tom Kocmi, Philipp Koehn, Nicholas Lourie, Christof Monz, Makoto Morishita, Masaaki Nagata, Ajay Nagesh, Toshiaki Nakazawa, Matteo Negri, Santanu Pal, Allahsera Auguste Tapo, Marco Turchi, Valentin Vydrin, and Marcos Zampieri. 2021. Findings of the 2021 conference on machine translation (WMT21). In *Proceedings of the Sixth Conference on Machine Translation*, pages 1–88, Online. Association for Computational Linguistics.

Antonios Anastasopoulos, Luisa Bentivogli, Marcely Z. Boito, Ondřej Bojar, Roldano Cattoni, Anna Currey, Georgiana Dinu, Kevin Duh, Maha Elbayad, Marcello Federico, Christian Federmann, Hongyu Gong, Roman Grundkiewicz, Barry Haddow, Benjamin Hsu, Dávid Javorský, Věra Kloudová, Surafel M. Lakew, Xutai Ma, Prashant Mathur, Paul McNamee, Kenton Murray, Maria Nădejde, Satoshi Nakamura, Matteo Negri, Jan Niehues, Xing Niu, Juan Pino, Elizabeth Salesky, Jiatong Shi, Sebastian Stüker, Katsuhito Sudoh, Marco Turchi, Yogesh Virkar, Alex Waibel, Changhan Wang, and Shinji Watanabe. 2022. FINDINGS OF THE IWSLT 2022 EVALUATION CAMPAIGN. In *Proceedings of the 19th International Conference on Spoken Language Translation (IWSLT 2022)*, Dublin, Ireland. Association for Computational Linguistics.

Antonios Anastasopoulos, Ondřej Bojar, Jacob Bremerman, Roldano Cattoni, Maha Elbayad, Marcello Federico, Xutai Ma, Satoshi Nakamura, Matteo Negri, Jan Niehues, Juan Pino, Elizabeth Salesky, Sebastian Stüker, Katsuhito Sudoh, Marco Turchi, Alexander Waibel, Changhan Wang, and Matthew Wiesner. 2021a. FINDINGS OF THE IWSLT 2021 EVALUATION CAMPAIGN. In *Proceedings of the 18th International Conference on Spoken Language Translation (IWSLT 2021)*, pages 1–29, Bangkok, Thailand (online). Association for Computational Linguistics.

Antonios Anastasopoulos, Ondřej Bojar, Jacob Bremerman, Roldano Cattoni, Maha Elbayad, Marcello Federico, Xutai Ma, Satoshi Nakamura, Matteo Negri, Jan Niehues, Juan Pino, Elizabeth Salesky, Sebastian Stüker, Katsuhito Sudoh, Marco Turchi, Alex Waibel, Changhan Wang, and Matthew Wiesner. 2021b. Findings of the IWSLT 2021 Evaluation Campaign. In *Proceedings of the 18th International Conference on Spoken Language Translation (IWSLT 2021)*, Online.

Ebrahim Ansari, Amittai Axelrod, Nguyen Bach, Ondřej Bojar, Roldano Cattoni, Fahim Dalvi, Nadir Durrani, Marcello Federico, Christian Federmann, Jiatao Gu, Fei Huang, Kevin Knight, Xutai Ma, Ajay Nagesh, Matteo Negri, Jan Niehues, Juan Pino, Elizabeth Salesky, Xing Shi, Sebastian Stüker, Marco Turchi, Alexander Waibel, and Changhan Wang. 2020. FINDINGS OF THE IWSLT 2020 EVALUATION CAMPAIGN. In *Proceedings of the 17th International Conference on Spoken Language Translation*, pages 1–34, Online. Association for Computational Linguistics.

Alexei Baevski, Yuhao Zhou, Abdelrahman Mohamed, and Michael Auli. 2020. wav2vec 2.0: A framework for self-supervised learning of speech representations. In *Advances in Neural Information Processing Systems 33: Annual Conference on Neural Information Processing Systems 2020, NeurIPS 2020, December 6-12, 2020, virtual.*

Parnia Bahar, Tobias Bieschke, and Hermann Ney. 2019. A Comparative Study on End-to-end Speech to Text Translation. In *Proceedings of International Workshop on Automatic Speech Recognition and Understanding (ASRU)*, pages 792–799, Sentosa, Singapore.

Parnia Bahar, Tobias Bieschke, Ralf Schlüter, and Hermann Ney. 2021a. Tight Integrated End-to-End Training for Cascaded Speech Translation. In *2021 IEEE Spoken Language Technology Workshop (SLT)*, pages 950–957.

Parnia Bahar, Patrick Wilken, Mattia A. Di Gangi, and Evgeny Matusov. 2021b. Without further ado: Direct and simultaneous speech translation by AppTek in 2021. In *Proceedings of the 18th International Conference on Spoken Language Translation (IWSLT 2021)*, pages 52–63, Bangkok, Thailand (online). Association for Computational Linguistics.

Sameer Bansal, Herman Kamper, Karen Livescu, Adam Lopez, and Sharon Goldwater. 2019. Pre-training on High-resource Speech Recognition Improves Low-resource Speech-to-text Translation. In *Proceedings of the 2019 Conference of the North American Chapter of the Association for Computational Linguistics: Human Language Technologies, Volume 1 (Long and Short Papers)*, pages 58–68, Minneapolis, Minnesota. Association for Computational Linguistics.

Ondřej Bojar, Christian Buck, Christian Federmann, Barry Haddow, Philipp Koehn, Johannes Leveling, Christof Monz, Pavel Pecina, Matt Post, Herve Saint-Amand, Radu Soricut, Lucia Specia, and Aleš Tamchyna. 2014. Findings of the 2014 workshop on statistical machine translation. In *Proceedings of the Ninth Workshop on Statistical Machine Translation*, pages 12–58, Baltimore, Maryland, USA. Association for Computational Linguistics.

Roldano Cattoni, Mattia A. Di Gangi, Luisa Bentivogli, Matteo Negri, and Marco Turchi. 2021. MuST-C: A multilingual corpus for end-to-end speech translation. *Computer Speech & Language*, 66:101155.

Mattia A. Di Gangi, Marco Gaido, Matteo Negri, and Marco Turchi. 2020. On Target Segmentation for Direct Speech Translation. In *Proceedings of the 14th Conference of the Association for Machine Translation in the Americas (AMTA 2020)*, pages 137–150, Virtual.

Marco Gaido, Mauro Cettolo, Matteo Negri, and Marco Turchi. 2021a. CTC-based compression for direct speech translation. In *Proceedings of the 16th Conference of the European Chapter of the Association for Computational Linguistics: Main Volume*, pages 690–696, Online. Association for Computational Linguistics.

Marco Gaido, Mattia A. Di Gangi, Matteo Negri, Mauro Cettolo, and Marco Turchi. 2020a. Contextualized Translation of Automatically Segmented Speech. In *Proc. Interspeech 2020*, pages 1471–1475.

Marco Gaido, Mattia A. Di Gangi, Matteo Negri, and Marco Turchi. 2020b. End-to-end speech-translation with knowledge distillation: FBK@IWSLT2020. In *Proceedings of the 17th International Conference on Spoken Language Translation*, pages 80–88, Online. Association for Computational Linguistics.

Marco Gaido, Mattia A. Di Gangi, Matteo Negri, and Marco Turchi. 2021b. On Knowledge Distillation for Direct Speech Translation . In *Proceedings of CLiC-IT 2020*, Online.

Marco Gaido, Matteo Negri, Mauro Cettolo, and Marco Turchi. 2021c. Beyond voice activity detection: Hybrid audio segmentation for direct speech translation. In *Proceedings of The Fourth International Conference on Natural Language and Speech Processing (ICNLSP 2021)*, pages 55–62, Trento, Italy. Association for Computational Linguistics.

Alex Graves, Santiago Fernández, Faustino J. Gomez, and Jürgen Schmidhuber. 2006. Connectionist Temporal Classification: Labelling Unsegmented Sequence Data with Recurrent Neural Networks. In *Proceedings of the 23rd international conference on Machine learning (ICML)*, pages 369–376, Pittsburgh, Pennsylvania.

Anmol Gulati, James Qin, Chung-Cheng Chiu, Niki Parmar, Yu Zhang, Jiahui Yu, Wei Han, Shibo Wang, Zhengdong Zhang, Yonghui Wu, and Ruoming Pang.

2020. Conformer: Convolution-augmented Transformer for Speech Recognition. In *Proc. Interspeech 2020*, pages 5036–5040.

Chi Han, Mingxuan Wang, Heng Ji, and Lei Li. 2021. Learning shared semantic space for speech-to-text translation. In *Findings of the Association for Computational Linguistics: ACL-IJCNLP 2021*, pages 2214–2225, Online. Association for Computational Linguistics.

François Hernandez, Vincent Nguyen, Sahar Ghannay, Natalia A. Tomashenko, and Yannick Estève. 2018. TED-LIUM 3: Twice as much data and corpus repartition for experiments on speaker adaptation. In *Speech and Computer - 20th International Conference, SPECOM 2018, Leipzig, Germany, September 18-22, 2018, Proceedings*, volume 11096 of *Lecture Notes in Computer Science*, pages 198–208. Springer.

Hirofumi Inaguma, Tatsuya Kawahara, and Shinji Watanabe. 2021. Source and target bidirectional knowledge distillation for end-to-end speech translation. In *Proceedings of the 2021 Conference of the North American Chapter of the Association for Computational Linguistics: Human Language Technologies*, pages 1872–1881, Online. Association for Computational Linguistics.

Javier Iranzo-Sánchez, Joan Albert Silvestre-Cerdà, Javier Jorge, Nahuel Roselló, Adrià Giménez, Albert Sanchis, Jorge Civera, and Alfons Juan. 2020. Europarl-ST: A Multilingual Corpus for Speech Translation of Parliamentary Debates. In *ICASSP 2020 - 2020 IEEE International Conference on Acoustics, Speech and Signal Processing (ICASSP)*, pages 8229–8233.

Yoon Kim and Alexander M. Rush. 2016. Sequence-level knowledge distillation. In *Proceedings of the 2016 Conference on Empirical Methods in Natural Language Processing*, pages 1317–1327, Austin, Texas. Association for Computational Linguistics.

Diederik P. Kingma and Jimmy Ba. 2015. Adam: A method for stochastic optimization. In *3rd International Conference on Learning Representations, ICLR 2015, San Diego, CA, USA, May 7-9, 2015, Conference Track Proceedings*.

Mingbo Ma, Liang Huang, Hao Xiong, Renjie Zheng, Kaibo Liu, Baigong Zheng, Chuanqiang Zhang, Zhongjun He, Hairong Liu, Xing Li, Hua Wu, and Haifeng Wang. 2019. STACL: Simultaneous translation with implicit anticipation and controllable latency using prefix-to-prefix framework. In *Proceedings of the 57th Annual Meeting of the Association for Computational Linguistics*, pages 3025–3036, Florence, Italy. Association for Computational Linguistics.

Xutai Ma, Mohammad Javad Dousti, Changhan Wang, Jiatao Gu, and Juan Pino. 2020a. SIMULEVAL: An evaluation toolkit for simultaneous translation. In *Proceedings of the 2020 Conference on Empirical Methods in Natural Language Processing: System Demonstrations*, pages 144–150, Online. Association for Computational Linguistics.

Xutai Ma, Juan Pino, and Philipp Koehn. 2020b. SimulMT to SimulST: Adapting simultaneous text translation to end-to-end simultaneous speech translation. In *Proceedings of the 1st Conference of the Asia-Pacific Chapter of the Association for Computational Linguistics and the 10th International Joint Conference on Natural Language Processing*, pages 582–587, Suzhou, China. Association for Computational Linguistics.

Vassil Panayotov, Guoguo Chen, Daniel Povey, and Sanjeev Khudanpur. 2015. Librispeech: An asr corpus based on public domain audio books. In *2015 IEEE International Conference on Acoustics, Speech and Signal Processing (ICASSP)*, pages 5206–5210.

Sara Papi, Marco Gaido, Matteo Negri, and Marco Turchi. 2021a. Dealing with training and test segmentation mismatch: FBK@IWSLT2021. In *Proceedings of the 18th International Conference on Spoken Language Translation (IWSLT 2021)*, pages 84–91, Bangkok, Thailand (online). Association for Computational Linguistics.

Sara Papi, Marco Gaido, Matteo Negri, and Marco Turchi. 2021b. Speechformer: Reducing information loss in direct speech translation. In *Proceedings of the 2021 Conference on Empirical Methods in Natural Language Processing*, pages 1698–1706, Online and Punta Cana, Dominican Republic.

Sara Papi, Marco Gaido, Matteo Negri, and Marco Turchi. 2022. Does simultaneous speech translation need simultaneous models?

Matt Post. 2018. A call for clarity in reporting BLEU scores. In *Proceedings of the Third Conference on Machine Translation: Research Papers*, pages 186–191, Brussels, Belgium. Association for Computational Linguistics.

Tomasz Potapczyk and Pawel Przybysz. 2020. SRPOL's system for the IWSLT 2020 end-to-end speech translation task. In *Proceedings of the 17th International Conference on Spoken Language Translation*, pages 89–94, Online. Association for Computational Linguistics.

Tomasz Potapczyk, Pawel Przybysz, Marcin Chochowski, and Artur Szumaczuk. 2019. Samsung's system for the IWSLT 2019 end-to-end speech translation task. In *Proceedings of the 16th International Conference on Spoken Language Translation*, Hong Kong. Association for Computational Linguistics.

Yi Ren, Jinglin Liu, Xu Tan, Chen Zhang, Tao Qin, Zhou Zhao, and Tie-Yan Liu. 2020. SimulSpeech: End-to-end simultaneous speech to text translation. In *Proceedings of the 58th Annual Meeting of the Association for Computational Linguistics*, pages 3787–3796, Online. Association for Computational Linguistics.

Rico Sennrich, Barry Haddow, and Alexandra Birch. 2016. Neural machine translation of rare words with subword units. In *Proceedings of the 54th Annual Meeting of the Association for Computational Linguistics (Volume 1: Long Papers)*, pages 1715–1725, Berlin, Germany. Association for Computational Linguistics.

David R. So, Wojciech Mańke, Hanxiao Liu, Zihang Dai, Noam Shazeer, and Quoc V. Le. 2021. Primer: Searching for efficient transformers for language modeling.

Emma Strubell, Ananya Ganesh, and Andrew McCallum. 2019. Energy and policy considerations for deep learning in NLP. In *Proceedings of the 57th Annual Meeting of the Association for Computational Linguistics*, pages 3645–3650, Florence, Italy. Association for Computational Linguistics.

Yun Tang, Juan Pino, Xian Li, Changhan Wang, and Dmitriy Genzel. 2021. Improving speech translation by understanding and learning from the auxiliary text translation task. In *Proceedings of the 59th Annual Meeting of the Association for Computational Linguistics and the 11th International Joint Conference on Natural Language Processing (Volume 1: Long Papers)*, pages 4252–4261, Online. Association for Computational Linguistics.

Chau Tran, Shruti Bhosale, James Cross, Philipp Koehn, Sergey Edunov, and Angela Fan. 2021. Facebook ai's wmt21 news translation task submission. In *Proc. of WMT*.

Ioannis Tsiamas, Gerard I Gállego, José AR Fonollosa, and Marta R Costa-jussà. 2022. Shas: Approaching optimal segmentation for end-to-end speech translation. *arXiv preprint arXiv:2202.04774*.

Changhan Wang, Juan Pino, Anne Wu, and Jiatao Gu. 2020a. CoVoST: A diverse multilingual speech-to-text translation corpus. In *Proceedings of The 12th Language Resources and Evaluation Conference*, pages 4197–4203, Marseille, France. European Language Resources Association.

Changhan Wang, Morgane Riviere, Ann Lee, Anne Wu, Chaitanya Talnikar, Daniel Haziza, Mary Williamson, Juan Pino, and Emmanuel Dupoux. 2021. VoxPopuli: A large-scale multilingual speech corpus for representation learning, semi-supervised learning and interpretation. In *Proceedings of the 59th Annual Meeting of the Association for Computational Linguistics and the 11th International Joint Conference on Natural Language Processing (Volume 1: Long Papers)*, pages 993–1003, Online. Association for Computational Linguistics.

Changhan Wang, Yun Tang, Xutai Ma, Anne Wu, Dmytro Okhonko, and Juan Pino. 2020b. fairseq s2t: Fast speech-to-text modeling with fairseq. In *Proceedings of the 2020 Conference of the Asian Chapter of the Association for Computational Linguistics (AACL): System Demonstrations*.

Chen Xu, Bojie Hu, Yanyang Li, Yuhao Zhang, Shen Huang, Qi Ju, Tong Xiao, and Jingbo Zhu. 2021. Stacked acoustic-and-textual encoding: Integrating the pre-trained models into speech translation encoders. In *Proceedings of the 59th Annual Meeting of the Association for Computational Linguistics and the 11th International Joint Conference on Natural Language Processing (Volume 1: Long Papers)*, pages 2619–2630, Online. Association for Computational Linguistics.

Xingshan Zeng, Liangyou Li, and Qun Liu. 2021. RealTranS: End-to-end simultaneous speech translation with convolutional weighted-shrinking transformer. In *Findings of the Association for Computational Linguistics: ACL-IJCNLP 2021*, pages 2461–2474, Online. Association for Computational Linguistics.

A Dataset Statisctics for Data Filtering

In this Section we report the histograms created when defining our data filtering mechanism (Section 2.2).

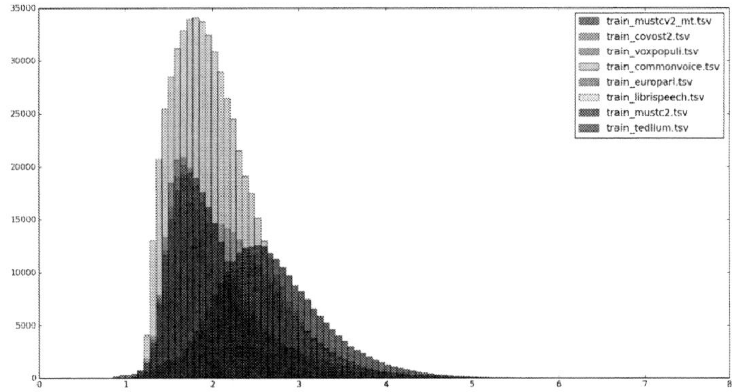

Figure 2: Histogram of the negative log-likelihood (NLL) of the samples for all the training set of the competition. The ST model used to estimate the NLL has been trained on all the data and was scoring 29.6 BLEU on MuST-C.

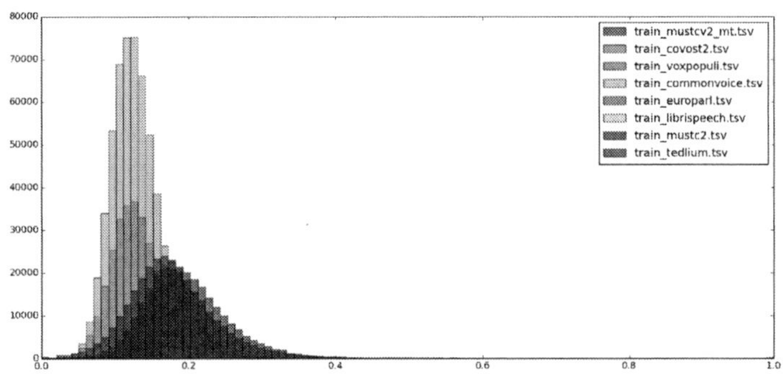

Figure 3: Histogram of the ratio between the number of target translation character and 10ms audio frames for all the training set of the competition.

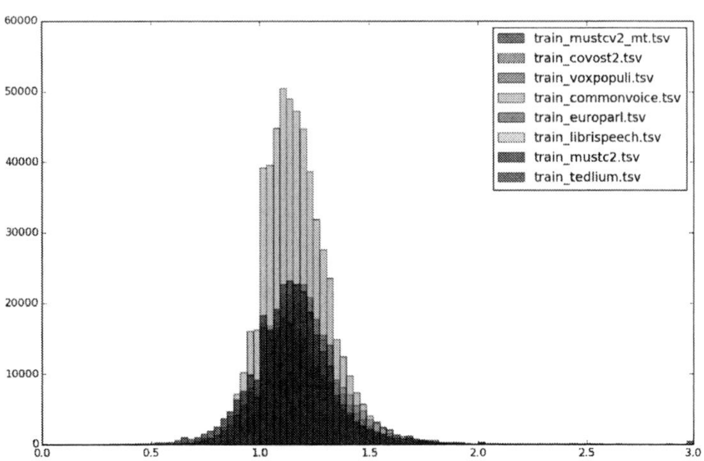

Figure 4: Histogram of the ratio between the number of characters in the target translation and the source punctuation-free transcript for all the training set of the competition.

Effective combination of pretrained models - KIT@IWSLT2022

Ngoc-Quan Pham[1] and **Tuan-Nam Nguyen**[1] and **Thai-Binh Nguyen**[1] and **Danni Liu**[2] and **Carlos Mullov**[1] and **Jan Niehues**[1] and **Alexander Waibel**[1,3]
[1]Karlsruhe Institute of Technology
[2]Maastricht University
[3]Carnegie Mellon University, Pittsburgh PA, USA
firstname.lastname@kit.edu
firstname.lastname@maastrichtuniversity.nl

Abstract

Pretrained models in acoustic and textual modalities can potentially improve speech translation for both Cascade and End-to-end approaches. In this evaluation, we aim at empirically looking for the answer by using the wav2vec, mBART50 and DeltaLM models to improve text and speech translation models. The experiments showed that the presence of these models together with an advanced audio segmentation method results in an improvement over the previous End-to-end system by up to 7 BLEU points. More importantly, the experiments showed that given enough data and modeling capacity to overcome the training difficulty, we can outperform even very competitive Cascade systems. In our experiments, this gap can be as large as 2.0 BLEU points, the same gap that the Cascade often led over the years.

1 Introduction

Speech translation (ST) has been the main theme of IWSLT for more than a decade and it goes without saying between the traditional Cascade approach and the recent End-to-end (E2E) possibility, the former has always been preferred. Being able to divide the complicated ST to smaller sub-problems: automatic recognition, (often) re-segmentation (Cho et al., 2017) and machine translation, the cascade approach has the advantage of using more data to separately optimize the components. The E2E, on the other hand, relies on a single network architecture that requires an explicit speech-translation dataset.

Over the years of participation, we observed that the performance gap between E2E and cascade is reduced (Anastasopoulos et al., 2021), and there are three negative factors that outweigh the advantages of having a single architecture without the problem of error propagation (Sperber and Paulik, 2020).

- Data utilization: the end2end model can only be directly trained on parallel speech translation data, which is often lacking compared to speech-transcription or text translation data. Previously the SLT models would require a necessary pre-training step with ASR in order to have comparable results with cascade (Bansal et al., 2018; Pham et al., 2020c).
- Modeling power. The transition from shallow LSTM-based models (Sperber et al., 2019) to Transformer-based models (Pham et al., 2020a) resulted in a big leap in model capacity and showed the potential of the E2E approach.
- Better audio segmentation. Decoding directly from long audio files is infeasible due to the expensive memory requirement and the presence of other distractions such as breaks, noise or music. Applying either cascade or E2E models absolutely requires an audio segmentation step performed by a voice activity detection system. While the cascade systems can handle imprecise cuts based on a re-segmentation process (Cho et al., 2017), the E2E lacks this ability to recover from this training-testing condition mismatch.

In our work, we massively improved our end-to-end SLT systems for English→German with up to 6 BLEU points by directly addressing the aforementioned weaknesses:

- Pretrained acoustic (Baevski et al., 2020) and language models (Tang et al., 2020) are incorporated in modeling. This allowed for transferring the knowledge during the pretraining processes which contain a massive amount of data. This effect is further enhanced when combined with the pseudo labels generated by machine translation.

Proceedings of the 19th International Conference on Spoken Language Translation (IWSLT 2022), pages 190 - 197
May 26-27, 2022

- By using the pretrained models, we fully utilized the large architectures that improved the results further. More importantly, the pretrained acoustic model directly extracts features from audio waveforms which is potentially an advantage compared to the manually extracted features in the previous systems.
- The audio segmentation component is changed into a full neural-based solution combined with pretraining (Tsiamas et al., 2022). The new solution is not only more accurate, but also directly optimized on TED Talks giving the translation model more precise and complete segmentations compared to the generic voice activity detectors.

Moreover, we also applied the same techniques to improve the Speech Recognition and Machine Translation components of the Cascade system. They also benefit from the above factors, albeit to a limited extent. Unlike previous years when the Cascade was always the better performing system, for the first time we selected the E2E as our primary submission.

For the current evaluation campaign (Anastasopoulos et al., 2022), we also expanded the SLT systems for two new directions: English→Chinese and English→Japanese, with both of the approaches available. The resulting system is also used in a simultaneous setting located in the same evaluation campaign (Polák et al., 2022).

2 Data

Speech Corpora. For training and evaluation of our ASR models, we used Mozilla Common Voice v7.0 (Ardila et al., 2019), Europarl (Iranzo-Sánchez et al., 2020), How2 (Sanabria et al., 2018), Librispeech (Panayotov et al., 2015), MuST-C v1 (Di Gangi et al., 2019), MuST-C v2 (Cattoni et al., 2021) and Tedlium v3 (Hernandez et al., 2018) dataset. The data split is presented in the following table 1.

3 Cascade System for Offline Speech Translation

We address the offline speech translation task by two main approaches, namely cascade and end-to-end. In the cascaded condition, the ASR module (Section 3.1) receives audio inputs and generates raw transcripts, which will then pass through a Segmentation module (Section 3.2) to formulate

Table 1: Summary of the English data-sets used for speech recognition

Corpus	Utterances	Speech data [h]
A: Training Data		
Common Voice	1225k	1667
Europarl	33k	85
How2	217k	356
Librispeech	281k	963
MuST-C v1	230k	407
MuST-C v2	251k	482
TEDLIUM	268k	482
B: Test Data		
Tedlium	1155	2.6
Librispeech	2620	5.4

well normalized inputs to our Machine Translation module (Section 3.3). The MT outputs are the final outputs of the cascade system. On the other hand, the end-to-end architecture is trained to directly translate English audio inputs into German text outputs (Section 3.4).

3.1 Speech Recognition

The speech recognition model is based on the wav2vec 2.0 architecture (Baevski et al., 2020) with a CTC decoder on top of the Transformer layers. The model is trained to output characters with a vocabulary of 30. Here we used the large version of Wav2vec 2.0 (24 hidden layers, hidden size is 1024), which was pre-trained on 53k hours of English audio data. The fine-tuning process used approximately 4.5k hours of audio (as illustrated in Table 1). The CTC decoder is supported by a 5-gram language model with a beam size of 100. The text corpus used to create the 5-gram model comes from the transcription label of the audio data.

3.2 Text Segmentation

The text segmentation in the cascaded pipeline serves as a normalization on the ASR output, which usually lacks punctuation marks and casing information. On the other hand, the machine translation system is often trained on well-written, high-quality bilingual data. Following the idea from (Nguyen et al., 2020), since punctuation and casing information always belong to words, we combine that info into 15 tags label (e.g **U. U, T! T$** ...). In which, punctuation has 5 types are **". , ! ? $"** (**$** stands for no punctuation), casing information has 3 types are **"T"** (uppercase the first character of word), **"U"** (uppercase all character of word), **"L"** (lowercase all character of word). Our text segmentation model will become a sequence tagging model. We fine tune a BERT base-uncased model (Devlin et al., 2018) to predict tag label for each word in the input. Model has 12 hidden layers and hidden size is 768. The Yelp Review Dataset (Zhang et al., 2015) is used for training this model.

3.3 Machine Translation

For the machine translation module, we first re-use the English→German machine translation model from our last year' submission to IWSLT (Pham et al., 2020b). More than 40 millions sentence pairs being extracted from TED, EPPS, NC, Common-Crawl, ParaCrawl, Rapid and OpenSubtitles corpora were used for training the model. In addition, 26 millions sentence pairs are generated from the back-translation technique by a German→English translation system. A large transformer architecture was trained with Relative Attention. We adapted to the in-domain by fine-tuning on TED talk data with stricter regularizations. The same adapted model was trained on noised data synthesized from the same TED data. The final model is the ensemble of the two.

To fully use the available resources this year, we also fine-tune pretrained DeltaLM (Ma et al., 2021). We use the "base" configuration with 12 encoder and 6 decoder layers. Similar to the approach above, we conduct a two-step fine-tuning, first on WMT data and then on TED transcript-translation parallel data (except for English→Chinese where we directly fine-tuned on TED due to computation constraints). We also use this MT system to generate synthetic data from TEDLIUM transcripts for training the end-to-end systems.

For English→Japanese, the MT model based on DeltaLM and trained using 11.3M sentences from JESC, JParaCrawl, KFTT, TED and WikiMatrix datasets. Similar to the English→Chinese model, this model is also further finetuned on TED.

4 End-to-End System

4.1 Corpora

For training, we use all of the data available in Table 2. Here, the Speech Translation is pre-filtered using an ASR model to remove the samples that have a high mismatch between the manual label and transcription output[1].

Because of the multilingual condition, we combine the datasets for Japanese and Chinese from MuST-C, CoVoST (Wang et al., 2020) to train multilingual systems. Moreover, we followed the success of generating synthetic labels for audio utterances (Pham et al., 2020b) and translated the transcripts of TEDLIUM into all three languages using the MT models. This process required us to reconstruct the punctuations for the transcripts (Sperber and Paulik, 2020) and the translation in general is relatively noisy and incomplete (due the to fact that the segmentations are not necessarily aligned into grammatically correct sentences).

Table 2: Training data for E2E translation models.

Data	Utterances	Total time
English→German		
MuST-C v1	228K	408h
MuST-C v2	250K	408h
Europarl	32K	60h
Speech Translation	142K	160h
TEDLIUM	268K	415h
CoVoST	272K	424h
English→Japanese		
MuST-C v2	328K	420h
CoVoST	232K	400h
TEDLIUM	268K	415h
English→Chinese		
MuST-C	350K	480h
CoVoST	232K	400h
TEDLIUM	268K	415h

During training, the validation data is the Development set of the MuST-C corpus. The reason is that the SLT testsets often do not have the aligned audio and translation, while training end-to-end models often rely on perplexity for early stopping.

4.2 Modeling

In order to fully utilize the pretrained acoustic and language models, we constructed the SLT architecture with the encoder based on the wav2vec 2.0 (Baevski et al., 2020) and the decoder based on the autoregressive language model pretrained with mBART50 (Tang et al., 2020).

wav2vec 2.0 is a Transformer encoder model which receives raw waveforms as input and generates high level representations. The architecture consists of two main components: first a convolution-based *feature extractor* downsamples long audio waveforms into features that have similar lengths with spectrograms. After that, a deep

[1]Here we used BLEU score as the metric.

Transformer encoder uses self-attention and feed-forward neural network blocks to transform the features without further downsampling.

During the self-supervised training process, the network is trained with a constrastive learning strategy (Baevski et al., 2020), in which the features (after being downsampled) are randomly masked and the model learns to predict the quantized latent representation of the masked time step as well as encouraging the model to diversify the quantization codebooks by maximizing their entropies.

During the supervised learning step, we freeze the feature extraction weights to save memory since the first layers are among the largest ones and fine-tune all of the weights in the Transformer encoders. Moreover, in order to make the model more robust against the fluctuation in absolute positions when it comes to audio signals, as well as the training-testing mismatched condition happening when we have to use a segmentation model to find audio segments during testing, we added the relative position encodings (Dai et al., 2019; Pham et al., 2020a) to alleviate this problem.

Here we used the same pretrained model with the speech recognizer, with the large architecture pretrained with $53k$ hours of unlabeled data.

mBART50 is an encoder-decoder Transformer-based language model. During training, instead of the typical language modeling setting of predicting the next word in the sequence, this model is trained to reconstruct a sequence from its noisy version (Lewis et al., 2019) and later extended to a multilingual version (Liu et al., 2020; Tang et al., 2020) in which the corpora from multiple languages are combined during training. mBART50 is the version that is pretrained on 50 languages.

Architecture wise, this model follows the Transformer encoder and decoder (Vaswani et al., 2017). During fine-tuning, we can combine the mBART50 decoder with encoder pretrained with the wav2vec 2.0 so that each component contains the knowledge of one modality. The cross-attention layers connecting the decoder with the encoder are the parts that require extensive fine-tuning in this case, due to the modality mismatch between pretraining and finetuning.

Eventually, the model is easily extensible to a multilingual scenario by training on the combination of the datasets. The mBART50 vocabulary contains language tokens for all three languages and can be used to control the language output (Ha et al., 2016).

4.3 Speech segmentation

As pointed out in (Tsiamas et al., 2022), the quality of audio segmentation has a big impact on the performance of the speech translation models, which are trained on utterances corresponding to full sentences, often manually aligned, and this rarely happens with an automatic segmentation system.

With the advantage of neural architectures and pretrained models, we follow the SHAS method (Tsiamas et al., 2022) to train a Transformer-based audio segmentation model on the MuST-C v2 corpus. Based on the high-level audio features generated by wav2vec 2.0, the model predicts the probability of each frame belonging to an utterance or not with cross-entropy. Afterwards, given the probabilities of the frames in an audio sequence (which are actually averaged over several rolls for more consistent accuracy), a segmentation algorithm called probabilistic DAC is used to aggressively cut the segments at the points with lowest probabilities, and then trim the segments to get probabilities higher than a set threshold.

We found this method to be much more effective than other voice activity detectors such as WebRTC-VAD (Wiseman, 2016). In the next experimental part, it will be shown that the audio segmentation quality is one of the most important factors helping the E2E system. Here we closely followed the original implementations and parameters to obtain the neural segmenter.

5 Experimental Results

5.1 Speech Recognition

The quality of our ASR system is measured on two testsets: TEDLIUM and Librispeech (clean). For comparison, we also provide the WER from the models trained without pre-training, including the Transformers (Pham et al., 2019), Conformers (Gulati et al., 2020) and LSTMs (Nguyen et al., 2019).

Table 3: WER on Libri and TEDLIUM test sets.

Data	Libri	TEDLIUM
Conformer-based	3.0	4.8
Transformer-based	3.2	4.9
LSTM-based	2.6	**3.9**
wav2vec 2.0	**1.1**	4.2

It is notable that the latest ASR system with pretraining is substantially better than the same architecture (but with less layers) on both Librispeech and TEDLIUM tests. While the improvement on TEDLIUM is 12.5%, we observed a significant 63% improvement on Librispeech, which is enabled by the large amount of read speech included in pretraining. The wav2vec 2.0 layer is also considerably larger than both Transformer variants.

Compared with the LSTMs, the wav2vec model is 57% better in Librispeech, yet the former reaches lower error rate in TEDLIUM. Since TED Talks accounts for the majority of the training data, pretraining on a large amount of read speech might not fully transfer to a more formal and spontaneous speech style.

5.2 Machine Translation

In Table 4, we report the performance of the machine translation systems described in Section 3.3. We first show results for English-German when: 1) translating directly from the ground-truth transcripts, and 2) translating from the ASR outputs (Section 5.1).

First, we see incorporating the pretrained DeltaLM (Ma et al., 2021) improves translation quality from the ground-truth by 0.9-1.5 BLEU. The gain carries over to the speech translation performance when cascading with the ASR model, yet at a smaller scale of 0.5-0.8 BLEU. This suggests that the MT quality still degrades when coping with noisy inputs from ASR transcripts.

For Chinese and Japanese, the two newly added language in this year's evaluation campaign, we evaluate on the MuST-C tst-COMMON transcript-translation data. The BLEU scores are 28.3 and 19.5 respectively[2].

Table 4: Performance of the machine translation module in BLEU↑.

Testset en→de	tst2015	tst2019	tst2020
From ground-truth			
MT2021	33.9	28.5	32.3
MT2022	34.8	30.0	33.2
From ASR			
MT2021	26.1	25.1	27.9
MT2022	26.9	25.9	28.4

[2]Using `tok.zh` and `tok.ja-mecab-0.996-IPA` respectively from sacreBLEU(Post, 2018)

5.3 End-to-end Offline Speech Translation

Given two new factors coming into play for the End-to-end models, namely pretrained models and audio segmentation, the models are tested on the static test which is the tst-COMMON set from the MuST-C corpus (Di Gangi et al., 2019) with the pre-segmented utterances and labels. This testset is available for all three languages. The whole system is tested on the IWSLT testsets without utterance boundaries and labels are only provided in paragraphs (each talk is contained in one paragraph). In this condition, only English→German tests are available.

The results on this test for all three languages are presented in Table 5. On English-German, overall we managed to improve the purely supervised model with Transformers (Pham et al., 2020a) by 2.6 BLEU points. Using the pretrained weights from wav2vec and mBART is very effective for an additional 1.6 BLEU points, while we found that the relative attention also contributed for a 0.7 BLEU points, and training the model in the multilingual setting is also slightly better.

Table 5: BLEU scores on tst-COMMON from MuST-C

Model	BLEU
English-German	
E2E 2021	30.6
wav2vec + mBART	32.2
wav2vec + rel + mBART	32.9
wav2vec + rel + mBART + multi	33.2
English-Chinese	
wav2vec + rel + mBART + multi	24.5
English-Japanese	
wav2vec + rel + mBART + multi	16.9

Table 6: ST: Translation performance in BLEU↑ on IWSLT testsets (re-segmentation required). Progressive results from this year and last year end-to-end (E2E) and cascade (CD) are provided.

Testset →	tst2015	tst2019	tst2020
E2E2021	22.13	20.43	23.20
CD2021	24.95	21.07	25.4
E2E2021 + SHAS	26.66	24.55	25.58
+W2V-MBART	26.64	26.31	28.66
+REL	27.27	26.58	29.11
+MULTI	27.65	26.84	29.2
+ENSEMBLE	**27.87**	**27.61**	**30.05**
CD2022	26.84	25.91	28.35

The final results on previous IWSLT testsets are presented in Table 6. First of all, the new segmentation method SHAS managed to improve the translation results of our previous year's submission by up to 4.4 BLEU points (as can be see on tst2015 and tst2019). By using a stronger model with wav2vec and mBART pretrained modules, the results are vastly improved by 2.2 and 3.1 BLEU points on tst2019 and tst2020. The performance is incrementally improved even further, by combining different techniques including relative attention, multilingual training and ensemble. Eventually, we obtain a result which is 7.8 BLEU points better than the last year's end-to-end submission.

The cascade system is also improved this year, by using the pretrained ASR, MT and better segmentation. On tst2020, we managed to improve the BLEU score by 3 points. However this enhancement pales against the E2E, and this is our first participation in which the E2E convincingly outperformed the Cascade system.

6 Conclusion

If the end-to-end models remained as a promising approach in the previous evaluation campaigns, it eventually blooms as the superior solution when the conditions are met to overcome its problems, namely training difficulty, segmentation issues and inefficient data usage. While the performance of the E2E system is now better, we can still believe that its far from being practical given the size of the model and the required presence of an audio segmenter. Moreover, the Cascade system is still necessary since it can provide a distillation tool for the E2E, via pseudolabels for better data utilization. The development of both approaches remains to be interesting awaiting the future achievement in multilingual and multimodal unsupervised and self-supervised training.

Acknowledgments

The projects on which this paper is based were funded by the Federal Ministry of Education and Research (BMBF) of Germany under the numbers 01IS18040A. The authors are responsible for the content of this publication.

References

Antonios Anastasopoulos, Luisa Bentivogli, Marcely Z. Boito, Ondřej Bojar, Roldano Cattoni, Anna Currey, Georgiana Dinu, Kevin Duh, Maha Elbayad, Marcello Federico, Christian Federmann, Hongyu Gong, Roman Grundkiewicz, Barry Haddow, Benjamin Hsu, Dávid Javorský, Věra Kloudová, Surafel M. Lakew, Xutai Ma, Prashant Mathur, Paul McNamee, Kenton Murray, Maria Nădejde, Satoshi Nakamura, Matteo Negri, Jan Niehues, Xing Niu, Juan Pino, Elizabeth Salesky, Jiatong Shi, Sebastian Stüker, Katsuhito Sudoh, Marco Turchi, Yogesh Virkar, Alex Waibel, Changhan Wang, and Shinji Watanabe. 2022. FINDINGS OF THE IWSLT 2022 EVALUATION CAMPAIGN. In *Proceedings of the 19th International Conference on Spoken Language Translation (IWSLT 2022)*, Dublin, Ireland. Association for Computational Linguistics.

Antonios Anastasopoulos, Ondřej Bojar, Jacob Bremerman, Roldano Cattoni, Maha Elbayad, Marcello Federico, Xutai Ma, Satoshi Nakamura, Matteo Negri, Jan Niehues, et al. 2021. Findings of the iwslt 2021 evaluation campaign. In *Proceedings of the 18th International Conference on Spoken Language Translation (IWSLT 2021)*, pages 1–29.

Rosana Ardila, Megan Branson, Kelly Davis, Michael Henretty, Michael Kohler, Josh Meyer, Reuben Morais, Lindsay Saunders, Francis M Tyers, and Gregor Weber. 2019. Common voice: A massively-multilingual speech corpus. *arXiv preprint arXiv:1912.06670*.

Alexei Baevski, Yuhao Zhou, Abdelrahman Mohamed, and Michael Auli. 2020. wav2vec 2.0: A framework for self-supervised learning of speech representations. *Advances in Neural Information Processing Systems*, 33:12449–12460.

Sameer Bansal, Herman Kamper, Karen Livescu, Adam Lopez, and Sharon Goldwater. 2018. Pre-training on high-resource speech recognition improves low-resource speech-to-text translation. *arXiv preprint arXiv:1809.01431*.

Roldano Cattoni, Mattia Antonino Di Gangi, Luisa Bentivogli, Matteo Negri, and Marco Turchi. 2021. Must-c: A multilingual corpus for end-to-end speech translation. *Computer Speech & Language*, 66:101155.

Eunah Cho, Jan Niehues, and Alex Waibel. 2017. NMT-based segmentation and punctuation insertion for real-time spoken language translation. In *Interspeech 2017*. ISCA.

Zihang Dai, Zhilin Yang, Yiming Yang, Jaime Carbonell, Quoc Le, and Ruslan Salakhutdinov. 2019. Transformer-XL: Attentive language models beyond a fixed-length context. In *Proceedings of the 57th Annual Meeting of the Association for Computational Linguistics (ACL)*.

Jacob Devlin, Ming-Wei Chang, Kenton Lee, and Kristina Toutanova. 2018. BERT: pre-training of deep bidirectional transformers for language understanding. *CoRR*, abs/1810.04805.

Mattia A. Di Gangi, Roldano Cattoni, Luisa Bentivogli, Matteo Negri, and Marco Turchi. 2019. MuST-C: a Multilingual Speech Translation Corpus. In *Proceedings of the Conference of the North American Chapter of the Association for Computational Linguistics (NAACL)*.

Anmol Gulati, James Qin, Chung-Cheng Chiu, Niki Parmar, Yu Zhang, Jiahui Yu, Wei Han, Shibo Wang, Zhengdong Zhang, Yonghui Wu, et al. 2020. Conformer: Convolution-augmented transformer for speech recognition. *arXiv preprint arXiv:2005.08100*.

Thanh-Le Ha, Jan Niehues, and Alexander Waibel. 2016. Toward multilingual neural machine translation with universal encoder and decoder. In *Proceedings of the 13th International Workshop on Spoken Language Translation (IWSLT 2016)*, Seattle, USA.

François Hernandez, Vincent Nguyen, Sahar Ghannay, Natalia Tomashenko, and Yannick Estève. 2018. Tedlium 3: twice as much data and corpus repartition for experiments on speaker adaptation. In *International Conference on Speech and Computer*, pages 198–208. Springer.

Javier Iranzo-Sánchez, Joan Albert Silvestre-Cerda, Javier Jorge, Nahuel Roselló, Adria Giménez, Albert Sanchis, Jorge Civera, and Alfons Juan. 2020. Europarl-st: A multilingual corpus for speech translation of parliamentary debates. In *ICASSP 2020-2020 IEEE International Conference on Acoustics, Speech and Signal Processing (ICASSP)*, pages 8229–8233. IEEE.

Mike Lewis, Yinhan Liu, Naman Goyal, Marjan Ghazvininejad, Abdelrahman Mohamed, Omer Levy, Ves Stoyanov, and Luke Zettlemoyer. 2019. Bart: Denoising sequence-to-sequence pre-training for natural language generation, translation, and comprehension. *arXiv preprint arXiv:1910.13461*.

Yinhan Liu, Jiatao Gu, Naman Goyal, Xian Li, Sergey Edunov, Marjan Ghazvininejad, Mike Lewis, and Luke Zettlemoyer. 2020. Multilingual denoising pre-training for neural machine translation. *Transactions of the Association for Computational Linguistics*, 8:726–742.

Shuming Ma, Li Dong, Shaohan Huang, Dongdong Zhang, Alexandre Muzio, Saksham Singhal, Hany Hassan Awadalla, Xia Song, and Furu Wei. 2021. Deltalm: Encoder-decoder pre-training for language generation and translation by augmenting pretrained multilingual encoders. *CoRR*, abs/2106.13736.

Thai Binh Nguyen, Quang Minh Nguyen, Thi Thu Hien Nguyen, Quoc Truong Do, and Chi Mai Luong. 2020. Improving Vietnamese Named Entity Recognition from Speech Using Word Capitalization and Punctuation Recovery Models. In *Proc. Interspeech 2020*, pages 4263–4267.

Thai-Son Nguyen, Sebastian Stueker, Jan Niehues, and Alex Waibel. 2019. Improving sequence-to-sequence speech recognition training with on-the-fly data augmentation. *arXiv preprint arXiv:1910.13296*.

Vassil Panayotov, Guoguo Chen, Daniel Povey, and Sanjeev Khudanpur. 2015. Librispeech: an asr corpus based on public domain audio books. In *2015 IEEE international conference on acoustics, speech and signal processing (ICASSP)*, pages 5206–5210. IEEE.

Ngoc-Quan Pham, Thanh-Le Ha, Tuan-Nam Nguyen, Thai-Son Nguyen, Elizabeth Salesky, Sebastian Stüker, Jan Niehues, and Alex Waibel. 2020a. Relative Positional Encoding for Speech Recognition and Direct Translation. In *Proc. Interspeech 2020*, pages 31–35.

Ngoc-Quan Pham, Thai-Son Nguyen, Thanh-Le Ha, Tuan-Nam Nguyen, Maximilian Awiszus, Felix Schneider, Sebastian Stüker, and Alexander Waibel. 2020b. Tkit's iwslt 2020 slt translation system. In *Proceedings of the 17th International Workshop on Spoken Language Translation (IWSLT 2020)*.

Ngoc-Quan Pham, Thai-Son Nguyen, Jan Niehues, Markus Muller, and Alex Waibel. 2019. Very deep self-attention networks for end-to-end speech recognition. *arXiv preprint arXiv:1904.13377*.

Ngoc-Quan Pham, Felix Schneider, Tuan Nam Nguyen, Thanh-Le Ha, Thai-Son Nguyen, Maximilian Awiszus, Sebastian Stüker, and Alex Waibel. 2020c. Kit's iwslt 2020 slt translation system. In *Proceedings of the 17th International Conference on Spoken Language Translation*, pages 55–61.

Peter Polák, Ngoc-Quan Ngoc, Tuan-Nam Nguyen, Danni Liu, Carlos Mullov, Jan Niehues, Ondřej Bojar, and Alexander Waibel. 2022. CUNI-KIT System for Smultaneous Speech Translation Task at IWSLT 2022. In *Proceedings of the 19th International Conference on Spoken Language Translation (IWSLT 2022)*, Dublin, Ireland. Association for Computational Linguistics.

Matt Post. 2018. A call for clarity in reporting BLEU scores. In *Proceedings of the Third Conference on Machine Translation: Research Papers*, pages 186–191, Brussels, Belgium. Association for Computational Linguistics.

Ramon Sanabria, Ozan Caglayan, Shruti Palaskar, Desmond Elliott, Loïc Barrault, Lucia Specia, and Florian Metze. 2018. How2: a large-scale dataset for multimodal language understanding. *arXiv preprint arXiv:1811.00347*.

Matthias Sperber, Graham Neubig, Jan Niehues, and Alex Waibel. 2019. Attention-passing models for robust and data-efficient end-to-end speech translation. *arXiv preprint arXiv:1904.07209*.

Matthias Sperber and Matthias Paulik. 2020. Speech translation and the end-to-end promise: Taking stock of where we are. *arXiv preprint arXiv:2004.06358*.

Yuqing Tang, Chau Tran, Xian Li, Peng-Jen Chen, Naman Goyal, Vishrav Chaudhary, Jiatao Gu, and Angela Fan. 2020. Multilingual translation with extensible multilingual pretraining and finetuning. *arXiv preprint arXiv:2008.00401*.

Ioannis Tsiamas, Gerard I Gállego, José AR Fonollosa, and Marta R Costa-jussà. 2022. Shas: Approaching optimal segmentation for end-to-end speech translation. *arXiv preprint arXiv:2202.04774*.

Ashish Vaswani, Noam Shazeer, Niki Parmar, Jakob Uszkoreit, Llion Jones, Aidan N Gomez, Łukasz Kaiser, and Illia Polosukhin. 2017. Attention is all you need. In *Advances in Neural Information Processing Systems*, pages 5998–6008.

Changhan Wang, Anne Wu, and Juan Pino. 2020. Covost 2 and massively multilingual speech-to-text translation. *arXiv preprint arXiv:2007.10310*.

John Wiseman. 2016. python-webrtcvad. `https://github.com/wiseman/py-webrtcvad`.

Xiang Zhang, Junbo Zhao, and Yann LeCun. 2015. Character-level Convolutional Networks for Text Classification . *arXiv:1509.01626 [cs]*.

The USTC-NELSLIP Offline Speech Translation Systems for IWSLT 2022

Weitai Zhang[1,2], Zhongyi Ye[2], Haitao Tang[2], Xiaoxi Li[2], Xinyuan Zhou[2],
Jing Yang[2], Jianwei Cui[1], Pan Deng[1], Mohan Shi[1], Yifan Song[1],
Dan Liu[1,2], Junhua Liu[1,2], and Lirong Dai[1]

[1]University of Science and Technology of China, Hefei, China
[2]iFlytek Research, Hefei, China
{zwt2021, danliu, jwcui, pdeng, smohan, yfsong}@mail.ustc.edu.cn
lrdai@ustc.edu.cn
{zyye7, xxli16, httang, xyzhou15, jingyang24, jhliu}@iflytek.com

Abstract

This paper describes USTC-NELSLIP's submissions to the IWSLT 2022 Offline Speech Translation task, including speech translation of talks from English to German, English to Chinese and English to Japanese. We describe both cascaded architectures and end-to-end models which can directly translate source speech into target text. In the cascaded condition, we investigate the effectiveness of different model architectures with robust training and achieve 2.72 BLEU improvements over last year's optimal system on MuST-C English-German test set. In the end-to-end condition, we build models based on Transformer and Conformer architectures, achieving 2.26 BLEU improvements over last year's optimal end-to-end system. The end-to-end system has obtained promising results, but it is still lagging behind our cascaded models.

1 Introduction

This paper describes the submission to IWSLT 2022 Offline Speech Translation task by National Engineering Laboratory for Speech and Language Information Processing (NELSLIP), University of Science and Technology of China, China.

For years, Spoken Language Translation (SLT) has been addressed by cascading an Automatic Speech Recognition (ASR) and a Machine Translation (MT) system. The ASR system processes source speech into source text and the MT system translates ASR output into text in target language independently. Recent trends rely on using a single neural network to directly translate the speech in source language into the text in target language without intermediate symbolic representations. The end-to-end paradigm shows an enormous potential to overcome some of the cascaded systems' problems, such as higher architectural complexity and error propagation (Duong et al., 2016; Berard et al., 2016; Weiss et al., 2017). Last year's results of IWSLT 2021 have confirmed that the performance of end-to-end models is approaching the results of cascaded solutions. The best end-to-end submission (under the same segmentation and training data conditions) is 2 BLEU points (22.6 vs 24.6) below the top-ranked system (Anastasopoulos et al., 2021).

In this work, we build machine translation systems with techniques like back translation (Sennrich et al., 2016a), domain adaptation and model ensemble, which have been proved to be effective practices in IWSLT and WMT (Akhbardeh et al., 2021). Besides, we further improve cascaded speech translation system performance with methods of self-training (Kim and Rush, 2016; Ren et al., 2020; Liu et al., 2019), speech synthesis (Shen et al., 2018), Supervised Hybrid Audio Segmentation (SHAS) (Tsiamas et al., 2022), etc.

In end-to-end condition, we initialize the encoder with the corresponding component of ASR models and the decoder with that of MT models respectively (Le et al., 2021). Methods used in cascaded systems and as much semi-supervised data as possible are utilized to improve end-to-end models' performance. Furthermore, we try to obtain a better performance with ensemble of cascaded and end-to-end models, which may accelerate the application of end-to-end models in industrial scenarios.

The remaining of the paper proceeds as follows. Section 2 describes speech recognition, speech-to-text translation (S2T for short) and text-to-text translation (T2T for short) data used in our experiments. Section 3 and Section 4 present our cascaded and end-to-end systems respectively, where the details about model architectures and techniques for training and inference will be described. The experimental settings and final results are shown in Section 5.

Proceedings of the 19th International Conference on Spoken Language Translation (IWSLT 2022), pages 198 - 207
May 26-27, 2022 ©2022 Association for Computational Linguistics

2 Datasets and Preprocessing

2.1 Speech Recognition Data

The speech recognition datasets used in our experiments are described in Table 1, in which Librispeech, MuST-C(v1, v2), TED Lium3, Europarl, VoxPopuli and CoVoST are available and used. After extract 40 dimensional log-mel filter bank features computed with a $25ms$ window size and a $10ms$ window shift, we train a baseline ASR model and filter training samples with WER$> 40\%$. Then we augment the speech data with speed perturbation, and over-sample TED/MuST-C corpus with the ratio used last year (Liu et al., 2021), which finally generate almost 8k hours of speech recognition corpora.

Corpus	Duration(h)	Sample Scale
Librispeech	960	1
Europarl	161	1
MuST-C(v1)	399	3
MuST-C(v2)	449	3
TED-LIUM3	452	3
CoVoST2	1985	1
VoxPopuli	1270	1

Table 1: Statistics of ASR Corpora.

We further extend two data augmentation methods: First, Adjacent voices are concatenated to generate longer training speeches; Second, we train a Glow-TTS (Casanova et al., 2021) model with MuST-C datasets and generate 24k hours of audio feature using sentences from EN→DE text translation corpora. The final training data for ASR is described in Table 2.

Data	Duration(h)
Raw data	8276
+ concat	16000
+ oversampling	32000
+ TTS	56000

Table 2: Overall training data for ASR.

2.2 Text Translation Corpora

We participate in translation of English to German, Chinese and Japanese. All available bilingual data and as much monolingual data as possible are used for training our systems. We apply language identification to retain sentences predicted as desired language, remove sentences longer than 250 tokens and with a source/target length ratio exceeding 3, filter sentences with lower scores based on baseline machine translation models. We use LTP4.0[1] (Che et al., 2020) for Chinese tokenization, MeCab morphological analyzer[2] for Japanese tokenization and moses for English tokenization. Then subwords are generated via Byte Pair Encoding (BPE) (Sennrich et al., 2016b) with 30k merge operations for each language direction. Table 3 lists statistics of parallel and monolingual data used for training our systems. The details are as follows.

EN→DE The bilingual data includes CommonCrawl, CoVoST2, Europarl, MuST-C(v1, v2), Librivox, News Commentary, Opensubtitles, Parawcrawl(v3, v5.1), Rapid, Wikimatrix-v1 and Wikititles-v2. A total of 151 million sentence pairs are available, 120 million pairs of which are reserved for training. The monolingual English and German data are mainly from News Commentary and News crawl.

EN→ZH Almost 50 million sentence pairs collected from CCMT Corpus, News Commentary, ParaCrawl, Wiki Titles, UN Parallel Corpus, WikiMatrix, Wikititles, MuST-C and CoVoST2 are used for training EN→ZH text MT. 50 million monolingual Chinese sentences are randomly extracted from News crawl and Common Crawl for Back Translation.

EN→JA We use 16 million sentence pairs from MuST-C, CoVoST2, TED Talk, JESC-v2, News Commentary, Paracrawl, Wikimatrix and Wikititles. 20 million Japanese monolingual sentences from News Commentary, News crawl and Common Crawl are randomly extracted for Back Translation.

	Parallel	Monolingual
EN-DE	120M	180M
EN-ZH	50M	50M
EN-JA	15.75M	20M

Table 3: Overall training data for text MT.

2.3 Speech Translation Corpora

The speech translation datasets used in our experiments are described in Table 4. MuST-C and CoVoST2 are available for speech translation (speech, transcription and translation included) in all three

[1] https://github.com/HIT-SCIR/ltp
[2] https://github.com/uenewsar/mecab

language directions, while Europarl is specifically available in EN→DE speech translation track.

We further extend two data augmentation methods: First, transcriptions of all speech recognition datasets are sent to a text translation model to generate text y' in target language, which is similar with sentence knowledge distillation. The generated y' with its corresponding speech are directly added to speech translation dataset (described as KD Corpus in Table 4). Second, we use the trained Glow-TTS model to generate audio feature from randomly selected sentence pairs from EN→DE, EN→ZH and EN→JA text translation corpora. The generated filter bank features and their corresponding target language text are used to expand our speech translation dataset (described as TTS Corpus in Table 4).

	Corpus	Duration(h)	Sample Scale
EN-DE	Europarl	161	2
	MuST-C	449	2
	CoVoST2	1094	2
	KD	16000	2
	TTS	24000	1
EN-ZH	MuST-C	593	2
	CoVoST2	1092	2
	KD	16000	2
	TTS	27000	1
EN-JA	MuST-C	282	2
	CoVoST2	988	2
	KD	16000	2
	TTS	13000	1

Table 4: Statistics of Speech Translation Corpora

3 Cascaded Speech Translation

3.1 Automatic Speech Recognition

Voice Activity Detection We use Supervised Hybrid Audio Segmentation (SHAS) (Tsiamas et al., 2022) to split long audios into shorter segments. SHAS is originally propsed to learn the optimal segmentation for speech translation. Experiments on MuST-C and mTEDx show that the translation of the segments produced by SHAS approaches the quality of the manual segmentation on 5 languages pairs. Hence, we use SHAS for both Voice Activity Detection in ASR and segmentation in Speech Translation, which means that we have no more segmentation operations and ASR outputs are directly sent to text machine translation component.

Besides, we propose a semantic VAD method as follows: 1) train a text segmentation model based on transformer; 2) re-segment ASR results into new sentences with complete semantic information; 3) use Force Alignment to align speech time stamp and ASR results; 4) re-segment voices into new fragments. We hope to seek a more friendly segmentation for machine translation.

Model Architecture We think representations sent to ASR encoder component are important, so we use three model architectures in ASR: VGG-Transformer (Mohamed et al., 2019), VGG-Conformer (Gulati et al., 2020) and GateCNN-Transformer (Dauphin et al., 2017) implemented on Fairseq, described as follows:

- VGG-Conformer: 2 layers of VGG and 12 layers of Conformer in encoder, 6 layers of Transformer in decoder. The embedding size is 512, the hidden size of FFN is 2048, and the attention head is 8.

- VGG-Transformer: 2 layers of VGG and 16 layers of Transformer in encoder, 6 layers of Transformer in decoder. The embedding size is 512, the hidden size of FFN is 4096, and the attention head is 8.

- GateCNN-Conformer: 6 layers of GateCNN and 12 layers of Conformer in encoder, 6 layers of Transformer in decoder. The embedding size is 512, the hidden size of FFN is 2048, and the attention head is 8.

The Specaugment technique (Park et al., 2019) is used to improve robustness, and Connectionist Temporal Classification (CTC) is added to make models converge better. Other training details are as follows: 1) We apply BPE to the transcripts with 30000 merge operations; 2) Arabic numerals are converted into corresponding English words; 3) Punctuation marks and uppercase are remained for fitting text machine translation; 4) We use Adam optimizer and adopt the default learning schedule in fairseq; 5) Model is trained on 32 Tesla V100 40G GPUs within 2 days; 6) We use ensemble decoding of several models with beamsize of 15 to produce final transcriptions; 7) Other parameters are default in Fairseq.

3.2 Neural Machine Translation

The machine translation models are based on Transformer (Vaswani et al., 2017) implemented on the Fairseq toolkit (Ott et al., 2019). Each single model is carried out on 16 NVIDIA V100 GPUs with default settings. Important techniques used in our experiments are: Back Translation, Sentence-level Knowledge Distillation, Domain Adaptation and Ensemble.

Back Translation Back-Translation (Sennrich et al., 2016a) is an effective way to improve the translation performance by translating target-side monolingual data to generate synthetic sentence pairs, which has been widely used in research and industrial scenarios. We train NMT models with bilingual data, and translate German/Chinese/Japanese sentences to English ones.

Knowledge Distillation Sentence-level Knowledge Distillation (Kim and Rush, 2016)(also known as self-training) is another useful technique to improve performance. We augment training data by translating English sentences to German/Chinese/Japanese using a trained NMT model.

Domain Adapatation As high-quality and domain-specific translation is crucial, fine-tuning the concatenation system on in-domain data shows the best performance (Saunders, 2021). To improve in-domain translation while do not decrease the quality of out-domain translation, we fine-tune the NMT model on a mix of in-domain data (MuST-C, TED-LIUM3, etc.) and random selected out-of-domain data until convergence. The speech recognition training data are also used as augmented in-domain self-training data by translating the labelled English sentences.

We also use Denoise-based approach (Wang et al., 2018) to measure and select data for domain MT and apply them to denoising NMT training. Denoising is concerned with a different type of data quality and tries to reduce the negative impact of data noise on MT training, in particular, neural MT (NMT) training.

Ensemble For each language direction, we train 4 variants based on Transformer big settings and the final model is the ensemble of the 4 models:

- E12D6: 12 layers for the encoder and 6 layers for the decoder. The embedding size is 1024, FFN size is 8192 and attention head is 16. All available corpora including bilingual, BT and FT data are used.
- E15D6: 15 layers for the encoder, 10% training data are randomly dropped and a different seed is set.
- E18D6: 18 layers for the encoder and 10-30% training data with lower machine translation scores are dropped.
- Macaron: A model with macaron architecture (Lu et al., 2019) based on data of E18D6. 36 layers for the encoder and FFN size is 2048.

3.3 Robust MT Training

To address the error propagation problem in cascaded ST, we propose a ASR output adaptation training method for improving MT model robustness against ASR errors. English transcriptions of all speech translation datasets are sent to a trained ASR model to generate text x' in source side, paired with the target side labels. We use 3 approaches to improve MT model's robustness detailed as follows: 1) We use the synthetic data to fine-tune MT model; 2) While fine-tuning, we add KL loss to prevent over-fitting; 3) we distill the model both by clean input and ASR output as showed in Figure 1.

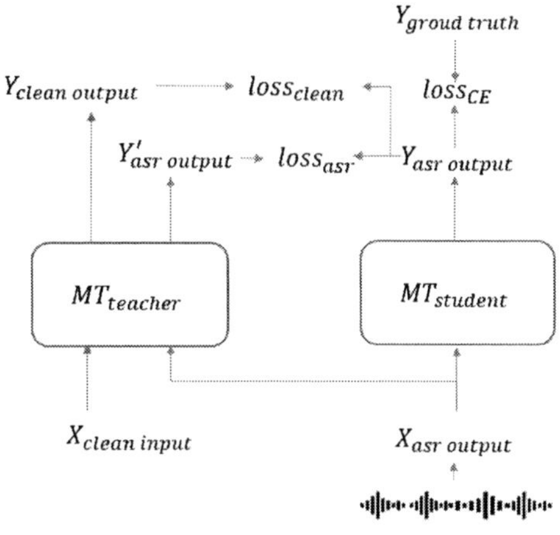

Figure 1: Overview of Robust MT Training.

4 End-to-End Speech Translation

As regards model architecture, we investigate 4 variants in end-to-end speech translation.

- VGG-C: The encoder is VGG-Conformer, initialized by ASR VGG-Conformer architecture.

The decoder is 6 layers of Transformer with embedding size of 1024, attention head of 16 and FFN size of 8192.

- VGG-C-init: The encoder is VGG-Conformer, initialized by ASR VGG-Conformer architecture. The decoder is 6 layers of Transformer, initialized by NMT E15D6 variant.
- VGG-T: The encoder is VGG-Transformer, initialized by ASR VGG-Transformer architecture. The decoder is 6 layers of Transformer with embedding size of 1024, attention head of 16 and FFN size of 8192.
- VGG-T-init: The encoder is VGG-Transformer, initialized by ASR VGG-Transformer architecture. The decoder is 6 layers of Transformer, initialized by NMT E15D6 variant.

5 Experiments

All our experiments are conducted using Fairseq toolkit (Ott et al., 2019). We use word error rate (WER) to evaluate the ASR models and report case-sensitive SacreBLEU scores for machine translation. Results of MuST-C tst-COMMON (tst-COM), IWSLT tst2018/tst2019/tst2020 are listed together, which can be compared as baselines for other researchers and participants in the future. We also present results of IWSLT 2022 testsets in the Appendix.

5.1 Automatic Speech Recognition

The overall experimental results about ASR is described in Table 6. We use SHAS as a segmentation tool in default for all testsets. We compare the results of different model architectures with and without TTS augmented training data, showed in line 1-6. In our experiments, TTS augmented data has consistent improvements in all three architectures, and an absolute gain of 0.42% accuracy is observed in GateCNN-Conformer, which makes GateCNN-Conformer with TTS augmented data performs best as a single model.

In line 7, we ensemble all 6 single models to gain a best result, where the WER is at an average of 5.32, and 0.69 lower than the best single model. For comparison with other works, we list the result of tst-COM with official segments in line 8, which performs better than concatenating the segments and using SHAS. In line 9, we present results with semantic SHAS (described in Sec. 3.1) based on the ensemble models, which shows that semantic SHAS is slightly worse and lagging behind SHAS by 0.13 in accuracy. In our final submissions, line 7 serves as the ASR part of our cascaded primary system, and line 9 serves as part of a contrastive system.

5.2 Speech Translation

For text machine translation, we use the Adam optimizer with $\beta_1 = 0.9$ and $\beta_2 = 0.98$. To speed up the training process, we conduct training with half precision floating point (FP16). We set max learning rate to $7e$-4 and warmup-steps to 8000. To improve model robustness, we set bpe dropout to 0.05, and mask 15% words in source and target inputs in accord with BERT. When fine tuning on in-domain datasets, we add KL loss with weight=1.0 to avoid over-fitting.

For end-to-end ST, the segmentation tool used is SHAS (to our knowledge, using semantic SHAS will not be considered as end-to-end). All available training data including TTS augmented data and knowledge distillation data described in Sec. 2.3 are used. We also fine-tune models on in-domain corpus for further improvements.

For tst-COM, we report results of both official segmentation and SHAS segmentation. Sacrebleu scores are computed by using automatic resegmentation of the hypothesis based on the reference translation by mwerSegmenter.

Effectiveness of Robust MT Training The experiment is conducted based on EN→DE cascaded speech translation track. We generate 1.38M sentences from 1500h speech translation datasets. Experimental results are described in Table 5. By comparing line 3 and line 6, our method can further gain 0.55 and 0.75 BLEU in tst-COM and tst2018 regardless of the impact of domain adaptation. Robust MT Training is adopted for training all our following systems.

EN→DE Experimental results are described in Table 7. In the first group of text MT results, line 2-5 show the effectiveness of model size, data clean and fine-tuning on in-domain datasets. We ensemble 4 different variants described in Sec. 3.2 and constitute results in line 6, which makes our text MT outperforming Volctrans's ensemble results (Zhao et al., 2021) by 1.85 BLEU in tst-COM.

In the second group of cascaded ST results, we present final results produced with ensemble ASR

#		tst-COM	tst2018
1	text MT	36.21	32.14
2	ASR→text MT	33.34	26.20
3	+finetune	34.11	28.41
4	Robust Training	34.21	27.62
5	+KL Loss	34.61	28.69
6	+KD Loss	34.66	29.16

Table 5: Experimental results of Robust MT Training.

in Table 6 and ensemble text MT in line 6 by SHAS and semantic SHAS respectively. By comparing line 8 and line 9, SHAS performs better in tst-COM and tst2018, while semantic SHAS performs better in tst2019 and tst2020. Results of tst-COM for speech translation contained in parenthesis are based on official segmentation, which means our cascaded system outperforms Volctrans's cascaded results (Zhao et al., 2021) by 2.72 BLEU in tst-COM. We observe more improvements in cascaded ST than text MT due to our better ASR system.

Regards end-to-end ST, we compare the results of different model architectures with and without TTS augmented training data, showed in line 11-16. From line 11-14, TTS augmented data has improvements by 0.43 BLEU in VGG-Conformer-init, while decrease the BLEU scores (0.09) in VGG-Conformer. Using NMT decoder for initialization brings consistent improvements with or without TTS data. In line 17, we ensemble all 6 single models with outperforming best single model by an average of 0.97 BLEU, but it is still lagging behind cascaded systems by 1.36 BLEU in tst-COM. Our end-to-end system outperforms KIT's end-to-end results (Nguyen et al., 2021) by 2.26 BLEU in tst-COM.

To investigate the effectiveness of ensemble of cascaded and end-to-end systems, we present the results in line 18 and 19 with SHAS and semantic SHAS respectively. We observe consistent and slight improvements in all testsets except tst-COM using SHAS. We submit systems of #8, #9, #17, #18, #19, with #8 as primary system in cascaded condition and #17 as primary system in end-to-end condition.

EN→ZH Experimental results are described in Table 8. Regards text MT, line 1-3 show the effectiveness of model size and data clean. We further improve performance with fine-tuning models on MuST-C and TED Talk corpus in line 4. Line 5 shows results of ensemble MT from 4 fine-tuned variants described in Sec. 3.2. In the second group of cascaded ST results, we present final results produced with ensemble ASR in Table 6 and ensemble text MT by SHAS and semantic SHAS respectively. Results of tst-COM for speech translation contained in parenthesis are based on official segmentation. Regards end-to-end ST, we train 4 different models based on conclusions from EN→DE end-to-end experiments. In line 12, we ensemble 4 single models and get 28.92 BLEU in tst-COM within official segmentation. Our final end-to-end ST result on tst-COM is still lagging behind cascaded system by 0.89 BLEU.

Same with EN→DE translation track, we present the ensemble results of cascaded systems and end-to-end systems in line 13 and 14 with SHAS and semantic SHAS respectively, which brings slight improvements comparing with cascaded system. We submit systems of #6, #7, #12, #13, #14, with #6 as primary system in cascaded condition and #12 as primary system in end-to-end condition.

EN→JA The overall experimental results is described in Table 9. Regards text MT, line 1-3 show the effectiveness of model size and data clean. We further improve performance with fine-tuning models on MuST-C and TED Talk corpus in line 4. Line 5 shows results of ensemble models from 4 fine-tuned variants described in Sec. 3.2. Line 6-7 present cascaded ST results with ASR outputs from ensemble models, which only decrease 0.25 BLEU on dev and 0.48 BLEU on tst-COM compared with text MT. The reason might be partly attributed to the fact that text MT BLEU is relatively lower and ASR errors have a smaller portion of all factors affecting the performance. While MuST-C training data and tst-COM have no punctuations in Japanese side, We think punctuations help people understand. We train a punctuation model based on transformer encoder, and add punctuations for translations. The performance decreases because of the mismatch between references and translations in punctuations.

Regards end-to-end ST, we train 4 different models based on conclusions from EN→DE end-to-end experiments. In line 12, we ensemble 4 models and get 18.61 BLEU in tst-COM with official segmentation. Our final end-to-end ST result on tst-COM is still lagging behind cascaded system by 2.89 BLEU. We submit systems of #6, #7, #8, #9, #12, with #6 as primary system in cascaded condition and #12 as primary system in end-to-end condition.

#	System	tst-COM	tst2018	tst2019	tst2020	avg
1	VGG-Conformer (w/ TTS)	3.66	8.56	5.28	7.23	6.18
2	VGG-Conformer (w/o TTS)	3.70	8.55	5.34	7.54	6.28
3	VGG-Transformer (w/ TTS)	**3.31**	8.39	5.58	7.43	6.18
4	VGG-Transformer (w/o TTS)	3.34	8.50	5.85	7.76	6.36
5	GateCNN-Conformer (w/ TTS)	4.06	7.87	5.14	6.98	6.01
6	GateCNN-Conformer (w/o TTS)	4.35	8.12	5.74	7.52	6.43
7	ensemble (1, 2, 3, 4, 5, 6, SHAS)	3.36	**7.30**	**4.59**	**6.03**	**5.32**
8	7 (w/o SHAS)	3.49	-	-	-	-
9	7 (w/ semantic SHAS)	3.54	7.26	4.89	6.10	5.45

Table 6: Overall experimental results of ASR. We present WER performance of tst-COM, tst2018, tst2019 and tst2020, and hope it can be compared as baselines in other works. For tst-COM, we concatenate the audios and segment with SHAS except for line 8.

#	Systems	tst-COM	tst2018	tst2019	tst2020
	Text MT				
1	Volctrans(ensemble) (Zhao et al., 2021)	(36.7)	-	-	-
2	base	32.65	29.02	26.90	-
3	clean+big	36.21	32.03	29.64	-
4	text MT	36.84	32.65	30.02	-
5	4+finetune	38.20	34.56	**31.86**	35.54
6	ensemble MT	**38.55**	**34.89**	31.82	**36.08**
	Cascaded ASR→MT				
7	Volctrans(ensemble) (Zhao et al., 2021)	(33.3)	-	-	-
8	ensemble ASR→6+SHAS	**34.73(36.02)**	**30.02**	29.25	32.15
9	+semantic SHAS	34.36*(36.02)	29.59	**29.40**	**32.44**
	End-to-End ST				
10	KIT (ensemble) (Nguyen et al., 2021)	(32.4)	-	-	-
11	VGG-C (w/o TTS)	31.81(33.37)	28.47	26.48	28.82
12	VGG-C-init (w/o TTS)	31.79(33.48)	28.44	26.70	29.17
13	VGG-C (w/ TTS)	31.58(32.78)	**29.00**	26.47	28.69
14	VGG-C-init (w/ TTS)	**32.39(33.74)**	28.98	**27.03**	**29.59**
15	VGG-T (w/ TTS)	31.37(32.72)	28.54	26.17	28.42
16	VGG-T-init (w/ TTS)	31.21(32.81)	28.68	26.23	28.67
17	Ensemble (11-16)	**33.23(34.66)**	**29.93**	**28.20**	**30.57**
	Ensemble of cascaded and e2e systems				
18	Ensemble(8, 17)	33.58(36.05)	**30.93**	**29.57**	32.15
19	Ensemble(8, 17)* +semantic SHAS	**34.47*(36.13)**	30.19	29.41	**32.50**

Table 7: Overall experimental results of EN→DE translation track. Results of tst-COM for speech translation contained in parenthesis are based on official segmentation which are comparable with previous works. Results with * are based on semantic SHAS, and others are based on SHAS. Weights of models in line 18 and 19 are different. We submitted 5 systems in EN→DE track with system ID in bold.

#	Systems	tst-COM
	Text MT	
1	base	23.26
2	clean+big	26.92
3	text MT	27.49
4	3+finetune	30.19
5	ensemble MT	**31.03**
	Cascaded ASR→MT	
6	ensemble ASR→5+SHAS	**29.68(29.81)**
7	+semantic SHAS	29.23(29.81)
	End-to-End ST	
8	VGG-C (w/ TTS)	28.34(28.60)
9	VGG-C-init (w/ TTS)	28.51(28.71)
10	VGG-T (w/ TTS)	27.91(28.41)
11	VGG-T-init (w/ TTS)	27.85(28.23)
12	Ensemble (8,9,10,11)	**28.78(28.92)**
	Ensemble of cascaded and e2e systems	
13	Ensemble(6, 12)	29.80(29.79)
14	+semantic SHAS	29.41(29.79)

Table 8: Overall experimental results of EN→ZH translation track. Results in parentheses are with official segmentation.

#	Systems	tst-COM
	Text MT	
1	base	15.44
2	clean+big	17.43
3	text MT	18.72
4	3+finetune	21.78
5	ensemble MT	**22.02**
	Cascaded ASR→MT	
6	ensemble ASR→5+SHAS	**21.25(21.50)**
7	+semantic SHAS	21.11(21.50)
8	6+punctuation model	19.29(18.81)
9	7+punctuation model	19.84(18.81)
	End-to-End ST	
8	VGG-C (w/o TTS)	17.72(17.71)
9	VGG-C-init (w/o TTS)	17.66(17.76)
10	VGG-C-init (w/ TTS)	**17.97(18.20)**
11	VGG-T-init (w/ TTS)	17.60(17.66)
12	Ensemble (8,9,10,11)	**18.62(18.61)**

Table 9: Overall experimental results of EN→JA translation track. Results in parentheses are with official segmentation.

6 Conclusion

This paper summarizes the results of IWSLT 2022 Offline Speech Translation task produced by the USTC-NELSLIP team. We investigate various model architectures and data augmentation approaches to build strong speech translation systems, both in cascaded condition and end-to-end condition. In our experiments, we demonstrate the effectiveness of Back Translation, Knowledge Distillation, Domain Adaptation, Ensemble, elegant segmentation. Our end-to-end model surpasses the last year's best system by 2.26 BLEU, but it is still lagging behind our cascaded model by an average of 1.73 BLEU scores on MuST-C test sets. As a note for future work, we would like to investigate the effectiveness of speech data augmentation and multi-modal representations in end-to-end speech translation.

References

Farhad Akhbardeh, Arkady Arkhangorodsky, Magdalena Biesialska, Ondřej Bojar, Rajen Chatterjee, Vishrav Chaudhary, Marta R. Costa-jussa, Cristina España-Bonet, Angela Fan, Christian Federmann, Markus Freitag, Yvette Graham, Roman Grundkiewicz, Barry Haddow, Leonie Harter, Kenneth Heafield, Christopher Homan, Matthias Huck, Kwabena Amponsah-Kaakyire, Jungo Kasai, Daniel Khashabi, Kevin Knight, Tom Kocmi, Philipp Koehn, Nicholas Lourie, Christof Monz, Makoto Morishita, Masaaki Nagata, Ajay Nagesh, Toshiaki Nakazawa, Matteo Negri, Santanu Pal, Allahsera Auguste Tapo, Marco Turchi, Valentin Vydrin, and Marcos Zampieri. 2021. Findings of the 2021 conference on machine translation (WMT21). In *Proceedings of the Sixth Conference on Machine Translation*, pages 1–88, Online. Association for Computational Linguistics.

Antonios Anastasopoulos, Ondřej Bojar, Jacob Bremerman, Roldano Cattoni, Maha Elbayad, Marcello Federico, Xutai Ma, Satoshi Nakamura, Matteo Negri, Jan Niehues, Juan Pino, Elizabeth Salesky, Sebastian Stüker, Katsuhito Sudoh, Marco Turchi, Alexander Waibel, Changhan Wang, and Matthew Wiesner. 2021. FINDINGS OF THE IWSLT 2021 EVALUATION CAMPAIGN. In *Proceedings of the 18th International Conference on Spoken Language Translation (IWSLT 2021)*, pages 1–29, Bangkok, Thailand (online). Association for Computational Linguistics.

Alexandre Berard, Olivier Pietquin, Christophe Servan, and Laurent Besacier. 2016. Listen and translate: A proof of concept for end-to-end speech-to-text translation. *CoRR*, abs/1612.01744.

Edresson Casanova, Christopher Shulby, Eren Gölge, Nicolas Michael Müller, Frederico Santos de Oliveira, Arnaldo Candido Jr., Anderson da Silva Soares, Sandra Maria Aluísio, and Moacir Antonelli Ponti. 2021. Sc-glowtts: An efficient zero-shot multi-speaker text-to-speech model. In *Interspeech 2021, 22nd Annual Conference of the International Speech Communication Association, Brno, Czechia, 30 August - 3 September 2021*, pages 3645–3649. ISCA.

Wanxiang Che, Yunlong Feng, Libo Qin, and Ting Liu. 2020. N-ltp: A open-source neural chinese language technology platform with pretrained models. *arXiv preprint arXiv:2009.11616*.

Yann N. Dauphin, Angela Fan, Michael Auli, and David Grangier. 2017. Language modeling with gated convolutional networks. In *Proceedings of the 34th International Conference on Machine Learning, ICML 2017, Sydney, NSW, Australia, 6-11 August 2017*, volume 70 of *Proceedings of Machine Learning Research*, pages 933–941. PMLR.

Long Duong, Antonios Anastasopoulos, David Chiang, Steven Bird, and Trevor Cohn. 2016. An attentional model for speech translation without transcription. In *Proceedings of the 2016 Conference of the North American Chapter of the Association for Computational Linguistics: Human Language Technologies*, pages 949–959, San Diego, California. Association for Computational Linguistics.

Anmol Gulati, James Qin, Chung-Cheng Chiu, Niki Parmar, Yu Zhang, Jiahui Yu, Wei Han, Shibo Wang, Zhengdong Zhang, Yonghui Wu, and Ruoming Pang. 2020. Conformer: Convolution-augmented transformer for speech recognition. In *Interspeech 2020, 21st Annual Conference of the International Speech Communication Association, Virtual Event, Shanghai, China, 25-29 October 2020*, pages 5036–5040. ISCA.

Yoon Kim and Alexander M Rush. 2016. Sequence-level knowledge distillation. *arXiv preprint arXiv:1606.07947*.

Hang Le, Florentin Barbier, Ha Nguyen, Natalia Tomashenko, Salima Mdhaffar, Souhir Gabiche Gahbiche, Benjamin Lecouteux, Didier Schwab, and Yannick Estève. 2021. ON-TRAC' systems for the IWSLT 2021 low-resource speech translation and multilingual speech translation shared tasks. In *Proceedings of the 18th International Conference on Spoken Language Translation (IWSLT 2021)*, pages 169–174, Bangkok, Thailand (online). Association for Computational Linguistics.

Dan Liu, Mengge Du, Xiaoxi Li, Yuchen Hu, and Lirong Dai. 2021. The USTC-NELSLIP systems for simultaneous speech translation task at IWSLT 2021. In *Proceedings of the 18th International Conference on Spoken Language Translation, IWSLT 2021, Bangkok, Thailand (online), August 5-6, 2021*, pages 30–38. Association for Computational Linguistics.

Yuchen Liu, Hao Xiong, Zhongjun He, Jiajun Zhang, Hua Wu, Haifeng Wang, and Chengqing Zong. 2019. End-to-end speech translation with knowledge distillation.

Yiping Lu, Zhuohan Li, Di He, Zhiqing Sun, Bin Dong, Tao Qin, Liwei Wang, and Tie-Yan Liu. 2019. Understanding and improving transformer from a multi-particle dynamic system point of view. *CoRR*, abs/1906.02762.

Abdelrahman Mohamed, Dmytro Okhonko, and Luke Zettlemoyer. 2019. Transformers with convolutional context for ASR. *CoRR*, abs/1904.11660.

Tuan Nam Nguyen, Thai Son Nguyen, Christian Huber, Ngoc-Quan Pham, Thanh-Le Ha, Felix Schneider, and Sebastian Stüker. 2021. KIT's IWSLT 2021 offline speech translation system. In *Proceedings of the 18th International Conference on Spoken Language Translation (IWSLT 2021)*, pages 125–130, Bangkok, Thailand (online). Association for Computational Linguistics.

Myle Ott, Sergey Edunov, Alexei Baevski, Angela Fan, Sam Gross, Nathan Ng, David Grangier, and Michael Auli. 2019. fairseq: A fast, extensible toolkit for sequence modeling. In *Proceedings of the 2019 Conference of the North American Chapter of the Association for Computational Linguistics (Demonstrations)*, pages 48–53, Minneapolis, Minnesota. Association for Computational Linguistics.

Daniel S. Park, William Chan, Yu Zhang, Chung-Cheng Chiu, Barret Zoph, Ekin D. Cubuk, and Quoc V. Le. 2019. Specaugment: A simple data augmentation method for automatic speech recognition. In *Interspeech 2019, 20th Annual Conference of the International Speech Communication Association, Graz, Austria, 15-19 September 2019*, pages 2613–2617. ISCA.

Yi Ren, Jinglin Liu, Xu Tan, Chen Zhang, Tao Qin, Zhou Zhao, and Tie-Yan Liu. 2020. SimulSpeech: End-to-end simultaneous speech to text translation. In *Proceedings of the 58th Annual Meeting of the Association for Computational Linguistics*, pages 3787–3796, Online. Association for Computational Linguistics.

Danielle Saunders. 2021. Domain adaptation and multi-domain adaptation for neural machine translation: A survey. *CoRR*, abs/2104.06951.

Rico Sennrich, Barry Haddow, and Alexandra Birch. 2016a. Improving neural machine translation models with monolingual data. In *Proceedings of the 54th Annual Meeting of the Association for Computational Linguistics (Volume 1: Long Papers)*, pages 86–96, Berlin, Germany. Association for Computational Linguistics.

Rico Sennrich, Barry Haddow, and Alexandra Birch. 2016b. Neural machine translation of rare words with subword units. In *Proceedings of the 54th Annual Meeting of the Association for Computational*

Linguistics (Volume 1: Long Papers), pages 1715–1725, Berlin, Germany. Association for Computational Linguistics.

Jonathan Shen, Ruoming Pang, Ron J Weiss, Mike Schuster, Navdeep Jaitly, Zongheng Yang, Zhifeng Chen, Yu Zhang, Yuxuan Wang, Rj Skerrv-Ryan, et al. 2018. Natural tts synthesis by conditioning wavenet on mel spectrogram predictions. In *2018 IEEE International Conference on Acoustics, Speech and Signal Processing (ICASSP)*, pages 4779–4783. IEEE.

Ioannis Tsiamas, Gerard I. Gállego, José A. R. Fonollosa, and Marta Ruiz Costa-jussà. 2022. Shas: Approaching optimal segmentation for end-to-end speech translation. *ArXiv*, abs/2202.04774.

Ashish Vaswani, Noam Shazeer, Niki Parmar, Jakob Uszkoreit, Llion Jones, Aidan N. Gomez, Lukasz Kaiser, and Illia Polosukhin. 2017. Attention is all you need. In *Advances in Neural Information Processing Systems 30: Annual Conference on Neural Information Processing Systems 2017, December 4-9, 2017, Long Beach, CA, USA*, pages 5998–6008.

Wei Wang, Taro Watanabe, Macduff Hughes, Tetsuji Nakagawa, and Ciprian Chelba. 2018. Denoising neural machine translation training with trusted data and online data selection. In *Proceedings of the Third Conference on Machine Translation: Research Papers, WMT 2018, Belgium, Brussels, October 31 - November 1, 2018*, pages 133–143. Association for Computational Linguistics.

Ron J. Weiss, Jan Chorowski, Navdeep Jaitly, Yonghui Wu, and Zhifeng Chen. 2017. Sequence-to-sequence models can directly transcribe foreign speech. *CoRR*, abs/1703.08581.

Chengqi Zhao, Zhicheng Liu, Jian Tong, Tao Wang, Mingxuan Wang, Rong Ye, Qianqian Dong, Jun Cao, and Lei Li. 2021. The volctrans neural speech translation system for IWSLT 2021. In *Proceedings of the 18th International Conference on Spoken Language Translation, IWSLT 2021, Bangkok, Thailand (online), August 5-6, 2021*, pages 64–74. Association for Computational Linguistics.

A Appendix

We present results of official test sets and progress test sets. For En→DE translation track, end-to-end model is lagging behind cascaded model by 1.4 BLEU on tst2022 and 1.8 BLEU on tst2021. Our best result surpasses the last year's best system by 4.4 BLEU, which means performant systems built with classical approaches are strongly competitive. In English to Japanese track, results with punctuations added performs better in ref2 and worse in ref1, mostly because of reference annotations.

#	ref2	ref1	both
8	26.7	23.9	37.6
9	26.3	23.7	37.1
17	25.3	22.9	35.7
18	26.6	23.8	37.4
19	26.2	23.7	37.0

Table 10: Offical BLEU results of IWSLT tst2022 in EN→DE speech translation track.

#	ref2	ref1	both
HW-TSC	24.6	20.3	34.0
8	28.9	24.1	40.3
9	29.0	23.8	40.1
17	27.2	23.0	38.4
18	29.0	23.9	40.3
19	28.8	23.7	39.8

Table 11: Offical BLEU results of IWSLT tst2021 in EN→DE speech translation track.

#	ref2	ref1	both
6	35.8	35.7	44.1
7	35.5	35.3	43.7
12	33.8	34.1	41.9
13	36.1	36.0	44.5
14	35.7	35.5	44.0

Table 12: Offical BLEU results of IWSLT tst2021 in EN→ZH speech translation track.

#	ref2	ref1	both
6	21.6	20.1	33.4
7	21.2	19.8	32.8
8	24.9	18.3	35.2
9	23.8	18.4	34.3
12	20.5	17.4	30.5

Table 13: Offical BLEU results of IWSLT tst2021 in EN→JA speech translation track.

The AISP-SJTU Simultaneous Translation System for IWSLT 2022

Qinpei Zhu[1] Renshou Wu[1] Guangfeng Liu[1] Xinyu Zhu[1] Xingyu Chen[2]
Yang Zhou[1] Qingliang Miao[1] Rui Wang[2] Kai Yu[1,2]
[1]AI Speech Co., Ltd., Suzhou, China
[2]Shanghai Jiao Tong University, Shanghai, China

Abstract

This paper describes AISP-SJTU's submissions for the IWSLT 2022 Simultaneous Translation task. We participate in the text-to-text and speech-to-text simultaneous translation from English to Mandarin Chinese. The training of the CAAT is improved by training across multiple values of right context window size, which achieves good online performance without setting a prior right context window size for training. For speech-to-text task, the best model we submitted achieves 25.87, 26.21, 26.45 BLEU in low, medium and high regimes on tst-COMMON, corresponding to 27.94, 28.31, 28.43 BLEU in text-to-text task.

1 Introduction

This paper describes the systems submitted by AI Speech Co., Ltd. (AISP) and Shanghai Jiaotong University (SJTU) for IWSLT 2022 Simultaneous Translation task. Two speech translation systems including cascade and end-to-end (E2E) for the Simultaneous Speech Translation track, and a simultaneous neural machine translation (MT) system for the text-to-text Simultaneous Translation track. The systems are focused on English to Mandarin Chinese language pair.

For simultaneous speech translation, recent work tends to fall into two categories, cascaded systems and E2E systems. And the cascaded system often outperforms the fully E2E approach. Only one work (Ansari et al., 2020; Anastasopoulos et al., 2021) shows that the E2E model can achieve better results than the cascaded model. In their work they introduce pre-training (Stoian et al., 2020; Dong et al., 2021; Wang et al., 2020b) and data augmentation techniques (Pino et al., 2020; Xu et al., 2021) to E2E models. Therefore, in this paper, we hope to optimize the speech translation model from two aspects. First, we aim to build a robust cascade model and learn best practices from WMT evaluation activities (Wu et al., 2020; Meng et al., 2020; Zeng et al., 2021), such as back translation (Sennrich et al., 2015; Edunov et al., 2018; Lample et al., 2017). Second, we explore various self-supervised learning methods and introduce as much semi-supervised data as possible towards finding the best practice of training cascaded speech-to-text (S2T) models. In our settings, ASR data, MT data, and monolingual text data are all considered in a progressively training framework. We only trained one E2E model, and its BLEU is 22.49 with 1272 AL. Due to the huge difference in the scale of training data from the cascaded model, E2E performance is far lower than that of the latter. The cascaded S2T final performance on the MuST-C V2 test set is 25.87, 26.21, 26.45 BLEU with low, medium and high regimes.

In addition, we also participate in the simultaneous text-to-text (T2T) task. Our system is based on an efficient wait-k model (Elbayad et al., 2020) and CAAT model (Liu et al., 2021b). We investigate large-scale knowledge distillation (Kim and Rush, 2016; Freitag et al., 2017) and back translation methods. Specially, we develop a multi-path training strategy, which enables a unified model serving different wait-k paths. All MT models are based on transformer (Vaswani et al., 2017). The organizers use the output of a streaming ASR system as input to the text-to-text system, and the results will be shown in the overview paper (Anastasopoulos et al., 2022).

The rest of this paper is organized as follows. Section 2 describes the details of the data preprocessing and augmentation. Section 3 describes the models used in our system and introduces details of the model structure and techniques used in training and inference. We present experimental results in Section 4 and related works in Section 5. Finally, the conclusion is given in Section 6.

Proceedings of the 19th International Conference on Spoken Language Translation (IWSLT 2022), pages 208 - 215
May 26-27, 2022 ©2022 Association for Computational Linguistics

Language	Corpus	Sentences
EN→ZH	WMT2019	20.1M
EN→ZH	WMT2020	20.7M
EN→ZH	WMT2021	42.3M
EN→ZH	OpenSubtitles2018	9.969M
EN→ZH	MuST-C	0.359M

Table 1: Statistics of text parallel datasets.

2 Data Preprocessing and Augmentation

2.1 Data Preprocessing

En-Zh Text Corpora We use English-Chinese (EN-ZH) parallel sentences from WMT2019, WMT2020, WMT2021, OpenSubtitles2018 and MuST-C for training. The statistics of the parallel data is shown in Table 1. Additionally, we select 15% of the Chinese monolingual corpora from News Crawl, News Commentary and Common Crawl for data augmentation. For EN-ZH language pairs, the filtering rules are as follows:

* Filter out sentences that contain long words over 40 characters or over 120 words.
* The word ratio between the source word and the target word must not exceed 1:3 or 3:1.
* Filter out the sentences that have invalid Unicode characters or HTML tags.
* Filter out the duplicated sentence pairs.

Finally, we filter the real and pseudo parallel corpora through a semantic matching model which is trained using limited data. The statistics of the text training data is shown in Table 2.

As for text preprocessing, we apply Moses tokenizer and SentencePiece with 32,000 merge operations on each side.

En-Zh Speech Corpora The speech datasets used in our systems are shown in Table 3, where MuST-C is speech-translation specific (speech, transcription and translation included), and Europarl, CoVoST2, LibriSpeech, TED-LIUM3 and VoxPopuli are speech-recognition specific (only speech and transcription). Kaldi (Ravanelli et al., 2019) is used to extract 80 dimensional log-mel filter bank features, which are computed with a 25ms window size and a 10 ms window shift, and specAugment (Park et al., 2019) are performed during training phase.

	EN→ZH
Bilingual Data	67.4M
Source Mono Data	200.5M
Target Mono Data	405.2M

Table 2: Statistics of the text training data.

Corpus	Frames	Aug	Snt
MuST-C	211M	599M	0.35M
Europarl	30M	80M	0.035M
CoVoST2	711M	202M	1.42M
LibriSpeech	131M	372M	0.1M
TED-LIUM3	163M	463M	0.26M
VoxPopuli	191M	543M	0.18M

Table 3: Statistics of raw and augmented speech corpora. Frames is the audio frames number of the raw data, and Aug is for the audio augmented data. Snt refers to the number of sentences corresponding to the raw audio data.

2.2 Text-to-Text Augmentation

For text-to-text machine translation, augmented data from monolingual corpora in source and target language are generated by knowledge distillation (Kim and Rush, 2016; Freitag et al., 2017) and back translation (Edunov et al., 2018) respectively. Moreover, we use automatic speech recognition (ASR) output utterances to improve MT's robustness.

Back-Translation Back-translation (Sennrich et al., 2015; Lample et al., 2017) is an effective way to improve the translation quality by leveraging a large amount of monolingual data and it has been widely used in WMT campaigns. In our setting, we add a "<BT>" tag to the source side of back-translated data to prevent overfitting on the synthetic data, which is also known as tagged back-translation (Caswell et al., 2019; Marie et al., 2020; Tong et al., 2021).

Knowledge Distillation Sequence-level knowledge distillation (Wang et al., 2021; Sun et al., 2020) is another useful technique to improve translation performance. We enlarge the training data by translating English sentences to Chinese using a good teacher model. Specifically, we trained an EN→ZH offline model based on the deep Transformer as a teacher model. And the beam-search strategy of beam-size 5 is used when translating the English source text into the Chinese target text.

ASR Output Adaptation Traditionally, the

output of ASR systems is lowercased with no punctuation marks, while the MT systems receive natural texts. In our system, we attempt to make our MT systems robust to these irregular texts. A simple method is to apply the same rules on the source side of the MT training set. However, empirical study shows this method causes translation performance degradation. Inspired by the tagged back-translation method (Caswell et al., 2019), we enhance the regular MT models with transcripts from both ASR systems and ASR datasets. An extra tag "<ASR>" indicates the irregular input. Note that the basic idea to bridge the gap between the ASR output and the MT input involves additional sub-systems, like case and punctuation restoration. In our cascaded system, we prefer to use fewer sub-systems, and we will conduct detailed comparison in our future work.

2.3 Speech-to-Text Augmentation

All datasets except MuST-C only contain speech and transcription data. For these datasets, an offline translation model (trained with constrained data) is used to generate Chinese pseudo sentences, which serves as augmented data for training E2E model. In addition, we augment each audio dataset by about 300% using the speed, volume and echo perturbation method as well, and for the CoVoST2 corpus, we augment by 30%. The details are shown in Table 3. Specifically, we first make two copies of all original audio except for CoVoST2. And then, the original audio of all datasets is mixed with all the augmented audio. Finally, we get these training data that are about 1:1 of the original and the augmented audio. Therefore, these training data naturally include the Chinese pseudo data mentioned above. Both ASR and E2E are trained on this training data.

3 Models

3.1 Dynamic-CAAT

Our simultaneous translation systems are based on Cross Attention Augmented Transducer (CAAT) (Liu et al., 2021b), which jointly optimizes the policy and translation model by considering all possible READ-WRITE simultaneous translation action paths. CAAT uses a novel latency loss whose expectation can be optimized by a forward-backward algorithm. Training with this latency loss ensures the controllable latency of CAAT simultaneous translation model. For speech-to-text task, CAAT process the streaming encoder for speech data by block processing with the right context and infinite left context. For text-2-text task, CAAT use conventional unidirectional transformer encoder for text data, which masking the self-attention to only consider previous time-steps.

We improve the training of the CAAT by multiple values of right context window size. Training along multiple right context window size achieves good online performance without setting a prior right context window size in model training. Compared to unidirectional encoder, models trained in this manner can use more source information. The encoder updates the encoder states when new source tokens are available, so that both the encoding of past source tokens and new source tokens are updated. We also show that it is possible to train a single model that is effective across a large range of latency levels.

3.2 Pre-trained LM

For ASR, great advances can be made through pre-training a language model (LM), such as BERT (Devlin et al., 2018), by using sufficient target-domain text (Gao et al., 2021). Inspired by these work, we re-train two language models based on BERT: an English LM and a Chinese LM, respectively for ASR and E2E. Unlike traditional BERT, these two LMs are unidirectional and can be regarded as a special predictor architecture of CAAT.

3.3 Text-to-Text Simultaneous Translation

Our text-to-text Simultaneous Systems are based on Dynamic-CAAT. We use the Dynamic-CAAT implemented based on Transformer, by dividing Transformer's decoder into predictor and joiner module. The predictor and joiner share the same number of transformer blocks as the conventional transformer decoder, while there are no cross-attention blocks in the predictor module and no self-attention blocks in the joiner module.

3.4 Speech-to-Text Simultaneous Translation

3.4.1 Cascaded Systems

The cascaded system includes two modules, simultaneous ASR and simultaneous text-to-text MT. Simultaneous MT system is built with Dynamic-CAAT proposed in Sec. 3.1. However, ASR system directly uses the original CAAT framework for training.

We adjust the range of AL through three hyper-parameters: K, B and P. Where K means the number of ASR output tokens is at least K more than the number of MT output tokens. B is the beam width of MT. P means that the probability of the token generated by the MT model must be greater than P.

The pre-trained LM for ASR is retrained by only using English text corpora descirbed in Sec. 2.1.

3.4.2 E2E Systems

E2E model is built on the original CAAT model. First, we train the E2E model with mixed real and pseudo paired speech-translation data and the scale of the pseudo data is about 1:1 to the real data. Second, pre-training ASR encoder and pre-training LM predictor are used to improve performance under restricted resources. Finally, we train E2E model using multitask learning (Wang et al., 2020a; Ma et al., 2020b; Tang et al., 2021), but didn't achieve the expected effect in this task.

Compared with the tens of millions of data in the MT model, the training data for E2E system is insufficient. So we just train E2E model with low regime, and the E2E model is only used to verify the effectiveness of the training methods.

4 Experiments

In our experiments, pre-norm Transformer-base(Xiong et al., 2020) is used as the offline baseline model to compare with the text-to-text models. The baseline model has 12 encoder layers and 6 decoder layers and it is trained only using bilingual data. We compare the baseline model with three text-to-text models: wait-k(Elbayad et al., 2020), efficient wait-k and Dynamic-CAAT. For speech-to-text task, we compare the results of ASR cascaded Dynamic-CAAT and efficient wait-k respectively. The details of models are summarized in Table 4.

Systems are evaluated with respect to quality and latency. Quality is evaluated with the standard BLEU metric (Papineni et al., 2002). Latency is evaluated with metric average lagging (AL), which is extended to the task of simultaneous speech translation from simultaneous machine translation (Ma et al., 2020d). We conduct all our experiments using Simuleval toolkit (Ma et al., 2020a) and report results for the submitted speech translation tasks. Latest 6 checkpoints of a single training process are averaged in our experiments. We also adopted FP16 mix-precision training to accelerate the training process with almost no loss in BLEU. All models are trained on 8 RTX A10 GPUs. All translation systems are followed by a post-processing module for Chinese punctuation.

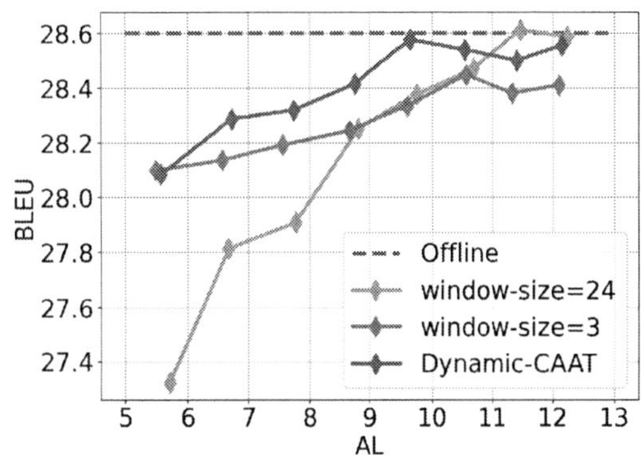

Figure 1: Effectiveness of Dynamic-CAAT

4.1 Effectiveness of Dynamic-CAAT

To demonstrate the effectiveness of Dynamic-CAAT, we compare it with CAAT with different right context window size. Offline results are used for reference, and the offline model has a latency of $AL = |x|$. Models are trained with a batch size of 32,000 token. Figure 1 presents the performance of models trained for a single right context window size w, with $w_{train} \in \{3, 24\}$. Each model is evaluated across different right context window size w, $w_{eval} \in \{4, 5, ..., 11\}$. From Figure 1 we observe that performance of model with $w = 24$ is worse than that of model with right window size $w = 3$, especially $w_{eval} \in \{4, 5, 6\}$). Meanwhile, we found that training on a small right context window size $w = 3$ can generalize well to other w. We note that jointly training on Dynamic right context window size w outperforms training on a single path.

4.2 Effectiveness of Pre-trained LM

We compare the results of the ASR and E2E systems with their respective LM methods. The implementation of our models are based on the CAAT code [1]. For both ASR and E2E tasks, we use specAugment (Park et al., 2019) with $F = 15, m_F = 2, T = 70, p = 0.2, m_T = 2$, and use Adam optimizer (Kingma and Ba, 2014) with $\beta_1 = 0.9$, $\beta_2 = 0.98$. We set max tokens as 20000

[1]https://github.com/danliu2/caat

Model	Encoder Layers	Decoder Layers/ Predictor Layers	Joiner Layers	Hidden Size	FFN
Offline	12	6	-	512	2048
wait-k	6	6	-	512	1024
efficient wait-k	6	6	-	1024	4096
Dynamic-CAAT	12	6	6	512	2048
ASR	12	6	6	512	2048
E2E	12	6	6	512	2048

Table 4: The details of several model architectures we used.

Models	tst-COMMON (WER / AL)	dev (WER / AL)
ASR-base	13.81 / 927	14.98 / 883
+LM	11.32 / 901	13.32 / 869
Models	**tst-COMMON (BLEU / AL)**	**dev (BLEU / AL)**
E2E-base	19.56 / 1304	17.62 / 1381
+LM	22.49 / 1272	19.71 / 1347

Table 5: Effectiveness of pre-trained LM.

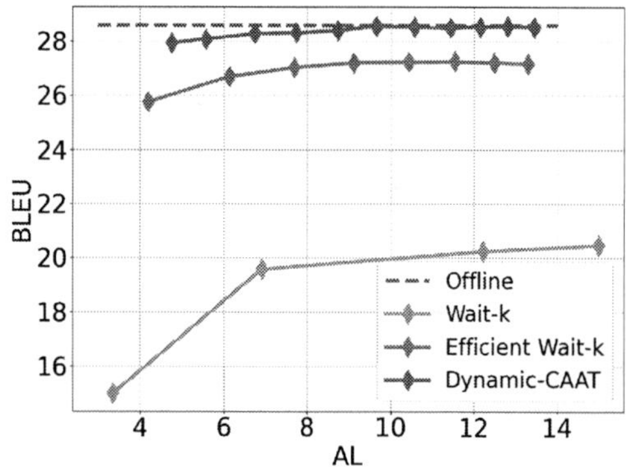

Figure 2: Latency-quality trade-offs of text-to-text simultaneous translation.

and update frequency as 8 during training. And during inference, the beam width is set to 5. Table 5 shows ASR and E2E experiment results. We observe that the ASR and E2E both outperform the baseline systems trained without pre-trained LM.

4.3 Text-to-Text Simultaneous Translation

In text-to-text simultaneous translation task, experiments are conducted on tst-COMMON test set. The latency is measured with the subword-level latency metric. We compare Dynamic-CAAT models with wait-k and efficient wait-k[2]. The results of

[2]https://github.com/elbayadm/attn2d

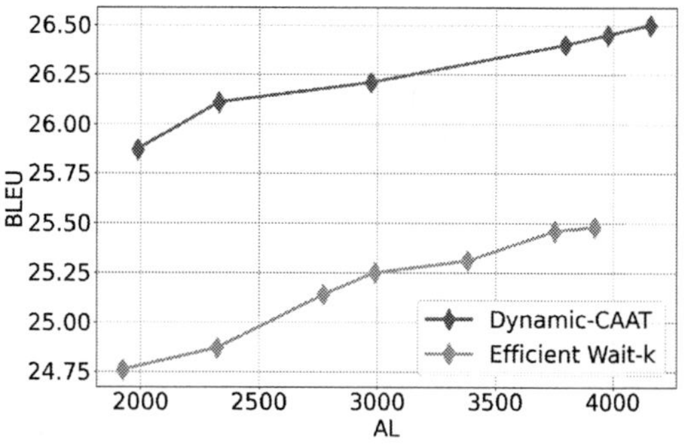

Figure 3: Latency-quality trade-offs of speech-to-text simultaneous translation.

text-to-text EN→ZH are shown in Figure 2. We can see that performance of Dynamic-CAAT is always better than that of wait-k and efficient wait-k, especially in low latency regime, and performance of Dynamic-CAAT is nearly equivalent to offline result.

And during inference, the "<ASR>" tag is added to the front of the ASR output and it can increase 0.2 bleu. For the text-to-text task, we set the beam width to 1.

4.4 Cascaded Speech translation

Under the cascaded setting, we paired two well-trained ASR and Dynamic-CAAT systems. The WER of ASR system's performance is 11.32 with 901 AL, and the cascaded system's results vary with the Dynamic-CAAT hyperparameters K, B, P. The range of K is 3 to 20. P is set to 0.35, and B is set to 1, however, when K is greater than 14, B is set to 6. For comparison, we use another text-to-text machine translation model, efficient wait-k. Performance of cascaded systems is shown in Figure 3. On the test set tst-COMMON from MuST-C v2, the cascaded system of Dynamic-CAAT achieves 25.87, 26.21, 26.45 BLEU with

1987, 2972, 3974 AL respectively. We also find that the BLEU value of Dynamic-CAAT is on average 1.0 higher than that of efficient wait-k in the same AL range.

5 Related Work

5.1 Data Augmentation

In terms of data scale, the amount of training data for speech translation is significantly smaller than that for text-to-text machine translation, and lack of data decreases performance of speech translation. As described in Section 2, based on the text-to-text MT model, sequence-level knowledge distillation and self-training are used to solve the problem of low performance of the speech translation model. This approach has also proven to be the most efficient way to utilize large amounts of ASR training data (Pino et al., 2020; Gaido et al., 2020). In addition, generating speech synthetic data is also effective for low-resource speech recognition tasks (Bansal et al., 2018; Ren et al., 2020).

5.2 Simultaneous Translation

Recent work on simultaneous translation (including S2T and T2T) can be roughly divided into two categories. The first category is represented by the wait-k method, which uses a fixed strategy for the READ/WRITE actions of simultaneous translation, and these models are easy to implement. The second category assumes that adaptive policies are superior to fixed policies, because adaptive policies can flexibly balance the tradeoff between translation quality and latency based on current context information. Research in this category includes supervise learning (Zheng et al., 2019), simultaneous translation decoding with adaptive policy (Zheng et al., 2020), and so on. In addition, researchers have also proposed a monotonic attention mechanism optimized for translation and policy for flexible policy, e.g., Monotonic Infinite Lookback (MILk) attention (Arivazhagan et al., 2019) and Monotonic Multihead Attention (MMA) (Ma et al., 2020c).

6 Conclusion

This paper summarizes the results of the shared tasks in the IWSLT 2022 produced by the AISP-SJTU team. In this paper, Dynamic-CAAT we used outperforms efficient wait-k, and its result is close to offline model in the case of $AL > 9$. From the experiments we also can see that the pre-trained language model plays a most important role in both ASR and E2E translation. Because of the huge difference in the amount of data, the performance of the E2E system is much lower than that of cascaded system. In the future, we hope to explore more effective data augmentation experiments applied to E2E translation. We hope that our practice can facilitate research work and industrial applications.

References

Antonios Anastasopoulos, Luisa Bentivogli, Marcely Z. Boito, Ondřej Bojar, Roldano Cattoni, Anna Currey, Georgiana Dinu, Kevin Duh, Maha Elbayad, Marcello Federico, Christian Federmann, Hongyu Gong, Roman Grundkiewicz, Barry Haddow, Benjamin Hsu, Dávid Javorský, Věra Kloudová, Surafel M. Lakew, Xutai Ma, Prashant Mathur, Paul McNamee, Kenton Murray, Maria Nădejde, Satoshi Nakamura, Matteo Negri, Jan Niehues, Xing Niu, Juan Pino, Elizabeth Salesky, Jiatong Shi, Sebastian Stüker, Katsuhito Sudoh, Marco Turchi, Yogesh Virkar, Alex Waibel, Changhan Wang, and Shinji Watanabe. 2022. FINDINGS OF THE IWSLT 2022 EVALUATION CAMPAIGN. In *Proceedings of the 19th International Conference on Spoken Language Translation (IWSLT 2022)*, Dublin, Ireland. Association for Computational Linguistics.

Antonios Anastasopoulos, Ondřej Bojar, Jacob Bremerman, Roldano Cattoni, Maha Elbayad, Marcello Federico, Xutai Ma, Satoshi Nakamura, Matteo Negri, Jan Niehues, Juan Pino, Elizabeth Salesky, Sebastian Stüker, Katsuhito Sudoh, Marco Turchi, Alexander Waibel, Changhan Wang, and Matthew Wiesner. 2021. FINDINGS OF THE IWSLT 2021 EVALUATION CAMPAIGN. In *Proceedings of the 18th International Conference on Spoken Language Translation (IWSLT 2021)*, pages 1–29, Bangkok, Thailand (online). Association for Computational Linguistics.

Ebrahim Ansari, Amittai Axelrod, Nguyen Bach, Ondřej Bojar, Roldano Cattoni, Fahim Dalvi, Nadir Durrani, Marcello Federico, Christian Federmann, Jiatao Gu, Fei Huang, Kevin Knight, Xutai Ma, Ajay Nagesh, Matteo Negri, Jan Niehues, Juan Pino, Elizabeth Salesky, Xing Shi, Sebastian Stüker, Marco Turchi, Alexander Waibel, and Changhan Wang. 2020. FINDINGS OF THE IWSLT 2020 EVALUATION CAMPAIGN. In *Proceedings of the 17th International Conference on Spoken Language Translation*, pages 1–34, Online. Association for Computational Linguistics.

Naveen Arivazhagan, Colin Cherry, Wolfgang Macherey, Chung-Cheng Chiu, Semih Yavuz, Ruoming Pang, Wei Li, and Colin Raffel. 2019. Monotonic infinite lookback attention for simultaneous machine translation. *arXiv preprint arXiv:1906.05218*.

Sameer Bansal, Herman Kamper, Karen Livescu, Adam Lopez, and Sharon Goldwater. 2018. Pre-training on high-resource speech recognition improves low-resource speech-to-text translation. *arXiv preprint arXiv:1809.01431*.

Isaac Caswell, Ciprian Chelba, and David Grangier. 2019. Tagged back-translation. *arXiv preprint arXiv:1906.06442*.

Jacob Devlin, Ming-Wei Chang, Kenton Lee, and Kristina Toutanova. 2018. BERT: pre-training of deep bidirectional transformers for language understanding. *CoRR*, abs/1810.04805.

Qianqian Dong, Rong Ye, Mingxuan Wang, Hao Zhou, Shuang Xu, Bo Xu, and Lei Li. 2021. Listen, understand and translate: Triple supervision decouples end-to-end speech-to-text translation. In *Proceedings of the AAAI Conference on Artificial Intelligence*, volume 35, pages 12749–12759.

Sergey Edunov, Myle Ott, Michael Auli, and David Grangier. 2018. Understanding back-translation at scale. *arXiv preprint arXiv:1808.09381*.

Maha Elbayad, Laurent Besacier, and Jakob Verbeek. 2020. Efficient wait-k models for simultaneous machine translation. *arXiv preprint arXiv:2005.08595*.

Markus Freitag, Yaser Al-Onaizan, and Baskaran Sankaran. 2017. Ensemble distillation for neural machine translation. *arXiv preprint arXiv:1702.01802*.

Marco Gaido, Mattia Antonino Di Gangi, Matteo Negri, and Marco Turchi. 2020. End-to-end speech-translation with knowledge distillation: Fbk@ iwslt2020. *arXiv preprint arXiv:2006.02965*.

Changfeng Gao, Gaofeng Cheng, Runyan Yang, Han Zhu, Pengyuan Zhang, and Yonghong Yan. 2021. Pre-training transformer decoder for end-to-end asr model with unpaired text data. In *ICASSP 2021 - 2021 IEEE International Conference on Acoustics, Speech and Signal Processing (ICASSP)*, pages 6543–6547.

Yoon Kim and Alexander M Rush. 2016. Sequence-level knowledge distillation. *arXiv preprint arXiv:1606.07947*.

Diederik P Kingma and Jimmy Ba. 2014. Adam: A method for stochastic optimization. *arXiv preprint arXiv:1412.6980*.

Guillaume Lample, Alexis Conneau, Ludovic Denoyer, and Marc'Aurelio Ranzato. 2017. Unsupervised machine translation using monolingual corpora only. *arXiv preprint arXiv:1711.00043*.

Bei Li, Yinqiao Li, Chen Xu, Ye Lin, Jiqiang Liu, Hui Liu, Ziyang Wang, Yuhao Zhang, Nuo Xu, Zeyang Wang, et al. 2019. The niutrans machine translation systems for wmt19. In *Proceedings of the Fourth Conference on Machine Translation (Volume 2: Shared Task Papers, Day 1)*, pages 257–266.

Dan Liu, Mengge Du, Xiaoxi Li, Yuchen Hu, and Lirong Dai. 2021a. The ustc-nelslip systems for simultaneous speech translation task at iwslt 2021. *arXiv preprint arXiv:2107.00279*.

Dan Liu, Mengge Du, Xiaoxi Li, Ya Li, and Enhong Chen. 2021b. Cross attention augmented transducer networks for simultaneous translation. In *Proceedings of the 2021 Conference on Empirical Methods in Natural Language Processing*, pages 39–55.

Xutai Ma, Mohammad Javad Dousti, Changhan Wang, Jiatao Gu, and Juan Pino. 2020a. Simuleval: An evaluation toolkit for simultaneous translation. *arXiv preprint arXiv:2007.16193*.

Xutai Ma, Juan Pino, and Philipp Koehn. 2020b. Simulmt to simulst: Adapting simultaneous text translation to end-to-end simultaneous speech translation. *arXiv preprint arXiv:2011.02048*.

Xutai Ma, Juan Miguel Pino, James Cross, Liezl Puzon, and Jiatao Gu. 2020c. Monotonic multihead attention. In *International Conference on Learning Representations*.

Xutai Ma, Juan Miguel Pino, and Philipp Koehn. 2020d. Simulmt to simulst: Adapting simultaneous text translation to end-to-end simultaneous speech translation. *CoRR*, abs/2011.02048.

Benjamin Marie, Raphael Rubino, and Atsushi Fujita. 2020. Tagged back-translation revisited: Why does it really work? In *Proceedings of the 58th Annual Meeting of the Association for Computational Linguistics*, pages 5990–5997.

Fandong Meng, Jianhao Yan, Yijin Liu, Yuan Gao, Xianfeng Zeng, Qinsong Zeng, Peng Li, Ming Chen, Jie Zhou, Sifan Liu, et al. 2020. Wechat neural machine translation systems for wmt20. *arXiv preprint arXiv:2010.00247*.

Kishore Papineni, Salim Roukos, Todd Ward, and Wei-Jing Zhu. 2002. Bleu: A method for automatic evaluation of machine translation. In *Proceedings of the 40th Annual Meeting on Association for Computational Linguistics*, ACL '02, page 311–318, USA. Association for Computational Linguistics.

Daniel S Park, William Chan, Yu Zhang, Chung-Cheng Chiu, Barret Zoph, Ekin D Cubuk, and Quoc V Le. 2019. Specaugment: A simple data augmentation method for automatic speech recognition. *arXiv preprint arXiv:1904.08779*.

Juan Pino, Qiantong Xu, Xutai Ma, Mohammad Javad Dousti, and Yun Tang. 2020. Self-training for end-to-end speech translation. *arXiv preprint arXiv:2006.02490*.

Mirco Ravanelli, Titouan Parcollet, and Yoshua Bengio. 2019. The pytorch-kaldi speech recognition toolkit. In *ICASSP 2019-2019 IEEE International Conference on Acoustics, Speech and Signal Processing (ICASSP)*, pages 6465–6469. IEEE.

Yi Ren, Jinglin Liu, Xu Tan, Chen Zhang, Tao Qin, Zhou Zhao, and Tie-Yan Liu. 2020. Simulspeech: End-to-end simultaneous speech to text translation. In *Proceedings of the 58th Annual Meeting of the Association for Computational Linguistics*, pages 3787–3796.

Rico Sennrich, Barry Haddow, and Alexandra Birch. 2015. Improving neural machine translation models with monolingual data. *arXiv preprint arXiv:1511.06709*.

Mihaela C Stoian, Sameer Bansal, and Sharon Goldwater. 2020. Analyzing asr pretraining for low-resource speech-to-text translation. In *ICASSP 2020-2020 IEEE International Conference on Acoustics, Speech and Signal Processing (ICASSP)*, pages 7909–7913. IEEE.

Haipeng Sun, Rui Wang, Kehai Chen, Masao Utiyama, Eiichiro Sumita, and Tiejun Zhao. 2020. Knowledge distillation for multilingual unsupervised neural machine translation. *arXiv preprint arXiv:2004.10171*.

Tzu-Wei Sung, Jun-You Liu, Hung-yi Lee, and Lin-shan Lee. 2019. Towards end-to-end speech-to-text translation with two-pass decoding. In *ICASSP 2019-2019 IEEE International Conference on Acoustics, Speech and Signal Processing (ICASSP)*, pages 7175–7179. IEEE.

Yun Tang, Juan Pino, Changhan Wang, Xutai Ma, and Dmitriy Genzel. 2021. A general multi-task learning framework to leverage text data for speech to text tasks. In *ICASSP 2021-2021 IEEE International Conference on Acoustics, Speech and Signal Processing (ICASSP)*, pages 6209–6213. IEEE.

Chengqi Zhao Zhicheng Liu Jian Tong, Tao Wang Mingxuan Wang, Rong Ye Qianqian Dong Jun Cao, and Lei Li. 2021. The volctrans neural speech translation system for iwslt 2021. *IWSLT 2021*, page 64.

Ashish Vaswani, Noam Shazeer, Niki Parmar, Jakob Uszkoreit, Llion Jones, Aidan N Gomez, Łukasz Kaiser, and Illia Polosukhin. 2017. Attention is all you need. *Advances in neural information processing systems*, 30.

Changhan Wang, Yun Tang, Xutai Ma, Anne Wu, Dmytro Okhonko, and Juan Pino. 2020a. fairseq s2t: Fast speech-to-text modeling with fairseq. *arXiv preprint arXiv:2010.05171*.

Chengyi Wang, Yu Wu, Shujie Liu, Ming Zhou, and Zhenglu Yang. 2020b. Curriculum pre-training for end-to-end speech translation. *arXiv preprint arXiv:2004.10093*.

Fusheng Wang, Jianhao Yan, Fandong Meng, and Jie Zhou. 2021. Selective knowledge distillation for neural machine translation. *arXiv preprint arXiv:2105.12967*.

Liwei Wu, Xiao Pan, Zehui Lin, Yaoming Zhu, Mingxuan Wang, and Lei Li. 2020. The volctrans machine translation system for wmt20. *arXiv preprint arXiv:2010.14806*.

Ruibin Xiong, Yunchang Yang, Di He, Kai Zheng, Shuxin Zheng, Chen Xing, Huishuai Zhang, Yanyan Lan, Liwei Wang, and Tie-Yan Liu. 2020. On layer normalization in the transformer architecture. *CoRR*, abs/2002.04745.

Chen Xu, Xiaoqian Liu, Xiaowen Liu, Laohu Wang, Canan Huang, Tong Xiao, and Jingbo Zhu. 2021. The niutrans end-to-end speech translation system for iwslt 2021 offline task. *arXiv preprint arXiv:2107.02444*.

Xianfeng Zeng, Yijin Liu, Ernan Li, Qiu Ran, Fandong Meng, Peng Li, Jinan Xu, and Jie Zhou. 2021. Wechat neural machine translation systems for wmt21. *arXiv preprint arXiv:2108.02401*.

Baigong Zheng, Kaibo Liu, Renjie Zheng, Mingbo Ma, Hairong Liu, and Liang Huang. 2020. Simultaneous translation policies: From fixed to adaptive. *arXiv preprint arXiv:2004.13169*.

Baigong Zheng, Renjie Zheng, Mingbo Ma, and Liang Huang. 2019. Simultaneous translation with flexible policy via restricted imitation learning. *arXiv preprint arXiv:1906.01135*.

The Xiaomi Text-to-Text Simultaneous Speech Translation System for IWSLT 2022

Bao Guo[1*] **Mengge Liu**[2*†] **Wen Zhang**[1] **Hexuan Chen**[1] **Chang Mu**[1]
Xiang Li[1] **Jianwei Cui**[1] **Bin Wang**[1] **Yuhang Guo**[2]
[1]Xiaomi AI Lab, Beijing, China
[2]Beijing Institute of Technology, Beijing, China
guobao@xiaomi.com 3120201046@bit.edu.cn
{zhangwen17,chenhexuan,muchang1,lixiang21}@xiaomi.com
{cuijianwei,wangbin11}@xiaomi.com guoyuhang@bit.edu.cn

Abstract

This system paper describes the Xiaomi Translation System for the IWSLT 2022 Simultaneous Speech Translation (noted as SST) shared task. We participate in the English-to-Mandarin Chinese Text-to-Text (noted as T2T) track. Our system is built based on the Transformer model with novel techniques borrowed from our recent research work. For the data filtering, language-model-based and rule-based methods are conducted to filter the data to obtain high-quality bilingual parallel corpora. We also strengthen our system with some dominating techniques related to data augmentation, such as knowledge distillation, tagged back-translation, and iterative back-translation. We also incorporate novel training techniques such as R-drop, deep model, and large batch training which have been shown to be beneficial to the naive Transformer model. In the SST scenario, several variations of `wait-k` strategies are explored. Furthermore, in terms of robustness, both data-based and model-based ways are used to reduce the sensitivity of our system to Automatic Speech Recognition (ASR) outputs. We finally design some inference algorithms and use the adaptive-ensemble method based on multiple model variants to further improve the performance of the system. Compared with strong baselines, fusing all techniques can improve our system by 2~3 BLEU scores under different latency regimes.

1 Introduction

In the IWSLT 2022 Evaluation Campaign, our team at Xiaomi AI Lab participates in one Simultaneous Speech Translation task (Anastasopoulos et al., 2022), which is the Text-to-Text track in English to Mandarin Chinese translation direction. We first introduce the techniques used in our final submitted system from four aspects: data, model, inference, and robustness.

Data-related techniques are introduced from two perspectives: data augmentation and domain-related data selection. For data augmentation, we employ technologies such as back-translation (BT) (Sennrich et al., 2016a), knowledge distillation (KD) (Kim and Rush, 2016), and iterative back-translation (Hoang et al., 2018) etc. to generate large-scale synthetic bilingual datasets, which have been proved to be very effective in the field of machine translation. We also use the technology of Tagged Back-Translation (TaggedBT) (Caswell et al., 2019), that is, prepending a reserved token <BT> to the beginning of the synthetic source sentence in the training set, so that the model could distinguish the originality of the source sentence. Meanwhile, the effects of different combinations of multiple training sets on the model performance are explored. For domain-related data selection, differences in the domains of the training and test sets can have a large negative impact on the results on the test sets. To make the model obtain domain-related knowledge as much as possible, we apply the LM-based data selection technique (Axelrod et al., 2011) to select high-quality and domain-related data from bilingual corpora.

In terms of model, since the submitted systems will be ranked by the translation quality with three latency regimes (low, medium, and high), participants are encouraged to submit multiple systems for each regime to provide more data points for latency-quality tradeoff analyses. Besides, we empirically believe that different models have different translation performance and inference latency on T2T tasks, and they can complement each other, so we build various advanced SST models (i.e. BASEDEEP and BIGDEEP), which are all based on deep Transformer model (Vaswani et al., 2017), but have been empirically proven to outperform the Transformer-Big model on the SST model. For

*Equal contribution.

† The work was done during the author's internship at Xiaomi.

Proceedings of the 19th International Conference on Spoken Language Translation (IWSLT 2022), pages 216 - 224
May 26-27, 2022 ©2022 Association for Computational Linguistics

the T2T track, the output of a streaming ASR system (usually prefix of the entire source sentence) will be fed into the SST system as input instead of the gold transcript. So we adopt the `wait-k` training strategy (Ma et al., 2019; Elbayad et al., 2020) to meet the scenario of simulating simultaneous translation. In addition, we also employ the R-Drop (Liang et al., 2021) and adaptive-ensemble techniques (Zheng et al., 2020) which have also been proven beneficial for translation models.

For inference, we empirically analyze the problems of our system in translation under low latency (e.g. when k is equal to 3) and propose a constrained decoding strategy to wait for some specific words or phrases to appear before translation, which can alleviate some translation issues of the `wait-k` model in low-latency situations as much as possible.

The input fed into the SST model is the output of the ASR system, and according to the statistics of previous researchers, the two error types homophones and words with a similar pronunciation account for a large proportion in the output of the ASR system. Therefore, in order to weaken the model's sensitivity to ASR output errors, we introduce methods to enhance the model's robustness to both error types: homophones or words with a similar pronunciation. Additionally, a char-to-subwords error correction model is further proposed to correct ASR errors before feeding into the translation model.

The remainder of this paper is organized as follows. We perform statistics on the data used and introduce pre-processing in Section 2. Section 3 and 4 elaborate our systems, the techniques employed, and evaluation, followed by the main experimental results and ablation studies reported in Section 5. Finally, we conclude this paper in Section 6.

2 Data

We introduce the data used in our system from the following three aspects: statistics, pre-processing and filtering.

Statistics. We use the allowed training sets, which include MuST-C v2.0 [1], CoVoST [2], TED corpus [3], OpenSubtitles2018 [4], and the bilingual corpus provided by WMT2021 [5]. We find that the four datasets MuST-C v2.0, CoVoST, TED corpus, and OpenSubtitles2018 are all datasets that are biased towards the oral domain, so we combined these four datasets as the training set in **Oral** domain. We also empirically treat WMT21 as the training set in the **News** domain. The statistical results of the original datasets are shown in Table 1. Among them, all the available bilingual corpora provided by WMT2021 includes: News Commentary v16 (0.32M) [6], Wiki Titles v3 (0.92M), UN Parallel Corpus V1.0 (15.9M), CCMT Corpus (8.9M), WikiMatrix (2.6M), Back-translated news (19.8M), and ParaCrawl v7.1 (14.2M). We use the `tst-COMMON` test set (including 2, 841 sentences) as the development set to validate our models.

Bilingual data		Size	Filtered
Oral	**MuST-C v2.0**	360K	7.8M
	CoVoST	870K	
	TED corpus	250K	
	OpenSubtitles2018	11.2M	
News	**WMT2021**	61.1M	45.3M
Total	-	75.32M	53.1M

Table 1: The statistical results of all available bilingual training sets.

Pre-processing. `Sacremoses` [7] is conducted to normalize and tokenize English sentences. We use the traditional and simplified conversion tool to convert traditional Chinese text to simplified, use the `jieba` [8] tool to segment Chinese sentences, and remove redundant spaces in the text.

Rule-based Filtering. The training set is filtered according to the following rules (the content in parentheses after each item indicates the number of sentence pairs remaining after the current step of filtering is performed):

- We remove duplicate sentence pairs and empty data in the training set (65.3M);
- We first use `fast_align` [9] to filter out sen-

[1]https://ict.fbk.eu/must-c/

[2]https://github.com/facebookresearch/covost

[3]https://wit3.fbk.eu/2017-01-c

[4]https://opus.nlpl.eu/OpenSubtitles2018.php

[5]https://www.statmt.org/wmt21/

[6]Numbers in parentheses indicate the number of parallel sentence pairs

[7]https://github.com/alvations/sacremoses

[8]https://github.com/fxsjy/jieba

[9]https://github.com/clab/fast_align

tence pairs with scores less than -7 and then use Language Identification (LangID) tool [10] to remove those sentence pairs that do not contain English or Chinese (55.9M);
- Sentence pairs in which more than 58% of the tokens in the source sentences appear in the target sentences are discarded (53.8M);
- Sentence pairs with a length ratio of source to target or a length ratio of target to source greater than 3.0, or sentence pairs containing sentences with a length of more than 100 tokens are discarded (53.1M).

The size statistics of the training set on domains **Oral** and **News** are shown in Table 1. The filtered training set on the two domains contains 53.1M sentence pairs, marked as s1 (as shown in Table 3).

Language-model-based Filtering. Drawing on the method of Axelrod et al. (2011), we train two 5-gram language models (denoted as lm^{in} and lm^{out}) on English sentences in the MuST-C v2.0 (oral domain) and s1 (news domain) training sets respectively. For each English sentence in s1, we use lm^{in} and lm^{out} to calculate ppl^{in} and ppl^{out} respectively. Sentence pairs in s1 are sorted in ascending order according to the value of $ppl^{in} - ppl^{out}$, and the first 30M are selected as the parallel corpus related to the oral domain. Finally, based on the pre-trained language model, s1 is filtered into a bilingual parallel corpus of size 30M related to the oral domain (**Fppl** shown in Table 3).

3 Configurations

3.1 Model Settings

For the implementation of Transformer, we use the code provided by fairseq[11] (Ott et al., 2019). The token-level batch size is set as about 250k on 8 GPUs for all the experiments. The learning rate is set as 1e-3 for all models, which is controlled by Adam optimizer (Kingma and Ba, 2014). To acquire strong baselines, dropout (Srivastava et al., 2014) is used and set as 0.05 for all the models. We use byte-pair encodings (BPE) (Sennrich et al., 2016b) with $32k$ for all models. All submitted models are trained by using s4 on 8 V100 GPUs or 8 A100 GPUs. For training each model, we run 100k steps and save the model every 2.5k steps with the early stop mechanism, which means that if there are 10 consecutive checkpoints with no improvement in BLEU on the development set, then the training is terminated. The sizes of English vocabulary and Chinese vocabulary are $33,512$ and $43,048$ respectively.

3.2 Evaluation

Following official automatic evaluation criteria, we use BLEU score (Papineni et al., 2002) to evaluate our system for translation quality. For translation latency, standard metrics average lagging (AL) (Ma et al., 2020) is applied for simultaneous machine translation. In order to simulate the speech-to-text translation latency for a text-to-text task, we also use the officially provided noisy test set `tst-COMMON` to simulate non-computation-aware AL (NCA-AL), which are decoded with the streaming ASR model and contain the source timestamps [12]. SimulEval [13] open-source tool is employed to calculate BLEU and AL.

	base_eadb	big_exdy
Encoder layers	a	x
Decoder layers	b	y
Embedding Dim	512	2048
FFN Dim	1024	4096
Number of Heads	8	16

Table 2: The configurations of our deep Transformer models. Note that the **base_eadb** model has an a-layer encoder and a b-layer decoder, the encoder and decoder of the **big_exdy** model have x and y layers respectively. "Dim" means the dimension size.

4 Techniques

In this section, we elaborate the models we use and the employed techniques.

4.1 Deep Architecture

Our submitted system uses two deep Transformer models, named base_eadb and big_exdy. We use the deep-norm technique proposed by Wang et al. (2022) to train the deep models. The base_eadb models we adopt contain an a-layer encoder and a b-layer decoder with `Transformer-base` setting. For big_exdy, we train deep Transformer models with an x-layer encoder and a y-layer decoder by leveraging `Transformer-big` setting. The detailed model configuration is shown in Table 2. Our

[10] https://github.com/saffsd/langid.py
[11] https://github.com/pytorch/fairseq
[12] https://github.com/facebookresearch/SimulEval/blob/main/docs/timestamps.md
[13] https://github.com/facebookresearch/SimulEval

Name	Oral (7.8M)	News (45.3M)	Fppl (30M)	Foral (6.5M)	Size
s1	P	P	-	-	53.1M
s2	P+TaggedBT+KD	P+TaggedBT+KD	-	-	150M
s3	-	-	1KD	2TaggedBTv1+3KDv1	48M
s4	-	-	1KD	2P+2TaggedBTv2+3KDv2	58M

Table 3: Four training sets obtained according to different combinations of datasets. The detailed description of **Oral** and **News** can be seen from Table 1. "P" means parallel data. "TaggedBT" represents tagged back-translation. The numbers in front of "TaggedBT" or "KD" denote the number of models used to conduct back-translation and knowledge distillation respectively. "v1" and "v2" respectively indicate that the first and second iteration of data augmentation on the data in the corresponding columns. For rows s3 and s4 of the **Fppl** column, the 1KD data is translated by using the en2zh_base_e25d6_s1 model.

final submitted system contains only 2 deep models: en2zh_base_e40d6 [14] and en2zh_big_e12d6, with 210M and 370M parameters, respectively.

4.2 R-Drop

All models are trained by using the R-Drop training algorithm with the weight α set to be 5. More detailed description of the R-Drop training algorithm can be found in paper Liang et al. (2021).

4.3 `Wait-k` Strategies

Based on the naive `wait-k` algorithm proposed by Ma et al. (2019), we build our systems and make inference by using two variants of the `wait-k` algorithm, the details are as follows.

Training. The first is effective `wait-k` proposed by Elbayad et al. (2020), which means a fixed `k` value is selected during training (named as `wait(k)`), and the models are trained to generate the target sentence concurrently with the source sentence, but always `k` words behind. The second is multi-path `wait-k` policies introduced by Elbayad et al. (2020), which dynamically and randomly select a value within the `k`-value interval (such as `[k, k+t]`) for each batch during training (named as `wait(k)-(k+t)`).

Inference. At inference, we use two strategies: `single-k` and adaptive-ensemble. For `single-k`, corresponding to efficient `wait-k`, a fixed value of `k` is set during decoding. When the number of source tokens read minus the number of target tokens output is greater than or equal to `k`, the decoding is performed to output a token. In addition, we conduct the `waitmore` strategy. Specifically, when the read words are prepositions, punctuation, and other meaningless words, we make $\mathrm{k}+1$, that is, wait for one more source token. When the source has been read, we switch to the regular model to do the rest of the decoding.

Another strategy is adaptive-ensemble. Specifically, for multiple `wait-k` models, we test their performance on each `k` value in the interval $[1, 19]$, and then determine the top three models corresponding to each `k` value according to the model confidence (log-probability). During the decoding process, the `k` value starts from 1, and the upper bound is 19. At the current value of `k`, the top three models corresponding to the `k` value are used for ensemble decoding, and the top-1 probability value in the probability distribution is used as the confidence. If it is higher than the preset threshold, the decoding result is output, otherwise, the value of `k` is incremented by 1. The settings are the same as Zheng et al. (2020).

4.4 Data Augmentation

Back-translation (BT) (Sennrich et al., 2016a) and knowledge distillation (KD) are very effective data augmentation methods for the naive NMT model [15]. Here we empirically use the TaggedBT technique proposed by Caswell et al. (2019), which has been validated and concluded to be superior to BT. In particular, we add a reserved tag <BT> at the beginning of the source sentence in the training data synthesized by BT, and the tag is treated in the same way as all other tokens. Given the success of Nguyen et al. (2020) and Wang et al. (2020), we also adopt the ensemble method based on data diversification. The details of our approach are as follows.

Based on s1, we first train three English-to-Chinese models and two Chinese-to-English mod-

[14] en2zh_base_e40d6 means the English-to-Chinese translation model including a 40-layer encoder and a 6-layer decoder with `Transformer-base` setting.

[15] Compared with the `wait-k` model, we refer to the original NMT model as the naive NMT model.

els. We translate the **Fppl** training set by using above 5 models, and construct two BT data (noted as 2TaggedBT) and three KD data (noted as 3KD), then merge **Fppl**, 2TaggedBT and 3KD before deduplication to build corpus s2. For the **Oral** training set, we use the existing model to translate English into Chinese and sort in descending order according to sentence-level BLEU, then save 6.5M parallel corpus (denoted as **Foral**). Similarly, we perform the first iteration on the **Foral** data, obtaining two BT data (2TaggedBTv1) and three KD data (3KDv1). We finally merge 1KD, 2TaggedBTv1, and 3KDv1 before deduplication to build corpus s3. Finally, we perform the second iteration (Hoang et al., 2018) on the **Foral** data to obtain two BT data (2TaggedBTv2) and three KD data (3KDv2). 1KD, two copies of **Foral** data, 2TaggedBTv2, and 3KDv2 are merged before deduplication to generate the training set s4.

Our final submission system contains the following deep models: en2zh_base_e40d6_s4 [16] and en2zh_big_e12d6_s4, both of which are trained on data s4.

4.5 Robustness to ASR Noise

We propose two methods to improve the robustness of the system to ASR output noise, and the two methods are orthogonal.

Synthetic Noise Generation. The training set **Foral** is further filtered to 5.6M based on the sentence-level BLEU score between candidate and reference. We randomly generate synthetic noise on the English sentences in the filtered **Foral** to form synthetic bilingual data, then merge it with the authentic bilingual data to obtain final bilingual data s5 (including 11M sentence pairs).

The specific process of generating noise is as follows: for a word w, the Double Metaphone[17] and CMU pronouncing dictionary[18] are first used to obtain the consonants of w, and then words with the same consonants will be clustered together to form cluster C_w, note that $w \notin C_w$. Finally, with a probability of 5%, we either insert a word after w, delete w, or replace w with the corresponding homophone, which is the word in C_w with the smallest edit distance from w. en2zh_base_e40d6_s4 and en2zh_big_e12d6_s4 are finetuned on s5.

Error Correction Model. For the specific scenario of streaming ASR, we construct examples based on English sentences in **Foral** to train an error correction model: 1) insert, delete, replace or reorder the characters in the words randomly, and generate two noisy datasets on the entire sentence pairs and one noisy dataset on the prefix pairs [19]; 2) use the method proposed by Lee et al. (2018) to generate the pronunciation sequence of each sentence (with spaces reserved), and train a model to generate subword sequences from the pronunciation sequence (BLEU score is 96), then we randomly insert or delete spaces on the pronunciation sequence to simulate the noise of speech segmentation, and use the trained model to decode the noisy pronunciation sequence, finally reserve the decoding result different from the original sentence (4M) as noise data; 3) up-sample 3 copies of the authentic bilingual data in the entire sentence part, then up-sample 2 copies of the authentic bilingual data in the prefix part, and finally merge all bilingual data (including 48M sentence pairs) and train a char-to-subwords Transformer model for error correction.

Models	BLEU
en2zh_big_e6d6_s1	28.05
en2zh_big_e6d6_s3	28.94
en2zh_big_e6d6_s4	28.97

Table 4: The effect of training sets constructed with different data augmentation strategies on model performance.

5 Experimental Results

5.1 Main Results

To verify the impact of each dataset on model performance, we train three en2zh_big_e6d6 models on s1, s3 and s4. Note that we also train a deep model en2zh_big_e36d6 on s2, and the result is 28.90, which is comparable to the en2zh_big_e6d6 model on s4. Therefore, due to the large amount of s2, we only use en2zh_big_e36d6_s2 for subsequent data filtering and construction. The experimental results are listed in Table 4. As can be seen that the domain-related data augmentation

[16] en2zh_base_e40d6_s4 means the English-to-Chinese translation model which contains 40-layer encoder and 6-layer decoder and adopts `Transformer-base` setting, the model is trained on s4.

[17] Double Metaphone is a phonetic algorithm for indexing words by their English pronunciation.

[18] `https://github.com/cmusphinx/cmudict`

[19] We randomly truncate the prefix of the sentence pair to make the model aware of the scenario of streaming ASR.

(**Foral**) boosts the baseline by 0.89 BLEU score, but the iterative data augmentation does not seem to bring more gains. In addition, we also explore iterative data augmentation on en2zh_base_e40d6_s4 model, and the improvement is also not particularly obvious (28.94->29.07), so our final submitted systems do not use iterative data augmentation. We argue that the effectiveness of iterative data augmentation is strongly related to both the training sets and the model architectures.

According to the official, the latency thresholds are determined by the NCA-AL, which represents the delay to the perfect real time system. We finally submit two systems, a single-model system for CA scenarios and another adaptive-ensemble system for NCA scenarios. More experimental results can be found in (Anastasopoulos et al., 2022).

Models	BLEU
en2zh_big_e6d6_s1	27.96
en2zh_big_e6d6_s1 + R-Drop	28.37
en2zh_big_e20d6_s1 + R-Drop	28.55
en2zh_big_e25d6_s1 + R-Drop	28.77

Table 5: The impact of R-Drop and deep models on translation quality on the clean `tst-COMMON` test set.

5.2 Validation of R-Drop and Deep Model

For this ablation study, we train several models on data s1 and use the clean development set to verify the effectiveness of the R-Drop technique and deep models. The experimental results are shown in Table 5. It can be seen that the R-Drop technology improves our strong baseline by 0.41 points, and the deep model further improves 0.4 BLEU scores. We employ both techniques in all subsequent experiments.

5.3 Choice of k value

We empirically choose the optimal `k`-value or `k`-value interval based on the quality-latency ratio (QLR) on the development set.

Firstly, we train multiple en2zh_big_e6d6 models on the training set s1 (including 53.1 sentence pairs) using different `k`-values under effective `wait-k` policy and different `k`-value intervals under multi-path `wait-k` policy [20], then explore the impact of different `k`-values and different `k`-value intervals on QLR of decoding development

[20]Effective and multi-path `wait-k` policies correspond to `wait(k)` and `wait(k)-(k+t)` as defined in the **Training** paragraph in Section 4.3, respectively.

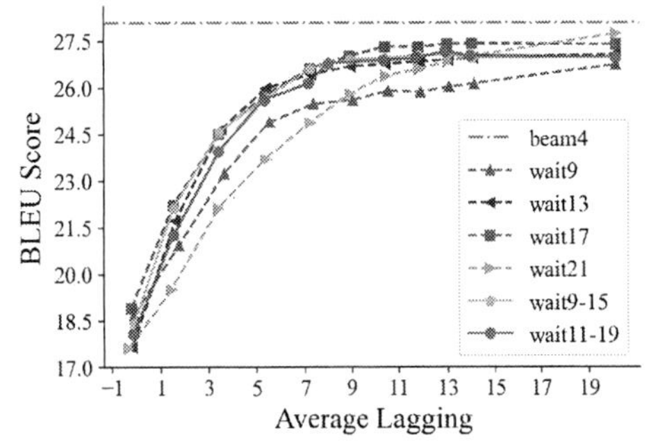

Figure 1: Comparison of QLR curves of different `wait-k` strategies on the development set. "beam4" denotes the naive decoding strategy with beam size 4.

set. For each policy, we test the BLEU scores under different average laggings on the development set, and draw the QLR curve, then compare the pros. and cons. of different strategies, as shown in Figure 1. As can be seen from Figure 1, when the value of k is too small or too large, the overall effect is relatively poor (for example, k=9 and k=21 correspond to the green and blue dashed lines in the figure, both of which are located at the bottom right). While wait17, wait9-15 and wait11-19 perform relatively well. Multi-path `wait-k` has almost the same effect as the effective `wait-k` policy, but has better robustness than the effective `wait-k`. Based on the above verification, our final submitted system includes the following 1 naive model and 6 `wait-k` models:

- en2zh_big_e12d6_s4
- en2zh_base_e40d6_s4_wait17
- en2zh_base_e40d6_s4_wait9-15
- en2zh_base_e40d6_s4_wait11-19
- en2zh_big_e12d6_s4_wait17
- en2zh_big_e12d6_s4_wait9-17
- en2zh_big_e12d6_s4_wait11-19

Models	BLEU
Baseline	19.02
+ Synthetic Noise Generation	19.23
+ Error Correction Model	20.28

Table 6: Performance comparison of different methods to improve the model's robustness to ASR noise.

5.4 Robustness to ASR Noise

We explore the performance of our two methods on the noisy `tst-COMMON` test set provided by the

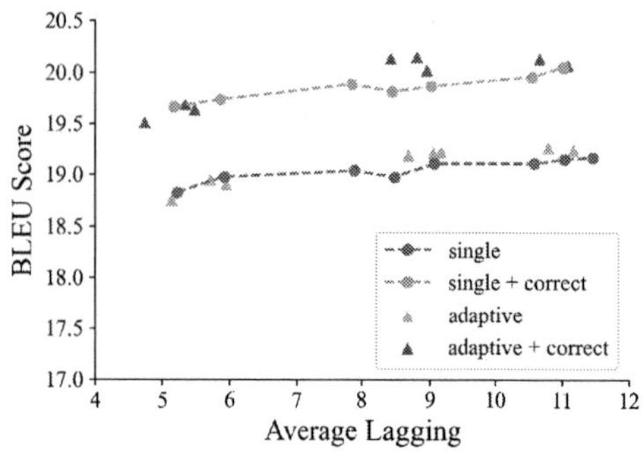

Figure 2: The benefits of the error correction model under the two inference strategies of single-k and adaptive-ensemble.

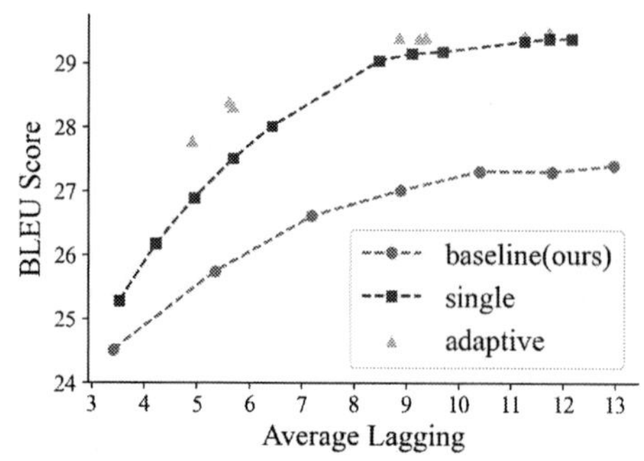

Figure 3: Comparison of QLR curves of baseline model, single-k decoding and adaptive-ensemble decoding on the development set.

official, and the results are shown in Table 6. It can be seen that the data-driven method has an improvement of 0.21 points compared to the baseline model. The error correction model is leveraged to correct the input before feeding the input into the translation model, which can further bring an improvement of 1.05 BLEU scores. We also verify the effect of the error correction model on the single model and ensemble model under different average laggings, the results are shown in Figure 2. It can be seen that the error correction model can significantly and consistently improve translation quality at both high and low latency, whether on single-k or adaptive-ensemble strategies.

5.5 Effect of Adaptive-ensemble

We use the inference strategy of single-k and adaptive-ensemble (introduced in the **Inference** paragraph in Section 4.3) to decode the development set, respectively, and then compare these two methods with the baseline model, and the results are shown in Figure 3. It can be seen that the QLR of the single-k strategy is significantly improved compared to the baseline model, and the adaptive-ensemble strategy brings further improvement.

6 Conclusion

We elaborate on the Xiaomi Text-to-Text Simultaneous Speech Translation System for the IWSLT 2022 in this paper. We first investigate the current mainstream techniques such as deep model and R-drop to construct a relatively strong baseline model, then explore various data augmentation techniques such as TaggedBT, KD, and iterative BT to further improve the translation quality of the deep model.

Then, we adopt the efficient `wait-k` strategy and the multi-path `wait-k` strategy to improve the translation quality of the system on the streaming output text which simulates the ASR output, and design some rule-based inference algorithms to remedy the obvious translation errors under low latency.

In order to alleviate the negative impact of the noise contained in the streaming ASR output on our system, we propose two error correction methods to improve the robustness of the model, so that the system has a significant improvement on the noisy inputs.

In the future, we will explore the effect of ways to mitigate exposure bias (Zhang et al., 2019) and pre-trained models, such as BERT (Devlin et al., 2019) and T5 (Raffel et al., 2020), on the text-to-text simultaneous speech translation task.

References

Antonios Anastasopoulos, Luisa Bentivogli, Marcely Z. Boito, Ondřej Bojar, Roldano Cattoni, Anna Currey, Georgiana Dinu, Kevin Duh, Maha Elbayad, Marcello Federico, Christian Federmann, Hongyu Gong, Roman Grundkiewicz, Barry Haddow, Benjamin Hsu, Dávid Javorský, Věra Kloudová, Surafel M. Lakew, Xutai Ma, Prashant Mathur, Paul McNamee, Kenton Murray, Maria Nădejde, Satoshi Nakamura, Matteo Negri, Jan Niehues, Xing Niu, Juan Pino, Elizabeth Salesky, Jiatong Shi, Sebastian Stüker, Katsuhito Sudoh, Marco Turchi, Yogesh Virkar, Alex Waibel, Changhan Wang, and Shinji Watanabe. 2022. FINDINGS OF THE IWSLT 2022 EVALUATION CAMPAIGN. In *Proceedings of the 19th International Conference on Spoken Language Translation (IWSLT 2022)*, Dublin, Ireland. Association for Computational Linguistics.

Amittai Axelrod, Xiaodong He, and Jianfeng Gao. 2011. Domain adaptation via pseudo in-domain data selection. In *Proceedings of the 2011 Conference on Empirical Methods in Natural Language Processing*, pages 355–362, Edinburgh, Scotland, UK. Association for Computational Linguistics.

Isaac Caswell, Ciprian Chelba, and David Grangier. 2019. Tagged back-translation. In *Proceedings of the Fourth Conference on Machine Translation (Volume 1: Research Papers)*, pages 53–63, Florence, Italy. Association for Computational Linguistics.

Jacob Devlin, Ming-Wei Chang, Kenton Lee, and Kristina Toutanova. 2019. BERT: Pre-training of deep bidirectional transformers for language understanding. In *Proceedings of the 2019 Conference of the North American Chapter of the Association for Computational Linguistics: Human Language Technologies, Volume 1 (Long and Short Papers)*, pages 4171–4186, Minneapolis, Minnesota. Association for Computational Linguistics.

Maha Elbayad, Laurent Besacier, and Jakob Verbeek. 2020. Efficient Wait-k Models for Simultaneous Machine Translation. In *Proc. Interspeech 2020*, pages 1461–1465.

Vu Cong Duy Hoang, Philipp Koehn, Gholamreza Haffari, and Trevor Cohn. 2018. Iterative back-translation for neural machine translation. In *Proceedings of the 2nd Workshop on Neural Machine Translation and Generation*, pages 18–24, Melbourne, Australia. Association for Computational Linguistics.

Yoon Kim and Alexander M. Rush. 2016. Sequence-level knowledge distillation. In *Proceedings of the 2016 Conference on Empirical Methods in Natural Language Processing*, pages 1317–1327, Austin, Texas. Association for Computational Linguistics.

Diederik P Kingma and Jimmy Ba. 2014. Adam: A method for stochastic optimization. *arXiv preprint arXiv:1412.6980*.

Younggun Lee, Suwon Shon, and Taesu Kim. 2018. Learning pronunciation from a foreign language in speech synthesis networks. *arXiv preprint arXiv:1811.09364*.

Xiaobo Liang, Lijun Wu, Juntao Li, Yue Wang, Qi Meng, Tao Qin, Wei Chen, Min Zhang, and Tie-Yan Liu. 2021. R-drop: Regularized dropout for neural networks. In *Advances in Neural Information Processing Systems*.

Mingbo Ma, Liang Huang, Hao Xiong, Renjie Zheng, Kaibo Liu, Baigong Zheng, Chuanqiang Zhang, Zhongjun He, Hairong Liu, Xing Li, Hua Wu, and Haifeng Wang. 2019. STACL: Simultaneous translation with implicit anticipation and controllable latency using prefix-to-prefix framework. In *Proceedings of the 57th Annual Meeting of the Association for Computational Linguistics*, pages 3025–3036, Florence, Italy. Association for Computational Linguistics.

Xutai Ma, Mohammad Javad Dousti, Changhan Wang, Jiatao Gu, and Juan Pino. 2020. SIMULEVAL: An evaluation toolkit for simultaneous translation. In *Proceedings of the 2020 Conference on Empirical Methods in Natural Language Processing: System Demonstrations*, pages 144–150, Online. Association for Computational Linguistics.

Xuan-Phi Nguyen, Shafiq Joty, Kui Wu, and Ai Ti Aw. 2020. Data diversification: A simple strategy for neural machine translation. In *Advances in Neural Information Processing Systems*, volume 33, pages 10018–10029. Curran Associates, Inc.

Myle Ott, Sergey Edunov, Alexei Baevski, Angela Fan, Sam Gross, Nathan Ng, David Grangier, and Michael Auli. 2019. fairseq: A fast, extensible toolkit for sequence modeling. In *Proceedings of the 2019 Conference of the North American Chapter of the Association for Computational Linguistics (Demonstrations)*, pages 48–53, Minneapolis, Minnesota. Association for Computational Linguistics.

Kishore Papineni, Salim Roukos, Todd Ward, and Wei-Jing Zhu. 2002. Bleu: a method for automatic evaluation of machine translation. In *Proceedings of the 40th Annual Meeting of the Association for Computational Linguistics*, pages 311–318, Philadelphia, Pennsylvania, USA. Association for Computational Linguistics.

Colin Raffel, Noam Shazeer, Adam Roberts, Katherine Lee, Sharan Narang, Michael Matena, Yanqi Zhou, Wei Li, and Peter J. Liu. 2020. Exploring the limits of transfer learning with a unified text-to-text transformer. *Journal of Machine Learning Research*, 21(140):1–67.

Rico Sennrich, Barry Haddow, and Alexandra Birch. 2016a. Improving neural machine translation models with monolingual data. In *Proceedings of the 54th Annual Meeting of the Association for Computational Linguistics (Volume 1: Long Papers)*, pages

86–96, Berlin, Germany. Association for Computational Linguistics.

Rico Sennrich, Barry Haddow, and Alexandra Birch. 2016b. Neural machine translation of rare words with subword units. In *Proceedings of the 54th Annual Meeting of the Association for Computational Linguistics (Volume 1: Long Papers)*, pages 1715–1725, Berlin, Germany. Association for Computational Linguistics.

Nitish Srivastava, Geoffrey Hinton, Alex Krizhevsky, Ilya Sutskever, and Ruslan Salakhutdinov. 2014. Dropout: A simple way to prevent neural networks from overfitting. *Journal of Machine Learning Research*, 15(56):1929–1958.

Ashish Vaswani, Noam Shazeer, Niki Parmar, Jakob Uszkoreit, Llion Jones, Aidan N Gomez, Ł ukasz Kaiser, and Illia Polosukhin. 2017. Attention is all you need. In *Advances in Neural Information Processing Systems*, volume 30. Curran Associates, Inc.

Hongyu Wang, Shuming Ma, Li Dong, Shaohan Huang, Dongdong Zhang, and Furu Wei. 2022. Deepnet: Scaling transformers to 1,000 layers. *arXiv preprint arXiv:2203.00555*.

Yiren Wang, Lijun Wu, Yingce Xia, Tao Qin, ChengXiang Zhai, and Tie-Yan Liu. 2020. Transductive ensemble learning for neural machine translation. *Proceedings of the AAAI Conference on Artificial Intelligence*, 34(04):6291–6298.

Wen Zhang, Yang Feng, Fandong Meng, Di You, and Qun Liu. 2019. Bridging the gap between training and inference for neural machine translation. In *Proceedings of the 57th Annual Meeting of the Association for Computational Linguistics*, pages 4334–4343, Florence, Italy. Association for Computational Linguistics.

Baigong Zheng, Kaibo Liu, Renjie Zheng, Mingbo Ma, Hairong Liu, and Liang Huang. 2020. Simultaneous translation policies: From fixed to adaptive. In *Proceedings of the 58th Annual Meeting of the Association for Computational Linguistics*, pages 2847–2853, Online. Association for Computational Linguistics.

NVIDIA NeMo Offline Speech Translation Systems for IWSLT 2022

Oleksii Hrinchuk[*], **Vahid Noroozi, Abhinav Khattar, Anton Peganov, Sandeep Subramanian, Somshubra Majumdar, Oleksii Kuchaiev**
NVIDIA, Santa Clara, CA

Abstract

This paper provides an overview of NVIDIA NeMo's speech translation systems for the IWSLT 2022 Offline Speech Translation Task. Our cascade system consists of 1) Conformer RNN-T automatic speech recognition model, 2) punctuation-capitalization model based on pre-trained T5 encoder, 3) ensemble of Transformer neural machine translation models fine-tuned on TED talks. Our end-to-end model has less parameters and consists of Conformer encoder and Transformer decoder. It relies on the cascade system by re-using its pre-trained ASR encoder and training on synthetic translations generated with the ensemble of NMT models. Our En→De cascade and end-to-end systems achieve 29.7 and 26.2 BLEU on the 2020 test set correspondingly, both outperforming the previous year's best of 26 BLEU.

1 Introduction

We participate in the IWSLT 2022 Offline Speech Translation Task (Anastasopoulos et al., 2022) for English→German and English→Chinese. Due to the limited amount of direct speech translation (ST) data, we mostly focused on building a strong cascade pipeline structured as follows:

- ASR model with Conformer (Gulati et al., 2020b) encoder and RNN-T (Graves, 2012) decoder trained with SpecAugment (Park et al., 2019) which transforms input audio into lower-cased text without punctuation.
- Punctuation-capitalization (PC) model with T5 (Raffel et al., 2019) encoder and classification head which transforms normalized ASR output into standard English text, more suitable for NMT model.
- Ensemble of 4 NMT Transformers (Vaswani et al., 2017) trained with back-translation and right-to-left distillation and fine-tuned on TED talks which translates English text into target language.

We also trained end-to-end models capitalizing on the pre-trained ASR encoder and synthetic translations obtained with the ensemble of NMT models. Our best end-to-end model consisting of Conformer encoder and Transformer decoder lags behind the best cascade by 2.7 BLEU on average, however, it might be preferred for some scenarios of limited resources or latency requirements.

Our systems are open-sourced as part of NVIDIA NeMo[1] framework (Kuchaiev et al., 2019).

2 Data

In this section, we describe the datasets used for training (Table 1). For evaluation, we used the development sets of Must-C v2, as well as the test sets from past IWSLT competitions.

ASR For training our ASR model, we used LibriSpeech (Panayotov et al., 2015), Mozilla Common Voice v6.1 (Ardila et al., 2019), TED-LIUM v3 (Hernandez et al., 2018), VoxPopuli v2 (Wang et al., 2021a), all available speech-to-English data from Must-C v2 (Cattoni et al., 2021) En-De/Zh/Ja datasets, ST-TED (Jan et al., 2018), and clean portion of Europarl-ST (Iranzo-Sánchez et al., 2020).

PC For training our punctuation-capitalization (PC) model, we combined 268M sentences from Europarl (Koehn, 2005), RAPID (Rozis and Skadiņš, 2017), TED (Cettolo et al., 2012), newscrawl, news-commentary English corpora used in WMT 2021 (Akhbardeh et al., 2021) and Wikipedia dump from WMT 2020. After that, we split the data into segments of up to 128 words ignoring sentence boundaries and removed all punctuation and capitalization.

[*]Correspondence to: ohrinchuk@nvidia.com

[1]https://github.com/NVIDIA/NeMo

Proceedings of the 19th International Conference on Spoken Language Translation (IWSLT 2022), pages 225 - 231
May 26-27, 2022

Table 1: Statistics of different datasets used for training. Synthetic datasets are marked with `typewriter` font.

Task	Dataset	Size	Time
ASR	LibriSpeech	281K	960
	CommonVoice v6.1	564K	901
	TED-LIUM v3	268K	454
	VoxPopuli v2	182K	523
	MuST-C v2 ASR	410K	728
MT De	WMT'21 bitext	60M	–
	`WMT'21 BT`	250M	–
	`WMT'21 R2L`	60M	–
MT Zh	WMT'21 bitext	42M	–
	OpenSubtitles	11M	–
	ST En→Zh	640K	1K
ST	MuST-C v2	251K	450
	CoVoST v2	290K	430
	ST-TED	172K	273
	Europarl-ST	33K	77
	`ASR synthetic`	1.3M	2.3K

MT For training our NMT models, we used all available bitext from WMT 2021 (Akhbardeh et al., 2021), as well as its right-to-left distillation and back-translated monolingual data (for En→De only), following Subramanian et al. (2021). After training, we fine-tuned our models on bitexts from Must-C v2 dataset.

ST For training our end-to-end ST models, we used Must-C v2, CoVoST v2 (Wang et al., 2020), ST-TED, and clean portion of Europarl-ST. In addition, we translated English transcripts from ASR datasets with unnormalized transcripts (all datasets, except for LibriSpeech and TED-LIUM v3) to obtain more speech-to-German data.

3 System

In this section, we describe the essential components of our cascade and end-to-end submissions.

Segmentation We relied on voice activity detection (VAD) to transform long TED talks from the evaluation datasets into smaller segments. Specifically, we used `WebRTC`[2] toolkit with frame duration, padding duration, and aggressive mode set to 30ms, 150ms, and 3, respectively. Following Inaguma et al. (2021), we then merged multiple short segments into longer chunks until there were no two segments shorter than a threshold $M_{dur} = 12$ms with the time interval between them below a threshold $M_{int} = 50$ms. We also experimented with other hyperparameters in the vicinity of these values but the resulting average BLEU score on IWSLT test datasets from previous years was lower.

[2]https://github.com/wiseman/py-webrtcvad

ASR We transcoded all audio data to mono-channel 16kHz wav format and normalized all the transcripts by removing capitalization and all punctuation marks except for apostrophe. We also discarded samples shorter than 0.2s and longer than 24s. As a result, our training dataset contained 1.9M audio segments with the total duration of 3800 hours.

We then trained a large version of conformer-transducer (Gulati et al., 2020a) with roughly 120M parameters, which uses RNN-T loss and decoder (Graves, 2012). The prediction network consists of a single layer of LSTM (Hochreiter and Schmidhuber, 1997) and the joint network is an MLP. All the hidden sizes in the decoder were set to 640.

PC Our punctuation-capitalization (PC) model consists of Transformer encoder initialized with pre-trained T5 (Raffel et al., 2019) and two classification heads — one for predicting punctuation and another for predicting capitalization. Capitalization head has two labels which correspond to whether the corresponding token needs to be upper-cased. Punctuation head has four labels for period, comma, question mark, and no punctuation which correspond to whether the corresponding token needs to be followed by a particular punctuation mark.

To do inference on the text of arbitrary length, we split it into segments of equal `segment length` and compute a sliding window (with a step `step`) product of token probabilities. To reduce prediction errors near the segment boundaries, we discard probabilities of `margin` tokens near the segment boundaries except for the left boundary of the first segment and the right boundary of the last segment. Table 2 illustrates how the described procedure works on a given fragment from Wikipedia.

NMT Our En→De text-to-text NMT models were based on NVIDIA NeMo's submission to the last year WMT'21 competition. We discarded all examples where a sentence in either language is

Table 2: Capitalization head inference on a text fragment from Wikipedia with the following parameters: `segment length` = 4, `step` = 1, `margin` = 1. Discarded probabilities near the segment boundaries are highlighted in red.

	bantam	sold	it	to	miramax	books
	bantam	sold	it	to		
U	0.9	0.1	0.1	0.2		
O	0.1	0.9	0.9	0.8		
		sold	it	to	miramax	
U		0.5	0.2	0.1	0.8	
O		0.5	0.8	0.9	0.2	
			it	to	miramax	books
U			0.1	0.1	0.8	0.6
O			0.9	0.9	0.2	0.4
	bantam	sold	it	to	miramax	books
U	0.9	0.1	.02	.01	0.8	0.6
O	0.1	0.9	.72	.81	0.2	0.4
	U	O	O	O	U	U
	Bantam	sold	it	to	Miramax	Books

longer than 250 tokens and where the length ratio between source and target exceeds 1.3. We also applied `langid` and `bicleaner` filtering following Subramanian et al. (2021). After such aggressive filtering, we ended up with 60M parallel sentences and 250M monolingual sentences for back-translation. We then trained four 24×6 NMT Transformers using different combinations of bitext, its right-to-left forward translation, and back-translated monolingual data.

Our En→Zh NMT model differs from En→De in that we used jieba tokenization and OpenCC traditional to simplified Chinese normalization, instead of Moses based tokenization and normalization. We used SentencePiece (Kudo and Richardson, 2018) tokenizer with shared vocabulary trained on a combination of English, Chinese and Japanese. We also did not do ensembling.

After training with news-only data, we additionally fine-tuned all our models on MuST-C v2 dataset which resulted in nearly 4 BLEU score boost on IWSLT test sets for En→De. The ensemble of four such models was used to generate synthetic translations for end-to-end ST model training.

To better adapt our cascade NMT models to possible punctuation-capitalization model artifacts, we altered the source side of fine-tuning dataset by normalizing it and running through the PC model.

End-to-end Our end-to-end model is Conformer encoder followed by Transformer decoder trained on pairs of English audio and German translation. After discarding all segments longer than 24s, we ended up with 740K segments with the total duration of 1180 hours. Adding synthetic translations of ASR datasets with unnormalized transcripts resulted in 2.06M segments with the total duration of 3450 hours.

4 Experiments

4.1 Setup

ASR We trained our Conformer-transducer ASR models for 300 epochs with the same architecture introduced in (Gulati et al., 2020a) for large model with AdamW (Loshchilov and Hutter, 2017) optimizer and Inverse Square Root Annealing (Vaswani et al., 2017) with 10K warmup steps and a maximum learning rate of 2×10^{-3}. Weight decay of 0.001 on all parameters was used for regularization. The effective batch size was set to 2K, and we could fit larger batch sizes via batch splitting for the RNN-T loss.

Time-Adaptive SpecAugment (Park et al., 2020) with 2 freq masks ($F = 27$) and 10 time masks ($T = 5\%$) is used as the augmentation scheme. We also used dropout of 0.1 for both the attention scores and intermediate activations. All predictions were made with greedy decoding and no external language model.

For the tokenizer, we trained and used an unigram SenetencePiece (Kudo and Richardson, 2018) with the vocabulary size of 1024. After training, we averaged the best 10 checkpoints based on the validation WER which led to a small boost in both the ASR (Table 3) and the resulting BLEU scores of the complete cascade (Table 4).

Table 3: Word error rate (WER) of the ASR model evaluated on different test datasets. Values in brackets correspond to evaluation on modified references with all numbers converted into their spoken form.

	Librispeech `test-other`	**MuST-C v2** `tst-COMMON`
Conf RNN-T	4.81	4.35 (2.51)
+ ckpt avg	4.65	4.21 (2.37)

Table 4: En→De BLEU scores calculated on IWSLT test sets from different years by using automatic re-segmentation of the hypothesis based on the reference translation by `mwerSegmenter` implemented in SLTev (Ansari et al., 2021). Avg Δ computes the improvement over the cascade baseline averaged over 7 test sets.

	2010	**2013**	**2014**	**2015**	**2018**	**2019**	**2020**	**AvgΔ**
Cascade systems								
Conf RNN-T + punct-capit + NMT	20.0	25.2	21.3	22.5	23.8	22.7	25.1	0
+ ASR checkpoint averaging	21.2	26.0	21.4	23.5	24.5	23.3	25.6	+0.7
+ NMT in-domain fine-tuning	24.5	31.3	26.1	27.6	27.6	26.4	28.8	+4.5
+ NMT repunctuated source	26.0	31.5	26.6	28.2	27.5	27.0	29.7	+5.1
+ NMT x4 ensembling	26.6	32.2	26.8	28.3	28.1	27.3	29.7	+5.5
End-to-end systems								
Conformer enc + Transformer dec	17.6	23.5	19.5	17.8	19.4	16.0	16.9	−4.3
+ ASR encoder init	19.8	25.5	21.6	22.4	22.4	20.4	21.7	−1.0
+ ASR synthetic data	24.5	30.0	25.2	25.3	24.9	24.1	26.2	+2.8
Text-to-text								
WMT'21 NMT model	33.3	35.6	31.7	33.5	31.0	28.6	32.4	+9.4
+ in-domain fine-tuning	35.7	41.2	36.2	38.1	34.7	31.7	35.0	+13.1

PC We trained our PC model for up to 400K updates using Adam optimizer (Kingma and Ba, 2014) and Inverse Square Root Annealing (Vaswani et al., 2017) with 12K warm-up steps and a maximum learning rate of 6×10^{-5}. Dropout of 0.1 was used for regularization.

Despite significant imbalance between no punctuation / capitalization and other classes, we trained with cross-entropy loss which showed to perform well in prior work (Courtland et al., 2020). We then computed F1 scores for both classification heads on IWSLT tst2019 dataset. Our high mean punctuation F1 score of 84.6 and capitalization F1 score of 92.6 suggest that the model does not suffer from the class imbalance inherent in the training data.

NMT We trained our NMT models (Transformer, 24×6 layers, $d_{\text{model}} = 1024$, $d_{\text{inner}} = 4096$, $n_{\text{heads}} = 16$) with Adam optimizer (Kingma and Ba, 2014) and Inverse Square Root Annealing (Vaswani et al., 2017) with 30K warmup steps and a maximum learning rate of 4×10^{-4}. The models were trained for a maximum for 450K steps with a dropout of 0.1 on intermediate activations and label smoothing with $\alpha = 0.1$.

After training, we finetuned all our base NMT models on MuST-C v2 for 3–4 epochs with an initial learning rate of 2×10^{-5}, linear annealing and no warmup.

End-to-end Our end-to-end models (17-layer Conformer encoder, 6-layer Transformer decoder, both with $d_{\text{model}} = 512$, $d_{\text{inner}} = 2048$, $n_{\text{heads}} = 8$) were trained for 50 epochs if starting from random initialization and for 30 epochs if using the pre-trained ASR encoder. Our vocabulary consists of 16384 YouTokenToMe[3] byte-pair-encodings trained on German transcripts of ST corpus.

4.2 Results

English-German Table 4 shows the performance of our baseline En→De system and its modifications on 7 different IWSLT test sets over the years. While all proposed modifications lead to clear improvements in BLEU scores, in-domain fine-tuning of NMT model contributes the most, adding almost 4 BLEU to both cascade and text-to-text.

End-to-end model trained on ST data lags behind the baseline cascade. Utilizing the pre-trained ASR encoder and additional synthetic translation data results in a significant boost of 7 BLEU score, however, the gap between end-to-end and best cascade is still 2.7 BLEU.

The difference of 7.6 BLEU between our best cascade and text-to-text translation of the ground truth transcripts suggests that there is still plenty of room for improvement on both ASR and PC parts of the cascade.

[3]https://github.com/VKCOM/YouTokenToMe

English-Chinese We evaluated our En→Zh submission on the development set of the MuST-C v2 dataset released by the competition organizers. Our cascade which differs by the NMT block only from the En→De cascade achieved 25.3 BLEU which improved to 26.7 BLEU after fine-tuning on re-punctuated in-domain data.

4.3 Discarded alternatives

When designing our submission, we explored a number of alternatives. They did not lead to clear improvement in preliminary experiments and, thus, were not included into the final submission.

ASR For our speech recognition part, we experimented with:

- other models, specifically, CitriNet (Majumdar et al., 2021) and Conformer-CTC;
- training on a subset of data (approximately 2.5K hours) with unnormalized transcripts to remove the necessity of using PC model;
- increasing model size by the factor of 1.5 for each parameter tensor.

Interestingly, using fully convolutional CitriNet model allowed us to transcribe the complete TED talks without need for audio segmentation. Unfortunately, the WER of this model was significantly higher than WER of more powerful Conformer-RNNT which resulted in worse overall performance.

PC For our punctuation-capitalization restoration part, we experimented with:

- training the described above PC model from scratch;
- initializing our encoder with BERT large (Devlin et al., 2019) and MBART50 (Liu et al., 2020) weights;
- replacing classification head with autoregressive seq-to-seq model following Cho et al. (2017).

NMT We experimented with more elaborate decoding mechanisms such as shallow fusion with external language model and noisy channel reranking (Yee et al., 2019) but got similar results at the cost of significant computation overhead. Note that both De language model and backward De→En model were not fine-tuned on in-domain data unlike the forward En→De model.

5 Conclusion

We present NVIDIA NeMo group's offline speech translation systems for En→De and En→Zh IWSLT 2022 Tasks.

Our *primary* cascade system consists of Conformer RNN-T ASR model, followed by Transformer-based PC and NMT models. To improve over the baseline, we utilize checkpoint averaging, in-domain fine-tuning, adaptation to PC artifacts, and ensembling. The resulting submission outperforms the last year's best (Wang et al., 2021b) by 3.7 BLEU on IWSLT 2020 test dataset. However, it is worth noting that this year more data was available for training.

Our *contrastive* end-to-end model consists of Conformer encoder and Transformer decoder and translates speech directly into the text in target language. The performance of such model trained on available ST data was almost 10 BLEU worse comparing to cascade. We managed to shrink this gap to 2.7 BLEU by capitalizing on strong ASR and NMT components of our cascade via pre-training and synthetic data generation. Due of its size and simplicity this model may be preferred for some scenarios, such as simultaneous speech translation.

Acknowledgments

The authors would like to thank Boris Ginsburg for many useful discussions over the course of this project and anonymous reviewers for their valuable feedback.

References

Farhad Akhbardeh, Arkady Arkhangorodsky, Magdalena Biesialska, Ondřej Bojar, Rajen Chatterjee, Vishrav Chaudhary, Marta R Costa-jussà, Cristina España-Bonet, Angela Fan, Christian Federmann, et al. 2021. Findings of the 2021 conference on machine translation (wmt21). In *Proceedings of the Sixth Conference on Machine Translation*, pages 1–88.

Antonios Anastasopoulos, Luisa Bentivogli, Marcely Z. Boito, Ondřej Bojar, Roldano Cattoni, Anna Currey, Georgiana Dinu, Kevin Duh, Maha Elbayad, Marcello Federico, Christian Federmann, Hongyu Gong, Roman Grundkiewicz, Barry Haddow, Benjamin Hsu, Dávid Javorský, Věra Kloudová, Surafel M. Lakew, Xutai Ma, Prashant Mathur, Paul McNamee, Kenton Murray, Maria Nădejde, Satoshi Nakamura, Matteo Negri, Jan Niehues, Xing Niu, Juan Pino, Elizabeth Salesky, Jiatong Shi, Sebastian Stüker, Katsuhito Sudoh, Marco Turchi, Yogesh Virkar, Alex Waibel, Changhan Wang, and Shinji Watanabe. 2022.

FINDINGS OF THE IWSLT 2022 EVALUATION CAMPAIGN. In *Proceedings of the 19th International Conference on Spoken Language Translation (IWSLT 2022)*, Dublin, Ireland. Association for Computational Linguistics.

Ebrahim Ansari, Ondřej Bojar, Barry Haddow, and Mohammad Mahmoudi. 2021. SLTEV: Comprehensive evaluation of spoken language translation. In *Proceedings of the 16th Conference of the European Chapter of the Association for Computational Linguistics: System Demonstrations*, pages 71–79, Online. Association for Computational Linguistics.

Rosana Ardila, Megan Branson, Kelly Davis, Michael Henretty, Michael Kohler, Josh Meyer, Reuben Morais, Lindsay Saunders, Francis M Tyers, and Gregor Weber. 2019. Common voice: A massively-multilingual speech corpus. *arXiv preprint arXiv:1912.06670*.

Roldano Cattoni, Mattia Antonino Di Gangi, Luisa Bentivogli, Matteo Negri, and Marco Turchi. 2021. Must-c: A multilingual corpus for end-to-end speech translation. *Computer Speech & Language*, 66:101155.

Mauro Cettolo, Christian Girardi, and Marcello Federico. 2012. Wit3: Web inventory of transcribed and translated talks. In *Conference of european association for machine translation*, pages 261–268.

Eunah Cho, Jan Niehues, and Alex Waibel. 2017. Nmt-based segmentation and punctuation insertion for real-time spoken language translation. In *Interspeech*, pages 2645–2649.

Maury Courtland, Adam Faulkner, and Gayle McElvain. 2020. Efficient automatic punctuation restoration using bidirectional transformers with robust inference. In *Proceedings of the 17th International Conference on Spoken Language Translation*, pages 272–279.

Jacob Devlin, Ming-Wei Chang, Kenton Lee, and Kristina Toutanova. 2019. BERT: Pre-training of deep bidirectional transformers for language understanding. In *Proceedings of the 2019 Conference of the North American Chapter of the Association for Computational Linguistics: Human Language Technologies, Volume 1 (Long and Short Papers)*, pages 4171–4186, Minneapolis, Minnesota. Association for Computational Linguistics.

Alex Graves. 2012. Sequence transduction with recurrent neural networks. *arXiv preprint arXiv:1211.3711*.

Anmol Gulati, James Qin, Chung-Cheng Chiu, Niki Parmar, Yu Zhang, Jiahui Yu, Wei Han, Shibo Wang, Zhengdong Zhang, Yonghui Wu, and Ruoming Pang. 2020a. Conformer: Convolution-augmented Transformer for speech recognition. In *Proceedings of Interspeech*, pages 5036–5040.

Anmol Gulati, James Qin, Chung-Cheng Chiu, Niki Parmar, Yu Zhang, Jiahui Yu, Wei Han, Shibo Wang, Zhengdong Zhang, Yonghui Wu, et al. 2020b. Conformer: Convolution-augmented transformer for speech recognition. *arXiv preprint arXiv:2005.08100*.

François Hernandez, Vincent Nguyen, Sahar Ghannay, Natalia Tomashenko, and Yannick Esteve. 2018. Tedlium 3: twice as much data and corpus repartition for experiments on speaker adaptation. In *International conference on speech and computer*, pages 198–208. Springer.

Sepp Hochreiter and Jürgen Schmidhuber. 1997. Long short-term memory. *Neural computation*, 9(8):1735–1780.

Hirofumi Inaguma, Brian Yan, Siddharth Dalmia, Pengcheng Guo, Jiatong Shi, Kevin Duh, and Shinji Watanabe. 2021. Espnet-st iwslt 2021 offline speech translation system. *arXiv preprint arXiv:2107.00636*.

Javier Iranzo-Sánchez, Joan Albert Silvestre-Cerda, Javier Jorge, Nahuel Roselló, Adria Giménez, Albert Sanchis, Jorge Civera, and Alfons Juan. 2020. Europarl-st: A multilingual corpus for speech translation of parliamentary debates. In *ICASSP 2020-2020 IEEE International Conference on Acoustics, Speech and Signal Processing (ICASSP)*, pages 8229–8233. IEEE.

Niehues Jan, Roldano Cattoni, Stüker Sebastian, Mauro Cettolo, Marco Turchi, and Marcello Federico. 2018. The iwslt 2018 evaluation campaign. In *Proceedings of IWSLT*, pages 2–6.

Diederik Kingma and Jimmy Ba. 2014. Adam: A method for stochastic optimization. *arXiv preprint arXiv:1412.6980*.

Philipp Koehn. 2005. Europarl: A parallel corpus for statistical machine translation. In *Proceedings of machine translation summit x: papers*, pages 79–86.

Oleksii Kuchaiev, Jason Li, Huyen Nguyen, Oleksii Hrinchuk, Ryan Leary, Boris Ginsburg, Samuel Kriman, Stanislav Beliaev, Vitaly Lavrukhin, Jack Cook, et al. 2019. Nemo: a toolkit for building ai applications using neural modules. *arXiv preprint arXiv:1909.09577*.

Taku Kudo and John Richardson. 2018. Sentencepiece: A simple and language independent subword tokenizer and detokenizer for neural text processing. *arXiv preprint arXiv:1808.06226*.

Yinhan Liu, Jiatao Gu, Naman Goyal, Xian Li, Sergey Edunov, Marjan Ghazvininejad, Mike Lewis, and Luke Zettlemoyer. 2020. Multilingual denoising pre-training for neural machine translation. *Transactions of the Association for Computational Linguistics*, 8:726–742.

Ilya Loshchilov and Frank Hutter. 2017. Decoupled weight decay regularization. *arXiv preprint arXiv:1711.05101*.

Somshubra Majumdar, Jagadeesh Balam, Oleksii Hrinchuk, Vitaly Lavrukhin, Vahid Noroozi, and Boris Ginsburg. 2021. Citrinet: Closing the gap between non-autoregressive and autoregressive end-to-end models for automatic speech recognition. *arXiv preprint arXiv:2104.01721*.

Vassil Panayotov, Guoguo Chen, Daniel Povey, and Sanjeev Khudanpur. 2015. Librispeech: an ASR corpus based on public domain audio books. In *Proceedings of ICASSP*, pages 5206–5210. IEEE.

Daniel S Park, William Chan, Yu Zhang, Chung-Cheng Chiu, Barret Zoph, Ekin D Cubuk, and Quoc V Le. 2019. Specaugment: A simple data augmentation method for automatic speech recognition. *arXiv preprint arXiv:1904.08779*.

Daniel S Park, Yu Zhang, Chung-Cheng Chiu, Youzheng Chen, Bo Li, William Chan, Quoc V Le, and Yonghui Wu. 2020. Specaugment on large scale datasets. In *ICASSP 2020-2020 IEEE International Conference on Acoustics, Speech and Signal Processing (ICASSP)*, pages 6879–6883. IEEE.

Colin Raffel, Noam Shazeer, Adam Roberts, Katherine Lee, Sharan Narang, Michael Matena, Yanqi Zhou, Wei Li, and Peter J Liu. 2019. Exploring the limits of transfer learning with a unified text-to-text transformer. *arXiv preprint arXiv:1910.10683*.

Roberts Rozis and Raivis Skadiņš. 2017. Tilde model-multilingual open data for eu languages. In *Proceedings of the 21st Nordic Conference on Computational Linguistics*, pages 263–265.

Sandeep Subramanian, Oleksii Hrinchuk, Virginia Adams, and Oleksii Kuchaiev. 2021. Nvidia nemo neural machine translation systems for english-german and english-russian news and biomedical tasks at wmt21. *arXiv preprint arXiv:2111.08634*.

Ashish Vaswani, Noam Shazeer, Niki Parmar, Jakob Uszkoreit, Llion Jones, Aidan N Gomez, Łukasz Kaiser, and Illia Polosukhin. 2017. Attention is all you need. In *Proceedings of NeurIPS*, pages 5998–6008.

Changhan Wang, Morgane Riviere, Ann Lee, Anne Wu, Chaitanya Talnikar, Daniel Haziza, Mary Williamson, Juan Pino, and Emmanuel Dupoux. 2021a. Voxpopuli: A large-scale multilingual speech corpus for representation learning, semi-supervised learning and interpretation. *arXiv preprint arXiv:2101.00390*.

Changhan Wang, Anne Wu, and Juan Pino. 2020. Covost 2 and massively multilingual speech-to-text translation. *arXiv preprint arXiv:2007.10310*.

Minghan Wang, Yuxia Wang, Chang Su, Jiaxin Guo, Yingtao Zhang, Yujia Liu, Min Zhang, Shimin Tao, Xingshan Zeng, Liangyou Li, et al. 2021b. The hwtsc's offline speech translation systems for iwslt 2021 evaluation. *arXiv preprint arXiv:2108.03845*.

Kyra Yee, Nathan Ng, Yann N Dauphin, and Michael Auli. 2019. Simple and effective noisy channel modeling for neural machine translation. *arXiv preprint arXiv:1908.05731*.

The NiuTrans's Submission to the IWSLT22 English-to-Chinese Offline Speech Translation Task

Yuhao Zhang[1], Canan Huang[1], Chen Xu[1], Xiaoqian Liu[1], Bei Li[1], Anxiang Ma[1,2], Tong Xiao[1,2] and Jingbo Zhu[1,2]
[1]NLP Lab, School of Computer Science and Engineering
Northeastern University, Shenyang, China
[2]NiuTrans Research, Shenyang, China
yoohao.zhang@gmail.com, xuchenneu@outlook.com
{maanxiang, xiaotong, zhujingbo}@mail.neu.edu.cn

Abstract

This paper describes NiuTrans's submission to the IWSLT22 English-to-Chinese (En-Zh) offline speech translation task. The end-to-end and bilingual system is built by constrained English and Chinese data and translates the English speech to Chinese text without intermediate transcription. Our speech translation models are composed of different pre-trained acoustic models and machine translation models by two kinds of adapters. We compared the effect of the standard speech feature (e.g. log Mel-filterbank) and the pre-training speech feature and try to make them interact. The final submission is an ensemble of three potential speech translation models. Our single best and ensemble model achieves 18.66 BLEU and 19.35 BLEU separately on MuST-C En-Zh tst-COMMON set.

1 Introduction

Speech translation is the task that transfers the speech input to the target language text. Comparing the cascade of automatic speech recognition (ASR) and machine translation (MT) systems, recently the end-to-end speech translation (E2E ST, for short ST) model arises more attention for its low latency and avoiding error propagation (Pino et al., 2020; Wang et al., 2020; Xu et al., 2021a; Indurthi et al., 2021). On the IWSLT21 offline speech translation task, the ST has shown its potential ability compared with cascade systems by using ASR and MT labeled data to pre-train modules of the ST model (Bahar et al., 2021). We explore that using different speech features and model architecture for the ST model can further lessen the gap with the cascade system. We design a model which fuses the two speech features to enrich speech information.

In our submission, we pre-train the machine translations model and choose the deep Transformer (Wang et al., 2019), ODE Transformer (Li et al., 2021a) and MBART (Liu et al., 2020) as MT backbone architectures. For the acoustic model, we use a progressive down-sampling method (PDS) and Wav2vec 2.0 (W2V) (Baevski et al., 2020). To integrate the pre-trained acoustic and textual model, we use the SATE method (Xu et al., 2021a) which adds an adapter between the acoustic and textual model. To utilize the model pre-trained by unlabeled data, such as W2V, and MBART, we purpose the multi-stage pre-training method toward ST (MSP) and add the MSP-Adapter to boost the ST performance. Manuscripts for the MSP and PDS are in preparation. We fuse the output feature of the PDS encoder and W2V with the multi-head attention of the decoder. The input of the former is a standard speech feature while the latter is a waveform. We evaluate the relation between the effect of the ensemble model and the diversity of model architecture.

Our best MT model reaches 19.76 BLEU and our ST model reaches 18.66 BLEU on the MuST-C En-ZH tst-COMMON set. While the ensemble model achieves 19.35 which shows the performance of ST can be further improved. The model that fuses two strong encoders does not outperform the model with a single encoder. We show the diversity of models is important during the ensemble stage. We find the bottleneck of our ST model is the de-noising and translating ability of MT modules.

2 Data

2.1 Data pre-processing

MT Due to the WMT21 task aiming at the news domain, we only choose the high-quality ones from WMT21 corpora. We fellow the Zhang et al. (2020) to clean parallel texts. The OpenSubtitle is the in-domain corpus but many translations do not match their source texts. We use the fast-align (Dyer et al.,

Proceedings of the 19th International Conference on Spoken Language Translation (IWSLT 2022), pages 232 - 238
May 26-27, 2022

Task	Corpus	Sentence	Hour
MT	CWMT	5.08M	-
	News commentary	0.29M	-
	UN	5.68M	-
	OpenSubtitle	4.14M	-
	Total	15.19M	-
ASR	Europarl-ST	0.03M	77
	Common Voice	0.28M	415
	VoxPopuil	0.18M	496
	LibriSpeech	0.28M	960
	TED LIUM	0.26M	448
	MuST-C V1	0.07M	137
	ST TED	0.16M	234
	MuST-C En-Zh	0.36M	571
	Total	1.61M	3338
ST	MuST-C En-Zh	0.35M	571

Table 1: Detail of labeled data

2013) to score all the sentence. We average the score by the length of the corresponding sentence and filter sentences below the score of -6.0. Since the news translation is always much longer than the spoken translation, we filter sentences with more than 100 words.

ASR Following the previous work (Xu et al., 2021b), we unify all the audio to the 16000 per second sample rate and single channel. The Common voice corpus consists of many noises, so we choose the cleaner part according to the CoVoST corpus. For the MuST-C V1 corpus, we remove repetitive items comparing the MuST-C En-Zh transcriptions. We use the Librispeech set to build the ASR system and then score the Common Voice, TED LIUM, and ST TED three corpora. The sentence that the WER is higher than 75% will be removed. We filter frames with lengths less than 5 or larger than 3000. We remove the utterances with the size of characters exceeding 400.

ST Since ST data is scarce, we only filter the data according to the frame lengths and the standard is the same as ASR. We segment the final test speech by the WebRTC VAD tool[1]. We control the size of the speech slices to make sure the length distribution is similar to the training set.

[1]https://github.com/wiseman/py-webrtcvad

Task	Corpus	Sentence	Hour
MT	TED	0.51M	-
ST	Europarl-ST	0.03M	77
	Common Voice	0.27M	415
	VoxPopuil	0.17M	496
	TED LIUM	0.26M	442
	MuST-C V1	0.06M	137
	ST TED	0.15M	233
	MuST-C En-Zh	0.35M	571
	Perturbation MuST-C En-Zh	0.71M	1142
	Total	2.03M	3513

Table 2: Detail of pseudo data

2.2 Data Augmentation

MT The MT is sensitive to the domain (Chu and Wang, 2018), so we only back-translate the monolingual data in the TED talk corpus as the pseudo parallel data.

ASR We only use the SpecAugment (Park et al., 2019) to mask the speech feature.

ST We use an MT model to translate transcriptions to build the pseudo tuple data. And we transform the MuST-C audio by speed rates of 0.9 and 1.1 to perturb the speech.

The Table 1 and Table 2 show the sizes of training data. We segment the English and Chinese text by Moses (Koehn et al., 2007) and NiuTrans (Xiao et al., 2012) separately. We use sentencepiece (Kudo and Richardson, 2018) to cut them to sub-word and the model is the same as MBART.

3 Model

We explore the performances of different ASR, MT, and adapter architectures. We experiment with three MT models, two ASR models and two adapters that integrate the MT and ASR to the ST model.

3.1 MT Model

The deep Transformer has been successfully used in translation task (Li et al., 2019). It deepens the encoder layer to obtain a stronger ability to model the source language. The ODE Transformer (Li et al., 2021a) also reached the state-of-art performance based on the vanilla deep model due to the efficient use of parameters. Since the output of

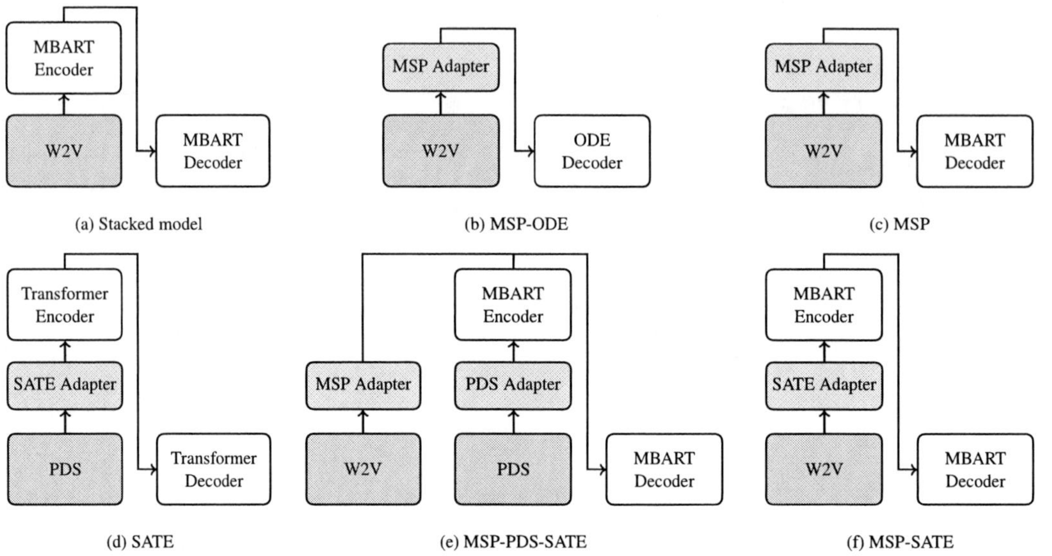

Figure 1: Overview of different ST models

the acoustic model consists of much noise, the Denoising self-encoding (DAE) model (e.g. MBART) can handle well about this situation. Further, the MBART pre-trained by lots of multilingual unlabeled data is helpful for the cross-lingual learning task. So we choose the above three models as our translation backbone models. Considering the output of the acoustic model does not contain the punctuation, we remove the punctuation in the source text before training the MT system. This operation is a little harmful to the MT model but does help the end-to-end system.

3.2 ASR Model

We use a progressive down-sampling method PDS for acoustic encoding based on Conformer which could improve the ASR performance. We also use the MSP method to fine-tune the W2V on the ASR task and can better bridge the gap between ASR and MT model. The input of the PDS model is the log Mel-filterbank feature while the W2V is based on waveform. Besides, acoustic models implement the relative position encoding (Dai et al., 2019).

3.3 ST Model

We combine the pre-trained modules with several adapters then fine-tune them with ST data. Besides the widely used Adapter consisting of a single hidden-layer feed-forward network (Bapna and Firat, 2019), we also use the SATE (Xu et al., 2021a) and MSP adapter. As Figure 1 shows, there are mainly six kinds of combined architecture we trained. Figure 1 (a) shows the W2V and MBART are stacked with the Adapter. The Figure 1 (b) and (c) show the W2V and MSP-adapter combined different MT decoders. The ST models composed with SATE adapter are shown in Figure 1 (d) and (f). As Figure 1 (e) shows, we fuse the output of two encoders which the input is filter-bank and waveform to make the different features interact. We use the cross multi-head attention of the decoder to extract two features and then average them.

4 Fine-tuning and Ensemble

To adjust the composed model to the ST task and a certain domain, we use the whole ST data to fine-tune the model. After coverage, we continue to train the model with only the MuST-C data set for domain adaptation.

We ensemble ST models by averaging distributions of model output. We search different combinations and numbers of models on the MuST-C set to investigate the influence of structural differences on the results of the ensemble model.

Since the final segmentation on the test set is inconsistent with the training set, we re-segment the training set by the same hyper-parameters as the test set. To get the reference of the audio, we implement the ensemble model to decode all the training audios and use the WER to re-cut the gold training paragraph into sentences. We utilize the new re-segment set to fine-tune the models.

Model	#Param	Dev	tst-COMMON
Baseline	54M	14.34	16.92
+parallel data	77M	16.48	18.74
+pseudo data	77M	16.81	18.74
+deep encoder	165M	16.91	19.76
ODE	104M	16.44	18.77
MBART	421M	16.04	18.12
Deep model	165M	16.23	18.96

Table 3: MT model measured by BLEU [%] metric

Model	#Param	Dev	tst-COMMON
PDS	127M	6.89	5.33
W2V	602M	4.89	5.31

Table 4: ASR model measured by WER [%] metric

Model	#Param	Dev	tst-COMMON
Single MT	165M	16.91	19.76
Transformer	30M	11.37	13.27
MSP	607M	14.96	17.19
+Pseudo data	607M	14.62	17.47
+Fine-tuning	607M	15.65	18.54
+Resegmentation	607M	15.26	18.41
+Ensemble	-	16.42	19.35

Table 5: ST model measured by BLEU [%] metric

Model	tst-COMMON	Ref2	Ref1	Both
MSP	26.7	-	-	-
Ensemble	29.1	32.3	33.2	40.5

Table 6: BLEU scores of ST models on MuST-C tst-COMMON and submitted tst2022 set. The scores are measured by the SLT.KIT toolkit.

5 Experiments

5.1 Experiment Settings

For the deep Transformer, we increased the encoder layers to 30 and keep the decoder 6 layers, the hidden size and FFN size is the same as the Transformer-base configuration. The ODE Transformer consisted of 18 encoder layers and 6 decoder layers. The pre-trained MBART consisted of a 12 layers encoder and a 12 layers decoder. All the models were trained with the pre-normalization operation. The size of the shared vocabulary was 44,144.

We used the pre-trained W2V model which does not fine-tune on the ASR task. We added the MSP-Adapter after the W2V and fine-tuned the model following the Baevski et al. (2020) fine-tuning configuration. During training on the ST set, we froze many parameters followed by Li et al. (2021b) to avoid catastrophic forgetting. The learning rate is set 3e-5 and we set drop and label smoothing at 0.2 to avoid over-fitting.

We implemented the early stop if the model does not promote for 8 times. We averaged the weights of the last 5 checkpoints for each training task. The beam size of inference was 8. All the MT and ST scores were calculated by multi-BLEU [2]. The ASR system was evaluated by word error rate (WER).

5.2 Results

MT Table 3 shows the MT results on the MuST-C dev and tst-COMMON set. Adding out-domain massive parallel data can significantly improve the performance. Though we add very few in-domain pseudo data, there is a +0.32 improvement on the dev set. The deep model gains +1.02 BLEU which significantly increases the ability of the MT model. To be consistent with the output of the acoustic model, we lowercase the English text and remove the punctuation. The MT results show a little degradation of performance while it is helpful for the end-to-end system. The MBART does not show its advantage compared with other methods. We conjecture that the exclusive model is better to deal with the Chinese translation task when there are dozen millions of clean parallel texts.

ASR There are two main architectures used for the ASR task. The PDS receives the log Mel-filterbank feature which is pre-processed while the input of W2V is the original sampling point of the waveform. Table 4 shows that W2V has much more parameters and achieves much better performance on the dev set. But the two models are comparable on the tst-COMMON set. This shows the W2V model is easy to over-fit.

ST Table 5 shows the MSP method which integrates pre-trained W2V and MBART modules to gain significant improvement compared with the vanilla Transformer model. We find directly adding pseudo data does not have an obvious effect. But after fine-tuning the MuST-C set, the improvement is significant. This shows the ST model is still

[2]https://github.com/moses-smt/mosesdecoder

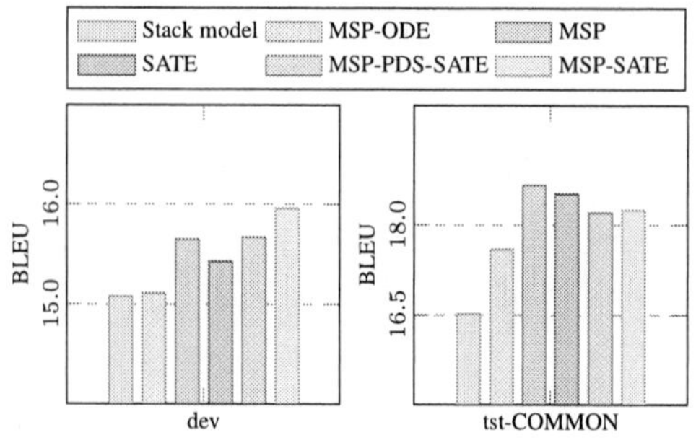

Figure 2: Comparison of the performance of the different models on MuST-C dev and tst-COMMON set

sensitive to the domain.

We compare the six combined architectures in Figure 2. Directly stacking two pre-trained models get the worst performance, this causes by the gap between the ASR and MT model. The ODE model has a stronger translation ability than the MBART, but the MSP-ODE does not outperform MSP on the ST task. We think it is due to the de-noising ability of the MBART since much noise such as silence exists in speech features. The MSP and the SATE get comparable performance on the tst-COMMON set and MSP-SATE which combined two methods gets the highest on the dev set. This proves the effect of MSP and SATE methods. We use the MSP-PDS-SATE to fuse two kinds of speech features and this model has about 900 million parameters. But the performance is not good enough. It needs to further explore how to make the pre-trained and original features interact.

To compare with other work conveniently, we provide some tst-COMMON results measured by official scripts [3] and each hypothesis is resegmented based on the reference by mwerSegmenter. The final results which are supplied by Anastasopoulos et al. (2022) in Table 6.

Ensemble The Table 5 shows the effect of ensemble model is also remarkable. We compared the performance of different combinations in Table 7. The fine-tuned model is likely over-fitting and we find the ensemble of the un-fine-tuned model is useful. We ensemble two models with much different architecture and the resulting gain is +0.56 improvement. We further add another different model but only gain slight improvement. We replace the MSP model with a worse model while the performance does not degenerate. This proves the ensemble model prefers the combination of models with a great difference and when the number of models increases, the performance of a single model does not matter.

[3] https://github.com/isl-mt/SLT.KIT/blob/master/scripts/evaluate/Eval.sh

Combination	tst-COMMON
MSP	18.66
MSP+MSP-UFT	18.99
MSP+SATE	19.22
MSP+SATE+MSP-SATE	19.35
MSP-UFT+SATE+MSP-SATE	19.34

Table 7: Ensemble model results measured by BLEU [%] metric. The MSP-UFT indicates the MSP model is un-fine-tuned.

6 Conclusions

This paper describes our submission to the IWSLT22 English to Chinese offline speech translation task. Our system is end-to-end and constrained. We pre-trained three types of machine translation models and two automatic speech recognition models. We integrate the acoustic and translation model on speech translation tasks by two types of adapters MSP and SATE. We fine-tune models to adapt domain and search for the best ensemble model for our submission. Our final system achieves 19.35 BLEU on MuST-C En-Zh tst-COMMON set.

Acknowledgments

This work was supported in part by the National Science Foundation of China (Nos. 61732005 and 61876035), the China HTRD Center Project (No. 2020AAA0107904) and Yunnan Provincial Major Science and Technology Special Plan Projects (Nos. 201902D08001905 and 202103AA080015). The authors would like to thank anonymous reviewers for their valuable comments. Thank Hao Chen and Jie Wang for processing the data.

References

Antonios Anastasopoulos, Luisa Bentivogli, Marcely Z. Boito, Ondřej Bojar, Roldano Cattoni, Anna Currey, Georgiana Dinu, Kevin Duh, Maha Elbayad, Marcello Federico, Christian Federmann, Hongyu Gong, Roman Grundkiewicz, Barry Haddow, Benjamin Hsu, Dávid Javorský, Věra Kloudová, Surafel M. Lakew, Xutai Ma, Prashant Mathur, Paul McNamee, Kenton Murray, Maria Nădejde, Satoshi Nakamura, Matteo Negri, Jan Niehues, Xing Niu, Juan Pino, Elizabeth Salesky, Jiatong Shi, Sebastian Stüker, Katsuhito Sudoh, Marco Turchi, Yogesh Virkar, Alex Waibel, Changhan Wang, and Shinji Watanabe. 2022. FINDINGS OF THE IWSLT 2022 EVALUATION CAMPAIGN. In *Proceedings of the 19th International Conference on Spoken Language Translation (IWSLT 2022)*, Dublin, Ireland. Association for Computational Linguistics.

Alexei Baevski, Yuhao Zhou, Abdelrahman Mohamed, and Michael Auli. 2020. wav2vec 2.0: A framework for self-supervised learning of speech representations. In *Advances in Neural Information Processing Systems*, volume 33, pages 12449–12460.

Parnia Bahar, Patrick Wilken, Mattia A. Di Gangi, and Evgeny Matusov. 2021. Without further ado: Direct and simultaneous speech translation by AppTek in 2021. In *Proceedings of the 18th International Conference on Spoken Language Translation (IWSLT 2021)*, pages 52–63, Bangkok, Thailand (online). Association for Computational Linguistics.

Ankur Bapna and Orhan Firat. 2019. Simple, scalable adaptation for neural machine translation. In *Proceedings of the 2019 Conference on Empirical Methods in Natural Language Processing and the 9th International Joint Conference on Natural Language Processing (EMNLP-IJCNLP)*, pages 1538–1548, Hong Kong, China. Association for Computational Linguistics.

Chenhui Chu and Rui Wang. 2018. A survey of domain adaptation for neural machine translation. In *Proceedings of the 27th International Conference on Computational Linguistics*, pages 1304–1319, Santa Fe, New Mexico, USA. Association for Computational Linguistics.

Zihang Dai, Zhilin Yang, Yiming Yang, Jaime Carbonell, Quoc Le, and Ruslan Salakhutdinov. 2019. Transformer-XL: Attentive language models beyond a fixed-length context. In *Proceedings of the 57th Annual Meeting of the Association for Computational Linguistics*, pages 2978–2988, Florence, Italy. Association for Computational Linguistics.

Chris Dyer, Victor Chahuneau, and Noah A. Smith. 2013. A simple, fast, and effective reparameterization of IBM model 2. In *Proceedings of the 2013 Conference of the North American Chapter of the Association for Computational Linguistics: Human Language Technologies*, pages 644–648, Atlanta, Georgia. Association for Computational Linguistics.

Sathish Indurthi, Mohd Abbas Zaidi, Nikhil Kumar Lakumarapu, Beomseok Lee, Hyojung Han, Seokchan Ahn, Sangha Kim, Chanwoo Kim, and Inchul Hwang. 2021. Task aware multi-task learning for speech to text tasks. In *ICASSP 2021 - 2021 IEEE International Conference on Acoustics, Speech and Signal Processing (ICASSP)*, pages 7723–7727.

Philipp Koehn, Hieu Hoang, Alexandra Birch, Chris Callison-Burch, Marcello Federico, Nicola Bertoldi, Brooke Cowan, Wade Shen, Christine Moran, Richard Zens, Chris Dyer, Ondřej Bojar, Alexandra Constantin, and Evan Herbst. 2007. Moses: Open source toolkit for statistical machine translation. In *Proceedings of the 45th Annual Meeting of the Association for Computational Linguistics Companion Volume Proceedings of the Demo and Poster Sessions*, pages 177–180, Prague, Czech Republic. Association for Computational Linguistics.

Taku Kudo and John Richardson. 2018. SentencePiece: A simple and language independent subword tokenizer and detokenizer for neural text processing. In *Proceedings of the 2018 Conference on Empirical Methods in Natural Language Processing: System Demonstrations*, pages 66–71, Brussels, Belgium. Association for Computational Linguistics.

Bei Li, Quan Du, Tao Zhou, Shuhan Zhou, Xin Zeng, Tong Xiao, and Jingbo Zhu. 2021a. Ode transformer: An ordinary differential equation-inspired model for neural machine translation. *arXiv preprint arXiv:2104.02308*.

Bei Li, Yinqiao Li, Chen Xu, Ye Lin, Jiqiang Liu, Hui Liu, Ziyang Wang, Yuhao Zhang, Nuo Xu, Zeyang Wang, Kai Feng, Hexuan Chen, Tengbo Liu, Yanyang Li, Qiang Wang, Tong Xiao, and Jingbo Zhu. 2019. The NiuTrans machine translation systems for WMT19. In *Proceedings of the Fourth Conference on Machine Translation (Volume 2: Shared Task Papers, Day 1)*, pages 257–266, Florence, Italy. Association for Computational Linguistics.

Xian Li, Changhan Wang, Yun Tang, Chau Tran, Yuqing Tang, Juan Pino, Alexei Baevski, Alexis Conneau, and Michael Auli. 2021b. Multilingual speech translation from efficient finetuning of pretrained models. In *Proceedings of the 59th Annual Meeting of the Association for Computational Linguistics and the 11th International Joint Conference on Natural Language Processing (Volume 1: Long Papers)*, pages 827–838, Online. Association for Computational Linguistics.

Yinhan Liu, Jiatao Gu, Naman Goyal, Xian Li, Sergey Edunov, Marjan Ghazvininejad, Mike Lewis, and Luke Zettlemoyer. 2020. Multilingual denoising pre-training for neural machine translation. *Transactions of the Association for Computational Linguistics*, 8:726–742.

Daniel S. Park, William Chan, Yu Zhang, Chung-Cheng Chiu, Barret Zoph, Ekin D. Cubuk, and Quoc V. Le. 2019. SpecAugment: A Simple Data Augmentation Method for Automatic Speech Recognition. In *Proc. Interspeech 2019*, pages 2613–2617.

Juan Pino, Qiantong Xu, Xutai Ma, Mohammad Javad Dousti, and Yun Tang. 2020. Self-Training for End-to-End Speech Translation. In *Proc. Interspeech 2020*, pages 1476–1480.

Chengyi Wang, Yu Wu, Shujie Liu, Ming Zhou, and Zhenglu Yang. 2020. Curriculum pre-training for end-to-end speech translation. In *Proceedings of the*

58th Annual Meeting of the Association for Computational Linguistics, pages 3728–3738, Online. Association for Computational Linguistics.

Qiang Wang, Bei Li, Tong Xiao, Jingbo Zhu, Changliang Li, Derek F. Wong, and Lidia S. Chao. 2019. Learning deep transformer models for machine translation. In *Proceedings of the 57th Annual Meeting of the Association for Computational Linguistics*, pages 1810–1822, Florence, Italy. Association for Computational Linguistics.

Tong Xiao, Jingbo Zhu, Hao Zhang, and Qiang Li. 2012. NiuTrans: An open source toolkit for phrase-based and syntax-based machine translation. In *Proceedings of the ACL 2012 System Demonstrations*, pages 19–24, Jeju Island, Korea. Association for Computational Linguistics.

Chen Xu, Bojie Hu, Yanyang Li, Yuhao Zhang, Shen Huang, Qi Ju, Tong Xiao, and Jingbo Zhu. 2021a. Stacked acoustic-and-textual encoding: Integrating the pre-trained models into speech translation encoders. In *Proceedings of the 59th Annual Meeting of the Association for Computational Linguistics and the 11th International Joint Conference on Natural Language Processing (Volume 1: Long Papers)*, pages 2619–2630, Online. Association for Computational Linguistics.

Chen Xu, Xiaoqian Liu, Xiaowen Liu, Tiger Wang, Canan Huang, Tong Xiao, and Jingbo Zhu. 2021b. The NiuTrans end-to-end speech translation system for IWSLT 2021 offline task. In *Proceedings of the 18th International Conference on Spoken Language Translation (IWSLT 2021)*, pages 92–99, Bangkok, Thailand (online). Association for Computational Linguistics.

Yuhao Zhang, Ziyang Wang, Runzhe Cao, Binghao Wei, Weiqiao Shan, Shuhan Zhou, Abudurexiti Reheman, Tao Zhou, Xin Zeng, Laohu Wang, Yongyu Mu, Jingnan Zhang, Xiaoqian Liu, Xuanjun Zhou, Yinqiao Li, Bei Li, Tong Xiao, and Jingbo Zhu. 2020. The NiuTrans machine translation systems for WMT20. In *Proceedings of the Fifth Conference on Machine Translation*, pages 338–345, Online. Association for Computational Linguistics.

The HW-TSC's Offline Speech Translation System for IWSLT 2022 Evaluation

Yinglu Li[1], Minghan Wang[1], Jiaxin Guo[1], Xiaosong Qiao[1], Yuxia Wang[2], Daimeng Wei[1], Chang Su[1], Yimeng Chen[1], Min Zhang[1], Shimin Tao[1], Hao Yang[1], Ying Qin[1]

[1]Huawei Translation Services Center, Beijing, China

[2]The University of Melbourne, Melbourne, Australia

{liyinglu,wangminghan,guojiaxin1,qiaoxiaosong,weidaimeng,suchang8,chenyimeng,zhangmin186,taoshimin,yanghao30,qinying}@huawei.com

yuxiaw@student.unimelb.edu.au

Abstract

This paper describes the HW-TSC's designation of the Offline Speech Translation System submitted for IWSLT 2022 Evaluation. We explored both cascade and end-to-end system on three language tracks (en-de, en-zh and en-ja), and we chose the cascade one as our primary submission. For the automatic speech recognition (ASR) model of cascade system, there are three ASR models including Conformer, S2T-Transformer and U2 trained on the mixture of five datasets. During inference, transcripts are generated with the help of domain controlled generation strategy. Context-aware reranking and ensemble based robustness enhancement strategy are proposed to produce better ASR outputs. For machine translation part, we pretrained three translation models on WMT21 dataset and fine-tuned them on in-domain corpora. Our cascade system shows more competitive performance than the known offline systems in the industry and academia.

1 Introduction

In recent years, end-to-end system and cascade system are fundamental pipelines for speech translation tasks. Traditional cascade system is comprised of continuing parts, automatic speech recognition (ASR) is responsible for generating transcripts from audios and machine translation model aims at translating ASR outputs from source language into target language. Obviously, the ASR part and MT part of this system are independent to some extent. Therefore, this paradigm enables people to utilise state-of-the-art ASR models and MT models and conduct experiments by different permutations and combinations. And those experiments can help us find the best combination of choice of ASR and MT model. ASR model like Conformer (Gulati et al., 2020) and S2T-Transformer (Synnaeve et al., 2019) are commonly used. MT models like Transformer (Vaswani et al., 2017) can be considered as a standard configuration.

On the contrary, there is also a disadvantage when applying cascade systems. The main aspect is that some important information such as the intonation and emphasis of speakers could not be explicitly expressed in the transcripts. This "missing information" might be the key to distinguish the gender of speaker, or the sarcasm and symbolism behind the texts. It means, there is a risk of losing important information under the condition of cascade system.

Correspondingly, end-to-end system preserves the competitive edge to learn the "missing information", because it is directly trained on the speech-to-text dataset without any transit process. Due to this property, end-to-end system has been paid attention in research and there is encouraging progress. For instance, Conformer (Gulati et al., 2020) can also be used in this task. However, there are some disadvantages for the end-to-end system. Firstly, due to the lack of large scale high quality bilingual speech translation datasets, training a productive end-to-end ST model can be non-trivial. Next, the mapping from speech space to the target language space is far more difficult than the mapping to the source language space, leading to greater demand on the scale of the training set.

This paper presents our work in IWSLT 2022 (Anastasopoulos et al., 2022) offline speech translation track. The main contribution of this paper can be summarized as follows:

1) We tested various combinations of ASR models, and finally found ensemble of Conformer and S2T-Transformer and filter by U2 can improve the ASR fluency and sentence expression.

2) Context-aware LM reranking can effectively improve the possibility to choose the best candidate in beam search.

Proceedings of the 19th International Conference on Spoken Language Translation (IWSLT 2022), pages 239 - 246
May 26-27, 2022 ©2022 Association for Computational Linguistics

Dataset	Number of Utterance	Duration(hrs)
LibriSpeech	281,241	960.85
MuST-C	340,421	590.67
IWSLT	170,229	254.41
CoVoST	1362,422	1802.52
TEDLIUM3	268,214	453.42

Table 1: Data statistics of our ASR corpora

Language	WMT Bilingual	In-domain Text
En-De	79M	459K
En-Zh	96M	590K
En-Ja	42M	552K

Table 2: Data statistics of our MT corpora

2 Method

2.1 Data Preparation and Preprocessing

There are five different datasets used in the training of our ASR models and ST models, such as MuST-C V2 (Cattoni et al., 2021), LibriSpeech(Panayotov et al., 2015), TED-LIUM 3 (Hernandez et al., 2018), CoVoST (Wang et al., 2020), IWSLT, as described in the left sub-plot of Figure 1. For the training dataset we extracted 80-dimensional filter bank features from the raw waveform firstly. Then, the dataset was cleaned in a fine-grained process. The training set was filtered on the criteria of absolute frame size (within 50 to 3000), number of tokens (within 1 to 150) and speed of the speech (within $\mu(\tau) \pm 4 \times \sigma(\tau)$), where $\tau = \frac{\text{\# frames}}{\text{\# tokens}}$. The detailed attributes such as the number of utterance and the duration of training datasets are shown in table 1. For test set, each TED talk was segmented into several utterances (no more than 20 seconds) with the officially provided segmentation tool (LIUM_SpkDiarization.jar).

We use the exactly same corpus to train our MT models following the configuration of (Wei et al., 2021), with the scale of the dataset showing in Tabel 2.

2.2 Automatic Speech Recognition

There are three types of basic ASR models Conformer (Gulati et al., 2020), S2T-Transformer (Synnaeve et al., 2019) and U2 (Zhang et al., 2020) used to recognize the speech and get transcripts. The first two models are standard autoregressive ASR models built upon the Transformer architecture (Vaswani et al., 2017). The last one is a unified model that can perform both streaming and non-streaming ASR, supported by the dynamic chunking training strategy (Zhang et al., 2020). During the training and decoding process, there are three important strategies we used to generate ASR results of these models as follows.

Domain controlled training and decoding By observing the corpus in the training set, we find that the style of text and the domain of the speech can be different between each dataset. Although the model is able to learn such difference implicitly, there are still some confusing patterns like case sensitivity and existence of punctuation that can not be easily learned. Therefore, we add the domain tag as the prefix token, acting as a known condition to guide the model to generate texts in required domain and style. It means, the model can learn the pattern given more prior knowledge. For example, the tag "<MC>" provides an instruction to the model to generate texts in the MuST-C style, or we can also use <LS> to make the model to generate LibriSpeech alike transcripts. The strategy also had a positive effect in our offline task submission of IWSLT 2021 (Wang et al., 2021). For Conformer and S2T-Transformer, since they are autoregressive generative models, we simply use the domain tag as the prefix token. However, this is not feasible for U2 with the CTC decoder. Therefore, we propose to first encode the domain tag with the input-embedding of the attention-based decoder of U2, then, adding the encoded tag to the down-sampled features element-wise, being together fed into attention layers of the encoder.

Context-aware LM reranking In order to take benefits from both Conformer and S2T-Transformer which has different model architecture, we ensemble them by averaging the predicted probabilities while generation. However, the ensemble doesn't solve a key problem comes from the independence assumption on each utterance. In other words, we translate each utterance in a TED talk speech independently without considering context information, which often cause inconsistent prediction on named entities such as person names. To this end, we adopt a language model (LM) to rerank beam candidates conditioned on a fixed length window of generated contexts.

Specifically, a Transformer-LM was trained on

Algorithm 1 Context-aware LM reranking

Require: ASR, LM, context length, beam size, utterance list: ϕ, Q, N, k, U
  Initialize: Context Buffer $C \leftarrow \{\}$
  Initialize: utterance index $i \leftarrow 0$
  while $i \neq |U| - 1$ **do**
    $\hat{Y}, P_\phi \leftarrow \phi(u_i, k)$: propose candidates
    if $i < N$ **then**
      $P_Q \leftarrow Q(\hat{Y}, C)$
    else
      $P_Q \leftarrow Q(\hat{Y}, C_{[-N:]})$
    end if
    $\hat{y}^* \leftarrow \arg\max_{\hat{y}} \sum_{m \in \{Q, \phi\}} w_m P_m$
    $C \leftarrow C \cup \{\hat{y}^*\}$
    $i \leftarrow i + 1$
  end while
  return C

the WMT21 monolingual English dataset, providing the perplexity score of each ASR beam candidate from the ensemble models by taking N previous generated sentence into account, ($N = 3$ obtains the best result). This method is commonly used to optimize document-level translation (Yu et al., 2020). A detailed explanation is presented in Algo 1 and the right sub-plot of Figure 1, which actually works like performing context-aware greedy search in the sentence-level. Besides the PPL (converted to the log probability) estimated by the LM, we also take the log probability of each beam candidate output by ASR models into account, combining them with a weighted sum (best combination searched in the experiment: $w_{LM} = 0.6, w_{ASR} = 0.4$).

Ensemble based robustness enhancement strategy Compared with ASR results generated from different ASR models, an interesting pattern can be found that U2 prefers to predict blank lines when facing with some hard samples. Hard samples, such as laughter and applause always confused S2T-Transformer and Conformer and they are more likely to output incorrectly. For instance, S2T-Transformer always outputs "*thank you very much indeed*" and Conformer generates "*There's many a slip, twixt cup and the lip.*" when the input is the audio which contained only the applause of audiences. This phenomenon can be explained by the reason that U2 is more robust to interference than S2T-Transformer and Conformer. Consequently, the strategy that U2 could be utilised to filter the noise of ASR results from Conformer and S2T-Transformer. In other words, we extracted the blank lines of prediction of U2 as the standard to correct the results of other two models. The process provides our system with more robustness to non-speech or background noise.

2.3 Machine Translation

In an cascade system, the input of machine translation (MT) model is the ASR results. In order to obtain the translated results, we use the WMT21 news corpora to train three individual MT models for each language (En-De, En-Zh, En-Ja). Then these MT models are fine-tuned on the combination of MuST-C and IWSLT dataset. After applying the MT models on the ensembling ASR results above, the final results, also called hypothesis were obtained in our experiment.

2.4 Multilingual E2E-ST

In the ene-to-end system, the ASR model and machine translation model trained on bilingual corpora are not the continents of the system. The E2E model can be directly trained on the bilingual/multilingual speech corpora. However, only MuST-C and COVOST provides the translation of some language pairs, which might not be enough. Therefor, we propose to use the MT model to generate translations in specific language for all ASR training corpora, and then combined them together including the ASR (English) text, tagged with domain and language abbreviations like "<MC_en>", "<LS_zh>", etc. This is commonly considered as sequence level knowledge distillation (KD) (Kim and Rush, 2016). Next, a multilingual speech translation (ST) model is trained on the corpora, which can be used in both ASR and translation in an end-to-end paradigm by giving required language and domain tag.

3 Experiments

3.1 Settings

Model Configurations Sentencepiece (Kudo and Richardson, 2018) is utilised for tokenization on ASR texts with a learned vocabulary restricted to 20000 sub-tokens. ASR models are configured as: $n_{\text{encoder\_layers}} = 16$, $n_{\text{decoder\_layers}} = 6$, $n_{\text{heads}} = 16$, $d_{\text{hidden}} = 1024$, $d_{\text{FFN}} = 4096$ for Conformer, $n_{\text{encoder\_layers}} = 12$, $n_{\text{decoder\_layers}} = 6$, $n_{\text{heads}} = 16$, $d_{\text{hidden}} = 1024$, $d_{\text{FFN}} = 4096$ for S2T-Transformer and $n_{\text{encoder\_layers}} = 12$, $n_{\text{decoder\_layers}} = 6$, $n_{\text{heads}} =$

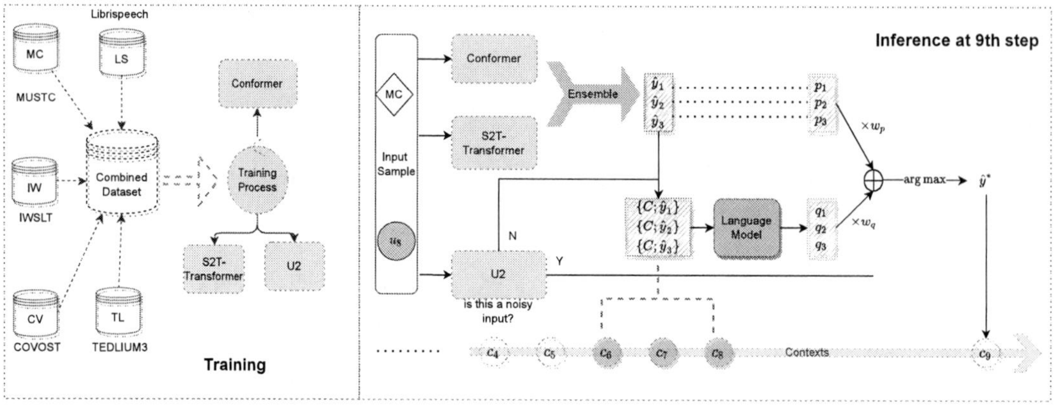

Figure 1: This figure presents the example of the training of our ASR models (left) as well as the inference of our cascade system (right). In the example of inference, input features and domain tags are feed into ASR models, being decoded by the ensemble of Conformer and S2T-Transformer and cleaned by U2. Then, beam candidates (k=3 here) are scored together with contexts (6 to 8) by the language model. Finally, the optimal candidate is selected according to modulated scores and becomes the new context.

ASR Model	CoVoST	MuST-C	TEDLIUM3	LibriSpeech
Conformer	11.27	6.31	5.33	4.39
S2T-Transformer	13.46	9.01	6.30	5.67
U2	14.68	9.71	11.93	5.79

Table 3: Comparison of wer scores of Conformer, S2T-Transformer and U2 trained on test sets of each individual dataset.

16, $d_{\text{hidden}} = 1024$, $d_{\text{FFN}} = 4096$ for U2. The NMT model has the standard Transformer-big configuration but with d_{FFN} set to 8192 (Ng et al., 2019). The language model is a standard Transformer language model with the configuration of: $n_{\text{layers}} = 12$, $n_{\text{heads}} = 16$, $d_{\text{hidden}} = 1024$, $d_{\text{FFN}} = 4096$. All models are implemented with `fairseq` (Ott et al., 2019).

During the training of ASR models, we set the batch size to the maximum of 20,000 frames per card. Inverse sqrt is used for lr scheduling with warm-up steps set to 10,000 and peak lr set as 5e-4. Adam is used as the optimizer. All ASR models are trained on 8 V100 GPUs for 50 epochs. Parameters for last 5 epochs are averaged. Audio features are normalized with utterance-level CMVN for Conformer and S2T-Transformer, and with global CMVN for U2. All audio inputs are augmented with spectral augmentation (Park et al., 2019).

We followed the work of Wei et al. (2021) on the pretraining of all NMT models. All of them are fine-tuned on in-domain corpus for 10 steps.

We use the toolkit from the SLT.KIT[1] for evaluation on all development set, which produces metrics including BLEU (Papineni et al., 2002), TER (Snover et al., 2006), BEER (Stanojevic and Sima'an, 2014) and CharacTER (Wang et al., 2016).

3.2 Results

Comparison of ASR models on each individual dataset We tested three ASR models (Conformer, U2 and S2T-Transformer) on four individual test sets, CoVoST, MuST-C, TEDLIUM and LibriSpeech. In Table 3, Conformer shows the best results in each column, which are 11.27, 6.31, 5.33 and 4.39 WERs in each dataset. It is obvious that Conformer has the significant advantage compared to other two models. However, after manually evaluating some samples, we find that Conformer is easier to over-fit the training corpora. Therefore, we decide to ensemble it with the S2T-Transformer during inference.

Comparison of our approach on past years' test sets In Table 4, we tested the performance of our cascade system on datasets of all past years, by providing 6 metrics evaluated by the SLT.KIT toolkit. By comparing these results with our last

[1] https://github.com/jniehues-kit/SLT.KIT

SET	BLEU	BLEU (last year)	TER	BEER	CharacTER	BLEU(ci)	TER(ci)
dev2010	27.19 (+1.19)	26.00	60.61	53.10	48.27	28.73	58.21
tst2010	27.51 (+1.14)	26.37	60.66	52.57	48.90	29.13	58.14
tst2013	29.38 (-0.51)	29.89	60.94	53.70	47.07	30.7	58.83
tst2014	28 (-0.03)	28.03	61.19	52.90	47.95	28.93	59.51
tst2015	24.06 (+0.86)	23.20	77.89	50.20	50.86	24.94	76.77
tst2018	23.12 (+0.99)	22.13	73.65	51.33	51.50	23.92	71.23
tst2019	25.92	-	62.11	52.22	48.96	27.13	60.08
tst2021 (En-De)	27.5/21.2/39.9						
tst2022 (En-De)	24.2/20.8/33.5						
tst2022 (En-Zh)	34.6/33.4/42.1						
tst2022 (En-Ja)	23.3/14.3/31.0						

Table 4: Overall results comparison on dev and test sets from 2010 to this year with the full use of our strategies (The results of 2010-2019 are all in En-De). For the column of BLEU, we also presents the improvements compared to our last year's BLEU score. The lower part of the table presents our submission results in this year, values from left to right are BLEU-ref1, BLEU-ref2 and BLEU both, respectively.

years' report (Wang et al., 2021), we find that our strategy used in this year provides significant improvements on most of datasets, demonstrating their efficiency.

In order to illustrate the difference between ASR results of Conformer, S2T-Transformer and U2, we choose some representative cases in Tab 5. Case 1 presents three sentences generated from three ASR models given an audio segment which only contains background music and applause. Obviously Conformer and S2T-Transformer both outputs wrong sentences, because nothing should be generated in the decoding process. Contrarily, U2 outputs the blank line which indicates the robustness of the model itself. Case 2 provides the transcripts that Conformer and S2T-Transformer outputs the correct results. However, U2 made some mistakes on uppercase and punctuation marks even though the contents are generally correct, which shows that U2 is not sensible with case or punctuation; This actually caused by the multi-modality problem (Gu et al., 2018), which is faced by all non-autoregressive generation models. Since the prediction of each token are independently modeled in U2 (conditional independence assumption used by the CTC decoder), the prediction of tokens with one-to-many mappings (usually referred to as capitalism or existence of punctuation) can be difficult to learn without visible contexts (compared to autoregressive models). Case 3 presents that the results of Conformer and S2T-Transformer contains different errors. The Conformer misunderstood the "an ex-boyfriend" for "a next boyfriend", and S2T Transformer made a mistake on "cuss words". By fixing the different mistakes, we successfully obtain the correct sentence in the ensemble results.

3.3 Ablation

Effectiveness of context-aware reranking We investigated and demonstrated whether the context-aware ASR reranking strategy works well and the results are indicated in Table 6. As we can see, we experimented the weight combination like $w_{\text{LM}} = \{0.0, 0.5, 0.6, 1.0\}$, $w_{\text{ASR}} = \{1.0, 0.5, 0.4, 0.0\}$, and several context length including $N = \{3, 4, 5\}$.

The higher the w_{LM} is, the more contribution does the LM provides to the scoring. The ablation study shows that context length at 3 is the best choice for reranking, since the results with context length at 4 or 5 both indicates lower BLEU scores. We suspect that longer contexts often misleads the scoring processing due to the unstable estimation of PPL on beam candidates of current utterance, resulting in non-convincing reranked results. Meanwhile, we find that the best combination of the weight on LM and ASR is 0.6 and 0.4, indicating that scoring only with LM cannot always produce promising estimation on the quality of the sentence.

Performance of Translation models We used the ASR results generated from Conformer on MuST-C tst-COMMON dataset to measure the performance of two text MT models and an end-to-end ST model, i.e. the MT model pretrained

	ASR model	Sentences
Case 1	Conformer	*There's many a slip, twixt cup and the lip.*
	S2T-Transformer	*Thank you very much indeed.*
	U2	-
	Ensemble	-
Case 2	Conformer	***And I** predict that in 10 years, we will lose our bees.*
	S2T-Transformer	***And I** predict that in 10 years, we will lose our bees.*
	U2	*and i predict that in ten years we will lose our bees*
	Ensemble	***And I** predict that in 10 years, we will lose our bees.*
Case 3	Conformer	*... the language that a next boyfriend taught you, where you learned all the **cuss** words ...*
	S2T-Transformer	*... the language that **an ex-boyfriend** taught you, where you learned all the cusp words ...*
	U2	*... the language that an ex-boy taught you or you learned all the cus words ...*
	Ensemble	*... the language that **an ex-boyfriend** taught you, where you learned all the **cuss** words ...*

Table 5: The table presents three cases to compare the difference when generating ASR results. Those words or sentences marked by underline represents the mistakes. Case 1 shows that U2 predict more robust result than Conformer and S2T-Transformer if the input audio is filled with applause; Case 2 shows the transcripts that Conformer and S2T outputs the correct results but U2 is not sensible with uppercase and punctuation marks; Case 3 presents that the results of Conformer and S2T-Transformer both contains error, but ensemble strategy successfully obtain the correct sentence.

Hyper-Parameters	N=3	N=4	N=5
$w_{\text{LM}} = 0.0, w_{\text{ASR}} = 1.0$		25.12	
$w_{\text{LM}} = 0.5, w_{\text{ASR}} = 0.5$	25.66	25.65	25.70
$w_{\text{LM}} = 0.6, w_{\text{ASR}} = 0.4$	**25.92**	25.76	25.73
$w_{\text{LM}} = 1.0, w_{\text{ASR}} = 0.0$	25.58	25.48	25.52

Table 6: This table shows the BLEU score evaluated on IWSLT tst2019 En-De dataset with different combination of LM reranking weight (w) and context length (N).

Model	En-De	En-Zh	En-Ja
Pretrained MT	33.1	24.1	14.8
In-domain FT MT	**33.3**	**24.6**	**15.1**
Multilingual E2E ST	30.8	22.3	13.0

Table 7: This table presents the BLEU score evaluated on MuST-C tst-COMMON dataset with our pretrained and in-domain fine-tuned MT model, note that the source texts comes from the same Conformer ASR model instead of the oracle text. The last row is performance of our end-to-end multilingual ST model evaluated with the speech input.

on WMT news corpora, the in-domain fine-tuned MT model and our multilingual ST model. The in-domain FT MT was trained on the combination of MuST-C and IWSLT text corpora, providing the best BLEU scores compared with other two models. The result demonstrates that the in-domain fine-tuning is effective to generate the reasonable translation hypothesis. On the other hand, End-to-End multilingual ST proves to be a competitive model since the results are relatively close to those of the baseline pretrained MT model. More importantly, the E2E ST was only trained once on the combination of all language pairs, without further fine-tuning on any of them.

4 Conclusion

This paper presents our offline speech translation systems in the IWSLT 2022 evaluation. We explored different strategies in the pipeline of building the cascade and end-to-end system. In the data preprocessing, we adopt efficient cleansing approaches to build the training set collected from different data sources. Domain controlled generation was used in the training and decoding of ASR models to fit the requirement of the evaluation test set. We also investigated the positive effect of context-aware LM reranking aiming at improving the quality and consistency of ASR outputs. Finally, we demonstrated that the cascade system consisted of reranking ASR system and MT model has the best performance than end-to-end system. In our future works, we would like to investigate more strategies on improving the consistency of ASR outputs beyond reranking, as well as better training and data augmentation strategies for end-to-end models.

References

Antonios Anastasopoulos, Luisa Bentivogli, Marcely Z. Boito, Ondřej Bojar, Roldano Cattoni, Anna Currey, Georgiana Dinu, Kevin Duh, Maha Elbayad, Marcello Federico, Christian Federmann, Hongyu Gong, Roman Grundkiewicz, Barry Haddow, Benjamin Hsu, Dávid Javorský, Věra Kloudová, Surafel M. Lakew, Xutai Ma, Prashant Mathur, Paul McNamee, Kenton Murray, Maria Nădejde, Satoshi Nakamura, Matteo Negri, Jan Niehues, Xing Niu, Juan Pino, Elizabeth Salesky, Jiatong Shi, Sebastian Stüker, Katsuhito Sudoh, Marco Turchi, Yogesh Virkar, Alex Waibel, Changhan Wang, and Shinji Watanabe. 2022. FINDINGS OF THE IWSLT 2022 EVALUATION CAMPAIGN. In *Proceedings of the 19th International Conference on Spoken Language Translation (IWSLT 2022)*, Dublin, Ireland. Association for Computational Linguistics.

Roldano Cattoni, Mattia Antonino Di Gangi, Luisa Bentivogli, Matteo Negri, and Marco Turchi. 2021. Must-c: A multilingual corpus for end-to-end speech translation. *Comput. Speech Lang.*, 66:101155.

Jiatao Gu, James Bradbury, Caiming Xiong, Victor O. K. Li, and Richard Socher. 2018. Non-autoregressive neural machine translation. In *6th International Conference on Learning Representations, ICLR 2018, Vancouver, BC, Canada, April 30 - May 3, 2018, Conference Track Proceedings*. OpenReview.net.

Anmol Gulati, James Qin, Chung-Cheng Chiu, Niki Parmar, Yu Zhang, Jiahui Yu, Wei Han, Shibo Wang, Zhengdong Zhang, Yonghui Wu, and Ruoming Pang. 2020. Conformer: Convolution-augmented transformer for speech recognition. In *Interspeech 2020, 21st Annual Conference of the International Speech Communication Association, Virtual Event, Shanghai, China, 25-29 October 2020*, pages 5036–5040. ISCA.

François Hernandez, Vincent Nguyen, Sahar Ghannay, Natalia A. Tomashenko, and Yannick Estève. 2018. TED-LIUM 3: Twice as much data and corpus repartition for experiments on speaker adaptation. In *Speech and Computer - 20th International Conference, SPECOM 2018, Leipzig, Germany, September 18-22, 2018, Proceedings*, volume 11096 of *Lecture Notes in Computer Science*, pages 198–208. Springer.

Yoon Kim and Alexander M. Rush. 2016. Sequence-level knowledge distillation. In *Proceedings of the 2016 Conference on Empirical Methods in Natural Language Processing, EMNLP 2016, Austin, Texas, USA, November 1-4, 2016*, pages 1317–1327. The Association for Computational Linguistics.

Taku Kudo and John Richardson. 2018. Sentencepiece: A simple and language independent subword tokenizer and detokenizer for neural text processing. In *Proceedings of the 2018 Conference on Empirical Methods in Natural Language Processing, EMNLP 2018: System Demonstrations, Brussels, Belgium, October 31 - November 4, 2018*, pages 66–71. Association for Computational Linguistics.

Nathan Ng, Kyra Yee, Alexei Baevski, Myle Ott, Michael Auli, and Sergey Edunov. 2019. Facebook fair's WMT19 news translation task submission. In *Proceedings of the Fourth Conference on Machine Translation, WMT 2019, Florence, Italy, August 1-2, 2019 - Volume 2: Shared Task Papers, Day 1*, pages 314–319. Association for Computational Linguistics.

Myle Ott, Sergey Edunov, Alexei Baevski, Angela Fan, Sam Gross, Nathan Ng, David Grangier, and Michael Auli. 2019. fairseq: A fast, extensible toolkit for sequence modeling. In *Proceedings of the 2019 Conference of the North American Chapter of the Association for Computational Linguistics: Human Language Technologies, NAACL-HLT 2019, Minneapolis, MN, USA, June 2-7, 2019, Demonstrations*, pages 48–53. Association for Computational Linguistics.

Vassil Panayotov, Guoguo Chen, Daniel Povey, and Sanjeev Khudanpur. 2015. Librispeech: An ASR corpus based on public domain audio books. In *2015 IEEE International Conference on Acoustics, Speech and Signal Processing, ICASSP 2015, South Brisbane, Queensland, Australia, April 19-24, 2015*, pages 5206–5210. IEEE.

Kishore Papineni, Salim Roukos, Todd Ward, and Wei-Jing Zhu. 2002. Bleu: a method for automatic evaluation of machine translation. In *Proceedings of the 40th Annual Meeting of the Association for Computational Linguistics, July 6-12, 2002, Philadelphia, PA, USA*, pages 311–318. ACL.

Daniel S. Park, William Chan, Yu Zhang, Chung-Cheng Chiu, Barret Zoph, Ekin D. Cubuk, and Quoc V. Le. 2019. Specaugment: A simple data augmentation method for automatic speech recognition. In *Interspeech 2019, 20th Annual Conference of the International Speech Communication Association, Graz, Austria, 15-19 September 2019*, pages 2613–2617. ISCA.

Matthew Snover, Bonnie Dorr, Richard Schwartz, Linnea Micciulla, and John Makhoul. 2006. A study of translation edit rate with targeted human annotation. In *Proceedings of the 7th Conference of the Association for Machine Translation in the Americas: Technical Papers*, pages 223–231.

Milos Stanojevic and Khalil Sima'an. 2014. Fitting sentence level translation evaluation with many dense features. In *Proceedings of the 2014 Conference on Empirical Methods in Natural Language Processing, EMNLP 2014, October 25-29, 2014, Doha, Qatar, A meeting of SIGDAT, a Special Interest Group of the ACL*, pages 202–206. ACL.

Gabriel Synnaeve, Qiantong Xu, Jacob Kahn, Edouard Grave, Tatiana Likhomanenko, Vineel Pratap, Anuroop Sriram, Vitaliy Liptchinsky, and Ronan Collobert. 2019. End-to-end ASR: from supervised to semi-supervised learning with modern architectures. *CoRR*, abs/1911.08460.

Ashish Vaswani, Noam Shazeer, Niki Parmar, Jakob Uszkoreit, Llion Jones, Aidan N. Gomez, Lukasz Kaiser, and Illia Polosukhin. 2017. Attention is all you need. In *Advances in Neural Information Processing Systems 30: Annual Conference on Neural Information Processing Systems 2017, December 4-9, 2017, Long Beach, CA, USA*, pages 5998–6008.

Changhan Wang, Anne Wu, and Juan Pino. 2020. Covost 2: A massively multilingual speech-to-text translation corpus.

Minghan Wang, Yuxia Wang, Chang Su, Jiaxin Guo, Yingtao Zhang, Yujia Liu, Min Zhang, Shimin Tao, Xingshan Zeng, Liangyou Li, Hao Yang, and Ying Qin. 2021. The hw-tsc's offline speech translation systems for IWSLT 2021 evaluation. *CoRR*, abs/2108.03845.

Weiyue Wang, Jan-Thorsten Peter, Hendrik Rosendahl, and Hermann Ney. 2016. Character: Translation edit rate on character level. In *Proceedings of the First Conference on Machine Translation, WMT 2016, colocated with ACL 2016, August 11-12, Berlin, Germany*, pages 505–510. The Association for Computer Linguistics.

Daimeng Wei, Zongyao Li, Zhanglin Wu, Zhengzhe Yu, Xiaoyu Chen, Hengchao Shang, Jiaxin Guo, Minghan Wang, Lizhi Lei, Min Zhang, Hao Yang, and Ying Qin. 2021. Hw-tsc's participation in the WMT 2021 news translation shared task. In *Proceedings of the Sixth Conference on Machine Translation, WMT@EMNLP 2021, Online Event, November 10-11, 2021*, pages 225–231. Association for Computational Linguistics.

Lei Yu, Laurent Sartran, Wojciech Stokowiec, Wang Ling, Lingpeng Kong, Phil Blunsom, and Chris Dyer. 2020. Better document-level machine translation with bayes' rule. *Trans. Assoc. Comput. Linguistics*, 8:346–360.

Binbin Zhang, Di Wu, Zhuoyuan Yao, Xiong Wang, Fan Yu, Chao Yang, Liyong Guo, Yaguang Hu, Lei Xie, and Xin Lei. 2020. Unified streaming and non-streaming two-pass end-to-end model for speech recognition. *CoRR*, abs/2012.05481.

The HW-TSC's Simultaneous Speech Translation System for IWSLT 2022 Evaluation

Minghan Wang[1], Jiaxin Guo[1], Yinglu Li[1], Xiaosong Qiao[1], Yuxia Wang[2], Zongyao Li[1], Chang Su[1], Yimeng Chen[1], Min Zhang[1], Shimin Tao[1], Hao Yang[1], Ying Qin[1]

[1]Huawei Translation Services Center, Beijing, China

[2]The University of Melbourne, Melbourne, Australia

{wangminghan,guojiaxin1,liyinglu,qiaoxiaosong,lizongyao,suchang8,chenyimeng,zhangmin186,taoshimin,yanghao30,qinying}@huawei.com

yuxiaw@student.unimelb.edu.au

Abstract

This paper presents our work in the participation of IWSLT 2022 simultaneous speech translation evaluation. For the track of text-to-text (T2T), we participate in three language pairs and build wait-k based simultaneous MT (SimulMT) model for the task. The model was pretrained on WMT21 news corpora, and was further improved with in-domain fine-tuning and self-training. For the speech-to-text (S2T) track, we designed both cascade and end-to-end form in three language pairs. The cascade system is composed of a chunking-based streaming ASR model and the SimulMT model used in the T2T track. The end-to-end system is a simultaneous speech translation (SimulST) model based on wait-k strategy, which is directly trained on a synthetic corpus produced by translating all texts of ASR corpora into specific target language with an offline MT model. It also contains a heuristic sentence breaking strategy, preventing it from finishing the translation before the the end of the speech. We evaluate our systems on the MUST-C tst-COMMON dataset and show that the end-to-end system is competitive to the cascade one. Meanwhile, we also demonstrate that the SimulMT model can be efficiently optimized by these approaches, resulting in the improvements of 1-2 BLEU points.

1 Introduction

Simultaneous speech/text translation (SimulST/SimulMT) applications are widely demanded in international communication scenarios such as conferences or live streaming.

From the perspective of system architecture, recent works on SimulST can be classified into cascade and end-to-end forms. Cascade systems are often composed of a streaming Automatic Speech Recognition (ASR) module and a steaming text-to-text machine translation module (MT). It might also contains other correction modules. The integration of these modules can be challenging, but the training of each can be beneficial from sufficient data resources. End-to-end approach is also a choice for SimulST, where translations can be directly generated from a unified model with the speech inputs, but bilingual speech translation datasets are still scarce resources.

From the perspective of simultaneous strategy, there is a fixed strategy which is represented by wait-k (Ma et al., 2019) and a flexible strategy such as monotonic attention (Arivazhagan et al., 2019). The fixed strategy is easier to implement but with inferior performance and the flexible one is more robust to the speed of speech but can be non-trivial in the implementation and training. Re-translation is also a strategy proposed recently for SimulMT system, which benefits from pre-trained MT models but often encounters with flicker (Arivazhagan et al., 2020; Sen et al., 2021).

The IWSLT 2022 SimulST shared task (Anastasopoulos et al., 2022) aims to provide a platform for participants to evaluate their approaches on both quality and latency. In this year, there are two sub-tracks, i.e. speech-to-text (S2T) and text-to-text (T2T), and three language directions including En-Zh, En-De and En-Ja in the evaluation. All submitted systems will be evaluated with the SimulEval (Ma et al., 2020a) tool, where BLEU (Papineni et al., 2002) and Average Lagging (AL) (Ma et al., 2020a) are used as metrics for ranking. Meanwhile, systems will be classified into three latency regimes (low, medium, high) with their AL, which are determined differently by the language pairs. The SimulEval formulates the simultaneous translation as a process where an agent should take "READ" or "WRITE" actions to control the progress of translation. A "READ" action allows the agent to get the latest source segments from the server. A "WRITE" action enables the agent to make prediction and send generated tokens back to server for scoring. Participants are required to implement their approaches under this framework.

Proceedings of the 19th International Conference on Spoken Language Translation (IWSLT 2022), pages 247 - 254
May 26-27, 2022

Dataset	Number of Utterance	Duration (hrs)
Librispeech	281,241	960.85
MuST-C	340,421	590.67
IWSLT	170,229	254.41
CoVoST	1362,422	1802.52
TEDLIUM3	268,214	453.42

Table 1: Data statistics of our ASR corpora

Language	WMT Bilingual	In-domain Text
En-De	79M	459K
En-Zh	96M	590K
En-Ja	42M	552K

Table 2: Data statistics of our MT corpora

In this paper, we present our work on the participation of all language directions for both S2T and T2T sub-tasks. For the T2T task, we start by modeling with the original wait-k model and optimizing it with in-domain fine-tuning and self-training (Gaido et al., 2020), resulting in large improvements on their performance. We experiment both cascade and end-to-end systems for the S2T task and find that the end-to-end one is quite competitive especially on the latency metric.

2 Method

2.1 Data Preparation & Pre-Processing

ASR Corpora We adopt exactly same data pre-processing pipeline to our offline task submission. Briefly, we combine 5 ASR (LibriSpeech(Panayotov et al., 2015), MuST-C V2 (Cattoni et al., 2021), CoVoST (Wang et al., 2020), TED-LIUM 3 (Hernandez et al., 2018) and IWSLT official dataset) corpora and perform strict cleansing based on absolute frame length (within 50 to 3000), number of tokens (within 1 to 150) and the speed of speech (within $\mu(\tau) \pm 4 \times \sigma(\tau)$, where $\tau = \frac{\text{\# frames}}{\text{\# tokens}}$) for all training utterances. There are basically 1% of noisy samples being filtered out.

MT corpora We follow the pipeline in (Wei et al., 2021) to pre-process the WMT 21 news corpora as well as the in-domain corpora (mixture of MUST-C and IWSLT). Statistics of our MT corpora are shown in Table 2.

2.2 ASR model

We adopt the U2 (Zhang et al., 2020) as the ASR module in our cascade system. U2, a framework that can be applied on standard Transformer (Vaswani et al., 2017) or Conformer (Gulati et al., 2020) architectures, is able to perform both streaming and non-streaming ASR. The major difference between U2 and other offline autoregressive ASR models is that it supports streaming with the help of the dynamic chunk training and decodes with a CTC decoder on the top of the encoder. The dynamic chunk training is achieved by dynamically applying a causal mask with different chunk size at the self-attention layer in the encoder. It is similar to the self-attention of an autoregressive decoder, but allowing the hidden representation to condition on some look-ahead contexts within the chunk. During inference, since the encoder hidden states is monotonically encoded chunk by chunk, the argmax decoding of CTC makes sure that tokens decoded in previous chunks are fixed, which successfully achieves streaming. Besides the CTC decoder, U2 also preserves the standard autoregressive (AR) Transformer decoder, and can be jointly trained with the CTC decoder to improve the stability of training. Originally, the AR decoder can be used to re-score CTC generated texts if prefix beam search is used to propose multiple candidates. However, we don't use the re-scoring in our system.

Since the decoding of arbitrary size of the chunk is learned with the dynamic chunk training, the latency of U2 can be freely determined by the chunk size used in the inference. The chunk size is also directly correlated to the performance, as it defines the volume of look-ahead contexts used in the current chunk.

2.3 Text to Text Model

Our T2T models are used in the T2T track and also as the translation module in the cascade system. It is a standard Transformer model with the wait-k strategy (Ma et al., 2019) for simultaneous decoding. For each language pair, we pre-train the wait-k T2T model on the WMT 2021 news corpora following similar settings as (Wei et al., 2021) to acquire the model $\mathcal{M}_1$. Then, we fine-tune it on the mixture of MuST-C and IWSLT corpora denoted as $\mathcal{C}_{\text{ind}}$, and obtain the domain adapted model $\mathcal{M}_2$. Although the domain transferring contributes some improvements, we find that it is not able to solve a key problem. Since the simultaneous decoding is only conditioned on partially observed context, there is a big gap between the training of offline MT models and SimulMT models, in which the re-ordered translations from unseen context can be significantly difficult for SimulMT models to learn.

To mitigate this problem, we propose to use self-training (Liu et al., 2021; Kim and Rush, 2016). Firstly, we translate the in-domain corpora $\mathcal{C}_{\text{ind}}$ with $\mathcal{M}_2$ and obtain $\mathcal{C}_{\text{ind}}'$, then, we fine-tune $\mathcal{M}_2$ on the mixture of $\mathcal{C}_{\text{ind}}$ and $\mathcal{C}_{\text{ind}}'$ and obtain $\mathcal{M}_3$. In this way, the self-distilled translations are more monotonic and easier to learn.

2.4 Cascade Speech to Text Model

Algorithm 1 Decoding of Cascade System

Require: ASR, T2T, chunk size,k: $\phi, \mathcal{M}, N_c, k$
  Initialize: Speech buffer $S \leftarrow \{\}$
  Initialize: ASR buffer $A \leftarrow \{\}$
  Initialize: MT buffer $H \leftarrow \{\}$
  Initialize: Frame position $p \leftarrow 0$
  Initialize: MT Finish writing chunk $e \leftarrow$ true
  while w is not </s> **do**
    if $|S| - p < N_c$ and e and not finish reading **then**
      READ next input s
      $S \leftarrow S \cup \{s\}$
    else
      $A \leftarrow \phi(S)$: decode all texts with ASR
      $p \leftarrow |S|$: move frame position
      if $|A| - |H| \geq k$ **then**
        decode with MT: $w \leftarrow \mathcal{M}(A)$
        $H \leftarrow H \cup \{w\}$
        $e \leftarrow (|A| - |H| < k)$
        WRITE w
      end if
    end if
  end while

Our cascade system is the integration of U2 and wait-k T2T model. When evaluating with SimulEval, U2 makes decisions mainly based on whether the input stream can fill a chunk, if not, it directly calls READ, otherwise, it transcribes audio inputs into English texts, and passes the entire sequence to the T2T model. The T2T model takes the output of U2 as inputs, and determines whether to read more based on the length difference between source and target sequence compared to k. Note that since U2 may decode several tokens in the latest chunk at once, we need to distinguish the read action of T2T model and ASR model. More specifically, when tokens decoded in the latest chunk from U2 exceeds the length difference of k for the T2T model, we need to let the T2T model decode for several steps instead of using the read action outputs by T2T model to read more audio frames, this will significantly increase the latency. Therefore, we introduce a flag e, representing whether the T2T model finishes its decoding process for all newly input tokens from current chunk. Algorithm 1 and Figure 1 describes the detailed process.

2.5 End-to-end Speech to Text Model

Besides the cascade system, we also explored the end-to-end (E2E) system. A key disadvantage to train an E2E system comes from the lack of large scale speech translation corpora. Therefore, we use the pre-trained MT model (trained on WMT21 News corpora) to create the knowledge distilled data (Kim and Rush, 2016) by translating all ASR corpora into required language, which significantly increases the scale of the training set.

There are two reasons that we use an offline MT model instead of our T2T model to generate the KD data. 1) the T2T model has lower performance compared to the offline model which may further limit the performance upper bound of the student model. 2) Decoding with T2T model is quite slower than the offline MT model.

For the E2E S2T model, we use the Conv-Transformer (Inaguma et al., 2020) with wait-k strategy of different k for each language. More specifically, we adopt similar configurations in (Ma et al., 2020b), where a pre-decision module is used to handle the large length gap between speech frames and target sentence, so that the wait-k algorithm can work properly with enough source information. Here we use the fixed pre-decision policy by pooling frames into a summarized feature vector for the wait-k decision every fixed number of frames (7 frames for all three models in our experiments).

During the evaluation with SimulEval, we found that E2E S2T model can easily predict the "</s>" when there is a silence interval in the speech. Although fed with more source inputs or applied with EOS penalty, the model is still incapable of translating samples into multiple sentences.

We suspect that the model is only trained on properly segmented utterances containing scarce samples with more than one sentence, but evaluated on samples with multiple sentences. This often causes the agent to send an incomplete translation to the server. To this end, we design a simple but efficient sentence breaking strategy to prevent the

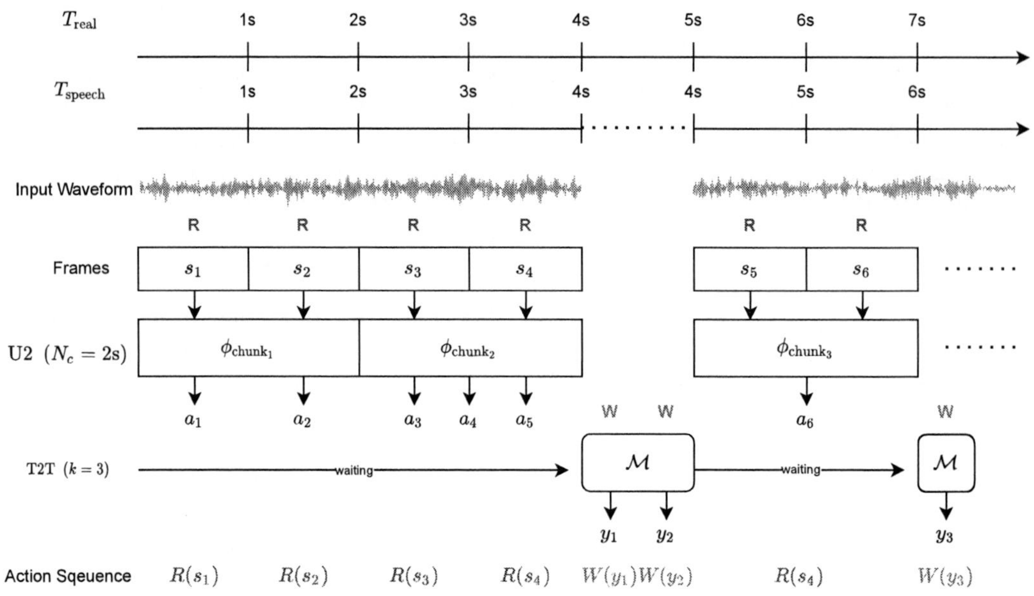

Figure 1: This figure presents an example of decoding with our cascade system, in which the the chunk size of U2 is set equivalent to 2s, the k for the wait-k T2T is set to 3. We plot the timeline of the real wall time and the speech time for a more cleared description. To present the collaboration of two models, we assume that decoding with U2 needs no time but decoding with wait-k T2T requires 0.5s per token.

agent from early stopping. In detail, when the decoder predict "</s>" as the next token, we check if the agent finishes reading source inputs. If it does, the "</s>" is the true ending of the speech, otherwise, it will be used as an ending of the sub-sentence, meaning that the "</s>" won't be sent back to the server, and the agent should keep translating until the entire speech is processed. The ending of a sub-sentence will also be used to clean the source input buffer and target context buffer, which means each sub-sentence is translated independently by the agent. We find this approach may in some extent introduce more latency since for each sub-sentence, the agent needs re-wait-k steps to start the generation, however, it is quite helpful to improve the performance on samples that might be mis-segmented with the original approach.

2.6 Domain Controlled Generation

As mentioned in section 2.1, we combine different corpora with different data source to create the united dataset, in which the domain and text style can be various. Directly training the model on the mixture of them can be harmful to the performance since some of these differences can't be easily captured from the speech inputs, so they should be considered as prior knowledge. Therefore, we reuse the strategy from our last year's work (Wang et al., 2021) by providing a domain tag as a known condition to control the generation style. This strategy is used in our E2E S2T model and ASR model. For the S2T model, we add the domain tag as the first token input to the decoder. For the ASR model, since we only use the CTC decoding, domain information needs to be provided at the encoder side. Therefore, we first encode the domain tag with the word embedding layer of the decoder to acquire its representation vector, then, we perform an element-wise sum with the down-sampled input features before feeding to encoder attention layers.

Since the test sets have similar distribution with MuST-C corpora in previous years, we control the model to generate MuST-C alike text by using the domain tag "<MC>" during the inference process.

3 Experiments

We conduct experiments on three types of systems including T2T, cascade S2T and E2E S2T. All systems are evaluated on the MuST-C tst-COMMON dataset for all three languages.

3.1 Setup

We adopt same configuration recipe to our offline submission on the training of the U2 model,

Language	k	Quality BLEU	Latency AL	AL_CA	AP	AP_CA	DAL	DAL_CA
En-De	k=3	24.98	2.66	-	0.66	-	4.14	-
	k=6	31.50	5.58	-	0.78	-	6.53	-
	k=15	33.38	11.12	-	0.93	-	11.87	-
En-Ja	k=6	8.55	1.74	-	0.67	-	5.70	-
	k=10	14.53	6.70	-	0.85	-	8.53	-
	k=14	14.26	9.75	-	0.92	-	10.95	-
En-Zh	k=6	22.53	2.93	-	0.71	-	5.40	-
	k=10	26.45	6.78	-	0.85	-	8.29	-
	k=14	27.54	9.53	-	0.92	-	10.60	-

Table 3: This table shows the results of our T2T models, where AL is computed with number of tokens.

Language	k	Quality BLEU	Latency AL	AL_CA	AP	AP_CA	DAL	DAL_CA
En-De	k=3	18.56	1959.58	2672.29	0.79	1.02	2411.61	3186.99
	k=6	23.90	2608.47	3490.75	0.87	1.18	3067.46	4110.86
	k=15	24.78	4020.55	5116.26	0.96	1.32	4312.52	5582.31
En-Ja	k=6	7.28	2215.07	2555.88	0.80	0.92	2620.34	2852.7
	k=10	12.16	2867.81	3262.79	0.92	1.06	3343.08	3675.45
	k=14	11.57	3365.65	3764.64	0.95	1.09	3811.56	4142.38
En-Zh	k=6	18.59	2119.71	2468.9	0.83	0.95	2603.03	2837.85
	k=10	22.50	2838.8	3207.05	0.92	1.05	3292.46	3573.82
	k=14	23.61	3424.94	3780.95	0.95	1.09	3782.05	4065.2

Table 4: This table shows the results of our cascade S2T models, where AL is computed with milliseconds.

where 80 dimensional Mel-Filter bank features are extracted from raw waveform, and being augmented with speed perturbation (Ko et al., 2015) and spectral augmentation (Park et al., 2019). The model is trained with the hyper-parameters ($n_{(encoder+decoder)\_layers}$ = 12 + 3, n_{heads} = 8, d_{hidden} = 512, d_{FFN} = 2048, $n_{\text{sub sampling}}$=4) for 50 epochs on 8 V100 GPUs. All ASR texts are tokenized with SPM (Kudo and Richardson, 2018) with the vocab size set as 20000.

For the T2T model, we train three models with different k for each language, where k=(3,6,15) for En-De, k=(6,10,14) for En-Zh, k=(6,10,14) for En-Ja. All of them are trained for 40 epochs with similar hyper-parameters ($n_{(encoder+decoder)\_layers}$ = 16 + 4, n_{heads} = 8, d_{hidden} = 512, d_{FFN} = 2048) while pre-training and 10 epochs for fine-tuning and self-training. For En-De and En-Ja, we use SPM for tokenization with vocab size set to 32k, and subword-nmt for En-Zh with vocab size set to 30k. Note that the vocabularies for T2T models are different from that for the ASR model, meaning that the outputs of ASR model in the cascade system need to be re-tokenized for T2T models.

Three S2T models are trained for each language with k=7 for En-De, k=14 for En-Zh and En-Ja. The hyper-parameters are: ($n_{(encoder+decoder)\_layers}$ = 12 + 6, n_{heads} = 8, d_{hidden} = 512, d_{FFN} = 2048) for all models. We train them for 50 epochs on the knowledge distilled dataset.

3.2 Results

T2T Table 3 shows the results of all T2T models, which are evaluated with the SimulEval with the oracle English texts as source inputs. We can see that for all language pairs, a large improvements can be obtained from low latency to medium latency by increasing k from 3 to 6 (En-De) or from 6 to 10 (En-Zh/Ja), but when increasing the latency

Language	k	Quality BLEU	Latency AL	AL_CA	AP	AP_CA	DAL	DAL_CA
En-De	k=7	22.13	2374.54	2831.08	0.86	0.99	2523.52	2990
En-Ja	k=14	12.82	1848.46	2369.75	0.94	1.09	3374.76	3796.14
En-Zh	k=14	20.38	1753.37	2240.23	0.94	1.09	3341.84	3762.65

Table 5: This table shows the results of our end-to-end S2T models, where AL is computed with milliseconds.

from medium to high, the profit is not that significant, demonstrating that the upper bound of wait-k models can be easily reached even with larger k.

Cascade S2T Table 4 presents result of our cascade S2T models, evaluated with the SimulEval by using utterance speech as inputs. Compared with the oracle inputs of T2T model, the performance of cascade S2T models often degrades 2-4 BLEU points when using the same T2T model due to the error propagation comes from the ASR model. We also find that the latency of our cascade systems are quite large although with relatively low k value. This can be explained from the example in Figure 1 where the wait-k model has to wait until the U2 reads 4 times and completes the decoding of chunk 2 (output 3 tokens), since the wait-k model can only decode when the the length difference satisfies the criteria of k. Unfortunately, this eventually increases the delay of y_1 and y_2 when computing the AL.

End-to-end S2T Table 5 are results from our E2E S2T models. Compared with cascade S2T models, the latency of E2E models can be better controlled since the latency offset caused by the collaboration of the ASR and T2T in the cascade system is not necessarily existed in the E2E model. Surprisingly, the performances of E2E models are also competitive to cascade systems, demonstrating that training the model on KD corpora is quite effective.

3.3 Ablation Study

To further explore the effect of fine-tuning and self-training on our T2T models, we present our experimental results on MuST-C tst-COMMON evaluated for the T2T task as described in Table 6. For all language pairs, in-domain fine-tuning brings 2+ BLEU points and self-training brings additional 1+ points.

Approach	En-De	En-Ja	En-Zh
Pre-training	29.21	11.21	23.14
+Fine-tuning	32.05	13.08	25.73
+Self-Training	33.38	14.26	27.54

Table 6: This table presents the improvements coming from applying each strategy during the training of T2T models. We only present results of models with k=15 for En-De, k=14 for En-Ja and En-Zh.

4 Conclusion

In this paper, we report our work in the IWSLT-2022 simultaneous speech translation evaluation. We explored 4 solutions with a cascade and end-to-end system on two sub-tracks and three language directions: 1) We evaluated the method of training a streaming ASR model U2 on the large scale mixed training corpora and inference with the domain controlled generation. 2) We explored the optimization of wait-k T2T models with self-training, and obtained positive results. 3) We tried to build a cascade S2T system by integrating the streaming ASR model with the wait-k T2T model, and compared it with our end-to-end approach. 4) We trained our end-to-end S2T model with knowledge distillation and found it to be competitive to our cascade approach.

In our future works, we will investigate more in terms of simultaneous strategies, efficient using of pretrained models, as well as better training schema with limited ST dataset.

References

Antonios Anastasopoulos, Luisa Bentivogli, Marcely Z. Boito, Ondřej Bojar, Roldano Cattoni, Anna Currey, Georgiana Dinu, Kevin Duh, Maha Elbayad, Marcello Federico, Christian Federmann, Hongyu Gong, Roman Grundkiewicz, Barry Haddow, Benjamin Hsu, Dávid Javorský, Věra Kloudová, Surafel M. Lakew, Xutai Ma, Prashant Mathur, Paul McNamee, Kenton Murray, Maria Nădejde, Satoshi Nakamura, Matteo Negri, Jan Niehues, Xing Niu, Juan Pino, Elizabeth Salesky, Jiatong Shi, Sebastian Stüker, Katsuhito Sudoh, Marco Turchi, Yogesh Virkar, Alex Waibel, Changhan Wang, and Shinji Watanabe. 2022. FINDINGS OF THE IWSLT 2022 EVALUATION CAMPAIGN. In *Proceedings of the 19th International Conference on Spoken Language Translation (IWSLT 2022)*, Dublin, Ireland. Association for Computational Linguistics.

Naveen Arivazhagan, Colin Cherry, Wolfgang Macherey, Chung-Cheng Chiu, Semih Yavuz, Ruoming Pang, Wei Li, and Colin Raffel. 2019. Monotonic infinite lookback attention for simultaneous machine translation. In *Proceedings of the 57th Conference of the Association for Computational Linguistics, ACL 2019, Florence, Italy, July 28- August 2, 2019, Volume 1: Long Papers*, pages 1313–1323. Association for Computational Linguistics.

Naveen Arivazhagan, Colin Cherry, Wolfgang Macherey, and George F. Foster. 2020. Retranslation versus streaming for simultaneous translation. In *Proceedings of the 17th International Conference on Spoken Language Translation, IWSLT 2020, Online, July 9 - 10, 2020*, pages 220–227. Association for Computational Linguistics.

Roldano Cattoni, Mattia Antonino Di Gangi, Luisa Bentivogli, Matteo Negri, and Marco Turchi. 2021. Must-c: A multilingual corpus for end-to-end speech translation. *Comput. Speech Lang.*, 66:101155.

Marco Gaido, Mattia Antonino Di Gangi, Matteo Negri, and Marco Turchi. 2020. End-to-end speech-translation with knowledge distillation: Fbk@iwslt2020. In *Proceedings of the 17th International Conference on Spoken Language Translation, IWSLT 2020, Online, July 9 - 10, 2020*, pages 80–88. Association for Computational Linguistics.

Anmol Gulati, James Qin, Chung-Cheng Chiu, Niki Parmar, Yu Zhang, Jiahui Yu, Wei Han, Shibo Wang, Zhengdong Zhang, Yonghui Wu, and Ruoming Pang. 2020. Conformer: Convolution-augmented transformer for speech recognition. In *Interspeech 2020, 21st Annual Conference of the International Speech Communication Association, Virtual Event, Shanghai, China, 25-29 October 2020*, pages 5036–5040. ISCA.

François Hernandez, Vincent Nguyen, Sahar Ghannay, Natalia A. Tomashenko, and Yannick Estève. 2018. TED-LIUM 3: Twice as much data and corpus repartition for experiments on speaker adaptation. In *Speech and Computer - 20th International Conference, SPECOM 2018, Leipzig, Germany, September 18-22, 2018, Proceedings*, volume 11096 of *Lecture Notes in Computer Science*, pages 198–208. Springer.

Hirofumi Inaguma, Shun Kiyono, Kevin Duh, Shigeki Karita, Nelson Yalta, Tomoki Hayashi, and Shinji Watanabe. 2020. Espnet-st: All-in-one speech translation toolkit. In *Proceedings of the 58th Annual Meeting of the Association for Computational Linguistics: System Demonstrations, ACL 2020, Online, July 5-10, 2020*, pages 302–311. Association for Computational Linguistics.

Yoon Kim and Alexander M. Rush. 2016. Sequence-level knowledge distillation. In *Proceedings of the 2016 Conference on Empirical Methods in Natural Language Processing, EMNLP 2016, Austin, Texas, USA, November 1-4, 2016*, pages 1317–1327. The Association for Computational Linguistics.

Tom Ko, Vijayaditya Peddinti, Daniel Povey, and Sanjeev Khudanpur. 2015. Audio augmentation for speech recognition. In *INTERSPEECH 2015, 16th Annual Conference of the International Speech Communication Association, Dresden, Germany, September 6-10, 2015*, pages 3586–3589. ISCA.

Taku Kudo and John Richardson. 2018. Sentencepiece: A simple and language independent subword tokenizer and detokenizer for neural text processing. In *Proceedings of the 2018 Conference on Empirical Methods in Natural Language Processing, EMNLP 2018: System Demonstrations, Brussels, Belgium, October 31 - November 4, 2018*, pages 66–71. Association for Computational Linguistics.

Dan Liu, Mengge Du, Xiaoxi Li, Yuchen Hu, and Lirong Dai. 2021. The USTC-NELSLIP systems for simultaneous speech translation task at IWSLT 2021. In *Proceedings of the 18th International Conference on Spoken Language Translation, IWSLT 2021, Bangkok, Thailand (online), August 5-6, 2021*, pages 30–38. Association for Computational Linguistics.

Mingbo Ma, Liang Huang, Hao Xiong, Renjie Zheng, Kaibo Liu, Baigong Zheng, Chuanqiang Zhang, Zhongjun He, Hairong Liu, Xing Li, Hua Wu, and Haifeng Wang. 2019. STACL: simultaneous translation with implicit anticipation and controllable latency using prefix-to-prefix framework. In *Proceedings of the 57th Conference of the Association for Computational Linguistics, ACL 2019, Florence, Italy, July 28- August 2, 2019, Volume 1: Long Papers*, pages 3025–3036. Association for Computational Linguistics.

Xutai Ma, Mohammad Javad Dousti, Changhan Wang, Jiatao Gu, and Juan Miguel Pino. 2020a. SIMULEVAL: an evaluation toolkit for simultaneous translation. In *Proceedings of the 2020 Conference on Empirical Methods in Natural Language Processing: System Demonstrations, EMNLP 2020 - Demos, Online, November 16-20, 2020*, pages 144–150. Association for Computational Linguistics.

Xutai Ma, Juan Miguel Pino, and Philipp Koehn. 2020b. Simulmt to simulst: Adapting simultaneous text translation to end-to-end simultaneous speech translation. In *Proceedings of the 1st Conference of the Asia-Pacific Chapter of the Association for Computational Linguistics and the 10th International Joint Conference on Natural Language Processing, AACL/IJCNLP 2020, Suzhou, China, December 4-7,*

2020, pages 582–587. Association for Computational Linguistics.

Vassil Panayotov, Guoguo Chen, Daniel Povey, and Sanjeev Khudanpur. 2015. Librispeech: An ASR corpus based on public domain audio books. In *2015 IEEE International Conference on Acoustics, Speech and Signal Processing, ICASSP 2015, South Brisbane, Queensland, Australia, April 19-24, 2015*, pages 5206–5210. IEEE.

Kishore Papineni, Salim Roukos, Todd Ward, and Wei-Jing Zhu. 2002. Bleu: a method for automatic evaluation of machine translation. In *Proceedings of the 40th Annual Meeting of the Association for Computational Linguistics, July 6-12, 2002, Philadelphia, PA, USA*, pages 311–318. ACL.

Daniel S. Park, William Chan, Yu Zhang, Chung-Cheng Chiu, Barret Zoph, Ekin D. Cubuk, and Quoc V. Le. 2019. Specaugment: A simple data augmentation method for automatic speech recognition. In *Interspeech 2019, 20th Annual Conference of the International Speech Communication Association, Graz, Austria, 15-19 September 2019*, pages 2613–2617. ISCA.

Sukanta Sen, Ulrich Germann, and Barry Haddow. 2021. The university of edinburgh's submission to the IWSLT21 simultaneous translation task. In *Proceedings of the 18th International Conference on Spoken Language Translation, IWSLT 2021, Bangkok, Thailand (online), August 5-6, 2021*, pages 46–51. Association for Computational Linguistics.

Ashish Vaswani, Noam Shazeer, Niki Parmar, Jakob Uszkoreit, Llion Jones, Aidan N. Gomez, Lukasz Kaiser, and Illia Polosukhin. 2017. Attention is all you need. In *Advances in Neural Information Processing Systems 30: Annual Conference on Neural Information Processing Systems 2017, December 4-9, 2017, Long Beach, CA, USA*, pages 5998–6008.

Changhan Wang, Anne Wu, and Juan Pino. 2020. Covost 2: A massively multilingual speech-to-text translation corpus.

Minghan Wang, Yuxia Wang, Chang Su, Jiaxin Guo, Yingtao Zhang, Yujia Liu, Min Zhang, Shimin Tao, Xingshan Zeng, Liangyou Li, Hao Yang, and Ying Qin. 2021. The hw-tsc's offline speech translation systems for IWSLT 2021 evaluation. *CoRR*, abs/2108.03845.

Daimeng Wei, Zongyao Li, Zhanglin Wu, Zhengzhe Yu, Xiaoyu Chen, Hengchao Shang, Jiaxin Guo, Minghan Wang, Lizhi Lei, Min Zhang, Hao Yang, and Ying Qin. 2021. Hw-tsc's participation in the WMT 2021 news translation shared task. In *Proceedings of the Sixth Conference on Machine Translation, WMT@EMNLP 2021, Online Event, November 10-11, 2021*, pages 225–231. Association for Computational Linguistics.

Binbin Zhang, Di Wu, Zhuoyuan Yao, Xiong Wang, Fan Yu, Chao Yang, Liyong Guo, Yaguang Hu, Lei Xie, and Xin Lei. 2020. Unified streaming and non-streaming two-pass end-to-end model for speech recognition. *CoRR*, abs/2012.05481.

MLLP-VRAIN UPV systems for the IWSLT 2022 Simultaneous Speech Translation and Speech-to-Speech Translation tasks

Javier Iranzo-Sánchez and **Javier Jorge** and **Alejandro Pérez-González-de-Martos**
Adrià Giménez and **Gonçal V. Garcés Díaz-Munío** and **Pau Baquero-Arnal**
Joan Albert Silvestre-Cerdà and **Jorge Civera** and **Albert Sanchis** and **Alfons Juan**
Machine Learning and Language Processing Group
Valencian Research Institute for Artificial Intelligence
Universitat Politècnica de València
Camí de Vera s/n, 46022 València, Spain

Abstract

This work describes the participation of the MLLP-VRAIN research group in the two shared tasks of the IWSLT 2022 conference: Simultaneous Speech Translation and Speech-to-Speech Translation. We present our streaming-ready ASR, MT and TTS systems for Speech Translation and Synthesis from English into German. Our submission combines these systems by means of a cascade approach paying special attention to data preparation and decoding for streaming inference.

1 Introduction

In this paper we describe the participation of the MLLP-VRAIN research group in the shared tasks of the *19th International Conference on Spoken Language Translation (IWSLT)*. We participated in two shared tasks: the *Simultaneous Speech Translation* and the (offline) *Speech-to-Speech Translation* tasks. The translation pair for both tasks was English to German. Our submission follows the cascade approach, with individual ASR, MT and TTS components. We use common ASR and MT models for both tasks, with additional latency restrictions for the Simultaneous task. In short, for the Simultaneous S2T task our system comprises a one-pass decoder ASR system based on the HMM-DNN approach with a chunk-based BLSTM AM combined with a Transformer LM, followed by a multi-k Transformer-based MT system. Regarding the S2S translation task, the aforementioned systems are followed by a non-autoregressive Conformer-based text-to-spectogram module, ending with a multi-band UnivNet neural vocoder to convert from the spectogram to the final audio wave.

This paper is structured as follows. Section 2 describes our participation in the *Simultaneous Speech Translation (ST)* task: the architecture and design decisions of the ASR and MT components in our cascade system, and the evaluation of the individual components as well as the speech translation system as a whole. Section 3 describes our participation in the *Speech-to-Speech (S2S) Translation* task, paying special attention to the speaker-adaptive TTS system specifically developed for this task. Our conclusions for the shared task are drawn in Section 4.

2 Simultaneous Speech Translation

2.1 ASR System Description

The acoustic model (AM) was trained using 3649 hours from resources listed in Table 4 in Appendix A. The evaluation sets were those provided with MuST-C v2.0: *tst-HE*, *tst-COMMON* and *dev*, for the English-German language pair. To train the AM we follow our training recipe for the DNN-HMM model, thoroughly described in Jorge et al. (2022). After this training pipeline we end up with a BLSTM network with 8 bidirectional hidden layers and 512 LSTM cells per layer and direction, with 10861 output labels (sub-phonetic units), trained with TensorFlow (Abadi et al., 2015). During inference, to enable streaming recognition, we perform a chunking-based processing of the input to carry out both feature normalization and feature scoring, as also described in Jorge et al. (2022).

Regarding the language model (LM), we trained a count-based model (n-gram) and a neural-based model (Transformer LM, TLM). For the former, we trained a 4-gram LM with KenLM (Heafield, 2011) using 1.3G sentences and 17G of running words (see Table 5 in Appendix A for a complete list of resources). For the latter, in order to alleviate the training time for this neural model, we selected a subset with the WIT3, MuST-C, and a random sample from the rest of the data up to 1G words. This TLM was trained using an adapted version of the FairSeq toolkit (Ott et al., 2019). The architecture is based on a 24-layer network with 768 units per layer, 4096-unit feed-forward neural

Proceedings of the 19th International Conference on Spoken Language Translation (IWSLT 2022), pages 255 - 264
May 26-27, 2022

network, 12 attention heads, and an embedding of 768 dimensions. These models were trained until convergence with batches limited to 512 tokens. Parameters were updated every 32 batches. During inference, Variance Regularization was applied to speed up the computation of TLM scores (Baquero-Arnal et al., 2020). Regarding the selected vocabulary, it comprises 300K words, with an OOV rate of about 0.3% on the selected dev sets. Lastly, we combined these acoustic and language models to perform a one-pass streaming recognition with our internal decoder implemented in TLK (del Agua et al., 2014).

2.2 MT System Description

The MT system must be ready to translate unpunctuated, lowercase ASR transcriptions. To prepare the MT system for this, the source side of the training data is pre-processed using the same approach as that applied to the LM training data (Iranzo-Sánchez et al., 2020a). Subword segmentation is based on the SentencePiece described in Kudo and Richardson (2018). Internally, 40k BPE operations are used, jointly learned on the source and target data, and the white-space sentence word separator symbol is used as a suffix to ease the decoding.

Most of our efforts this year have been focused on data preparation, selection and filtering. We have considered the following setups for training our models:

- *Baseline* data setup: For this configuration, we use all of the WMT20 news translation task data (Barrault et al., 2020), Europarl-ST (Iranzo-Sánchez et al., 2020b), MuST-C v2 (Di Gangi et al., 2019) and the TED corpus (Cettolo et al., 2012a), for a total of 48M sentence pairs used for training.
- *WMT21*: We use WMT21 news translation task (Akhbardeh et al., 2021) data instead of WMT20, for a total of 97M sentence pairs used for training.
- *OpenSubtitles*: Add the OpenSubtitles 2018 (Lison and Tiedemann, 2016) to the training data. This adds an additional 22M sentence pairs to the training data.
- *Bicleaner*: We use the Bicleaner and Bifixer tools (Ramírez-Sánchez et al., 2020) to filter the training data. We use the v1.4 pre-trained model published by the Bitextor team to score the sentences, and we do not run the LM component during filtering. We filter the sentences using two values for the filtering threshold, 0.3 and 0.5, so sentences with a score lower than the threshold are discarded before training.
- *Clean ups.*: In order to increase the proportion of clean data used by the model during training, we take those parallel corpora that contain document-level information (TED, news-commentary, Wikititles, rapid, Europarl, Europarl-ST and MuST-C), and upsample them by a factor of 5. Our expectation is that corpora which contain entire documents can be more reliable that sentence pairs extracted from other sources.
- *[ASR]-half*: Using this configuration, we prepend a new special token [ASR] to the source text sequence to be translated during inference. Additionally, during training, only half of the data is pre-processed following the ASR recipe, and we append the special [ASR] tag to it. The other half of the data keeps its original casing and punctuation. Ideally, this would allow the model to learn how to translate ASR output, while at the same time having access to some information about capitalization and casing during training. This setup is inspired in Zhao et al. (2021), but the authors used a different pre-processing schema.

All our models are based on the Transformer BIG architecture (Vaswani et al., 2017). We use the Adam optimizer, learning rate 5e-4 with an inverse square root decay, and train for a total of 1M batches of 16k tokens each. After training finishes, we carry out domain adaptation by finetuning on the MuST-C train data for 5000 updates or until the dev perplexity stops improving.

For training simultaneous MT models, we use the multi-k approach (Elbayad et al., 2020), because it achieves competitive results while at the same time provides us with the flexibility of adjusting the latency at inference time. By default, a random k is used for each batch, sampled between 1 and the length of the longest sentence included in the batch. We also tried training with a smaller k upper bound to check whether the quality improves in low-latency scenarios.

During decoding, we use beam search with a beam size of 6 for the offline model, whereas we

Table 1: PPL and WER figures for the *dev* and *tst-HE/CO(MMON)* sets with 4-gram model and TLM.

		dev	*tst-HE*	*tst-CO*
PPL	4-gram	117	117	106
	TLM	54	54	55
WER	4-gram	7.8	7.2	9.5
	TLM	5.8	5.3	7.3

Table 2: WER figures varying the window size (in ms) of the look-ahead context of the chunk-based BLSTM.

look-ahead window	250	500	1000	1500
dev	6.9	5.8	5.6	5.6
tst-HE	6.6	5.3	5.1	5.0
tst-COMMON	9.3	7.3	7.0	7.1

use speculative beam-search (Zheng et al., 2019) with a beam size of 4 for simultaneous models. Higher beam values significantly increased decoding costs for a negligible increase in quality. In order to speed-up decoding, we first compute how many w words we need to generate based on the wait-k policy. Then, we carry out speculative beam-search by generating hypothesis with a maximum length of $w \cdot a + b + 1$ subwords, where a and b are two hyperparameters optimized on the dev set. If this first search does not generate the w words we need, we carry out a second search with a maximum hypothesis length of 150 subwords.

2.3 ASR System Evaluation

First, we carried out a comparative evaluation in terms of perplexity (PPL) and Word Error Rate (WER) between the 4-gram model and the TLM on the MuST-C.v2 dev set *dev* and the test sets, *tst-HE* and *tst-COMMON*. Table 1 shows PPL and WER figures on dev and test sets having validated and fine-tuned hyperparameters on the dev set. It is worth noting how roughly halving perplexity involves a consistent WER reduction of about 23-25%.

Next, with the best setup from the previous experiment (using TLM) we performed another set of evaluations to explore the impact of the size of the window for the acoustic look-ahead context on WER. For this comparison, we considered values of 250, 500, 1000, and 1500 ms of future context for the chunk-based BLSTM. Table 2 illustrates the resulting WER when the look-ahead context is modified. As expected, providing more future context allows the model to deliver more accurate scores, reducing the WER. Indeed, increasing this context results in a WER reduction of about 20% the cost of increasing the latency from 250 to 1000 ms.

2.4 MT System Evaluation

As in the ASR system, we also use the MuST-C.v2 dev set in order to validate and fine-tune hyperparameters. Additionally, we report results on the MuST-C.v2 tst-COMMON set, as well as on the IWSLT 2015 and 2018 test sets, using the BLEU score (Papineni et al., 2002).

Table 3 shows BLEU figures of a conventional offline system and a range of simultaneous multi-k systems trained on the data setups described in Section 2.2. These results correspond to the fine-tuned models using the in-domain MuST-C data, which results in a consistent improvement across all training setup. For the sake of comparison on the Baseline data setup between the offline and simultaneous system, the simultaneous multi-k system was evaluated when running inference in offline mode ($k = 100$). The ranking of training data setups for multi-k systems with $k \in \{1, 3, 6, 15\}$ on inference time was the same.

As observed in Table 3, the unidirectional encoder used for training the multi-k system (system #2) results in a small quality degradation when compared with the offline model (system #1), similarly to what was observed in (Iranzo-Sánchez et al., 2022). Adding OpenSubtitles to the data (system #3) shows some improvements across the evaluation sets. The use of the *[ASR]-half* pre-processing scheme (system 4) shows a promising 1.7 BLEU increase on MuST-C tst-COMMON, but it does not convey to other evaluation sets. Other tentative configurations using the *[ASR]-half* approach did not improve over non-*[ASR]-half* results.

With regards to systems using WMT21 data (systems #5-7), it is surprising to see that the additional data does not seem to improve results across the board, even if we use filtering, when compared to the baseline data configuration. Additional experiments are needed on this regard, but a possible explanation is that the smaller baseline dataset is more in-domain than the larger WMT21 set, perhaps due to the speech corpora being a bigger portion of the training data.

Based on our intuition behind the results provided by systems #5-7, we ran an additional experiment combining the WMT21 with data upsampling

Table 3: BLEU scores of offline and multi-k MT systems for different training data setups on MuST-C.v2 *dev* and *tst*-CO(MMON), and IWSLT 2015 and 2018 test sets.

#	System	*dev*	*tst*-CO	tst2015	tst2018
1	Offline Baseline	33.0	33.8	33.4	31.6
2	Multi-k Baseline	32.2	32.8	32.3	30.7
3	+ OpenSubtitles	**32.3**	33.3	**33.2**	30.7
4	+ [ASR]-half	31.4	**34.5**	30.4	28.8
5	+ WMT21	31.9	32.6	32.5	30.2
6	+ Bicleaner (tr=0.3)	31.7	32.6	32.5	31.0
7	+ Bicleaner (tr=0.5)	31.8	32.3	32.8	30.9
8	+ Clean ups. & OpenSubtitles	32.2	32.9	32.6	**31.1**

and the OpenSubtitles2018 corpora (system #8, see Section 2.2). This configuration obtained better results than systems #4-7, and even outperformed system #2 on tst2018. Based on the results on the dev set, we selected systems #3 and #8 for further experimentation.

The default implementation of the multi-k system samples a random k each batch, with a maximum k value of the longest sentence in the batch. In our case, we discard before training all sentences longer than 100 words. This means that the model trains across multiple latency regimes, and in some batches is actually training with the same restrictions as an offline model. Thus, it might be beneficial to train with a smaller upper value of k, in order to encourage better translation quality for low-latency regimes. We trained a new system #3 with a maximum k of 20 subwords and study its trade-off between latency measured as Average Lagging (AL) (Ma et al., 2019) and BLEU compared with the conventional system #3 (maximum k=100) in Figure 1. As shown, no performance improvement at low latency when training with a smaller k threshold is observed, and therefore we decided not to use the multi-k system trained with maximum $k = 20$.

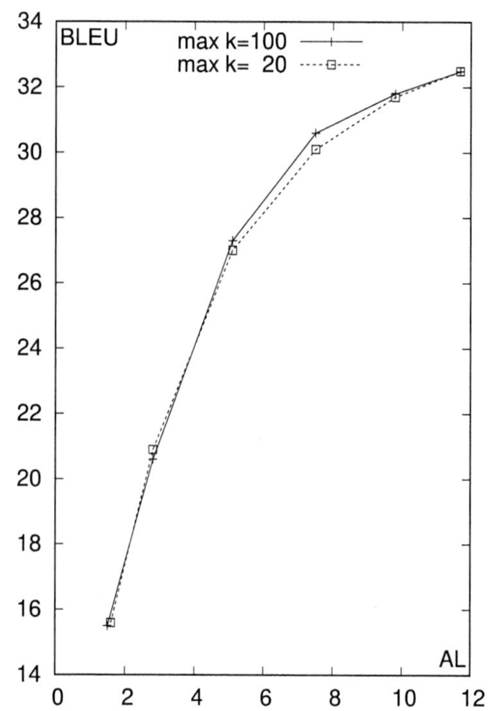

Figure 1: BLEU versus AL for maximum values of $k \in \{20, 100\}$ for multi-k system #3 measured on MuST-C.v2 *tst*-COMMON.

2.5 Simultaneous S2T System Evaluation

Based on the previously described ASR and MT systems, we now move into optimizing the decoding hyper-parameters of the joint cascade system. For the ASR component, we optimized the pruning parameters, that is, the grammar scale factor, the beam and the number of active hypotheses at both sub-phonetic and word level, as well as the recombination limit and the look-ahead acoustic context. As described before all experiments were carried out using the TLM model, since no differences on computational AL were found between both language models. For the MT component, we optimized the inference time k, and the a and b hyperparameters of the speculative beam search.

The goal is to obtain the best hyperparameter combination that satisfies the AL thresholds defined in the simultaneous task, $1000, 2000$, and 4000. Our cascade systems operates approximately at Real-Time Factor of 0.5, so we first run a wide hyperparameter sweep using *tst*-HE, which is a smaller dataset than *tst*-COMMON. The results are shown in Figure 2.

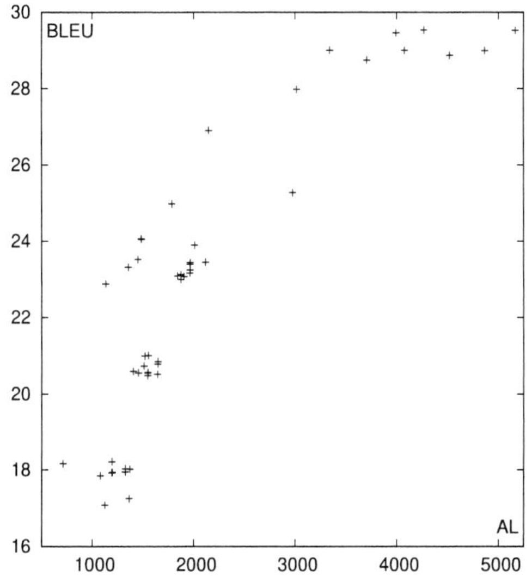

Figure 2: BLEU vs AL for different hyperparameter configurations of our simultaneous ST system measured on MuST-C.v2 *tst*-HE.

It can be observed how the choice of hyperparameters is critical in order to maximize the quality of the system, as there are differences of up to 4 BLEU points between systems that have the same latency. We found it significantly hard to obtain a system with AL$\leq$ 1000, as our ASR decoder with a TLM takes a long time to consolidate hypothesis. We came up with a strategy in order to be able to submit a low-latency system, so that every time a new transcribed word is consolidated, we also send the unconsolidated part of the top scoring hypothesis to the MT system. Using this strategy, our hope is that if the unconsolidated hypothesis do not show a lot of variation, the latency of the cascade system can be significantly reduced in exchange for a small degradation of translation quality. We tested this strategy as well as our best performing systems (#3 and #8) on tst-COMMON, and report BLEU versus AL in Figure 3.

Figure 3 shows how we were able to stay below the AL$=$ 1000 threshold thanks to using the ASR unconsolidated hypothesis. Based on these results, our final submission to the shared task are shown in Figure 3 as filled points, with system #8 submitted as *System 1, Primary*, and system #3 submitted as *System 2, Contrastive*.

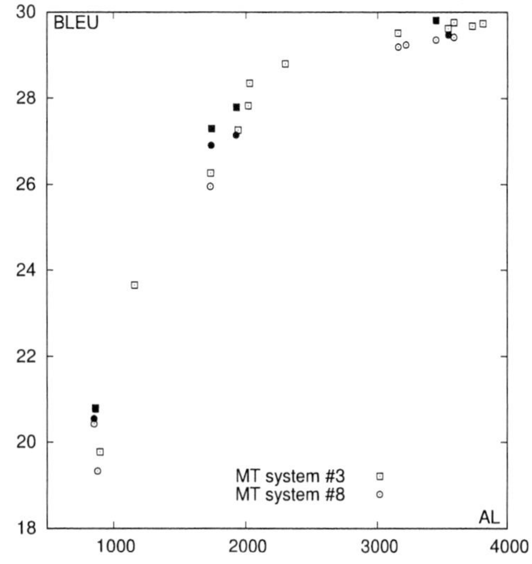

Figure 3: BLEU vs AL for different configurations of simultaneous ST systems measured on MuST-C.v2 tst-COMMON. Filled points were included in our submission to the shared task.

3 Speech-to-Speech Translation

In this section we describe our submission to the Speech-to-Speech translation track, in which we include a speaker-adaptive TTS module to our previously described cascaded Speech Translation system. Thus, we reuse the ASR and MT models developed for the Simultaneous Speech Translation task, though imposing a less restrictive pruning setup. This involves, in brief, more look-ahead context and a wider search space for the ASR system described in Section 2.1, and using the offline MT system instead of the simultaneous multi-k MT system referred to in Section 2.2. Therefore, the remaining of this section will describe the additional TTS module included to carry out the final text-to-audio conversion of the S2S pipeline.

3.1 TTS System Description

In the context of the S2S translation task, for many applications the TTS module should not only be able to produce high quality natural sounding synthetic speech in a predefined set of voices, but ideally also be capable of mimicking the voice characteristics of the original speaker in the target language (e.g. male or female). To that end, our proposed TTS model follows the transfer learning approach to zero-shot speaker adaptation or multi-speaker TTS (Doddipatla et al., 2017; Jia et al., 2018; Cooper et al., 2020; Casanova et al., 2021), where an auxiliary speaker encoder model trained on a speaker classification task is leveraged to compute speaker embeddings from reference utterances both during training and inference.

Our speaker encoder model follows the modified ResNet-34 residual network architecture (He et al., 2016) from Chung et al. (2018), which is being widely used for speaker recognition tasks with excellent results (Xie et al., 2019; Chung et al., 2020b). However, similar to Chung et al. (2020a) we halve the number of filters in each residual block with respect to the original ResNet-34 architecture to reduce computational costs and avoid over-fitting when trained on relatively small datasets. The model is trained on a speaker classification task on the TED-LIUM v3 dataset (Hernandez et al., 2018), which contains 452 hours of transcribed speech data from 2351 TED conference talks given by 2028 unique speakers. To reduce class imbalance, we limit the number of audio segments per speaker to 50. We trim leading and trailing silence, apply a pre-emphasis filter with a coefficient of 0.97 and extract 64-dim log-mel spectrograms from training samples. During training, we also perform on-the-fly audio data augmentation such as randomly adding Gaussian noise, reverberations, dynamic range compression and frequency masking in order to help generalization to different audio recording conditions. Mean and variance normalization is performed by adding an instance normalization layer to the spectrogram inputs. The model is trained to minimize the Angular Prototypical loss (Chung et al., 2020b), in which we set $M = 2$ where M is the number of samples per speaker in each mini-batch. We use the Adam optimizer with a fixed learning rate of 0.0005 and train the model for 100K steps using a mini-batch size of 300 samples (150 different speakers), each comprising 2.5 seconds.

Our TTS model follows the two-stage approach to end-to-end neural text-to-speech. It is comprised of a non-autoregressive Conformer-based *text-to-spectrogram* network and a *spectrogram-to-wave* multi-band UnivNet (Jang et al., 2021; Yang et al., 2020) neural vocoder. We extract phoneme durations by means of a forced-aligner auto-encoder model trained on the same data as in de Martos et al. (2021). The Conformer encoder and decoder blocks follow the modifications proposed in Liu et al. (2021). First, the Swish activation function is replaced with ReLU for better generalization, particularly on long sentences. Second, the depthwise convolution is placed before the self-attention module for faster convergence. Finally, the linear layers in feed-forward modules are replaced by convolution layers.

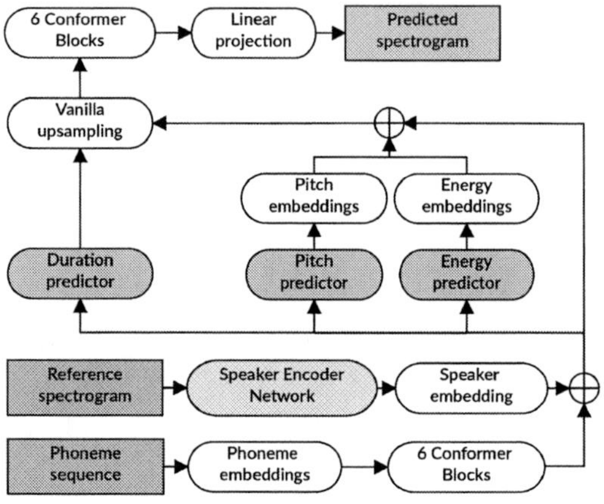

Figure 4: Speaker-adaptive Conformer text-to-spectrogram network architecture.

Figure 4 depicts the speaker-adaptive text-to-spectrogram network architecture. The encoder and decoder modules consist of 6 Conformer blocks with attention dimension 384 and a kernel size of 1536 for convolutional feed-forward modules. The speaker encoder model is used to extract 256-dim speaker embeddings which are linearly projected and added to the encoder hidden states. The variance adaptor modules (duration, pitch and energy predictors) follow the convolutional architecture in Ren et al. (2021) with 2, 5 and 2 layers, respectively. The pitch prediction is done similarly as in Łańcucki (2020), where frame-wise F_0 values are first converted to the logarithmic domain and averaged over every input symbol using phoneme durations. Then, predicted (ground truth during training) phoneme-level pitch values are projected and added to the encoder hidden states by means of a 1-D convolution.

The text-to-spectrogram model is trained on the LibriVoxDeEn dataset (Beilharz et al., 2020), comprising 547 hours (487 hours after silence trimming) of sentence-aligned audios from German audio books. We down-sample all audios to 16kHz and compute 100-bin log-mel spectrograms with Hann windowing, 50ms window length, 12.5ms hop size and 1024 point Fourier transform. Phoneme sequences are extracted from normalized text transcriptions using the eSpeak NG[1] tool. Frame-wise pitch (F_0) values are estimated using the WORLD vocoder toolkit (MORISE et al., 2016; Morise et al., 2009). The model is optimized to minimize a combination of the $\ell 1$ loss and the SSIM (Structural SIMilarity index measure) (Wang et al., 2004) between reference and predicted spectrograms. Additionally, auxiliary $\ell 1$ losses are used also for the duration, pitch and energy variance prediction modules between reference and predicted values. An auxiliary $\ell 1$ loss between standard deviation values of target and predicted pitch contours (F_0 values) is used to encourage the pitch predictor produce less flattened prosody as the result of training on a huge variety of speakers. We train the model using the Adam optimizer for 500K steps on a NVIDIA RTX 3090 GPU with a batch size of 12 and a learning rate of 0.0001 with a linear ramp up for the first 5000 steps.

Finally, a 4-band UnivNet vocoder is trained to generate 24kHz audios from 16kHz spectrograms. UnivNet is a recent GAN-based vocoder that has been shown to produce high quality speech of comparable quality to best performing GAN vocoders such as HiFi-GAN (Su et al., 2020) while bringing an improved inference speed of about $1.5\times$. The model is trained on the LibriVoxDeEn 16kHz ground truth spectrograms and 22kHz original audios (up-sampled to 24kHz for simplicity) with a batch size of 64 distributed along 4 GPUs for 1M steps. Then, the text-to-spectrogram model is used to compute ground truth aligned spectrograms using reference phoneme durations, pitch and energy values, and the vocoder model is fine-tuned on the predicted spectrograms for an additional 100K steps.

4 Conclusions

The MLLP-VRAIN research group has participated in the Simultaneous Speech Translation and Speech-to-Speech Translation tasks using our state-of-the art streaming-ready cascade systems. Under the cascade approach, each individual component has been described and evaluated, as well as the joint cascade system.

The results show that the cascade approach remains a flexible and powerful solution for ST tasks, yet at the same time there is a great deal of hyper-parameter optimization that needs to be carried out in order to properly integrate the different components. The use of unconsolidated ASR hypothesis has enabled very low-latency translation in exchange for a small decrease in quality. In terms of future work, we would like to further study the use of partial hypothesis by the MT system and other downstream components, as a means of improving the quality-latency tradeoff.

[1] http://espeak.sourceforge.net

Acknowledgements

The research leading to these results has received funding from the European Union's Horizon 2020 research and innovation programme under grant agreements no. 761758 (X5Gon) and 952215 (TAILOR), and Erasmus+ Education programme under grant agreement no. 20-226-093604-SCH (EXPERT); the Government of Spain's grant RTI2018-094879-B-I00 (Multisub) funded by MCIN/AEI/10.13039/501100011033 & "ERDF A way of making Europe", and FPU scholarships FPU18/04135; and the Generalitat Valenciana's research project Classroom Activity Recognition (ref. PROMETEO/2019/111).

References

News Crawl corpus (WMT workshop) 2015. http://www.statmt.org/wmt15/translation-task.html.

Martín Abadi et al. 2015. TensorFlow: Large-scale machine learning on heterogeneous systems.

Farhad Akhbardeh, Arkady Arkhangorodsky, Magdalena Biesialska, Ondrej Bojar, Rajen Chatterjee, Vishrav Chaudhary, Marta R. Costa-jussà, Cristina España-Bonet, Angela Fan, Christian Federmann, Markus Freitag, Yvette Graham, Roman Grundkiewicz, Barry Haddow, Leonie Harter, Kenneth Heafield, Christopher Homan, Matthias Huck, Kwabena Amponsah-Kaakyire, Jungo Kasai, Daniel Khashabi, Kevin Knight, Tom Kocmi, Philipp Koehn, Nicholas Lourie, Christof Monz, Makoto Morishita, Masaaki Nagata, Ajay Nagesh, Toshiaki Nakazawa, Matteo Negri, Santanu Pal, Allahsera Auguste Tapo, Marco Turchi, Valentin Vydrin, and Marcos Zampieri. 2021. Findings of the 2021 conference on machine translation (WMT21). In *Proc of WMT*, pages 1–88.

Pau Baquero-Arnal, Javier Jorge, Adrià Giménez, Joan Albert Silvestre-Cerdà, Javier Iranzo-Sánchez, Alberto Sanchís, Jorge Civera Saiz, and Alfons Juan-Císcar. 2020. Improved Hybrid Streaming ASR with Transformer Language Models. In *Proc. of Interspeech*, pages 2127–2131.

Loïc Barrault, Ondrej Bojar, Fethi Bougares, Rajen Chatterjee, Marta R. Costa-jussà, Christian Federmann, Mark Fishel, Alexander Fraser, Yvette Graham, Paco Guzman, Barry Haddow, Matthias Huck, Antonio Jimeno-Yepes, Philipp Koehn, André Martins, Makoto Morishita, Christof Monz, Masaaki Nagata, Toshiaki Nakazawa, and Matteo Negri, editors. 2020. *Proceedings of the Fifth Conference on Machine Translation*.

Benjamin Beilharz, Xin Sun, Sariya Karimova, and Stefan Riezler. 2020. Librivoxdeen: A corpus for german-to-english speech translation and speech recognition. In *Proc. of LREC*.

Edresson Casanova, Christopher Shulby, Eren Gölge, Nicolas Michael Müller, Frederico Santos de Oliveira, Arnaldo Candido Jr., Anderson da Silva Soares, Sandra Maria Aluisio, and Moacir Antonelli Ponti. 2021. SC-GlowTTS: An Efficient Zero-Shot Multi-Speaker Text-To-Speech Model. In *Proc. of Interspeech*, pages 3645–3649.

Mauro Cettolo, Christian Girardi, and Marcello Federico. 2012a. WIT^3: Web Inventory of Transcribed and Translated Talks. In *Proc. of EAMT*, pages 261–268.

Mauro Cettolo, Christian Girardi, and Marcello Federico. 2012b. Wit3: Web inventory of transcribed and translated talks. In *Proc. of EAMT*, pages 261–268.

Joon Son Chung, Jaesung Huh, and Seongkyu Mun. 2020a. Delving into VoxCeleb: Environment Invariant Speaker Recognition. In *Proc. Odyssey 2020 The Speaker and Language Recognition Workshop*, pages 349–356.

Joon Son Chung, Jaesung Huh, Seongkyu Mun, Minjae Lee, Hee-Soo Heo, Soyeon Choe, Chiheon Ham, Sunghwan Jung, Bong-Jin Lee, and Icksang Han. 2020b. In Defence of Metric Learning for Speaker Recognition. In *Proc. of Interspeech*, pages 2977–2981.

Joon Son Chung, Arsha Nagrani, and Andrew Zisserman. 2018. VoxCeleb2: Deep Speaker Recognition. In *Proc. of Interspeech*, pages 1086–1090.

Erica Cooper, Jeff Lai, Yusuke Yasuda, Fuming Fang, Xin Wang, Nanxin Chen, and Junichi Yamagishi. 2020. Zero-shot multi-speaker text-to-speech with state-of-the-art neural speaker embeddings. In *Proc. of ICASSP*, pages 6184–6188.

Alejandro Pérez-González de Martos, Albert Sanchis, and Alfons Juan. 2021. Vrain-upv mllp's system for the blizzard challenge 2021. *arXiv preprint arXiv:2110.15792*.

M.A. del Agua et al. 2014. The translectures-UPV toolkit. In *Advances in Speech and Language Technologies for Iberian Languages*, pages 269–278.

Mattia A. Di Gangi, Roldano Cattoni, Luisa Bentivogli, Matteo Negri, and Marco Turchi. 2019. MuST-C: a Multilingual Speech Translation Corpus. In *Proc. of NAACL-HLT*, pages 2012–2017.

Rama Doddipatla, Norbert Braunschweiler, and Ranniery Maia. 2017. Speaker Adaptation in DNN-Based Speech Synthesis Using d-Vectors. In *Proc. of Interspeech*, pages 3404–3408.

Maha Elbayad, Laurent Besacier, and Jakob Verbeek. 2020. Efficient Wait-k Models for Simultaneous Machine Translation. In *Proc. of Interspeech*, pages 1461–1465.

Kaiming He, Xiangyu Zhang, Shaoqing Ren, and Jian Sun. 2016. Deep residual learning for image recognition. In *Proc. of CVPR*, pages 770–778.

Kenneth Heafield. 2011. Kenlm: Faster and smaller language model queries. In *Proc. of WMT*, page 187–197.

François Hernandez, Vincent Nguyen, Sahar Ghannay, Natalia Tomashenko, and Yannick Estève. 2018. Ted-lium 3: Twice as much data and corpus repartition for experiments on speaker adaptation. In *Speech and Computer*, pages 198–208.

Javier Iranzo-Sánchez, Jorge Civera, and Alfons Juan. 2022. From simultaneous to streaming machine translation by leveraging streaming history. *arXiv preprint arXiv:2203.02459*.

Javier Iranzo-Sánchez, Adrià Giménez, Joan Albert Silvestre-Cerdà, Pau Baquero, Jorge Civera, and Alfons Juan. 2020a. Direct Segmentation Models for Streaming Speech Translation. In *Proc. of EMNLP*, pages 2599–2611.

Javier Iranzo-Sánchez, Joan Albert Silvestre-Cerdà, Javier Jorge, Nahuel Roselló, Adrià Giménez, Albert Sanchis, Jorge Civera, and Alfons Juan. 2020b. Europarl-ST: A Multilingual Corpus For Speech Translation Of Parliamentary Debates. In *Proc. of ICASSP*, pages 8229–8233.

Won Jang, Dan Lim, Jaesam Yoon, Bongwan Kim, and Juntae Kim. 2021. UnivNet: A Neural Vocoder with Multi-Resolution Spectrogram Discriminators for High-Fidelity Waveform Generation. In *Proc. of Interspeech*, pages 2207–2211.

Ye Jia et al. 2018. Transfer Learning from Speaker Verification to Multispeaker Text-To-Speech Synthesis. In *Proc. of NIPS*, pages 4485–4495.

Javier Jorge, Adrià Giménez, Joan Albert Silvestre-Cerdà, Jorge Civera, Albert Sanchis, and Alfons Juan. 2022. Live streaming speech recognition using deep bidirectional lstm acoustic models and interpolated language models. *IEEE/ACM Transactions on Audio, Speech, and Language Processing*, 30:148–161.

Philipp Koehn. 2005. Europarl: A Parallel Corpus for Statistical Machine Translation. In *Proc. of MT Summit*, pages 79–86.

Taku Kudo and John Richardson. 2018. Sentencepiece: A simple and language independent subword tokenizer and detokenizer for neural text processing. In *Proc. of EMNLP: System Demonstrations*, pages 66–71.

Pierre Lison and Jörg Tiedemann. 2016. OpenSubtitles2016: Extracting large parallel corpora from movie and TV subtitles. In *Proc. of LREC*, pages 923–929.

Yanqing Liu, Zhihang Xu, Gang Wang, Kuan Chen, Bohan Li, Xu Tan, Jinzhu Li, Lei He, and Sheng Zhao. 2021. Delightfultts: The microsoft speech synthesis system for blizzard challenge 2021. *arXiv preprint arXiv:2110.12612*.

Mingbo Ma, Liang Huang, Hao Xiong, Renjie Zheng, Kaibo Liu, Baigong Zheng, Chuanqiang Zhang, Zhongjun He, Hairong Liu, Xing Li, Hua Wu, and Haifeng Wang. 2019. STACL: Simultaneous translation with implicit anticipation and controllable latency using prefix-to-prefix framework. In *Proc. of ACL*, pages 3025–3036. ACL.

Masanori Morise, Hideki Kawahara, and Haruhiro Katayose. 2009. Fast and reliable f0 estimation method based on the period extraction of vocal fold vibration of singing voice and speech. In *Audio Engineering Society Conference: 35th International Conference: Audio for Games*. Audio Engineering Society.

Masanori MORISE, Fumiya YOKOMORI, and Kenji OZAWA. 2016. World: A vocoder-based high-quality speech synthesis system for real-time applications. *IEICE Transactions on Information and Systems*, E99.D(7):1877–1884.

Mozilla. 2022. Commonvoice 6.1.

Myle Ott, Sergey Edunov, Alexei Baevski, Angela Fan, Sam Gross, Nathan Ng, David Grangier, and Michael Auli. 2019. fairseq: A fast, extensible toolkit for sequence modeling. In *Proc. of NAACL-HLT*, pages 48–53.

V. Panayotov et al. 2015. Librispeech: an ASR corpus based on public domain audio books. In *Proc. of ICASSP*, pages 5206–5210.

Kishore Papineni, Salim Roukos, Todd Ward, and Wei-Jing Zhu. 2002. Bleu: a Method for Automatic Evaluation of Machine Translation. In *Proc. of ACL*, pages 311–318.

Gema Ramírez-Sánchez, Jaume Zaragoza-Bernabeu, Marta Bañón, and Sergio Ortiz Rojas. 2020. Bifixer and bicleaner: two open-source tools to clean your parallel data. In *Proc. of EAMT*, pages 291–298.

Yi Ren, Chenxu Hu, Xu Tan, Tao Qin, Sheng Zhao, Zhou Zhao, and Tie-Yan Liu. 2021. Fastspeech 2: Fast and high-quality end-to-end text to speech. In *Proc. of ICLR*.

Ramon Sanabria, Ozan Caglayan, Shruti Palaskar, Desmond Elliott, Loïc Barrault, Lucia Specia, and Florian Metze. 2018. How2: a large-scale dataset for multimodal language understanding. In *Proceedings of the Workshop on Visually Grounded Interaction and Language (ViGIL)*. NeurIPS.

Holger Schwenk, Vishrav Chaudhary, Shuo Sun, Hongyu Gong, and Francisco Guzmán. 2021. Wiki-Matrix: Mining 135M parallel sentences in 1620 language pairs from Wikipedia. In *Proc. of EACL*, pages 1351–1361.

Jiaqi Su, Zeyu Jin, and A. Finkelstein. 2020. Hifi-gan: High-fidelity denoising and dereverberation based on speech deep features in adversarial networks. In *Proc. of Interspeech*.

Jörg Tiedemann. 2012. Parallel data, tools and interfaces in opus. In *Proc. of LREC*.

Ashish Vaswani, Noam Shazeer, Niki Parmar, Jakob Uszkoreit, Llion Jones, Aidan N. Gomez, Lukasz Kaiser, and Illia Polosukhin. 2017. Attention is all you need. In *Proc. of NIPS*, pages 5998–6008.

Zhou Wang, Alan Bovik, Hamid Sheikh, and Eero Simoncelli. 2004. Image quality assessment: From error visibility to structural similarity. *Image Processing, IEEE Transactions on*, 13:600 - 612.

Weidi Xie, Arsha Nagrani, Joon Son Chung, and Andrew Zisserman. 2019. Utterance-level aggregation for speaker recognition in the wild. In *Proc. of ICASSP*, pages 5791–5795.

Geng Yang et al. 2020. Multi-band MelGAN: Faster Waveform Generation for High-Quality Text-to-Speech. *arXiv preprint arXiv:2005.05106*.

Chengqi Zhao, Zhicheng Liu, Jian Tong, Tao Wang, Mingxuan Wang, Rong Ye, Qianqian Dong, Jun Cao, and Lei Li. 2021. The volctrans neural speech translation system for IWSLT 2021. In *Proc. of IWSLT*, pages 64–74.

Renjie Zheng, Mingbo Ma, Baigong Zheng, and Liang Huang. 2019. Speculative beam search for simultaneous translation. In *Proc. of EMNLP-IJCNLP*, pages 1395–1402.

Michał Ziemski, Marcin Junczys-Dowmunt, and Bruno Pouliquen. 2016. The united nations parallel corpus v1. 0. In *Proc. of LREC*, pages 3530–3534.

Adrian Łańcucki. 2020. Fastpitch: Parallel text-to-speech with pitch prediction. *arXiv preprint arXiv:2006.06873*.

A Appendix: ASR resources

Table 4: Transcribed speech resources, with the sets used and total hours per set and globally. (tr=train, d=dev, t=test, v=val, do/to=dev-other/test-other)

Set	Hours
CommonVoice 6.1	
(Mozilla, 2022) (v)	1668.0
Librispeech(tr+do+to)	
(Panayotov et al., 2015)	970.1
MuST-C v2.0(tr en-{de,ja,zh})	
(Di Gangi et al., 2019)	608.2
How2	
(Sanabria et al., 2018)(tr+v+d)	304.5
Europarl-ST v1.1 (tr+d+t)	
(Iranzo-Sánchez et al., 2020b)	98.7
Total	3649.6

Table 5: Text resources used to train the ngram LM.

Set	Sent (K)	Words (M)
News discussions	635117.8	8317.1
News crawl (new)	274930.0	6029.9
Open Subs 18		
(Lison and Tiedemann, 2016)	439507.3	2429.2
WikiMatrix v1		
(Schwenk et al., 2021)	19422.8	2107.5
UN Parallel Corpus V1.0		
(Ziemski et al., 2016)	14517.5	308.4
Europarl v10		
(Koehn, 2005)	2317.3	56.3
News Commentary		
(Tiedemann, 2012) v1	646.8	14.1
LibriSpeech	287.0	9.5
CommonVoice 6.1	613.5	6.3
MuST-C v2.0	389.3	6.3
How2	191.6	3.4
Europarl-ST v1.1	36.0	0.9
WIT3		
(Cettolo et al., 2012b)	14.6	0.2
Total	1387991.6	17522.1

Pretrained Speech Encoders and Efficient Fine-tuning Methods for Speech Translation: UPC at IWSLT 2022

Ioannis Tsiamas*, **Gerard I. Gállego***, **Carlos Escolano**, **José A. R. Fonollosa**, **Marta R. Costa-jussà**
TALP Research Center, Universitat Politècnica de Catalunya, Barcelona
{ioannis.tsiamas,gerard.ion.gallego,carlos.escolano
jose.fonollosa,marta.ruiz}@upc.edu

Abstract

This paper describes the submissions of the UPC Machine Translation group to the IWSLT 2022 Offline Speech Translation and Speech-to-Speech Translation tracks. The offline task involves translating English speech to German, Japanese and Chinese text. Our Speech Translation systems are trained end-to-end and are based on large pretrained speech and text models. We use an efficient fine-tuning technique that trains only specific layers of our system, and explore the use of adapter modules for the non-trainable layers. We further investigate the suitability of different speech encoders (wav2vec 2.0, HuBERT) for our models and the impact of knowledge distillation from the Machine Translation model that we use for the decoder (mBART). For segmenting the IWSLT test sets we fine-tune a pretrained audio segmentation model and achieve improvements of 5 BLEU compared to the given segmentation. Our best single model uses HuBERT and parallel adapters and achieves 29.42 BLEU at English-German MuST-C tst-COMMON and 26.77 at IWSLT 2020 test. By ensembling many models, we further increase translation quality to 30.83 BLEU and 27.78 accordingly. Furthermore, our submission for English-Japanese achieves 15.85 and English-Chinese obtains 25.63 BLEU on the MuST-C tst-COMMON sets. Finally, we extend our system to perform English-German Speech-to-Speech Translation with a pretrained Text-to-Speech model.

1 Introduction

In the last few years, *end-to-end* (or *direct*) Speech Translation (ST) models have gained popularity in the research community. These systems differ from the classical *cascade* ones in their architecture, where instead of concatenating an Automatic Speech Recognition (ASR) model and a Machine Translation (MT) system, they directly translate speech into the target language without an intermediate transcription. This approach solves some limitations of cascade ST systems, like error propagation and slow inference times. But on the other hand, such approaches require more data to be competitive, which are not as abundant as ASR and MT data (Sperber and Paulik, 2020). However, the performance gap between the two approaches has become very small in the last years (Bentivogli et al., 2021), with end-to-end approaches having the best performances for the IWSLT 2020 test set in the last two evaluation campaigns (Ansari et al., 2020; Anastasopoulos et al., 2021).

Following this research trend, we participate in the Offline Speech Translation task of IWSLT 2022 (Anastasopoulos et al., 2022) with end-to-end systems that are built on top of our last year's submission (Gállego et al., 2021). The approach we follow is to leverage large pretrained speech and text models, in order to reduce the required amount of data usually needed to train competitive end-to-end ST systems (§2.1). As a speech encoder, we consider wav2vec 2.0 (Baevski et al., 2020) and HuBERT (Hsu et al., 2021), both already fine-tuned on English ASR data. As a text decoder, we use an mBART50 (Tang et al., 2020) fine-tuned on multilingual MT (one-to-many). These two modules are coupled with a *length adaptor* block, that reduces the length discrepancy. Although powerful, combining these modules results in a substantially large system, that is hard to train on normal hardware, given its computational and memory requirements. We thus follow a minimalistic fine-tuning strategy Li et al. (2021), which trains only specific modules in the network (§2.2). In addition, we extend this approach by adding *parallel adapters* (He et al., 2022) to the frozen layers (§2.3). We also explore the use of *knowledge distillation* (Hinton et al., 2015) from MT (Liu et al., 2019; Gaido et al., 2020) with mBART as the teacher (§2.4). Finally, we use SHAS (Tsiamas et al., 2022) to approximate

*Equal contribution

Proceedings of the 19th International Conference on Spoken Language Translation (IWSLT 2022), pages 265 - 276
May 26-27, 2022 ©2022 Association for Computational Linguistics

the optimal segmentation for the IWSLT test sets (§5).

In summary, our contributions with this work are: (1) We perform a comparison of wav2vec 2.0 and HuBERT for building an ST model. (2) We extend the fine-tuning strategy proposed by Li et al. (2021) with parallel adapters. (3) We study the effect of Knowledge Distillation for ST, in the context of pre-trained models.

2 Methodology

In this section, we describe the main parts of the proposed system 1, along with our approach for knowledge distillation and the Text-to-Speech model.

2.1 Pretrained modules

Our system is initialized with two pretrained models, an ASR encoder and an MT decoder. These two components were originally trained with self-supervised learning (SSL) strategies, and then fine-tuned with supervised learning on the ASR and MT tasks, respectively. Following, we describe these models, and we give details on how we couple them to build an ST system.

Speech Encoders We experiment with two different pretrained speech encoders: wav2vec 2.0 (Baevski et al., 2020) and HuBERT (Hsu et al., 2021). Thanks to the SSL pretraining, these models can achieve very competitive results with only a few labelled data points. Both speech encoders are based on the same architecture. The first block consists of a stack of seven 1D convolutional layers, which extract features from the raw waveform input. Next, a Transformer encoder (Vaswani et al., 2017) further processes these features, and extracts contextualized representations. The main difference between these two speech encoders lies on the pretraining strategy they follow. On the one hand, wav2vec 2.0 is pretrained to identify the true speech representation from a masked time step, by solving a contrastive task on quantized representations. On the other hand, HuBERT predicts the masked time steps by computing the loss against pseudo-labels, which are obtained from an iterative offline clustering.

Text Decoder We use the decoder of mBART to initialize the decoder of our system (Liu et al., 2020). Similarly to the speech encoders, mBART is also pretrained with SSL and then fine-tuned for a downstream task. It follows the same strategy used to pretrain BART (Lewis et al., 2020), but in this case, the model is trained with multilingual data. Concretely, it is trained as a denoising autoencoder, with the objective of reconstructing the original text input, which has been intentionally corrupted. After pre-training, mBART can be fine-tuned with supervised data on the (multilingual) MT task.

Length Adaptor To build our system, we combine two components that were designed for different modalities. Hence, there is a length discrepancy between the actual encoder representations and the ones expected by the decoder. To reduce this gap, we introduce a simple module to shorten the sequence length of the encoder outputs (Li et al., 2021). The length adaptor is a stack of convolutional layers that reduces the sequence length by 8, thus achieving a better coupling of the two main blocks.

2.2 LNA Fine-tuning

The LayerNorm and Attention (LNA) fine-tuning strategy consists of just training some specific layers in an ST system initialized by pretrained speech and text models. By avoiding a full fine-tuning, it is feasible to train the combination of these massive pretrained components in a time and memory efficient way. Specifically, we use the version of this strategy that fine-tunes the layer normalization, the encoder self-attention and the decoder cross-attention layers. LNA fine-tuning approaches the results of a full fine-tuning, while training just the 20% of the total parameters (Li et al., 2021).

2.3 Parallel Adapters

Although LNA fine-tuning has been shown to yield very competitive results, it almost entirely neglects the feed-forward blocks in the Transformer, where lie most of the parameters of every layer. Recent studies have unveiled the contribution of these blocks in promoting concepts in the vocabulary space (Geva et al., 2022). Hence, totally freezing them could hinder the performance of the system in a new domain. Instead of fine-tuning the parameters of a layer, another popular approach is to use adapters (Houlsby et al., 2019; Le et al., 2021) to approximate its output. An adapter module is a feed-forward network with a bottleneck dimension and ReLU activation. In this research, we use adapters to compliment the LNA fine-tuning technique (§2.2) by adding adapters to the (frozen) feed-

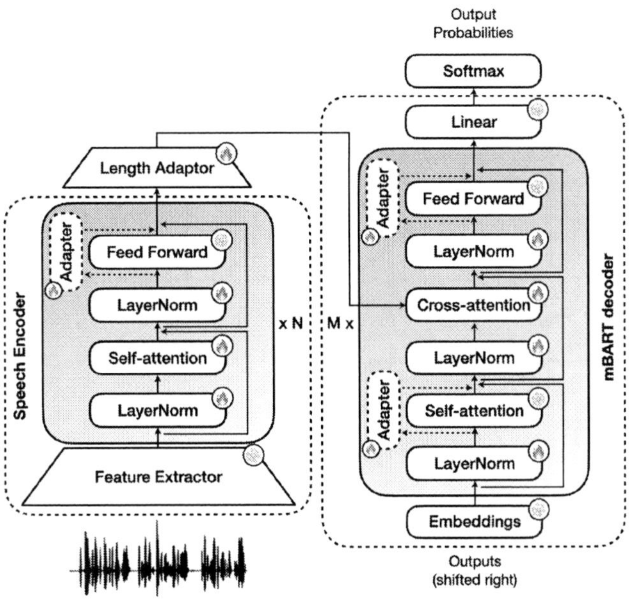

Figure 1: System overview. Fire indicates that a block is fine-tuned, and snowflake that it is frozen.

forward layers of the transformer layers. We also add them to the (frozen) decoder self-attention layers, since the number of extra parameters are negligible. Following He et al. (2022), we used adapters with a scaled parallel insertion form, which was found to provide higher performance gains than with a sequential insertion.

2.4 Knowledge Distillation

Apart from efficient fine-tuning methods, we experimented with using knowledge distillation (KD) (Hinton et al., 2015), which has been successfully applied for training an end-to-end ST model (student) (Liu et al., 2019; Gaido et al., 2020), by transferring knowledge from a pretrained MT model (teacher). The effectiveness of KD stems from the fact that the MT task is less complex than the ST task, and thus the student can benefit from learning the teacher distribution. In this work, we are using word-level KD, where the output probabilities of the MT model act as soft labels for the ST model. The loss is a weighted sum of the standard Cross Entropy and the Kullback-Leibler (KL) divergence between the student and teacher output distributions. The importance of each term in the loss is controlled by a hyperparameter $\lambda \in (0, 1)$. Since we are initializing the decoder of our models with the mBART decoder, we are also using it as the teacher for KD. Following (Gaido et al., 2020), we extract the top-k output probabilities with mBART offline and thus there is no additional computational impact during training with KD, while it also does not affect negatively the learning process (Tan et al., 2019; Gaido et al., 2020) Due to extracting only the top-k logits from the teacher, the teacher distribution tends to be sharper than normal, and thus we used a temperature $T > 1$, to soften it.

3 Data

3.1 Datasets

To train our models we used data from three speech translation datasets, MuST-C v2 (Di Gangi et al., 2019), Europarl-ST (Iranzo-Sánchez et al., 2020) and CoVoST-2 (Wang et al., 2020). More specifically, we used the English-German (en-de), English-Japanese (en-ja) and English-Chinese (en-zh) from MuST-C and CoVoST, and the en-de from Europarl-ST. MuST-C is based on TED talks, Europarl-ST on the European Parliament proceedings, and CoVoST is derived from the Common Voice (Ardila et al., 2020) corpus. Since only MuST-C has in-domain data, we used the dev and tst-COMMON splits for development and testing, while from Europarl-ST and CoVoST, we used their respective dev and test splits as additional training data. Furthermore, the IWSLT test sets of 2019 and 2020 (Niehues et al., 2019; Ansari et al., 2020), which do not have ground truth segmentations, serve as development data for en-de. Finally, we submit our predictions for the IWSLT test set of 2021 (en-de) (Anastasopoulos et al., 2021) and the test sets of 2022 (en-de, en-ja, en-zh) (Anastasopoulos et al., 2022).

Dataset	en-de	en-ja	en-zh
MuST-C v2	436	526	545
Europarl-ST †	83	-	-
CoVoST 2 †	413	413	413
Total	942	939	958

Table 1: Training data measured in hours. †: train, dev and test splits are considered.

3.2 Data Filtering

We removed examples with duration longer than 25 seconds to avoid memory issues. To ensure that our training data are of high quality, we applied two stages of filtering by either modifying the transcriptions and translations (text filtering) or to completely removing an example (speech filtering).

Text filtering. We applied this filtering in both the transcription and translation of each example, and the process is different for each dataset. For MuST-C we removed the speaker names, that are in-audible and usually appear at the beginning of the sentences when multiple speakers are active in a talk. We also removed events like "Laughter" and "Applause" that are not expected to be generated by our ST systems during evaluation. For Europarl-ST we converted the number format to match the one in MuST-C, by using commas as the thousands-separator in large numbers instead of spaces. No specific text filtering is applied on the CoVoST data. Finally, to minimize the differences between the datasets, we applied punctuation and spacing normalization with Sacremoses[1].

Speech filtering. To identify and remove noisy examples, that would potentially hurt the performance of our models, we applied speech filtering on all source audios in our training data. We performed ASR inference with a pretrained wav2vec 2.0[2] using the Transformers library (Wolf et al., 2020), and removed the examples that had a word error rate (WER) higher than 0.75. WER was calculated after removing punctuation and multiple spaces, lower-casing the ground-truth transcriptions and converting numbers from digits to their spelled-out words format. The average WER per dataset was 0.141 for MuST-C, 0.175 and 0.152 for CoVoST, and the speech-filtering process resulted in removing 1.5% of MuST-C, 1% of Europarl-ST and 2% of CoVoST.

3.3 Data Augmentation

To enrich and diversify our data, we perform audio augmentation. This process is done on-the-fly during training using WavAugment (Kharitonov et al., 2021). Each training example has a probability of 0.8 to be augmented, in which case the *tempo* and *echo* effects are applied. Modifying the tempo of an audio allows our ST models to adapt to speeches of different speeds, while the echo effect simulates the echoing that is present in large rooms, where usually TED talks take place. The tempo augmentation parameter is sampled uniformly in the range of (0.85, 1.3), while the echo-delay and echo-decay parameters, which control the echo augmentation, are sampled from the ranges of (20, 200) and (0.05, 0.2) respectively.

4 Experiments

Here we describe the experiments we carried out in this work with their implementation details.

4.1 Experimental Setup

LNA-wav2vec. We build on top of our submission to IWSLT 2021 (Gállego et al., 2021), where we combined a wav2vec 2.0 encoder, with an mBART decoder, and the whole system is trained with the LNA technique. This year, we reproduce this experiment, with two main differences. First, we perform a hyperparameter tuning for the learning rate and use the entire CoVoST dataset (out-of-domain) instead of sub-sampling it.

LNA-HuBERT. In the next experiment, we explore the effect that different speech encoders bring in our system. Thus, we initialize the speech encoder of our ST model, with HuBERT.

LNA-Adapters. Last year, we found it to be beneficial, to use an adapter, at the output of the speech encoder. We expand this idea, and perform an experiment where we instead of using a single adapter, we use scaled parallel adapters in all frozen sublayers of our system. These are the feed-forward layers of both the encoder and decoder, as well as

[1] https://github.com/alvations/sacremoses

[2] https://huggingface.co/facebook/wav2vec2-large-960h-lv60-self

the self-attention layers in the decoder, that are not part of the LNA fine-tuning.

KD. For the next experiment, we use knowledge distillation from mBART, where the loss of the ST model during training is a weighted sum of the standard cross entropy and the KL divergence between the MT and ST output distributions. We also explored the trade-off between the two loss functions, by tuning the λ parameter that controls it.

Apart from the aforementioned experiments, we apply checkpoint averaging, where we average around the best checkpoint of an experiment (**ckpt AVG**). Furthermore, we continue fine-tuning for few more epochs on only the in-domain data of MuST-C, while also using smaller data augmentation probability (**in-domain FT**). Finally, since the aforementioned experiments have core differences, we hypothesize that they are diverse enough to benefit from ensembling. We experiment with ensemble decoding from various combinations of our best models (**Ensemble**).

4.2 Implementation Details

All our models use the same architectures for the encoder and the decoder. The encoder is either initialized with wav2vec 2.0[3] or HuBERT[4] and are composed of a 7-layer convolutional feature extractor and 24-layer Transformer encoder. Both were pretrained with 60k hours of untranscribed speech from Libri-Light (Kahn et al., 2020), and fine-tuned for ASR with 960 hours of labeled data from Librispeech (Panayotov et al., 2015). The wav2vec 2.0 version we use was also fine-tuned with pseudo-labels (Xu et al., 2020). The decoder is initialized from mBART[5] that has been fine-tuned for multilingual MT, including English to German, Japanese and Chinese. Its decoder is a 12-layer Transformer. The feature extractor of the encoder has 512 channels, kernel sizes of (10, 3, 3, 3, 3, 2, 2) and strides of (5, 2, 2, 2, 2, 2, 2). Each layer in the Transformer encoder and decoder has a dimensionality of 1024, feed-forward dimension of 4096, 16 heads, ReLU activations, and use pre-layer normalization. The length adaptor between the encoder and decoder is a 3-layer convolutional network with 1024 channels, stride of 2 and uses GLU activations. The embedding layer and the linear projection weights of the decoder are shared, and has a size of 250,000. For the experiment with adapters, we are using scaled parallel adapters with a dimensionality of 512 and a scaling factor of 4 (He et al., 2022).

The inputs to the model are waveforms of 16kHz sampling rate, which are normalized to zero mean and unit variance. During training, each source audio is augmented (before normalization) with a probability of 0.8. We train bilingual models on all data of Table 1, with maximum source length of 400,000 and target length of 1024 tokens. We use gradient accumulation and data parallelism to achieve a batch size of approximately 32 million tokens. We use Adam (Kingma and Ba, 2014) with $\beta_1 = 0.99$, $\beta_2 = 0.98$ and base learning rate of $2.5 \cdot 10^{-4}$, which we found in preliminary experiments to be better, compared to the learning rate of 10^{-4} that we used last year (Gállego et al., 2021). The learning rate is controlled by a tri-stage scheduler with phases of 0.15, 0.15 and 0.7 for warm-up, hold and decay accordingly, while the initial and final learning rate has a scale of 0.01 compared to base. Sentence averaging and gradient clipping of 20 are used. We applied dropout of 0.1 before every non-frozen layer, and use time masking for spans of length 10 with probability of 0.2 and channel masking for spans of length 20 with probability of 0.1 in the output of the encoder feature extractor.

The loss is the cross-entropy with label smoothing of 0.2. For the experiments that additionally use KD, the loss is a weighted sum of the standard cross-entropy (no label smoothing) and the KL divergence between the teacher and student distributions, controlled by a hyperparameter λ, which we tune in (0, 1). The teacher distribution for each step is extracted offline with mBART[6] using the Transformers library. We keep the top-8 indices, and both the teacher and student distributions are additionally modified with temperature $T = 1.3$ (Gaido et al., 2020).

For in-domain fine-tuning, we train only on data from MuST-C, and lower the probability of augmentation to 0.2. We train for an additional 4

[3] https://dl.fbaipublicfiles.com/fairseq/wav2vec/wav2vec2_vox_960h_new.pt

[4] https://dl.fbaipublicfiles.com/hubert/hubert_large_ll60k_finetune_ls960.pt

[5] https://dl.fbaipublicfiles.com/fairseq/models/mbart50/mbart50.ft.1n.tar.gz

[6] https://huggingface.co/facebook/mbart-large-50-one-to-many-mmt

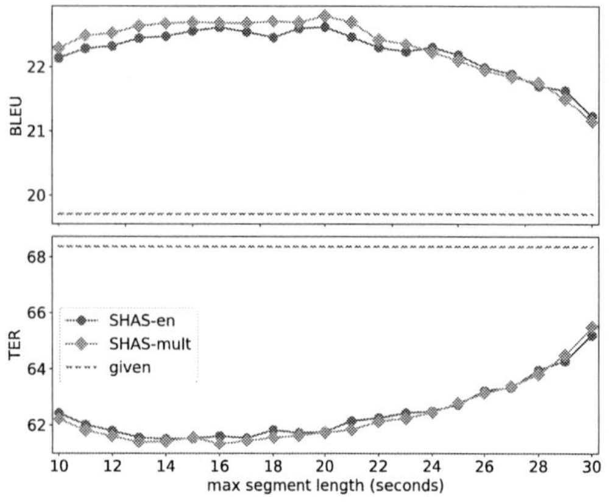

Figure 2: BLEU(↑) and TER(↓) in IWSLT test 2019 for different parameters of max-segment-length for the English and multilingual SHAS methods. With dashed lines are the results for the given segmentation.

epochs with a learning rate of 10^{-5}. The learning rate is increased from $5 \cdot 10^{-7}$ for the first 15% of the training and then decays for the rest of the training.

After training, we pick the best checkpoint according to the BLEU (Papineni et al., 2002) on the development set of MuST-C and average 5 checkpoints around it. For generation, we use a beam search of 5. We used one of our base experiments (LNA-HuBERT) with learning rate of 10^{-4}), to fine-tune SHAS on the 2019 IWLST test set (Niehues et al., 2019) and then use the best configuration to segment the test sets of 2020, 2021 and 2022 (Ansari et al., 2020; Anastasopoulos et al., 2021, 2022). We choose our best model based on the BLEU of the 2019 test set and report results on MuST-C tst-COMMON and the IWSLT test set of 2020. For choosing the best segmentation (§5), apart from BLEU, we additionally evaluate with TER (Snover et al., 2006). Our models are implemented in fairseq (Ott et al., 2019) and are trained using NVIDIA apex[7] and 16 floating point precision. The code for our experiments is available in a public repository[8].

5 Audio Segmentation

Although our training data contain ground truth segmentations derived from strong punctuation of the transcriptions, the IWSLT test sets, are unsegmented and thus require an intermediate step of audio segmentation, before applying our ST models. Past evaluation campaigns of IWSLT have shown light to the importance of accurate audio segmentation for end-to-end ST, where top-performing participants used their own segmentation algorithms to get large improvements in translation quality. For our submission, we are using SHAS, a segmentation method that can effectively learn the manual segmentation from a labelled speech corpus (Tsiamas et al., 2022). It relies on a segmentation frame classifier and a probabilistic Divide-and-Conquer (pDAC) algorithm to obtain the segmentation for a given audio. The frame classifier is a Transformer encoder with a binary classification layer, that predicts the splitting frames in the audio using as inputs contextual representations extracted with a frozen XLS-R (Babu et al., 2021). The pDAC segmentation algorithm is based on the method of (Potapczyk and Przybysz, 2020) and progressively splits on the frames of the lowest probability, until all resulting segments are shorter than a pre-specified max-segment-length parameter. Segmentations created with SHAS approach the translation quality of the manual segmentation on the en-de tst-COMMON set of MuST-C v2.0, retaining 95% of the manual BLEU.

We used the public implementation of SHAS[9] and tested two available pretrained models for the frame classifiers, one trained on English source audio from MuST-C v2 and a multilingual which is additionally trained on Spanish, French, Portuguese, and Italian data from mTEDx (Salesky et al., 2021). We obtain the frame probabilities for the audios of the 2019 IWSLT test set (Niehues et al., 2019) with the English and multilingual classifiers, and then used the pDAC algorithm with a varying max-segment-length to segment them. To find the best parameters, we maximize the translation quality of the segmentation by the following process: (1) Translate the resulting segments with our ST model, (2) align the translations with the references using the mwerSegmenter tool (Matusov et al., 2005) and (3) compute the BLEU and TER scores.

In figure 2 we observe that values of max-segment-length in the range of 14 and 20 seconds for pDAC, result in the best segmentation, with BLEU scores of 22.5 and TER scores of 61.5. Additionally, in that range, SHAS with a multilingual classifier performs better than the English

[7] https://github.com/NVIDIA/apex
[8] https://github.com/mt-upc/iwslt-2022
[9] https://github.com/mt-upc/SHAS

one, with small improvements of approximately 0.2 BLEU. The highest BLEU score overall is obtained with the multilingual classifier and at max-segment-length of 20 seconds, but given that there is an increase in the TER score, we decided to continue with max-segment-length of 16 seconds, which seems to have more consistent results. Thus, for our final results (§6) for the test sets of 2019 and 2020, as well as for our submissions for 2021 and 2022, we used SHAS with the multilingual classifier and a max-segment-length of 16 seconds (SHAS-mult-16). Due to the absence of available test sets to fine-tune SHAS for the Japanese and Chinese, we also use SHAS-mult-16 to segment the en-ja and en-zh IWSLT 2022 test sets.

6 Results

In this section, we analyze the results of our experiments. We base our experimentation on the en-de language pair, to compare the results with our last year's submission (Gállego et al., 2021; Anastasopoulos et al., 2021). Hence, first we analyze the results for this language pair (Table 2) and then present the results for en-ja and en-zh (Table 3).

6.1 English-German

In our main results for en-de (Table 2), we also include our last year's submission (row 0). In (1), we repeat the same experiment, with the main differences being an increase of the learning rate to $2.5 \cdot 10^{-4}$, no sub-sampling of the CoVoST data, and using SHAS for the segmentation of the IWLST data at inference. These changes are already providing us an increase of 2.3 BLEU in MuST-C and 3 BLEU at IWSLT tst2019. In (2), we substitute the wav2vec 2.0 encoder for a HuBERT encoder, which brings further improvements of 0.6 to 0.8 BLEU in all test sets. With the addition of adapters (3a), we observe improvements in the IWSLT test sets but a drop in MuST-C. We hypothesize that complimenting LNA with adapters (§2.3) results in overfitting in MuST-C, but at the same time, the additional parameters provide an extra flexibility to the model regarding data from different segmentation (IWSLT test sets). With checkpoint averaging (3b), we get improvements in all test sets, providing the overall best results from a single model. Next, we apply knowledge distillation (4a), which initially results in a slight drop for the IWSLT test sets and in an increase in MuST-C (as compared to 3a). We believe that, since knowledge distillation from MT (§2.4) uses manually segmented data (MuST-C), those are the data that could benefit from it (§6.3). With in-domain fine-tuning and checkpoint averaging (4b, 4c), we get small improvements of 0.2 BLEU in all test sets. By ensembling our two best models (5a), we get improvements in all test sets. Finally, since our models are diverse enough (speech encoder, adapters, knowledge distillation), we ensemble all four of them (5c) and obtain our best results, with 30.83 BLEU on MuST-C tst-COMMON, and 25.39, 27.78 on the 2019 and 2020 test IWSLT test sets. The segmentation algorithm also plays a key role in the performance of our models, with improvements of 4 to 5.5 BLEU in all experiments, as compared to the given one.

6.2 English-Japanese & English-Chinese

From the results of en-ja and en-zh (Table 3), we observe that similarly to en-de, the addition of adapters brings a slight drop in performance for MuST-C. Still, we hypothesize that this would turn into an increase for the unsegmented IWSLT test sets, although we cannot confirm it since there are no data available from previous editions. Moreover, we noticed that MT with mBART performed worse than our ST model (11.63 BLEU for en-ja and 19.51 BLEU for en-zh on dev), meaning that knowledge distillation would most likely cause a drop in performance. Therefore, we do not perform KD for those languages. Finally, we ensemble the two models (after checkpoint averaging), with which we obtain on tst-COMMON 15.85 BLEU for en-ja and 25.63 BLEU for en-zh.

6.3 Analysis on Knowledge Distillation

We carry out an analysis on knowledge distillation, to better understand its impact to our system (Table 2, row 4). Specifically, we analyze the trade-off between the standard cross entropy and the teacher-student KL divergence, by varying the lambda in [0.25, 0.5, 0.75, 1]. In figure 3 we provide the BLEU scores for the dev and tst-COMMON sets of MuST-C and the IWSLT test sets of 2019 and 2020, which are segmented with SHAS-mult-16. We also provide the results for an experiment that does not use KD, but instead of the standard cross entropy, it was trained with the label-smoothed one. We also provide the performance of the MT teacher (dashed line) on the dev set of MuST-C, which can be seen as an upper bound for the student. Firstly, we observe that relying completely on the teacher

		Dataset	MuST-C		IWSLT			
		split	dev	tst-COMMON	tst2019		tst2020	
		segmentation			given	SHAS	given	SHAS
0		LNA-wav2vec (Gállego et al., 2021)	26.76	26.23	17.25	20.06	-	-
1		LNA-wav2vec	29.08	28.50	18.37	23.03	19.61	25.33
2		LNA-HuBERT	28.97	29.27	19.02	23.72	20.09	25.61
3	a	LNA-Adapters-HuBERT	28.92	28.53	19.51	24.07	20.66	26.35
	b	↪ ckpt AVG	29.41	**29.42**	**20.48**	**24.88**	**21.19**	**26.77**
4	a	LNA-Adapters-HuBERT-KD	**29.44**	28.79	19.37	23.74	20.25	26.10
	b	↪ in-domain FT	29.43	28.97	19.52	23.87	20.67	26.17
	c	↪ ckpt AVG	29.42	28.87	19.71	23.92	20.93	26.32
5	a	Ensemble (3b, 4c)	30.07	30.33	20.51	24.98	21.85	27.38
	b	Ensemble (3b, 4c, 2)	30.33	30.44	**<u>20.69</u>**	25.34	22.30	27.61
	c	Ensemble (3b, 4c, 2, 1)	**<u>30.53</u>**	**<u>30.83</u>**	20.65	**<u>25.39</u>**	**<u>22.40</u>**	**<u>27.78</u>**

Table 2: BLEU scores for en-de MuST-C and IWSLT sets. In bold are the best scores by single models, and in underlined bold are the best scores overall. LNA-wav2vec (Gállego et al., 2021) uses a different segmentation algorithm and results are not available for tst2020.

Language Pair	en-ja		en-zh	
split	dev	test	dev	test
LNA-HuBERT	**12.45**	15.20	**22.55**	24.84
↪ ckpt AVG (a)	12.32	15.36	22.28	**24.95**
LNA-Adapters-HuBERT	12.26	14.89	22.29	24.48
↪ ckpt AVG (b)	12.07	**15.46**	22.07	24.85
Ensemble (a, b)	**<u>12.45</u>**	**<u>15.85</u>**	**<u>22.98</u>**	**<u>25.63</u>**

Table 3: BLEU scores on dev and test (tst-COMMON) sets of MuST-C v2 for en-ja and en-zh. In bold are the best scores by single models, and in underlined bold are the best scores overall.

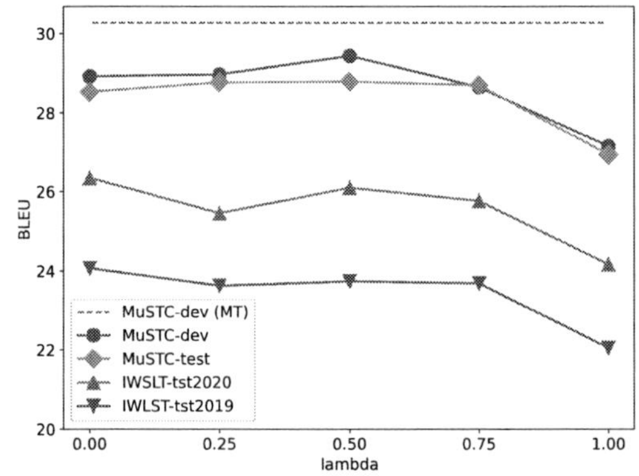

Figure 3: BLEU scores for knowledge distillation with varying lambda for en-de. IWSLT test sets are segmented with SHAS-mult-16.

degrades the translation quality in all sets. This is contrary to previous research suggesting that $\lambda = 1$ is optimal (Liu et al., 2019). This conflicting results likely stems from the small differences between our ST and MT models, which in dev set of MuST-C is approximately 1.5 BLEU, while in (Liu et al., 2019) the gap is more than 10 BLEU. Secondly, we observe that there is an increase in BLEU when the ST model is trained with a mixture of the two losses for MuST-C ($\lambda = 0.5$), but there is a drop for the IWSLT test sets. We believe that these differences are a consequence of the training-testing segmentation mismatch, where the MuST-C sets have the same segmentation as the training data, while for IWSLT sets, this segmentation is only approximated with SHAS. This difference is expected to make it harder for the ST model to utilize the MT knowledge from the ground truth segmentations.

6.4 Submission Results

In Table 4 we present our results on the official test sets of IWSLT 2022 (Anastasopoulos et al., 2022). All test sets were segmented with SHAS (§5), and the models used are the best ensembles for each language (Tables 2, 3). For the en-de test set of 2021 (Anastasopoulos et al., 2021), we obtain a BLEU of 24.5 (ref-1)[10]. This result, compared to the ones of IWSLT 2021 (Anastasopoulos et al., 2021), stands 2.7 BLEU above our submission (Gállego et al., 2021), 1.9 BLEU above the best end-to-end submission (Bahar et al., 2021) and only 0.1 BLEU

[10] IWSLT systems were ranked with this reference in 2021.

IWSLT test set	BLEU		
	ref-1	ref-2	both
en-de 2021	24.5	20.9	34.8
en-de 2022	23.0	20.8	32.3
en-ja 2022	15.1	15.6	24.7
en-zh 2022	29.2	29.9	36.4

Table 4: Official submission results for en-de (2021, 2022) and en-ja, en-zh (2022). BLEU is measured for two different references and for both together. Different models are used for each language. For en-de we used Ensemble of Table 2 - row 5c and for en-ja and en-zh the Ensembles of Table 3.

below the best overall[11]. For the test sets of 2022 we obtain 23 BLEU for en-de, 15.1 BLEU for en-ja and 29.2 BLEU for en-zh. The reader can refer to Anastasopoulos et al. (2022) for a comparison with the other submitted systems.

7 Speech-to-Speech

We have also submitted our system to the Speech-to-Speech (S2S) translation task[12], by building a cascade system. This is composed of the main end-to-end Speech-to-Text translation model and a Text-to-Speech (TTS) system. We used a pretrained[13] VITS model (Kim et al., 2021) for synthesizing the German speech. It is based on normalizing flows (Rezende and Mohamed, 2015), adversarial training and a stochastic duration predictor. It is capable of generating speech in different pitches and rhythms, resulting in more natural sounding audio utterances.

8 Conclusions

We described the submission of the UPC Machine Translation group for the IWSLT 2022 Offline ST and Speech-to-Speech tasks. Our system is end-to-end and leverages ASR and MT pretrained models to initialize the encoder and decoder. Due to the large size of the system, we employed efficient fine-tuning methods that train only specific layers and provide evidence that the addition of parallel adapters to the non-trainable layers can bring further improvements. We showed that a HuBERT encoder is more suitable than wav2vec 2.0 for our system and brings improvements in all test sets. We also explored the use of knowledge distillation, which provided only minor improvements to the test sets with ground-truth segmentations, most likely because the MT model was borderline better than our ST model. Additionally, we show that the SHAS method provides high-quality segmentations of the IWSLT test sets, bringing improvements up to 5 BLEU compared to the given segmentation. Our best single model, uses a HuBERT encoder and LNA with parallel adapters, and achieved 29.42 BLEU on MuST-C tst-COMMON set, and 24.88 and 26.77 BLEU on IWSLT 2019 and IWSLT 2020 test sets. We ensembled 4 different systems for our final submission, which further increased the BLEU in the aforementioned sets by 1 to 1.5 points. We also described our submissions for the English-Japanese and English-Chinese pairs that scored 15.85 and 25.63 MuST-C tst-COMMON. Finally, we also submitted a Speech-to-Speech system, by using a pretrained German TTS model to the generated translations.

For future work, we are planning to explore more pretrained speech encoders and text decoders, and dive deeper into the ways that we can optimally combine them and efficiently fine-tune for end-to-end ST. We will also investigate how to gain the most from an MT teacher, in such scenarios where there is a small gap between the MT and the ST models.

[11]Cascade system by HW-TSC, no paper available

[12]Results not available at time of submission, the reader can refer to Anastasopoulos et al. (2022)

[13]`https://github.com/jmp84/vits`

Acknowledgements

This work was supported by the project ADAVOICE, PID2019-107579RB-I00 / AEI / 10.13039/501100011033

References

Antonios Anastasopoulos, Luisa Bentivogli, Marcely Z. Boito, Ondřej Bojar, Roldano Cattoni, Anna Currey, Georgiana Dinu, Kevin Duh, Maha Elbayad, Marcello Federico, Christian Federmann, Hongyu Gong, Roman Grundkiewicz, Barry Haddow, Benjamin Hsu, Dávid Javorský, Věra Kloudová, Surafel M. Lakew, Xutai Ma, Prashant Mathur, Paul McNamee, Kenton Murray, Maria Nădejde, Satoshi Nakamura, Matteo Negri, Jan Niehues, Xing Niu, Juan Pino, Elizabeth Salesky, Jiatong Shi, Sebastian Stüker, Katsuhito Sudoh, Marco Turchi, Yogesh Virkar, Alex Waibel, Changhan Wang, and Shinji Watanabe. 2022. FINDINGS OF THE IWSLT 2022 EVALUATION CAMPAIGN. In *Proceedings of the 19th International Conference on Spoken Language Translation (IWSLT 2022)*, Dublin, Ireland. Association for Computational Linguistics.

Antonios Anastasopoulos, Ondřej Bojar, Jacob Bremerman, Roldano Cattoni, Maha Elbayad, Marcello Federico, Xutai Ma, Satoshi Nakamura, Matteo Negri, Jan Niehues, Juan Pino, Elizabeth Salesky, Sebastian Stüker, Katsuhito Sudoh, Marco Turchi, Alex Waibel, Changhan Wang, and Matthew Wiesner. 2021. Findings of the IWSLT 2021 Evaluation Campaign. In *Proceedings of the 18th International Conference on Spoken Language Translation (IWSLT 2021)*, Online.

Ebrahim Ansari, Amittai Axelrod, Nguyen Bach, Ondrej Bojar, Roldano Cattoni, Fahim Dalvi, Nadir Durrani, Marcello Federico, Christian Federmann, Jiatao Gu, Fei Huang, Kevin Knight, Xutai Ma, Ajay Nagesh, Matteo Negri, Jan Niehues, Juan Pino, Elizabeth Salesky, Xing Shi, Sebastian Stüker, Marco Turchi, Alexander H. Waibel, and Changhan Wang. 2020. FINDINGS OF THE IWSLT 2020 EVALUATION CAMPAIGN. In *Proceedings of the 17th International Conference on Spoken Language Translation, IWSLT 2020, Online, July 9 - 10, 2020*, pages 1–34. Association for Computational Linguistics.

R. Ardila, M. Branson, K. Davis, M. Henretty, M. Kohler, J. Meyer, R. Morais, L. Saunders, F. M. Tyers, and G. Weber. 2020. Common voice: A massively-multilingual speech corpus. In *Proceedings of the 12th Conference on Language Resources and Evaluation (LREC 2020)*, pages 4211–4215.

Arun Babu, Changhan Wang, Andros Tjandra, Kushal Lakhotia, Qiantong Xu, Naman Goyal, Kritika Singh, Patrick von Platen, Yatharth Saraf, Juan Pino, et al. 2021. XLS-R: Self-supervised Cross-lingual Speech Representation Learning at Scale. *arXiv preprint arXiv:2111.09296*.

Alexei Baevski, Yuhao Zhou, Abdelrahman Mohamed, and Michael Auli. 2020. wav2vec 2.0: A framework for self-supervised learning of speech representations. In *Advances in Neural Information Processing Systems*, volume 33, pages 12449–12460. Curran Associates, Inc.

Parnia Bahar, Patrick Wilken, Mattia A. Di Gangi, and Evgeny Matusov. 2021. Without further ado: Direct and simultaneous speech translation by AppTek in 2021. In *Proceedings of the 18th International Conference on Spoken Language Translation (IWSLT 2021)*, pages 52–63, Bangkok, Thailand (online). Association for Computational Linguistics.

Luisa Bentivogli, Mauro Cettolo, Marco Gaido, Alina Karakanta, Alberto Martinelli, Matteo Negri, and Marco Turchi. 2021. Cascade versus direct speech translation: Do the differences still make a difference? In *Proceedings of the 59th Annual Meeting of the Association for Computational Linguistics and the 11th International Joint Conference on Natural Language Processing (Volume 1: Long Papers)*, pages 2873–2887, Online. Association for Computational Linguistics.

Mattia A. Di Gangi, Roldano Cattoni, Luisa Bentivogli, Matteo Negri, and Marco Turchi. 2019. MuST-C: a Multilingual Speech Translation Corpus. In *Proceedings of the 2019 Conference of the North American Chapter of the Association for Computational Linguistics: Human Language Technologies, Volume 1 (Long and Short Papers)*, pages 2012–2017, Minneapolis, Minnesota. Association for Computational Linguistics.

Marco Gaido, Mattia A. Di Gangi, Matteo Negri, and Marco Turchi. 2020. End-to-end speech-translation with knowledge distillation: FBK@IWSLT2020. In *Proceedings of the 17th International Conference on Spoken Language Translation*, pages 80–88, Online. Association for Computational Linguistics.

Gerard I. Gállego, Ioannis Tsiamas, Carlos Escolano, José A. R. Fonollosa, and Marta R. Costa-jussà. 2021. End-to-end speech translation with pre-trained models and adapters: UPC at IWSLT 2021. In *Proceedings of the 18th International Conference on Spoken Language Translation (IWSLT 2021)*, pages 110–119, Bangkok, Thailand (online). Association for Computational Linguistics.

Mor Geva, Avi Caciularu, Kevin Ro Wang, and Yoav Goldberg. 2022. Transformer feed-forward layers build predictions by promoting concepts in the vocabulary space. *arXiv preprint arXiv:2203.14680*.

Junxian He, Chunting Zhou, Xuezhe Ma, Taylor Berg-Kirkpatrick, and Graham Neubig. 2022. Towards a unified view of parameter-efficient transfer learning. In *International Conference on Learning Representations*.

Geoffrey E. Hinton, Oriol Vinyals, and Jeffrey Dean. 2015. Distilling the knowledge in a neural network. *ArXiv*, abs/1503.02531.

Neil Houlsby, Andrei Giurgiu, Stanislaw Jastrzebski, Bruna Morrone, Quentin De Laroussilhe, Andrea Gesmundo, Mona Attariyan, and Sylvain Gelly. 2019. Parameter-efficient transfer learning for NLP. In *Proceedings of the 36th International Conference on Machine Learning*, volume 97 of *Proceedings of Machine Learning Research*, pages 2790–2799. PMLR.

Wei-Ning Hsu, Benjamin Bolte, Yao-Hung Hubert Tsai, Kushal Lakhotia, Ruslan Salakhutdinov, and Abdelrahman Mohamed. 2021. Hubert: Self-supervised speech representation learning by masked prediction of hidden units. *IEEE/ACM Transactions on Audio, Speech, and Language Processing*, 29:3451–3460.

Javier Iranzo-Sánchez, Joan Albert Silvestre-Cerdà, Javier Jorge, Nahuel Roselló, Adrià Giménez, Albert Sanchis, Jorge Civera, and Alfons Juan. 2020. Europarl-st: A multilingual corpus for speech translation of parliamentary debates.

J. Kahn, M. Rivière, W. Zheng, E. Kharitonov, Q. Xu, P. E. Mazaré, J. Karadayi, V. Liptchinsky, R. Collobert, C. Fuegen, T. Likhomanenko, G. Synnaeve, A. Joulin, A. Mohamed, and E. Dupoux.

2020. Libri-light: A benchmark for asr with limited or no supervision. In *ICASSP 2020 - 2020 IEEE International Conference on Acoustics, Speech and Signal Processing (ICASSP)*, pages 7669–7673. https://github.com/facebookresearch/libri-light.

Eugene Kharitonov, Morgane Rivière, Gabriel Synnaeve, Lior Wolf, Pierre-Emmanuel Mazaré, Matthijs Douze, and Emmanuel Dupoux. 2021. Data augmenting contrastive learning of speech representations in the time domain. In *2021 IEEE Spoken Language Technology Workshop (SLT)*, pages 215–222.

Jaehyeon Kim, Jungil Kong, and Juhee Son. 2021. Conditional variational autoencoder with adversarial learning for end-to-end text-to-speech. In *Proceedings of the 38th International Conference on Machine Learning*, volume 139 of *Proceedings of Machine Learning Research*, pages 5530–5540. PMLR.

Diederik P. Kingma and Jimmy Ba. 2014. Adam: A method for stochastic optimization.

Hang Le, Juan Pino, Changhan Wang, Jiatao Gu, Didier Schwab, and Laurent Besacier. 2021. Lightweight adapter tuning for multilingual speech translation. In *Proceedings of the 59th Annual Meeting of the Association for Computational Linguistics and the 11th International Joint Conference on Natural Language Processing (Volume 2: Short Papers)*, pages 817–824, Online. Association for Computational Linguistics.

Mike Lewis, Yinhan Liu, Naman Goyal, Marjan Ghazvininejad, Abdelrahman Mohamed, Omer Levy, Veselin Stoyanov, and Luke Zettlemoyer. 2020. BART: Denoising sequence-to-sequence pre-training for natural language generation, translation, and comprehension. In *Proceedings of the 58th Annual Meeting of the Association for Computational Linguistics*, pages 7871–7880, Online. Association for Computational Linguistics.

Xian Li, Changhan Wang, Yun Tang, Chau Tran, Yuqing Tang, Juan Pino, Alexei Baevski, Alexis Conneau, and Michael Auli. 2021. Multilingual speech translation from efficient finetuning of pretrained models. In *Proceedings of the 59th Annual Meeting of the Association for Computational Linguistics and the 11th International Joint Conference on Natural Language Processing (Volume 1: Long Papers)*, pages 827–838.

Yinhan Liu, Jiatao Gu, Naman Goyal, Xian Li, Sergey Edunov, Marjan Ghazvininejad, Mike Lewis, and Luke Zettlemoyer. 2020. Multilingual denoising pre-training for neural machine translation. *Transactions of the Association for Computational Linguistics*, 8:726–742.

Yuchen Liu, Hao Xiong, Jiajun Zhang, Zhongjun He, Hua Wu, Haifeng Wang, and Chengqing Zong. 2019. End-to-End Speech Translation with Knowledge Distillation. In *Proc. Interspeech 2019*, pages 1128–1132.

Evgeny Matusov, Gregor Leusch, Oliver Bender, and Hermann Ney. 2005. Evaluating Machine Translation Output with Automatic Sentence Segmentation. In *Proceedings of the Second International Workshop on Spoken Language Translation*, Pittsburgh, Pennsylvania, USA.

J. Niehues, R. Cattoni, S. Stüker, M. Negri, M. Turchi, Elizabeth Salesky, Ramon Sanabria, Loïc Barrault, Lucia Specia, and Marcello Federico. 2019. The iwslt 2019 evaluation campaign. In *Proceedings of the 16th International Workshop on Spoken Language Translation*.

Myle Ott, Sergey Edunov, Alexei Baevski, Angela Fan, Sam Gross, Nathan Ng, David Grangier, and Michael Auli. 2019. fairseq: A fast, extensible toolkit for sequence modeling. In *Proceedings of NAACL-HLT 2019: Demonstrations*.

Vassil Panayotov, Guoguo Chen, Daniel Povey, and Sanjeev Khudanpur. 2015. Librispeech: An asr corpus based on public domain audio books. In *2015 IEEE International Conference on Acoustics, Speech and Signal Processing (ICASSP)*, pages 5206–5210.

Kishore Papineni, Salim Roukos, Todd Ward, and Wei-Jing Zhu. 2002. Bleu: a method for automatic evaluation of machine translation. In *Proceedings of the 40th Annual Meeting of the Association for Computational Linguistics*, pages 311–318, Philadelphia, Pennsylvania, USA. Association for Computational Linguistics.

Tomasz Potapczyk and Pawel Przybysz. 2020. SRPOL's System for the IWSLT 2020 End-to-End Speech Translation Task. In *Proceedings of the 17th International Conference on Spoken Language Translation*, pages 89–94, Online. Association for Computational Linguistics.

Danilo Rezende and Shakir Mohamed. 2015. Variational inference with normalizing flows. In *Proceedings of the 32nd International Conference on Machine Learning*, volume 37 of *Proceedings of Machine Learning Research*, pages 1530–1538, Lille, France. PMLR.

Elizabeth Salesky, Matthew Wiesner, Jacob Bremerman, Roldano Cattoni, Matteo Negri, Marco Turchi, Douglas W. Oard, and Matt Post. 2021. Multilingual tedx corpus for speech recognition and translation. In *Proceedings of Interspeech*.

Matthew Snover, Bonnie Dorr, Rich Schwartz, Linnea Micciulla, and John Makhoul. 2006. A study of translation edit rate with targeted human annotation. In *Proceedings of the 7th Conference of the Association for Machine Translation in the Americas: Technical Papers*, pages 223–231, Cambridge, Massachusetts, USA. Association for Machine Translation in the Americas.

Matthias Sperber and Matthias Paulik. 2020. Speech translation and the end-to-end promise: Taking stock of where we are. In *Proceedings of the 58th Annual Meeting of the Association for Computational Linguistics*, pages 7409–7421, Online. Association for Computational Linguistics.

Xu Tan, Yi Ren, Di He, Tao Qin, and Tie-Yan Liu. 2019. Multilingual neural machine translation with knowledge distillation. In *International Conference on Learning Representations*.

Yuqing Tang, Chau Tran, Xian Li, Peng-Jen Chen, Naman Goyal, Vishrav Chaudhary, Jiatao Gu, and Angela Fan. 2020. Multilingual translation with extensible multilingual pretraining and finetuning. *arXiv preprint arXiv:2008.00401*.

Ioannis Tsiamas, Gerard I. Gállego, José A. R. Fonollosa, and Marta R. Costa-jussà. 2022. Shas: Approaching optimal segmentation for end-to-end speech translation.

Ashish Vaswani, Noam Shazeer, Niki Parmar, Jakob Uszkoreit, Llion Jones, Aidan N Gomez, Ł ukasz Kaiser, and Illia Polosukhin. 2017. Attention is all you need. In *Advances in Neural Information Processing Systems*, volume 30. Curran Associates, Inc.

Changhan Wang, Anne Wu, and Juan Pino. 2020. Covost 2: A massively multilingual speech-to-text translation corpus. *arXiv preprint arXiv:2007.10310*.

Thomas Wolf, Lysandre Debut, Victor Sanh, Julien Chaumond, Clement Delangue, Anthony Moi, Pierric Cistac, Tim Rault, Rémi Louf, Morgan Funtowicz, Joe Davison, Sam Shleifer, Patrick von Platen, Clara Ma, Yacine Jernite, Julien Plu, Canwen Xu, Teven Le Scao, Sylvain Gugger, Mariama Drame, Quentin Lhoest, and Alexander M. Rush. 2020. Transformers: State-of-the-art natural language processing. In *Proceedings of the 2020 Conference on Empirical Methods in Natural Language Processing: System Demonstrations*, pages 38–45, Online. Association for Computational Linguistics.

Qiantong Xu, Alexei Baevski, Tatiana Likhomanenko, Paden Tomasello, Alexis Conneau, Ronan Collobert, Gabriel Synnaeve, and Michael Auli. 2020. Self-training and pre-training are complementary for speech recognition. *arXiv preprint arXiv:2010.11430*.

CUNI-KIT System for Simultaneous Speech Translation Task at IWSLT 2022

Peter Polák[1] and **Ngoc-Quan Ngoc**[2] and **Tuan-Nam Nguyen**[2] and **Danni Liu**[3]
Carlos Mullov[2] and **Jan Niehues**[2] and **Ondřej Bojar**[1] and **Alexander Waibel**[2,4]
polak@ufal.mff.cuni.cz
[1] Charles University
[2] Karlsruhe Institute of Technology
[3] Maastricht University
[4] Carnegie Mellon University

Abstract

In this paper, we describe our submission to the Simultaneous Speech Translation at IWSLT 2022. We explore strategies to utilize an offline model in a simultaneous setting without the need to modify the original model. In our experiments, we show that our onlinization algorithm is almost on par with the offline setting while being $3\times$ faster than offline in terms of latency on the test set. We also show that the onlinized offline model outperforms the best IWSLT2021 simultaneous system in medium and high latency regimes and is almost on par in the low latency regime. We make our system publicly available.[1]

1 Introduction

This paper describes the CUNI-KIT submission to the Simultaneous Speech Translation task at IWSLT 2022 (Anastasopoulos et al., 2022) by Charles University (CUNI) and Karlsruhe Institute of Technology (KIT).

Recent work on end-to-end (E2E) simultaneous speech-to-text translation (ST) is focused on training specialized models specifically for this task. The disadvantage is the need of storing an extra model, usually a more difficult training and inference setup, increased computational complexity (Han et al., 2020; Liu et al., 2021) and risk of performance degradation if used in offline setting (Liu et al., 2020a).

In this work, we base our system on a robust multilingual offline ST model that leverages pretrained wav2vec 2.0 (Baevski et al., 2020) and mBART (Liu et al., 2020b). We revise the onlinization approach by Liu et al. (2020a) and propose an improved technique with a fully controllable quality-latency trade-off. We demonstrate that without any change to the offline model, our simultaneous system in the mid- and high-latency regimes is on par with the offline performance. At the same time, the model outperforms previous IWSLT systems in medium and high latency regimes and is almost on par in the low latency regime. Finally, we observe a problematic behavior of the average lagging metric for speech translation (Ma et al., 2020) when dealing with long hypotheses, resulting in negative values. We propose a minor change to the metric formula to prevent this behavior.

Our contribution is as follows:

- We revise and generalize onlinization proposed by Liu et al. (2020a); Nguyen et al. (2021) and discover parameter enabling quality-latency trade-off,
- We demonstrate that one multilingual offline model can serve as simultaneous ST for three language pairs,
- We demonstrate that an improvement in the offline model leads also to an improvement in the online regime,
- We propose a change to the average lagging metric that avoids negative values.

2 Related Work

Simultaneous speech translation can be implemented either as a (hybrid) cascaded system (Kolss et al., 2008; Niehues et al., 2016; Elbayad et al., 2020; Liu et al., 2020a; Bahar et al., 2021) or an end-to-end model (Han et al., 2020; Liu et al., 2021). Unlike for the offline speech translation where cascade seems to have the best quality, the end-to-end speech translation offers a better quality-latency trade-off (Ansari et al., 2020; Liu et al., 2021; Anastasopoulos et al., 2021).

End-to-end systems use different techniques to perform simultaneous speech translation. Han et al. (2020) uses wait-k (Ma et al., 2019) model and metalearning (Indurthi et al., 2020) to alleviate

[1] https://hub.docker.com/repository/docker/polape7/cuni-kit-simultaneous

Proceedings of the 19th International Conference on Spoken Language Translation (IWSLT 2022), pages 277 - 285
May 26-27, 2022 ©2022 Association for Computational Linguistics

the data scarcity. Liu et al. (2020a) uses a unidirectional encoder with monotonic cross-attention to limit the dependence on future context. Other work (Liu et al., 2021) proposes Cross Attention augmented Transducer (CAAT) as an extension of RNN-T (Graves, 2012).

Nguyen et al. (2021) proposed a hypothesis stability detection for automatic speech recognition (ASR). The *shared prefix* strategy finds the longest common prefix in all beams. Liu et al. (2020a) explore such strategies in the context of speech recognition and translation. The most promising is the longest common prefix of two consecutive chunks. The downside of this approach is the inability to parametrize the quality-latency trade-off. We directly address this in our work.

3 Onlinization

In this section, we describe the onlinization of the offline model and propose two ways to control the quality-latency trade-off.

3.1 Incremental Decoding

Depending on the language pair, translation tasks may require reordering or a piece of information that might not be apparent until the source utterance ends. In the offline setting, the model processes the whole utterance at once, rendering the strategy most optimal in terms of quality. If applied in online mode, this ultimately leads to a large latency. One approach to reducing the latency is to break the source utterance into chunks and perform the translation on each chunk.

In this paper, we follow the incremental decoding framework described by Liu et al. (2020a). We break the input utterance into small fixed-size chunks and decode each time after we receive a new chunk. After each decoding step, we identify a stable part of the hypothesis using *stable hypothesis detection*. The stable part is sent to the user ("committed" in the following) and is no longer changed afterward (i.e., no retranslation).[2] Our current implementation assumes that the whole speech input fits into memory, in other words, we are only adding new chunks as they are arriving. This simplification is possible because the evaluation of the shared task is performed on segmented input, on individual utterances. With each newly arrived input chunk, the decoding starts with forced decoding of the already committed tokens and continues with beam search decoding.

3.2 Chunk Size

Speech recognition and translation use chunking for simultaneous inference with various chunk sizes ranging from 300 ms to 2 seconds (Liu, 2020; Nguyen et al., 2021) although the literature suggests that the turn-taking in conversational speech is shorter, around 200 ms (Levinson and Torreira, 2015). We investigate different chunk sizes in combination with various stable hypothesis detection strategies. As we document later, the chunk size is the principal factor that controls the quality-latency trade-off.

3.3 Stable Hypothesis Detection

Committing hypotheses from incomplete input presents a possible risk of introducing errors. To reduce the instability and trade time for quality, we employ a *stable hypothesis detection*. Formally, we define a function $prefix(W)$ that, given a set of hypotheses (i.e., W^c_{all} if we want to consider the whole beam or W^c_{best} for the single best hypothesis obtained during the beam search decoding of the c-th chunk), outputs a stable prefix. We investigate several functions:

Hold-n (Liu et al., 2020a) Hold-n strategy selects the best hypothesis in the beam and deletes the last n tokens from it:

$$\text{prefix}(W^c_{best}) = W_{0:\max(0,|W|-n)}, \qquad (1)$$

where W^c_{best} is the best hypothesis obtained in the beam search of c-th chunk. If the hypothesis has only n or fewer tokens, we return an empty string.

LA-n Local agreement (Liu et al., 2020a) displays the agreeing prefixes of the two consecutive chunks. Unlike the hold-n strategy, the local agreement does not offer any explicit quality-latency trade-off. We generalize the strategy to take the agreeing prefixes of n consecutive chunks.

During the first $n-1$ chunks, we do not output any tokens. From the n-th chunk on, we identify the longest common prefix of the best hypothesis of the n consecutive chunks:

$$\text{prefix}(W^c_{best}) = \begin{cases} \varnothing, & \text{if } c < n, \\ \text{LCP}(W^{c-n+1}_{best}, ..., W^c_{best}), & \text{otherwise,} \end{cases} \qquad (2)$$

[2]This is a requirement for the evaluation in the Simultaneous Speech Translation task at IWSLT 2022.

where $LCP(\cdot)$ is longest common prefix of the arguments.

SP-n Shared prefix (Nguyen et al., 2021) strategy displays the longest common prefix of all the items in the beam of a chunk. Similarly to the LA-n strategy, we propose a generalization to the longest common prefix of all items in the beams of the n consecutive chunks:

$$\text{prefix}(W^c_{all}) = \begin{cases} \varnothing, & \text{if } c < n, \\ \text{LCP}(W^{c-n+1}_{\text{beam } 1\ldots B}, \ldots, W^{c}_{\text{beam } 1\ldots B}), & \text{otherwise,} \end{cases} \tag{3}$$

i.e., all beam hypotheses $1, ..., B$ (where B is the beam size) of all chunks $c - n + 1, ..., c$.

3.4 Initial Wait

The limited context of the early chunks might result in an unstable hypothesis and an emission of erroneous tokens. The autoregressive nature of the model might cause further performance degradation in later chunks. One possible solution is to use longer chunks, but it inevitably leads to a higher latency throughout the whole utterance. To mitigate this issue, we explore a lengthening of the first chunk. We call this strategy an initial wait.

4 Experiments Setup

In this section, we describe the onlinization experiments.

4.1 Evaluation Setup

We use the SimulEval toolkit (Ma et al., 2020). The toolkit provides a simple interface for evaluation of simultaneous (speech) translation. It reports the quality metric BLEU (Papineni et al., 2002; Post, 2018) and latency metrics Average Proportion (AP, Cho and Esipova 2016), Average Lagging (AL, Ma et al. 2019), and Differentiable Average Lagging (DAL, Cherry and Foster 2019) modified for speech source.

Specifically, we implement an `Agent` class. We have to implement two important functions: `policy(state)` and `predict(state)`, where `state` is the state of the agent (e.g., read processed input, emitted tokens, ...). The policy function returns the action of the agent: (1) `READ` to request more input, (2) `WRITE` to emit new hypothesis tokens.

We implement the `policy` as specified in Algorithm 1. The default action is `READ`. If there is a new chunk, we perform the inference and use the $prefix(W^c)$ function to find the stable prefix. If there are new tokens to display (i.e., $|prefix(W^c)| > |prefix(W^{c-1})|$), we return the `WRITE` action. As soon as our agent emits an end-of-sequence (EOS) token, the inference of the utterance is finished by the SimulEval. We noticed that our model was emitting the EOS token quite often, especially in the early chunks. Hence, we ignore the EOS if returned by our model and continue the inference until the end of the source.[3]

Algorithm 1 Policy function

```
Require: state
  if state.new_input > chunk_size then
    hypothesis ← predict(state)
    if |hypothesis| > 0 then
      return WRITE
    end if
  end if
  return READ
```

4.2 Speech Translation Models

In our experiments, we use two different models. First, we do experiments with a monolingual *Model A*, then for the submission, we use a multilingual and more robust *Model B*.[4]

Model A is the KIT IWSLT 2020 model for the Offline Speech Translation task. Specifically, it is an end-to-end English to German Transformer model with relative attention. For more described description, refer to Pham et al. (2020b).

4.2.1 Multilingual Model

For the submission, we use a multilingual Model B. We construct the SLT architecture with the encoder based on the wav2vec 2.0 (Baevski et al., 2020) and the decoder based on the autoregressive language model pretrained with mBART50 (Tang et al., 2020).

wav2vec 2.0 is a Transformer encoder model which receives raw waveforms as input and generates high-level representations. The architecture consists of two main components: first, a

[3]This might cause an unnecessary increase in latency, but it might be partially prevented by voice activity detection.

[4]We also did experiments with a dedicated English-German model similar to Model B (i.e., based on wav2vec and mBART), but it performed worse both in offline and online setting compared to the multilingual version.

convolution-based *feature extractor* downsamples long audio waveforms into features that have similar lengths with spectrograms.After that, a deep Transformer encoder uses self-attention and feed-forward neural network blocks to transform the features without further downsampling.

During the self-supervised training process, the network is trained with a contrastive learning strategy (Baevski et al., 2020), in which the already downsampled features are randomly masked and the model learns to predict the quantized latent representation of the masked time step.

During the supervised learning step, we freeze the feature extraction weights to save memory since the first layers are among the largest ones. We fine-tune all of the weights in the Transformer encoder. Moreover, to make the model more robust to the fluctuation in absolute positions and durations when it comes to audio signals,we added the relative position encodings (Dai et al., 2019; Pham et al., 2020a) to alleviate this problem.[5]

Here we used the same pretrained model with the speech recognizer, with the large architecture pretrained with $53k$ hours of unlabeled data.

mBART50 is an encoder-decoder Transformer-based language model. During training, instead of the typical language modeling setting of predicting the next word in the sequence, this model is trained to reconstruct a sequence from its noisy version (Lewis et al., 2019) and later extended to a multilingual version (Liu et al., 2020b; Tang et al., 2020) in which the corpora from multiple languages are combined during training. mBART50 is the version that is pretrained on 50 languages.

The mBART50 model follows the Transformer encoder and decoder (Vaswani et al., 2017). During fine-tuning, we combine the mBART50 decoder with the wav2vec 2.0 encoder, where both encoder and decoder know one modality. The cross-attention layers connecting the decoder with the encoder are the parts that require extensive fine-tuning in this case, due to the modality mismatch between pretraining and fine-tuning.

Finally, we use the model in a multilingual setting, i.e., for English to Chinese, German, and Japanese language pairs by training on the combination of the datasets. The mBART50 vocabulary contains language tokens for all three languages and can be used to control the language output (Ha et al., 2016).

For more details on the model refer to Pham et al. (2022).

4.3 Test Data

For the onlinization experiments, we use MuST-C (Cattoni et al., 2021) `tst-COMMON` from the v2.0 release. We conduct all the experiments on the English-German language pair.

5 Experiments and Results

In this section, we describe the experiments and discuss the results.

5.1 Chunks Size

We experiment with chunk sizes of 250 ms, 500 ms, 1s, and 2 s. We combine the sizes of the chunks with different partial hypothesis selection strategies. The results are shown in Figure 1.

The results document that the chunk size parameter has a stronger influence on the trade-off than different prefix strategies. Additionally, this enables constant trade-off strategies (e.g., LA-2) to become flexible.

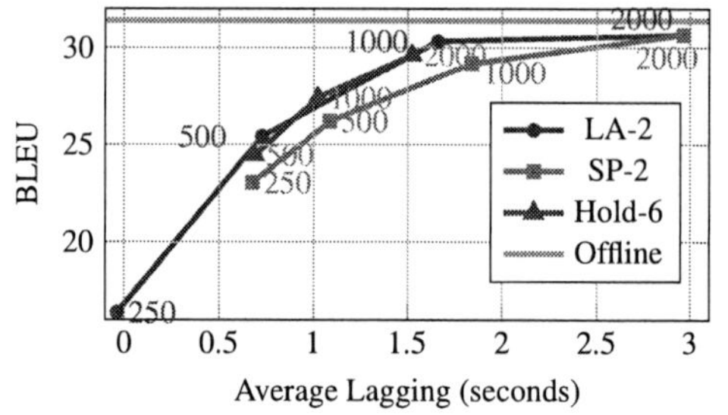

Figure 1: Quality-latency trade-off of different chunk sizes combined with different stable hypothesis detection strategies. The number next to the marks indicates chunk size in milliseconds.

5.2 Stable Hypothesis Detection Strategies

We experiment with three strategies: hold-n (withholds last n tokens), shared prefix (SP-n; finds the longest common prefix of all beams in n consecutive chunks) and local agreement (LA-n; finds the longest common prefix of the best hypothesis in n consecutive chunks). For hold-n, we select $n = 3, 6, 12$; for SP-n, we select $n = 1, 2$ ($n = 1$ corresponds to the strategy by Nguyen et al. (2021)); for LA-n we select $n = 2, 3, 4$ ($n = 2$

[5]This has the added advantage of better generalization in situations where training and testing data are segmented differently.

corresponds to the strategy by Liu et al. (2020a)). The results are in Figures 2 and 3.

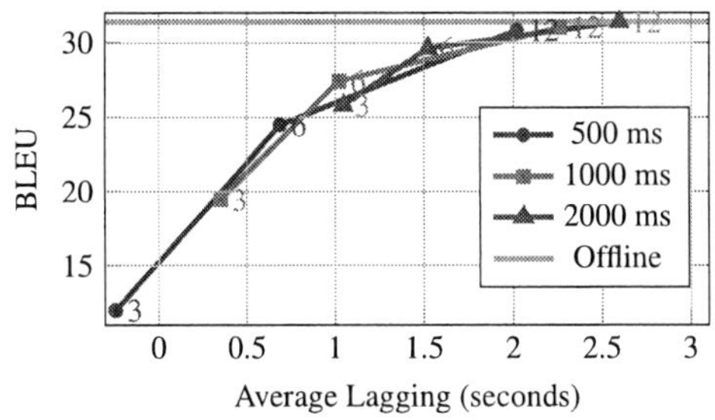

Figure 2: Quality-latency trade-off of hold-n strategy with different values of n. The number next to the marks indicates n. Colored lines connect results with equal chunk size.

Hold-n The results suggest (see Figure 2) that the hold-n strategy can use either n or chunk size to control the quality-latency trade-off with equal effect. The only exception seems to be too low $n <= 3$, which slightly underperforms the options with higher n and shorter chunk size.

Local agreement (LA-n) The local agreement seems to outperform all other strategies (see Figure 3). LA-n for all n follows the same quality-latency trade-off line. The advantage of LA-2 is in reduced computational complexity compared to the other LA-n strategies with $n > 2$.

Shared prefix (SP-n) SP-1 strongly underperforms other strategies in quality (see Figure 3). While the SP-1 strategy performs well in the ASR task (Nguyen et al., 2021), it is probably too lax for the speech translation task. The generalized and more conservative SP-2 performs much better. Although, the more relaxed LA-2, which considers only the best item in the beam, has a better quality-latency trade-off curve than the more conservative SP-2.

5.3 Initial Wait

As we could see in Section 5.1, the shorter chunk sizes tend to perform worse. One of the reasons might be the limited context of the early chunks.[6] To increase the early context, we prolong the first chunk to 2 seconds.

The results are in Table 1. We see a slight (0.3 BLEU) increase in quality for a chunk size of 250 ms, though the initial wait does not improve the BLEU and a considerable increase in the latency.

Initial wait	Chunk size	BLEU	AL	AP	DAL
	250	16.34	-35.97	0.66	1435.06
0	500	25.40	727.55	0.73	1791.21
	1000	30.29	1660.59	0.83	2662.18
	250	16.60	358.35	0.74	2121.54
2000	500	25.42	952.15	0.77	2142.53
	1000	30.29	1654.77	0.83	2657.48

Table 1: Quality-latency trade-off of the LA-2 strategy with and without the initial wait.

The performance seems to be influenced mainly by the chunk size. The reason for smaller chunks' under-performance might be caused by (1) acoustic uncertainty towards the end of a chunk (e.g., words often get cut in the middle), or (2) insufficient information difference between two consecutive chunks.

This is supported by the observation in Figure 3. Increasing the number of consecutive chunks (i.e., increasing the context for the decision) considered in the local agreement strategy (LA-2, 3, 4), improves the quality, while it adds latency.

5.4 Negative Average Lagging

Interestingly, we noticed that some of the strategies achieved negative average lagging (e.g., LA-2 in Section 5.1) with a chunk size of 250 ms has AL of -36 ms). After a closer examination of the outputs, we found that the negative AL is in utterances where the hypothesis is significantly longer than the reference. Recall the average latency for speech input defined by Ma et al. (2020):

$$\text{AL}_{\text{speech}} = \frac{1}{\tau'(|\mathbf{X}|)} \sum_{i=1}^{\tau'(|\mathbf{X}|)} d_i - d_i^*, \tag{4}$$

where $d_i = \sum_{k=1}^{j} T_k$, j is the index of raw audio segment that has been read when generating y_i, T_k is duration of raw audio segment, $\tau'(|\mathbf{X}|) = \min\{i|d_i = \sum_{j=1}^{|\mathbf{X}|} T_j\}$ and d_i^* are the delays of an ideal policy:

$$d_i^* = (i-1) \times \sum_{j=1}^{|\mathbf{X}|} T_j \,/ |\mathbf{Y}^*|, \tag{5}$$

where $\mathbf{Y}^*$ is reference translation.

If the hypothesis is longer than the reference, then $d_i^* > d_i$, making the sum argument in Equation (4) negative. On the other hand, if we use the length of the hypothesis instead, then a shorter

[6]If we translated a non-pre-segmented input, this problem would be limited only onetime to the beginning of the input.

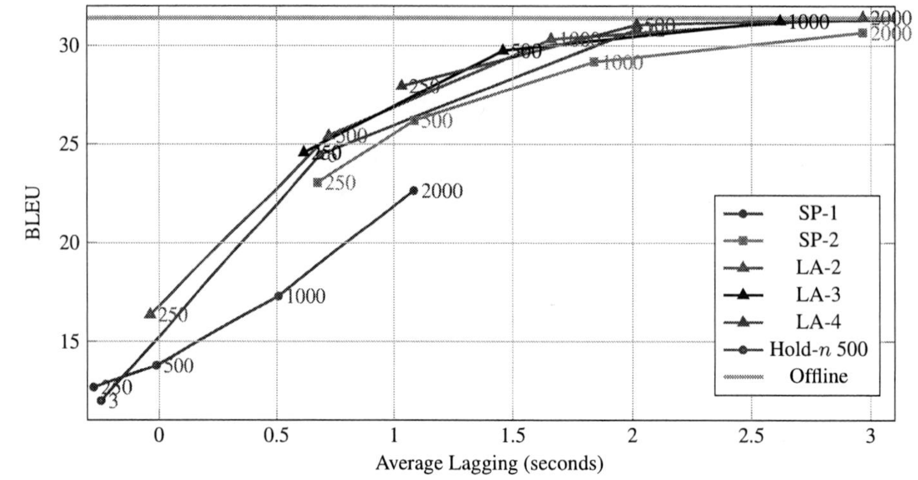

Figure 3: Quality-latency trade-off of shared prefix (SP-n) and local agreement (LA-n) with different n and chunk size.

hypothesis would benefit.[7] We, therefore, suggest using the maximum of both to prevent the advantage of either a shorter or a longer hypothesis:

$$d_i^* = (i-1) \times \sum_{j=1}^{|\mathbf{X}|} T_j \;/ max(|\mathbf{Y}|, |\mathbf{Y}^*|). \quad (6)$$

6 Submitted System

In this section, we describe the submitted system. We follow the allowed training data and pretrained models and therefore our submission is *constrained* (see Section 4.2.1 for model description).

For stable hypothesis detection, we decided to use the local agreement strategy with $n = 2$. As shown in Section 5.2, the LA-2 has the best latency-quality trade-off along with other LA-n strategies. To achieve the different latency regimes, we use various chunk sizes, depending on the language pair. We decided not to use larger $n > 2$ to control the latency, as it increases the computation complexity while having the same effect as using a different chunk size. The results on MuST-C tst-COMMON are in Table 2. The quality-latency trade-off is in Figure 4.

From Table 2 and Figure 4, we can see that the proposed method works well on two different models and various language pairs. We see that an improvement in the offline model (offline BLEU of 31.36 and 33.14 for Model A and B, respectively) leads to improvement in the online regime.

[7]Ma et al. (2019) originally used the hypothesis length in the Equation (5) and then Ma et al. (2020) suggested to use the reference length instead.

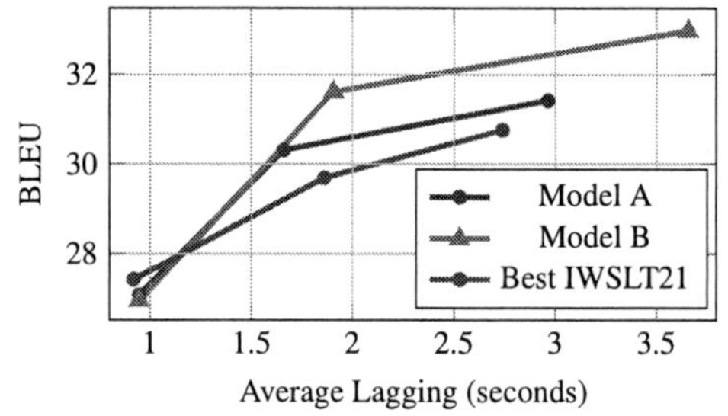

Figure 4: Quality-latency trade-off on English-German tst-COMMON of our two models: a dedicated English-German model trained from scratch (Model A) and a multilingual model based on wav2vec and mBART (Model B). We also include the best IWSLT 2021 system (USTC-NELSLIP (Liu et al., 2021)).

Finally, we see that our method beats the best IWSLT 2021 system (USTC-NELSLIP (Liu et al., 2021)) in medium and high latency regimes using both models (i.e., a model trained from scratch and a model based on pretrained wav2vec and mBART), and is almost on par in the low latency regime (Model A is losing 0.35 BLEU and Model B is losing 0.47 BLEU).

6.1 Computationally Aware Latency

In this paper, we do not report any computationally aware metrics, as our implementation of Transformers is slow. Later, we implemented the same onlinization approach using wav2vec 2.0 and mBART from Huggingface Transformers (Wolf et al., 2020). The new implementation reaches faster than real-time inference speed.

Model	Language pair	Latency regime	Chunk size	BLEU	AL	AP	DAL
Best IWSLT21 system	En-De	Low	-	27.40	920	0.68	1420
		Medium	-	29.68	1860	0.82	2650
		High	-	30.75	2740	0.90	3630
Model A	En-De	Low	600	27.05	947	0.76	1993
		Medium	1000	30.30	1660	0.84	2662
		High	2000	31.41	2966	0.93	3853
		Offline	-	31.36	5794	1.00	5794
Model B	En-De	Low	500	26.93	945	0.77	2052
		Medium	1000	31.60	1906	0.86	2945
		High	2500	32.98	3663	0.96	4452
		Offline	-	33.14	5794	1.00	5794
	En-Ja	Low	1000	16.84	2452	0.90	3212
		Medium	2400	16.99	3791	0.97	4296
		High	3000	16.97	4140	0.98	4536
		Offline	-	16.88	5119	1.00	5119
	En-Zh	Low	800	23.69	1761	0.85	2561
		Medium	1500	24.29	2788	0.93	3500
		High	2500	24.56	3669	0.97	4212
		Offline	-	24.54	5119	1.00	5119

Table 2: Results of the older model used for the experiments (Model A) and the submitted system (Model B) on the MuST-C v2 tst-COMMON. We also include the best IWSLT 2021 system (USTC-NELSLIP (Liu et al., 2021)).

7 Conclusion

In this paper, we reviewed onlinization strategies for end-to-end speech translation models. We identified the optimal stable hypothesis detection strategy and proposed two separate ways of the quality-latency trade-off parametrization. We showed that the onlinization of the offline models is easy and performs almost on par with the offline run. We demonstrated that an improvement in the offline model leads to improved online performance. We also showed that our method outperforms a dedicated simultaneous system. Finally, we proposed an improvement in the average latency metric.

Acknowledgments

This work has received support from the project "Grant Schemes at CU" (reg. no. CZ.02.2.69/0.0/0.0/19_073/0016935), the grant 19-26934X (NEUREM3) of the Czech Science Foundation, the European Union's Horizon 2020 Research and Innovation Programme under Grant Agreement No 825460 (ELITR), and partly supported by a Facebook Sponsored Research Agreement "Language Similarity in Machine Translation".

References

Antonios Anastasopoulos, Luisa Bentivogli, Marcely Z. Boito, Ondřej Bojar, Roldano Cattoni, Anna Currey, Georgiana Dinu, Kevin Duh, Maha Elbayad, Marcello Federico, Christian Federmann, Hongyu Gong, Roman Grundkiewicz, Barry Haddow, Benjamin Hsu, Dávid Javorský, Věra Kloudová, Surafel M. Lakew, Xutai Ma, Prashant Mathur, Paul McNamee, Kenton Murray, Maria Nădejde, Satoshi Nakamura, Matteo Negri, Jan Niehues, Xing Niu, Juan Pino, Elizabeth Salesky, Jiatong Shi, Sebastian Stüker, Katsuhito Sudoh, Marco Turchi, Yogesh Virkar, Alex Waibel, Changhan Wang, and Shinji Watanabe. 2022. FINDINGS OF THE IWSLT 2022 EVALUATION CAMPAIGN. In *Proceedings of the 19th International Conference on Spoken Language Translation (IWSLT 2022)*, Dublin, Ireland. Association for Computational Linguistics.

Antonios Anastasopoulos, Ondřej Bojar, Jacob Bremerman, Roldano Cattoni, Maha Elbayad, Marcello Federico, Xutai Ma, Satoshi Nakamura, Matteo Negri, Jan Niehues, Juan Pino, Elizabeth Salesky, Sebastian Stüker, Katsuhito Sudoh, Marco Turchi, Alexander Waibel, Changhan Wang, and Matthew Wiesner. 2021. FINDINGS OF THE IWSLT 2021 EVALUATION CAMPAIGN. In *Proceedings of the 18th International Conference on Spoken Language Translation (IWSLT 2021)*, pages 1–29, Bangkok, Thailand (online). Association for Computational Linguistics.

Ebrahim Ansari, Amittai Axelrod, Nguyen Bach, Ondřej Bojar, Roldano Cattoni, Fahim Dalvi, Nadir Durrani, Marcello Federico, Christian Federmann, Jiatao Gu, Fei Huang, Kevin Knight, Xutai Ma, Ajay Nagesh, Matteo Negri, Jan Niehues, Juan Pino, Elizabeth Salesky, Xing Shi, Sebastian Stüker, Marco Turchi, Alexander Waibel, and Changhan Wang. 2020. FINDINGS OF THE IWSLT 2020 EVALUATION CAMPAIGN. In *Proceedings of the 17th International Conference on Spoken Language Translation*, pages 1–34, Online. Association for Computational Linguistics.

Alexei Baevski, Yuhao Zhou, Abdelrahman Mohamed,

and Michael Auli. 2020. wav2vec 2.0: A framework for self-supervised learning of speech representations. *Advances in Neural Information Processing Systems*, 33:12449–12460.

Parnia Bahar, Patrick Wilken, Mattia A. Di Gangi, and Evgeny Matusov. 2021. Without further ado: Direct and simultaneous speech translation by AppTek in 2021. In *Proceedings of the 18th International Conference on Spoken Language Translation (IWSLT 2021)*, pages 52–63, Bangkok, Thailand (online). Association for Computational Linguistics.

Roldano Cattoni, Mattia Antonino Di Gangi, Luisa Bentivogli, Matteo Negri, and Marco Turchi. 2021. Must-c: A multilingual corpus for end-to-end speech translation. *Computer Speech & Language*, 66:101155.

Colin Cherry and George Foster. 2019. Thinking slow about latency evaluation for simultaneous machine translation. *arXiv preprint arXiv:1906.00048*.

Kyunghyun Cho and Masha Esipova. 2016. Can neural machine translation do simultaneous translation? *arXiv preprint arXiv:1606.02012*.

Zihang Dai, Zhilin Yang, Yiming Yang, Jaime Carbonell, Quoc Le, and Ruslan Salakhutdinov. 2019. Transformer-XL: Attentive language models beyond a fixed-length context. In *Proceedings of the 57th Annual Meeting of the Association for Computational Linguistics (ACL)*.

Maha Elbayad, Ha Nguyen, Fethi Bougares, Natalia Tomashenko, Antoine Caubrière, Benjamin Lecouteux, Yannick Estève, and Laurent Besacier. 2020. ON-TRAC consortium for end-to-end and simultaneous speech translation challenge tasks at IWSLT 2020. In *Proceedings of the 17th International Conference on Spoken Language Translation*, pages 35–43, Online. Association for Computational Linguistics.

Alex Graves. 2012. Sequence transduction with recurrent neural networks. *arXiv preprint arXiv:1211.3711*.

Thanh-Le Ha, Jan Niehues, and Alexander Waibel. 2016. Toward multilingual neural machine translation with universal encoder and decoder. In *Proceedings of the 13th International Workshop on Spoken Language Translation (IWSLT 2016)*, Seattle, USA.

Hou Jeung Han, Mohd Abbas Zaidi, Sathish Reddy Indurthi, Nikhil Kumar Lakumarapu, Beomseok Lee, and Sangha Kim. 2020. End-to-end simultaneous translation system for IWSLT2020 using modality agnostic meta-learning. In *Proceedings of the 17th International Conference on Spoken Language Translation*, pages 62–68, Online. Association for Computational Linguistics.

Sathish Indurthi, Houjeung Han, Nikhil Kumar Lakumarapu, Beomseok Lee, Insoo Chung, Sangha Kim, and Chanwoo Kim. 2020. End-end speech-to-text translation with modality agnostic meta-learning. In *ICASSP 2020 - 2020 IEEE International Conference on Acoustics, Speech and Signal Processing (ICASSP)*, pages 7904–7908.

Muntsin Kolss, Stephan Vogel, and Alex Waibel. 2008. Stream decoding for simultaneous spoken language translation. In *Ninth Annual Conference of the International Speech Communication Association.*

Stephen C Levinson and Francisco Torreira. 2015. Timing in turn-taking and its implications for processing models of language. *Frontiers in psychology*, 6:731.

Mike Lewis, Yinhan Liu, Naman Goyal, Marjan Ghazvininejad, Abdelrahman Mohamed, Omer Levy, Ves Stoyanov, and Luke Zettlemoyer. 2019. Bart: Denoising sequence-to-sequence pre-training for natural language generation, translation, and comprehension. *arXiv preprint arXiv:1910.13461*.

Dan Liu, Mengge Du, Xiaoxi Li, Yuchen Hu, and Lirong Dai. 2021. The USTC-NELSLIP systems for simultaneous speech translation task at IWSLT 2021. In *Proceedings of the 18th International Conference on Spoken Language Translation (IWSLT 2021)*, pages 30–38, Bangkok, Thailand (online). Association for Computational Linguistics.

Danni Liu. 2020. Low-latency end-to-end speech recognition with enhanced readability. Master's thesis, Maastricht University.

Danni Liu, Gerasimos Spanakis, and Jan Niehues. 2020a. Low-Latency Sequence-to-Sequence Speech Recognition and Translation by Partial Hypothesis Selection. In *Proc. Interspeech 2020*, pages 3620–3624.

Yinhan Liu, Jiatao Gu, Naman Goyal, Xian Li, Sergey Edunov, Marjan Ghazvininejad, Mike Lewis, and Luke Zettlemoyer. 2020b. Multilingual denoising pre-training for neural machine translation. *Transactions of the Association for Computational Linguistics*, 8:726–742.

Mingbo Ma, Liang Huang, Hao Xiong, Renjie Zheng, Kaibo Liu, Baigong Zheng, Chuanqiang Zhang, Zhongjun He, Hairong Liu, Xing Li, et al. 2019. Stacl: Simultaneous translation with implicit anticipation and controllable latency using prefix-to-prefix framework. In *Proceedings of the 57th Annual Meeting of the Association for Computational Linguistics*, pages 3025–3036.

Xutai Ma, Mohammad Javad Dousti, Changhan Wang, Jiatao Gu, and Juan Pino. 2020. Simuleval: An evaluation toolkit for simultaneous translation. In *Proceedings of the 2020 Conference on Empirical Methods in Natural Language Processing: System Demonstrations*, pages 144–150.

Thai-Son Nguyen, Sebastian Stüker, and Alex Waibel. 2021. Super-Human Performance in Online Low-Latency Recognition of Conversational Speech. In *Proc. Interspeech 2021*, pages 1762–1766.

Jan Niehues, Thai Son Nguyen, Eunah Cho, Thanh-Le Ha, Kevin Kilgour, Markus Müller, Matthias Sperber, Sebastian Stüker, and Alex Waibel. 2016. Dynamic Transcription for Low-Latency Speech Translation. In *Proc. Interspeech 2016*, pages 2513–2517.

Kishore Papineni, Salim Roukos, Todd Ward, and Wei-Jing Zhu. 2002. Bleu: a method for automatic evaluation of machine translation. In *Proceedings of the 40th annual meeting of the Association for Computational Linguistics*, pages 311–318.

Ngoc-Quan Pham, Thanh-Le Ha, Tuan-Nam Nguyen, Thai-Son Nguyen, Elizabeth Salesky, Sebastian Stüker, Jan Niehues, and Alex Waibel. 2020a. Relative Positional Encoding for Speech Recognition and Direct Translation. In *Proc. Interspeech 2020*, pages 31–35.

Ngoc-Quan Pham, Tuan-Nam Nguyen, Thai-Binh Nguyen, Danni Liu, Carlos Mullov, Jan Niehues, and Alexander Waibel. 2022. Effective combination of pretrained models - KIT@IWSLT2022. In *Proceedings of the 19th International Conference on Spoken Language Translation (IWSLT 2022)*, Dublin, Ireland. Association for Computational Linguistics.

Ngoc-Quan Pham, Felix Schneider, Tuan Nam Nguyen, Thanh-Le Ha, Thai-Son Nguyen, Maximilian Awiszus, Sebastian Stüker, and Alex Waibel. 2020b. Kit's iwslt 2020 slt translation system. In *Proceedings of the 17th International Conference on Spoken Language Translation*, pages 55–61.

Matt Post. 2018. A call for clarity in reporting bleu scores. In *Proceedings of the Third Conference on Machine Translation: Research Papers*, pages 186–191.

Yuqing Tang, Chau Tran, Xian Li, Peng-Jen Chen, Naman Goyal, Vishrav Chaudhary, Jiatao Gu, and Angela Fan. 2020. Multilingual translation with extensible multilingual pretraining and finetuning. *arXiv preprint arXiv:2008.00401*.

Ashish Vaswani, Noam Shazeer, Niki Parmar, Jakob Uszkoreit, Llion Jones, Aidan N Gomez, Łukasz Kaiser, and Illia Polosukhin. 2017. Attention is all you need. In *Advances in Neural Information Processing Systems*, pages 5998–6008.

Thomas Wolf, Lysandre Debut, Victor Sanh, Julien Chaumond, Clement Delangue, Anthony Moi, Pierric Cistac, Tim Rault, Rémi Louf, Morgan Funtowicz, Joe Davison, Sam Shleifer, Patrick von Platen, Clara Ma, Yacine Jernite, Julien Plu, Canwen Xu, Teven Le Scao, Sylvain Gugger, Mariama Drame, Quentin Lhoest, and Alexander M. Rush. 2020. Transformers: State-of-the-art natural language processing. In *Proceedings of the 2020 Conference on Empirical Methods in Natural Language Processing: System Demonstrations*, pages 38–45, Online. Association for Computational Linguistics.

NAIST Simultaneous Speech-to-Text Translation System for IWSLT 2022

Ryo Fukuda†, Yuka Ko†, Yasumasa Kano†, Kosuke Doi†, Hirotaka Tokuyama†, Sakriani Sakti†‡, Katsuhito Sudoh†, Satoshi Nakamura†

†Nara Institute of Science and Technology, Japan

‡Japan Advanced Institute of Science and Technology, Japan

fukuda.ryo.fo3@is.naist.jp

Abstract

This paper describes NAIST's simultaneous speech translation systems developed for IWSLT 2022 Evaluation Campaign. We participated the speech-to-speech track for English-to-German and English-to-Japanese. Our primary submissions were end-to-end systems using adaptive segmentation policies based on Prefix Alignment.

1 Introduction

This paper describes NAIST's submissions to IWSLT 2022 (Anastasopoulos et al., 2022) Simultaneous Speech Translation track. We participated the speech-to-speech track for English-to-German (En-De) and English-to-Japanese (En-Ja) using our end-to-end simultaneous machine translation (SimulMT) systems.

SimulMT based on neural machine translation (NMT) has achieved a large success in recent years. There are two different SimulMT approaches depending on the policy that determines READ (waiting for speech input) and WRITE (writing text output) actions: *fixed* and *adaptive*. Fixed policies are usually implemented by simple rules (Dalvi et al., 2018; Ma et al., 2019; Fukuda et al., 2021; Sen et al., 2021). They are simple yet often effective, but they sometimes make inappropriate decisions due to large word order differences, pauses, and so on. In contrast, adaptive policies decide READ or WRITE actions flexibly taking current context into account (Zheng et al., 2019a,b, 2020; Liu et al., 2021). They can be more effective than fixed policies in end-to-end speech-to-speech SimulMT because it is difficult to define fixed policies for speech input.

In our systems, we use Bilingual Prefix Alignment (Kano et al., 2022), which extracts alignment between bilingual prefix pairs in the training time, for prefix-to-prefix translation in SimulMT. The Bilingual Prefix Alignment is applied to extract

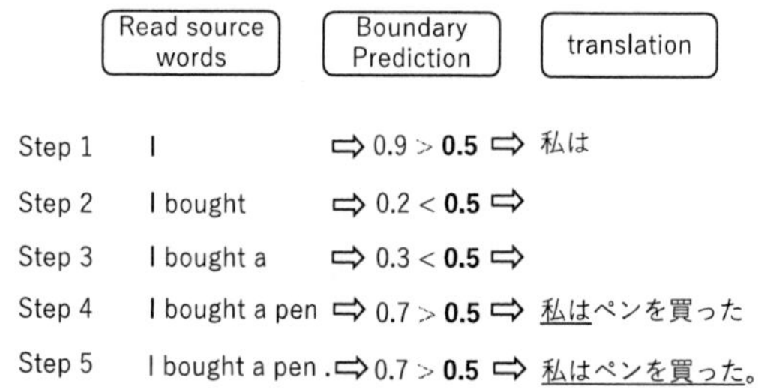

Figure 1: A brief overview of our prefix-to-prefix translation process (Kano et al., 2022) from English to Japanese. The threshold of boundary probability is 0.5 in this example. Underlined parts are the forced output prefixes.

prefix pairs of source language speech and target language translations. We also use the prefix pairs to train a boundary prediction model for an adaptive speech segmentation policy. Our system showed some improvements against wait-k baselines on the development data, in all the latency regimes in both En-De and En-Ja.

2 Simultaneous Speech Translation based on Bilingual Prefix Alignment

We developed simultaneous speech translation (SimulST) based on offline speech translation (ST). Our SimulST system translates an incrementally-growing source language speech prefix into the target language. When the system detects a segment boundary in source language speech, the latest segment is translated taking its input and translation history into account. The ST model is basically the same as an offline one, and we used it to translate an input prefix speech segment from the beginning. However, we constrained the translation prefix by the results in the previous time step. The constraint is implemented by a forced decoding with a given translation prefix. Figure 1 shows an example of whole translation process, but we input the speech prefixes with fixed number of frames. Please refer

Proceedings of the 19th International Conference on Spoken Language Translation (IWSLT 2022), pages 286 - 292
May 26-27, 2022 ©2022 Association for Computational Linguistics

to (Kano et al., 2022) for details of Bilingual Prefix Alignment.

For this system, we need an ST model using an ST corpus consisting of source language speech segments and corresponding translations in the target language. We then fine-tune the offline ST model with prefix pairs of source language speech and target language translations obtained using Bilingual Prefix Alignment. We also need a boundary predictor to segment source language speech adaptively as SimulMT policies. In this section, we present how to extract prefix pairs (2.1) and build the boundary predictor (2.2).

2.1 Extracting Prefix Pairs

Suppose we already have an offline ST model trained using an ST corpus and are going to extract prefix pairs for a speech segment in the source language (S). First, we extract the speech prefixes with τ, 2τ, 3τ, ... frames. Then, for each speech prefix S_{prefix}, we translate it into $\hat{T}_{prefix}$ using the offline ST model. Finally, we compare $\hat{T}_{prefix}$ with $\hat{T}_{offline}$, which is a translation of the entire speech segment. If $\hat{T}_{prefix}$ appears as a prefix of $\hat{T}_{offline}$, we extact $(S_{prefix}, \hat{T}_{prefix})$ as a prefix pair. We apply this process to all the source prefixes. Here, we use a forced decoding with the previously extracted prefix $\hat{T}_{prefix}$ to obtain latter prefix translations and update $\hat{T}_{offline}$ to extract consistent prefix translations. We may obtain the same target prefix with different source prefixes within a given speech segment. We just extract the first appearance and ignore the rest with longer speech prefixes in such cases. The procedure above sometimes extracts *unbalanced* prefix pairs, in which a source language prefix does not fully match its target language speech counterpart. Such unbalanced prefix pairs frequently appear between English and Japanese and cause the degradation of the translation performance. We use a simple heuristic rule to filter out them based on the length ratio between source language speech and target language translation. We exclude prefix pairs in which the length ratio len_s/len_t exceeds $maxratio$, where len_s is the length of S_{prefix} (in the number of frames) and len_t is the length of $\hat{T}_{prefix}$ (in the number of words).

2.2 Boundary Predictor

In inference, the SimulST system incrementally reads source speech and predicts a segment boundary in every τ frames.

To train the boundary predictor, we prepare pairs of a speech prefix and the corresponding binary label sequence extracted from the training data. One source language speech derives many speech prefixes in τ, 2τ, 3τ, ... frames. Suppose we extracted 2τ- and 5τ-frame speech prefixes from the same utterance, for example. We assign a label sequence with τ `0`s followed τ `1`s to the 2τ-frame prefix, which means we should predict a boundary in the second τ frames but not in the first τ frames. For the 5τ-frame prefix, we assign a label sequence where the second and fifth τ-frame parts are filled with `1`s and the rest with `0`s, consistently with the 2τ-frame prefix. In addition, we also extracted speech prefixes where the last τ-frame part is not a boundary. For example, the last τ-frame part of the 3τ- and 4τ-frame speech prefixes is filled with `0`s in this case. The boundary predictor is trained using weighted cross-entropy loss normalized in inverse proportional to the number of appearances of each label.

During inference, the boundary predictor predicts a boundary in every τ frames as a binary classification output. The prediction is made on every frames in the τ-frame segment, so we obtain τ binary classification outputs. If the proportion of label `1` here is larger than or equals to λ_{thre}, the predictor makes a decision of *boundary*, otherwise *non-boundary*.

3 Primary System

We developed SimulST systems for two language pairs: English-to-German (En-De) and English-to-Japanese (En-Ja). We implemented both our systems based on fairseq[1] (Ott et al., 2019).

3.1 End-to-end Speech Translation

3.1.1 Data

We used MuST-C v2 (Di Gangi et al., 2019), a multilingual ST corpus extracted from TED talks subtitles. Each dataset consists of triplets of segmented English speech, transcripts, and target language translations. The En-De and En-Ja datasets contained about 250k and 330k segments, respectively. As acoustic features, we used 80-dimensional log Mel filter bank (FBANK) with global-level cepstral mean and variance normalization (CMVN) applied.

[1] `https://github.com/pytorch/fairseq/commit/acf312418e4718996a103d67bd57516938137a7d`

We applied with Byte Pair Encoding (BPE) to split the sentences into subwords using SentencePiece (Kudo and Richardson, 2018), with a vocabulary of 20,000 subwords shared across the source and target languages.

3.1.2 Model

We used the Transformer implementation of fairseq to build the models. We trained the ASR model using the English speech-text pairs and then trained the ST model using the ASR model for the parameter initialization. The architecture of ASR and ST models were the same. The encoder consisted of a 2D-convolution layer that reduces the sequence length to a quarter, and 12 transformer encoder layers. The decoder consisted of six transformer decoder layers. We set the embedding dimensions and the feed-forward dimensions to 256 and 2,048 and used four attention heads for both the encoder and decoder. The model was trained using Adam with an initial learning rate of 0.0005 with warmup updates of 10,000. In the En-De ASR and ST models and the En-Ja ASR model, we performed the dropout probability of 0.1 and set early stopping patience to 16. In the En-Ja ST model, we set the dropout probability of 0.2 and set early stopping patience to 32.

The ST model training was in two steps. We first trained the ST model using entire segment pairs from the MuST-C. We then fine-tuned the model using bilingual prefix pairs extracted using Bilingual Prefix Alignment (2.1).

3.1.3 Evaluation

We evaluated the models with BLEU and Average Lagging (AL) (Ma et al., 2019) using SimulEval (Ma et al., 2020) on MuST-C v2 tst-COMMON. For En-De, we evaluated on the best ST model based on the dev set, and for En-Ja, we evaluated on the checkpoint averaged ST model in last 10 epochs. Our proposed models were decoded with beam search (beam size=10).

3.2 Implementation Details of the Proposed Method

3.2.1 Data Extraction

We extracted training data for the ST model and the boundary prediction model by using Bilingual Prefix Alignment described in section 2. We set $\tau = 100$ and tried $maxratio = \{\text{None}, 80, 40, 20\}$.

System	BLEU	AL
Offline	21.04	-
Baseline		
wait-1	3.66	844.45
wait-5	11.49	1684.13
wait-17	18.80	3786.07
Proposed (λ_{thre})		
low (0.1)†	17.54	990.32
medium (0.47)	19.15	1859.56
high (0.68)	19.50	3896.67

Table 1: The main results of our systems on En-De tst-COMMON. † uses $T = 48$ frames as an input unit.

System	BLEU	AL
Offline	11.6	-
Baseline		
wait-7	4.76	2369.68
wait-17	8.46	3723.65
wait-27	9.55	4421.75
Proposed (λ_{thre})		
low (0.0)	9.26	2185.51
medium (0.36)	9.90	3946.02
high (0.4)	10.22	4733.65

Table 2: The main results of our systems on En-Ja tst-COMMON. The FT model was the best model with data filtering approach.

3.2.2 Boundary Predictor

We trained the boundary predictor using the extracted source language speech prefixes. The boundary predictor consisted of a 2D-convolution layer reducing the sequence length to $\tau/4$ (25 frames), a unidirectional LSTM layer, and an output linear layer that gives label probabilities $\hat{x}_n \in R^2$ at the n-th frame of the convolution layer. We set the embedding dimensions and the hidden state dimensions of the LSTM layer to 256 and 512. The model was trained using Adam with an initial learning rate of 0.0001, warmup updates of 4,000 and early stopping patience of 8. During inference, we tried several values of voting threshold λ_{thre} between 0.0 to 1.0 to adjust for latency and BLEU tradeoffs.

4 Experiments

We conducted comparative experiments with wait-k (Ma et al., 2019). For baseline wait-k, we tried k ranging from 1 to 19 at two intervals for En-De and 5 to 31 at two intervals (excluding 29) for En-Ja.

Metrics	En-De	En-Ja
Accuracy	0.678	0.679
Precision	0.646	0.480
Recall	0.490	0.009
F1	0.557	0.017

Table 3: The evaluation results of boundary predictor models on prefix pairs of tst-COMMON dataset in $\lambda_{thre} = 0.5$.

Following the default wait-k setting in fairseq, one unit for k was set to 280 frames. For examples, when $k = 3$, after reading 3×280 frames, the model would WRITE and READ alternately.

4.1 Main Results

Table 1 shows the best results of the proposed and baseline SimulMT systems in En-De with low (AL $\leq$ 1,000), medium (AL $\leq$ 2,000), and high (AL $\leq$ 4,000) latency regimes. Table 2 shows the counterpart in En-Ja with low (AL $\leq$ 2,500), medium (AL $\leq$ 4,000), and high (AL $\leq$ 5,000) latency regimes. In both language pairs, our model outperformed the baselines with all the latency regimes. In particular, the proposed method showed a significant improvement of more than 10 points in BLEU in En-De with low latency regime. On the other hand, the improvement for En-Ja was smaller than in En-De. One possible reason was the performance difference of the boundary predictor, which depends on the difference between source and target languages. Table 3 shows the results of the boundary predictor on prefix pairs of tst-COMMON dataset with $\lambda_{thre} = 0.5$. For both language pairs, the accuracy was under 68%, suggesting the difficulty of binary classification at the acoustic frame level. Especially, the recall of En-Ja boundary predictor was extremely low, which means that its output predictions were almost 0 (READ) in $\lambda_{thre} = 0.5$. The small λ_{thre} value was required to output label 1 (WRITE) frequently on En-Ja, compared to En-De, as shown in Tables 1 and 2.

4.2 Effectiveness of Fine-tuning

Figure 2 shows the results of wait-k baselines, a model fine-tuned with bilingual prefix pairs (FT) and a model without fine-tuning (w/o FT). Figure 3 shows the counterparts in En-Ja. In En-De, the fine-tuned model worked better than the non fine-tuned model in the range of AL $\leq$ 4,000. The performance gap between proposed models and wait-k models in the low latency ranges were larger than those in the high latency ranges. On the other hand, the non-fine-tuned model worked better than the fine-tuned model in the very large latency ranges with AL > 4000. Both of them outperformed the baseline wait-k models consistently in BLEU. The fine-tuned model achieved higher BLEU scores at the cost of the larger latency, compared to the non-fine-tuned and wait-k models.

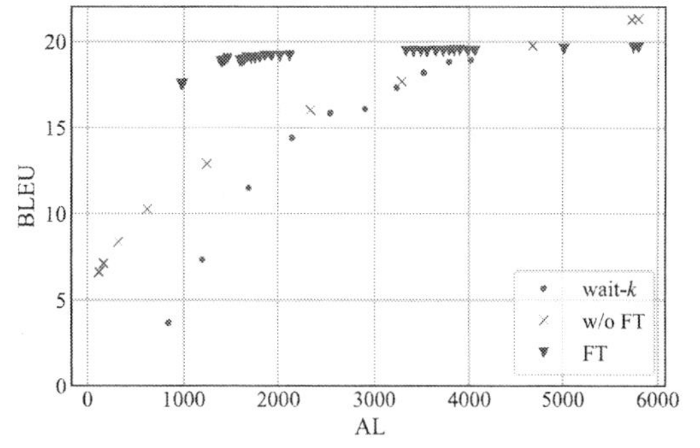

Figure 2: The BLEU and AL results of FT, w/o FT and baseline in En-De. The two FT points in low latency regime (AL$\leq$1000) were evaluated in $T = 48$ frames on $\lambda_{thre} = \{0.0, 0.1\}$.

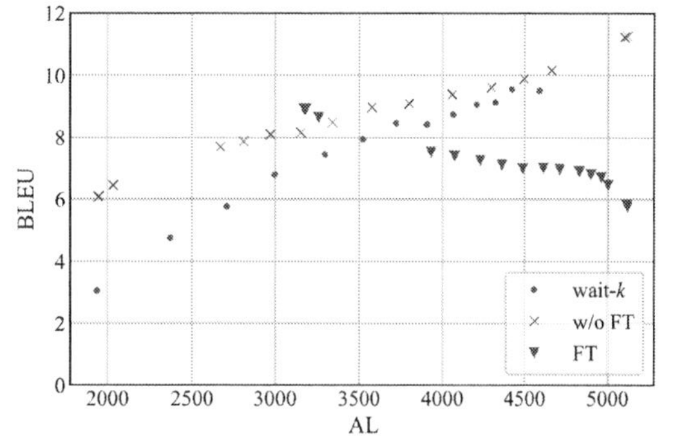

Figure 3: The BLEU and AL results of FT, w/o FT and baseline in En-Ja. The FT model was fine-tuned with non-filtered prefix pairs.

In En-Ja, the scores of the non-fine-tuned model were better than those of wait-k baselines with all the latency regimes. The performance improvements of the non-fine-tuned model against wait-k models in the low latency ranges were larger than those in the high latency ranges. However, the scores of the fine-tuned model were worse than those of wait-k models and the non-fine-tuned model almost everywhere. It suggests the failure of appropriate fine-tuning in En-Ja.

Figure 4: Examples of extracted prefix pairs on En-Ja containing unbalanced pairs whose target prefix is too short.

Filter ($maxratio$)	# samples (% removed)
None	642,426 (0%)
80	583,986 (9.1%)
40	447,517 (30.3%)
20	161,309 (74.9%)

Table 4: The samples size of En-Ja prefix alignment data filtered by $maxratio$. $maxratio$ indicates ratio between source speech frames size and target hypothesis tokens length.

	Offline (hyp/ref)
w/o FT	11.6 (0.885)
FT + Filter ($maxratio$)	
None	6.0 (0.515)
80	6.4 (0.530)
40	8.0 (0.609)
20	10.9 (0.796)

Table 5: The En-Ja FT BLEU results on offline with filtered prefix alignment data. hyp/ref indicates ratio between hypothesis length and reference length.

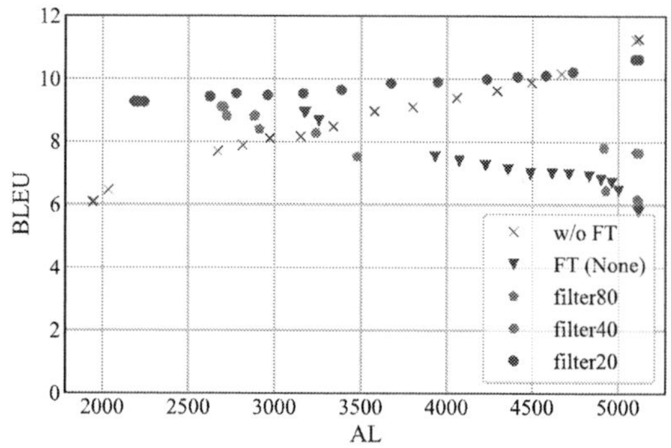

Figure 5: The En-Ja BLEU and AL results of w/o FT models and FT models. The FT models were fine-tuned with filtered prefix alignment data.

4.2.1 Data Filtering for English-Japanese

In contrast to En-De, the fine-tuned model was inferior to the non-fine-tuned and wait-k models in En-Ja. We expected that under-translation would degrade the performance because the fine-tuning used prefix pairs of a long source language speech prefix and a short target language text segment. It would be due to differences in sentence structures between English and Japanese. Since English and German are subject-verb-object (SVO) languages, the English prefix speech frames and the German prefix tokens can be aligned without long-distance reordering. For example, the pair dataset of English frames and German tokens {English prefix frames, German prefix tokens} would consist of {S, S}, {SV, SV}, {SVO, SVO}. On the other hand, since Japanese is a subject-object-verb (SOV) language, the difference in sentence structures between them causes the difficulty in aligning prefixes. For example, the prefix pairs of English speech and Japanese text {English prefix frames, Japanese prefix tokens} would consist of {S, S}, {SV, S}, {SVO, SOV}. Such an unbalanced pair like {SV, S} would make the fine-tuned model prefer inappropriately short outputs. Figure 4 shows examples of prefix pairs extracted using Bilingual Prefix Alignment to fine-tune the ST model. Bilingual Prefix Alignment extracted unbalanced pairs $(S_{prefix}, \hat{T}_{prefix})$ whose target prefix is too short. For example, a source speech prefix of 300 frames (about three seconds) is paired with a target prefix of only two subwords, which obviously does not match.

We applied simple data filtering described in 2.1 for En-Ja. Table 4 shows the prefix alignment dataset with the filtering. The filtering can reduce the unbalanced pairs of data that consists of long source speech frames and short target tokens. It would alleviate the model to generate too short sequences. Table 5 shows the results of the fine-tuned model with the filtered prefix pairs. Table 5 shows the BLEU improvement from no filter setting (None) to larger $maxratio$ filter setting with alleviating the gap between hypothesis length and reference length (*hyp/ref*). Figure 5 shows the results of the fine-tuned (FT) models with filtered prefix alignment dataset. FT (None) was worse than the non-fine-tuned model in the latency ranges with AL > 3500. The scores by the fine-tuned model using filtered data on $maxratio = 80$ (filter80) were almost the same as FT (None) model's. Decreasing $maxratio$ to 20 significantly improved BLEU scores. It suggests selective use of the fine-tuning data alleviated the under-translation problem for distant language pairs.

5 Conclusions

In this paper, we described our SimulST systems in English-to-German and English-to-Japanese. The proposed method uses prefix alignment data to fine-tune the offline ST model and train boundary predictor that judges when to READ and WRITE. Our models achieved some improvements compared to the wait-k baselines in every latency regime in both English-to-German and English-to-Japanese.

Acknowledgement

Part of this work was supported by JSPS KAKENHI Grant Number JP21H05054.

References

Antonios Anastasopoulos, Luisa Bentivogli, Marcely Z. Boito, Ondřej Bojar, Roldano Cattoni, Anna Currey, Georgiana Dinu, Kevin Duh, Maha Elbayad, Marcello Federico, Christian Federmann, Hongyu Gong, Roman Grundkiewicz, Barry Haddow, Benjamin Hsu, Dávid Javorský, Věra Kloudová, Surafel M. Lakew, Xutai Ma, Prashant Mathur, Paul McNamee, Kenton Murray, Maria Nădejde, Satoshi Nakamura, Matteo Negri, Jan Niehues, Xing Niu, Juan Pino, Elizabeth Salesky, Jiatong Shi, Sebastian Stüker, Katsuhito Sudoh, Marco Turchi, Yogesh Virkar, Alex Waibel, Changhan Wang, and Shinji Watanabe. 2022. FINDINGS OF THE IWSLT 2022 EVALUATION CAMPAIGN. In *Proceedings of the 19th International Conference on Spoken Language Translation (IWSLT 2022)*, Dublin, Ireland. Association for Computational Linguistics.

Fahim Dalvi, Nadir Durrani, Hassan Sajjad, and Stephan Vogel. 2018. Incremental decoding and training methods for simultaneous translation in neural machine translation. In *Proceedings of the 2018 Conference of the North American Chapter of the Association for Computational Linguistics: Human Language Technologies, Volume 2 (Short Papers)*, pages 493–499, New Orleans, Louisiana. Association for Computational Linguistics.

Mattia A. Di Gangi, Roldano Cattoni, Luisa Bentivogli, Matteo Negri, and Marco Turchi. 2019. MuST-C: a Multilingual Speech Translation Corpus. In *Proceedings of the 2019 Conference of the North American Chapter of the Association for Computational Linguistics: Human Language Technologies, Volume 1 (Long and Short Papers)*, pages 2012–2017, Minneapolis, Minnesota. Association for Computational Linguistics.

Ryo Fukuda, Yui Oka, Yasumasa Kano, Yuki Yano, Yuka Ko, Hirotaka Tokuyama, Kosuke Doi, Sakriani Sakti, Katsuhito Sudoh, and Satoshi Nakamura. 2021. NAIST English-to-Japanese simultaneous translation system for IWSLT 2021 simultaneous text-to-text task. In *Proceedings of the 18th International Conference on Spoken Language Translation (IWSLT 2021)*, pages 39–45, Bangkok, Thailand (online). Association for Computational Linguistics.

Yasumasa Kano, Katsuhito Sudoh, and Satoshi Nakamura. 2022. Simultaneous neural machine translation with prefix alignment. In *Proceedings of the 19th International Conference on Spoken Language Translation (IWSLT 2022)*, Dublin, Ireland. Association for Computational Linguistics.

Taku Kudo and John Richardson. 2018. Sentencepiece: A simple and language independent subword tokenizer and detokenizer for neural text processing. In *EMNLP (Demonstration)*.

Dan Liu, Mengge Du, Xiaoxi Li, Ya Li, and Enhong Chen. 2021. Cross attention augmented transducer networks for simultaneous translation. In *Proceedings of the 2021 Conference on Empirical Methods in Natural Language Processing*, pages 39–55, Online and Punta Cana, Dominican Republic. Association for Computational Linguistics.

Mingbo Ma, Liang Huang, Hao Xiong, Renjie Zheng, Kaibo Liu, Baigong Zheng, Chuanqiang Zhang, Zhongjun He, Hairong Liu, Xing Li, Hua Wu, and Haifeng Wang. 2019. STACL: Simultaneous translation with implicit anticipation and controllable latency using prefix-to-prefix framework. In *Proceedings of the 57th Annual Meeting of the Association for Computational Linguistics*, pages 3025–3036, Florence, Italy. Association for Computational Linguistics.

Xutai Ma, Mohammad Javad Dousti, Changhan Wang, Jiatao Gu, and Juan Pino. 2020. SIMULEVAL: An evaluation toolkit for simultaneous translation. In *Proceedings of the 2020 Conference on Empirical Methods in Natural Language Processing: System Demonstrations*, pages 144–150, Online. Association for Computational Linguistics.

Myle Ott, Sergey Edunov, Alexei Baevski, Angela Fan, Sam Gross, Nathan Ng, David Grangier, and Michael Auli. 2019. fairseq: A fast, extensible toolkit for sequence modeling. In *Proceedings of the 2019 Conference of the North American Chapter of the Association for Computational Linguistics (Demonstrations)*, pages 48–53, Minneapolis, Minnesota. Association for Computational Linguistics.

Sukanta Sen, Ulrich Germann, and Barry Haddow. 2021. The University of Edinburgh's submission to the IWSLT21 simultaneous translation task. In *Proceedings of the 18th International Conference on Spoken Language Translation (IWSLT 2021)*, pages 46–51, Bangkok, Thailand (online). Association for Computational Linguistics.

Baigong Zheng, Kaibo Liu, Renjie Zheng, Mingbo Ma, Hairong Liu, and Liang Huang. 2020. Simultaneous translation policies: From fixed to adaptive. In *Proceedings of the 58th Annual Meeting of the Association for Computational Linguistics*, pages 2847–2853, Online. Association for Computational Linguistics.

Baigong Zheng, Renjie Zheng, Mingbo Ma, and Liang Huang. 2019a. Simpler and faster learning of adaptive policies for simultaneous translation. In *Proceedings of the 2019 Conference on Empirical Methods in Natural Language Processing and the 9th International Joint Conference on Natural Language Processing (EMNLP-IJCNLP)*, pages 1349–1354, Hong Kong, China. Association for Computational Linguistics.

Baigong Zheng, Renjie Zheng, Mingbo Ma, and Liang Huang. 2019b. Simultaneous translation with flexible policy via restricted imitation learning. In *Proceedings of the 57th Annual Meeting of the Association for Computational Linguistics*, pages 5816–5822, Florence, Italy. Association for Computational Linguistics.

The HW-TSC's Speech to Speech Translation System for IWSLT 2022

Jiaxin Guo[1], Yinglu Li[1], Minghan Wang[1], Xiaosong Qiao[1], Yuxia Wang[2], Hengchao Shang[1], Chang Su[1], Yimeng Chen[1], Min Zhang[1], Shimin Tao[1], Hao Yang[1], Ying Qin[1]

[1]Huawei Translation Services Center, Beijing, China

[2]The University of Melbourne, Melbourne, Australia

{guojiaxin1,liyinglu,wangminghan,qiaoxiaosong,
shanghengchao, suchang8,chenyimeng,zhangmin186,
taoshimin,yanghao30,qinying}@huawei.com

yuxiaw@student.unimelb.edu.au

Abstract

The paper presents the HW-TSC's pipeline and results of Offline Speech to Speech Translation for IWSLT 2022. We design a cascade system consisted of an ASR model, machine translation model and TTS model to convert the speech from one language into another language(en-de). For the ASR part, we find that better performance can be obtained by ensembling multiple heterogeneous ASR models and performing reranking on beam candidates. And we find that the combination of context-aware reranking strategy and MT model fine-tuned on the in-domain dataset is helpful to improve the performance. Because it can mitigate the problem that the inconsistency in transcripts caused by the lack of context. Finally, we use VITS model provided officially to reproduce audio files from the translation hypothesis.

1 Introduction

In this year, there is only one track in the speech to speech translation task which is the English to German translation (En-De) (Anastasopoulos et al., 2022). The audio files in English are given in the dataset, and we are required to produce the audio files in German. In recent research of speech to speech task, there are basically two paradigms with respect to the system architecture, which are cascade and end-to-end. And the cascade pipeline composed by an ASR model, a MT model and a TTS model is commonly used, because this system is more mature than end-to-end one. The advantage of this pipeline is that each module of the system can be a state-of-the-art one trained on sufficient independent corpora. It also allows us to perform experiments with different combinations of ASR models, MT models and TTS models. But compared to end-to-end system, this cascade system may not capture all information like accent of speakers, emotion, etc.

End-to-End system like S2UT is introduced in (Lee et al., 2021), which can be directly trained on speech to speech dataset with the help of text generation as the auxiliary task. However, we didn't adopt this approach due to the insufficiency of available corpora.

Dataset	Number of Utterance	Duration(hrs)
LibriSpeech	281,241	960.85
MuST-C	340,421	590.67
IWSLT	170,229	254.41
CoVoST	1362,422	1802.52
TEDLIUM3	268,214	453.42

Table 1: Data statistics of our ASR corpora

For the ASR model, we tried Conformer (Gulati et al., 2020), S2T Transformer (Synnaeve et al., 2019) and U2(Zhang et al., 2020), and obtained three types of ASR results.

In translation, inconsistency of translation of same words in the context is a common difficulty. This is caused by the flaw of conventional translation that treats each sentence independently in a documents, ignoring surrounding contexts. For example, a family name in English can be translated in different ways in Chinese. Because Chinese transcripts comes from transliteration, and there are lots of words share same pronunciation but different spelling. This may cause the ambiguity in transcripts, which is hard for readers to understand. To solve the problem, we propose the context-aware reranking strategy in translation, essentially an approach to adapt sentence-level MT models into document-level translation scenarios. It aims to generate the best candidate by taking previous contexts into account and reranking with scores estimated by all models.

2 Method

2.1 Data Preprocessing

We consider five datasets as our training set of ASR models, which are MuST-C V2 (Cattoni et al.,

Proceedings of the 19th International Conference on Spoken Language Translation (IWSLT 2022), pages 293 - 297
May 26-27, 2022 ©2022 Association for Computational Linguistics

Language	WMT Bilingual	In-domain Text
En-De	79M	459K
En-Zh	96M	590K
En-Ja	42M	552K

Table 2: Data statistics of our MT corpora

Algorithm 1 Context-aware Translation reranking

Require: MT, MT', LM, context length, beam size, utterance list: $\mathcal{F}, \mathcal{G}, \mathcal{Q}, N, k, S$
  Initialize: Context Buffer $C \leftarrow \{\}$
  Initialize: source text index $i \leftarrow 0$
  while $i \neq |S| - 1$ **do**
    $\hat{Y}, P_{\text{f}} \leftarrow \mathcal{F}(u_i, k)$: propose candidates
    $P_{\text{g}} \leftarrow \mathcal{G}(u_i, \hat{Y})$: scoring with MT'
    if $i < N$ **then**
      $P_{\text{q}} \leftarrow \mathcal{Q}(\hat{Y}, C)$
    else
      $P_{\text{q}} \leftarrow \mathcal{Q}(\hat{Y}, C_{[-N:]})$
    end if
    $\hat{y}^* \leftarrow \arg\max_{\hat{y}} \sum m \in \{f, g, q\} w_m \log P_m$
    $C \leftarrow C \cup \{\hat{y}^*\}$
    $i \leftarrow i + 1$
  end while
  return C

2021), LibriSpeech(Panayotov et al., 2015), TED-LIUM 3 (Hernandez et al., 2018), CoVoST (Wang et al., 2020) and IWSLT. The statistical description is shown in Table 1. The CoVoST dataset has the longest duration and the largest number of utterances.

In the first step, we load the waveform of audio files as tensors and extract the 80-dimensional filter bank features of them. Because the encoder and decoder of a Transformer (Vaswani et al., 2017) model can only process limited size of sequences, we restrict the frame size of input speeches to the range of 50 to 3000, and the number of tokens should be no more than 150. At the same time, we calculate the speed of the speech by length of references and frame size of each sample. This metric could help us find those speech with small frame size but large number of tokens, or vice versa, which should be considered as outliers. So we choose the speech with the speed within $\mu(\tau) \pm 4 \times \sigma(\tau)$, where $\tau = \frac{\text{\# frames}}{\text{\# tokens}}$. Through these process pipeline in fine-grained level, we obtain the cleaned training set.

For the test set, we use the official dataset provided audios in the task. We also use the MuST-C dev, tst-COMMON and tst-HE set to evaluate our model so that they can be compared easily with other approaches.

For the training set of MT models, we follow the configuration and preprocessing procedures as (Wei et al., 2021), and the scale of the dataset is shown in Table 2.

2.2 Automatic Speech Recognition

We apply Conformer (Gulati et al., 2020) and S2T-Transformer (Synnaeve et al., 2019) to predict the fundamental results in an ensemble approach, and clean the predicted candidates with the U2 model (Zhang et al., 2020). All of these models are trained on the united dataset with the domain controlled training/generation (Wang et al., 2021). We ensemble the ASR result of the two models, and some results have been corrected in the post-processing. Sometimes both Conformer and S2T-Transformer makes errors in the recognising process, except the errors appeared in different position. For example, in a same sentence, the Conformer would recognise the "ex-boyfriend" as "next boyfriend" incorrectly, and the S2T-Transformer may misidentify "the cuss words" as "the cusp words". Through ensembling, these errors can be eliminated and results can be improved. We proved that the ensembling of these heterogeneous ASR models can in some what extent improve the possibility of choosing the correct answer.

Meanwhile, we find that two autoregressive models both have the drawback of producing meaningless sentences when acoustic inputs are applause or laughing from the audience. In this situation, U2 presents the stability and robustness in predicting those audio without real utterances. So, we use U2 as the criteria to filter the ensemble results comes from Conformer and S2T-Transformer. It means, for each sample, we predict with U2 first and see if the prediction is a blank line, if it is, we directly use it as the output, otherwise, we predict the sample again with the ensembled model mentioned above. This is the key to apply U2, but it would not change any other prediction of ensemble results.

After the cleaning process of U2, results are more anti-interference to the sample that filled with laughter or meaningless natural noise.

Test set	Approach	BLEU	ChrF	TER	Perf. Drop
dev	Oracle	32.1	0.61	0.534	21.4%
	TTS	25.12 (-6.98)	0.58 (-0.03)	0.585 (+0.051)	
tst-HE	Oracle	34.0	0.63	0.498	28.82%
	TTS	24.2 (-9.8)	0.56 (-0.07)	0.609 (+0.111)	
tst-COMMON	Oracle	31.2	0.63	0.550	21.80%
	TTS	24.4 (-6.8)	0.57 (-0.06)	0.627 (+0.077)	

Table 3: This table presents our overall performance evaluated on MuST-C dev, tst-HE and tst-COMMON set. Oracle stands for directly evaluating translation outputs of the MT model. TTS stands for evaluating on the transcripts predicted from the TTS output. Note that all results are evaluated without punctuation and with lower-casing since the wav2vec ASR model is only able to predict in that form. The column "Perf. Drop" statistics the drop of BLEU when applied with TTS.

2.3 Translation Models

We use the WMT21 news corpora to train the MT model in En-De direction, then, use the combination of MuST-C and IWSLT dataset to fine-tune the pretrained model.

2.4 Context-aware MT reranking

Following the work in (Yu et al., 2020) that utilises the noisy channel model (Brown et al., 1993) in document-level translation, we adopted similar strategy to improve the translation with longer context information. However, we make some simplification on the decoding process and the scoring function. More specifically, we restrict the context to a sliding window that only taking a fixed size of sentences into account when applying the LM scoring:

$$\begin{aligned}\mathcal{O}(x, y^{-N:}, y^i) =& w_{\text{MT}} \log p_{\text{MT}}(y^i|x^i) \\ &+ w_{\text{LM}} \log p_{\text{LM}}(y^i|y^{-N:}) \\ &+ w_{\text{MT'}} \log p_{\text{MT'}}(x^i|y^i) \quad (1)\end{aligned}$$

where N is the context length, w are weights for each component. The decoding process is also simplified into a greedy search instead of sentence-level beam search as described in Algo 1. During inference, we find that the test set is exactly same as the tst2022-en-de used in the offline, therefore, we manually regroup ASR outputs back to documents and translate them with this approach.

2.5 Text to Speech

In a cascade speech to speech translation system, text to speech (TTS) is the final module to convert translations into speech. We use the pretrained VITS (Kim et al., 2021) model for this procedure. VITS adapts variatoinal inference augmented with normalizing flows and an adversarial training process, largely improving the quality of generated speech. During inference process we only need to provide German texts, and use the model to produce raw audio files with 22kHz sample rate.

3 Experiments

3.1 Setup

In the training of our ASR models, we use the sentencepiece model (Kudo and Richardson, 2018) for tokenization with vocab size=20000. Configurations of ASR models are exactly same to our offline submission. We follow the recipe of (Wei et al., 2021) to train our NMT models in both directions, as well as the language model. All MT models are also fine-tuned on in-domain corpora for additional 10 epochs. We implemented all models with `fairseq` (Ott et al., 2019).

The automatic evaluation of our S2S system is achieved by calculating metrics on the re-transcribed outputs from our system. Specifically, an officially assigned ASR model: "wav2vec2-large-xlsr-53-german" (Baevski et al., 2020) is used to transcribe the TTS generated audio files back to texts first. Then, they are used for the evaluation with automatic tools performed in text-level. This significantly reduces the difficulty of evaluation but still preserves the fairness. We use BLEU (Papineni et al., 2002), ChrF (Popovic, 2015) and TER (Snover et al., 2006) as evaluation metrics in our experiments.

3.2 Results

Because the speech cannot be directly compared to transcripts, we have to convert the speech into transcripts by the Wav2vec ASR model. We tested

ASR Model	CoVoST	MuST-C	TEDLIUM3	LibriSpeech
w/ Domain Tag	11.27	6.31	5.33	4.39
wo/ Domain Tag	17.56	15.58	8.72	7.98

Table 4: Comparison of wer scores of ASR model trained on dataset with domain tag or not.

the score of BLEU, ChrF and TER by evaluating the translation outputs of MT model and the re-transcribed results of final outputs from TTS. And those scores can be seen in Table 3. Note that before computing evaluation metrics, we applied some normalizing process to make the results of Oracle and TTS comparable. More specifically, since the re-transcribed text from the wav2vec model is lower-cased and has no punctuation, we also perform lower-casing and removing of punctuation for Oracle hypothesis and the references. Finally, we evaluate metrics on Oracle and TTS hypothesis towards the normalized references.

From the experimental results on three sub sets of MuST-C, we have some interesting findings. Through the process of TTS and re-ASR, the BLEU score and ChrF score has both decreased by about 7+ and 0.05+, and the TER score increased by 0.07+. This trend appears in both three test sets, demonstrating that there might be serious information loss in this process. However, further conclusions can only be drawn from the human evaluation.

3.3 Ablation

Effectiveness of domain controlled generation We test whether the domain tag prefix is useful for the performance of model, and the results are shown in Table 4. There are four domain tag used in our new dataset, including "<MC>", "<LS>", "<TL>" and "<CV>". All these prefix represents the abbreviations of each dataset. Compared with the results of model fed by dataset without using any domain prefix tags, the model trained on the tagged dataset has the better performance. This essentially benefits from the extra prior information provided by the domain prefix tags. In detail, domain tags provides more latent information that cannot be easily captured in raw audios, making the generation more deterministic. Meanwhile, this allows us to control the generation style in our demanded domain, being closer to the reference. So, the domain tag prefix effectively improves the performance of our model.

4 Conclusion

In the paper, we elaborate the cascade system for this Speech to Speech task. There are several strategies we applied to improve the system, including domain-tag prefix and the context-aware reranking strategy. We did some experiments to verify the reliability of those strategies for a cascade system, and we also made some analysis from the theoretical level. In the future, we are going to explore the feasibility of the end-to-end system, since it might reduce the negative impact of information loss on system performance.

References

Antonios Anastasopoulos, Luisa Bentivogli, Marcely Z. Boito, Ondřej Bojar, Roldano Cattoni, Anna Currey, Georgiana Dinu, Kevin Duh, Maha Elbayad, Marcello Federico, Christian Federmann, Hongyu Gong, Roman Grundkiewicz, Barry Haddow, Benjamin Hsu, Dávid Javorský, Věra Kloudová, Surafel M. Lakew, Xutai Ma, Prashant Mathur, Paul McNamee, Kenton Murray, Maria Nădejde, Satoshi Nakamura, Matteo Negri, Jan Niehues, Xing Niu, Juan Pino, Elizabeth Salesky, Jiatong Shi, Sebastian Stüker, Katsuhito Sudoh, Marco Turchi, Yogesh Virkar, Alex Waibel, Changhan Wang, and Shinji Watanabe. 2022. FINDINGS OF THE IWSLT 2022 EVALUATION CAMPAIGN. In *Proceedings of the 19th International Conference on Spoken Language Translation (IWSLT 2022)*, Dublin, Ireland. Association for Computational Linguistics.

Alexei Baevski, Yuhao Zhou, Abdelrahman Mohamed, and Michael Auli. 2020. wav2vec 2.0: A framework for self-supervised learning of speech representations. In *Advances in Neural Information Processing Systems 33: Annual Conference on Neural Information Processing Systems 2020, NeurIPS 2020, December 6-12, 2020, virtual.*

Peter F. Brown, Stephen Della Pietra, Vincent J. Della Pietra, and Robert L. Mercer. 1993. The mathematics of statistical machine translation: Parameter estimation. *Comput. Linguistics*, 19(2):263–311.

Roldano Cattoni, Mattia Antonino Di Gangi, Luisa Bentivogli, Matteo Negri, and Marco Turchi. 2021. Must-c: A multilingual corpus for end-to-end speech translation. *Comput. Speech Lang.*, 66:101155.

Anmol Gulati, James Qin, Chung-Cheng Chiu, Niki Parmar, Yu Zhang, Jiahui Yu, Wei Han, Shibo Wang,

Zhengdong Zhang, Yonghui Wu, and Ruoming Pang. 2020. Conformer: Convolution-augmented transformer for speech recognition. In *Interspeech 2020, 21st Annual Conference of the International Speech Communication Association, Virtual Event, Shanghai, China, 25-29 October 2020*, pages 5036–5040. ISCA.

François Hernandez, Vincent Nguyen, Sahar Ghannay, Natalia A. Tomashenko, and Yannick Estève. 2018. TED-LIUM 3: Twice as much data and corpus repartition for experiments on speaker adaptation. In *Speech and Computer - 20th International Conference, SPECOM 2018, Leipzig, Germany, September 18-22, 2018, Proceedings*, volume 11096 of *Lecture Notes in Computer Science*, pages 198–208. Springer.

Jaehyeon Kim, Jungil Kong, and Juhee Son. 2021. Conditional variational autoencoder with adversarial learning for end-to-end text-to-speech. In *Proceedings of the 38th International Conference on Machine Learning, ICML 2021, 18-24 July 2021, Virtual Event*, volume 139 of *Proceedings of Machine Learning Research*, pages 5530–5540. PMLR.

Taku Kudo and John Richardson. 2018. Sentencepiece: A simple and language independent subword tokenizer and detokenizer for neural text processing. In *Proceedings of the 2018 Conference on Empirical Methods in Natural Language Processing, EMNLP 2018: System Demonstrations, Brussels, Belgium, October 31 - November 4, 2018*, pages 66–71. Association for Computational Linguistics.

Ann Lee, Peng-Jen Chen, Changhan Wang, Jiatao Gu, Xutai Ma, Adam Polyak, Yossi Adi, Qing He, Yun Tang, Juan Miguel Pino, and Wei-Ning Hsu. 2021. Direct speech-to-speech translation with discrete units. *CoRR*, abs/2107.05604.

Myle Ott, Sergey Edunov, Alexei Baevski, Angela Fan, Sam Gross, Nathan Ng, David Grangier, and Michael Auli. 2019. fairseq: A fast, extensible toolkit for sequence modeling. In *Proceedings of the 2019 Conference of the North American Chapter of the Association for Computational Linguistics: Human Language Technologies, NAACL-HLT 2019, Minneapolis, MN, USA, June 2-7, 2019, Demonstrations*, pages 48–53. Association for Computational Linguistics.

Vassil Panayotov, Guoguo Chen, Daniel Povey, and Sanjeev Khudanpur. 2015. Librispeech: An ASR corpus based on public domain audio books. In *2015 IEEE International Conference on Acoustics, Speech and Signal Processing, ICASSP 2015, South Brisbane, Queensland, Australia, April 19-24, 2015*, pages 5206–5210. IEEE.

Kishore Papineni, Salim Roukos, Todd Ward, and Wei-Jing Zhu. 2002. Bleu: a method for automatic evaluation of machine translation. In *Proceedings of the 40th Annual Meeting of the Association for Computational Linguistics, July 6-12, 2002, Philadelphia, PA, USA*, pages 311–318. ACL.

Maja Popovic. 2015. chrf: character n-gram f-score for automatic MT evaluation. In *Proceedings of the Tenth Workshop on Statistical Machine Translation, WMT@EMNLP 2015, 17-18 September 2015, Lisbon, Portugal*, pages 392–395. The Association for Computer Linguistics.

Matthew Snover, Bonnie Dorr, Richard Schwartz, Linnea Micciulla, and John Makhoul. 2006. A study of translation edit rate with targeted human annotation. In *Proceedings of the 7th Conference of the Association for Machine Translation in the Americas: Technical Papers*, pages 223–231.

Gabriel Synnaeve, Qiantong Xu, Jacob Kahn, Edouard Grave, Tatiana Likhomanenko, Vineel Pratap, Anuroop Sriram, Vitaliy Liptchinsky, and Ronan Collobert. 2019. End-to-end ASR: from supervised to semi-supervised learning with modern architectures. *CoRR*, abs/1911.08460.

Ashish Vaswani, Noam Shazeer, Niki Parmar, Jakob Uszkoreit, Llion Jones, Aidan N. Gomez, Lukasz Kaiser, and Illia Polosukhin. 2017. Attention is all you need. In *Advances in Neural Information Processing Systems 30: Annual Conference on Neural Information Processing Systems 2017, December 4-9, 2017, Long Beach, CA, USA*, pages 5998–6008.

Changhan Wang, Anne Wu, and Juan Pino. 2020. Covost 2: A massively multilingual speech-to-text translation corpus.

Minghan Wang, Yuxia Wang, Chang Su, Jiaxin Guo, Yingtao Zhang, Yujia Liu, Min Zhang, Shimin Tao, Xingshan Zeng, Liangyou Li, Hao Yang, and Ying Qin. 2021. The hw-tsc's offline speech translation systems for IWSLT 2021 evaluation. *CoRR*, abs/2108.03845.

Daimeng Wei, Zongyao Li, Zhanglin Wu, Zhengzhe Yu, Xiaoyu Chen, Hengchao Shang, Jiaxin Guo, Minghan Wang, Lizhi Lei, Min Zhang, Hao Yang, and Ying Qin. 2021. Hw-tsc's participation in the WMT 2021 news translation shared task. In *Proceedings of the Sixth Conference on Machine Translation, WMT@EMNLP 2021, Online Event, November 10-11, 2021*, pages 225–231. Association for Computational Linguistics.

Lei Yu, Laurent Sartran, Wojciech Stokowiec, Wang Ling, Lingpeng Kong, Phil Blunsom, and Chris Dyer. 2020. Better document-level machine translation with bayes' rule. *Trans. Assoc. Comput. Linguistics*, 8:346–360.

Binbin Zhang, Di Wu, Zhuoyuan Yao, Xiong Wang, Fan Yu, Chao Yang, Liyong Guo, Yaguang Hu, Lei Xie, and Xin Lei. 2020. Unified streaming and non-streaming two-pass end-to-end model for speech recognition. *CoRR*, abs/2012.05481.

CMU's IWSLT 2022 Dialect Speech Translation System

Brian Yan[1] **Patrick Fernandes**[1,2] **Siddharth Dalmia**[1] **Jiatong Shi**[1]
Yifan Peng[3] **Dan Berrebbi**[1] **Xinyi Wang**[1] **Graham Neubig**[1] **Shinji Watanabe**[1,4]
[1]Language Technologies Institute, Carnegie Mellon University, USA
[2]Instituto Superior Técnico & LUMLIS (Lisbon ELLIS Unit), Portugal
[3]Electrical and Computer Engineering, Carnegie Mellon University, USA
[4]Human Language Technology Center of Excellence, Johns Hopkins University, USA
{byan, pfernand, sdalmia, jiatongs}@cs.cmu.edu

Abstract

This paper describes CMU's submissions to the IWSLT 2022 dialect speech translation (ST) shared task for translating Tunisian-Arabic speech to English text. We use additional paired Modern Standard Arabic data (MSA) to directly improve the speech recognition (ASR) and machine translation (MT) components of our cascaded systems. We also augment the paired ASR data with pseudo translations via sequence-level knowledge distillation from an MT model and use these artificial triplet ST data to improve our end-to-end (E2E) systems. Our E2E models are based on the Multi-Decoder architecture with searchable hidden intermediates. We extend the Multi-Decoder by orienting the speech encoder towards the target language by applying ST supervision as hierarchical connectionist temporal classification (CTC) multi-task. During inference, we apply joint decoding of the ST CTC and ST autoregressive decoder branches of our modified Multi-Decoder. Finally, we apply ROVER voting, posterior combination, and minimum bayes-risk decoding with combined N-best lists to ensemble our various cascaded and E2E systems. Our best systems reached 20.8 and 19.5 BLEU on test2 (blind) and test1 respectively. Without any additional MSA data, we reached 20.4 and 19.2 on the same test sets.

1 Introduction

In this paper, we present CMU's Tunisian-Arabic to English ST systems submitted to the IWSLT 2022 dialectal ST track (Anastasopoulos et al., 2022). One of our goals is to investigate dialectal transfer from large MSA ASR and MT corpora to improve Tunisian-Arabic ST performance. We also view this task as setting for extending the sequence-level knowledge distillation (SeqKD) (Kim and Rush, 2016), E2E Multi-Decoder architecture (Dalmia et al., 2021), and system combination methods in our IWSLT 2021 offline ST systems (Inaguma et al., 2021b).

In particular, our contributions are the following:

1. Dialectal transfer from large paired MSA corpora to improve ASR and MT systems (§3.1)
2. MT SeqKD on MSA ASR data for artificial ST triplets to improve E2E ST systems (§3.2.2)
3. Multi-Decoder with hierarchical CTC training for target-oriented speech encodings (§3.2.3)
4. Multi-Decoder with CTC beam search hypothesis re-scoring during ST inference (§3.2.4)
5. Multi-Decoder with surface and posterior-level guidance from external models (§3.3.1)
6. Joint minimum bayes-risk decoding as an ensembling method (§3.3.2)

Results on the blind test set, test2, and ablations on the provided test set, test1, demonstrate the overall efficacy of our systems and the relative contributions of the aforementioned techniques (§5).

2 Task Description and Data Preparation

The Arabic language is not a monolith. Of its estimated 400 million native speakers, many speak in colloquial dialects such as, Tunisian-Arabic, that have relatively less standard orthographic rules and smaller ASR and MT corpora compared to formal MSA (Hussein et al., 2022). Both of these realities present challenges to building effective ST systems, and as such the dialectal speech translation shared task is an important venue for tackling these research problems.

Table 1 shows the corpora relevant to the shared task. The IWSLT22-Dialect corpus consists of ST triplets where 160 hours of 8kHz conversational Tunisian-Arabic speech are annotated with transcriptions and also translated into English. The MGB2 corpus (Ali et al., 2016) consists of 1100 hours of 16kHz broadcast MSA speech and the corresponding transcriptions. The OPUS corpus

Proceedings of the 19th International Conference on Spoken Language Translation (IWSLT 2022), pages 298 - 307
May 26-27, 2022

	#Hours	#Sentence	
	of Speech	Arabic	English
IWSLT22-Dialect	160	0.2M	0.2M
MGB2	1100	1.1M	-
OPUS	-	42M	42M

Table 1: Statistics for the three corpora included in the IWSLT 2022 dialect ST shared task. IWSLT22-Dialect has triplets of speech, source Arabic transcription, and target English translation. MGB2 and OPUS have only pairs for ASR and MT respectively.

(Tiedemann et al., 2020) consists of 42M MSA-English translation pairs across several domains. Any systems that use MGB2 or OPUS data for pre-training, fine-tuning, or any other purpose are designated as *dialect transfer* systems.[1]

Following the shared task guidelines, punctuation is removed and English text is lowercased. Buckwalter one-to-one transliteration of Arabic text (Habash et al., 2007) was applied to help non-Arabic speakers with ASR output interpretation. English sentences were tokenized with the `tokenizer.perl` script in the Moses toolkit (Koehn et al., 2007) for training and detokenized for scoring. Language-specific sentencepiece vocabularies were created using the byte pair encoding (BPE) algorithm (Sennrich et al., 2016) with the `sentencepiece` toolkit.[2] Speech data was up-sampled by a factor of 3 using 0.9 and 1.1 speed perturbation ratios (Ko et al., 2015). The IWSLT22-Dialect data was upsampled to 16kHz for consistency using the `sox` toolkit[3].

3 Proposed Methods

In this section, we describe our cascaded (§3.1) and E2E systems (§3.2). Then we describe methods for integrating both approaches §3.3.

3.1 Cascaded ASR→MT Systems

3.1.1 ASR

To train ASR models for our cascaded system, we use the ESPnet (Watanabe et al., 2018) framework. Our ASR architecture is based on hybrid CTC/attention approach (Watanabe et al., 2017) with a Conformer encoder (Gulati et al., 2020). The Conformer, which employs convolutions to model local patterns and self-attention to model long-range context, has shown to be effective on both ASR and E2E ST tasks (Guo et al., 2020; Inaguma et al., 2021b). We also use a bidirectional LSTM (Hochreiter and Schmidhuber, 1997; Graves and Schmidhuber, 2005) language model (LM) to re-score beam search hypotheses during inference. We ensemble multiple ASR systems with varying hyper-parameters using Recognizer Output Voting Error Reduction (ROVER) with minimal word-level edit-distance alignment (Fiscus, 1997).

3.1.2 MT

To train MT models for our cascaded system, we use the Fairseq (Ott et al., 2019) framework to train transformers encoder-decoder models (Vaswani et al., 2). To mitigate the exposure bias of training with ground-truth data and using ASR outputs at test time, we introduce *ASR mixing*, where during training, for each sample in the training set, the model maximizes the log-likehood of translation from both the *ground-truth source* and the *ASR source* from an ASR system. This is possible because we have triplet data for training set as well. We use the same system used in the cascaded system to generate ASR outputs for the training set. We ensemble multiple MT systems with varying random seeds using posterior combination of hypotheses during beam search.

We also train an MT model using the ESPnet toolkit (Watanabe et al., 2018) as an auxiliary model used for posterior combinations with our E2E ST systems as described in §3.3.1. These models use BPE vocabulary sizes that are optimal for E2E ST, which we found empirically to be smaller than for MT.

3.1.3 Direct Dialectal Transfer

To leverage MSA annotated speech data to improve our ASR system, we select a subset of the MGB2 data as an augmentation set to be added to the IWSLT22-Dialect data. We first use an ASR model trained on IWSLT22-Dialect data only to compute the cross-entropy of the utterances in the MGB2 data. We then select a percentage of the MGB2 utterances with the lowest cross-entropy. Similar cross-entropy based data selection has shown to effectively reduce noise resulting from domain mismatches in language modeling (Moore and Lewis, 2010) and MT (Junczys-Dowmunt, 2018). After pre-training on the mixture

[1]We do not use self-supervised representations, morphological analyzers, or any other resources reliant on data other than the three aforementioned corpora.

[2]`https://github.com/google/sentencepiece`

[3]`http://sox.sourceforge.net`

of MGB2 and IWSLT22-Dialect data, we then fine-tune on IWSLT22-Dialect data only.

To leverage the MSA translation data to improve our MT system, we use the OPUS corpus, cleaning sentences longer than 200 subwords. This results in about 30M sentence pairs of training data for MSA-English. We then train a larger transformer for 20 epochs on this training data. We the use fine-tune this model on the IWSLT22-Dialect data.

3.2 E2E ST Systems

3.2.1 Multi-Decoder Architecture

Multi-decoder model (Dalmia et al., 2021) is an end-to-end sequence model that exploits decomposition of a complex task into simpler tasks in it's model design. For speech translation it decomposes the task into ASR and MT sub-nets while maintaining the end-to-end differentiability. To train Multi-Decoder models, we modified the ESPnet framework (Watanabe et al., 2018).

As shown in figure 1.a, the speech signal, $X = \{\mathbf{x}_t \in \mathbb{R}^D | t = 1, ..., T\}$, is mapped to encoder representations by the *Speech Encoder* which are then in turn mapped autoregressively to decoder representations corresponding to the source language transcription, $Y^{\text{ASR}} = \{y_l^{\text{ASR}} \in \mathcal{V} | l = 1, ..., L\}$, by the *ASR Decoder*. These *ASR Decoder* representations, referred to as searchable hidden intermediates, are passed to the downstream *ST Encoder-Decoder*. In order to avoid error-propagation, the *ST Decoder* performs cross-attention over both the *Speech Encoder* and *ST Encoder* representations. The network is optimized with multi-tasking on cross-entropy losses for both the source and target languages, $\mathcal{L}_{\text{CE}}^{\text{ASR}}$ and $\mathcal{L}_{\text{CE}}^{\text{ST}}$ respectively, along with a CTC (Graves, 2012) loss $\mathcal{L}_{\text{CTC}}^{\text{ASR}}$:

$$\mathcal{L} = \lambda_1 \mathcal{L}_{\text{CE}}^{\text{ASR}} + \lambda_2 \mathcal{L}_{\text{CTC}}^{\text{ASR}} + \lambda_3 \mathcal{L}_{\text{CE}}^{\text{ST}} \quad (1)$$

where λ's are used for interpolation. During inference, the CTC branch of the *Speech Encoder* is also used to re-score beam search hypotheses produced by the *ASR Decoder*, following the Hybrid CTC/Attention method (Watanabe et al., 2017).

Inaguma et al. (2021a) showed that sampling CTC output instead of always using ground truth previous token helps the Multi-Decoder model. With a CTC sampling rate of 0.2, which means that with a probability of 0.2 we would use the CTC output instead of the ground truth during training. This simulates the inference condition where there would be ASR errors. We found this technique to be particularly helpful for this dataset.

3.2.2 SeqKD Dialectal Transfer

Our Multi-Decoder training objective, equation 1, assumes that each speech signal is annotated with both a source language transcription and target language translation. In order to include additional paired MSA data into this training regime, we first generate artificial speech, transcript, and translation triplets. To do so, we first build a MSA MT model using the OPUS data. We then generate pseudo-translations for the paired MGB2 data by feeding the MSA transcriptions as inputs to the MT model. This method is based on SeqKD Kim and Rush (2016) and can be considered as a dialectal application of MT to ST knowledge-distillation. We mix a percentage of the pseudo-translated data using the same cross-entropy based methodology as decribed in §3.1.3 with the Tunisian-Arabic data during training. We refer to this data augmentation as *MT SeqKD* in future sections.

3.2.3 Hierarchical Speech Encoder

CTC loss is often used as auxiliary loss in attention based encoder decoder models (Watanabe et al., 2017). It helps the attention based decoder by inducing monotonic alignment with the encoder representations (Kim et al., 2017). In this work, we extend this idea by creating a hierarchical encoder that customizes the ordering of the encoder for the individual sub-tasks by using auxiliary CTC loss at each sub-task. Here, we use an auxiliary CTC loss with ASR targets and another CTC loss with ST targets. As shown in figure 1.b, the first 12 layers of the *Speech Encoder* produce ASR CTC alignments, $Z^{\text{ASR}} = \{z_n^{\text{ASR}} \in \mathcal{V} \cup \{\varnothing\} | n = 1, ..., N\}$, while the final 6 layers produce ST CTC alignments, $Z^{\text{ST}} = \{z_n^{\text{ST}} \in \mathcal{V} \cup \{\varnothing\} | n = 1, ..., N\}$, where $\cup\{\varnothing\}$ denotes the blank emission. This creates a hierarchical encoder structure similar to (Sanabria and Metze, 2018; Lee and Watanabe, 2021; Higuchi et al., 2021). The Multi-Decoder with hierarchical encoder is optimized with an additional ST CTC loss, $\mathcal{L}_{\text{CTC}}^{\text{ST}}$:

$$\mathcal{L} = \lambda_1 \mathcal{L}_{\text{CE}}^{\text{ASR}} + \lambda_2 \mathcal{L}_{\text{CTC}}^{\text{ASR}} + \lambda_3 \mathcal{L}_{\text{CE}}^{\text{ST}} + \lambda_4 \mathcal{L}_{\text{CTC}}^{\text{ST}} \quad (2)$$

Note that the *ST Decoder* now performs cross-attention *Speech Encoder* representations that are oriented towards the target language.

3.2.4 Joint CTC/Attention Decoding for ST

The ST CTC branch of the *Speech Encoder* introduced in the previous section allows us to apply

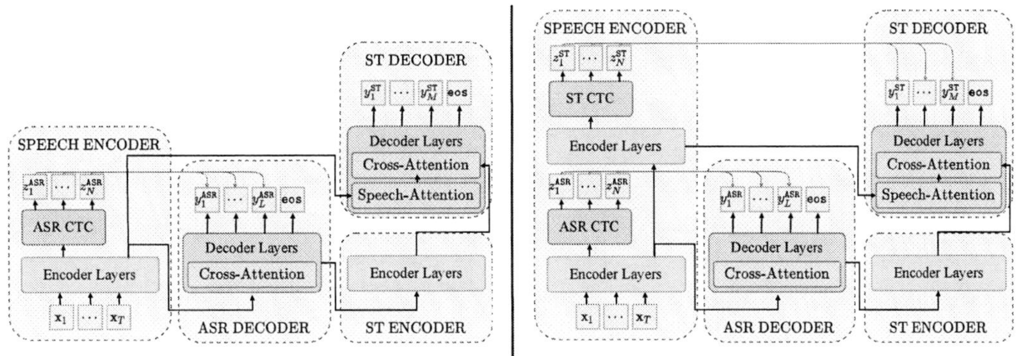

(a) Multi-Decoder **(b) Multi-Decoder w/ Hierarchical Encoder + CTC/Attn ST Decoding**

Figure 1: The left side presents the original Multi-Decoder architecture with searchable hidden intermediates produced by the *ASR Decoder*. The red lines indicate joint CTC/Attention decoding of beam search hypotheses produced by an autoregressive decoder. The right side presents a modified Multi-Decoder with both a hierarchical ASR to ST *Speech Encoder* optimized via CTC objectives and joint CTC/Attention ST inference.

joint CTC/Attention decoding using the one-pass beam search algorithm (Watanabe et al., 2017) during ST inference as well. Although previously only applied to ASR decoding, we found that joint CTC/Attention inference for the *ST Decoder* beam search hypotheses were beneficial in this task. Deng et al. (2022) show that joint modeling of CTC/Attention is effective for short contexts of blockwise streaming ST; as far as we know, our work is the first to show the benefit on long context. Our conjecture is that speech to translation transduction with attention mechanisms, as in the original Multi-Decoder, contains irregular alignments between the acoustic information and the target sequence. The hierarchical encoder and joint CTC/Attention decoding methods may alleviate these irregularities by enforcing greater monotonicity. We refer to the Multi-Decoder with hierarchical encoder and joint CTC/Attentionn ST decoding as the *Hybrid Multi-Decoder* in future sections.

3.3 Integrating E2E and Cascaded Systems

3.3.1 Guiding Multi-Decoder Representations

Since the Multi-Decoder (Dalmia et al., 2021) uses hidden representations from the autoregressive *ASR Decoder*, we can perform search and retrieval over this intermediate stage of the model. Dalmia et al. (2021) showed that ST quality improves by using beam search and external models like LMs to improve the representations the ASR sub-task level. We believe this an important property to have when building models for complex sequence tasks like speech translation, as often there is additional data present for the sub-tasks like ASR and MT. In this work, we help guide our Multi-Decoder model to retrieve better decoder representations by using external ASR and MT models.

We experimented with two approaches: 1) posterior level guidance and 2) surface level guidance. The former is similar in concept to posterior combination for model ensembling during inference as described in (Inaguma et al., 2021b), however the Multi-Decoder allows us to incorporate both an external ASR and MT model due to the searchable hidden intermediates whereas a vanilla encoder-decoder ST model would only be compatible with an external MT model. This method requires beam search over both ASR and MT/ST for multiple models. Alternatively, surface level guidance can avoid this expensive search over the ASR intermediates by instead retrieving the hidden representations for an ASR surface sequence produced externally.

We use the ROVER ASR outputs described in §3.1.1 as surface level guides for the Multi-Decoder's ASR intermediates and found this to be more effective than posterior combination with external ASR models. We refer to this method of retrieval as *ROVER intermediates* in future sections. Since ROVER is based on minimal edit-distance alignment, we did not find it compatible with translation sequences. For the *ST Decoder*, we use posterior combination with external ST and MT models and refer to this as *ST/MT Posterior Combination* in future sections.

3.3.2 Minimum Bayes-Risk

Rather than finding the most likely translation, Minimum Bayes-Risk (MBR) decoding aims to find the translation that maximizes the expected *utility* (equivalently, that minimizes *risk*, (Kumar and Byrne, 2002, 2004; Eikema and Aziz, 2020)). Let $\bar{\mathcal{Y}}_{\text{cands}}$, $\bar{\mathcal{Y}}_{\text{samples}}$ be sets containing N *candidate* hypotheses and M *sample* hypothesis. This sets can be obtained from one or multiple model by, for example sampling or taking the top beams in beam search. Let $u(y^*, y)$ be an utility function measuring the similarity between a hypothesis y and a reference y (we only consider BLEU in this work). MBR decoding seeks for

$$\hat{y}_{\text{MBR}} = \underset{y \in \bar{\mathcal{Y}}_{\text{cands}}}{\arg\max} \underbrace{\mathbb{E}_{Y \sim p_\theta(y|x)}[u(Y, y)]}_{\approx \frac{1}{M}\sum_{j=1}^{M} u(y^{(j)}, y)}, \quad (3)$$

We experimented with using MBR as a technique for system combination, in two forms:

- *True*: the stronger system (the E2E) is used to generate the N candidates $\bar{\mathcal{Y}}_{\text{cands}}$ and the weaker system (the Cascaded system) is used to generate M samples $\bar{\mathcal{Y}}_{\text{samples}}$. This means that the outputs will guaranteed to generated by the E2E system.
- *Joint*: in this case, both the E2E and the Cascaded generate N hypotheses, with are then concatenated to make both the candidate set and sample set $\bar{\mathcal{Y}}_{\text{samples}} = \bar{\mathcal{Y}}_{\text{cands}}$, with $|\bar{\mathcal{Y}}_{\text{cands}}| = 2N$

We explored using beam search and nucleus sampling (Holtzman et al., 2019) with different p values for both generating candidates and generating samples to compute the expectation over. Overall we found that, for both settings, using beam search to generate hypothesis for the E2E model and nucleus sampling with $p = 0.9$ for the cascaded system yield the best results. We use $N = M = 50$ for both settings.

4 Experimental Setup

ASR: We extracted 80-channel log-mel filterbank coefficients computed with 25-ms window size and shifted every 7-ms with 3-dimensional pitch features.[4] The features were normalized by the mean and the standard deviation calculated on the entire training set. We applied SpecAugment (Park et al., 2019) with mask parameters $(m_T, m_F, T, F) = (5, 2, 27, 0.5)$ and bi-cubic time-warping. We use a BPE vocabulary size of 1000. Our encoder has 2 CNN blocks followed by 12 Conformer blocks following (Guo et al., 2020). Each CNN block consisted of a channel size of 256 and a kernel size of 3 with a stride of 2×2, which resulted in time reduction by a factor of 4. Our decoder has 6 Transformer blocks. In both encoder and decoder blocks, the dimensions of the self-attention layer d_{model} and feed-forward network d_{ff} were set to 256 and 2048, respectively. The number of attention heads H was set to 8. The kernel size of depthwise separable convolution in Conformer blocks was set to 31. We optimized the model with the joint CTC/attention objective with a CTC weight of 0.3. We also used CTC and LM scores during decoding. Models were trained for 60 epochs. We averaged the model parameters of the 10 best epoch checkpoints by validation loss. Our LM is a BLSTM with 4 layers and 2048 unit dimension. Beam search is performed with beam size 20, CTC weight 0.2, and LM weight 0.1.

MT: We use SentencePiece (Kudo and Richardson, 2018) with the Byte-pair Encoding algorithm (Sennrich et al., 2016). We experimented with various vocabularies sizes and found that 4000 vocabulary size to be the best for small models. For the pretrained model, we use a vocabulary size of 16000. The small transformer model used for the non-dialect submissions has 512 embedding dimensions, 1024 feedforward dimensions, 6 layers and 4 heads on each layer on both encoder/decoder. The large transformer model used for dialect transfer has 1024 embedding dimensions, 4096 feedforward dimensions, 6 layers and 16 heads on each layer on both encoder/decoder. Models were trained with early stopping by validation loss. We averaged the model parameters of the last 5 epoch checkpoints. Unless otherwise specified, we use beam search with beam size of 5 and no length penalty in beam search.

Multi-Decoder: We use the same feature extraction as for ASR. We use separate BPE vocabularies for source and target, both of size 1000. The ASR sub-net of the Multi-Decoder is also the same as our ASR configuration, allowing for pre-trained initialization of the ASR encoder, decoder, and CTC. The hierarchical encoder adds 6 additional Trans-

[4] 7-ms shift was found to be helpful due to the presence of many short utterances in the IWSLT22-Dialect data.

ID	Model Type / Name	Dialect Transfer	test1 WER(↓)
A1	ASR Conformer	✗	50.4
A2	+ ROVER Comb.	✗	48.1
A3	ASR Conformer	✓	50.0
A4	+ ROVER Comb.	✓	**47.5**
			MT BLEU(↑)
B1	MT Transformer (Fairseq)	✗	21.8
B2	+ Posterior Comb.	✗	22.8
B3	MT Transformer (Fairseq)	✓	22.4
B4	+ Posterior Comb.	✓	**23.6**
B5	MT Transformer (ESPnet)	✗	21.0

Table 2: Results of the ASR and MT components of our cascaded systems, as measured by % WER and BLEU score on the provided test1 set. ROVER and posterior combinations were applied to ASR and MT respectively.

former layers to the original 12 Conformer layers. The MT sub-net of the Multi-Decoder has a 2 layer Transformer encoder and a 6 layer Transformer decoder. This second encoder has no convolutional subsampling. The MT sub-net has the same d_{model} and d_{ff} as the ASR sub-net. We optimized the model a CTC weight of 0.3 and an ASR weight of 0.3. Models were trained for 40 epochs. We averaged the model parameters of the 10 best epoch checkpoints by validation loss. Beam search over the ASR-subnet uses the same setting as for ASR. Beam search over the MT-subnet uses beam size 5/10 with CTC weight 0.3/0.1 for the basic/dialect conditions. Length penalty 0.1 was used for all cases.

5 Results and Analyses

5.1 Submitted Shared Task Systems

Figure 2 shows the results for ASR and MT systems used as part of the cascaded system as evaluated by WER and BLEU score respectively on the provided test set, test1. Dialectal transfer provides a moderate boosts of 0.4% and 0.6% WER without ROVER and with ROVER respectively. Notably, WER's for all systems are relatively high despite a moderate amount of training data; this is perhaps due to the non-standard orthographic form of the Tunisian-Arabic transcriptions.[5] Another possible cause for the high WER is the conversational nature of the data, which may require normalization similar to the Switchboard dataset (Godfrey et al., 1992). For the MT systems, we see that posterior combination leads to over 1 BLEU point improvements when translating ground-truth source sentences. Interestingly, while there is some benefit from the dialectic transfer, the benefits are relatively small, yielding an additional 0.8 BLEU for the ensembled models. This might be due to the domain mismatch between the Tunisian-Arabic data and MSA data.

Figure 3 shows the results of our cascaded, E2E, and integrated cascaded/E2E systems on both the blind shared task test set, test2, and on the provided test set, test1. The *Hybrid Multi-Decoder* outperforms the *ASR Mixing Cascade* by 1.3 and 0.9 BLEU on test1 without and with dialectal transfer respectively. Both models are boosted by the use of ROVER. The benefit of ROVER for models without dialectal transfer (0.3 BLEU) was larger than for models with dialectal transfer (0.1 BLEU), showing some diminishing returns from isolated improvements of the ASR component of the overall ST task. Posterior combination provided boosts in the range of 0.5-0.8 BLEU across the models. Finally, the *Minimum Bayes Risk Ensembling* yielded additional gains of 0.6-1.3 BLEU. The differences between the final *Minimum Bayes Risk Ensembling* systems and the best single systems without any external model integration are 1.5 and 1.3 BLEU without and without dialectal transfer respectively.

5.2 Ablation Studies

To show the individual contributions of our various methods, we present in this section several ablations. First, we show in figure 4 the impact of dialectal transfer from MGB2 data on ASR (as described in §3.1.3) and on E2E ST (as described in §3.2.2). As subset of MGB2 data selected via the cross-entropy filter outperformed a randomly selected subset, although both were better than when no MGB2 data was included. Since the IWSLT22-Dialect utterances were shorter than the MGB2 utterances on average, one effect of the cross-entropy filter was the removal of long utterances which appeared to benefit the model. We found that using up to 25% of the MGB2 data was best for ASR. For ST, both 25% and 50% of the MGB2 data with *MT SeqKD* yielded 0.5 BLEU gains, which is slightly less than the 0.8 BLEU gains that our cascaded systems obtained from dialectal transfer. This suggests some that there our *MT SeqKD* method may be improved in the future.

Next, in figure 5 we show the results MT and ST

[5] We found that the WER's decreased by about 4% when removing diacritics from the hypothesis and the reference.

ID	Type	Model Name	Child System(s)	Dialect Transfer	test1 BLEU(↑)	test2 BLEU(↑)
C1	Cascade	ASR Mixing Cascade	A1,B1	✗	16.4	-
C2	Cascade	+ ASR Rover Comb.	A2,B1	✗	16.7	-
C3	Cascade	+ MT Posterior Comb.	A2,B2	✗	17.5	18.6
C4	Cascade	ASR Mixing Cascade	A3,B3	✓	17.3	-
C5	Cascade	+ ASR Rover Comb.	A4,B3	✓	17.4	-
C6	Cascade	+ MT Posterior Comb.	A4,B4	✓	**17.9**	**19.4**
D1	E2E ST	Hybrid Multi-Decoder	-	✗	17.7	-
D2	Mix	+ ROVER Intermediates	A2	✗	18.1	19.1
D3	Mix	+ ST/MT Posterior Comb.	A2,B5	✗	18.7	19.7
D4	E2E ST	Hybrid Multi-Decoder	-	✓	18.2	-
D5	Mix	+ ROVER Intermediates	A4	✓	18.3	19.5
D6	Mix	+ ST/MT Posterior Comb.	A4,B5	✓	**18.9**	**19.8**
E1	Mix	Min. Bayes-Risk Ensemble	C3,D3	✗	19.2	20.4
E2	Mix	Min. Bayes-Risk Ensemble	C6,D6	✓	**19.5**	**20.8**

Table 3: Results of our cascaded, E2E, and integrated cascaded/E2E systems as measured by BLEU score on the blind test2 and provided test1 sets. *Dialect Transfer* indicates the use of either MGB2 or OPUS data. Rover, posterior combinations, and minimum bayes-risk ensembling were applied to both cascaded and E2E systems, with *Child System(s)* indicating the inputs to the resultant systems combinations.

Task	MGB2 Training Data	test1 WER(↓)
ASR	none	53.1
ASR	8% w/ random select	52.7
ASR	8% w/ CE filter	**52.4**
ASR	25% w/ CE filter	**52.4**
ASR	50% w/ CE filter	53.0
ASR	75% w/ CE filter	53.5
		BLEU(↑)
ST	none	16.6
ST	25% w/ CE filter + MT SeqKD	**17.1**
ST	50% w/ CE filter + MT SeqKD	**17.1**

Table 4: Ablation study on the effects of additional MGB2 data on ASR and ST performance as measured by WER and BLEU on the test1 set respectively.

Model Name	test1 ST BLEU(↑)	test1 MT BLEU(↑)
MT Transformer	16.2	20.9
+ ASR Mixing Training	**16.7**	**21.8**

Table 5: Ablation study on the effects of ASR mixing on ST and MT as measured by BLEU on the test1 set.

systems trained with and without *ASR mixing* (as described in §3.1.2), both in the cascaded setting and using ground-truth source sentences. Overall we see that *ASR mixing* helps improving the cascaded system. Surprisingly this also improves results for the translating from ground-truth source sentences. We hypothesise that *ASR mixing* acts as a form of regularization for the orthographic inconsistencies in the source transcriptions due to the conversational nature of Tunisian-Arabic.

In table 6, we show the effects of the *ASR CTC Sampling*, *Hierarchical Encoder*, and *Joint CTC/Attention ST Decoding* modifications to the original Multi-Decoder (as described in §3.2). We found that each of these techniques boosts the overall performance and we also found their effects to be additive. Table 6 also shows the performance of a vanilla encoder-decoder for comparison, which performed significantly worse than the Multi-Decoder. Due to time limitations, we did not submit the Multi-Decoder with hierarchical encoder, joint CTC/Attention ST decoding, and ASR CTC sampling for shared task evaluation, but this was our strongest single system as evaluated on the test1 set.

Finally, Figure 7 shows the results for the two

Model Name	test1 BLEU(↑)
Encoder-Decoder	16.0
Multi-Decoder	17.1
+ ASR CTC Sampling	17.6
+ Hierarchical Encoder	17.9
+ Joint CTC/Attn ST Decoding (D4)	18.2
+ ASR CTC Sampling	**18.4**

Table 6: Ablation study on the effects of ASR CTC sampling, hierarchical encoder, and joint CTC/Attn ST decoding as measured by BLEU on the test1 set.

Model Name	MBR Method	Dialect Transfer	test1 BLEU(↑)	test2 BLEU(↑)
MBR Ensemble	True	✗	19.0	20.1
MBR Ensemble (E1)	Joint	✗	**19.2**	**20.4**
MBR Ensemble	True	✓	19.3	20.7
MBR Ensemble (E2)	Joint	✓	**19.5**	**20.8**

Table 7: Comparison of the true vs. joint methods for minimum bayes-risk ensembling as measured by BLEU on the test1 and test2 sets.

different settings for system combination through MBR (as described in §3.3.2). Using the *Joint* setting where the hypothesis from both system are considered as both candidates/samples leads to the best translations compared to the *True* setting. Figure 8 shows that while effective for maximizing BLEU score, MBR did not improve according to human evaluation.[6]

6 Conclusion

In this paper, we have presented CMU's dialect speech translation systems for IWSLT 2022. Our systems encompass various techniques across cascaded and E2E approaches. Of the techniques we presented, the hierarchical encoder and joint CTC/Attention ST decoding modifications to the Multi-Decoder and the minimum bayes-risk ensembling were amongst the most impactful. In future work, we seek to formalize these methods with additional theoretical and experimental backing, including extensions to other corpora and tasks such as pure MT.

[6]Human evaluation methodology is detailed in (Anastasopoulos et al., 2022)

Model Name	test2 BLEU(↑)	test2 DA Ave. / z-score(↑)
Hybrid Multi-Decoder (D6)	19.8	66.5 / 0.119
MBR Ensemble (E2)	**20.8**	66.5 / 0.114

Table 8: Human evaluation results, as measured by DA average and z-score, showing the impact of maximizing BLEU score via minimum bayes-risk ensembling.

Acknowledgements

Brian Yan and Shinji Watanabe are supported by the Human Language Technology Center of Excellence. This work used the Extreme Science and Engineering Discovery Environment (XSEDE) (Towns et al., 2014), which is supported by National Science Foundation grant number ACI-1548562; specifically, the Bridges system (Nystrom et al., 2015), as part of project cis210027p, which is supported by NSF award number ACI-1445606, at the Pittsburgh Supercomputing Center. We'd also like to thank Soumi Maiti, Tomoki Hayashi, and Koshak for their contributions.

References

Ahmed Ali, Peter Bell, James Glass, Yacine Messaoui, Hamdy Mubarak, Steve Renals, and Yifan Zhang. 2016. The mgb-2 challenge: Arabic multi-dialect broadcast media recognition. In *2016 IEEE Spoken Language Technology Workshop (SLT)*, pages 279–284. IEEE.

Antonios Anastasopoulos, Luisa Bentivogli, Marcely Z. Boito, Ondřej Bojar, Roldano Cattoni, Anna Currey, Georgiana Dinu, Kevin Duh, Maha Elbayad, Marcello Federico, Christian Federmann, Hongyu Gong, Roman Grundkiewicz, Barry Haddow, Benjamin Hsu, Dávid Javorský, Věra Kloudová, Surafel M. Lakew, Xutai Ma, Prashant Mathur, Paul McNamee, Kenton Murray, Maria Nădejde, Satoshi Nakamura, Matteo Negri, Jan Niehues, Xing Niu, Juan Pino, Elizabeth Salesky, Jiatong Shi, Sebastian Stüker, Katsuhito Sudoh, Marco Turchi, Yogesh Virkar, Alex Waibel, Changhan Wang, and Shinji Watanabe. 2022. FINDINGS OF THE IWSLT 2022 EVALUATION CAMPAIGN. In *Proceedings of the 19th International Conference on Spoken Language Translation (IWSLT 2022)*, Dublin, Ireland. Association for Computational Linguistics.

Siddharth Dalmia, Brian Yan, Vikas Raunak, Florian Metze, and Shinji Watanabe. 2021. Searchable hidden intermediates for end-to-end models of decomposable sequence tasks. In *Proceedings of the 2021 Conference of the North American Chapter of the Association for Computational Linguistics: Human*

Language Technologies, pages 1882–1896, Online. Association for Computational Linguistics.

Keqi Deng, Shinji Watanabe, Jiatong Shi, and Siddhant Arora. 2022. Blockwise streaming transformer for spoken language understanding and simultaneous speech translation. *arXiv preprint arXiv:2204.08920*.

Bryan Eikema and Wilker Aziz. 2020. Is MAP decoding all you need? the inadequacy of the mode in neural machine translation. In *Proceedings of the 28th International Conference on Computational Linguistics*, pages 4506–4520, Barcelona, Spain (Online). International Committee on Computational Linguistics.

J.G. Fiscus. 1997. A post-processing system to yield reduced word error rates: Recognizer output voting error reduction (rover). In *1997 IEEE Workshop on Automatic Speech Recognition and Understanding Proceedings*, pages 347–354.

John J Godfrey, Edward C Holliman, and Jane McDaniel. 1992. Switchboard: Telephone speech corpus for research and development. In *Acoustics, Speech, and Signal Processing, IEEE International Conference on*, volume 1, pages 517–520. IEEE Computer Society.

Alex Graves. 2012. Connectionist temporal classification. In *Supervised sequence labelling with recurrent neural networks*, pages 61–93. Springer.

Alex Graves and Jürgen Schmidhuber. 2005. Framewise phoneme classification with bidirectional lstm and other neural network architectures. *Neural Networks*, 18(5):602–610. IJCNN 2005.

Anmol Gulati, James Qin, Chung-Cheng Chiu, Niki Parmar, Yu Zhang, Jiahui Yu, Wei Han, Shibo Wang, Zhengdong Zhang, Yonghui Wu, and Ruoming Pang. 2020. Conformer: Convolution-augmented Transformer for speech recognition. In *Proceedings of Interspeech*, pages 5036–5040.

Pengcheng Guo, Florian Boyer, Xuankai Chang, Tomoki Hayashi, Yosuke Higuchi, Hirofumi Inaguma, Naoyuki Kamo, Chenda Li, Daniel Garcia-Romero, Jiatong Shi, et al. 2020. Recent developments on ESPnet toolkit boosted by Conformer. *arXiv preprint arXiv:2010.13956*.

Nizar Habash, Abdelhadi Soudi, and Timothy Buckwalter. 2007. On arabic transliteration. In *Arabic computational morphology*, pages 15–22. Springer.

Yosuke Higuchi, Keita Karube, Tetsuji Ogawa, and Tetsunori Kobayashi. 2021. Hierarchical conditional end-to-end asr with ctc and multi-granular subword units. *ArXiv*, abs/2110.04109.

Sepp Hochreiter and Jürgen Schmidhuber. 1997. Long short-term memory. *Neural computation*, 9(8):1735–1780.

Ari Holtzman, Jan Buys, Maxwell Forbes, and Yejin Choi. 2019. The curious case of neural text degeneration. *CoRR*, abs/1904.09751.

Amir Hussein, Shinji Watanabe, and Ahmed Ali. 2022. Arabic speech recognition by end-to-end, modular systems and human. *Computer Speech & Language*, 71:101272.

Hirofumi Inaguma, Siddharth Dalmia, Brian Yan, and Shinji Watanabe. 2021a. Fast-md: Fast multi-decoder end-to-end speech translation with non-autoregressive hidden intermediates. *2021 IEEE Automatic Speech Recognition and Understanding Workshop (ASRU)*, pages 922–929.

Hirofumi Inaguma, Brian Yan, Siddharth Dalmia, Pengcheng Gu, Jiatong Shi, Kevin Duh, and Shinji Watanabe. 2021b. Espnet-st iwslt 2021 offline speech translation system. In *IWSLT*.

Marcin Junczys-Dowmunt. 2018. Dual conditional cross-entropy filtering of noisy parallel corpora. In *Proceedings of the Third Conference on Machine Translation: Shared Task Papers*, pages 888–895.

Suyoun Kim, Takaaki Hori, and Shinji Watanabe. 2017. Joint ctc-attention based end-to-end speech recognition using multi-task learning. In *2017 IEEE international conference on acoustics, speech and signal processing (ICASSP)*, pages 4835–4839. IEEE.

Yoon Kim and Alexander M. Rush. 2016. Sequence-level knowledge distillation. In *Proceedings of the 2016 Conference on Empirical Methods in Natural Language Processing*, pages 1317–1327, Austin, Texas. Association for Computational Linguistics.

Tom Ko, Vijayaditya Peddinti, Daniel Povey, and Sanjeev Khudanpur. 2015. Audio augmentation for speech recognition. In *Proceedings of Interspeech*, pages 3586–3589.

Philipp Koehn, Hieu Hoang, Alexandra Birch, Chris Callison-Burch, Marcello Federico, Nicola Bertoldi, Brooke Cowan, Wade Shen, Christine Moran, Richard Zens, Chris Dyer, Ondřej Bojar, Alexandra Constantin, and Evan Herbst. 2007. Moses: Open source toolkit for statistical machine translation. In *Proceedings of the 45th Annual Meeting of the Association for Computational Linguistics Companion Volume Proceedings of the Demo and Poster Sessions*, pages 177–180, Prague, Czech Republic. Association for Computational Linguistics.

Taku Kudo and John Richardson. 2018. SentencePiece: A simple and language independent subword tokenizer and detokenizer for neural text processing. In *Proceedings of the 2018 Conference on Empirical Methods in Natural Language Processing: System Demonstrations*, pages 66–71, Brussels, Belgium. Association for Computational Linguistics.

Shankar Kumar and William Byrne. 2002. Minimum bayes-risk word alignments of bilingual texts. In *Proceedings of the ACL-02 Conference on Empirical Methods in Natural Language Processing - Volume 10*, EMNLP '02, page 140–147, USA. Association for Computational Linguistics.

Shankar Kumar and William Byrne. 2004. Minimum Bayes-risk decoding for statistical machine translation. In *Proceedings of the Human Language Technology Conference of the North American Chapter of the Association for Computational Linguistics: HLT-NAACL 2004*, pages 169–176, Boston, Massachusetts, USA. Association for Computational Linguistics.

Jaesong Lee and Shinji Watanabe. 2021. Intermediate loss regularization for ctc-based speech recognition. In *ICASSP 2021 - 2021 IEEE International Conference on Acoustics, Speech and Signal Processing (ICASSP)*, pages 6224–6228.

Robert C Moore and William Lewis. 2010. Intelligent selection of language model training data. In *Proceedings of the ACL 2010 conference short papers*, pages 220–224.

Nicholas A Nystrom, Michael J Levine, Ralph Z Roskies, and J Ray Scott. 2015. Bridges: a uniquely flexible hpc resource for new communities and data analytics. In *Proceedings of the 2015 XSEDE Conference: Scientific Advancements Enabled by Enhanced Cyberinfrastructure*, pages 1–8.

Myle Ott, Sergey Edunov, Alexei Baevski, Angela Fan, Sam Gross, Nathan Ng, David Grangier, and Michael Auli. 2019. fairseq: A fast, extensible toolkit for sequence modeling. In *Proceedings of the 2019 Conference of the North American Chapter of the Association for Computational Linguistics (Demonstrations)*, pages 48–53, Minneapolis, Minnesota. Association for Computational Linguistics.

Daniel S Park, William Chan, Yu Zhang, Chung-Cheng Chiu, Barret Zoph, Ekin D Cubuk, and Quoc V Le. 2019. SpecAugment: A simple data augmentation method for automatic speech recognition. In *Proceedings of Interspeech*, pages 2613–2617.

Ramon Sanabria and Florian Metze. 2018. Hierarchical multitask learning with ctc. In *2018 IEEE Spoken Language Technology Workshop (SLT)*, pages 485–490. IEEE.

Rico Sennrich, Barry Haddow, and Alexandra Birch. 2016. Neural machine translation of rare words with subword units. In *Proceedings of the 54th Annual Meeting of the Association for Computational Linguistics (Volume 1: Long Papers)*, pages 1715–1725, Berlin, Germany. Association for Computational Linguistics.

Jörg Tiedemann, Santhosh Thottingal, et al. 2020. Opus-mt–building open translation services for the world. In *Proceedings of the 22nd Annual Conference of the European Association for Machine Translation*. European Association for Machine Translation.

J. Towns, T. Cockerill, M. Dahan, I. Foster, K. Gaither, A. Grimshaw, V. Hazlewood, S. Lathrop, D. Lifka, G. D. Peterson, R. Roskies, J. R. Scott, and N. Wilkins-Diehr. 2014. Xsede: Accelerating scientific discovery. *Computing in Science & Engineering*, 16(5):62–74.

Ashish Vaswani, Noam Shazeer, Niki Parmar, Jakob Uszkoreit, Llion Jones, Aidan N Gomez, Ł ukasz Kaiser, and Illia Polosukhin. 2. Attention is all you need. In *Advances in Neural Information Processing Systems*, volume 30. Curran Associates, Inc.

Shinji Watanabe, Takaaki Hori, Shigeki Karita, Tomoki Hayashi, Jiro Nishitoba, Yuya Unno, Nelson Enrique Yalta Soplin, Jahn Heymann, Matthew Wiesner, Nanxin Chen, Adithya Renduchintala, and Tsubasa Ochiai. 2018. ESPnet: End-to-end speech processing toolkit. In *Proceedings of Interspeech*, pages 2207–2211.

Shinji Watanabe, Takaaki Hori, Suyoun Kim, John R. Hershey, and Tomoki Hayashi. 2017. Hybrid ctc/attention architecture for end-to-end speech recognition. *IEEE Journal of Selected Topics in Signal Processing*, 11(8):1240–1253.

ON-TRAC Consortium Systems for the IWSLT 2022 Dialect and Low-resource Speech Translation Tasks

Marcely Zanon Boito[1], **John Ortega**[2], **Hugo Riguidel**[2], **Antoine Laurent**[2], **Loïc Barrault**[2], **Fethi Bougares**[3], **Firas Chaabani**[3], **Ha Nguyen**[1,5], **Florentin Barbier**[4], **Souhir Gahbiche**[4], **Yannick Estève**[1]

[1]LIA - Avignon University, France, [2]LIUM - Le Mans University, France
[3]ELYADATA - Tunis, Tunisia, [4]Airbus - France, [5]LIG - Grenoble Alpes University
contact email: `yannick.esteve at univ-avignon.fr`

Abstract

This paper describes the ON-TRAC Consortium translation systems developed for two challenge tracks featured in the Evaluation Campaign of IWSLT 2022: low-resource and dialect speech translation. For the Tunisian Arabic-English dataset (low-resource and dialect tracks), we build an end-to-end model as our joint primary submission, and compare it against cascaded models that leverage a large fine-tuned wav2vec 2.0 model for ASR. Our results show that in our settings pipeline approaches are still very competitive, and that with the use of transfer learning, they can outperform end-to-end models for speech translation (ST). For the Tamasheq-French dataset (low-resource track) our primary submission leverages intermediate representations from a wav2vec 2.0 model trained on 234 hours of Tamasheq audio, while our contrastive model uses a French phonetic transcription of the Tamasheq audio as input in a Conformer speech translation architecture jointly trained on automatic speech recognition, ST and machine translation losses. Our results highlight that self-supervised models trained on smaller sets of target data are more effective to low-resource end-to-end ST fine-tuning, compared to large off-the-shelf models. Results also illustrate that even approximate phonetic transcriptions can improve ST scores.

1 Introduction

The vast majority of speech pipelines are developed for and in *high-resource* languages, a small percentage of languages for which there is a large amount of annotated data freely available (Joshi et al., 2020). However, the assessment of systems' performance only on high-resource settings can be problematic because it fails to reflect the real-world performance these approaches will have in diverse and smaller datasets.

In this context, the IWSLT 2022 (Anastasopoulos et al., 2022) proposes two interesting shared tasks: low-resource and dialect speech translation (ST). The former aims to assess the exploitability of current translation systems in data scarcity settings. The latter focuses on the assessment of the systems capabilities in *noisy* settings: different dialects are mixed in a single dataset of spontaneous speech. For the low-resource task, this year's language pairs are: Tamasheq-French and Tunisian Arabic-English. The latter is also used, in constrained conditions, for the dialect task.

This paper reports the ON-TRAC consortium submissions for the mentioned tasks. The ON-TRAC Consortium is composed of researchers from three French academic laboratories, LIA (Avignon University), LIUM (Le Mans University) and LIG (University Grenoble Alpes), together with two industrial partners: Airbus France and ELYDATA. Our systems for the dialect task focus on the comparison between cascaded and end-to-end approaches for ST. For the low-resource task, we focus on the leveraging of models based on self-supervised learning (SSL), and on the training of ST models with joint automatic speech recognition (ASR), machine translation (MT) and ST losses.

This paper is organized as follows. Section 2 presents the related work. The experiments with the Tunisian Arabic-English dataset for low-resource and dialect ST tasks are presented in Section 3. Results for the Tamasheq-French dataset for the low-resource track are presented in Section 4. Section 5 concludes this work.

2 Related work

Before the introduction of *direct* or *end-to-end* ST models (Berard et al., 2016; Weiss et al., 2017), the ST task was approached as a *cascaded* problem: the speech is transcribed using an ASR model, and the transcriptions are used to train a classic MT model. The limitations of this approach include the need for extensive transcriptions of the speech

Proceedings of the 19th International Conference on Spoken Language Translation (IWSLT 2022), pages 308 - 318
May 26-27, 2022

signal, and the error propagation between ASR and MT modules. In comparison to that, end-to-end ST models propose a simpler encoder-decoder architecture, removing the need for intermediate representations of the speech signal. Although at first, cascaded models were superior in performance compared to end-to-end models, results from recent IWSLT campaigns illustrate how end-to-end models have been closing this gap (Ansari et al., 2020; Bentivogli et al., 2021; Anastasopoulos et al., 2021). Moreover, the joint optimization of ASR, MT and ST losses in end-to-end ST models was shown to increase overall performance (Le et al., 2020; Sperber et al., 2020).

SSL models for speech processing are now a popular foundation blocks in speech pipelines (Schneider et al., 2019; Hsu et al., 2021; Baevski et al., 2019, 2020). These models are large trainable networks with millions, or even billions (Babu et al., 2021), of parameters that are trained on unlabeled audio data only. The goal of training these models is providing a powerful and reusable abstraction block, which is able to process raw audio in a given language or in multilingual settings (Conneau et al., 2020; Babu et al., 2021), producing a richer audio representation for the downstream tasks to train with, compared to surface features such as MFCCs or filterbanks. Recent work found considerable performance gains and/or state-of-the-art performance by including these blocks in their target tasks, and more importantly, the final models can be trained with a smaller amount of labeled data, increasing the *accessibility* of current approaches for speech processing (Kawakami et al., 2020; Schneider et al., 2019; Hsu et al., 2021; Baevski et al., 2019, 2020).[1]

3 Tunisian Arabic-English Experiments

In this section we present our experiments for translating Tunisian Arabic to English in the context of the dialect and low-resource tasks from IWSLT 2022. Section 3.1 describes the data used in our experiments.

We investigate two types of ST architectures: end-to-end architectures (Section 3.3), and pipeline models (Section 3.2). For the latter, we include the obtained ASR results. For both, results on the ST tasks are presented in Section 3.4.

[1]Recent benchmarks for SSL models can be found in Evain et al. (2021b,a); wen Yang et al. (2021); Conneau et al. (2022).

3.1 Data

The Tunisian Arabic dataset (LDC2022E01) use in our experiments was developed and provided by LDC[2] to the IWSLT 2022 participants. It comprises 383 h of Tunisian conversational speech with manual transcripts, from which 160 h are also translated into English. Thus, it is a three-way parallel corpus (audio, transcript, translation). This LDC data consistitutes *basic condition* of the dialect task. Arabic dialects are the informal form of communication in the everyday life in the Arabic world. Tunisian Arabic is one of several Arabic dialects: there is no standard written Arabic form for this language that is shared by all Tunisian speakers. Nevertheless, the transcripts of Tunisian conversations of the LDC2022E01 Tunisian Arabic dataset follow the rules of the Tunisian Arabic CODA – Conventional Orthography for Dialectal Arabic.

For the *dialect adaptation condition*, we use in addition to the LDC2022E01 dataset, the MGB2 dataset (Ali et al., 2016), which is composed of 1,200 h of broadcast news audio recordings in modern standard Arabic (MSA) from Aljazeera TV programs. These recordings are associated to captions with no timing information: they are not verbatims of the speech content, and can be an approximation. The MGB2 dataset also contains the automatic transcriptions generated by the Qatar Computing Research Institute (QCRI) ASR system. This external dataset is used for training our ASR systems.

3.2 Pipeline ST

For our pipeline ST models, we experiment with two different ASR architectures, presented in Section 3.2.1. We also train two MT models, presented in Section 3.2.2.

3.2.1 ASR system

End-to-end ASR model. Our end-to-end ASR system is implemented on the SpeechBrain toolkit (Ravanelli et al., 2021). It is composed of a wav2vec 2.0 module, a 1024-dimension dense hidden layer with a Leaky ReLU activation function, and a softmax output layer. The weights of the wav2vec 2.0 module were initialized from the XLSR-53 model released by Meta (Conneau et al., 2020). The CTC loss function (Graves et al., 2006) was used during the training process, and two different instances of Adam (Kingma and Ba, 2015) optimizers were used to manage the weight updates:

[2]`https://www.ldc.upenn.edu/`

System	Description	valid	test
primary	E2E w/o LM	41.1	45.1
not submitted	HMM/TDNN	50.3	-
post-evaluation	E2E + 5-gram	38.3	41.5

Table 1: Results for Tunisian Arabic ASR systems in terms of WER. Submissions to the low-resource track.

one dedicated to the wav2vec 2.0 module, the other one to the two additional layers. The output of the end-to-end model is based on characters.

The training of our model is separated in two stages. First, we train an end-to-end ASR model in MSA using the MGB2 data. To process this data, we used a dictionary of 95 characters (i.e. 95-dimensional output layer). Among the 1,200 h of speech associated to captions and automatic transcripts in the MGB2 dataset, we keep only the audio segments for which the captions and the automatic transcripts are strictly the same. This corresponds to roughly 820 h of speech.

Once our model in standard Arabic is trained, we use it to initialize our final Tunisian Arabic ASR model. The architecture is kept the same, excluding the 34-dimensional output layer, and we randomly reinitialise the weights of the 2 last layers. In other words, we keep only the weights of the ASR MGB2 fine-tuned wav2vec 2.0 model, performing *transfer learning* from MSA to Tunisian Arabic. We then train the end-to-end ASR model on the Tunisian audio data of the LDC2022E01 dataset and its normalized transcription. Lastly, we train a 5-gram language model (LM) on the normalized transcriptions.

Hybrid HMM/TDNN ASR system. In addition to the end-to-end ASR system describe above, we train a Kaldi-based system (Povey et al., 2011). The acoustic model uses chain models with the TDNN architecture and 40-dimensional high-resolution MFCCs extracted from frames of 25 ms length and 10 ms shift, applying usual data augmentation methods: speed perturbation at rates of 0.9, 1.0, and 1.1, and spectral augmentation. We employ a graphemic lexicon of 88k words, and we use a 3-gram LM built using the *SRILM* toolkit (Stolcke, 2002) with the Kneser-Ney smoothing. This 3-gram LM is trained using the transcripts of the training set and the vocabulary covering all the words of the graphemic lexicon.

ASR performance. Tunisian Arabic ASR results for 3 different models are presented in Table 1. The primary system is the end-to-end ASR model described above, without LM rescoring. The second row presents the result for the hybrid HMM/TDNN system. Due to its lower performance on the validation data in comparison to the end-to-end system, we decided to not submit this system. The last row presents the results for the end-to-end ASR with the 5-gram LM, a post-evaluation result.

3.2.2 MT model

We train two MT models using the *fairseq* toolkit (Ott et al., 2019). The first model (**contrastive1**) is an bi-LSTM model from Luong et al. (2015), trained using the `lstm_luong_wmt_en_de` recipe[3]. Both encoder and decoder consists of 4 LSTM layers, and the input is at the sub-word level using a BPE vocabulary of 8,000 units, trained on the target language.

The second model (**contrastive2**) is a fully convolutional model following the `fconv_wmt_en_fr`[4] sequence-to-sequence architecture from Gehring et al. (2017). It consists of 15 encoder and decoder layers, working on the sub-word level with input and output vocabularies of 4,000 BPE units.

3.3 End-to-end ST

The end-to-end ST model is a Conformer model (Gulati et al., 2020) based on the *Espnet* toolkit (Watanabe et al., 2018). This system is trained using 80-channel log-mel filterbank features computed on a 25 ms window with a 10 ms shift. We also use speed perturbation at ratio 0.9, 1.0, 1.1 and *SpecAugment* (Park et al., 2019) with 2 frequency masks and 5 time masks. In addition, a global Cepstral Mean and Variance Normalization (CMVN) technique is applied on the top of our features.

Our Conformer model consists of a 6-block Conformer encoder and a 6-block Transformer decoder. We use 1,000 BPE as the modeling units. The model is trained for 100 epochs and the last 10 best checkpoints are averaged to create the final model.

System	Track	Description	valid	test
primary	LR/D	End-to-end	12.2	12.4
contrastive1	LR	Cascade	15.1	13.6
contrastive2	LR	Cascade	12.8	11.3
post-evaluation	LR	Cascade	16.0	14.4

Table 2: Results for Tunisian Arabic to English translation systems in terms of %BLEU for low-resource (LR) and dialect (D) tracks.

3.4 Results

Table 2 presents our ST results for dialect and low-resource tracks. Our primary system for both tracks is the end-to-end system presented in Section 3.3. The two pipeline systems, *contrastive1* and *contrastive2*, are composed by the end-to-end ASR model, and they vary on the MT model used (presented in Section 3.2.2). Since ASR models use external data (MGB2), these submissions are for the low-resource track only. Finally, the *post-evaluation* model is the composition of the *post-evaluation* end-to-end ASR model from Section 3.2.1, and the MT model from *contrastive1*.

We observe that our cascaded models are very competitive compared against our end-to-end model (primary submission): our best ST result is obtained using the *contrastive1*. The *post-evaluation* model, which adds an 5-gram LM on the end-to-end ASR module, achieves even better scores. We believe that part of the reason this model is effective is the addition of the data in MSA from the MGB2 dataset, that is used to pre-train the end-to-end ASR model. Thus, the comparison between our cascaded and end-to-end models is not exactly fair, as out end-to-end model is trained on less data.

Moreover, we would like to highlight that although this dataset is offered as part of the *low-resource* track, we do not consider this setting to be one of data scarcity: 160 h of translated speech are available. We do, however, find this dataset to be extremely complex to work with. That is because there are multiple regional dialects from Tunisia mixed in the data, which makes the ST task harder. These regional dialects differ mainly on their accent, but sometimes also in terms of vocabulary and expression.

[3]https://fairseq.readthedocs.io/en/latest/_modules/fairseq/models/lstm.html

[4]https://fairseq.readthedocs.io/en/latest/models.html

Nonetheless, we find that the real challenge for processing this data comes from its nature. This dataset is a collection of telephonic conversations, where the acoustic conditions can be sometimes very challenging: some phone calls are made from mobile phones in very noisy environments, and sometimes some portions of audio recordings are saturated because of sudden high audio input gain.

By computing the WER on each audio recording in the validation set using our best ASR model, we observe that the lowest one achieved is 18.3%, while the highest one is 88.5%. Thus, we achieve a global WER of 38.3% (*post-evaluation* in Table 1), with a standard deviation is 12.3%. This illustrates the high variability in terms of audio quality that might exist in this dataset.

4 Tamasheq-French Experiments

In this section we present our experiments for the Tamasheq-French dataset in the context of the low-resource ST track. This dataset, recently introduced in Boito et al. (2022), contains 17 h of speech in the Tamasheq language, which corresponds to 5,829 utterances translated to French. Additional audio data was also made available through the *Niger-Mali audio collection*: 224 h in Tamasheq and 417 h in geographically close languages (French from Niger, Fulfulde, Hausa, and Zarma).[5] For all this data, the speech style is radio broadcasting, and the dataset presents no transcription.

Our experiments are separated in two different investigation branches:

1. The exploitation of SSL wav2vec 2.0 models (Baevski et al., 2020) for low-resource direct speech-to-text translation;
2. The production of *approximate* phonetic transcriptions for attenuating the challenge of training in low-resource settings.

We start by presenting the models proposed for the first branch: the SSL models pre-trained and/or fine-tuned for Tamasheq in Section 4.1, the *pipeline* experiments that use wav2vec 2.0 models as feature extractors in Section 4.2, and our primary system, an end-to-end architecture that directly fine-tunes a wav2vec 2.0 model, in Section 4.3. Section 4.4 focuses on the second branch of experiments, presenting our contrastive model that is

[5]https://demo-lia.univ-avignon.fr/studios-tamani-kalangou/

based on the joint optimization of ASR, MT and ST losses. This is made possible by the use of a French ASR system for generating an approximated phonetic transcription of the Tamasheq audio. In Section 4.5, we present and discuss our results, and lastly, Section 4.6 describes some less-successful experiments.

4.1 SSL models

Pre-trained models. We train two wav2vec 2.0 *base* models using the Niger-Mali audio collection. The *Tamasheq-only* model uses the 224 h in Tamasheq, and the *Niger-Mali* model uses all the data available: 641 h in five languages. Additionally, we include in the training data for both models the 19 h present in the *full* release of the Tamasheq-French corpus.[6] Therefore, both models are pre-trained on the target data. For training them, we use the same hyperparameters from the original wav2vec 2.0, as well as the original *fairseq* (Ott et al., 2019) implementation. These models are trained until 500k updates on 16 Nvidia Tesla V100 (32GB), and they are available for download at HuggingFace.[7]

Fine-tuned models. We experiment with the 7K large French wav2vec 2.0 model (LB-FR-7K) from the *LeBenchmark* (Evain et al., 2021b), and the multilingual XLSR-53 (Conneau et al., 2020). Both models are fine-tuned on the 243 h of Tamasheq (224 h +19 h) for approximately 20k updates on 4 Nvidia Tesla V100 (32GB). Finally, using the Tamasheq-only model, we also experiment fine-tuning it for the ASR task in MSA (primary ASR model from Section 3.2).

4.2 Pipeline SSL+ST models

Our models are very close to the recipe for low-resource ST from wav2vec 2.0 features described in Evain et al. (2021a). We use the *fairseq s2t* toolkit (Wang et al., 2020) for training an end-to-end ST Transformer model (Vaswani et al., 2017) with 4 heads, dimensionality of 256, inner projection of 1,024, 6 encoder and 3 encoder layers. The Transformer is preceded by a 1D convolutional layer (k=5, stride=2) for down-projecting the wav2vec 2.0 large (1,024) or base (768) features into the Transformer input dimensionality. These models are trained for 500 epochs using the Adam optimizer (Kingma and Ba, 2015) with 10k warm-up steps. For decoding, we use beam search with a beam size of 5. For these models and the ones from Section 4.3, we generate a 1k unigram vocabulary for the French text using *Sentencepiece* (Kudo and Richardson, 2018), with no pre-tokenization.

Lastly, we include baseline results that replace wav2vec 2.0 features by 80-dimensional mel filterbank (MFB) features. In this setting, the CNN preceding the transformer encoder is identical from the one in Evain et al. (2021a).

4.3 End-to-end SSL+ST models

Training an end-to-end ST model from a pre-trained speech encoder was first proposed in Li et al. (2021). In this work, our end-to-end ST model is similar to the end-to-end ASR model presented in Section 3.2.1. It is also implemented on *SpeechBrain*, and it comprises a wav2vec 2.0 as speech encoder, followed by a linear projection, and the Transformer Decoder from Section 4.2. The weights for the wav2vec 2.0 speech encoder are initialized from one of the models in Section 4.2, and the model is trained on the NLL loss. As in Section 3.2, two different instances of the Adam optimizer manage the weight updates: one dedicated to the wav2vec 2.0 module, the other one to the following layers.

Inspired by the layer-wise investigation for wav2vec 2.0 models described in Pasad et al. (2021), we explore reducing the number of layers in the Transformer encoder that is internal to the wav2vec 2.0 module. This is based on their finding that the Transformer encoder behaves in an auto-encoder fashion and therefore, the intermediate representations might contain a higher level of abstraction from the speech signal. In their work, they show that re-initializing the weights of the final Transformer Encoder layers increases performance in ASR fine-tuning.

Different from that, we propose to remove these layers altogether, which we believe is beneficial for low-resource ST fine-tuning for two reasons. First, a reduced wav2vec 2.0 module will still have considerable capacity for encoding the speech, and second, this reduction in number of trainable parameters might facilitate training.

For implementing this model, we simply drop the N final encoder layers from our training graph, keeping the final projection. We refer to this architecture as *W2V-N+ST*, where N is the number

[6] https://github.com/mzboito/IWSLT2022_Tamasheq_data

[7] https://huggingface.co/LIA-AvignonUniversity

of layers, starting from the first, kept during ST training.

4.4 End-to-end ASR+ST models

We investigate a ST architecture that jointly optimizes ST, MT and ASR losses, as in Le et al. (2020). For this evaluation campaign however, no Tamasheq transcript nor phonetic transcription was provided, so we create an approximate phonetic transcription (Section 4.4.1) that we use in our end-to-end joint system for ST (Section 4.4.2).

4.4.1 Phonetic transcription for Tamasheq

The Tamasheq is a Tuareg language spoken by around 500 thousand speakers, mainly from northern Mali. Its phonological system contains 5 vowels (+2 short vowels) and approximately 21 consonants if we ignore the 6 consonants of Arabic origin that are of marginal use (mostly for loanwords) (Heath, 2005). This leads to a set of 26 phonemes. Almost all of those phonemes appear to occur in French, which contains 36 phonemes, 16 vowels, 17 consonants and 3 glides.

This motivates to use a phonetizer pretrained on French in order to "transcribe" the Tamasheq signal into a sequence of pseudo-Tamasheq phonemes. A phonetic force alignment using a pre-trained Kaldi (Povey et al., 2011) chain-TDNN acoustic model was used, followed by an ASR system trained using ESPNet (Watanabe et al., 2018). The model is trained on MFB features, and it uses 12 blocks of Conformer (Gulati et al., 2020) encoders, followed by 6 blocks of Transformer decoders. It uses a hybrid loss between attention mechanism and CTC (Graves et al., 2006).

The French corpus is composed of approximately 200 h coming from ESTER1&2 (Galliano et al., 2009), REPERE (Giraudel et al., 2012) and VERA (Goryainova et al., 2014). No LM was used, and the phoneme error rate achieved on the ESTER2 test corpus is of 7,7% (silences are not ignored).

We highlight that there is no simple automatic way to evaluate the quality of the phonetic transcriptions we generated on Tamasheq. We however, manually verified some transcriptions and confirmed that they seemed to be of overall good quality.

System	Description	valid	test
primary	E2E, W2V-6+ST	8.34	5.70
contrastive	E2E, ASR+ST	6.40	5.04
contrastive2	pipeline, W2V-ASR+ST	3.62	3.17
contrastive3	pipeline, W2V-FT+ST	2.94	2.57
baseline	pipeline	2.22	1.80

Table 3: Results for the pipeline and end-to-end (E2E) Tamasheq-French ST systems in terms of %BLEU score. The first two rows present our submitted systems, while the reminder are complementary post-evaluation results.

4.4.2 Architecture

The system is based on the *ESPNet2* (Inaguma et al., 2020) ST recipe.[8] This end-to-end model is made of 12 blocks of conformer encoders (hidden size of dimension 1024), followed by 3 blocks of transformer decoders (hidden size of dimension 2048). Input features are 512-dimensional MFB features extracted from the wave signal.

Three losses are jointly used for training, as described in Equation 1. There, $\mathcal{L}_{ST}$ is the loss for Tamasheq speech to French text translation; $\mathcal{L}_{MT}$ is the loss for Tamasheq pseudo-phonetic transcription to French text translation; and $\mathcal{L}_{ASR}$ is the loss for Tamasheq speech to Tamasheq pseudo-phonetic transcription.

$$\mathcal{L} = 0.3 \times \mathcal{L}_{ST} + 0.5 \times \mathcal{L}_{MT} + 0.2 \times \mathcal{L}_{ASR} \quad (1)$$

4.5 Results

Results are presented in Table 3. Our primary submission (W2V-6+ST) uses the Tamasheq-only wav2vec 2.0 base model, with only 6 transformer encoder layers (from a total of 12). Results with different numbers of layers are present in the Appendix A.1. Our contrastive submission is the end-to-end model from Section 4.4. Finally, the three last rows present complementary results, including a baseline trained on MFB features, and two pipeline models. The *contrastive2* uses the Tamasheq-only wav2vec 2.0 model fine-tuned for the Arabic ASR task from Section 3.2 as feature extractor, while *contrastive3* extracts features from the Niger-Mali wav2vec 2.0 base model fine-tuned on Tamasheq. Other pipeline SSL+ST models achieved lower scores, and their results are grouped in Appendix A.2.

[8] `https://github.com/espnet/espnet/tree/master/espnet2/st`

Looking at our results, and concentrating on SSL models, we notice that models that use wav2vec 2.0 as feature extractor (*contrastive2* and *contrastive3*) achieve better performance compared to a baseline using MFB features. However, this finding does not hold for the wav2vec 2.0 large models fine-tuned on Tamasheq (XLSR-53 and LB-FR-7K), which scored as poorly as our baseline (results in Appendix A.2). We find this result surprising, specially in the case of the multilingual model (XLSR-53). This could mean that these large models are not useful as feature extractors for low-resource settings, even after task-agnostic fine-tuning on the target language.

Regarding the fine-tuning procedure, as in Evain et al. (2021a), we notice that ASR fine-tuning is more beneficial to ST than task-agnostic fine-tuning: *contrastive2* achieves better scores compared to *contrastive3*. We find this result interesting, considering that the ASR fine-tuning performed in this case did not targeted Tamasheq, but MSA. This could mean that, when languages are sufficiently similar, ASR fine-tuning in a different language could be performed for increasing the performance on a low-resource language without transcripts.

Regarding our primary system, we found better results by reducing the amount of trainable encoder layers inside the wav2vec 2.0 module. We also investigated freezing it partially or entirely during end-to-end ST training, but this resulted in performance decrease in the validation set.

Regarding the different wav2vec 2.0 models trained (Section 4.1), and focusing on our primary model, we find that similar to pipeline SSL+ST models, we achieved our best results with base architectures (Tamasheq-only and Niger-Mali). Close seconds to the performance obtained with our primary model (on the validation set) were the models using the same wav2vec 2.0 modules from *contrastive2* and *contrastive3*.

These results indicate that having a dedicated wav2vec 2.0 model trained on the target or on close languages is indeed better than fine-tuning large monolingual (LB-FR-7K) or multilingual (XLSR-53) models.[9] This is particularly interesting considering that the Tamasheq-only model is trained with only 234 h of speech, whereas XLSR-53 learned from approximately 56 thousand of hours. We believe that more investigation is necessary in order to confirm the observed trend. Finally, we find the gap between the primary's performance in validation and test sets surprising, and we intend to investigate this further as well.

Concluding, the *contrastive* model we propose in our submission presents a different approach for low-resource ST. By creating an approximate transcription of the Tamasheq audio, we are able to train more effectively, reaching a performance close to our primary model for the test set. This illustrates how transcriptions can be an effective form of increasing performance in low-resource settings, even when these are automatically generated. A possible extension of this work would be the combination of our primary and contrastive models: by inserting the primary's wav2vec 2.0 speech encoder into the training framework from the contrastive model, one can hypothesize that we could achieve even better scores.

4.6 Other Approaches

XLS-R ST model. During development, we tried to apply XLS-R for translation (Babu et al., 2021), using the implementation available on the HuggingFace.[10] In this approach, we aimed to use the pre-trained model, that is trained on 21 source languages with one target language (English), called *wav2vec2-xls-r-300m-21-to-en* to first translate the Tamasheq validation set to English. Then, as a second step, to translate the English system output to French. However, we observed that the decoder, based on a mBART (Liu et al., 2020), repeated several groups of tokens during decoding of up to hundreds of times. For example, the phrase: "the sun was shining in the sky" for the sentence: "In the evening, the sun was shining in the sky, and the sun was shining in the sky..." was repeated 32 times. This illustrates that out-of-shelf models can still fail to provide decent results in zero-shot settings.

ST fine-tuning for large wav2vec 2.0 models. All end-to-end models described in Section 4.3 are trained on a single Nvidia Tesla V100 (32GB). This limited our investigation using large wav2vec 2.0 models, since these only fit in this size of GPU after extreme reduction of the decoder network. Therefore, we find difficult to assess if the inferior performance of these large end-to-end models is

[9] By *close* we mean: (1) languages that are geographically close and with a known degree of lexical borrowing; (2) similar speech style and recording settings.

[10] https://huggingface.co/facebook/wav2vec2-xls-r-300m-21-to-en

due to the architecture size, or due to the speech representation produced by the wav2vec 2.0 models. In any case, reducing the number of encoder layers, and freezing some of the initial ones, resulted in better performance. The attained scores were however still inferior compared to pipeline models.

5 Conclusion

In this paper we presented our results for two IWSLT 2022 tasks: dialect and low-resource ST. Focusing on the Tunisian Arabic-English dataset (dialect and low-resource tasks), we trained an end-to-end ST model as primary submission for both tasks, and contrastive cascaded models that used external data in MSA for the low-resource track. Our cascaded models turned out to outperform slightly our end-to-end model, which we believe might be due to the additional 820 h of data in MSA that was used to pre-train our end-to-end ASR model. Finally, we observe a considerable variability in our ASR results, hinting that the quality of this dataset might be mixed.

Our experiments with the Tamasheq-French dataset (low-resource task) included the training and application of wav2vec 2.0 models for ST as either feature extractors or speech encoders. We find the latter to be more beneficial: by fine-tuning half of a wav2vec 2.0 base model trained on the Tamasheq language on the ST task, we achieve our best results. Between our findings regarding the use of SSL models for low-resource ST, we highlight two interesting points: first, we find that fine-tuning wav2vec 2.0 models for the ASR task turns out to be effective even when the fine-tuning and target languages are not the same. Second, we disappointingly observe that large models perform poorly in this low-resource setting, even after fine-tuning in the target language. These last results hint that it might be more beneficial to train wav2vec 2.0 in smaller sets of unlabeled target data (or in related languages in the same speech settings) than fine-tuning massive off-the-shelf SSL models.

Concluding, we also investigated the generation of approximate transcriptions on Tamasheq by using a French ASR model. Using these transcriptions to jointly constrain an end-to-end ST model on ASR, MT and ST losses, we achieved our second best reported results. This illustrates that even automatically generated approximate transcriptions can reduce the challenge of performing ST in low-resource settings.

Acknowledgements

This work was funded by the French Research Agency (ANR) through the ON-TRAC project under contract number ANR-18-CE23-0021. It was also partially funded by the European Commission through the SELMA project under grant number 957017. It used HPC resources from GENCI-IDRIS: grants 2020-A0111012991, 2021-AD011013317, 2021-AD011013331 and 2021-AD011012527. The authors would like to thank Daniel Luzzati from LIUM for his help on the Tamasheq phonological system.

References

Ahmed Ali, Peter Bell, James Glass, Yacine Messaoui, Hamdy Mubarak, Steve Renals, and Yifan Zhang. 2016. The mgb-2 challenge: Arabic multi-dialect broadcast media recognition. In *2016 IEEE Spoken Language Technology Workshop (SLT)*, pages 279–284. IEEE.

Antonios Anastasopoulos, Loïc Barrault, Luisa Bentivogli, Marcely Zanon Boito, Ondřej Bojar, Roldano Cattoni, Anna Currey, Georgiana Dinu, Kevin Duh, Maha Elbayad, Yannick Estéve, Marcello Federico, Christian Federmann, Souhir Gahbiche, Hongyu Gong, Roman Grundkiewicz, Barry Haddow, Benjamin Hsu, Dávid Javorský, Věra Kloudová, Surafel M. Lakew, Xutai Ma, Prashant Mathur, Paul McNamee, Kenton Murray, Maria Nădejde, Satoshi Nakamura, Matteo Negri, Jan Niehues, Xing Niu, John Ortega, Juan Pino, Elizabeth Salesky, Jiatong Shi, Sebastian Stüker, Katsuhito Sudoh, Marco Turchi, Yogesh Virkar, Alex Waibel, Changhan Wang, and Shinji Watanabe. 2022. FINDINGS OF THE IWSLT 2022 EVALUATION CAMPAIGN. In *Proceedings of the 19th International Conference on Spoken Language Translation (IWSLT 2022)*, Dublin, Ireland. Association for Computational Linguistics.

Antonios Anastasopoulos, Ondřej Bojar, Jacob Bremerman, Roldano Cattoni, Maha Elbayad, Marcello Federico, Xutai Ma, Satoshi Nakamura, Matteo Negri, Jan Niehues, Juan Pino, Elizabeth Salesky, Sebastian Stüker, Katsuhito Sudoh, Marco Turchi, Alexander Waibel, Changhan Wang, and Matthew Wiesner. 2021. FINDINGS OF THE IWSLT 2021 EVALUATION CAMPAIGN. In *Proceedings of the 18th International Conference on Spoken Language Translation (IWSLT 2021)*, pages 1–29, Bangkok, Thailand (online). Association for Computational Linguistics.

Ebrahim Ansari, Amittai Axelrod, Nguyen Bach, Ondřej Bojar, Roldano Cattoni, Fahim Dalvi, Nadir Durrani, Marcello Federico, Christian Federmann, Jiatao Gu, et al. 2020. Findings of the iwslt 2020 evaluation campaign. In *Proceedings of the 17th International Conference on Spoken Language Translation*, pages 1–34.

Arun Babu, Changhan Wang, Andros Tjandra, Kushal Lakhotia, Qiantong Xu, Naman Goyal, Kritika Singh, Patrick von Platen, Yatharth Saraf, Juan Pino, et al. 2021. Xls-r: Self-supervised cross-lingual speech representation learning at scale. *arXiv preprint arXiv:2111.09296*.

Alexei Baevski, Michael Auli, and Abdelrahman Mohamed. 2019. Effectiveness of self-supervised pretraining for speech recognition. *arXiv preprint arXiv:1911.03912*.

Alexei Baevski, Yuhao Zhou, Abdelrahman Mohamed, and Michael Auli. 2020. wav2vec 2.0: A framework for self-supervised learning of speech representations. *Advances in Neural Information Processing Systems*, 33:12449–12460.

Luisa Bentivogli, Mauro Cettolo, Marco Gaido, Alina Karakanta, Alberto Martinelli, Matteo Negri, and Marco Turchi. 2021. Cascade versus direct speech translation: Do the differences still make a difference? *CoRR*, abs/2106.01045.

Alexandre Berard, Olivier Pietquin, Christophe Servan, and Laurent Besacier. 2016. Listen and translate: A proof of concept for end-to-end speech-to-text translation. *CoRR*, abs/1612.01744.

Marcely Zanon Boito, Fethi Bougares, Florentin Barbier, Souhir Gahbiche, Loïc Barrault, Mickael Rouvier, and Yannick Estéve. 2022. Speech resources in the tamasheq language. *Language Resources and Evaluation Conference (LREC)*.

Alexis Conneau, Alexei Baevski, Ronan Collobert, Abdelrahman Mohamed, and Michael Auli. 2020. Unsupervised cross-lingual representation learning for speech recognition. *arXiv preprint arXiv:2006.13979*.

Alexis Conneau, Ankur Bapna, Yu Zhang, Min Ma, Patrick von Platen, Anton Lozhkov, Colin Cherry, Ye Jia, Clara Rivera, Mihir Kale, et al. 2022. Xtreme-s: Evaluating cross-lingual speech representations. *arXiv preprint arXiv:2203.10752*.

Solène Evain, Ha Nguyen, Hang Le, Marcely Zanon Boito, Salima Mdhaffar, Sina Alisamir, Ziyi Tong, Natalia Tomashenko, Marco Dinarelli, Titouan Parcollet, et al. 2021a. Task agnostic and task specific self-supervised learning from speech with *LeBenchmark*. In *Thirty-fifth Conference on Neural Information Processing Systems Datasets and Benchmarks Track (Round 2)*.

Solène Evain, Ha Nguyen, Hang Le, Marcely Zanon Boito, Salima Mdhaffar, Sina Alisamir, Ziyi Tong, Natalia Tomashenko, Marco Dinarelli, Titouan Parcollet, Alexandre Allauzen, Yannick Estève, Benjamin Lecouteux, François Portet, Solange Rossato, Fabien Ringeval, Didier Schwab, and Laurent Besacier. 2021b. *LeBenchmark*: A Reproducible Framework for Assessing Self-Supervised Representation Learning from Speech. In *Interspeech*, pages 1439–1443.

Sylvain Galliano, Guillaume Gravier, and Laura Chaubard. 2009. The ester 2 evaluation campaign for the rich transcription of french radio broadcasts. In *Tenth Annual Conference of the International Speech Communication Association*.

Jonas Gehring, Michael Auli, David Grangier, Denis Yarats, and Yann N. Dauphin. 2017. Convolutional sequence to sequence learning. *CoRR*, abs/1705.03122.

Aude Giraudel, Matthieu Carré, Valérie Mapelli, Juliette Kahn, Olivier Galibert, and Ludovic Quintard. 2012. The repere corpus: a multimodal corpus for person recognition. In *LREC*, pages 1102–1107.

Maria Goryainova, Cyril Grouin, Sophie Rosset, and Ioana Vasilescu. 2014. Morpho-syntactic study of errors from speech recognition system. In *LREC*, volume 14, pages 3050–3056.

Alex Graves, Santiago Fernández, Faustino Gomez, and Jürgen Schmidhuber. 2006. Connectionist temporal classification: labelling unsegmented sequence data with recurrent neural networks. In *Proceedings of the 23rd international conference on Machine learning*, pages 369–376.

Anmol Gulati, James Qin, Chung-Cheng Chiu, Niki Parmar, Yu Zhang, Jiahui Yu, Wei Han, Shibo Wang, Zhengdong Zhang, Yonghui Wu, and Ruoming Pang. 2020. Conformer: Convolution-augmented Transformer for Speech Recognition. In *Proc. Interspeech 2020*, pages 5036–5040.

Jeffrey Heath. 2005. *A Grammar of Tamashek (Tuareg of Mali)*. Walter de Gruyter, Berlin.

Wei-Ning Hsu, Benjamin Bolte, Yao-Hung Hubert Tsai, Kushal Lakhotia, Ruslan Salakhutdinov, and Abdelrahman Mohamed. 2021. Hubert: Self-supervised speech representation learning by masked prediction of hidden units. *IEEE/ACM Transactions on Audio, Speech, and Language Processing*, 29:3451–3460.

Hirofumi Inaguma, Shun Kiyono, Kevin Duh, Shigeki Karita, Nelson Yalta, Tomoki Hayashi, and Shinji Watanabe. 2020. ESPnet-ST: All-in-one speech translation toolkit. In *Proceedings of the 58th Annual Meeting of the Association for Computational Linguistics: System Demonstrations*, pages 302–311, Online. Association for Computational Linguistics.

Pratik Joshi, Sebastin Santy, Amar Budhiraja, Kalika Bali, and Monojit Choudhury. 2020. The state and fate of linguistic diversity and inclusion in the NLP world. In *Proceedings of the 58th Annual Meeting of the Association for Computational Linguistics*.

Kazuya Kawakami, Luyu Wang, Chris Dyer, Phil Blunsom, and Aaron van den Oord. 2020. Learning robust and multilingual speech representations. In *EMNLP*, pages 1182–1192, Online. Association for Computational Linguistics.

Diederik P. Kingma and Jimmy Ba. 2015. Adam: A method for stochastic optimization. In *ICLR 2015, Conference Track Proceedings*.

Taku Kudo and John Richardson. 2018. Sentencepiece: A simple and language independent subword tokenizer and detokenizer for neural text processing. *arXiv preprint arXiv:1808.06226*.

Hang Le, Juan Pino, Changhan Wang, Jiatao Gu, Didier Schwab, and Laurent Besacier. 2020. Dual-decoder transformer for joint automatic speech recognition and multilingual speech translation. *arXiv preprint arXiv:2011.00747*.

Xian Li, Changhan Wang, Yun Tang, Chau Tran, Yuqing Tang, Juan Pino, Alexei Baevski, Alexis Conneau, and Michael Auli. 2021. Multilingual speech translation from efficient finetuning of pretrained models. In *Proceedings of the 59th Annual Meeting of the Association for Computational Linguistics and the 11th International Joint Conference on Natural Language Processing (Volume 1: Long Papers)*, pages 827–838, Online. Association for Computational Linguistics.

Yinhan Liu, Jiatao Gu, Naman Goyal, Xian Li, Sergey Edunov, Marjan Ghazvininejad, Mike Lewis, and Luke Zettlemoyer. 2020. Multilingual denoising pre-training for neural machine translation. *Transactions of the Association for Computational Linguistics*, 8:726–742.

Thang Luong, Hieu Pham, and Christopher D. Manning. 2015. Effective approaches to attention-based neural machine translation. In *Proceedings of the 2015 Conference on Empirical Methods in Natural Language Processing*, pages 1412–1421, Lisbon, Portugal. Association for Computational Linguistics.

Myle Ott, Sergey Edunov, Alexei Baevski, Angela Fan, Sam Gross, Nathan Ng, David Grangier, and Michael Auli. 2019. fairseq: A fast, extensible toolkit for sequence modeling. In *NAACL (Demonstrations)*, pages 48–53, Minneapolis, Minnesota. Association for Computational Linguistics.

Daniel S Park, William Chan, Yu Zhang, Chung-Cheng Chiu, Barret Zoph, Ekin D Cubuk, and Quoc V Le. 2019. Specaugment: A simple data augmentation method for automatic speech recognition. *arXiv preprint arXiv:1904.08779*.

Ankita Pasad, Ju-Chieh Chou, and Karen Livescu. 2021. Layer-wise analysis of a self-supervised speech representation model. *arXiv preprint arXiv:2107.04734*.

Daniel Povey, Arnab Ghoshal, Gilles Boulianne, Lukas Burget, Ondrej Glembek, Nagendra Goel, Mirko Hannemann, Petr Motlicek, Yanmin Qian, Petr Schwarz, et al. 2011. The Kaldi speech recognition toolkit. In *IEEE Workshop on automatic speech recognition and understanding*.

Mirco Ravanelli, Titouan Parcollet, Peter Plantinga, Aku Rouhe, Samuele Cornell, Loren Lugosch, Cem Subakan, Nauman Dawalatabad, Abdelwahab Heba, Jianyuan Zhong, Ju-Chieh Chou, Sung-Lin Yeh, Szu-Wei Fu, Chien-Feng Liao, Elena Rastorgueva, François Grondin, William Aris, Hwidong Na, Yan Gao, Renato De Mori, and Yoshua Bengio. 2021. SpeechBrain: A general-purpose speech toolkit. ArXiv:2106.04624.

Steffen Schneider, Alexei Baevski, Ronan Collobert, and Michael Auli. 2019. wav2vec: Unsupervised pre-training for speech recognition. *arXiv preprint arXiv:1904.05862*.

Matthias Sperber, Hendra Setiawan, Christian Gollan, Udhyakumar Nallasamy, and Matthias Paulik. 2020. Consistent transcription and translation of speech. *Transactions of the Association for Computational Linguistics*, 8:695–709.

Andreas Stolcke. 2002. Srilm-an extensible language modeling toolkit. In *Seventh international conference on spoken language processing*.

Ashish Vaswani, Noam Shazeer, Niki Parmar, Jakob Uszkoreit, Llion Jones, Aidan N Gomez, Łukasz Kaiser, and Illia Polosukhin. 2017. Attention is all you need. *Advances in neural information processing systems*, 30.

Changhan Wang, Yun Tang, Xutai Ma, Anne Wu, Dmytro Okhonko, and Juan Pino. 2020. fairseq s2t: Fast speech-to-text modeling with fairseq. *arXiv preprint arXiv:2010.05171*.

Shinji Watanabe, Takaaki Hori, Shigeki Karita, Tomoki Hayashi, Jiro Nishitoba, Yuya Unno, Nelson Enrique Yalta Soplin, Jahn Heymann, Matthew Wiesner, Nanxin Chen, Adithya Renduchintala, and Tsubasa Ochiai. 2018. ESPnet: End-to-end speech processing toolkit. In *Proceedings of Interspeech*, pages 2207–2211.

Ron J. Weiss, Jan Chorowski, Navdeep Jaitly, Yonghui Wu, and Zhifeng Chen. 2017. Sequence-to-Sequence Models Can Directly Translate Foreign Speech. In *Proc. Interspeech 2017*, pages 2625–2629.

Shu wen Yang, Po-Han Chi, Yung-Sung Chuang, Cheng-I Jeff Lai, Kushal Lakhotia, Yist Y. Lin, Andy T. Liu, Jiatong Shi, Xuankai Chang, Guan-Ting Lin, Tzu-Hsien Huang, Wei-Cheng Tseng, Ko tik Lee, Da-Rong Liu, Zili Huang, Shuyan Dong, Shang-Wen Li, Shinji Watanabe, Abdelrahman Mohamed, and Hung yi Lee. 2021. SUPERB: Speech Processing Universal PERformance Benchmark. In *Interspeech*, pages 1194–1198.

A Tamasheq-French Experiments

A.1 ST fine-tuning from intermediate layers

# layers	valid	test
12 (all)	3.68	2.34
11	4.40	3.21
10	5.96	4.11
9	7.32	5.40
8	7.64	5.64
7	8.29	**6.00**
6	**8.34**	5.70
5	7.88	5.13
4	6.54	4.02

Table 4: Post-evaluation results for the end-to-end W2V-N+ST models from Section 4.3, using different N values (number of layers). All models were trained using the Tamasheq-only wav2vec 2.0 base model. Best results in bold.

A.2 Pipeline SSL+ST Results

W2V model	Fine-tuning	valid	test
LB-FR-7K	-	2.36	1.80
LB-FR-7K	Task-agnostic	2.48	1.92
XLSR-53	-	2.05	1.42
XLSR-53	Task-agnostic	1.99	1.91
Tamasheq-only	-	2.99	2.42
Tamasheq-only	ASR (Arabic)	**3.62**	**3.17**
Niger-Mali	-	2.81	2.68
Niger-Mali	Task-agnostic	2.94	2.57

Table 5: Post-evaluation results for the pipeline SSL+ST models from Section 4.2. Task-agnostic corresponds to the fine-tuning on 243 h of Tamasheq, as described in Section 4.1. Best results in bold.

JHU IWSLT 2022 Dialect Speech Translation System Description

Jinyi Yang[†*] **Amir Hussein**[†*] **Matthew Wiesner**[‡] **Sanjeev Khudanpur**[†‡]
[†]Johns Hopkins University
[‡] Human Language Technology Center of Excellence
{jyang126,ahussei6,wiesner,khudanpur}@jhu.edu

Abstract

This paper details the Johns Hopkins speech translation (ST) system used in the IWLST2022 dialect speech translation task. Our system uses a cascade of automatic speech recognition (ASR) and machine translation (MT). We use a Conformer model for ASR systems and a Transformer model for machine translation. Surprisingly, we found that while using additional ASR training data resulted in only a negligible change in performance as measured by BLEU or word error rate (WER), aggressive text normalization improved BLEU more significantly. We also describe an approach, similar to back-translation, for improving performance using synthetic dialect source text produced from source sentences in mismatched dialects.

1 Introduction

In this paper we describe the JHU dialect speech translation submissions and their development. Dialects are varieties of a language spoken by a group of people, often in a specific geographic location. In many languages, standard rules of pronunciation, orthography and syntax, but also available data resources are drawn from a single dominant dialect. A challenge for all language technologies, including automatic speech recognition (ASR), machine translation (MT), and speech translation (ST), is how to deal with non-standard dialects for which no formal orthography, grammar, or even data exist. Because many dialects are rarely if ever written, evaluation of ASR and MT on dialect speech is not even particularly well defined. However, there are no such problems evaluating speech translation on dialect speech, which here refers to the task of producing target language text from source language audio inputs.

A focus of both the dialect speech translation task and our system development, is how to leverage available resources from the standard dialect to improve performance on non-standard dialects. The dialect translation task focuses specifically on Tunisian Arabic.

Arabic and its dialects lie on a *dialect continuum* unified by a single standardized dialect, Modern standard Arabic (MSA) (Badawi et al., 2013). MSA is the primary language of *formal* and *written* communications (e.g. news broadcasts, parliaments and religion). However, most native Arabic speakers use local *dialects* in daily life, which generally lack a standard written form. Certain dialects, such as Algerian, Tunisian, and Moroccan Arabic also have strong Romance, and Berber substrates, and may exhibit a high degree of code-switching, especially with French.

Traditionally, speech translation systems have been built by cascading ASR and MT models to form a speech translation chain (Dixon et al., 2011). However, the more recent end-to-end approach (Berard et al., 2016; Weiss et al., 2017), which directly translates the source speech to target text, is appealing for this task since since both ASR and MT are ill-defined for unwritten spoken dialects, and there were relatively large amounts of translated speech ($\sim$160 hrs). We found, somewhat surprisingly during initial experimentation (See rows 1,2 of Table 7), that cascaded systems outperformed their end-to-end counterparts. For this reason, we focused on building cascaded systems. We leave diagnosis of the worse performance of the end-to-end systems to future work.

Our systems incorporated three improvements over the provided baseline. 1. We aggressively normalized the Tunisian Arabic transcripts, which led to improved MT performance. 2. We use additional MSA bi-text by pretraining models on these data using a shared BPE model with a large number of BPE units for both the MSA and Tunisian data. 3. We show that training on synthetic Tunisian source sentences instead of the MSA source sentences provides small improvements.

*Equal contribution.

Proceedings of the 19th International Conference on Spoken Language Translation (IWSLT 2022), pages 319 - 326
May 26-27, 2022 ©2022 Association for Computational Linguistics

2 The Dialect Speech Translation Task

The dialect speech translation task permitted submissions using models trained assuming different resource constraints, called: (A) basic, (B) dialect adaptation, and (C) unconstrained. We refer to these conditions as (A), (B) and (C) in the rest of the paper.

2.1 Data description

The total amount of data for the three conditions is listed in Table 1, with details of train, development and test1 sets in Table 2.

The development and test1 sets are provided by the organizers. The data are 3-way parallel: Tunisian Arabic transcripts and English translations are available for each Tunisian Arabic audio utterance. We use the development set for model comparison and hyperparameter tuning, and the test1 set for evaluating our ST systems. Finally, the task organizers provided a blind evaluation set (test2) during the evaluation period for final comparison of submissions. We used the test2 set to generate English translations, which were scored by the organizers.

For condition (C), we explored using pretrained audio representations trained only on additional unlabeled audio. However, we applied the exact same MT models as used in conditions (A) and (B).

3 Methods

We model the speech translation problem as a two step process. First, input audio is converted to source language text via an ASR model. Next, an MT model, which may have been trained on entirely different data from the ASR model, is used to translate the ASR output transcript into target language sentences. This model is known as a cascade model.

While cascade models suffer from a few well known problems, such as compounding error and inability to make direct use of the acoustic signal to improve translation quality, their modularity facilitates training on and incorporation of additional resources such as transcribed speech, bi-text, monolingual text, and unlabeled source language audio. We describe how we used these available resources to train the ASR and MT models in our ST cascade in each data condition.

3.1 ASR

Condition (A). We train our ASR model using the Tunisian Arabic audio and transcripts from the training set.

Condition (B). The MGB-2 data from condition (B) is used to train a large scale MSA conformer. The parameters of our conformer model are adopted from (Hussein et al., 2022). Then the pretrained model is fine-tuned on the Tunisian training data from condition (A). There are several sources of domain mismatch since the Tunisian data is sampled at 8KHz from telephone channel and the MGB-2 is sampled at 16KHz from broadcast news. As a result in this work we compare between two domain matching strategies for pre-training and fine-tuning: 1) Pretrain on 16KHz microphone data and fine-tune on up-sampled 16KHz telephone data, 2) Pretrain on down-sampled 8KHz microphone data and fine-tune on 8KHz telephone data.

Condition (C). We use the pretrained Wav2Vec2 multilingual model, XLSR-53 (Conneau et al., 2021) and fine-tune with the training data from condition (A). This model was trained on unlabeled speech in 53 languages, but notably, 1,000+hr of telephone conversations in 17 languages. There are some read prompts in Arabic, as well as a significant amount of French, which we suspect makes this model a better suited starting point for a Tunisian dialect ASR system.

3.2 MT

We use a transformer architecture for our MT models in condition (A) and (B). The model sizes are adjusted according to the amount of training data. We did not train MT models with extra data from condition (C).

Condition (A). We use the training data from condition (A). Two Byte-pair encoding (BPE) models were separately trained for Tunisian and English and applied to train, development and test1 sets. The trained model is referred as "*Ta2En-basic*".

Condition (B). We used two adaptation approaches. The first one is fine-tuning. We combine the Tunisian and MSA text to train a universal Arabic BPE model and use it to encode all the Arabic text. We also combine the English text from condition (A) and (B) to train an English BPE model and encode all the English text; an MT model, which

Condition	ASR	MT
(A) Basic	166 hours of manually transcribed Tunisian speech	~212 k lines of manually translated English from Tunisian
(B) Dialect adaptation	1200 hours of Modern Standard Arabic (MSA) broadcast news speech with transcripts from MGB-2 (Ali et al., 2016)	~42,000k lines of bitext in MSA-English for MT from the organizers (downloaded from OPUS (Tiedemann, 2012)
(C) Unconstrained	any English, Arabic dialects, or multilingual models beyond English and Arabic	any English, Arabic dialects, or multilingual models beyond English and Arabic

Table 1: Data for different conditions, provided by the organizers.

	ASR (hours)	MT (lines)
train (condition A)	160	~202k
train (condition B)	1200+160	~42M
dev	3.0	3833
test1	3.3	4204
test2	3.6	4288

Table 2: Details for train, dev and test1 sets for condition (A) and (B).

we call "*Msa2En*", is trained with MSA-English data from condition (B). The *Msa2En* model is then fine-tuned with the Tunisian-English data from condition (A), and called "*Msa2En-tune*".

The second method additionally tries to reduce the domain mismatch between conditions (B) and (A). Let $p_\theta(y_t \mid y_s)$, be an MT model with parameters, θ, trained on MSA-English bi-text, that generates English target sentences, y_t, conditioned on source sentences, y_s. Let $p(y_s)$ denote the marginal density over MSA source sentences. Let $q(y_s)$ denote the marginal density over Tunisian Arabic source sentences, and let us assume that the conditional density, $p(y_t \mid y_s)$, between English and MSA sentences, is the same as between English and Tunisian sentences. A good model should ideally then minimize

$$\mathbb{E}_{q(y_s)}\left[D(p(y_t \mid y_s) \parallel p_\theta(y_t \mid y_s))\right], \quad (1)$$

the expected value of the KL-divergence between the model posteriors and ground-truth Tunisian data over the Tunisian data. However, when training on the MSA data, the model is instead trained using

$$\mathbb{E}_{p(y_s)}\left[D(p(y_t \mid y_s) \parallel p_\theta(y_t \mid y_s))\right], \quad (2)$$

i.e, with the empirical MSA data marginal density, $p(y_s)$, instead of the Tunisian marginal, $q(y_s)$. We can reduce this dialect mismatch in training by using an extra back-translation model (Sennrich et al., 2016) to convert MSA text to Tunisian. Formally, we use this back-translation model, $q_\phi(y_s|y'_s)$, with parameters, ϕ, to generate samples that approximate draws from $q(y_s)$. We therefore propose to train our model to minimize

$$\mathbb{E}_{q_\phi(y_s|y'_s)}\left[D(p(y_t \mid y_s) \parallel p_\theta(y_t \mid y_s))\right]. \quad (3)$$

Because we have extra bi-text instead of simply monolingual text, we can choose to either back-translate the MSA source text to Tunisian, using English as a pivot language (i.e., y'_s is an MSA sentence), or we can back-translate directly from the English target text (i.e, $y'_s = y_t$). We trained both back-translation models, but ultimately trained using the MSA to Tunisian model following the steps below:

- Train an English to MSA MT model using the data from Table 2 condition (B). This model is referred to as "*En2Msa*",
- Translate the English from condition (A) to MSA, using the "*En2Msa*" model from the previous step. Thus, we obtain the paired Tunisian-MSA translation data, while the Tunisian are manually transcribed and the MSA are machine-translated.
- Train an MSA to Tunisian MT model, which we call "*Msa2Ta*", i.e., $q_\phi(y|y')$, with training data from the previous step.
- Translate the MSA from condition (B) to Tunisian, using the "*Msa2Ta*" model from the previous step from which we obtain around 42,000k pairs of Tunisian-English MT data.
- Train a Tunisian to English model with the data obtained from the previous step, referred as "*Ta2En-bt*".

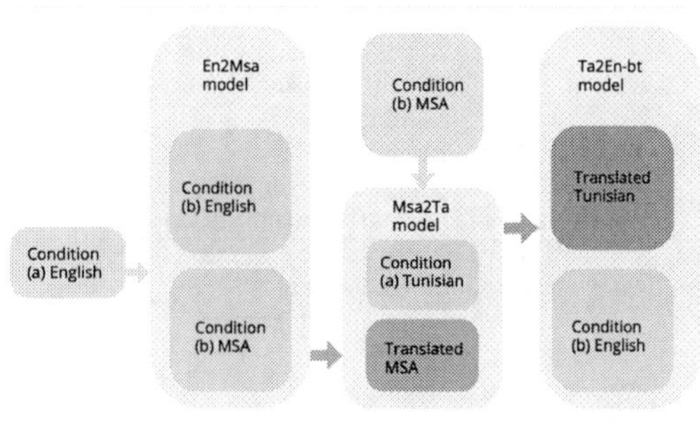

Figure 1: Generation of the back-translation model, $q_\phi\left(y_s \mid y_s'\right)$, used in our MT system. The En2Msa model is trained using the Condition (b) bi-text. The target English data from Condition (a) is passed through the En2Msa model to generate Condition (a) MSA source sentences (Translated MSA). We train an Msa2Ta model, i.e., $q_\phi\left(y_s \mid y_s'\right)$, using the Condition (a) Tunisian and Translated MSA. All Condition (b) MSA data is converted to Tunisian (Translated Tunisian). The final Ta2En-bt model is trained using the Translated Tunisian data as source sentences instead of the original Condition (b) MSA data.

- Fine-tune the above model, with data from condition (A), this model is referred to as "*Ta2En-bt-tune*".

The steps are illustrated in Figure 1, except the last step for fine-tuning.

We attempted to benchmark the different back-translation approaches by comparing the *En2Msa* + *Msa2Ta* cascade on the dev and test1 sets against the simpler, direct *En2Ta* approach using a single "*En2Ta*" model trained using the transcripts and translations from condition (A). However, the comparison is not completely fair. We also report performance of the *En2Msa* model on the condition (B) development and test sets, which each contains 40,000 randomly selected sentences from the six subsets from OPUS. Results are shown in table 3.

First, we see that the *En2Msa* model performs fairly well, with a BLEU score above 30, which is significantly higher than translation from English to Tunisian (row $En2Ta$). Next, comparing the rows $En2Ta$ and $Msa2Ta$, it appears that direct translation from English to Tunisian performs better. However, the *Msa2Ta* model may appear to perform artificially worse due to domain mismatch between the condition (B) and (A) English targets, as well as due to compounding errors from the sequential use of the 2 translation models, *En2Msa*, and *Msa2Ta*. We will conduct a "real" evaluation of our "Msa2Ta" model using ground-truth MSA-TA data (rather than synthetic MSA) in future work.

Model	dev	test1
En2Msa	31.7	31.4
En2Ta	14.2	12.1
Msa2Ta	10.6	10.6

Table 3: BLEU scores evaluating the back-translation quality of the En2Msa, En2Ta and Msa2Ta models.

4 Experiments

To test our approach, we conducted experiments on the ASR, MT, and ST tasks. In all experiments, unless otherwise stated we performed additional text normalization in order to reduce some of the orthographic variation in the Tunisian transcripts. In all experiments and for all languages / dialects, we remove punctuation, using the scripts provided by the organizer.[1]

For both Tunisian and MSA, we convert eastern Arabic digits to western Arabic digits, and remove diacritics and single character words. We also perform Alif/Ya/Ta-Marbuta normalization, which removes distinctions within three sets of characters that are often written inconsistently in dialect Arabic and even sometimes in modern standard Arabic: Alif forms (A = ا ,أ , إ, آ), Ya forms (y = ي , Y = ى, and Ta-Marbuta forms (p = ة , h = ه). For English, we keep all the text in lowercase, as the evaluation is performed on lowercased English text, and we use MOSES (Koehn et al., 2007) for text tokenization. It is difficult to assess the normalization affect on the quality of the ASR. However, we can measure its effect on the downstream task of translation, described in section 4.2.

4.1 ASR experiments

We tested to what extent additional MSA resources might benefit the ASR performance on the Tunisian dialect data. All models for conditions (A) and (B) are trained using Espnet (Watanabe et al., 2018) using the hybrid attention / CTC architecture (Watanabe et al., 2017) and decoding (Hori et al., 2017).

Baseline-small. We improve the Baseline end-to-end conformer model provided by the organizer[2] by reducing its number of parameters: BPE units 1000 -> 500, CNN sub-sampling kernel 31 -> 15. This

[1] https://github.com/kevinduh/iwslt22-dialect

[2] https://github.com/espnet/espnet/blob/master/egs2/iwslt22_dialect/asr1

model is trained with only the Tunisian data from condition (A). The details of the Baseline-small architecture are provided in Table 4.

MGB-tune. The provided MGB-2 data from condition (B) was used to pretrain a large conformer model, with parameters parameters adopted from (Hussein et al., 2022) as shown in Table 4. Then the pretrained model is fine-tuned on Tunisian data from condition (A) by updating all model parameters with $1/10$ of the learning rate that was used during the training similar to (Hussein et al., 2021). The original MGB-2 dataset comes with very long segments >100 seconds. We noticed that training on these segments was preventing the model from converging. As a result we used a better MGB-2 segmentation from (Mubarak et al., 2021) which has segments of maximum length of 15 seconds.

Table 4: Values of Baseline-small hyperparameters CNN: refers to CNN module kernel, Att: attention, Enc: encoder, Dec: decoder, and FF: fully connected layer

Model	BPE	Att heads	CNN	Enc layers	Dec layers	d^k	FF units
Baseline-small	500	4	15	8	4	512	2048
MGB-tune	5000	8	31	12	6	512	2048

MGB2-tune-trans is a pretrained transformer (Hussein et al., 2022) on 16KHz MGB-2 and then fine-tuned. This is the state-of-the-art ASR transformer model on MGB-2 test set.

MGB2-tune-conf is a conformer trained on MGB-2 16KHz. The training hyperparameters are similar to the *MGB2-tune-trans* model.

MGB2-tune-best is the same model structure as *MGB2-tune-conf*, except that the MGB-2 speech recordings are down sampled from 16KHz to 8KHz.

Wav2Vec2. For the unconstrained submissions we fine-tuned the self-supervised, Wav2Vec2 model XLSR-53. We fine-tune these models, generally following the method described in (Baevski et al., 2020): we added a single additional linear layer at the output of the XLSR-53 model corresponding to the number of BPE units, and fine-tuned using the CTC loss on the the normalized target transcripts. Baevski et al. (2020), only use character outputs, but since many vowels are not written in Arabic, we opted to instead use a small number of BPE units (400, which is roughly the number of digraphs in Arabic) so that hidden vowels might be modeled by surrounding context. As in (Baevski et al., 2020), we froze only the feature-extractor, i.e., the convolutional layers in the model during fine-tuning. We trained with the Adam optimizer, using a learning rate of 1e-05, with 8000 warmup steps, after which the learning rate was decayed exponentially with a decay rate of 1e-05. We used a gradient threshold of 5.0, and a weight decay of 1e-06.

We decode using a WFST decoder for CTC models (Miao et al., 2015) implemented in k2.[3] We trained a 3-gram language model on the Tunisian transcripts, and used a "pronunciation" lexicon mapping words to BPE units. We augmented the fixed vocabulary with the BPE units themselves, which enables the decoder to decode OOVs (about 5% of the tokens), by taking back-off transitions in the language model.

Looking at rows "(A) Baseline" and "(C) Wav2Vec2-tune" in Table 5, we see that fine-tuning the XLSR-53 model provided very marginal gains over the baseline model.

	MGB-2		TA	
Model	dev	test	dev	test1
(A) Baseline	-	-	40.8	45.2
(A) Baseline-small	-	-	40.8	44.8
(B) MGB2-tune-trans	14.6	14.2	40.5	44.1
(B) MGB2-tune-conf	**13.0**	**13.2**	40.1	44.9
(B) MGB2-tune-best	**13.0**	13.3	**38.8**	**43.8**
(C) Wav2Vec2-tune	-	-	40.6	44.5

Table 5: WER (%) of ASR models.

The best ASR peformance on the TA test1 set is achieved by *MGB2-tune-best*. This model is a large conformer model pre-trained on down-sampled 8KHz MGB-2 data and fine-tuned on the Tunisian training data. The *MGB2-tune-conf* model achieves (to our knowledge) a new state-of-the-art on the MGB-2 dataset, with relative improvements of 10% on dev and 7% on the test MGB-2, comparing to *MGB2-tune-trans*.

4.2 MT experiments

We train the MT models as described in Section 3.2, with Fairseq (Ott et al., 2019). We use Sacrebleu (Post, 2018) to compute the case-insensitive (all text in lowercase) BLEU (Papineni et al., 2002) scores for the dev and test1 sets. We test models using either the manual, source language transcript ("Gold Source"), or the ASR output ("ASR Source"), as shown in Table 7. The "ASR Source"

[3]https://github.com/k2-fsa/k2

for all the MT models in Table 7 was generated by ASR model "*(A) Baseline*" for fair comparison among MT models.

Condition	A	B
Encoder layers	6	6
Encoder embed dim	512	512
Encoder ffn embed dim	1024	2048
Encoder attn heads	4	8
Decoder layers	6	6
Decoder embed dim	512	512
Decoder ffn embed dim	1024	2048
Decoder attn heads	4	8

Table 6: MT model parameters. (* "ffn": feed-forward; "attn": attention)

	Gold Source		ASR Source	
Model	dev	test1	dev	test1
(A*) Ta2En-e2e, raw	-	-	16.7	13.7
(A*) Ta2En-basic, raw	24.7	20.9	18.1	15.3
(A) Ta2En-basic	25.3	21.2	18.7	16.1
(B) Msa2En	3.5	2.8	-	-
(B) Msa2En-tune	27.4	**24.2**	19.8	17.0
(B) Ta2En-bt	12.1	11.2	-	-
(B) Ta2En-bt-tune	**27.6**	**24.2**	**19.9**	**17.2**
(B) Ta2En-bt-tune, best	**<u>29.0</u>**	**<u>25.0</u>**	**<u>20.5</u>**	**<u>17.8</u>**

Table 7: BLEU scores of various MT models using either the gold reference transcripts or ASR hypotheses. **Bold** values indicate the best among comparable results. **<u>Bold and underlined</u>** values are the best overall results using different hyperparameters.

Ta2En-basic. The model parameters can be found in Table 6 Condition (A). We use 4000 BPE units for Tunisian Arabic, and 4000 BPE units for English. We train with the Adam optimizer (Kingma and Ba, 2015); each batch contains maximum 4096 tokens; the maxiumum learning rate is 5e-04, attained after 4000 warm-up steps, and then decayed according to an inverse square root scheduler; we use dropout probability of 0.3; the model is trained for 50 epochs.

We first evaluate the effects of Arabic text normalization. Without text normalization, as shown in Table 7 *(A∗) Ta2En-basic,raw*, the BLEU scores are consistently worse on both dev and test1 sets regardless of the input source (gold vs. ASR). Therefore, we use normalized Arabic text for all the other MT experiments. This simple pre-processing was the greatest source of improvement that did not involve training on additional bi-text, or hyper-parameter tuning.

Msa2En and Msa2En-tune. The model parameters can be found in Table 6 Condition (B). We use 2000 BPE units for the combined MSA and Tunisian Arabic, and 2000 BPE units for the combined English from conditions (A) and B. The hyper-parameters are identical to those used when training "Ta2En-basic", except that we increase the batch size to maximum 20000 tokens. When fine-tuning, we reduce the maximum learning rate to 4e-05, and the batch size to 2048 tokens.

Comparing rows *(B) Msa2En* and *(B) Msa2En-tune* in Table 7, we see a large improvement in BLEU scores from this fine-tuning procedure, which is reasonable, since direct application of the *(B) Msa2En* without fine-tuning results in significant dialect and domain mismatch. However, comparing rows *(B) Msa2En-tune* and *(A) Ta2En-basic*, we see that pre-training on unrelated data and fine tuning with in domain data improves the MT performance on both dev and test1 sets.

Ta2En-bt and Ta2En-bt-tune. We then examine to what extent back-translation of MSA source sentences to synthetic Tunisian Arabic text improves adaptation of the MSA MT system. We use the same BPE models as the one used for *Msa2En*, as well as the model parameters and training hyper-parameters. The tuning hyper-parameters are the same as used for the *Msa2En-tune*.

An interesting finding, comparing the *Msa2En* and *Ta2En-bt* models, neither of which is fine-tuned on any Tunisian-English data, is that the *Ta2En-bt* performs, on average, ~8 BLEU better on the dev and test1 set, which indicates that our method to reduce dialect mismatch between MSA and Tunisian is helpful. After fine tuning, the *Ta2En-bt-tune* still shows some marginal improvement over the *Msa2En-tune* model.

Ta2En-bt-tune, best The training and tuning data are exactly the same as the one used for the *Ta2En-bt-tune*, except that we increased the BPE units from 2000 to 32, 000, for both Tunisian and English. We also increased the model size, using the model parameters according to the original implementation (Vaswani et al., 2017). This model gave the best MT performance on both dev and test1 sets.

	MT Model							
	(A) Ta2En-basic			(B) Msa2En-tune		(B) Ta2En-bt-tune, best		
ASR Model	dev	test1	test2	dev	test1	dev	test1	test2
(A) Baseline	18.7	16.1	**17.1**	19.8	17.0	20.7	17.8	**18.9**
(B) MGB2-tune-conf	18.7	15.8	-	19.7	16.9	20.5	17.6	-
(B) MGB2-tune-best	19.1	16.3	-	20.0	17.4	20.7	18.0	-
(C) Wav2Vec2-tune	18.3	15.6	-	19	16.9	20.3	17.5	**18.7**

Table 8: BLEU scores on the dev, test1 and test2. For the submission, for the basic condition, we use ASR model "(A) Baseline" and MT model "(A) Ta2En-basic"; for the dialect adaptation condition, we use ASR model "(A) Baseline" and MT model "(B) Ta2En-bt-tune,best"; for the unconstrained condition, we use ASR model "(C) Wav2Vec2-tune" and MT model "(B) Ta2En-bt-tune,best". The BLEU scores for the evaluation set are in bold text.

4.3 ST experiments

For our cascaded ST system, we chose the ASR and MT models that gave the best BLEU scores on the dev set in each condition. During the evaluation period, we ran our ST system and generated translations of the blind evaluation set (test2); the BLEU scores on this set were calculated by the organizers and provided to our team. The results are listed in Table 8.

For the "Basic condition" submission, we used ASR model: "*(A) Baseline*" and MT model: "*(A) Ta2En-basic*". For the "Dialect adaptation condition" submission, we used ASR model: "*(A) Baseline*" and MT model: "*(B) Ta2En-bt-tune, best*". For the "Unconstrained condition" submission, we used ASR model: "*(C) Wav2Vec2-tune*" and MT model: "*(B) Ta2En-bt-tune, best*".

Note that we actually have better ST performance with ASR model "*(B) MGB2-tune-best*", consistently with all MT model combinations. However, the training of this ASR model was only completed after the evaluation period, therefore we did not use it for our final submission.

5 Conclusion

We have detailed the our submission for the IWSLT 2022 dialect speech translation task. We briefly compared end-to-end to cascaded systems and found that cascaded models were slightly outperforming their end-to-end counterparts despite, a relative abundance of training data.

We demonstrated that increased text normalization, and back-translation to reduce dialect mismatch improved speech translation performance. Finally, we described two ways of using extra mismatched dialect resources and found surprisingly that using additional unlabeled data through the use of the XLSR-53 model resulted in only small improvements. Using additional large labeled MSA resources resulted in slight improvements to the ASR, and modest improvements in MT.

Future work should expand upon the back-translation results to determine the optimal method for minimizing the dialect mismatch when augmenting training with additional bi-text.

6 Acknowledgments

We would like to thank Dr. Ahmed Ali, and Dr. Shammur Chowdhury for their support and guidance as well as the Qatar Computing Research Institute (QCRI) more broadly for providing some of the computational resources that made this work possible.

References

Ahmed M. Ali, Peter Bell, James R. Glass, Yacine Messaoui, Hamdy Mubarak, Steve Renals, and Yifan Zhang. 2016. The mgb-2 challenge: Arabic multi-dialect broadcast media recognition. *2016 IEEE Spoken Language Technology Workshop (SLT)*, pages 279–284.

El Said Badawi, Michael Carter, and Adrian Gully. 2013. *Modern written Arabic: A comprehensive grammar*. Routledge.

Alexei Baevski, Yuhao Zhou, Abdelrahman Mohamed, and Michael Auli. 2020. wav2vec 2.0: A framework for self-supervised learning of speech representations. *Advances in Neural Information Processing Systems*, 33:12449–12460.

Alexandre Berard, Olivier Pietquin, Christophe Servan, and Laurent Besacier. 2016. Listen and translate: A proof of concept for end-to-end speech-to-text translation. *ArXiv*, abs/1612.01744.

Alexis Conneau, Alexei Baevski, Ronan Collobert, Abdel rahman Mohamed, and Michael Auli. 2021. Unsupervised cross-lingual representation learning for speech recognition. In *Interspeech*.

Paul R. Dixon, Andrew Finch, Chiori Hori, and Hideki Kashioka. 2011. Investigation of the effects of ASR tuning on speech translation performance. In *Proceedings of the 8th International Workshop on Spoken Language Translation: Evaluation Campaign*, pages 167–174, San Francisco, California.

Takaaki Hori, Shinji Watanabe, and John Hershey. 2017. Joint CTC/attention decoding for end-to-end speech recognition. In *Proceedings of the 55th Annual Meeting of the Association for Computational Linguistics (Volume 1: Long Papers)*, pages 518–529, Vancouver, Canada. Association for Computational Linguistics.

Amir Hussein, Shammur Chowdhury, and Ahmed Ali. 2021. Kari: Kanari/qcri's end-to-end systems for the interspeech 2021 indian languages code-switching challenge. *arXiv preprint arXiv:2106.05885*.

Amir Hussein, Shinji Watanabe, and Ahmed Ali. 2022. Arabic speech recognition by end-to-end, modular systems and human. *Computer Speech & Language*, 71:101272.

Diederik P. Kingma and Jimmy Ba. 2015. Adam: A method for stochastic optimization. *CoRR*, abs/1412.6980.

Philipp Koehn, Hieu Hoang, Alexandra Birch, Chris Callison-Burch, Marcello Federico, Nicola Bertoldi, Brooke Cowan, Wade Shen, Christine Moran, Richard Zens, Chris Dyer, Ondřej Bojar, Alexandra Constantin, and Evan Herbst. 2007. Moses: Open source toolkit for statistical machine translation. In *Proceedings of the 45th Annual Meeting of the Association for Computational Linguistics Companion Volume Proceedings of the Demo and Poster Sessions*, pages 177–180, Prague, Czech Republic. Association for Computational Linguistics.

Yajie Miao, Mohammad Abdelaziz Gowayyed, and Florian Metze. 2015. Eesen: End-to-end speech recognition using deep rnn models and wfst-based decoding. *2015 IEEE Workshop on Automatic Speech Recognition and Understanding (ASRU)*, pages 167–174.

Hamdy Mubarak, Amir Hussein, Shammur Absar Chowdhury, and Ahmed Ali. 2021. QASR: QCRI aljazeera speech resource a large scale annotated Arabic speech corpus. In *Proceedings of the 59th Annual Meeting of the Association for Computational Linguistics and the 11th International Joint Conference on Natural Language Processing (Volume 1: Long Papers)*, pages 2274–2285, Online. Association for Computational Linguistics.

Myle Ott, Sergey Edunov, Alexei Baevski, Angela Fan, Sam Gross, Nathan Ng, David Grangier, and Michael Auli. 2019. fairseq: A fast, extensible toolkit for sequence modeling. In *Proceedings of the 2019 Conference of the North American Chapter of the Association for Computational Linguistics (Demonstrations)*, pages 48–53, Minneapolis, Minnesota. Association for Computational Linguistics.

Kishore Papineni, Salim Roukos, Todd Ward, and Wei-Jing Zhu. 2002. Bleu: a method for automatic evaluation of machine translation. In *Proceedings of the 40th Annual Meeting of the Association for Computational Linguistics*, pages 311–318, Philadelphia, Pennsylvania, USA. Association for Computational Linguistics.

Matt Post. 2018. A call for clarity in reporting BLEU scores. In *Proceedings of the Third Conference on Machine Translation: Research Papers*, pages 186–191, Brussels, Belgium. Association for Computational Linguistics.

Rico Sennrich, Barry Haddow, and Alexandra Birch. 2016. Improving neural machine translation models with monolingual data. In *Proceedings of the 54th Annual Meeting of the Association for Computational Linguistics (Volume 1: Long Papers)*, pages 86–96, Berlin, Germany. Association for Computational Linguistics.

Jörg Tiedemann. 2012. Parallel data, tools and interfaces in opus. In *LREC*.

Ashish Vaswani, Noam Shazeer, Niki Parmar, Jakob Uszkoreit, Llion Jones, Aidan N Gomez, ukasz Kaiser, and Illia Polosukhin. 2017. Attention is all you need. In *Advances in Neural Information Processing Systems*, volume 30. Curran Associates, Inc.

Shinji Watanabe, Takaaki Hori, Shigeki Karita, Tomoki Hayashi, Jiro Nishitoba, Yuya Unno, Nelson Yalta, Jahn Heymann, Matthew Wiesner, Nanxin Chen, Adithya Renduchintala, and Tsubasa Ochiai. 2018. Espnet: End-to-end speech processing toolkit. *ArXiv*, abs/1804.00015.

Shinji Watanabe, Takaaki Hori, Suyoun Kim, John R. Hershey, and Tomoki Hayashi. 2017. Hybrid ctc/attention architecture for end-to-end speech recognition. *IEEE Journal of Selected Topics in Signal Processing*, 11:1240–1253.

Ron J. Weiss, Jan Chorowski, Navdeep Jaitly, Yonghui Wu, and Z. Chen. 2017. Sequence-to-sequence models can directly translate foreign speech. In *INTERSPEECH*.

Controlling Translation Formality Using Pre-trained Multilingual Language Models

Elijah Rippeth* and **Sweta Agrawal*** and **Marine Carpuat**
Department of Computer Science
University of Maryland
{erip,sweagraw,marine}@cs.umd.edu

Abstract

This paper describes the University of Maryland's submission to the Special Task on Formality Control for Spoken Language Translation at IWSLT, which evaluates translation from English into 6 languages with diverse grammatical formality markers. We investigate to what extent this problem can be addressed with a *single multilingual model*, simultaneously controlling its output for target language and formality. Results show that this strategy can approach the translation quality and formality control achieved by dedicated translation models. However, the nature of the underlying pre-trained language model and of the finetuning samples greatly impact results.

1 Introduction

While machine translation (MT) research has primarily focused on preserving meaning across languages, linguists and lay-users alike have long known that pragmatic-preserving communication is an important aspect of the problem (Hovy, 1987). To address one dimension of this, several works have attempted to control aspects of formality in MT (Sennrich et al., 2016; Feely et al., 2019; Schioppa et al., 2021). Indeed, this research area was formalized as formality-sensitive machine translation (FSMT) by Niu et al. (2017), where the translation is not only a function of the source segment but also the desired target formality. The lack of gold translation with alternate formality for supervised training and evaluation has lead researchers to rely on manual evaluation and synthetic supervision in past work (Niu and Carpuat, 2020). Additionally, these works broadly adapt to formal and informal registers as opposed to specifically controlling grammatical formality.

The Special Task on Formality Control on Spoken Language Translation provides a new benchmark by contributing high-quality training datasets

Source: **Do you like$_1$** Legos? **did you$_2$** ever play with them as a child or even later?

German Informal: **Magst du$_1$** Legos? **Hast du$_2$** jemals als Kind mit ihnen gespielt oder sogar später?

German Formal: **Mögen Sie$_1$** Legos? **Haben Sie$_2$** jemals als Kind mit ihnen gespielt oder sogar später?

Table 1: Contrastive formal and informal translations into German. Grammatical formality markers are bolded and aligned via indices.

for diverse languages (Nădejde et al., 2022). In this task, a source segment in English is paired with two references which are minimally contrastive in grammatical formality, one for each formality level (formal and informal; Table 1). Training and test samples are provided in the domains of "telephony data" and "topical chat" (Gopalakrishnan et al., 2019) for four language pairs (English-{German (DE), Spanish (ES), Hindi (HI), Japanese(JA)}) and a test dataset for two additional "zero-shot" (ZS) language pairs (EN-{Russian (RU), Italian (IT)}). Markers of grammatical formality vary across these languages. Personal pronouns and verb agreement mark formality in many Indo-European languages (e.g., DE, HI, IT, RU, ES), while in JA, Korean (KO) and other languages, distinctions can be more extensive (e.g., using morphological markers) to express polite, respectful, and humble speech.

In this work, we investigate how to control grammatical formality in MT for many languages with minimal resources. Specifically, we ask whether a single multilingual model can be finetuned to translate in the appropriate formality for any of the task languages. We introduce additive vector interventions to encode style on top of mT5-large (Xue et al., 2021) and mBART-large (Liu et al., 2020), and investigate the impact of finetuning on varying types of gold and synthetic samples to minimize reliance on manual annotation.

* equal contribution.

Proceedings of the 19th International Conference on Spoken Language Translation (IWSLT 2022), pages 327 - 340
May 26-27, 2022 ©2022 Association for Computational Linguistics

2 Method

Given an input sequence x, we design a *single model* that produces an output

$$y^* = \arg\max p(y|x, l, f; \theta_{LM}, \theta_F)$$

for any language l and formality level f considered in this task. The bulk of its parameters θ_{LM} are initialized with a pre-trained multilingual language model. A small number of additional parameters θ_F enable formality control. All parameters are finetuned for formality-controlled translation.

2.1 Multilingual Language Models

We experiment with two underlying multilingual models: 1) **mT5-large**[1] — a multilingual variant of T5 that is pre-trained on the Common Crawl-based dataset covering 101 languages and 2) **mBART-large**[2] — a Transformer encoder-decoder which supports multilingual machine translation for 50 languages. While mBART-large is pre-trained with parallel and monolingual supervision, mT5-large uses only monolingual dataset during the pre-training phase. Following standard practice, mT5 controls the output language, l, via prompts ("Translate to German"), and mBART replaces the beginning of sequence token in the decoder with target language tags (<2xx>).

2.2 Additive Formality Control

While large-scale pre-trained language models have shown tremendous success in multiple monolingual and multilingual controlled generation (Zhang et al., 2022) and style transfer tasks, their application to controlled cross-lingual text generation have been limited. Few-shot style-transfer approaches (Garcia et al., 2021; Riley et al., 2021; Krishna et al., 2022) hold the promise of minimal supervision but perform poorly on low-resource settings and their outputs lack diversity.

A popular way of introducing control when generating text with a particular style attribute is *tagging*, where the desired control tags (e.g., <2formal>) are appended to the source or the target sequence. However, as discussed in Schioppa et al. (2021), this approach has several limitations, including but not limited to the necessity of including the control tokens in the vocabulary at the start of the training, which restricts the enhancement of pre-trained models with controllability.

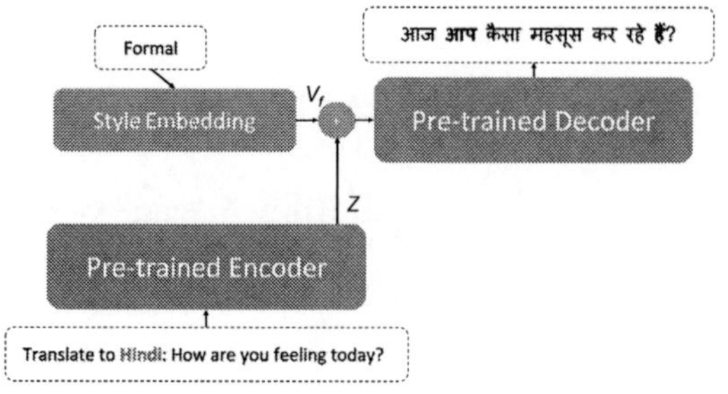

Figure 1: Controlling the output formality of a multilingual language model with additive interventions.

We introduce formality control by adapting the vector-valued interventions proposed by Schioppa et al. (2021) for machine translation (MT), as illustrated in Figure 1. Formally, given source text x, a formality level f, an encoder E and decoder D, parameterized by θ_{LM}, and a style embedding layer (Emb) parameterized by θ_F with the same output dimension as E, we have

$$Z = E(x), \quad V = \text{Emb}(f)$$
$$y = D(Z + V)$$

Our formality levels can take values corresponding to formal, informal, and "neutral" translations, the last of which is used to generate "generic" translations in which there is no difference in the grammatical formality of the translation of the source if translated formally or informally. Unlike Schioppa et al. (2021) who use a zero-vector as their neutral vector, we learn a separate vector.

2.3 Finetuning

Finetuning each multilingual model requires triplets of the form (x, y, f) for each available target language, l, where x, y and f are the source text, the reference translation and the formality label corresponding to the reference translation respectively. The loss function is then given by:

$$\mathcal{L} = \sum_{(x,y,l,f)} \log p(y|x, l, f; \theta_{LM}, \theta_F) \quad (1)$$

Given *paired contrastive* training samples of the form (X, Y_f, Y_{if}), as provided by the shared task, the loss decomposes into balanced formal and informal components, but does not explicitly exploit

[1]24 layers with 1024 sized embeddings, 2816 FFN embedding dimension, and 16 heads for both encoder and decoder.

[2]12 layers with 1024 sized embeddings, 4096 FFN embedding dimension, and 16 heads for both encoder and decoder.

Language	Size		Length			Style		
	Train	Test	Source	Formal	Informal	Avg. TER	# Phrasal	# Neutral
EN-DE	400	600	22.78	24.68	24.57	0.126	1.89	23
EN-ES	400	600	22.72	22.64	22.60	0.089	1.56	49
EN-HI	400	600	22.90	25.92	25.92	0.068	1.57	68
EN-JA	1000	600	24.61	32.43	30.80	0.165	2.47	20

Table 2: Shared Task Data Statistics: We use "13a" tokenization for all languages except Japanese for which we use "ja-mecab" implemented in the sacrebleu library.

the fact that Y_i and Y_f align to the same input:

$$\mathcal{L} = \sum_{(x,y_f,l)} \log p(y_f|x,l,f;\theta_{LM},\theta_F) + \sum_{(x,y_{if},l)} \log p(y_{if}|x,l,if;\theta_{LM},\theta_F) \quad (2)$$

2.4 Synthetic Supervision

Since paired contrastive samples are expensive to obtain, we explore the use of synthetic training samples to replace or complement them. This can be done either by automatically annotating naturally occurring bitext for formality, which yields formal and informal samples, and additionally by rewriting the translation to alter its formality to obtain paired contrastive samples. The second approach was used by Niu and Carpuat (2020) to control the register of MT output. However, since this shared task targets grammatical formality and excludes other markers of formal vs. informal registers, we focus on the first approach, thus prioritizing control on the nature of the formality markers in the output over the tighter supervision provided by paired contrastive samples.

Given a translation example (x, y), we predict a silver-standard formality label (f) for the target y using two distinct approaches:

- Rules (ES, DE, IT, RU): We label formality using heuristics based on keyword search, dependency parses, and morphological features. We use spaCy (Honnibal et al., 2020) to (non-exhaustively) retrieve documents that imply a necessarily formal, necessarily informal, or ambiguously formal label. In the case of an ambiguously formal label, we treat it as unambiguously formal (for examples, see B). The complete set of rules for each of the languages are included in the Appendix Table 12. While simple to implement, these heuristics privilege precision over recall, and risk biasing the synthetic data to the few grammatical aspects they encode.
- Classifiers (HI, JA, IT, RU): We train a binary formal vs. informal classifier on the shared task data (HI, JA) and on the synthetic data (IT, RU). Unlike rules, they can also be transferred in a zero-shot fashion to new languages, and might be less biased toward precision when well-calibrated.

3 Evaluation Settings

Data The shared task provides English source segments paired with two contrastive reference translations, one for each formality level (informal and formal) for four language pairs: EN-{DE, ES, JA, HI} in the *supervised* setting and two language pairs: EN-{RU, IT} in the *zero-shot* setting. The sizes and properties of the datasets for the supervised language pairs are listed in Table 2. Formal texts tend to be longer and more diverse than informal texts for JA compared to other language pairs. The percentage of neutral samples (same formal and informal outputs) vary from 2% (in JA) to 17% (in HI). In the *zero-shot* setting, 600 test samples are released for the two language pairs (RU, IT).

During development, the last 50 paired contrastive examples from each domain are set aside as a validation set for each of the supervised languages (TASK DEV) and use the remaining samples for training (TASK TRAIN).

Metrics We evaluate the translation quality of the detruecased detokenized outputs from each systems using **BLEU** (Papineni et al., 2002) and **COMET** (Rei et al., 2020). We use the 13A tokenizer to report SACREBLEU[3] scores for all languages, except Japanese, for which we use the JA-MECAB. We also report the official **formality accuracy** (ACC.). Given a set of hypotheses H, sets of corresponding phrase-annotated formal references F and informal

[3]https://pypi.org/project/sacrebleu/2.0.0/

Model	Target Language	Size	Source
	JA	15K	JParaCrawl (Morishita et al., 2020)
	HI	13K	CCMatrix (Schwenk et al., 2021b)
Synthetic Finetuned	IT, RU	15K	Paracrawl v8 (Bañón et al., 2020)
	DE	15K	CommonCrawl, Europarl v7 (Koehn, 2005)
	ES	15K	CommonCrawl, Europarl v7, UN (Ziemski et al., 2016)
	DE,ES,IT,RU	20M	Paracrawl v9
Bilingual Baselines	HI	0.7M	CCMatrix
	JA	3.2M	Wikimatrix (Schwenk et al., 2021a), JESC (Pryzant et al., 2018)

Table 3: Data sources from which unlabeled formality parallel examples are sampled for EN-X for training the *Synthetic Finetuned* and the *Bilingual* baselines.

references IF, and a function ϕ yielding phrase-level contrastive terms from a reference, the task-specific evaluation metric is defined as follows:

$$match_f = \sum_j \mathbb{1}\left[\phi(F_j) \in H_j \wedge \phi(IF_j) \notin H_j\right]$$

$$match_i = \sum_j \mathbb{1}\left[\phi(F_j) \notin H_j \wedge \phi(IF_j) \in H_j\right]$$

$$acc_j = \frac{match_j}{match_f + match_i}, \quad j \in \{f, i\}$$

We note that the task accuracy is a function of the number of *matches* in the hypotheses, not the number of *expected* phrases, i.e. $match_f + match_{if} \leq \|H\|$ and discuss the implications in the Appendix (Section C).

4 Experimental Conditions

We compare multilingual models, where a single model is used to generate formal and informal translations for all languages with bilingual models trained for each language pair, as detailed below.

4.1 Multilingual Models

Data We consider three finetuning settings:

- **Gold finetuned**: the model is finetuned only on *paired contrastive* shared task data (400 to 1000 samples per language pair).
- **Synthetic finetuned**: the model is finetuned on *synthetic silver-labelled triplets* (up to 7500 samples per formality level and language as described below).
- **Two-pass finetuned**: the *Synthetic finetuned* model is further finetuned on a mixture of gold data and 1000 examples re-sampled from the synthetic training set for unseen languages, which we use to avoid catastrophic forgetting from the silver finetuning stage.

Synthetic samples are drawn from multiple data sources (3), sampling at most 7500 examples for each language and formality level. [4] The formality labels are predicted as described in 2.4. Rule-based predictors directly give a label. With classifiers, we assign the formal label if $P(\text{formal}|y) \geq 0.85$ and informal if $P(\text{formal}|y) \leq 0.15$.

We additionally compare with the translations generated from the base mBART-large model with no finetuning, referred to as the "*formality agnostic m*BART-*large*".

Training settings We finetune mT5-large and mBART-large with a batch size of 2 and 8 respectively for 10 and 3 epochs respectively. We mask the formality labels used to generate vector-valued interventions with a probability of 0.2. The mT5-large model — "*synthetic finetuned m*T5-*large*" — is trained for an additional 5 epochs, with a batch size of 2 on a mixture of task data for seen languages and a subset of the sampled synthetic data for unseen languages. Again, we mask the formality tag with probability 0.2 except in the case of unseen languages where the formality tag is masked with probability 1.0, resulting in the "*two-pass finetuned m*T5-*large*" model.

Formality Classifiers Following Briakou et al. (2021), we finetune XLM-R on binary classification between formal and informal classes, using the shared task datasets for each of the supervised language pairs (DE, ES, JA, HI) and synthetic datasets for zero-shot language pairs (RU, IT). We treat the "neutral" samples as both "formal" and "informal" when training the classifiers. We use the Adam optimizer, a batch size of 32, and a learning rate of 5×10^{-3} to finetune for 3 epochs. We report

[4] We do not experiment with varying the sizes of the synthetic dataset due to the time constraints and leave it to the future work.

SAMPLES	TO	EN-DE BLEU	EN-DE ACC.	EN-HI BLEU	EN-HI ACC.	EN-JA BLEU	EN-JA ACC.	EN-ES BLEU	EN-ES ACC.
Paired Contrastive	F	35.0	**100**	28.7	98.7	33.1	95.3	32.6	**100**
Unpaired Triplets	F	**35.5**	**100**	**31.6**	**100**	**39.6**	**100**	**35.5**	**100**
Paired Contrastive	IF	32.7	98.5	26.4	98.3	32.3	**100**	33.8	**100**
Unpaired Triplets	IF	**35.9**	**98.6**	**30.9**	**98.4**	**40.3**	**100**	**39.6**	97.9

Table 4: Results on the TASK DEV split when training *Additive mT5-large* with and without contrastive examples: Sample diversity from Unpaired triplets improve BLEU and Accuracy over paired contrastive samples.

DATA	EN-DE	EN-HI	EN-JA	EN-ES
Paired Contrastive	0.397	0.371	0.421	0.505
Unpaired Triplets	0.459	0.415	0.460	0.580

Table 5: Results on the TASK DEV split: TER between generated formal and informal sentences.

the accuracy of the learned classifiers trained on the TASK TRAIN dataset in Appendix Table 14.

4.2 Bilingual Models

We consider two types of bilingual models:

1. **Formality Agnostic:** These models were released by the shared task organizers. Each model is bilingual and trained on a sample of 20 million lines from the Paracrawl Corpus (V9) using the Sockeye NMT toolkit. Models use big transformers with 20 encoder layers, 2 decoder layers, SSRU's in place of decoder self-attention, and large batch training.

2. **Formality Specific (Gold):** We finetune the models in [1] to generate a formal model and an informal model for each language pair (except the zero-shot language pairs).

The effective capacity of the bilingual, formality specific models is 3.14B parameters.Each model has 314M parameters, resulting in $(314 \times 2 \times 4) =$ 2.5B parameters for the four supervised languages (DE, ES, HI, JA) and two pre-trained models $(314 \times 2) =$ 628M parameters for the unseen languages (RU, IT).This is significantly larger than the capacities of our single multilingual models (Additive mT5-large: 1.25B, Additive mBART-large: 610M).

5 System Development Results

During system development, we explore the impact of different types of training samples and finetuning strategies on translation quality and formality accuracy on TASK DEV.

Contrastive Samples We estimate the benefits of fine-tuning on informal vs. formal translations of the same inputs for this task. We train two variants of the `gold finetuned mT5-large` model using 50% of the paired contrastive samples and 100% of the unpaired triplets (i.e., selecting one formality level per unique source sentence) from the TASK TRAIN samples (Table 4). Results show that sample diversity resulting from unpaired triplets leads to better translation quality as measured by BLEU (Average Gain: Formal +3.2. Informal +5.38), without compromising on the formality accuracy. Training with paired samples result in lower TER between formal and informal output compared to unpaired triplets (Table 5), suggesting that the outputs generated by the model trained on paired samples are more contrastive. This further motivates our `two-pass finetuned` model which uses gold contrastive samples on the final stage of finetuning to bias the model towards generating contrastive MT outputs.

While TASK DEV is too small to make definitive claims, we report our system development results in Tables 6 and 7. We observe that finetuning on gold contrastive examples (`gold-finetuned`) improves the translation quality and accuracy of the translation models (`formality-agnostic`), highlighting the importance of limited but high-quality in-domain supervision on the resulting models. Further, each of the `mT5-large` models improves in translation quality with additional data and training. While the results are dramatic due to size of both TASK TRAIN and TASK DEV, the trends validate the approach to augment both mBART-large and the mT5-large with additive interventions to control formality.

6 Official Results

Submissions We submit five variants of multilingual models (numbered **[1-5]** in Tables 8-11),

Model	EN-DE BLEU	EN-DE COMET	EN-DE Acc.	EN-ES BLEU	EN-ES COMET	EN-ES Acc.	EN-JA BLEU	EN-JA COMET	EN-JA Acc.	EN-HI BLEU	EN-HI COMET	EN-HI Acc.
Bilingual												
Formality Agnostic	33.2	0.432	33.8	41.3	0.675	24.5	13.0	-0.093	25.6	27.8	0.464	96.5
Formality Specific (Gold)	49.1	0.539	100.0	56.0	0.790	100.0	26.0	0.242	89.1	37.5	0.694	100.0
Multilingual Model												
mBART-large												
Formality Agnostic	33.3	0.295	68.9	27.0	0.120	56.5	18.3	-0.016	71.9	20.7	0.340	88.4
Gold Finetuned	42.8	0.462	95.9	41.1	0.548	97.7	24.7	0.326	89.4	29.6	0.678	95.6
mT5-large												
Gold Finetuned	53.3	0.260	**100.0**	53.5	0.427	**100.0**	49.8	0.645	98.1	43.5	0.359	**100.0**
Synthetic Finetuned	64.5	0.557	**100.0**	50.7	0.345	**100.0**	58.5	0.837	97.7	61.2	0.844	**100.0**
Two-pass Finetuned	**86.8**	**0.824**	**100.0**	**88.2**	**1.070**	**100.0**	**68.3**	**0.980**	**100.0**	**70.4**	**0.975**	**100.0**

Table 6: Results on the TASK DEV split in the ***formal*** *supervised* setting. ACC.: *formal* accuracy.

Model	EN-DE BLEU	EN-DE COMET	EN-DE Acc.	EN-ES BLEU	EN-ES COMET	EN-ES Acc.	EN-JA BLEU	EN-JA COMET	EN-JA Acc.	EN-HI BLEU	EN-HI COMET	EN-HI Acc.
Bilingual												
Formality Agnostic	37.2	0.470	66.2	45.8	0.691	75.5	13.5	-0.096	74.4	23.7	0.436	3.5
Formality Specific (Gold)	48.4	0.557	98.5	55.1	0.813	95.7	22.6	0.182	97.8	36.3	0.675	91.5
Multilingual Model												
mBART-large												
Formality Agnostic	29.3	0.262	31.1	26.3	0.101	43.5	16.2	-0.036	28.1	18.7	0.330	11.6
Gold Finetuned	39.6	0.456	76.5	40.4	0.582	95.3	21.6	0.289	72.7	27.7	0.631	82.8
mT5-large												
Gold Finetuned	52.8	0.232	**100.0**	53.8	0.513	**100.0**	47.3	0.617	**100.0**	41.7	0.144	**100.0**
Synthetic Finetuned	66.0	0.563	**100.0**	57.6	0.530	**100.0**	59.0	0.813	98.5	57.7	0.761	**100.0**
Two-pass Finetuned	**86.6**	**0.843**	**100.0**	**87.7**	**1.081**	**100.0**	**69.5**	**0.976**	**100.0**	**70.1**	**0.957**	**100.0**

Table 7: Results on the TASK DEV split in the ***informal*** *supervised* setting. ACC.: *informal* accuracy.

and compare them to the bilingual models built on top of the organizers' baselines. We first discuss results on the official test split for the *supervised* setting (Tables 8, 9). To better understand the degree of overall control afforded, we also report the average scores of the formal and informal settings in Table 10 before turning to the *zero-shot* setting in Table 11.

Multilingual Approach The best multilingual models (`[1]` & `[4]`) consistently outperform the `bilingual formality-agnostic` baselines, improving both translation quality (Worst-case gain in Average BLEU: Formal (+1.67), Informal: (+3.7)) and formality accuracy (Worst-case gain in Average ACC.: Formal (+40.38), Informal: (+31.6)). They approach the quality of formal and informal bilingual systems, but the gap in translation quality and formality accuracy varies across languages. While for DE and ES, there is a large difference in translation quality (approx. 10 BLEU points) between the multilingual models and the bilingual baselines, the multilingual models consistently get higher formality accuracy across language pairs and style directions and also perform comparably with the bilingual models in matching the translation quality for HI and JA. We attribute these differences to the amount of training data used across the language pairs (HI: 0.7M to DE 20M). This is an encouraging result, since the bilingual approach uses a much larger language-specific parameter budget and bitext for training than the all purpose multilingual models, which can benefit from transfer learning across languages.

mBART vs. mT5 The `gold finetuned` `mBART-large` model achieves the best overall translation quality among the multilingual variants as expected given that mBART-large is pre-trained on parallel text. Its translation quality is higher than that of mT5-large models according to BLEU and COMET for all languages except HI (informal), which could be attributed to the nature and amount of pre-training data used for HI. Its formality accuracy is in the 90's and within 5 percentage

	EN-DE			EN-ES			EN-JA			EN-HI		
	BLEU	COMET	ACC.	BLEU	COMET	ACC.	BLEU	COMET	ACC.	BLEU	COMET	ACC.
Bilingual Models												
Formality Agnostic	33.0	0.472	53.6	37.5	0.646	37.9	14.9	-0.102	23.3	**26.5**	**0.519**	98.8
Formal Gold Finetuned	**45.9**	**0.557**	**100.0**	**48.6**	**0.734**	**98.4**	**26.0**	**0.290**	**87.1**	23.0	0.303	**98.9**
Multilingual Models												
mBART-large												
Formality Agnostic	35.1	0.344	83.6	26.9	0.210	67.8	18.3	0.051	**93.4**	20.1	0.383	93.5
[4] Gold Finetuned	**38.6**	**0.484**	93.6	38.3	**0.549**	96.7	**26.1**	**0.397**	78.2	29.7	**0.691**	98.5
mT5-large												
[3] Gold Finetuned	7.9	-1.472	**100.0**	5.2	-1.340	97.0	8.9	-0.792	88.5	3.9	-1.152	**99.6**
[2] Synthetic Finetuned	22.1	0.076	92.4	28.1	0.274	86.5	16.3	-0.086	84.5	22.6	0.305	99.5
[1] Two-pass Finetuned	37.0	0.302	99.4	**38.6**	0.509	**99.5**	24.7	0.273	86.3	**29.9**	0.471	99.4

Table 8: Results on the official test split in the ***formal*** *supervised* setting. Best scores from multilingual and bilingual systems are **bolded**. Our official submissions to the shared task are numbered [1-4].

MODEL	EN-DE			EN-ES			EN-JA			EN-HI		
	BLEU	COMET	ACC.	BLEU	COMET	ACC.	BLEU	COMET	ACC.	BLEU	COMET	ACC.
Bilingual Models												
Formality Agnostic	32.3	0.476	46.4	40.4	0.672	62.1	15.5	-0.094	76.7	20.8	0.493	1.2
Formality Specific (Gold)	**43.5**	**0.559**	**90.0**	**48.2**	**0.762**	**92.9**	**23.5**	**0.272**	**98.7**	**31.2**	**0.724**	**92.1**
Multilingual Models												
mBART-large												
Formality Agnostic	28.4	0.299	16.4	25.3	0.205	32.2	16.2	0.032	6.6	16.7	0.370	6.5
[4] Gold Finetuned	**36.1**	**0.472**	77.4	**38.3**	**0.549**	82.7	**22.8**	**0.346**	88.0	27.6	**0.670**	64.7
mT5-large												
[3] Gold Finetuned	7.3	-1.424	96.0	5.9	-1.295	**96.1**	7.2	-0.795	**98.9**	2.7	-1.205	96.5
[2] Synthetic Finetuned	21.7	0.046	91.4	28.2	0.337	91.6	13.6	-0.135	83.3	17.8	0.277	8.3
[1] Two-pass Finetuned	35.9	0.301	**96.5**	38.0	0.539	93.2	22.3	0.252	97.5	**29.2**	0.439	**98.7**

Table 9: Results on the official test split in the ***informal*** *supervised* setting. Best scores from multilingual and bilingual systems are **bolded**. Our official submissions to the shared task are numbered [1-4].

points to the highest score for all languages except Japanese (78.2%) in the formal direction. In the informal direction, the gap between mBART-large and the best system on formality accuracy is larger across the board (Average Acc.: +19.3), suggesting that finetuning on gold data cannot completely recover an informal translation despite generally strong performance in formal translations.

Finetuning strategies Results show that the combination of synthetic and gold data is crucial to help the mT5-large-based model learn to translate and mark formality appropriately. Finetuning only on the gold data leads to overfitting: the model achieves high formality accuracy scores, but poor translation quality (BLEU < 10). Manual inspection of mT5-large-based system outputs suggests that translations often include tokens in the wrong language (Appendix Table 13). Finetuning on synthetic data improves translation quality substantially compared to gold data only (Average gain in BLEU: Formal (+15.8), Informal (+14.6)). Two-pass finetuning improves formality control (Average gain in ACC.: Formal (+5.43), Informal (+27.85)), with additional translation quality improvement across the board over synthetic-finetuned model (Average gain in BLEU: Formal (+10.27), Informal (+11.03); COMET: Formal (+0.247), Informal (+0.252)). While we primarily focused on the impact of synthetic supervision on mT5-large, we believe a similar investigation using mBART-large would yield interesting results and leave this as future work.

Performance across languages While the higher resource language pairs (DE, ES) achieve better translation quality (in BLEU and COMET) over the relatively lower resource languages (HI, JA), the formality accuracy is more comparable across the language pairs for the multilingual models

Model	EN-DE			EN-ES			EN-JA			EN-HI		
	BLEU	COMET	Acc.	BLEU	COMET	Acc.	BLEU	COMET	Acc.	BLEU	COMET	Acc.
Bilingual Models												
Formality Agnostic	32.7	0.474	50.0	39.0	0.659	50.0	15.2	-0.100	50.0	23.7	0.506	50.0
Formality Specific (Gold)	**44.7**	**0.558**	**95.0**	**48.4**	**0.748**	**95.7**	**24.8**	**0.281**	**92.9**	**27.1**	**0.513**	**95.5**
Multilingual Models												
*m*BART-*large*												
Formality Agnostic	31.8	0.322	50.0	26.1	0.207	50.0	17.3	0.041	50.0	18.4	0.377	50.0
[4] Gold Finetuned	**37.4**	**0.478**	85.5	**38.3**	**0.549**	89.7	**24.5**	**0.371**	83.1	28.7	**0.680**	81.6
*m*T5-*large*												
[3] Gold Finetuned	7.6	-1.448	**98.0**	5.6	-1.317	**96.6**	8.1	-0.794	**93.7**	3.3	-1.179	98.1
[2] Synthetic Finetuned	21.9	0.061	91.9	28.2	0.305	89.1	15.0	-0.111	83.9	20.2	0.291	53.9
[1] Two-pass Finetuned	36.5	0.301	**98.0**	**38.3**	0.524	96.4	23.5	0.263	91.9	**29.6**	0.455	**99.1**

Table 10: Averaged formal and informal results on the official test split in the *supervised* setting. Best scores from multilingual and bilingual systems are **bolded**. Our official submissions to the shared task are numbered `[1-4]`.

Model	To Formal						To Informal					
	EN-IT			EN-RU			EN-IT			EN-RU		
	BLEU	COMET	Acc.	BLEU	COMET	Acc.	BLEU	COMET	Acc.	BLEU	COMET	Acc.
Bilingual baselines	37.0	0.557	4.5	27.9	0.220	93.3	44.2	0.618	95.5	22.0	0.169	6.7
[1] mT5-large (ZS)	27.6	0.306	32.8	22.7	0.123	**100.0**	32.6	0.379	**97.9**	17.0	0.058	1.1
[4] mBART-large (ZS)	**30.2**	**0.545**	38.7	**26.2**	**0.275**	**100.0**	**35.0**	**0.597**	95.9	**20.8**	**0.203**	**13.8**
[5] mT5-large (FS)	27.1	0.302	**49.7**	20.7	0.007	**100.0**	31.2	0.346	93.3	15.5	-0.050	1.8

Table 11: Results on the official test split for the *zero-shot* setting. Our official submissions to the shared task are numbered `[1-5]`.

(standard deviation: mT5-large (4), mBART-large (10)). We can observe that the task accuracy is lowest (< 90%) when translating to formal Japanese. By inspection, we observe three broad classes of errors: 1) lexical choice, 2) cross-script matching, 3) ambiguity in politeness levels (Feely et al., 2019). Lexical choice is invariant in machine translation and is occasionally a valid error in the case of mistranslation, so we focus on the latter two error cases. Japanese has three writing systems and false positives in formality evaluation can occur when surface forms do not match as in the case of 面白い which can also be written as おもしろい (gloss: 'interesting'). Finally, there are cases in which the system and reference formality mismatch but can both be interpreted as formal (e.g., 働きます vs. 働く; gloss: 'work' (polite) vs. 'work' (formal)).

Zero-Shot We observe limited zero-shot transfer of grammatical formality to unseen languages (Table 11). For both `mBART-large` and `mT5-large` models, the EN-IT performance is biased towards informal translations, while EN-RU is biased in the formal direction. In the case of EN-IT, both mBART-large and mT5-large almost always interpret the English second person pronoun as second person *plural* when translating to formal, exploiting the ambiguity of English on the source side. By contrast, when generating informal translations, pronouns are typically preserved as singular. In comparison, with mT5-large-based translations into RU, we see almost unanimous preference toward the formal, likely due to sampling bias when curating the synthetic training set. We also observe that mBART-large prefers to translate in a formal manner irrespective of desired target. In addition, when mBART-large fails to account for the target formality, it often generates paraphrases of the formal target. These strong preferences might be symptoms of systematic differences in formality across languages in the training data of these models. Finally, the use of silver standard formality labels ("fully supervised" setting (FS)) does not improve over the zero-shot approach, with similar observations of mT5-large-based translations as outlined above. We observe that in the case of EN-RU, there is a higher incidence of code-switched translations. This may indicate noise introduced in the automatic labeling process and requires further examination in future work.

7 Related Work

Most MT approaches only indirectly capture the style properties of the target text. While efforts have been made to generate better outputs in their pragmatic context via controlling formality (Sennrich et al., 2016; Feely et al., 2019; Niu and Carpuat, 2020; Schioppa et al., 2021), complexity (Marchisio et al., 2019; Agrawal and Carpuat, 2019), gender (Rabinovich et al., 2017), these studies only focus a single language pair. Due to the paucity of style annotated corpora, zero-shot style transfer within and across languages has received a lot of attention. However, adapting pre-trained large-scale language models during inference using only a few examples (Garcia et al., 2021; Riley et al., 2021; Krishna et al., 2022) limits their transfer ability and the diversity of their outputs. While prior works use pre-trained language models like BERT, GPT to intialize θ_{LM} for improving translation quality (Guo et al., 2020; Zhu et al., 2019), in this work, we focus on adapting sequence-to-sequence multilingual models for controlled generation of a desired formality and study style transfer in multilingual supervised and zero-shot settings.

8 Conclusion

We present the University of Maryland's submission which examines the performance of a single multilingual model allowing control of both target language and formality. Results show that while multilingual FSMT models lag behind large, bilingual, formality-specific models in terms of MT quality, they show stronger formality control performance across all the language pairs. Furthermore, while synthetic unpaired triplets help `mT5-large` with FSMT performance and the two-stage finetuning process improves MT quality and contrastive task performance, `mBART-large` still outperforms this class of models, likely due to its large amount of pre-training supervision.

In future work, we suggest a deeper investigation of potentially confounding roles in the study of FSMT, such as the impact of formal register as compared to grammatical formality in training data. We also suggest a thorough analysis of *what* is transferred in the zero-shot setting. Finally, we recommend an audit of underlying pre-training and finetuning data sources for pre-trained multilingual models, which we believe hinder zero-shot formality transfer for EN-IT and EN-RU in which a single formality is strongly preferred.

References

Sweta Agrawal and Marine Carpuat. 2019. Controlling text complexity in neural machine translation. In *Proceedings of the 2019 Conference on Empirical Methods in Natural Language Processing and the 9th International Joint Conference on Natural Language Processing (EMNLP-IJCNLP)*, pages 1549–1564, Hong Kong, China. Association for Computational Linguistics.

Marta Bañón, Pinzhen Chen, Barry Haddow, Kenneth Heafield, Hieu Hoang, Miquel Esplà-Gomis, Mikel L. Forcada, Amir Kamran, Faheem Kirefu, Philipp Koehn, Sergio Ortiz Rojas, Leopoldo Pla Sempere, Gema Ramírez-Sánchez, Elsa Sarrías, Marek Strelec, Brian Thompson, William Waites, Dion Wiggins, and Jaume Zaragoza. 2020. ParaCrawl: Web-scale acquisition of parallel corpora. In *Proceedings of the 58th Annual Meeting of the Association for Computational Linguistics*, pages 4555–4567, Online. Association for Computational Linguistics.

Eleftheria Briakou, Sweta Agrawal, Joel Tetreault, and Marine Carpuat. 2021. Evaluating the evaluation metrics for style transfer: A case study in multilingual formality transfer. In *Proceedings of the 2021 Conference on Empirical Methods in Natural Language Processing*, pages 1321–1336, Online and Punta Cana, Dominican Republic. Association for Computational Linguistics.

Weston Feely, Eva Hasler, and Adrià de Gispert. 2019. Controlling Japanese honorifics in English-to-Japanese neural machine translation. In *Proceedings of the 6th Workshop on Asian Translation*, pages 45–53, Hong Kong, China. Association for Computational Linguistics.

Xavier Garcia, Noah Constant, Ankur Parikh, and Orhan Firat. 2021. Towards continual learning for multilingual machine translation via vocabulary substitution. In *Proceedings of the 2021 Conference of the North American Chapter of the Association for Computational Linguistics: Human Language Technologies*, pages 1184–1192, Online. Association for Computational Linguistics.

Karthik Gopalakrishnan, Behnam Hedayatnia, Qinlang Chen, Anna Gottardi, Sanjeev Kwatra, Anu Venkatesh, Raefer Gabriel, and Dilek Hakkani-Tür. 2019. Topical-Chat: Towards Knowledge-Grounded Open-Domain Conversations. In *Proc. Interspeech 2019*, pages 1891–1895.

Junliang Guo, Zhirui Zhang, Linli Xu, Hao-Ran Wei, Boxing Chen, and Enhong Chen. 2020. Incorporating bert into parallel sequence decoding with adapters. *Advances in Neural Information Processing Systems*, 33:10843–10854.

Matthew Honnibal, Ines Montani, Sofie Van Landeghem, and Adriane Boyd. 2020. spaCy: Industrial-strength Natural Language Processing in Python.

Eduard Hendrik Hovy. 1987. *Generating Natural Language under Pragmatic Constraints*. Ph.D. thesis, USA. AAI8729079.

Philipp Koehn. 2005. Europarl: A parallel corpus for statistical machine translation. In *Proceedings of Machine Translation Summit X: Papers*, pages 79–86, Phuket, Thailand.

Kalpesh Krishna, Deepak Nathani, Xavier Garcia, Bidisha Samanta, and Partha Talukdar. 2022. Few-shot controllable style transfer for low-resource multilingual settings.

Yinhan Liu, Jiatao Gu, Naman Goyal, Xian Li, Sergey Edunov, Marjan Ghazvininejad, Mike Lewis, and Luke Zettlemoyer. 2020. Multilingual denoising pre-training for neural machine translation. *Transactions of the Association for Computational Linguistics*, 8:726–742.

Kelly Marchisio, Jialiang Guo, Cheng-I Lai, and Philipp Koehn. 2019. Controlling the reading level of machine translation output. In *Proceedings of Machine Translation Summit XVII: Research Track*, pages 193–203, Dublin, Ireland. European Association for Machine Translation.

Makoto Morishita, Jun Suzuki, and Masaaki Nagata. 2020. JParaCrawl: A large scale web-based English-Japanese parallel corpus. In *Proceedings of the 12th Language Resources and Evaluation Conference*, pages 3603–3609, Marseille, France. European Language Resources Association.

Xing Niu and Marine Carpuat. 2020. Controlling neural machine translation formality with synthetic supervision. In *Proceedings of the AAAI Conference on Artificial Intelligence*, volume 34, pages 8568–8575.

Xing Niu, Marianna Martindale, and Marine Carpuat. 2017. A study of style in machine translation: Controlling the formality of machine translation output. In *Proceedings of the 2017 Conference on Empirical Methods in Natural Language Processing*, pages 2814–2819, Copenhagen, Denmark. Association for Computational Linguistics.

Maria Nădejde, Anna Currey, Benjamin Hsu, Xing Niu, Marcello Federico, and Georgiana Dinu. 2022. CoCoA-MT: A dataset and benchmark for Contrastive Controlled MT with application to formality. In *Findings of the Association for Computational Linguistics: NAACL 2022*, Seattle, USA. Association for Computational Linguistics.

Kishore Papineni, Salim Roukos, Todd Ward, and Wei-Jing Zhu. 2002. Bleu: a method for automatic evaluation of machine translation. In *Proceedings of the 40th Annual Meeting of the Association for Computational Linguistics*, pages 311–318, Philadelphia, Pennsylvania, USA. Association for Computational Linguistics.

Reid Pryzant, Youngjoo Chung, Dan Jurafsky, and Denny Britz. 2018. JESC: Japanese-English subtitle corpus. In *Proceedings of the Eleventh International Conference on Language Resources and Evaluation (LREC 2018)*, Miyazaki, Japan. European Language Resources Association (ELRA).

Ella Rabinovich, Raj Nath Patel, Shachar Mirkin, Lucia Specia, and Shuly Wintner. 2017. Personalized machine translation: Preserving original author traits. In *Proceedings of the 15th Conference of the European Chapter of the Association for Computational Linguistics: Volume 1, Long Papers*, pages 1074–1084, Valencia, Spain. Association for Computational Linguistics.

Ricardo Rei, Craig Stewart, Ana C Farinha, and Alon Lavie. 2020. COMET: A neural framework for MT evaluation. In *Proceedings of the 2020 Conference on Empirical Methods in Natural Language Processing (EMNLP)*, pages 2685–2702, Online. Association for Computational Linguistics.

Parker Riley, Noah Constant, Mandy Guo, Girish Kumar, David Uthus, and Zarana Parekh. 2021. TextSETTR: Few-shot text style extraction and tunable targeted restyling. In *Proceedings of the 59th Annual Meeting of the Association for Computational Linguistics and the 11th International Joint Conference on Natural Language Processing (Volume 1: Long Papers)*, pages 3786–3800, Online. Association for Computational Linguistics.

Andrea Schioppa, David Vilar, Artem Sokolov, and Katja Filippova. 2021. Controlling machine translation for multiple attributes with additive interventions. In *Proceedings of the 2021 Conference on Empirical Methods in Natural Language Processing*, pages 6676–6696, Online and Punta Cana, Dominican Republic. Association for Computational Linguistics.

Holger Schwenk, Vishrav Chaudhary, Shuo Sun, Hongyu Gong, and Francisco Guzmán. 2021a. WikiMatrix: Mining 135M parallel sentences in 1620 language pairs from Wikipedia. In *Proceedings of the 16th Conference of the European Chapter of the Association for Computational Linguistics: Main Volume*, pages 1351–1361, Online. Association for Computational Linguistics.

Holger Schwenk, Guillaume Wenzek, Sergey Edunov, Edouard Grave, Armand Joulin, and Angela Fan. 2021b. CCMatrix: Mining billions of high-quality parallel sentences on the web. In *Proceedings of the 59th Annual Meeting of the Association for Computational Linguistics and the 11th International Joint Conference on Natural Language Processing (Volume 1: Long Papers)*, pages 6490–6500, Online. Association for Computational Linguistics.

Rico Sennrich, Barry Haddow, and Alexandra Birch. 2016. Controlling politeness in neural machine translation via side constraints. In *Proceedings of the 2016 Conference of the North American Chapter of the Association for Computational Linguistics: Human

Language Technologies, pages 35–40, San Diego, California. Association for Computational Linguistics.

Linting Xue, Noah Constant, Adam Roberts, Mihir Kale, Rami Al-Rfou, Aditya Siddhant, Aditya Barua, and Colin Raffel. 2021. mT5: A massively multilingual pre-trained text-to-text transformer. In *Proceedings of the 2021 Conference of the North American Chapter of the Association for Computational Linguistics: Human Language Technologies*, pages 483–498, Online. Association for Computational Linguistics.

Hanqing Zhang, Haolin Song, Shaoyu Li, Ming Zhou, and Dawei Song. 2022. A survey of controllable text generation using transformer-based pre-trained language models. *arXiv preprint arXiv:2201.05337*.

Jinhua Zhu, Yingce Xia, Lijun Wu, Di He, Tao Qin, Wengang Zhou, Houqiang Li, and Tieyan Liu. 2019. Incorporating bert into neural machine translation. In *International Conference on Learning Representations*.

Michał Ziemski, Marcin Junczys-Dowmunt, and Bruno Pouliquen. 2016. The United Nations parallel corpus v1.0. In *Proceedings of the Tenth International Conference on Language Resources and Evaluation (LREC'16)*, pages 3530–3534, Portorož, Slovenia. European Language Resources Association (ELRA).

A Rules for Synthetic Data Curation

LANG	Formal	Informal
en-de	(P=2 $\in$ M and Num=Plural $\in$ M) or PP=Sie	P=2 $\in$ M and Num=Plural $\notin$ M
en-es	P=2 $\in$ M and Form=Polite $\in$ M	P=2 $\in$ M and Num=Singular $\in$ M and Form=Polite $\notin$ M
en-it	PP=voi or PP=lei	PP=tu
en-ru	PP=Вы	PP=ты

Table 12: Rules for extracting formal and informal sentences for each language pair from existing bitext. P: Person; PP: Personal pronoun; N: Number; $x \in M$ indicates that some token within the sentence has morphological features matching x as produced by spaCy.

B Glosses

B.1 Necessarily formal

Appropriate pronouns with accompanying conjugation imply the sentence is grammatically formal.

(1) ¿Cuándo nació usted? (Spanish)
When born you (form.)?
'When were you (form.) born?'

(2) Woher kommen Sie? (German)
Where from come you (form.)?
'Where are you (form.) from?'

B.2 Necessarily informal

Appropriate pronouns with accompanying conjugation imply the sentence is grammatically informal. Note that Spanish is pro-drop, which relaxes the requirement on personal pronouns.

(3) ¿Cuándo naciste (tú)? (Spanish)
When born you (inf.)?
'When were you (inf.) born?'

(4) Woher kommst du? (German)
Where from come you (inf.)?
'Where are you (inf.) from?'

B.3 Ambiguously formal

Because Spanish is pro-drop, personal pronouns can be omitted depending on context. Since formal conjugations are shared with neutral third person subjects, this leaves ambiguity when the pronoun is dropped. For sake of gloss, we use $\emptyset$ to indicate a dropped pronoun.

(5) ¿Cuándo nació $\emptyset$?
When born {you (form.), he, she, it}?
'When {were you (form.), was {he, she, it}} born?'

C Official Evaluation

We report the number of examples labeled as FORMAL, INFORMAL, NEUTRAL, OTHER by the formality scorer for the best multilingual models (`[1, 4]`) and the baseline systems for each language pair and formality direction. As described in 3, the accuracy is computed based on *realized* matches, which excludes examples labelled as NEUTRAL and OTHER. Figure 2 shows that the number of these excluded NEUTRAL samples can range from 15% to 43%.

D Example Outputs

Source: Wow, that's awesome! Who is your favorite Baseball team? I like my Az team lol

German Formal Hypothesis: Wow, das ist toll! Wer ist Ihr Lieblings- Baseballteam? Ich mag meine Az-Team lol.

German Formal Reference: Wow, das ist fantastisch! Welches ist Ihr Lieblingsbaseballteam? Ich stehe auf mein AZ-Team lol.

German Informal Hypothesis: Wow, das ist toll! Wer ist dein Lieblings野球team? Ich mag meine Az Team lol.

German Informal Reference: Wow, das ist fantastisch! Welches ist dein Lieblingsbaseballteam? Ich stehe auf mein AZ-Team lol.

Table 13: Contrastive outputs from English-German. Note that there is not only variety in lexical choice between references and hypotheses, but also between hypotheses of varying formality (i.e., 野球 is "baseball" in Japanese)

E Accuracy of Formality Classifiers

We report the accuracy of the learned classifiers on the TASK TRAIN dataset in Table 14.

LANGUAGE	Accuracy	
	Formal	Informal
en-de	98%	99%
en-es	99%	92%
en-ja	98%	98%
en-hi	96%	95%

Table 14: Accuracy of trained formality classifiers on the TASK DEV dataset.

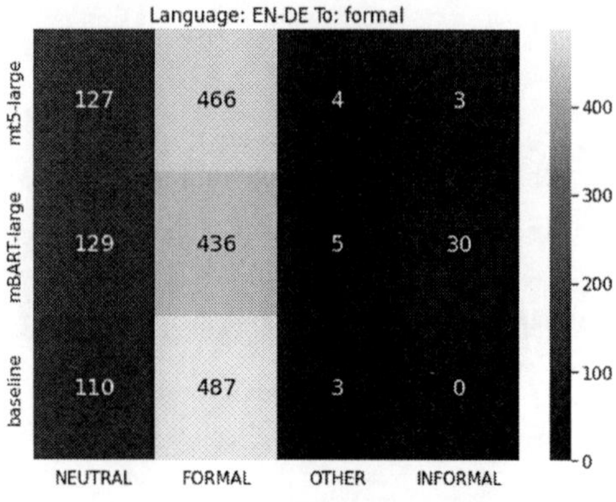

(a)

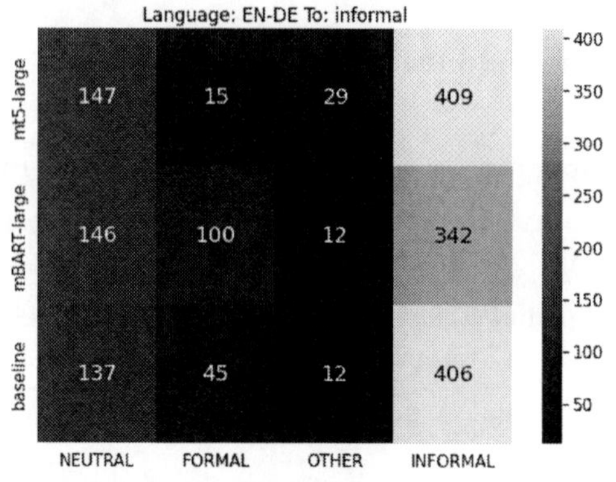

(b)

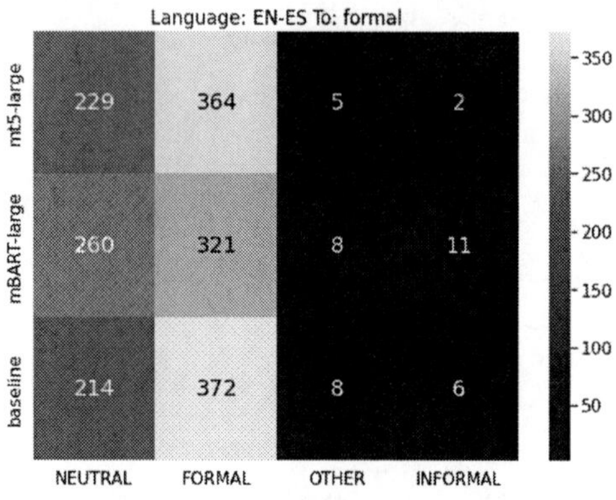

(c)

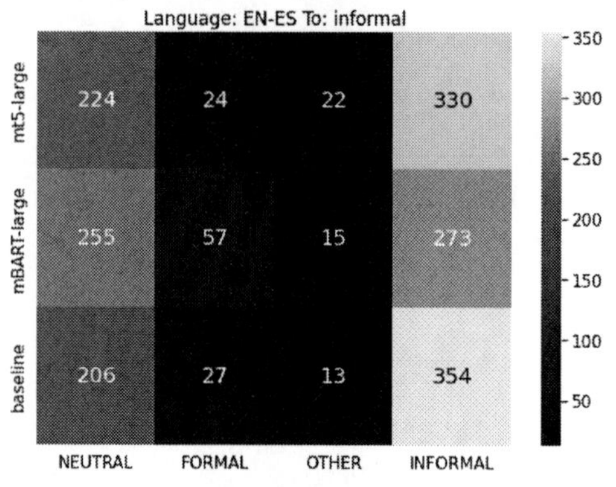

(d)

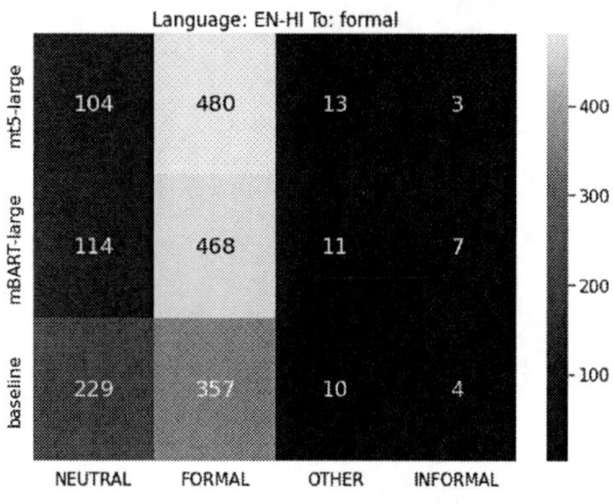

(e)

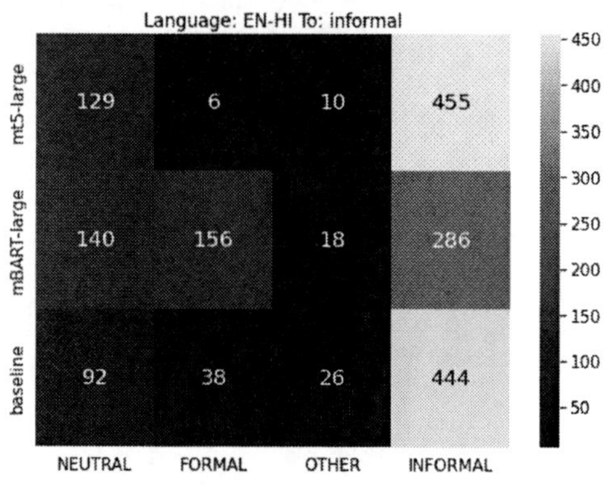

(f)

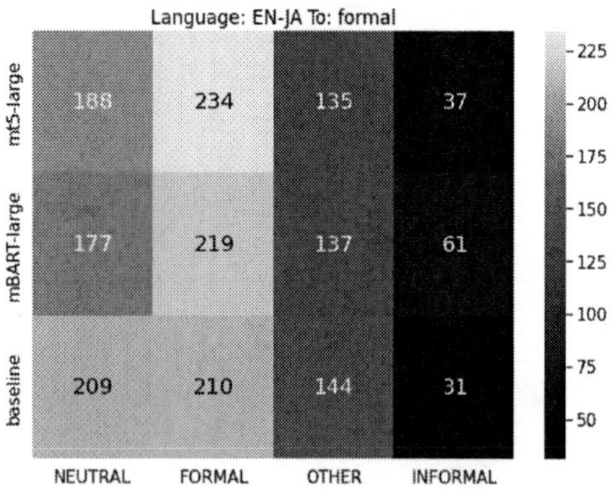

(g)

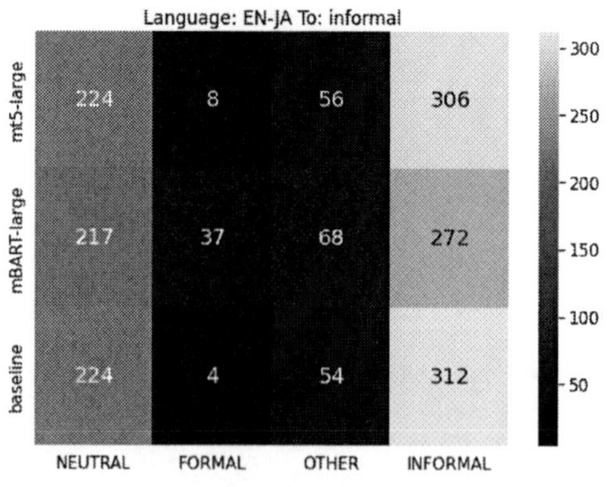

(h)

Figure 2: Class Distribution for the baseline, mBART-large and mT5-large systems for all the supervised language pairs.

Controlling Formality in Low-Resource NMT with Domain Adaptation and Re-Ranking: SLT-CDT-UoS at IWSLT2022

Sebastian T. Vincent, Loïc Barrault, Carolina Scarton
Department of Computer Science, University of Sheffield
Regent Court, 211 Portobello, Sheffield, S1 4DP, UK
{stvincent1, l.barrault, c.scarton}@shef.ac.uk

Abstract

This paper describes the SLT-CDT-UoS group's submission to the first Special Task on Formality Control for Spoken Language Translation, part of the IWSLT 2022 Evaluation Campaign. Our efforts were split between two fronts: data engineering and altering the objective function for best hypothesis selection. We used language-independent methods to extract formal and informal sentence pairs from the provided corpora; using English as a pivot language, we propagated formality annotations to languages treated as zero-shot in the task; we also further improved formality controlling with a hypothesis re-ranking approach. On the test sets for English-to-German and English-to-Spanish, we achieved an average accuracy of .935 within the constrained setting and .995 within unconstrained setting. In a zero-shot setting for English-to-Russian and English-to-Italian, we scored average accuracy of .590 for constrained setting and .659 for unconstrained.

1 Introduction

Formality-controlled machine translation enables the system user to specify the desired formality level at input so that the produced hypothesis is expressed in a formal or informal style. Due to discrepancies between different languages in formality expression, it is often the case that the same source sentence has several plausible hypotheses, each aimed at a different audience; leaving this choice to the model may result in an inappropriate translation.

This paper describes our team's submission to the first Special Task on Formality Control in SLT at IWSLT 2022 (Anastasopoulos et al., 2022), where the objective was to achieve control over binary expression of formality in translation (enable the translation pipeline to generate formal or informal translations depending on user input). The task evaluated translations from English (EN) into German (DE), Spanish (ES), Russian (RU), Italian (IT), Japanese (JA) and Hindi (HI). Among these, EN-{RU,IT} were considered zero-shot; for other pairs, small paired formality-annotated corpora were provided. The task ran in two settings: **constrained** (limited data and pre-trained model resources) and **unconstrained** (no limitations on either resource). Submissions within both the constrained and unconstrained track were additionally considered in two categories: full supervision and zero-shot.

Our submission consisted of four primary systems, one for each track/subtrack combination, and we focused on the EN-{DE,ES,RU,IT} language directions. We were interested in leveraging the provided formality-annotated triplets $(src, tgt_{\text{formal}}, tgt_{\text{informal}})$ to extract sufficiently large annotated datasets from the permitted training corpora, without using language-specific resources or tools. We built a multilingual translation model in the given translation directions and fine-tuned it on our collected data. Our zero-shot submissions used fine-tuning data only for the non-zero-shot pairs. To boost the formality control (especially within the constrained track), we included a formality-focused hypothesis re-ranking step. Our submissions to both tracks followed the same concepts, with the unconstrained one benefitting from larger corpora, and thus more fine-tuning data.

In Section 2 we describe our submission to the constrained track, including the data extraction step (Section 2.2, 2.3). Our approach begins with extending this small set to cover more samples by extracting them from the allowed corpora. We use a language-independent approach of domain adaptation for this. Then, we extract samples for the zero-shot pairs (EN-{RU,IT}) based on data collected for (EN-{DE,ES}). We then experiment with re-ranking the top n model hypotheses with a formality-focused objective function. Within our systems, we provide the formality information as a *tag* appended to the input of the model. Throughout the paper we use $\mathbb{F}$ to denote the *formal* style

Proceedings of the 19th International Conference on Spoken Language Translation (IWSLT 2022), pages 341 - 350
May 26-27, 2022

and $\mathbb{I}$ to denote the *informal* style.

All our models submitted to the "supervised" subtracks achieved an average of $+.284$ accuracy point over a baseline for all EN-{DE,ES,RU,IT} test sets, while the "zero-shot" models achieved an average improvement of .124 points on the EN-{RU,IT} test sets. Our work highlights the potential of both data adaptation and re-ranking approaches in attribute control for NMT.

2 Constrained Track

The MuST-C textual corpus (Di Gangi et al., 2019) with quantities listed in Table 1 was the only data source allowed within the constrained track, alongside the IWSLT corpus of formality-annotated sentences (Nadejde et al., 2022). MuST-C is a collection of transcribed TED talks, all translated from English. The IWSLT data itself came from two domains: telephone conversations and topical chat (Gopalakrishnan et al., 2019). The data was additionally manually annotated at phrase level for formal and informal phrases, and the organisers provided an evaluation tool `scorer.py` which, given a set of hypotheses, used these annotations to match sought formal or informal phrases, yielding an accuracy score when the number of correct matches is greater than the number of incorrect matches[1]. This scorer skips test cases where no matches are found in the hypotheses.

In all our experiments we used the multilingual Transformer model architecture provided within `fairseq` (Ott et al., 2019). For our pre-training data we used the full MuST-C corpus. We applied SentencePiece (Kudo and Richardson, 2018) to build a joint vocabulary of 32K tokens across all languages. We list the model specifications in Table 2. Pre-training lasts 100K iterations or 63 epochs. We average checkpoints saved at roughly the last 10 epochs.

2.1 Formality Controlling

Once the model was pre-trained, we fine-tuned it on the supervised data to control the desired formality of the hypothesis with a *tagging* approach (Sennrich et al., 2016), whereby a formality-indicating tag is appended to the source input. This method has been widely used in research in various controlling tasks (e.g. Johnson et al., 2017; Vanmassenhove et al., 2018; Lakew et al., 2019).

[1] `https://github.com/amazon-research/contrastive-controlled-mt/blob/main/IWSLT2022/scorer.py`, accessed 8 April 2022.

2.2 Automatic Extraction of Formal and Informal Data

Since our approach was strongly dependent on the availability of labelled data, our initial efforts focused on making the training corpus larger by extracting sentence pairs with formal and informal target sentences from the provided MuST-C corpus. We made the assumption that similar sentences would correspond to a similar formality level. Thus, we decided to use the data selection approach to select the most similar sentence pairs from the out-of-domain corpus (MuST-C) to both the formal and informal sides of the IWSLT corpus, which we consider our in-domain data (each side separately).

Specifically, let $G = (G_{src}, G_{tgt})$ be the out-of-domain corpus (MuST-C), and let $S_{\mathbb{F}} = (S_{src}, S_{tgt,\mathbb{F}})$ and $S_{\mathbb{I}} = (S_{src}, S_{tgt,\mathbb{I}})$ be the in-domain corpora (IWSLT). For simplicity, let us focus on adaptation to $S_{\mathbb{F}}$.

Our adaptation approach focuses on the target-side sentences because the IWSLT corpus is paired (for each English sentence there is a formal and informal variant in the target language). The approach builds a vocabulary of non-singleton tokens from $S_{tgt,\mathbb{F}}$, then builds two language models: LM_S from $S_{tgt,\mathbb{F}}$ and LM_G from a random sample of 10K sentences from G_{tgt}; both language models use the originally extracted vocabulary. Then, we calculate the sentence-level perplexity $PP(LM_G, G_{tgt})$ and $PP(LM_S, G_{tgt})$. Finally, the sentence pairs within G are ranked by

$$PP(LM_S, G_{tgt}) - PP(LM_G, G_{tgt}).$$

Let $G_{sorted\_by\_\mathbb{F}}$, $G_{sorted\_by\_\mathbb{I}}$ denote the resulting corpora sorted by the perplexity difference. The intuition behind this approach is that sentences which use a certain formality will naturally rank higher on the ranked list for that formality, due to similarities in the used vocabulary.

To obtain the formal and informal corpora from the sorted data, we needed to decide on a criterion. Let $\mathbb{F}_{pos}$ and $\mathbb{I}_{pos}$ be the position of a sentence pair in the formal/informal ranking, respectively. Our first approach was simple: let C denote the size of the out-of-domain corpus; we implemented an $Assign_\theta$ function which, for a $\theta \in [0, C)$, assigned a label to the sentence pair (src, tgt), using the following rules:

$$Assign_\theta \begin{cases} \mathbb{F}, & \text{if } \mathbb{F}_{pos} < \theta < \mathbb{I}_{pos}; \\ \mathbb{I}, & \text{if } \mathbb{I}_{pos} < \theta < \mathbb{F}_{pos}; \\ None, & \text{otherwise.} \end{cases}$$

Corpus	EN-DE		EN-ES		EN-IT		EN-RU	
MuST-C (v1.2)	229.7K		265.6K		253.6K		265.5K	
IWSLT-22	0.8K		0.8K		–		–	
Formality-annotated	$\mathbb{F}$	$\mathbb{I}$	$\mathbb{F}$	$\mathbb{I}$	$\mathbb{F}$	$\mathbb{I}$	$\mathbb{F}$	$\mathbb{I}$
INFEREASY	8.6K	8.6K	6.7K	6.7K	36.6K	36.6K	38.3K	38.3K
INFERFULL	13.7K	9.5K	10.5K	4.5K	11.4K	13.5K	12.0K	14.1K
+ZERO SHOT ON EN-{RU,IT}	13.7K	9.5K	10.5K	4.5K	0K	0K	0K	0K
+IWSLT-22	14.1K	9.9K	10.9K	4.9K	11.4K	13.5K	12.0K	14.1K

Table 1: Corpora containing training data used in the constrained track. Values indicate number of sentence pairs after preprocessing.

```
CUDA_VISIBLE_DEVICES 0,1,2,3
-finetune-from-model *
-max-update *
-ddp-backend=legacy_ddp
-task multilingual_translation
-arch multilingual_transformer_iwslt_de_en
-lang-pairs en-de,en-es,en-ru,en-it
-encoder-langtok tgt
-share-encoders
-share-decoder-input-output-embed
-optimizer adam
-adam-betas '(0.9, 0.98)'
-lr 0.0005
-lr-scheduler inverse_sqrt
-warmup-updates 4000
-warmup-init-lr '1e-07'
-label-smoothing 0.1
-criterion label_smoothed_cross_entropy
-dropout 0.3
-weight-decay 0.0001
-save-interval-updates *
-keep-interval-updates 10
-no-epoch-checkpoints
-max-tokens 1000
-update-freq 2
-fp16
```

Table 2: Parameters of `fairseq-train` for pre-training and fine-tuning all models. The starred ($\star$) parameters depend on the track/subtrack and can be found in the paper description or in the implementation.

We condition assignment on both positional lists since common phrases such as (*Yes! – Ja!*) may rank high on both sides, but should not get included in either corpus. We determine θ empirically by selecting a value that yields the most data as a result. These values were selected dynamically for each language pair, and resulted in $\theta = 0.45\mathcal{C}$ for EN-DE and $\theta = 0.5\mathcal{C}$ for EN-ES. We refer to this approach as INFEREASY.

We quickly observed that the selection method needed to take into account the relative ranking of a sentence pair for both formalities. To illustrate this, let $\theta = 50$, the number of sentences $n = 100$; a sentence pair with rankings $\mathbb{F}_{pos} = 49, \mathbb{I}_{pos} = 51$ will get included in the formal corpus, but with $\mathbb{F}_{pos} = 1, \mathbb{I}_{pos} = 50$ it will not, because $\mathbb{I}_{pos}$ is in the top k for the informal set, even though the relative difference between the two positions is large. To amend this, we introduced a classification by *relative position difference*: for any sentence pair with positions $(\mathbb{F}_{pos}, \mathbb{I}_{pos})$ we classify it as formal if $\mathbb{F}_{pos} - \mathbb{I}_{pos} > \alpha$. We determine α empirically: using $0.05\mathcal{C}$ and $0.2\mathcal{C}$ as the lower and upper bound, respectively, for several values α in range we compute a language model from the resulting data and calculate average perplexity $PP(\text{LM}_{Corpus(\alpha)}, \text{IWSLT})$. We select the α value which minimises this perplexity. We refer to this approach as INFERFULL.

2.3 Generalisation for Zero-Shot Language Pairs

For two language pairs (EN-{RU,IT}) no supervised training data was provided, meaning we could only use the IWSLT corpus and our inferred data from EN-{DE,ES} to obtain data for these pairs. We decided to focus on comparisons on the source (EN) side, meaning we could not use the IWSLT corpus as it was paired. One observation we made at this point was that, contrary to intuition, the same source sentences within the MuST-C corpus had different formality expressions in the German and Spanish corpora, respectively.

Let EN-DEXES be a corpus of triplets of sentences $(src_{\text{EN}}, tgt_{\text{DE}}, tgt_{\text{ES}})$ obtained by identifying English sentences which occur in both the EN-DE and EN-ES corpora. Since there are many such sentences in the MuST-C corpus, the EN-DEXES contains 85.72% of sentence pairs from the EN-DE and 74.13% of pairs from the EN-ES corpus. After marking the target sides of the EN-DEXES corpus for formality with INFERFULL, we quantified in how many cases both languages get the same label (formal of informal), and in how many cases they get a different label (Table 3). Out of all annotated triplets, only 5.8% triplets were annotated in both target languages; this is a significantly smaller fraction than expected. Within that group, almost 60% triplets had matching annotations. This implies that the same English sentence can sometimes (approx. 2 out of 5 times in our case) be expressed with different formality in the target language in the same discourse situation.

EN-DE	EN-ES	Count	% of annotated
$\mathbb{F}$	$\mathbb{F}$	845	2.85%
$\mathbb{I}$	$\mathbb{I}$	233	0.78%
$\mathbb{F}$	$\mathbb{I}$	381	0.95%
$\mathbb{I}$	$\mathbb{F}$	362	1.22%
$\mathbb{F}$	$\emptyset$	10851	36.54%
$\mathbb{I}$	$\emptyset$	7805	26.29%
$\emptyset$	$\mathbb{F}$	6567	22.12%
$\emptyset$	$\mathbb{I}$	2749	9.26%

Table 3: Context combinations for the EN-DEXES triplet extracted from the MuST-C dataset. "$\emptyset$" denotes "no context".

Given the non-zero count of triplets with matching formalities, we make another assumption: namely that the English sentences of the triplets with matching formalities may be of "strictly formal" or "strictly informal" nature, meaning the translations of at least some of those sentences to Russian and Italian may express the same formality. To extract formal and informal sentences for the zero-shot pairs, we adapted the original method, but this time using English as a pivot to convey the formality information. As the in-domain corpus, we used the English sentences whose German and Spanish translations were both labelled as formal or both as informal, respectively (columns 1, 2 in Table 3). We ranked the EN-RU and EN-IT corpora by their source sentences' similarity to that intersection (using the perplexity difference as before).

To infer the final corpora with the INFERFULL method, we used the α which yielded corpora of similar quantity to the ones for EN-{DE,ES}, since we could not determine that value empirically.

2.4 Relative Frequency Model for Reranking: FORMALITYRERANK

We observed that even when a model gets the formality wrong in its best hypothesis, the correct answer is sometimes found within the *n* best hypotheses, but at a lower position. We hypothesised that by re-ranking the n-best list according to a criterion different from the beam search log probability we could push the hypothesis with the correct formality to the first position.

We performed an oracle experiment with `scorer.py` to obtain an upper bound on what can be gained by re-scoring the n-best list perfectly: we generated k-best hypotheses for $k \in \{1, 5, 10, 20, 30, ..100\}^2$ and from each list of k hypotheses we selected the first hypothesis (if any) which `scorer.py` deemed of correct formality. The results (Table 4) show that as we expand the list of hypotheses, among them we can find more translations of correct formality, up to a .959 average accuracy (+.106 w.r.t. the model) for $k = 100$. The column "# Cases" shows that on average in up to 21 cases a hypothesis of the correct formality could be found with re-ranking. Finally, for any k, selecting the hypotheses with the correct formality (Oracle) in place of the most probable ones does (Model) not decrease translation quality, and may improve it (column "BLEU").

k	Accuracy Model	Accuracy Oracle	δ_{to_best}	# Cases	BLEU Model	BLEU Oracle
1	.838	.838	0.00	0.00	25.28	25.28
5	.858	.892	1.79	7.00	24.80	24.80
10	.857	.913	2.66	11.50	25.10	25.53
20	.853	.921	3.46	13.75	24.74	25.15
30	.851	.930	5.75	16.00	24.68	25.06
40	.853	.936	7.84	16.75	24.88	25.24
50	.853	.944	9.64	18.25	24.84	25.20
60	.852	.950	11.78	19.75	24.71	25.04
70	.852	.950	12.08	19.75	24.71	25.04
80	.852	.952	12.78	20.25	24.72	25.04
90	.852	.954	13.58	20.50	24.72	25.04
100	.853	.959	14.66	21.25	24.72	25.04

Table 4: Results of the oracle experiment. The used model was *constrained* and trained with the INFERFULL method, provided values are averaged across the development set. δ_{to_best} describes the average distance to the first hypothesis of correct formality for cases where the most probable hypothesis is incorrect. The column "# Cases" quantifies that phenomenon.

To re-rank the hypotheses we built a simple relative frequency model from the IWSLT data. For each term $t_i \in \mathcal{T}$ we calculated its occurrence counts $\mathbb{F}_{count}$ in the *formal* set and $\mathbb{I}_{count}$ in the *informal* set. Let $count(t_i) = \mathbb{F}_{count}(t_i) + \mathbb{I}_{count}(t_i)$. Since we wished to focus on terms differentiating

[2]We capped the search at $k = 100$ due to long inference times for higher k values.

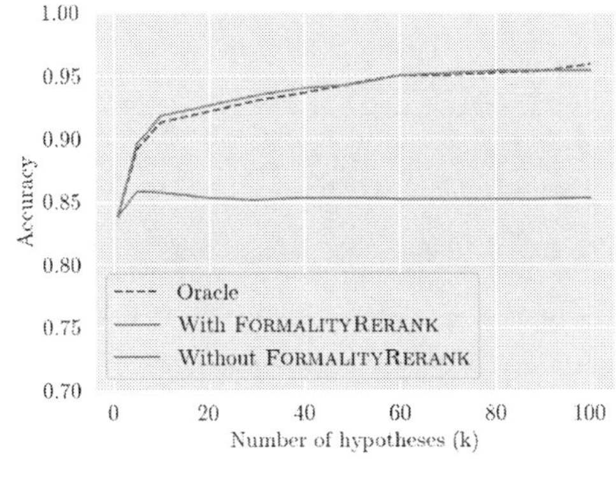

Figure 1: Validation accuracy plot showing the effect of applying FORMALITYRERANK to a list of k model hypotheses.

the two sets, we calculated the count difference ratio and used it as the weight β:

$$\beta(t_i) = \frac{|\mathbb{F}_{count}(t_i) - \mathbb{I}_{count}(t_i)|}{\max_{t_k \in \mathcal{T}} |\mathbb{F}_{count}(t_k) - \mathbb{I}_{count}(t_k)|}$$

We additionally nullified probabilities for terms for which the difference of the number of occurrences in the formal and informal sets was lower than the third of total occurrences:

$$\kappa(t_i) = \begin{cases} 0, & \text{if } \frac{|\mathbb{F}_{count}(t_i) - \mathbb{I}_{count}(t_i)|}{\mathbb{F}_{count}(t_i) + \mathbb{I}_{count}(t_i)} < 0.33^3; \\ 1, & \text{otherwise} \end{cases}$$

The probabilities could now be calculated as

$$p(\mathbb{F}|t_i) = \frac{\mathbb{F}_{count}(t_i)}{count(t_i)} * \beta(t_i) * \kappa(t_i)$$

$$p(\mathbb{I}|t_i) = \frac{\mathbb{I}_{count}(t_i)}{count(t_i)} * \beta(t_i) * \kappa(t_i)$$

For a hypothesis Y, a source sentence S and contexts $c, \hat{c} \in \{\mathbb{F}, \mathbb{I}\}, c \neq \hat{c}$, our objective function in translation thus became

$$p(Y|X, c) = p(Y|X) + p(c|Y) - p(\hat{c}|Y)$$

where

$$p(c|Y) = \sum_i p(c|y_i)$$

Figure 1 shows how validation accuracy increases when this method is used, and that the model is now able to match the oracle accuracy for nearly every k. For $k = 100$ the average improvement in accuracy is .102. The effect of model's accuracy sometimes surpassing the oracle accuracy (e.g. for $k = 30$) is a by-product of slight sample size variations: the evaluation script `scorer.py` depends on phrase matches, and a sample is only counted for evaluation if a hypothesis has at least one phrase match against the formality-annotated reference.

2.5 Model Selection: BESTACCAVERAGING

We fine-tuned each model for 100K iterations on the MuST-C corpus with formality tags appended to relevant sentences. We then evaluated every checkpoint (saved each epoch) with `scorer.py` on IWSLT data. Our initial approach to selecting a model assumed averaging the last 10 checkpoints from training. We experimented with an alternative method to finding which checkpoints to average: we first computed the accuracy on the IWSLT dataset for each checkpoint, and then selected a window of 10 consecutive checkpoints with the highest average accuracy (BESTACCAVERAGING).

2.6 Development Results

We report the validation results in Table 5. The first result we observed was that in both language pairs the pre-trained model (a strong baseline) learned a **dominant** formality: formal for EN-DE (.853 accuracy to .147) and informal for EN-ES (.632 accuracy to .368).

We observed that both methods (INFEREASY and INFERFULL) yield consistently better accuracy for dominant formalities than non-dominant ones. Nevertheless, with INFERFULL we obtain an average +.474 accuracy points over the baseline for non-dominant formalities; INFEREASY fails to learn meaningful control for non-dominant formalities. Based on these results we focused out later efforts on INFERFULL alone.

Continuing with INFERFULL, we noticed a significant improvement of up to +.223 accuracy points for (EN-DE, $\mathbb{I}$) when using FORMALITYRERANK on top of standard beam search ($k = 100$) without impacting the translation quality. Finally, BESTACCAVERAGING helped bring the average accuracy score up to .961 without impacting translation quality.

2.7 Submitted Models

Based on the validation results, we submitted two models to the constrained track: to the *full supervision* subtrack, we submitted the INFERFULL model with FORMALITYRERANK ($k = 100$) and

	MuST-C (BLEU)				IWSLT (Accuracy)				
	EN-DE	EN-ES	EN-RU	EN-IT	EN-DE $\mathbb{F}$	EN-DE $\mathbb{I}$	EN-ES $\mathbb{F}$	EN-ES $\mathbb{I}$	Mean
Pre-trained	**30.7**	39.7	19.5	**31.3**	.853	.147	.368	.632	.500
INFEREASY	30.1	39.3	19.9	31.1	.967	.167	.376	.595	.526
INFERFULL	30.1	**39.8**	19.8	31.2	.978	.637	.854	.963	.858
+FORMALITYRERANK	30.1	**39.8**	19.8	31.2	**1.000**	.860	**.968**	**.990**	.955
+BESTACCAVERAGING	30.3	39.6	**20.0**	31.2	**1.000**	**.899**	.956	**.990**	**.961**

Table 5: Results on the **development** sets for models built within the constrained track.

BESTACCAVERAGING upgrades; for the *zero-shot* subtrack, we fine-tuned an alternative version of the model where we skipped the EN-{RU,IT} fine-tuning data, effectively making inference for these zero-shot pairs[4]. We used the same augments as in *full supervision*.

3 Unconstrained Track

Our submission for the unconstrained track largely copies the constrained track one, but is applied to a larger training corpus.

3.1 Data Collection and Preprocessing

We collect all datasets permitted by the organisers for our selected language pairs, including:

- **MuST-C (v1.2)** (Di Gangi et al., 2019),
- **Paracrawl (v9)** (Bañón et al., 2020),
- **WMT Corpora** (from the News Translation task) (Barrault et al., 2021):
  - **NewsCommentary (v16)** (Tiedemann, 2012),
  - **CommonCrawl** (Smith et al., 2013),
  - **WikiMatrix** (Schwenk et al., 2021),
  - **WikiTitles (v3)** (Barrault et al., 2020),
  - **Europarl (v7, v10)** (Koehn, 2005),
  - **UN (v1)** (Ziemski et al., 2016),
  - **Tilde Rapid** (Rozis and Skadiņš, 2017),
  - **Yandex**[5].

We list data quantities as well as availability for all language pairs in Table 6. We preprocessed the WMT and Paracrawl corpora: for both we first ran a simple rule-based heuristic of removing sentence pairs with sentences longer than 250 tokens, and with a source-target ratio greater than 1.5; removing non-ASCII characters on the English side, pruning some problematic sentences (e.g. links). We normalised punctuation using the script from Moses (Koehn et al., 2007). We removed cases where either sentence is empty or where the source is the same as the target. Finally, we asserted that the case (lower/upper) of the first characters must be the same between source and target and that if either sentence ends in a punctuation mark, its counterpart must end in the same one. As the last step, we removed identical and very similar sentence pairs.

After the initial preprocessing, we ran the *Bi-Cleaner* tool (Ramírez-Sánchez et al., 2020) on each corpus; the algorithm assigns a confidence score $\in [0, 1]$ to each pair, measuring whether the sentences are good translations of each other, effectively removing potentially noisy sentences. We removed all sentence pairs from the corpora which scored below 0.7 confidence. The final training data quantities are reported in Table 6.

3.2 Data Labelling

Before we applied the same method to obtain fine-tuning data for the unconstrained track, we observed that many sentence pairs in this corpus are not dialogue, and hence useless for fine-tuning. As the first step, we used the original perplexity-based re-ranking algorithm to prune the unconstrained corpus. We used the MuST-C corpus as in-domain and all the unconstrained data as out-of-domain. We truncated the unconstrained set to the top 5M sentences most like the MuST-C data. We then applied INFERFULL with α threshold adapted to the data volume. The resulting data quantities can be found in the last row of Table 6.

[4] We labelled a small random sample of training data with a random formality tag so the model learned to recognise the symbol as part of the input.

[5] `https://translate.yandex.ru/corpus?lang=en`, accessed 4 Apr 2022.

Corpus	EN-DE		EN-ES		EN-IT		EN-RU	
MuST-C (v1.2)	0.23M		0.27M		0.25M		0.27M	
Paracrawl (v9)	278.31M		269.39M		96.98M		5.38M	
NewsCommentary v16	0.40M		0.38M		0.09M		0.34M	
CommonCrawl	2.40M		1.85M		–		0.88M	
WikiMatrix	5.47M		–		–		3.78M	
WikiTitles (v3)	1.47M		–		–		1.19M	
Europarl (v7|v10)	1.83M		1.97M		1.91M		–	
UN (v1)	–		11.20M		–		–	
Tilde Rapid	1.03M		–		–		–	
Yandex	–		–		–		1M	
Total								
Raw	291.14M		285.06M		99.23M		12.84M	
Preprocessed	76.99M		91.29M		36.99M		3.86M	
	$\mathbb{F}$	$\mathbb{I}$	$\mathbb{F}$	$\mathbb{I}$	$\mathbb{F}$	$\mathbb{I}$	$\mathbb{F}$	$\mathbb{I}$
Formality-annotated	216.5K	187.2K	111.8K	129.7K	101.0K	172.0K	195.9K	218.4K

Table 6: Corpora containing training data used in the unconstrained experiments. Values indicate number of sentence pairs after preprocessing.

3.3 Pre-training and Fine-tuning

We used an identical model architecture to the one from the constrained track but extended the training time: we pre-trained for 1.5M iterations (approx. 1.5 epochs) and fine-tuned for 0.25M iterations (approx. 47 epochs). For fine-tuning, we used the MuST-C corpus (to maintain high translation quality) concatenated with the inferred formality-annotated data (to learn formality control). We applied FORMALITYRERANK with $k = 50$, but not BESTACCAVERAGING as we found that the differences in average accuracy for most checkpoints is minimal (and nears 100); instead, we averaged the last 10 checkpoints.

3.4 Development Results

The development results (Table 7) surpassed those achieved in the constrained track, presumably thanks to richer corpora extracted for both formalities. INFERFULL yielded near-perfect accuracy for all sets but (EN-DE, $\mathbb{I}$), and applying FORMALITYRERANK effectively brought all scores up to a mean accuracy of .999. Our pre-trained model for this track achieved lower BLEU scores than for the constrained track, which is explained by the test set coming from the same domain as the constrained training data.

3.5 Submitted model

Similarly to the constrained track, we submit two models to the unconstrained track: to the *full supervision* subtrack, we submit the INFERFULL model with FORMALITYRERANK ($k = 50$); for the *zero-shot* subtrack, we fine-tune an alternative version of that in which we skip the EN-{RU,IT} fine-tuning data, effectively making inference for these pairs zero shot.

4 Final Results

We report the final evaluation results in Table 8 (translation quality) and Table 9 (formality control). In the latter we also provide the performance of our baseline (pre-trained) model for reference.

Within the constrained track, we achieved near-ideal accuracy for the dominant formality for each language pair (between .961 and 1.000) with the supervised model. Scores for non-dominant formalities are weaker but still impressive for EN-{DE,ES} with an average of .880. Our best model for EN-{RU,IT} improved by .193 accuracy points over the baseline. The models submitted to the unconstrained track again achieved an impressive average accuracy of .992 for dominant formality; additionally, performance for non-dominant formality in EN-{DE,ES} improved significantly w.r.t. the constrained model, also averaging .992. This means that with enough training data our methods were capable of matching the performance on a minority class w.r.t. a majority class.

Finally, contrary to the constrained track, the *unconstrained-zero-shot* model achieved the best accuracy for zero-shot pairs, to an average of .659.

	MuST-C (BLEU)				IWSLT (Accuracy)				
					EN-DE		EN-ES		
	EN-DE	EN-ES	EN-RU	EN-IT	$\mathbb{F}$	$\mathbb{I}$	$\mathbb{F}$	$\mathbb{I}$	Mean
Pre-trained	28.9	39.5	18.5	29.3	.634	.366	.215	.785	.500
INFERFULL	**32.3**	**40.8**	**20.4**	**32.0**	.990	**1.000**	.952	.991	.983
+FORMALITYRERANK	**32.3**	**40.8**	**20.4**	**32.0**	**1.000**	**1.000**	**.995**	**1.000**	**.999**

Table 7: Results on the **development** sets for models built within the unconstrained track.

Model name	BLEU				COMET			
	EN-DE	EN-ES	EN-RU	EN-IT	EN-DE	EN-ES	EN-RU	EN-IT
constrained-supervised (1)	31.50	36.53	21.41	33.28	.4477	.6076	.3311	.5676
constrained-zero-shot (2)	31.25	36.65	21.43	33.15	.4368	.6108	.3298	.5525
unconstrained-supervised (3)	32.50	36.98	22.01	33.56	.4972	.6349	.3846	.5927
unconstrained-zero-shot (4)	32.47	36.83	21.45	33.12	.4851	.6209	.3565	.5623

Table 8: Translation quality results on the **test** sets for all submitted models. Numbers in brackets indicate number of model submitted.

Model name	EN-DE		EN-ES		EN-RU		EN-IT	
	$\mathbb{F}$	$\mathbb{I}$	$\mathbb{F}$	$\mathbb{I}$	$\mathbb{F}$	$\mathbb{I}$	$\mathbb{F}$	$\mathbb{I}$
constrained-pre-trained	.885	.115	.457	.543	.951	.049	.149	.851
constrained-supervised (1)	1.000	.886	.874	.980	.981	.234	.349	.961
constrained-zero-shot (2)	–	–	–	–	.981	.154	.294	.929
unconstrained-pre-trained	.745	.255	.323	.677	.964	.036	.052	.948
unconstrained-supervised (3)	1.000	1.000	.981	1.000	.992	.136	.188	.980
unconstrained-zero-shot (4)	–	–	–	–	.995	.142	.512	.986

Table 9: Accuracy results on the **test** data as measured by `scorer.py`.

5 Conclusions

Overall results suggest that it is easy for a pre-trained translation model to learn controlled expression of the dominant type within a dichotomous phenomenon while learning to render the less-expressed type is significantly harder, especially in a low-resource scenario. Our methods applied to the supervised language pairs (English-to-German, English-to-Spanish) worked near unfailingly, but using English as a pivot language to propagate formality information did not help achieve similar results for the zero-shot pairs.

We suspect that the significant accuracy gains from FORMALITYRERANKING may have been partially due to formality in the studied language pairs itself being expressed primarily via certain token words such as the honorific *Sie* in German creating a *pivot* effect (Fu et al., 2019). As such, it may be of interest for future research to study such methods applied to more complex phenomena, such as grammatical expression of gender.

Finally, results for the EN-{RU,IT} language pairs may not have been as good as expected because we used the inferred data from the constrained track to build the relative frequency model, but the inferred data turned out to be not as high quality as we expected. Future work may investigate a robust solution to this problem of propagating formality via a source (pivot) language to extract training data for other language pairs.

Code used for our implementation can be accessed at `https://github.com/st-vincent1/iwslt_formality_slt_cdt_uos/`.

Acknowledgements

This work was supported by the Centre for Doctoral Training in Speech and Language Technologies (SLT) and their Applications funded by UK Research and Innovation [grant number EP/S023062/1].

References

Antonios Anastasopoulos, Luisa Bentivogli, Marcely Z Boito, Ondřej Bojar, Roldano Cattoni, Anna Currey, Georgiana Dinu, Kevin Duh, Maha Elbayad, Marcello Federico, Christian Federmann, Hongyu Gong, Roman Grundkiewicz, Barry Haddow, Benjamin Hsu, Dávid Javorský, Věra Kloudová, Surafel M Lakew, Xutai Ma, Prashant Mathur, Paul McNamee, Kenton Murray, Maria N\uadejde, Satoshi Nakamura, Matteo Negri, Jan Niehues, Xing Niu, Juan Pino, Elizabeth Salesky, Jiatong Shi, Sebastian Stüker, Katsuhito Sudoh, Marco Turchi, Yogesh Virkar, Alex Waibel, Changhan Wang, and Shinji Watanabe. 2022. FINDINGS OF THE IWSLT 2022 EVALUATION CAMPAIGN. In *Proceedings of the 19th International Conference on Spoken Language Translation (IWSLT 2022)*, Dublin, Ireland. Association for Computational Linguistics.

Marta Bañón, Pinzhen Chen, Barry Haddow, Kenneth Heafield, Hieu Hoang, Miquel Esplà-Gomis, Mikel L. Forcada, Amir Kamran, Faheem Kirefu, Philipp Koehn, Sergio Ortiz Rojas, Leopoldo Pla Sempere, Gema Ramírez-Sánchez, Elsa Sarrías, Marek Strelec, Brian Thompson, William Waites, Dion Wiggins, and Jaume Zaragoza. 2020. ParaCrawl: Web-scale acquisition of parallel corpora. In *Proceedings of the 58th Annual Meeting of the Association for Computational Linguistics*, pages 4555–4567, Online. Association for Computational Linguistics.

Loïc Barrault, Magdalena Biesialska, Ondřej Bojar, Marta R. Costa-jussà, Christian Federmann, Yvette Graham, Roman Grundkiewicz, Barry Haddow, Matthias Huck, Eric Joanis, Tom Kocmi, Philipp Koehn, Chi-kiu Lo, Nikola Ljubešić, Christof Monz, Makoto Morishita, Masaaki Nagata, Toshiaki Nakazawa, Santanu Pal, Matt Post, and Marcos Zampieri. 2020. Findings of the 2020 conference on machine translation (WMT20). In *Proceedings of the Fifth Conference on Machine Translation*, pages 1–55, Online. Association for Computational Linguistics.

Loic Barrault, Ondrej Bojar, Fethi Bougares, Rajen Chatterjee, Marta R. Costa-jussa, Christian Federmann, Mark Fishel, Alexander Fraser, Markus Freitag, Yvette Graham, Roman Grundkiewicz, Paco Guzman, Barry Haddow, Matthias Huck, Antonio Jimeno Yepes, Philipp Koehn, Tom Kocmi, Andre Martins, Makoto Morishita, and Christof Monz, editors. 2021. *Proceedings of the Sixth Conference on Machine Translation*. Association for Computational Linguistics, Online.

Mattia A. Di Gangi, Roldano Cattoni, Luisa Bentivogli, Matteo Negri, and Marco Turchi. 2019. MuST-C: a Multilingual Speech Translation Corpus. In *Proceedings of the 2019 Conference of the North American Chapter of the Association for Computational Linguistics: Human Language Technologies, Volume 1 (Long and Short Papers)*, pages 2012–2017, Minneapolis, Minnesota. Association for Computational Linguistics.

Yao Fu, Hao Zhou, Jiaze Chen, and Lei Li. 2019. Rethinking text attribute transfer: A lexical analysis. In *Proceedings of the 12th International Conference on Natural Language Generation*, pages 24–33, Tokyo, Japan. Association for Computational Linguistics.

Karthik Gopalakrishnan, Behnam Hedayatnia, Qinlang Chen, Anna Gottardi, Sanjeev Kwatra, Anu Venkatesh, Raefer Gabriel, and Dilek Hakkani-Tür. 2019. Topical-Chat: Towards Knowledge-Grounded Open-Domain Conversations. In *Proc. Interspeech 2019*, pages 1891–1895.

Melvin Johnson, Mike Schuster, Quoc V. Le, Maxim Krikun, Yonghui Wu, Zhifeng Chen, Nikhil Thorat, Fernanda Viégas, Martin Wattenberg, Greg Corrado, Macduff Hughes, and Jeffrey Dean. 2017. Google's Multilingual Neural Machine Translation System: Enabling Zero-Shot Translation. *Transactions of the Association for Computational Linguistics*, 5:339–351.

Philipp Koehn. 2005. Europarl: A Parallel Corpus for Statistical Machine Translation. In *Conference Proceedings: the tenth Machine Translation Summit*, pages 79–86, Phuket, Thailand. AAMT, AAMT.

Philipp Koehn, Hieu Hoang, Alexandra Birch, Chris Callison-Burch, Marcello Federico, Nicola Bertoldi, Brooke Cowan, Wade Shen, Christine Moran, Richard Zens, Chris Dyer, Ondřej Bojar, Alexandra Constantin, and Evan Herbst. 2007. Moses: Open source toolkit for statistical machine translation. In *Proceedings of the 45th Annual Meeting of the Association for Computational Linguistics Companion Volume Proceedings of the Demo and Poster Sessions*, pages 177–180, Prague, Czech Republic. Association for Computational Linguistics.

Taku Kudo and John Richardson. 2018. SentencePiece: A simple and language independent subword tokenizer and detokenizer for neural text processing. In *Proceedings of the 2018 Conference on Empirical Methods in Natural Language Processing: System Demonstrations*, pages 66–71, Brussels, Belgium. Association for Computational Linguistics.

Surafel Melaku Lakew, Mattia Di Gangi, and Marcello Federico. 2019. Controlling the Output Length of Neural Machine Translation. *arXiv*.

Maria Nadejde, Anna Currey, Benjamin Hsu, Xing Niu, Marcello Federico, and Georgiana Dinu. 2022. CoCoA-MT: A Dataset and Benchmark for Contrastive Controlled MT with Application to Formality. In *Findings of the Association for Computational Linguistics: NAACL 2022*, Seattle, USA. Association for Computational Linguistics.

Myle Ott, Sergey Edunov, Alexei Baevski, Angela Fan, Sam Gross, Nathan Ng, David Grangier, and Michael Auli. 2019. fairseq: A fast, extensible toolkit for sequence modeling. In *Proceedings of the 2019 Conference of the North American Chapter of the Association for Computational Linguistics (Demonstrations)*, pages 48–53, Minneapolis, Minnesota. Association for Computational Linguistics.

Gema Ramírez-Sánchez, Jaume Zaragoza-Bernabeu, Marta Bañón, and Sergio Ortiz Rojas. 2020. Bifixer and bicleaner: two open-source tools to clean your parallel data. In *Proceedings of the 22nd Annual Conference of the European Association for Machine Translation*, pages 291–298, Lisboa, Portugal. European Association for Machine Translation.

Roberts Rozis and Raivis Skadiņš. 2017. Tilde MODEL - multilingual open data for EU languages. In *Proceedings of the 21st Nordic Conference on Computational Linguistics*, pages 263–265, Gothenburg, Sweden. Association for Computational Linguistics.

Holger Schwenk, Vishrav Chaudhary, Shuo Sun, Hongyu Gong, and Francisco Guzmán. 2021. WikiMatrix: Mining 135M parallel sentences in 1620 language pairs from Wikipedia. In *Proceedings of the 16th Conference of the European Chapter of the Association for Computational Linguistics: Main Volume*, pages 1351–1361, Online. Association for Computational Linguistics.

Rico Sennrich, Barry Haddow, and Alexandra Birch. 2016. Controlling politeness in neural machine translation via side constraints. *2016 Conference of the North American Chapter of the Association for Computational Linguistics: Human Language Technologies, NAACL HLT 2016 - Proceedings of the Conference*, pages 35–40.

Jason R. Smith, Herve Saint-Amand, Magdalena Plamada, Philipp Koehn, Chris Callison-Burch, and Adam Lopez. 2013. Dirt cheap web-scale parallel text from the Common Crawl. In *Proceedings of the 51st Annual Meeting of the Association for Computational Linguistics (Volume 1: Long Papers)*, pages 1374–1383, Sofia, Bulgaria. Association for Computational Linguistics.

Jörg Tiedemann. 2012. Parallel data, tools and interfaces in OPUS. In *Proceedings of the Eighth International Conference on Language Resources and Evaluation (LREC'12)*, pages 2214–2218, Istanbul, Turkey. European Language Resources Association (ELRA).

Eva Vanmassenhove, Christian Hardmeier, and Andy Way. 2018. Getting gender right in neural machine translation. *Proceedings of the 2018 Conference on Empirical Methods in Natural Language Processing, EMNLP 2018*, pages 3003–3008.

Michał Ziemski, Marcin Junczys-Dowmunt, and Bruno Pouliquen. 2016. The United Nations parallel corpus v1.0. In *Proceedings of the Tenth International Conference on Language Resources and Evaluation (LREC'16)*, pages 3530–3534, Portorož, Slovenia. European Language Resources Association (ELRA).

Improving Machine Translation Formality Control with Weakly-Labelled Data Augmentation and Post Editing Strategies

Danial Zhang*, Jiang Yu*, Pragati Verma*, Ashwinkumar Ganesan* & Sarah Campbell
Alexa AI, Amazon
{dyz, janyu, vpragati, gashwink, srh}@amazon.com

Abstract

This paper describes Amazon Alexa AI's implementation for the IWSLT 2022 shared task on formality control. We focus on the unconstrained and supervised task for en→hi (Hindi) and en→ja (Japanese) pairs where very limited formality annotated data is available. We propose three simple yet effective post editing strategies namely, T-V conversion, utilizing a verb conjugator and seq2seq models in order to rewrite the translated phrases into formal or informal language. Considering nuances for formality and informality in different languages, our analysis shows that a language-specific post editing strategy achieves the best performance. To address the unique challenge of limited formality annotations, we further develop a formality classifier to perform *weakly-labelled* data augmentation which automatically generates synthetic formality labels from large parallel corpus. Empirical results on the IWSLT formality testset have shown that proposed system achieved significant improvements in terms of formality accuracy while retaining BLEU score on-par with baseline.

1 Introduction

Although neural machine translation (NMT) models have achieved state-of-the-art results with high BLEU scores[1], given a language pair, they are trained on generic parallel corpora that are extracted from various open source datasets such as the Europarl corpus (Koehn; Iranzo-Sánchez et al., 2019). These datasets make an implicit assumption that there is a single translation in the target language to a sentence from the source language. But the style of the language generated, through which meaning is conveyed, is also important (Heylighen et al., 1999). Thus, there is a need to control certain attributes of the text generated in a target language such as politeness or formality.

In this paper, we present our system for the IWSLT 2022 formality control task for machine translation.[2] We focus on the unconstrained and supervised scenario for en→hi and en→ja language pairs. In the proposed system, we explore post editing strategies that correct or alter textual formality once the translation has been completed. Post editing strategies can be language specific or language agnostic. We propose three strategies, T-V conversion (deterministically converting the informal or T-form of a pronoun to its corresponding formal or V-form) , verb conjugation, and a seq2seq model that learns to transform input text to be of a formal or informal nature. The T-V conversion and verb conjugation are language-specific strategies that are applied to en→hi, and en→ja pairs respectively. These two methods are compared against an alternative seq2seq model (Enarvi et al., 2020) that is language agnostic. We show that compared to a baseline translation model provided in task, a finetuned mBART model (Liu et al., 2020) with language-specific rule-based post editing significantly improved the baseline model performance and achieved the best formality control accuracy and BLEU score.

A unique challenge in this IWSLT Formality shared task is data sparsity - only few hundred formality annotated samples are available for finetuning the formality controlled NMT model. Therefore, we further devise a data augmentation method, utilizing linguistic cues to automatically annotate a small seed set of target (i.e., Hindi and Japanese) texts with formality labels. Then the seed set is utilized to train a multilingual text formality classifier that can further mine massive parallel corpus to find extra formality annotated data. We found such weakly-labeled data augmentation strategy significantly improved en→ja performance.

The paper is organized into the following sec-

*Equal contribution.

[1] http://nlpprogress.com/english/machine_translation.html

[2] https://iwslt.org/2022/formality

Proceedings of the 19th International Conference on Spoken Language Translation (IWSLT 2022), pages 351 - 360
May 26-27, 2022 ©2022 Association for Computational Linguistics

T-form (Informal)	V-form (Formal)	Translation
तुम	आप	you
तुम्हारा	आपका	your
तुम्हें	आपको	to you

Table 1: Examples of T-V distinction in Hindi.

tions: §2 describes each method, §3 shows the performance of each method and language it is applied to and §4 discusses the prior work on formality.

2 System Design

2.1 Task Definition

In this submission, we focus on unconstrained and supervised formality control machine translation task. Formally, given a source segment $\boldsymbol{X} = \{x_1, x_2, ..., x_m\}$, and a formality level $l \in \{\text{formal, informal}\}$, the goal is to find the model characterized by parameters $\boldsymbol{\Theta}$ that generates the most likely translation $\boldsymbol{Y} = \{y_1, y_2, ..., y_n\}$ corresponding to the formality level:

$$\boldsymbol{Y} = \arg\max_{Y_l} P(\boldsymbol{X}, l; \boldsymbol{\Theta}) \quad (1)$$

The overall architecture and workflow of the proposed system is described in Figure 1. We present the design of each component below.

2.2 NMT & Formality Finetuning

We took a two-step process to finetune the formality controlled NMT model. First, we pretrain a generic NMT model using a large-scale parallel corpus. We chose two model architectures for building the NMT model - 1) the provided Transformer-based pretrained model implemented using Sockeye[3], and 2) a mBART model implemented using fairseq.[4] We described the datasets used and finetuning details of the NMT models in §3.1.

2.3 Post Editing

We explore three post editing strategies that rewrite the hypotheses generated for the formal/informal translations from the formality controlled NMT models.

T-V Conversion

Many languages use honorifics to convey varying levels of politeness, social distance, courtesy, differences in age, etc. between addressor and addressee in a conversation. Even though the use of honorifics is not the only way to convey register (Wardhaugh, 1986), it is a way to ascertain register in sentences where pronouns are explicitly mentioned. The T-V distinction (Brown and Gilman, 1960) is a convention followed by many languages wherein different pronouns are used to convey familiarity or formality. In languages following this T-V distinction, it is applied to most pronouns of *address*, along with their verb conjugations. For sentences explicitly having pronouns of address, it is possible to write a simple, albeit noisy regex-based classifier to deterministically recognize the form (T-form or informal form; V-form or formal form) of the pronoun and thus output the grammatical register of the sentence in question. Examples of such T-V classification for Hindi is shown in Table 6.

For post editing using the T-V distinction in Hindi, we use a deterministic map of pronouns of address in T-form and their corresponding V-form in Hindi. For Hindi, this mapping is almost one-to-one, i.e. the map can be flipped along the horizontal axis to map V-form keys to T-form values without any loss in fidelity. This map can simply be looked up in the correct direction, and the values substituted for the keys in order to do a post-edit. We note that this method can be somewhat noisy as it only takes the pronouns of address into account and not the corresponding verb agreement. However, in our experiments this method has worked well in situations where some noise can be tolerated, such as post editing mistakes made by a predictive model, use in data augmentation, etc. The rules for T-V conversion and vice-versa are given in Appendix A.

Verb Conjugation

Apart from pronoun-based T-V form distinction, formality distinctions can be further encoded with verb morphology. For example, the word "to write" in Japanese 書く (kaku) can be transformed into its formal/polite form as 書きます (kakimasu). One complexity is that the conjugation of each verb depends on the class of the verb as well as its syntactic context in the sentence. For example, the verb "write!" 書け (kake) has the same stem "書" as 書く, yet its formal form is 書いてください (kaite kudasai). To address this issue, we first apply morphological analyzer that jointly identifies the verb and its corresponding verb class, as well as it Part-of-Speech Tag. Then dictionary rules adopted from (Feely et al., 2019a) are applied

[3]https://github.com/awslabs/sockeye

[4]https://github.com/pytorch/fairseq

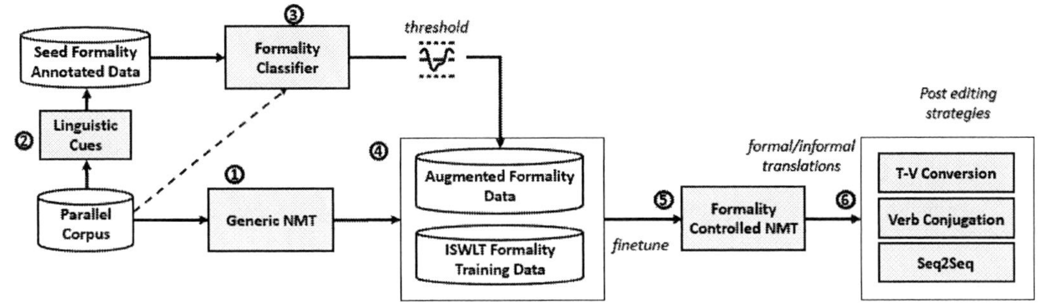

Workflow Description. ① Parallel NMT corpus is used to train a generic NMT model. ② We leverage linguistic cues (dictionaries of formality indicators) to extract formal/informal target segments in the parallel corpus, and use then as seed formality annotated training data. ③ The seed training data is used to train a multilingual formality classifier which then during inference time, automatically labels the formality in the unannotated parallel corpus. ④ The segments that have prediction confidence >95%, together with the seed formality annotated data is selected as augmented formality data. ⑤ The augmented formality data and the provided IWSLT formality training data together finetune the NMT model for the formality control task. ⑥ Finally, the translation output of the formality controlled NMT model is further processed by one of three post editing strategies.

Figure 1: System Architecture Overview

to convert the verb into its formal/informal counterparts. In the proposed system, we applied verb conjugation for en→ja, and used Kytea[5] as the morphological analyzer.

Using Sequence-to-Sequence Model

Similar to neural machine translations architectures, post editing can be performed by a sequence-to-sequence model where the input is informal or formal while the output is the opposite. In our work, we experiment with transformer based pointer network from Enarvi et al. (2020).[6] The architecture, originally used for text summarizing, modifies the NMT transformer architecture from Vaswani et al. (2017) with a copy attention mechanism. In tasks where the input and output dictionary are highly similar such grammatical error correction or formality, copy attention allows the model to replicate parts of the input while autoregressing the output sequence (See et al., 2017). The main benefit of using such a post editing model is that it can be consistently applied across languages i.e. it is **language agnostic** and does not need any language specific editing methods compared to prior approaches.

In our implementation, we use the transformer pointer network that is part of the fairseq package and additionally finetune a pretrained mBART (Liu et al., 2020) with the formal-informal parallel corpus provided in this task and monolingual data from the standard translation corpus. For the monolingual data, the source and target sequences are the same (we copy the source text to the target), allowing the model to be trained as an auto-encoder (pre-training the copy attention mechanism). We add two tokens i.e. __F__ at the end of formal sentences and __IF__ at the end of informal sentences to provide a signal to the model of the formality change intent similar to Niu et al. (2018). These tokens are added only to the training data from the formality control corpus provided in this task while the monolingual data remains unchanged. The model is trained in two phases. The first phase pretrains the model as an auto-encoder. The second phase finetunes the model to perform the formality change.

For en→hi, we use the target language corpus from Kunchukuttan et al. (2018) while for en→ja, we reuse the corpus from Morishita et al. (2020). A subset of $20,000$ Hindi or Japanese sequences are randomly sampled from the dataset.

2.4 Augment Weakly-Labeled Data

We further explore data augmentation technique to tackle the very limited access to formality annotated data. We propose to build a formality classifier that automatically labels an unannotated text as "formal" or "informal". The formality classifier can be trained using a set of seed training data with rule-based automatic annotations. In particular, we apply the T-V distinction technique for en→hi to automatically annotate Hindi texts in the en→hi parallel corpus as "formal" or "informal". Note that not all Hindi texts have T-V in-

[5]http://www.phontron.com/kytea/

[6]https://github.com/pytorch/fairseq/tree/main/examples/pointer_generator

dicators, therefore, only a small subset from the parallel corpus are labelled. Similarly, for en→ja, we follow the technique in Feely et al. (2019b), where we search for Japanese sentences that have more than one verb that indicates formality, and annotate these sentences accordingly. Tables 6-8 in Appendix summarize the T-V rule for en→hi and formality-indicating verbs for en→ja that were used to generate seed training data.

Using the formality labeled texts, we train a multilingual text classifier using multilingual Bert implemented with SimpleTransformers.[7] Then given the text classifier, we automatically label each target segments in the unannotated parallel corpus as formal or informal, which will be used during formality control finetuning. To ensure the quality of the formality label, we only select the annotated sentences that have a prediction score higher than a predefined threshold of 0.95. During formality finetuning, we upsampled the formality training data to a 1:1 ratio compared to the automatically annotated data. We summarize the size of the augmented data as well as the formality classifier accuracy in Appendix C.

3 Experiments

3.1 Training Details

The NMT model is first finetuned using a large parallel corpus. For the en→hi pair, we use IIT Bombay English-Hindi parallel corpus (Kunchukuttan et al., 2017) that contains 1.6 Million segments for training. For en→ja, we use two parallel corpora - WikiMatrix (Schwenk et al., 2019) and JParaCrawl (Morishita et al., 2019). When finetuning the mBART models for both en→hi and en→ja formality tasks, we set the following hyperparameters: maximum tokens = 512, drop out = 0.3, learning rate is 3e-05 for en→ja and 3e-04 for en→hi, random seed = 222, attention-dropout = 0.1, weight-decay = 0.0. The model is trained for a total of $20,000$ updates for en→ja and $160,000$ updates for en→hi, and the first 500 updates are used as warmup steps. The model is trained using Adam Optimizer (Kingma and Ba, 2015) with β_1 = 0.9. β_2 = 0.98, and ϵ = 1e-06. For the alternative Transformer-based NMT architecture, we pretrained the model with the same dataset, using the same model architecture and setup as the WMT14 en-de Transformer model (Gehring et al., 2017).

[7] https://simpletransformers.ai/

We further finetune the NMT models using the IWSLT Formality dataset for 1,000 steps for both language pairs. We chose a small number of training steps for this finetuning step to avoid overfitting the model and maintain a balanced BLEU score on the generic NMT performance.

3.2 Evaluation Dataset & Metrics

We evaluate the proposed system using the novel *IWSLT Formality Dataset* from Nădejde et al. (2022), which is part of the shared IWSLT task. This dataset comprises of source segments paired with two contrastive reference translations, one for each formality level (informal and formal). Since the reference was not disclosed during submission, we used a random sample of 25% of the training set as validation data and another non-overlapping 25% of the training set as test data. We report the BLEU score (Post, 2018) for measuring machine translation quality. We also report the formality control accuracy leveraging phrase-level formality annotations.[8] We use training / test dataset from both domains, i.e., telephony and topical-chats (Gopalakrishnan et al., 2019).

3.3 Results & Findings

The performance of all candidates are presented in Table 2. We make the following observations. First, compared to the pretrained base model, finetuning strategies significantly improved both BLEU score and formality accuracy. Moreover, the rule-based post editing strategy significantly improves the formality accuracy as compared to the finetuned model without post editing, while maintaining on-par BLEU scores. In particular, the formal accuracy improved from 93.9% to 95.5%, whereas the informal accuracy improved from 98.1% to 100% for the en→ja pair. For en→hi, the formal accuracy already reached 100% accuracy without post editing. Therefore, post editing was only performed to improve the informal accuracy where we observe a huge improvement from 84.4% to 97.8%.

For the seq2seq model-based post editing strategy, we only change formal text to informal text. The hypothesis generated is assumed to be formal and then post editing is applied to make it informal when necessary. Hence, the performance of the model for formal translation is the same

[8] https://github.com/amazon-research/contrastive-controlled-mt/tree/main/IWSLT2022#evaluation

	Formal BLEU		Informal BLEU		Formal Accuracy		Informal Accuracy	
	en→hi	en→ja	en→hi	en→ja	en→hi	en→ja	en→hi	en→ja
Base$_{\text{TRF}}$	19.2	13.0	15.9	13.5	0.982	0.256	0.018	0.744
Base$_{\text{mBART}}$	22.0	19.4	20.3	16.9	0.857	0.585	0.143	0.415
Finetuned$_{\text{TRF}}$	21.8	23.1	17.5	20.7	**1.000**	0.763	0.844	0.854
Finetuned$_{\text{mBART}}$	**33.7**	27.8	32.7	23.6	**1.000**	0.939	0.973	0.981
Finetuned$_{\text{TRF}}$ + Augmentation	17.1	22.1	14.5	18.3	**1.000**	0.776	0.714	0.931
Finetuned$_{\text{mBART}}$ + Augmentation	29.6	**27.9**	25.4	23.7	**1.000**	**0.962**	**1.000**	**1.000**
Finetuned$_{\text{TRF}}$ + Rule-based Editing	21.8	23.2	17.4	20.7	**1.000**	0.789	0.978	0.935
Finetuned$_{\text{mBART}}$ + Rule-based Editing	**33.7**	27.7	**32.9**	23.9	**1.000**	0.955	0.987	**1.000**
Finetuned$_{\text{TRF}}$ + Model-Based Editing	21.8*	10.4	20.4	20.7*	**1.000***	0.594	0.972	0.854*
Finetuned$_{\text{mBART}}$ + Model-Based Editing	**33.7***	27.8*	30.9	**25.8**	**1.000***	0.939*	1.000	0.262

Table 2: **Summary of overall performance.** The **Base** model is the pretrained translation model available through sockeye (Domhan et al., 2020). The **Finetuned** model represents the model finetuned on the IWSLT dataset provided. We utilize two different types of encoder-decoder models. **TRF** is the Transformer-based translation model available from sockeye, while **mBART** is the multilingual BART model. We provide results with data augmentation and post editing strategies that include rule-base editing (T-V conversion or verb conjugation) and model-based editing (using mBART transformers from Enarvi et al. (2020)). * represents the type that is generated directly by the **Finetuned$_{\text{mBART/TRF}}$** model without post editing.

as Finetuned$_{\text{mBART}}$, while the informal accuracy and BLEU score changes. We observe that in case of Japanese, the model improves the BLEU score from 23.1 to 25.8 but the informal output's accuracy score is low at 26.2%. For Hindi, the BLEU score is 30.9 while informal accuracy is 1.00%. Analysis of generated informal sentences shows that the model arbitrarily creates copies of text segments (repetition), leading to a reduced BLEU score.

We also observe that the data augmentation strategy improves the en→ja pair significantly, resulting in formal accuracy increased from 93.9% to 96.2%, and informal accuracy increases from 98.1% to 100%. In contrast, the data augmentation causes degradation on the formality accuracy for en→hi and did not improve the BLEU score. This may be due to the noisy seed training data where we used single T-V pronoun matching heuristics for Hindi to select formal/informal seed data instead of using a more complete set of heuristics including verb conjugation matching together with T-V pronoun matching. For Japanese however, the annotations are more accurate as we only select seed data that contains *multiple* formality indicating verbs.

While applying post editing strategies, we made an observation that using different conversion directions lead to very different results as indicated in Table 3. In particular, we found that uni-directional conversions, including formal→formal (i.e., convert formal hypothesis to formal) and informal→informal perform much better than cross-directional conversions such as formal→informal (i.e.,convert formal hypothesis to informal) and informal→formal. This is expected due to the typically high precision but low recall of rule-based formality conversions (Feely et al., 2019a), meaning that it cannot capture all formality pairs during the conversion, causing degraded accuracy.

Direction	BLEU		Accuracy	
	en→hi	en→ja	en→hi	en→ja
Formal hypothesis	23.5	23.8	0.896	0.789
Formal → Formal	**24.2**	**23.7**	**0.982**	**0.810**
Informal → Formal	23.7	21.6	0.981	0.612
Informal hypothesis	21.4	20.4	0.353	0.935
Informal → Informal	**22.3**	**20.5**	**0.902**	**1.000**
Formal → Informal	22.3	18.8	0.775	0.581

Table 3: Rule-based Post Editing Effect w.r.t. Conversion Directions. → represents the direction in which post editing happens.

	Testset	BLEU	COMET
en→hi	newstest2014	38.9	0.8741
en→ja	newstest2020	19.4	0.3783

Table 4: Generic NMT performance.

Finally, we report the performance of our submitted system on generic NMT test set, and blind IWSLT test set in Table 4 and Table 5 as required by the task. For en→hi, our submitted system employed finetuned mBART + data augmentation strategy which demonstrated the best performance on the development set. For en→ja, the submitted system employs finetuned mBART + data augmentation + post editing (verb conjugation). We have observed that the formality accuracy improvements are consistent with the observation in

	Formal BLEU		Informal BLEU		Formal Accuracy		Informal Accuracy	
	en→hi	**en→ja**	**en→hi**	**en→ja**	**en→hi**	**en→ja**	**en→hi**	**en→ja**
Finetuned$_{\text{mBART}}$	30.3	27.1	29.3	24.6	0.989	0.858	0.919	0.949
Our System	27.7	28.9	22.6	25.1	0.998	0.888	0.993	0.988

Table 5: Formality control performance on blind submission.

Table 2. Specifically, compared to the finetuned mBART candidate system, we observed 0.09% formal and 7.4% informal absolute accuracy improvements for en→hi. For en→ja, we observed 3.0% formal and and 3.9% informal absolute accuracy improvements. These results indicate the effectiveness of the proposed post editing and data augmentation strategies. We observed en→ja improved BLEU score as well. Interestingly, we observed that the proposed system for en→hi had worse BLEU score compared to the finetuned mBART model. One potential cause of this is that the formality augmented data for en→hi came from a different domain than the test set which is conversational in nature. We can potentially improve the BLEU score by augmenting the training data with more conversational data or up-sampling the IWSLT formality data during training. We leave these directions for future improvement.

4 Background

The task of controlling formality in the output of machine translation has drawn much attention in recent MT architectures. Earlier approaches are rule-based systems where non-linguistic information such as speaker profile and gender information is used to personalized MT with gender/speaker-specific data (Rabinovich et al., 2016; Michel and Neubig, 2018). More recently, Niu et al. (2017) coined the term Formality Sensitive Machine Translation (FSMT), and proposed lexical formality models to control the level of formality of MT output by selecting phrases of that are most similar to a desired formality level from the k-best list during decoding. Alternatively, a popular formality control approach is by leveraging side constraints in NMT where a style tag (e.g., <Formal>/<Informal>) is attached to the beginning of each source example, and the NMT model is forced to "pay attention to" these style tags during translation (Sennrich et al., 2016; Niu and Carpuat, 2020).

Formality control for machine translation is closely related to formality transfer (FT), which is the task of automatically transforming text in one formality style (e.g., "informal") into another (e.g., polite) (Niu et al., 2018). The FT task usually takes a seq2seq-like approach (Zhang et al., 2020) given parallel corpus such as Grammarly' s Yahoo Answers Formality Corpus (GYAFC) (Rao and Tetreault, 2018). These FT models are often applied as a rewriting mechanism after the MT outputs are generated. Recently, Niu et al. (2018) proposed a novel multi-task model that jointly perform FT and FSMT. Honorifics based post editing approaches have also been widely deployed for formality control tasks. A widespread instance of using honorifics to determine register is the grammatical T-V distinction (Brown and Gilman, 1960), distinguishing between the informal (Latin *Tu*) and the formal (Latin *Vos*). Alternatively, verb conjugation combined with syntactic parsing has been used to alter the inflection of the main verb of the sentence to achieve multiple levels of formality (Feely et al., 2019a).

5 Conclusion

In this paper, we target improving the machine translation formality control performance given limited formality annotated training data. We explored three different strategies including rule-based post editing, seq2seq point networks, and formality classifier-based augmentation. We found that data augmentation using formality classifier significantly improved formality accuracy on en→ja pair. We also found that post editing strategies on top of finetuned mBART models are simple and effective ways to improve the formality control performance. Results on the IWSLT testset have indicated performance improvements in terms of formality accuracy in both en→hi and en→ja pairs while retaining on-par BLEU score.

References

R. Brown and A. Gilman. 1960. The pronouns of power and solidarity. In T. A. Sebeok, editor, *Style in*

Language, pages 253–276. MIT Press, Cambridge, Mass.

Tobias Domhan, Michael Denkowski, David Vilar, Xing Niu, Felix Hieber, and Kenneth Heafield. 2020. The sockeye 2 neural machine translation toolkit at AMTA 2020. In *Proceedings of the 14th Conference of the Association for Machine Translation in the Americas (Volume 1: Research Track)*, pages 110–115, Virtual. Association for Machine Translation in the Americas.

Seppo Enarvi, Marilisa Amoia, Miguel Del-Agua Teba, Brian Delaney, Frank Diehl, Stefan Hahn, Kristina Harris, Liam McGrath, Yue Pan, Joel Pinto, Luca Rubini, Miguel Ruiz, Gagandeep Singh, Fabian Stemmer, Weiyi Sun, Paul Vozila, Thomas Lin, and Ranjani Ramamurthy. 2020. Generating medical reports from patient-doctor conversations using sequence-to-sequence models. In *Proceedings of the First Workshop on Natural Language Processing for Medical Conversations*, pages 22–30, Online. Association for Computational Linguistics.

Weston Feely, Eva Hasler, and Adrià de Gispert. 2019a. Controlling japanese honorifics in english-to-japanese neural machine translation. In *Proceedings of the 6th Workshop on Asian Translation*, pages 45–53.

Weston Feely, Eva Hasler, and Adrià de Gispert. 2019b. Controlling japanese honorifics in english-to-japanese neural machine translation. In *Proceedings of the 6th Workshop on Asian Translation*, pages 45–53. Association for Computational Linguistics.

Jonas Gehring, Michael Auli, David Grangier, Denis Yarats, and Yann N Dauphin. 2017. Convolutional sequence to sequence learning. In *International Conference on Machine Learning*, pages 1243–1252. PMLR.

Karthik Gopalakrishnan, Behnam Hedayatnia, Qinlang Chen, Anna Gottardi, Sanjeev Kwatra, Anu Venkatesh, Raefer Gabriel, and Dilek Hakkani-Tür. 2019. Topical-Chat: Towards Knowledge-Grounded Open-Domain Conversations. In *Proc. Interspeech 2019*, pages 1891–1895.

Francis Heylighen, Jean Marc Dewaele, and Léo Apostel. 1999. Formality of language: definition, measurement and behavioral determinants.

Javier Iranzo-Sánchez, Joan Albert Silvestre-Cerdà, Javier Jorge, Nahuel Roselló, Adrià Giménez, Albert Sanchis, Jorge Civera, and Alfons Juan. 2019. Europarl-st: A multilingual corpus for speech translation of parliamentary debates.

Diederik P. Kingma and Jimmy Ba. 2015. Adam: A method for stochastic optimization. In *3rd International Conference on Learning Representations, ICLR 2015, San Diego, CA, USA, May 7-9, 2015, Conference Track Proceedings*.

Philipp Koehn. Europarl: A parallel corpus for statistical machine translation.

Anoop Kunchukuttan, Pratik Mehta, and Pushpak Bhattacharyya. 2017. The iit bombay english-hindi parallel corpus. *arXiv preprint arXiv:1710.02855*.

Anoop Kunchukuttan, Pratik Mehta, and Pushpak Bhattacharyya. 2018. The IIT Bombay English-Hindi parallel corpus. In *Proceedings of the Eleventh International Conference on Language Resources and Evaluation (LREC 2018)*, Miyazaki, Japan. European Language Resources Association (ELRA).

Yinhan Liu, Jiatao Gu, Naman Goyal, Xian Li, Sergey Edunov, Marjan Ghazvininejad, Mike Lewis, and Luke Zettlemoyer. 2020. Multilingual denoising pre-training for neural machine translation. *CoRR*, abs/2001.08210.

Paul Michel and Graham Neubig. 2018. Extreme adaptation for personalized neural machine translation. *arXiv preprint arXiv:1805.01817*.

Makoto Morishita, Jun Suzuki, and Masaaki Nagata. 2019. Jparacrawl: A large scale web-based english-japanese parallel corpus. *arXiv preprint arXiv:1911.10668*.

Makoto Morishita, Jun Suzuki, and Masaaki Nagata. 2020. JParaCrawl: A large scale web-based English-Japanese parallel corpus. In *Proceedings of The 12th Language Resources and Evaluation Conference*, pages 3603–3609, Marseille, France. European Language Resources Association.

Xing Niu and Marine Carpuat. 2020. Controlling neural machine translation formality with synthetic supervision. In *Proceedings of the AAAI Conference on Artificial Intelligence*, volume 34, pages 8568–8575.

Xing Niu, Marianna Martindale, and Marine Carpuat. 2017. A study of style in machine translation: Controlling the formality of machine translation output. In *Proceedings of the 2017 Conference on Empirical Methods in Natural Language Processing*, pages 2814–2819.

Xing Niu, Sudha Rao, and Marine Carpuat. 2018. Multi-task neural models for translating between styles within and across languages. *arXiv preprint arXiv:1806.04357*.

Maria Nădejde, Anna Currey, Benjamin Hsu, Xing Niu, Marcello Federico, and Georgiana Dinu. 2022. CoCoA-MT: A dataset and benchmark for Contrastive Controlled MT with application to formality. In *Findings of the Association for Computational Linguistics: NAACL 2022*, Seattle, USA. Association for Computational Linguistics.

Matt Post. 2018. A call for clarity in reporting BLEU scores. In *Proceedings of the Third Conference on Machine Translation: Research Papers*, pages 186–191, Belgium, Brussels. Association for Computational Linguistics.

Ella Rabinovich, Shachar Mirkin, Raj Nath Patel, Lucia Specia, and Shuly Wintner. 2016. Personalized machine translation: Preserving original author traits. *arXiv preprint arXiv:1610.05461*.

Sudha Rao and Joel Tetreault. 2018. Dear sir or madam, may i introduce the gyafc dataset: Corpus, benchmarks and metrics for formality style transfer. *arXiv preprint arXiv:1803.06535*.

Holger Schwenk, Vishrav Chaudhary, Shuo Sun, Hongyu Gong, and Francisco Guzmán. 2019. Wikimatrix: Mining 135m parallel sentences in 1620 language pairs from wikipedia. *arXiv preprint arXiv:1907.05791*.

Abigail See, Peter J. Liu, and Christopher D. Manning. 2017. Get to the point: Summarization with pointer-generator networks. *CoRR*, abs/1704.04368.

Rico Sennrich, Barry Haddow, and Alexandra Birch. 2016. Controlling politeness in neural machine translation via side constraints. In *Proceedings of the 2016 Conference of the North American Chapter of the Association for Computational Linguistics: Human Language Technologies*, pages 35–40.

Ashish Vaswani, Noam Shazeer, Niki Parmar, Jakob Uszkoreit, Llion Jones, Aidan N Gomez, Ł ukasz Kaiser, and Illia Polosukhin. 2017. Attention is all you need. In *Advances in Neural Information Processing Systems*, volume 30. Curran Associates, Inc.

R Wardhaugh. 1986. *Introduction to Sociolinguistics* , 2nd edition. Wiley Series in Probability and Statistics. Cambridge: Blackwell.

Yi Zhang, Tao Ge, and Xu Sun. 2020. Parallel data augmentation for formality style transfer. *arXiv preprint arXiv:2005.07522*.

Appendix

A T-V conversion

Following tables 6 and 7, provide a list of rules applied to the dataset in order to change formality. Table 6 provides rules to change the language from informal to formal, while table 7 performs the inverse.

T-form (Informal)	V-form (Formal)
"तुम्हें"	"आपको"
"तुमको"	"आपको"
"तुम्हारे"	"आपके"
"तुम्हारा"	"आपका"
"तुम्हारी"	"आपकी"
"तुम"	"आप"
" हो "	" हैं "

Table 6: Rules for converting T-form to V-form for Hindi. The order of applying the rules is significant, along with the spaces within quotes, if present.

V-form (Formal)	T-form (Informal)
"आपको"	"तुम्हें"
"आपके"	"तुम्हारे"
"तुम्हारे"	"आपके"
"आपका"	"तुम्हारा"
"आपकी"	"तुम्हारी"
"आप "	"तुम "
" हैं "	" हो "

Table 7: Rules for converting V-form to T-form for Hindi. The order of applying the rules is significant, along with the spaces within quotes, if present.

B Formality-indicating verbs for Japanese

	Formality-indicating verbs
Formal	ございます, いらっしゃいます, おります, なさいます, 致します, ご覧になります, おいでになります, 伺います, 参ります, 存知します, 存じ上げます, 召し上がります, 頂く, 頂きます, 頂いて, 差しあげます, 下さいます, おっしゃいます, 申し上げます, 拝見します, お目に掛かります
Informal	だ, だった, じゃない, じゃなかった, だろう, だから, だけど, だって, だっけ, そうだ, ようだ

Table 8: Indicating verbs for generating seed training data for en→ja formality classifier.

C Formality Classifier Accuracy and Data Sizes

		Precision	Recall	F1
en→hi	Formal	0.802	0.757	0.779
	Informal	0.776	0.827	0.801
en→ja	Formal	0.885	0.817	0.850
	Informal	1.0	0.852	0.920

Table 9: Formality classifier accuracy using IWSLT formality testset as groundtruth.

	Seed	Unlabeled	Augmented
en→hi	142,900	1,667,803	142,900*
en→ja	9,856	13,956,005	26,294

Table 10: Weakly labeled data sizes. *Due to the relatively poor performance of the formality classifier for en→hi, only the seed training data was used for data augmentation.

D Post Editing Seq2seq Model

Following are details about the post editing model utilized to perform formality change. We use a base model architecture from Enarvi et al. (2020). As described in §2.3, the transformer model is trained in two phases, viz., pretraining with monolingual language data and then finetuning the formality control dataset.

Following are the hyper-parameters with which the model is trained and later inference is performed:

Hyperparameter	Value
Tokenizer	Sacremoses
Pointer layers	-2
Pointer head	2
Pointer markers	1000
Label Smoothing	0.1
Weight Decay	0.0
Learning Rate	0.001
Batch Size	512
Total Number of Updates	20000

Table 11: **Hyperparameters of Post Editing model.** The table shows values of hyperparameters that are manually set. All other parameters are set to their default value in the package. *Pointer layers* are the attention layers being pointed to and *Pointer head* denotes the number of attention heads used.

HW-TSC's Participation in the IWSLT 2022 Isometric Spoken Language Translation

Zongyao Li, Jiaxin Guo, Daimeng Wei, Hengchao Shang, Minghan Wang, Ting Zhu, Zhanglin Wu, Zhengzhe Yu, Xiaoyu Chen, Lizhi Lei, Hao Yang, Ying Qin
Huawei Translation Service Center, Beijing, China
`{lizongyao,guojiaxin1,weidaimeng,shanghengchao,wangminghan, zhuting20,wuzhanglin2,yuzhengzhe,chenxiaoyu35, leilizhi,yanghao30,qinying}@huawei.com`

Abstract

This paper presents our submissions to the IWSLT 2022 Isometric Spoken Language Translation task. We participate in all three language pairs (English-German, English-French, and English-Spanish) under the constrained setting, and submit an English-German result under the unconstrained setting. We use the standard Transformer model as the baseline and obtain the best performance via one of its variants that shares the decoder input and output embedding. We perform detailed pre-processing and filtering on the provided bilingual data. Several strategies are used to train our models, such as Multilingual Translation, Back Translation, Forward Translation, R-Drop, Average Checkpoint, and Ensemble. We experiment on three methods for biasing the output length: i) conditioning the output to a given target-source length-ratio class; ii) enriching the transformer positional embedding with length information and iii) length control decoding for non-autoregressive translation etc. Our submissions achieve 30.7, 41.6 and 36.7 BLEU respectively on the tst-COMMON test sets for English-German, English-French, English-Spanish tasks and 100% comply with the length requirements.

1 Introduction

This paper introduces our submissions to the IWSLT 2022 Isometric Spoken Language Translation task. To train our models, we perform multiple data filtering strategies to enhance data quality. In addition, we leverage Multilingual model (Johnson et al., 2017), Forward (Wu et al., 2019) and Back Translation (Edunov et al., 2018), and R-Drop (Wu et al., 2021) strategies to further enhance training effects. We also adopt Length Token (Lakew et al., 2019), Length Encoding (Takase and Okazaki, 2019) and Non-Autoregressive Translation (NAT) to further enhance system performances. We compare and contrast different strategies in light of our experiment results and conduct analysis accordingly.

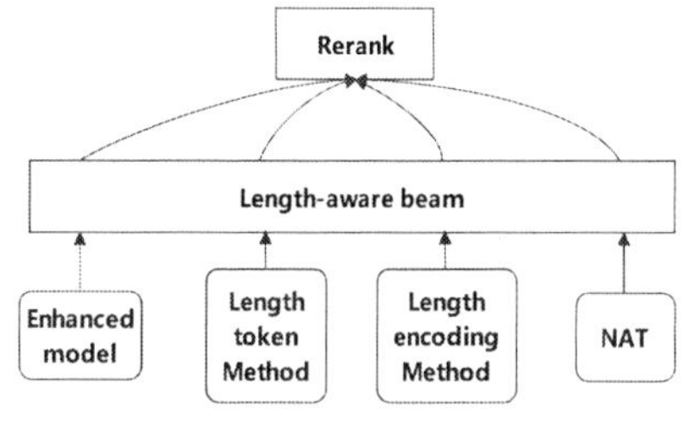

Figure 1: The training process for the IWSLT 2022 Isometric Spoken Language Translation.

The overall training process is illustrated in Figure 1. Section 2 focuses on our training techniques, including model architecture, data processing and training strategies. Section 3 describes our experiment settings and training process. Section 4 presents the experiment results while section 5 analyzes the effects of different model enhancement and length control strategies on the quality and length of translation outputs.

2 Method

2.1 Model Architecture

2.1.1 Autoregressive NMT Model

Transformer-based model with the self-attention mechanism (Vaswani et al., 2017) has achieved the state-of-the-art translation performance. The Transformer architecture is a standard encoder-decoder model. The encoder can be viewed as a stack of N layers, including a self-attention sub-layer and a feed-forward (FFN) sub-layer. The decoder shares a similar architecture as the encoder but integrates an encoder-decoder attention sub-layer to capture the mapping between two languages.

For autoregressive translation (AT) models we trained in this shared task, Transformer-Base architecture is used, which features 6-layer encoder, 6-layer decoder, 512 dimensions of word vec-

Proceedings of the 19th International Conference on Spoken Language Translation (IWSLT 2022), pages 361 - 368
May 26-27, 2022

tor, 2048-hidden-state, 8-head self-attention, post-norm, share decoder input, and output embedding.

2.1.2 Non-autoregressive NMT Model

Non-autoregressive models generate all outputs in parallel and break the dependency between output tokens. For AT models, EOS (end of sentence) token is used to indicate the end of a sentence and thus determines the length of the sequence. On the contrary, for NAT models, the output length should be predicted in advance. We believe such mechanism is more suitable for this task.

CMLM (Ghazvininejad et al., 2019) adopts a masked language model to progressively generate the sequence from entirely masked inputs and has achieved stunning performance among non-autoregressive NMT models. HI-CMLM (Wang et al., 2021a) extends CMLM using a novel heuristic hybrid strategy, i.e. fence-mask, to improve the translation quality of short texts and speed up early-stage convergence. In the constrained task, HI-CMLM is used, which features 6-layer encoder, 6-layer decoder, 512 dimensions of word vector, 1024-hidden-state, and 4-head self-attention.

AT and NAT models have distinctive superiorities and drawbacks in terms of performance and latency. We try to combine the two strategies into one model, hoping to leverage advantages of both. Diformer (Wang et al., 2021b) (Directional Transformer), with a newly introduced direction variable, is a unified framework that jointly models Autoregressive and Non-autoregressive settings into three generation directions (left-to-right, right-to-left and straight). It works by controlling the prediction of each token to have specific dependencies under that direction. In the unconstrained task, Diformer is used, which features 6-layer encoder, 6-layer decoder, 512 dimensions of word vector, 2048-hidden-state, and 8-head self-attention.

2.2 Data Processing and Augmentation

As for the constrained task, we use only the officially provided data, MuST-C v1.2. As for the unconstrained task, we additionally apply WMT2014 data to the English-German task for NAT model training.

2.2.1 Data Filtering

We perform the following steps to cleanse all data:

- Filter out repeated sentences (Khayrallah and Koehn, 2018; Ott et al., 2018).
- Convert XML escape characters.
- Normalize punctuations using Moses (Koehn et al., 2007).
- Delete HTML tags, non-UTF-8 characters, unicode characters and invisible characters.
- Filter out sentences with mismatched parentheses and quotation marks; sentences of which punctuation exceeds 30%; sentences with the character-to-word ratio greater than 12 or less than 1.5; sentences of which the source-to-target token ratio higher than 3 or lowers than 0.3; sentences with more than 120 tokens.
- Apply langid (Joulin et al., 2016b,a) to filter sentences in other languages.
- Use fast-align (Dyer et al., 2013) to filter sentence pairs with poor alignment, and about 10% of the data is filtered out.

Language pair	Raw data	Data filtering
en-de	229.7K	211.1K
en-fr	275.1K	253.9K
en-es	265.6K	247.8K

Table 1: Data sizes before and after filtering.

Data sizes before and after filtering are listed in Table 1.

2.2.2 Data Diversification

Nguyen et al. (2020) introduce Data Diversification, a simple but effective strategy to enhance neural machine translation (NMT) performance. It diversifies the training data by using the predictions of multiple forward and backward models and then merging the generated text with the original dataset on which the final NMT model is trained.

In terms of back translation, we adopt top-k sampling to translate data (BT sampling). With regard to forward translation, we translate data using beam search. Through sampling, we ensure that the sizes of data generated by forward and back translation are relatively equal. In this paper, we refer to the combination of forward and backward translation sampling as FBTS.

Inspired by Iterative Joint Training (Zhang et al., 2018), we first adopt multiple copies of BT sampling data for model training in this task. Then, we further perform model augmentation training by merging multiple copies of FBTS data generated by the optimized model with the authentic bilingual data. Since model performance (Zhang et al., 2019) will be affected due to length control, we generate a great amount of synthetic parallel data to enrich data diversity, in hope of minimizing the effect of length control.

2.2.3 Data Distillation and Self-Distillation Mixup Training

Knowledge distillation trains a student model to perform better by learning from a stronger teacher model. This method has been proved effective for NAT models training by Zhou et al. (2019). In this work, we use enhanced AT models as teacher models to generate distilled data, and use self-distillation mixup training (Guo et al., 2021) strategy to train the NAT student models.

2.3 Model Augmentation

2.3.1 Multilingual Model

Johnson et al. (2017) proposes a simple solution that uses a single neural machine translation model to translate across multiple languages, without architecture changes. The model introduces an artificial token at the beginning of the input sentence to specify the required target language. All languages use a shared vocabulary. No additional parameters are required. The experiments surprisingly show that such model design can achieve better translation qualities across languages. In the task, we use only constrained data of the particular language pair for training. Taking en2de as an example, we use only English-to-German and German-to-English data.

2.3.2 R-Drop Training

R-Drop (Wu et al., 2021) uses a simple dropout twice method to construct positive samples for comparative learning, significantly improving the experimental results in supervised tasks. We apply R-Drop with $a = 5$ to regularize the model so as to prevent over-fitting.

2.3.3 Ensemble

Model ensemble is a widely used technique in previous WMT workshops (Garmash and Monz, 2016), which enhances the performance by combining the predictions of several models at each decoding step. We train multiple models (generally four models) by shuffling training data and perform ensemble decoding with the above models in the inference phase.

2.4 Output Length Control

As described in the task, we define length compliance (LC) as the percentage of translations in a given test set falling in a predefined length threshold of ±10% of the number of characters in the source sentence.

2.4.1 Length Token

Lakew et al. (2019) classify bi-text into three classes based on the target-to-source character ratio (LR) of each sample (s; t) pair. The labels are defined based on LR thresholds: $short < 0.9 < normal < 1.1 < long$ in our experiment. We prepend the length token $v \epsilon \{short; normal; long\}$ at the beginning of the source sentence during training. The desired v is prepended on the input sentence during inference.

2.4.2 Length Encoding

Takase and Okazaki (2019) propose a simple but effective extension of sinusoidal positional encoding to constrain the length of outputs generated by a neural encoder-decoder model. We adopt the length-ratio positional encoding (LRPE) method mentioned in the paper. LRPE is expected to generate sentences of any length even if sentences of exact lengths are not included in the training data.

2.4.3 Length-control decoding for NAT

Traditional NAT models predict the output token numbers first and then generate all output tokens in parallel. Some prior work (Wang et al., 2021c) has analyzed how length prediction influences the performance of NAT. To further improve the length compliance, we propose length-control decoding (LCD), which sets the length of the target tokens as that of the source tokens. We assume that if the source and target sentences have the same number of tokens, their sentence lengths are also approximately the same.

2.4.4 Length-aware beam

In order to get better translation results, we generate n-best hypotheses with a multi-model ensemble. In this task, beam-size is set to 12, so that 12 candidate outputs are generated for one source sentence, among which we select the one that comply with the +-10% length requirements. The candidate output with the least loss value is selected when all the 12 outputs fail to meet the length requirement. This method is called length-aware beam (LAB).

2.4.5 Rerank

We try various strategies in our experiments. With LAB strategy, each model has its own trade off on quality and length control. We ensemble several models of which BLEU is better on tst-COMMON test sets to score all the candidate outputs. Based on the scores, we rerank the candidates to select the best one.

3 Settings

3.1 Experiment Settings

We use the open-source fairseq (Ott et al., 2019) for training. BERTScore is used to measure system performances and the script officially provided is used to calculate the output lengths in the task. Each model is trained using 8 GPUs. The size of each batch is set to 2048, parameter update frequency to 2, and learning rate to 5e-4. The number of warmup steps is 4000, and the dropout is 0.3. We share vocabulary for source and target languages, and sizes of the vocabularies for English-German, English-French and English-Spanish are 30k, 27k, and 30k respectively. We use early stopping when validation loss stops improving and apply checkpoint averaging on last 5 checkpoints. In the inference phase, the beam-size is 12 and the length penalty is set to 0.6.

3.2 System Process

Our overall training strategy is to train a baseline model, conduct enhanced training with techniques such as multilingual translation, R-Drop, and data augmentation. After obtaining the optimized model, we add length token to the training data, adopt length encoding to the model, and use non-autoregressive decoding to control the output length. In addition, we ensemble multiple models to achieve the submitted results. Our training process is as follows:

1) We preprocess the training data using methods mentioned in section 2.2.1 and train four models using Multilingual Translation and R-Drop strategies with shuffled training data.

2) We perform data augmentation as described in section 2.2.2. We train four models with bilingual data and BT sampling data generated by the models mentioned in step 1. Then, we perform FBTS data augmentation on the basis of the enhanced models and train four more models. For the constrained setting, we use both source and target sides of the bilingual data to generate four copies of forward and backward translated pseudo bi-texts (one model generates one copy), respectively.

3) We add length token to authentic and synthetic parallel data as described in section 2.4.1, and train four models to ensemble. We also train a model using length encoding, as mentioned in section 2.4.2.

4) We train the NAT models using the method described in section 2.4.3 with authentic bilingual data and synthetic parallel data generated in step 2).

5) We average the last five checkpoints and perform separate inference on each model, and then ensemble the models. We change length token $(long, normal, short)$ for models using Length Token strategy to generate multiple results.

6) We use the method described in section 2.4.4 and 2.4.5 rerank hypotheses generated from models trained by different strategies to get the final results.

4 Experiment Result

Table 2 lists the results of our submissions on the tst-COMMON test sets. The baseline models, trained on transformer-base architecture, achieve the poorest performances on BLEU and rather poor performance on LC. Our enhanced models (Enhanced), trained with data and model augmentation strategies, achieve the highest BLEU scores (33.3, 45.9, 37.1) but the lowest LC scores (36.9, 36.6, 57.9) on the three language pairs. Len-tok models are trained with Length Token strategy and the length token is set to $normal$, and an improvement on LC has been witnessed. Len-control decoding for nat models uses NAT Decoding. Length-aware beam strategy is demonstrated useful for all of the three types of models as we witness significant improvements on LC for those models by using the strategy. Rerank1 reranks hypotheses from the enhanced and Len-tok models; Rerank2 reranks hypotheses from the enhanced and len-control decoding for nat models; and Rerank3 reranks hypotheses from all of the three types of models. Accord-

Pairs	English-German				English-French				English-Spanish			
System	BLEU	F1	LR	LC	BLEU	F1	LR	LC	BLEU	F1	LR	LC
Baseline	28.9	0.828	1.12	41.0	35.6	0.812	1.22	33.1	30.5	0.809	1.11	44.0
Enhanced	**33.3**	**0.842**	1.14	36.9	**45.9**	**0.872**	1.14	36.6	**37.1**	**0.850**	1.04	57.9
+LAB	33.0	0.838	1.10	68.6	45.4	0.869	1.13	50.5	36.9	0.848	1.03	72.1
Len-tok	32.1	0.835	1.06	54.7	44.1	0.866	1.09	49.1	36.8	0.848	1.02	66.8
+LAB	31.2	0.830	**1.04**	80.8	42.9	0.859	1.07	73.s1	37.1	0.845	1.01	84.2
NAT	30.4	0.829	1.04	83.5	42.3	0.848	1.05	82.3	36.1	0.830	1.01	89.9
+LAB	29.8	0.826	1.05	**89.0**	41.6	0.848	1.05	**87.3**	35.9	0.833	1.01	**93.7**
Rerank1	30.7	0.830	1.03	99.8	41.5	0.851	1.03	98.7	36.8	0.845	1.01	98.9
Rerank2	29.9	0.829	1.02	100	40.9	0.849	1.02	100	36.0	0.844	1.01	100
Rerank3	30.7	0.830	1.04	**100**	41.6	0.851	**1.02**	**100**	36.7	0.845	**1.01**	**100**

Table 2: Experimental results of our submitted system. (F1 is short for BERTScore F1.)

Pairs	English-German				English-French				English-Spanish			
System	BLEU	F1	LR	LC	BLEU	F1	LR	LC	BLEU	F1	LR	LC
Enhanced	33.0	0.838	1.10	68.6	45.4	0.869	1.13	50.5	36.9	0.848	1.03	72.1
LT-normal	31.2	0.830	1.04	80.8	42.9	0.859	1.07	73.1	37.1	0.845	1.01	84.2
LT-short	27.2	0.818	0.94	82.0	38.0	0.845	0.98	85.3	36.3	0.841	0.95	83.3
LT-long	32.6	0.839	1.15	45.4	44.9	0.864	1.17	42.8	35.0	0.844	1.07	66.1
LRPC	28.0	0.822	1.06	79.3	40.6	0.843	1.04	78.7	34.8	0.842	1.00	90.5

Table 3: The experimental results of length token and encoding method.

ing to our experiment results, Rerank3 achieves the best BLEU and BERTScore scores and 100% comply with the length requirement. For details about the blind-test results submitted, see appendix A.

5 Analysis

5.1 Data Augmentation and Model Augmentation to Enhance Model Performance

Our experiment results demonstrate that model augmentation has positive effects on model performances. Table 4 lists the BLEU scores on the tst-COMMON test sets. Compared with the baseline models, other models obtain much higher BLEU on English-German, English-French and English-Spanish tasks. Our experiment on English-German task shows that strategies such as multilingual translation, decoder input and output embedding (Tied-embed) sharing, R-Drop, BT sampling, and FBTS, have significant impact on translation quality. Meanwhile, ensemble strategy can only result in little improvement due to the limited size of the training data. The final BLEU scores of en2de, en2fr, and en2es are 33.3, 45.9, and 37.1 respectively.

Strategy	En2de	En2fr	En2es
Baseline	28.9	35.6	30.5
+Tied-embed	29.5	-	-
+Multilingual	29.9	-	-
+R-Drop	30.6	43.0	34.3
+BT sampling	32.0	45.1	36.9
+FBTS	33.1	45.9	37.0
+Ensemble	**33.3**	**45.9**	**37.1**

Table 4: The experimental results of Model Augmentation.

5.2 Length Token and Length Encoding to Control Output Length

Our experiment demonstrates that the length token method is useful to control the output length. In order to enrich the diversity of results, we decode models using token $\{short; normal; long\}$ and LAB strategy, which correspond to LT-short, LT-normal and LT-long respectively. Table 3 shows that LT-normal model has the best overall quality. LT-short model leads to significantly shortened outputs and poor performance. LT-long model generates long outputs with relatively good performance. The above results further illustrate the shortening the length of outputs is the root cause of translation

Pairs	English-German				English-French				English-Spanish			
System	BLEU	F1	LR	LC	BLEU	F1	LR	LC	BLEU	F1	LR	LC
Enhanced	33.3	0.842	1.14	36.9	45.9	0.872	1.14	36.6	37.1	0.850	1.04	57.9
NAT	31.6	0.835	1.06	62.5	43.1	0.860	1.08	60.6	36.6	0.837	1.01	68.0
+LCD	30.4	0.829	1.04	83.5	42.3	0.848	1.05	82.3	36.1	0.830	1.01	89.9
+LAB	29.8	0.826	1.05	89.0	41.6	0.848	1.05	87.3	35.9	0.833	1.01	93.7
Unconstrained NAT	28.8	0.825	1.02	96.3	-	-	-	-	-	-	-	-

Table 5: The experimental result of Length-control decoding for NAT.

Pairs		English-German			
System	**Strategy**	BLEU	F1	LR	LC
Enhanced	LAB	33.0	0.838	1.10	68.6
LT-normal	LAB	31.2	0.830	1.04	80.8
LT-short	LAB	27.2	0.818	0.94	82.0
LT-long	LAB	32.6	0.839	1.15	45.4
NAT	LCD+LAB	29.8	0.826	1.05	89.0
Rerank1	-	30.7	0.830	1.03	99.8
Rerank3	-	30.7	0.830	1.04	100

Table 6: The experimental result of LAB and Rerank Method.

quality degradation. Although the LRPC method can dynamically adjust the length of the output, it negatively affects the translation quality, so we do not use the LRPC method in our submissions.

5.3 NAT to Control Output Length

Our experiments show that the model trained with NAT strategy can predict the output length based on the source length, so it outperforms the model trained with AT strategy on LC measurement, but underperforms the AT model on BLEU measurement. Table 5 illustrates that LCD strategy produces significantly improved LC scores but decreased BLEU scores. The LAB strategy leads to further improved LC scores but slightly decreased BLEU scores.

The unconstrained NAT model is trained along with the WMT14 English-German training data and fine-tuned with MuST-C. We witness significant improvements on LR and LC after increasing the data size. We believe data diversity is the reason for such improvement.

5.4 Effect of Length-aware beam and Rerank on Result

Table 2 shows that all systems achieve much higher LC scores when they are trained using LAB strategy. However, table 6 presents systems trained with various output length controlling methods without the rerank. Models without reranking can only achieve 89% LC at most. 100% LC can only be achieved by reranking all the above systems to minimize the deterioration of translation quality.

6 Conclusion

This paper presents HW-TSC's submission to IWSLT 2022 Isometric Spoken Language Translation Task. In general, we explore data and model augmentation methods, and achieve huge increases in BLEU scores when comparing with baseline models. In terms of length compliance, we use strategies such as Length Token, Length Encoding, NAT, Length-Aware Beam and Rerank. Our systems obtain 30.7, 41.6 and 36.7 BLEU respectively on the tst-COMMON test sets for English-German, English-French, English-Spanish tasks and 100% comply with the length requirements.

References

Chris Dyer, Victor Chahuneau, and Noah A. Smith. 2013. A simple, fast, and effective reparameterization of IBM model 2. In *Human Language Technologies: Conference of the North American Chapter of the Association of Computational Linguistics, Proceedings, June 9-14, 2013, Westin Peachtree Plaza Hotel, Atlanta, Georgia, USA*, pages 644–648.

Sergey Edunov, Myle Ott, Michael Auli, and David Grangier. 2018. Understanding back-translation at scale. In *Proceedings of the 2018 Conference on Empirical Methods in Natural Language Processing, Brussels, Belgium, October 31 - November 4, 2018*, pages 489–500.

Ekaterina Garmash and Christof Monz. 2016. Ensemble learning for multi-source neural machine translation. In *Proceedings of COLING 2016, the 26th International Conference on Computational Linguistics: Technical Papers*, pages 1409–1418.

Marjan Ghazvininejad, Omer Levy, Yinhan Liu, and Luke Zettlemoyer. 2019. Mask-predict: Parallel decoding of conditional masked language models. *arXiv preprint arXiv:1904.09324*.

Jiaxin Guo, Minghan Wang, Daimeng Wei, Hengchao Shang, Yuxia Wang, Zongyao Li, Zhengzhe Yu, Zhanglin Wu, Yimeng Chen, Chang Su, Min Zhang, Lizhi Lei, Shimin Tao, and Hao Yang. 2021. Self-distillation mixup training for non-autoregressive neural machine translation. *CoRR*, abs/2112.11640.

Melvin Johnson, Mike Schuster, Quoc V Le, Maxim Krikun, Yonghui Wu, Zhifeng Chen, Nikhil Thorat, Fernanda Viégas, Martin Wattenberg, Greg Corrado, et al. 2017. Google's multilingual neural machine translation system: Enabling zero-shot translation. *Transactions of the Association for Computational Linguistics*, 5:339–351.

Armand Joulin, Edouard Grave, Piotr Bojanowski, Matthijs Douze, Hérve Jégou, and Tomas Mikolov. 2016a. Fasttext.zip: Compressing text classification models. *arXiv preprint arXiv:1612.03651*.

Armand Joulin, Edouard Grave, Piotr Bojanowski, and Tomas Mikolov. 2016b. Bag of tricks for efficient text classification. *arXiv preprint arXiv:1607.01759*.

Huda Khayrallah and Philipp Koehn. 2018. On the impact of various types of noise on neural machine translation. *arXiv preprint arXiv:1805.12282*.

Philipp Koehn, Hieu Hoang, Alexandra Birch, Chris Callison-Burch, Marcello Federico, Nicola Bertoldi, Brooke Cowan, Wade Shen, Christine Moran, Richard Zens, et al. 2007. Moses: Open source toolkit for statistical machine translation. In *Proceedings of the 45th annual meeting of the association for computational linguistics companion volume proceedings of the demo and poster sessions*, pages 177–180.

Surafel Melaku Lakew, Mattia Di Gangi, and Marcello Federico. 2019. Controlling the output length of neural machine translation. *arXiv preprint arXiv:1910.10408*.

Xuan-Phi Nguyen, Shafiq Joty, Kui Wu, and Ai Ti Aw. 2020. Data diversification: A simple strategy for neural machine translation. *Advances in Neural Information Processing Systems*, 33:10018–10029.

Myle Ott, Michael Auli, David Grangier, and Marc'Aurelio Ranzato. 2018. Analyzing uncertainty in neural machine translation. In *International Conference on Machine Learning*, pages 3956–3965. PMLR.

Myle Ott, Sergey Edunov, Alexei Baevski, Angela Fan, Sam Gross, Nathan Ng, David Grangier, and Michael Auli. 2019. fairseq: A fast, extensible toolkit for sequence modeling. *arXiv preprint arXiv:1904.01038*.

Sho Takase and Naoaki Okazaki. 2019. Positional encoding to control output sequence length. *arXiv preprint arXiv:1904.07418*.

Ashish Vaswani, Noam Shazeer, Niki Parmar, Jakob Uszkoreit, Llion Jones, Aidan N Gomez, Łukasz Kaiser, and Illia Polosukhin. 2017. Attention is all you need. In *Advances in neural information processing systems*, pages 5998–6008.

Minghan Wang, Jiaxin Guo, Yuxia Wang, Yimeng Chen, Chang Su, Daimeng Wei, Min Zhang, Shimin Tao, and Hao Yang. 2021a. HI-CMLM: improve CMLM with hybrid decoder input. In *Proceedings of the 14th International Conference on Natural Language Generation, INLG 2021, Aberdeen, Scotland, UK, 20-24 September, 2021*, pages 167–171. Association for Computational Linguistics.

Minghan Wang, Jiaxin Guo, Yuxia Wang, Daimeng Wei, Hengchao Shang, Chang Su, Yimeng Chen, Yinglu Li, Min Zhang, Shimin Tao, and Hao Yang. 2021b. Diformer: Directional transformer for neural machine translation. *CoRR*, abs/2112.11632.

Minghan Wang, Guo Jiaxin, Yuxia Wang, Yimeng Chen, Su Chang, Hengchao Shang, Min Zhang, Shimin Tao, and Hao Yang. 2021c. How length prediction influence the performance of non-autoregressive translation? In *Proceedings of the Fourth BlackboxNLP Workshop on Analyzing and Interpreting Neural Networks for NLP*, pages 205–213, Punta Cana, Dominican Republic. Association for Computational Linguistics.

Lijun Wu, Juntao Li, Yue Wang, Qi Meng, Tao Qin, Wei Chen, Min Zhang, Tie-Yan Liu, et al. 2021. R-drop: regularized dropout for neural networks. *Advances in Neural Information Processing Systems*, 34.

Lijun Wu, Yiren Wang, Yingce Xia, Tao Qin, Jianhuang Lai, and Tie-Yan Liu. 2019. Exploiting monolingual data at scale for neural machine translation. In *Proceedings of the 2019 Conference on Empirical Methods in Natural Language Processing and the 9th International Joint Conference on Natural Language Processing (EMNLP-IJCNLP)*, pages 4207–4216.

Tianyi Zhang, Varsha Kishore, Felix Wu, Kilian Q Weinberger, and Yoav Artzi. 2019. Bertscore: Evaluating text generation with bert. *arXiv preprint arXiv:1904.09675*.

Zhirui Zhang, Shujie Liu, Mu Li, Ming Zhou, and Enhong Chen. 2018. Joint training for neural machine translation models with monolingual data. In *Thirty-Second AAAI Conference on Artificial Intelligence*.

Chunting Zhou, Graham Neubig, and Jiatao Gu. 2019. Understanding knowledge distillation in non-autoregressive machine translation. *arXiv preprint arXiv:1911.02727*.

A Blind-test result

Table 7 presents the blind-test results for our submissions. isometric-slt-01, 02, 03, and 04 indicates Rerank1, Rerank2, Rerank3, and unconstrained

Pairs	English-German				English-French				English-Spanish			
System	BLEU	F1	LR	LC	BLEU	F1	LR	LC	BLEU	F1	LR	LC
isometric-slt-01	18.0	0.744	1.25	99.5	30.8	0.768	1.18	99.5	30.4	0.784	1.15	99.5
isometric-slt-02	17.8	0.753	1.18	100	27.8	0.763	1.17	100	28.7	0.788	1.15	100
isometric-slt-03	17.9	0.740	1.28	99.5	31.5	0.765	1.19	98.0	29.9	0.784	1.18	96.5
isometric-slt-04	20.2	0.759	1.03	96.0	-	-	-	-	-	-	-	-

Table 7: The experimental result of blind-test.

NAT results in our experiments. isometric-slt-03 post-processes punctuation over-translated, and as a result, it cannot 100% meets the length requirements.

AppTek's Submission to the IWSLT 2022 Isometric Spoken Language Translation Task

Patrick Wilken
AppTek
Aachen, Germany
pwilken@apptek.com

Evgeny Matusov
AppTek
Aachen, Germany
ematusov@apptek.com

Abstract

To participate in the Isometric Spoken Language Translation Task of the IWSLT 2022 evaluation, constrained condition, AppTek developed neural Transformer-based systems for English-to-German with various mechanisms of length control, ranging from source-side and target-side pseudo-tokens to encoding of remaining length in characters that replaces positional encoding. We further increased translation length compliance by sentence-level selection of length-compliant hypotheses from different system variants, as well as rescoring of N-best candidates from a single system. Length-compliant back-translated and forward-translated synthetic data, as well as other parallel data variants derived from the original MuST-C training corpus were important for a good quality/desired length trade-off. Our experimental results show that length compliance levels above 90% can be reached while minimizing losses in MT quality as measured in BERT and BLEU scores.

1 Introduction

In this paper, we describe AppTek's submission to the IWSLT 2022 Isometric Spoken Language Translation evaluation (Anastasopoulos et al., 2022). Our goal was to create a system that produces translations which are within 10% of the source sentence length, but have similar levels of quality as a baseline system translations without length control. AppTek participated in the constrained condition with an English-to-German neural machine translation (NMT) system that we describe in Section 2. The system was extended with 5 different length control methods, which we explain in detail in Section 3. We also created synthetic data with back-translation, forward-translation, as well as a novel data augmentation method of synonym replacement. All three methods are described in Section 4. Our experimental results on the MuST-C tst-COMMON test set and the official evaluation test set are presented in Section 5, including ablation studies that prove the effectiveness of synthetic data and noisy length encoding for a better trade-off between length compliance and MT quality. We summarize our findings in Section 6.

2 Baseline system

2.1 Data

We follow the constrained condition of the IWSLT Isometric SLT task and use only English-to-German TED-talk data from the MuST-C corpus (Di Gangi et al., 2019). The corpus contains 251K sentence pairs with 4.7M and 4.3M English and German words, respectively.

We apply minimal text pre-processing, mainly consisting of normalization of quotes and dashes. 2K sentences that have mismatching digits or parentheses in source and target were filtered out.

We use a joint English and German SentencePiece model (Kudo and Richardson, 2018), trained on the whole corpus using a vocabulary size of 20K, to split the data into subwords.

2.2 Neural NMT model

In preliminary experiments we tried several Transformer model configurations, including *base* and *big* from the original paper (Vaswani et al., 2017), a 12 encoder and decoder layer variant of *base*, and a "deep" 20 encoder layer version with halved feed-forward layer dimension in the encoder and only 4 attention heads. These attempts to optimize the model architecture for the given, rather low resource task did not yield a better architecture than Transformer *big*, which we end up using in all our experiments.

We however find an increased dropout rate of 0.3 and an increased label smoothing of 0.2 to be crucial. We further optimize the model by sharing the parameters of the source and target embeddings as well as the softmax projection matrix.

Proceedings of the 19th International Conference on Spoken Language Translation (IWSLT 2022), pages 369 - 378
May 26-27, 2022

In all experiments we use two translation factors (García-Martínez et al., 2016) on both the source and target side to represent the casing of the subwords and the binary decision whether a subword is attached to the previous subword (Wilken and Matusov, 2019). This allows for explicit sharing of information between closely related variants of a subword and reduces the model vocabulary size.

All models are trained on a single GPU for 162 to 198 epochs of 100K sentence pairs each in less than two days. We use batches of 1700 subwords and accumulate gradients over 8 subsequent batches. The global learning rate of the Adam optimizer is increased linearly from 3×10^{-5} to 3×10^{-4} in the first 10 epochs and then decreased dynamically by factor 0.9 each time perplexity on the MuST-C dev set increases during 4 epochs. For decoding we use beam search with a beam size of 12.

We train the Transformer models using RETURNN (Doetsch et al., 2017; Zeyer et al., 2018), which is a flexible neural network toolkit based on Tensorflow (Abadi et al., 2015). Automation of the data processing, training and evaluation pipelines is implemented with Sisyphus (Peter et al., 2018).

3 Length control methods

In this work we perform an extensive evaluation of different ways to control the length of the translations generated by the NMT model, all applied to the same baseline Transformer *big* model.

3.1 N-best rescoring

A simple method to achieve length compliant translation is to generate N-best lists and select translation hypotheses from the lists that adhere to the desired length constraints. Saboo and Baumann (2019) and Lakew et al. (2021) compute a linear combination of the original MT model score and a length-related score to reorder the N-best list. In this work, we simply extract the translation from the N-best list with the best MT score that has a character count within a 10% margin of the source character count and fall back to the first best hypothesis if there is no such translation. This approach is tailored towards the evaluation condition of the IWSLT Isometric SLT task where length compliance within a 10% margin is a binary decision and the absolute length difference is not considered.

While N-best rescoring has the advantage of being applicable to any NMT model that uses beam search, it is outperformed by learned length control methods because in many cases there is no length compliant translation in the N-best list, and also because learned methods are able to shorten the translation in a more semantically meaningful way. However, we use N-best rescoring on top of other methods to further improve length compliance, as done by Lakew et al. (2021).

3.2 Length class token

Lakew et al. (2019) introduce a special token at the start of the source sentence to control translation length. For this, the training data is classified into difference length classes based on the target-to-source ratio measured in number of characters. In this work we use two variants of length classes:

1. 3 length bins representing "too short", "length compliant" and "too long". Length compliant here means the number of characters in source and target differs by less than 10%;
2. 7 length bins from "extra short" to "extra long", such that an approximately equal number of training sentence pairs falls into each bin.

The first option is focused on isometric MT, i.e. equal source and target length, while the second option offers a more fine-grained length control.

In addition, we analyze the difference of adding the token to the source versus the target side. Adding the token on the target side has the advantage of offering the option to not enforce a length class at inference time and instead let the model perform an unbiased translation. This is especially important in a commercial setting where costs can be saved by deploying a single model for general and isometric MT.

3.2.1 Length ROVER

A system that takes a length class as input can produce multiple different translations of a given source sentence. To maximize the chance for length compliant translations, we produce translations of the whole test set for each of the length bins and then, for each sentence, select the hypothesis which adheres to the length constraint. We refer to this as length ROVER, in analogy to the automatic speech recognition system combination technique called ROVER (Fiscus, 1997). If multiple length bins produce a length compliant translation, precedence is determined by the corpus-level translation quality scores for the different length bins. If no bin produces a length compliant translation the bin with the best corpus-level translation quality is used as fallback.

As we use a target-side length token, we can let the model predict the length token instead of forcing one. This usually leads to the best corpus-level translation quality. We include this freely decoded translation in the length ROVER.

When applying the length ROVER to the 7-bin model, we exclude the bins corresponding to the longest and shortest translations as those rarely lead to length compliant translations but generally to degraded translation quality. The same is true for the "too short" and "too long" bins in the 3-bin model, which is why we do not use the length ROVER for this model.

3.3 Length encoding

We adopt length-difference positional encoding (LDPE) from Takase and Okazaki (2019). It replaces the positional encoding in the transformer decoder, which usually encodes the absolute target position, with a version that "counts down" from a desired output length L_{forced} to zero. At each decoding step the available remaining length is an input to the decoder and thus the model learns to stop at the right position. In training, L_{forced} is usually set to the reference target length L_{target}, while at inference time it can be set as desired. For isometric MT, setting it to the source length $L_{\text{forced}} = L_{\text{source}}$ is the natural choice.

The original work of Takase and Okazaki (2019) uses a character-level decoder, which means that the number of decoding steps equals the translation length, assuming the latter is measured in number of characters. Using subwords (Sennrich et al., 2016) as the output unit of the decoder is more common in state-of-the-art systems (Akhbardeh et al., 2021). In this case, one can either encode the target length in terms of number of subword tokens (Liu et al., 2020; Niehues, 2020; Buet and Yvon, 2021), or keep the character-level encoding which however requires subtracting the number of characters in the predicted subword token in each decoding step (Lakew et al., 2019). The former has the disadvantage that the number of subword tokens is a less direct measure of translation length, especially for the case of the IWSLT Isometric SLT task where length compliance is measured in terms of number of characters. The second option is more exact but arguably a bit more complex to implement. In this work we compare results for both methods.

In contrast to (Lakew et al., 2019) we do not combine standard token-level positional encoding and character-level length encoding, instead we only use the latter.

3.3.1 Length perturbation

For both the token-level and character-level version we add random noise to the encoded translation length L_{forced} during training (Oka et al., 2020). We find that this is necessary to make the model robust to the mismatch between training, where the target length is taken from a natural translation, and inference, where the enforced target length is a free parameter. Especially in the case of character-length encoding one cannot expect that a high-quality translation with a given exact character count exists. As opposed to Oka et al. (2020), who add a random integer to the token-level target length sampled from a fixed interval, e.g. $[-4, 4]$, we chose a relative +/-10% interval:

$$L_{\text{forced}} \sim U\left(\lfloor 0.9 \cdot L_{\text{target}} \rceil, \lfloor 1.1 \cdot L_{\text{target}} \rceil\right) \quad (1)$$

Here, $U(n, m)$ denotes the discrete uniform distribution in the interval $[n, m]$, and $\lfloor \cdot \rceil$ denotes rounding to the nearest integer. This is in line with the +/-10% length compliance condition used in the evaluation. The length difference subtracted in each decoder step is left unaltered, which means counting down will stop at a value that in general is different from zero.

3.3.2 Second-pass length correction

Length encoding as described above does not result in a length compliant translation in all cases. The reasons for this are: 1. general model imperfections, intensified by the small size of the training data in the constrained track; 2. the noise added to the target length in training (although it is within the "allowed" 10% range); 3. for the case of token-level length encoding, an equal number of source and target tokens does not necessarily mean an equal number of characters.

We therefore perform a second decoding pass for those sentences where the first pass does not generate a length compliant translation. In this second pass, instead of attempting to enforce $L_{\text{forced}} = L_{\text{source}}$, we make a correction by multiplying by the source-to-target ratio observed in the first pass (measured in tokens or characters, depending on the unit used for length encoding):

$$L_{\text{forced}}^{\text{2-pass}} = \left\lfloor L_{\text{source}} \cdot \frac{L_{\text{source}}}{L_{\text{target}}^{\text{1-pass}}} \right\rceil \quad (2)$$

$L_{\text{target}}^{\text{1-pass}}$ is the first pass translation length, $\lfloor \cdot \rceil$ denotes rounding. That way, an over-translation of factor r in the first pass will be counteracted by "aiming" at a translation length of $1/r$ of the source length in the second pass.

This procedure could be applied iteratively, one could even run a grid search of many different values for L_{forced} until a length compliant translation is generated. We refrain from doing so as we find it to be impracticable in real-world applications.

4 Synthetic data

We expand the original MuST-C data with synthetic data of different types, all derived from the given MuST-C corpus.

First, we include a copy of the data[1] in which two consecutive sentences from the same TED talk are concatenated into one. Since many segments in the original data are short, this helps to learn more in-context translations. Then, we also include a copy of the data where the English side is preprocessed by lowercasing, removing punctuation marks and replacing digits, monetary amounts and other entities with their spoken forms. This helps to adjust to the spoken style of TED talks and imperfections in the (manual) transcriptions of the training and evaluation data.

We also use 82K bilingual phrase pairs extracted from word-aligned MuST-C data, as described below, as training instances.

4.1 Word synonym replacement

To enrich the training data with more examples of length-compliant translations, we experiment with a novel technique of replacing a few randomly selected source (English) words in a given sentence pair with their synonyms which are shorter/longer in the number of characters, so that the resulting modified synthetic sentence is closer to being length compliant. Whereas in an unconstrained conditions the synonyms can come from WordNet or other sources, in the constrained track we rely on synonyms extracted from a bilingual lexicon. The replacement of a source word with a synonym in a given sentence pair happens only if it is aligned to a target word, for which another word translation exists in the bilingual lexicon.

The word alignment and bilingual word lexicon extraction is performed on the lowercased MuST-C corpus itself using FastAlign (Dyer et al., 2013). The bilingual lexicon is filtered to contain entries with the costs (negative log of the word-level translation probability) of 50 or lower.

We apply the synonym replacements only to sentence pairs for which the target sentence is not length-compliant with the source. We first generate multiple versions of modified source sentences for these data, which all differ in the choice of randomly selected words that are to be replaced with synonyms and in the actual synonyms selected for replacement (also at random). Each word in a sentence has a 0.5 chance of being considered for replacement (regardless of whether it has synonyms as defined above or not), and the replacement is done with (at most) one of 3 synonym candidates with the highest lexicon probability which have fewer or more characters than the word being replaced, depending on whether the length of the original sentence was too long or too short.

From the resulting data (ca. 1M sentences), we keep only those modified source sentences for which the BERT F1 score (Zhang et al., 2020) with respect to the original (unmodified) source sentence is 0.94 or higher. In this way we try to make sure that the meaning of the modified source sentence stays very close to the original meaning. This way, only 192K sentences are kept, which are then paired with the original target (German) sentences to form a synthetic synonym replacement parallel corpus.

4.2 Back-translated data

We train the reverse, German-to-English system with 7 length bins and source length token as described in Section 3 using the same architecture and settings as for the English-to-German system. We then use this system to translate the MuST-C corpus from German to English, generating 7 translations of each sentence for each of the 7 bins. From these data, we keep all back-translations which make the corresponding German sentence length-compliant. This resulted in a back-translated corpus of 172K sentence pairs.

[1] Including, if applicable, the synthetic data described below.

#		tst-COMMON v2 BLEU	BERT	LC	blind test BLEU	BERT	LC
0	**baseline** *(no length control)*	32.0	84.00	44.03	19.2	77.94	45.50
1	**source-side token, 3 bins**	31.3	83.94	51.59	20.6	78.40	62.50
2	+ N-best rescoring	30.5	83.60	78.41	20.1	77.78	81.50
3	**target-side token, 3 bins**	31.4	83.88	50.12	19.7	78.37	53.50
4	+ N-best rescoring	30.7	83.58	77.40	18.3	77.43	82.50
	target-side token, 7 bins						
5	predicted token *(no length control)*	32.0	84.00	45.23	18.3	77.55	46.50
6	+ N-best rescoring	31.1	83.75	71.20	18.9	77.38	72.50
7	M token	31.7	83.99	49.19	19.1	78.24	56.00
8	+ N-best rescoring	31.0	83.74	76.39	18.6	77.68	81.00
9	S token	30.5	83.73	62.95	18.9	78.05	59.00
10	+ N-best rescoring	29.8	83.38	87.64	18.9	77.52	85.50
11	XS token	28.1	83.09	72.13	18.2	77.81	68.00
12	+ N-best rescoring	27.8	82.91	92.21	17.8	77.32	90.00
13	ROVER over XS to XL	29.0	83.35	80.66	17.5	77.59	76.50
14	+ N-best rescoring	28.0	82.94	94.19	17.6	77.09	93.00
15	ROVER over S to L	31.1	83.83	66.90	18.2	77.76	65.50
16	+ N-best rescoring	30.0	83.38	88.57	18.7	77.32	86.50
17	**length encoding (tokens)**	31.5	83.91	48.57	19.6	77.45	55.50
18	+ 2-pass length correction	30.0	83.42	68.14	19.5	77.75	75.50
19	+ N-best rescoring	30.9	83.66	72.36	19.3	77.47	80.50
20	+ 2-pass length correction	29.5	83.12	88.41	19.0	76.95	92.00
21	**length encoding (characters)**	30.7	83.57	63.64	20.1	78.27	73.00
22	+ 2-pass length correction	29.3	82.89	89.50	19.2	77.55	90.50
23	+ N-best rescoring	30.0	83.24	88.10	19.2	77.22	95.50
24	+ 2-pass length correction	29.2	82.76	98.14	18.8	76.80	98.00

Table 1: English→German translation results for MuST-C tst-COMMON and the IWSLT 2022 Isometric SLT blind test. All values in %. LC = length compliance within 10% in number of characters. All systems are based on the same Transformer *big* model. Length bins of the 7-bin system are referred to as XXS, XS, S, M, L, XL and XXL from short to long. For explanation of N-best rescoring, ROVER, and 2-pass length correction refer to Section 3.

4.3 Forward-translated data

In addition to back-translated data, we also augmented our training corpus with forward-translated data. For this, we generated translations using our English-to-German system with 7 length bins and a source length token for each of the length classes. Then, we kept only those translations which turned out to be length-compliant with the corresponding source sentence. The resulting synthetic corpus has 213K sentence pairs.

5 Experimental results

Table 1 presents results for all length control methods explored in this work. We evaluate on MuST-C tst-COMMON v2[2] and the blind test set provided by the shared task organizers using the official scoring script[3]. As a measure of MT quality it computes BLEU (Papineni et al., 2002; Post, 2018) and BERT F1 score (Zhang et al., 2020). Length compliance (LC) is calculated as the proportion of translations that have a character count which differs by 10% or less from the number of characters in the source sentence. For this, spaces are not counted and sentences with less than 10 characters are ignored. References for the blind test set were made available only after development of the systems. Line 0 in Table 1 corresponds to a system trained without any of the length control methods from Section 3. All systems use all synthetic data as described in Section 4 if not stated otherwise.

5.1 Length token systems

Rows 1 to 4 of Table 1 show results for the 3-bin length token systems. The "length compliant" bin is used for all translations. (When used on the target side it is enforced as the first decoding step.) Overall, we observe no major differences between a source-side and target-side length token in both LC and MT quality scores. Synthetic data and selection of the length bin alone leads to length compliant translations in about 50% of cases (rows 1 and 3). This shows that the model has to compromise between translation quality and length and that a length token is not a strong enough signal to enforce the corresponding length class in all cases.

[2]The official evaluation uses tst-COMMON v1. Differences in metric scores are minor though.

[3]Blind test set and scoring script are published under `https://github.com/amazon-research/isometric-slt`.

N-best rescoring, i.e. selection of a length compliant translation from the beam search output of size 12, can improve LC to 78% on tst-COMMON but comes at the cost of a loss in translation quality by 0.8% BLEU and 0.3% BERTScore absolute.

The 7-bin system shown in rows 5 to 16 offers a greater variety of trade-off points. We refer to the 7 length bins with size labels from "XXS" to "XXL". The target-to-source ratio boundaries for equally sized bins in terms of training examples are computed to be 0.90, 0.98, 1.02, 1.06, 1.10, and 1.23. This means the desired 1.0 ratio for isometric MT falls into the "S" bin.

Row 5 shows the scores achieved when not forcing any length token. This configuration leads to the same quality on tst-COMMON as the baseline system, namely 32.0% BLEU and 84.0% BERTScore. This indicates that the model is able to predict the right length class corresponding to an unbiased translation. Setting the length token to either "M", "S" or "XS" offers different trade-offs between translation quality and length compliance. Interestingly, the "XS" class has a higher LC than the class "S" which should represent translations with a target-to-source ratio closer to 1. Again, this shows that the effect of length tokens is in conflict with general translation quality, which is optimal when not skipping any information present in the source. A more extreme length class has to be chosen to achieve the desired amount of compression. In all cases N-best rescoring has the same effect as observed for the 3-bin systems, namely a higher LC at the cost of worse translation quality. All length classes not shown in the table lead to either clearly worse LC or quality scores.

The outputs for different length tokens, possibly after N-best rescoring, can be combined with the length ROVER. As mentioned in Section 3.2.1, we exclude the extreme length classes. We consider two variants: excluding the bins with shortest and longest translations, or excluding the *two* shortest and longest. As expected, both variants lead to more length compliant translations in the combined output. However, they provide different trade-offs: while the first variant (rows 13, 14) can achieve 94% length compliance on tst-COMMON, translation quality drops to similarly low values as observed for the "XS" length class. The second variant is more conservative and achieves only 89% length compliance, but preserves higher BLEU and BERT scores.

5.2 Length encoding systems

Rows 17 to 24 of Table 1 show the results of systems trained with length encoding as described in Section 3.3. They are also trained using 3 length bins and a "length compliant" token is forced on the target side, we however observe no significant differences to not using the token.

Using the source length as input to the decoder ($L_{\text{forced}} = L_{\text{source}}$), the token-level length encoding model (row 17) does not achieve a higher LC value than the length token systems (49%), while the model with character-level length encoding (row 21) is able to produce compliant translations in 64% of the cases. Doing a length-corrected second decoding pass is very effective for both systems. This shows that the decoder input L_{forced} has a strong impact on the model output, however has to be adjusted to get the desired output length. In Section 3.3.1 we give explanations for such imperfections. In addition, similar to the case of length tokens, we attribute this to the fact that in training the desired length is always conform with the reference translation, while at inference time the model often has to compress its output to fulfill the length constraints, which might require a more extreme value for the targeted length L_{forced}.

N-best rescoring can be applied on top to achieve a further large increase in length compliance[4]. This indicates that there is length variety in the N-best list that at least in part can be attributed to the noise added through length perturbation (Section 3.3.1). The resulting character-level length encoding system in row 24 achieves the overall best length compliance value of 98.14%.

5.3 System selection

To select systems for our submission, in Figure 1 we visualize the inherent trade-off between length compliance and translation quality for the systems from Table 1. We look at BERT scores as they were announced to be the main MT quality metric for the evaluation. We chose system 16, the 7-bin length token system using the length ROVER, as our primary submission. As contrastive submissions we include systems 2 (3 length bins using source-side token), 14 (ROVER variation of the primary submission) and 24 (character-level length encoding with second-pass length correction). All submissions use N-best rescoring. As it can be

[4]First-best translation length of first pass is used for length correction, N-best rescoring only applied in the second pass.

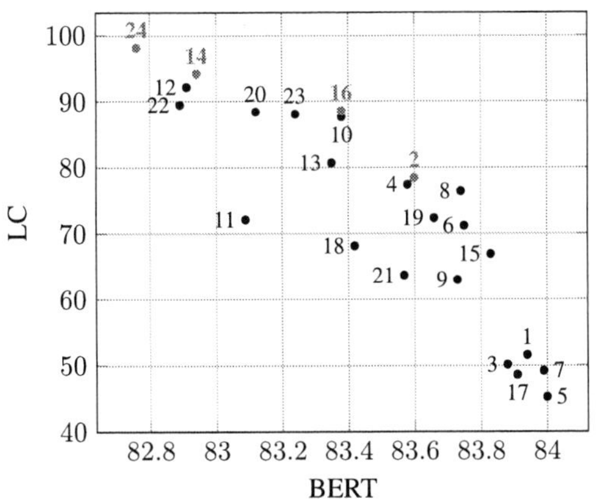

Figure 1: Visualization of length compliance (LC) vs. BERTScore trade-offs on MuST-C tst-COMMON for systems taken from Table 1. Data point labels are the row numbers (#) from Table 1. Submitted systems are labeled in bold blue.

seen, the different length control methods are all able to provide useful trade-off points. While only length encoding can achieve a near perfect length compliance, length token-based methods can offer a good compromise that preserves more of the baseline MT performance.

5.4 Ablation study

For a selected subset of the systems we show the contribution of the most important types of synthetic data used in our systems (Section 4), as well as the effect of length perturbation (Section 3.3.1).

5.4.1 Effect of synthetic data

Comparison of the first two rows of Table 2 shows that taking away synthetic data created using word synonym replacement (Section 4.1) from the 7-bin length token system causes a slight degradation of the BLEU score and no significant change of BERT and length compliance score on tst-COMMON. We consistently observe the same tendencies when taking other configurations of the 7-bin system from Table 1 as baseline (not shown here). This indicates that synonym replacement has some positive effect on MT quality as a data augmentation method, but fails to lead to the desired effect of improved length compliance. This could also in part be explained by the fact that in our experiment setting, removing synonym data resulted in the increased relative proportion of length-compliant back- and forward-translated data.

Removing also the back- and forward-translated data from training leads to a consistent drop in all quality metrics on tst-COMMON. In particular, length compliance becomes worse, even in the considered case that uses the length ROVER and N-best rescoring. When training the length-unbiased system of row 5, Table 1 without synthetic data LC even drops from 45.27 to 30.70 (not shown in Table 2). This shows that length-compliant back- and forward-translated data clearly has the desired effect of learning isometric translation and it is still noticeable when combined with other length control methods. Also for the length encoding model (row 8) we observe a similar positive effect of the synthetic data, despite the translation length being predominantly determined by the length value fed into the decoder.

On the blind test set we observe contradicting results. For this we can provide no better explanation than referring to statistical randomness. In Table 1 one can see that ranking of independently trained neural models (e.g. rows 1, 3, 5, 17 and 21) disagrees on the two test sets, which we attribute to the small size of 200 lines of the blind test set. In fact, according to paired bootstrap resampling computed with SacreBLEU (Post, 2018), the large difference of 1.3 BLEU between row 1 and 2 of Table 2 is not statistically significant with $p < 0.05$, and the 95% confidence interval of row 1 is 2.8 BLEU.

5.4.2 Effect of length perturbation

Without length perturbation the character-level length encoding model is able to produce length compliant translations in almost all cases, as can be seen in Row 7 of Table 2, without the need for subsequent steps like N-best rescoring or second-pass length correction. This however comes at the cost of a severe drop in translation quality as measured in both BLEU and BERT score. When comparing to row 24 of Table 1 it is apparent that the system trained with length perturbation and using the above-mentioned methods can achieve a similar high level of length compliance while offering a better translation quality by 2.6% BLEU and 1.1% BERT F1 score absolute.

A similar drop in translation quality due to lack of length perturbation can be observed for the case of token-level length encoding comparing rows 4 and 5 of Table 2. The gain in LC from training without noise is outperformed by the combination of N-best rescoring and second-pass length correction applied to the baseline system (row 20, Table 1). Notably, even without noise in training token-level

#		tst-COMMON v2			blind test		
		BLEU	BERT	LC	BLEU	BERT	LC
	target-side token, 7 bins						
1	Row 16, Table 1	30.0	83.38	88.57	18.7	77.32	86.50
2	+ no synonym replacement	29.6	83.41	88.41	20.0	77.58	88.50
3	+ no back-/forward-translation	29.5	83.20	87.48	19.5	77.49	87.50
	length encoding (tokens)						
4	Row 19, Table 1	30.9	83.66	72.36	19.3	77.47	80.50
5	+ no length perturbation	28.6	82.32	76.12	18.3	74.51	81.00
	length encoding (characters)						
6	Row 21, Table 1	30.7	83.57	63.64	20.1	78.27	73.00
7	+ no length perturbation	26.6	81.66	98.26	18.4	76.07	99.00
8	+ no synonyms replacement, no back-/forward-translation	30.0	83.37	61.94	19.8	77.86	75.50

Table 2: Ablation study results. All values in %.

length encoding does not surpass a length compliance value of 80%. This shows that the number of subwords is not accurate enough as a measure of length when targeting a precise character count.

6 Conclusion

In this paper, we described AppTek's neural MT system with length control that we submitted to the IWSLT 2022 Isometric Spoken Translation Evaluation. We showed that by using length-compliant synthetic data, as well as encoding the desired translation length in various ways, we can significantly increase the length compliance score, while at the same time limiting the loss of information as reflected in only slightly lower BERT scores. As one of the best methods for real-time production settings not involving system combination, N-best list rescoring or 2-pass search, the modified positional encoding that counts the desired length in characters achieves the best quality/length compliance trade-off in our experiments. We attribute this to more fine-grained length control capabilities of this system as compared to systems that use source-side or target-side length pseudo-tokens.

References

Martín Abadi, Ashish Agarwal, Paul Barham, Eugene Brevdo, Zhifeng Chen, Craig Citro, Greg S. Corrado, Andy Davis, Jeffrey Dean, Matthieu Devin, Sanjay Ghemawat, Ian Goodfellow, Andrew Harp, Geoffrey Irving, Michael Isard, Yangqing Jia, Rafal Jozefowicz, Lukasz Kaiser, Manjunath Kudlur, Josh Levenberg, Dandelion Mané, Rajat Monga, Sherry Moore, Derek Murray, Chris Olah, Mike Schuster, Jonathon Shlens, Benoit Steiner, Ilya Sutskever, Kunal Talwar, Paul Tucker, Vincent Vanhoucke, Vijay Vasudevan, Fernanda Viégas, Oriol Vinyals, Pete Warden, Martin Wattenberg, Martin Wicke, Yuan Yu, and Xiaoqiang Zheng. 2015. TensorFlow: Large-scale machine learning on heterogeneous systems. Software available from tensorflow.org.

Farhad Akhbardeh, Arkady Arkhangorodsky, Magdalena Biesialska, Ondřej Bojar, Rajen Chatterjee, Vishrav Chaudhary, Marta R. Costa-jussa, Cristina España-Bonet, Angela Fan, Christian Federmann, Markus Freitag, Yvette Graham, Roman Grundkiewicz, Barry Haddow, Leonie Harter, Kenneth Heafield, Christopher Homan, Matthias Huck, Kwabena Amponsah-Kaakyire, Jungo Kasai, Daniel Khashabi, Kevin Knight, Tom Kocmi, Philipp Koehn, Nicholas Lourie, Christof Monz, Makoto Morishita, Masaaki Nagata, Ajay Nagesh, Toshiaki Nakazawa, Matteo Negri, Santanu Pal, Allahsera Auguste Tapo, Marco Turchi, Valentin Vydrin, and Marcos Zampieri. 2021. Findings of the 2021 conference on machine translation (WMT21). In *Proceedings of the Sixth Conference on Machine Translation*, pages 1–88, Online. Association for Computational Linguistics.

Antonios Anastasopoulos, Luisa Bentivogli, Marcely Z. Boito, Ondřej Bojar, Roldano Cattoni, Anna Currey, Georgiana Dinu, Kevin Duh, Maha Elbayad, Marcello Federico, Christian Federmann, Hongyu Gong, Roman Grundkiewicz, Barry Haddow, Benjamin Hsu, Dávid Javorský, Věra Kloudová, Surafel M. Lakew, Xutai Ma, Prashant Mathur, Paul McNamee, Kenton Murray, Maria Nădejde, Satoshi Nakamura, Matteo Negri, Jan Niehues, Xing Niu, Juan Pino, Elizabeth Salesky, Jiatong Shi, Sebastian Stüker, Katsuhito Sudoh, Marco Turchi, Yogesh Virkar, Alex Waibel, Changhan Wang, and Shinji Watanabe. 2022. FINDINGS OF THE IWSLT 2022 EVALUATION CAMPAIGN. In *Proceedings of the 19th International Conference on Spoken Language Translation (IWSLT 2022)*, Dublin, Ireland. Association for Computational Linguistics.

François Buet and François Yvon. 2021. Toward genre adapted closed captioning. In *Interspeech 2021*, pages 4403–4407. ISCA.

Mattia A Di Gangi, Roldano Cattoni, Luisa Bentivogli, Matteo Negri, and Marco Turchi. 2019. Must-c: a multilingual speech translation corpus. In *Proceedings of the 2019 Conference of the North American*

Chapter of the Association for Computational Linguistics: Human Language Technologies, Volume 1 (Long and Short Papers), pages 2012–2017.

Patrick Doetsch, Albert Zeyer, Paul Voigtlaender, Ilia Kulikov, Ralf Schlüter, and Hermann Ney. 2017. Returnn: The rwth extensible training framework for universal recurrent neural networks. In *2017 IEEE International Conference on Acoustics, Speech and Signal Processing (ICASSP)*, pages 5345–5349. IEEE.

Chris Dyer, Victor Chahuneau, and Noah A. Smith. 2013. A simple, fast, and effective reparameterization of IBM model 2. In *Proceedings of the 2013 Conference of the North American Chapter of the Association for Computational Linguistics: Human Language Technologies*, pages 644–648, Atlanta, Georgia. Association for Computational Linguistics.

J.G. Fiscus. 1997. A post-processing system to yield reduced word error rates: Recognizer output voting error reduction (rover). In *1997 IEEE Workshop on Automatic Speech Recognition and Understanding Proceedings*, pages 347–354.

Mercedes García-Martínez, Loïc Barrault, and Fethi Bougares. 2016. Factored neural machine translation architectures. In *Proceedings of the 13th International Conference on Spoken Language Translation*, Seattle, Washington D.C. International Workshop on Spoken Language Translation.

Taku Kudo and John Richardson. 2018. SentencePiece: A simple and language independent subword tokenizer and detokenizer for neural text processing. In *Proceedings of the 2018 Conference on Empirical Methods in Natural Language Processing: System Demonstrations*, pages 66–71, Brussels, Belgium. Association for Computational Linguistics.

Surafel M Lakew, Marcello Federico, Yue Wang, Cuong Hoang, Yogesh Virkar, Roberto Barra-Chicote, and Robert Enyedi. 2021. Machine translation verbosity control for automatic dubbing. In *ICASSP 2021-2021 IEEE International Conference on Acoustics, Speech and Signal Processing (ICASSP)*, pages 7538–7542. IEEE.

Surafel Melaku Lakew, Mattia Di Gangi, and Marcello Federico. 2019. Controlling the output length of neural machine translation. In *Proceedings of the 16th International Conference on Spoken Language Translation*, Hong Kong. Association for Computational Linguistics.

Danni Liu, Jan Niehues, and Gerasimos Spanakis. 2020. Adapting end-to-end speech recognition for readable subtitles. In *Proceedings of the 17th International Conference on Spoken Language Translation*, pages 247–256, Online. Association for Computational Linguistics.

Jan Niehues. 2020. Machine translation with unsupervised length-constraints. In *Proceedings of the 14th Conference of the Association for Machine Translation in the Americas (Volume 1: Research Track)*, pages 21–35, Virtual. Association for Machine Translation in the Americas.

Yui Oka, Katsuki Chousa, Katsuhito Sudoh, and Satoshi Nakamura. 2020. Incorporating noisy length constraints into transformer with length-aware positional encodings. In *Proceedings of the 28th International Conference on Computational Linguistics*, pages 3580–3585, Barcelona, Spain (Online). International Committee on Computational Linguistics.

Kishore Papineni, Salim Roukos, Todd Ward, and Wei-Jing Zhu. 2002. Bleu: a method for automatic evaluation of machine translation. In *Proceedings of the 40th Annual Meeting of the Association for Computational Linguistics*, pages 311–318, Philadelphia, Pennsylvania, USA. Association for Computational Linguistics.

Jan-Thorsten Peter, Eugen Beck, and Hermann Ney. 2018. Sisyphus, a workflow manager designed for machine translation and automatic speech recognition. In *Proceedings of the 2018 Conference on Empirical Methods in Natural Language Processing: System Demonstrations*, pages 84–89, Brussels, Belgium. Association for Computational Linguistics.

Matt Post. 2018. A call for clarity in reporting bleu scores. In *Proceedings of the Third Conference on Machine Translation: Research Papers*, pages 186–191.

Ashutosh Saboo and Timo Baumann. 2019. Integration of dubbing constraints into machine translation. In *Proceedings of the Fourth Conference on Machine Translation (Volume 1: Research Papers)*, pages 94–101, Florence, Italy. Association for Computational Linguistics.

Rico Sennrich, Barry Haddow, and Alexandra Birch. 2016. Neural machine translation of rare words with subword units. In *Proceedings of the 54th Annual Meeting of the Association for Computational Linguistics (Volume 1: Long Papers)*, pages 1715–1725, Berlin, Germany. Association for Computational Linguistics.

Sho Takase and Naoaki Okazaki. 2019. Positional encoding to control output sequence length. In *Proceedings of the 2019 Conference of the North American Chapter of the Association for Computational Linguistics: Human Language Technologies, Volume 1 (Long and Short Papers)*, pages 3999–4004, Minneapolis, Minnesota. Association for Computational Linguistics.

Ashish Vaswani, Noam Shazeer, Niki Parmar, Jakob Uszkoreit, Llion Jones, Aidan N Gomez, Łukasz Kaiser, and Illia Polosukhin. 2017. Attention is all you need. *Advances in neural information processing systems*, 30.

Patrick Wilken and Evgeny Matusov. 2019. Novel applications of factored neural machine translation. *arXiv preprint arXiv:1910.03912*.

Albert Zeyer, Tamer Alkhouli, and Hermann Ney. 2018. RETURNN as a generic flexible neural toolkit with application to translation and speech recognition. In *Proceedings of ACL 2018, System Demonstrations*, pages 128–133, Melbourne, Australia. Association for Computational Linguistics.

Tianyi Zhang, Varsha Kishore, Felix Wu, Kilian Q. Weinberger, and Yoav Artzi. 2020. Bertscore: Evaluating text generation with bert. In *International Conference on Learning Representations*.

Hierarchical Multi-task learning framework for Isometric-Speech Language Translation

Aakash Bhatnagar and **Nidhir Bhavsar**
Navrachana University
Vadodara, India
(18124526,1803488)@nuv.ac.in

Muskaan Singh and **Petr Motlicek**
IDIAP Research Institute,
Martigny, Switzerland
(msingh,petr.motlicek)@idiap.ch

Abstract

This paper presents our submission for the shared task on isometric neural machine translation at International Conference on Spoken Language Translation (IWSLT). There are numerous state-of-art models for translation problems. However, these models lack any length constraint to produce short or long outputs from the source text. This paper proposes a hierarchical approach to generate isometric translation on the MUST-C dataset. We achieve a BERTscore of 0.85, a length ratio of 1.087, a BLEU score of 42.3, and a length range of 51.03%. On the blind dataset provided by the task organizers, we obtained a BERTscore of 0.80, a length ratio of 1.10, and a length range of 47.5%. We have made our code public hee https://github.com/aakash0017/Machine-Translation-ISWLT.

1 Introduction

Reaching a worldwide audience is a critical aspect of audio-visual content localization. This automation necessitates source language speech translation and seamless integration of target language speech with the original visual information. The uniqueness of this task is to generate length-controlled outputs. A significant application of isometric translation is in automatic dubbing, where the most crucial part is to sync the length of translated subtitles with the audio of the source language. These types of translations give a holistic experience to the user while reading the translated sentences. This paper will explain our hierarchical architecture for generating such isometric outputs.

Initially, we experimented with a verbosity-controlled multi-task model. We used two prompt types: (i) task prompt and (ii) length prompt. The task prompt decides what task the model should perform. For example, an empty prompt means that the model will receive English inputs and generate translated French outputs, whereas "para" prompt means that the model will receive french input and generate paraphrased French sentences. Para prompt always accompanies a length prompt that ensures that the paraphrased output is of the desired length. To illustrate, if the initial translated output of the model falls short of the source text, we will append the prompt: "para long." This prompt will help the model paraphrase this generated output to an optimal length. We experimented with various combinations of this translate-paraphrasing approach. Finally, our best architectures consist of three separately trained models for translation and paraphrasing. We use Helsinki OPUS-MT and Google's MT5 for machine translation & paraphrasing, respectively, while Google translation API for short-length sentences. We use MUST-C v1.2 FR and PAWS-X EN-FR datasets to train these models.

2 Shared Task Overview

This task entails creating translations that are similar in length to the source. The shared task's outcome can help with the following issues: auto standardized dubbing to achieve coupling between the source and target speech, improved subtitling to fit the translated content into a specified video frame, layout constrained translation to control the generated text to fit in the document tables or database fields, and more general simultaneous speech translation for ease of reading or listening. Participants in the shared task can create text-to-text MT systems for languages such as German (De), French (Fr), and Spanish (Es) using either the MUST-C or

Proceedings of the 19th International Conference on Spoken Language Translation (IWSLT 2022), pages 379 - 385
May 26-27, 2022 ©2022 Association for Computational Linguistics

WMT datasets.

3 Background

Our approach towards controlling the output length of translated sequences is based on the recent advancement in the transformer architecture (16) towards multi-task training.

3.1 Transformer

With the advent of transfer learning techniques in NLP through transformer-based models like T5 (11) have become more unified & can convert all text-based language problems into text-to-text formats. Trained on Datasets like C4, these models have achieved state-of-the-art performances for text generation tasks like summarization, question-answering & machine translation, to be precise. At its core, these models constitute a sequence-to-sequence architecture that can process sequences using only attention & feed-forward networks—partitioned into Block of Encoders and Decoder, each of which comprises multi-headed attention.

3.2 Few shot learning

As described in Brown et al. (2), fine-tuning a model for machine translation using a pre-trained model has been the most common approach in recent years, which involves updating the weights of a pre-trained model by training on a supervised dataset specific to the desired task. Typically thousands to hundreds of thousands of labeled examples are used. The main disadvantages are the need for a new giant dataset for every task, the potential for poor generalization out-of-distribution, and the potential to exploit spurious features of the training data, potentially resulting in an unfair comparison with human performance. However, on the contrary, few-shot learning refers to the setting where the model is given a few demonstrations of the task at inference time. This works by giving K examples of context and completion, and then one final example of context, with the model expected to provide the completion.

4 System Overview

In this section, we will explain our architecture in detail. As mentioned in the above sections, we implement a hierarchical architecture consisting of 3 separate models. Our model is a complex fusion of two distinct functionalities, resulting in a differentiated pipeline that adds to improved performance for text generation tasks. The entirety of the model is fragmented into neural machine translation and a text paraphrasing system. While the former converts text from the source (En) to target (Fr) language, the latter, which is trained independently of the NMT model, assists in deforming the generated text into a more useful form specific to the task. Additionally, we are also using Google's translation API for short-length sentences.

4.1 Translation Module

This module uses Helsinki OPUS-MT (15) for neural machine translation. The model is pre-trained using the MarianMT framework (5), a stable production-ready NMT toolbox with efficient training and decoding capabilities, and is trained on freely available parallel corpora collected in the large bitext repository OPUS (14). The pre-trained version of the OPUS-MT model has six self-attentive layers in both the encoder and decoder networks and eight attention heads in each layer. We use verbosity control during fine-tuning. While training, we use three length prompts: "long," "short," and "normal" and one task prompt i.e. a empty string. The task prompt is defined as per the task (translation) in the module and length prompts are defined by the t Length-Ratio (LR) between the source and target texts. These prompts are appended to the input text, thus, allowing the model to recognize and differentiate key attributes governed by the Length Compliance (LC) matrix. The range of the LR ratio we use while selecting the prompts is mentioned in the equation 1.

$$f\left(x\right)=\begin{cases} short, & LR<0.95 \\ normal, & 0.95\leq LR\geq 1.05 \\ long, & LR>1.05 \end{cases}$$

(1)

$$f^{'}\left(x\right)=\begin{cases} para\ long, & LR<0.95 \\ para\ short, & LR>1.05 \end{cases}$$

(2)

We experiment with the OPUS-MT model on two different datasets: WMT (1) and MUST-C (4). After experimentation, we decided to use MUST-C as it gave the most optimal results. OPUS-MT model, however, does not have any length-control mechanism. To fine-tune the model for isometric

Source Text (EN)	Target Text (FR)	SL	TL	LR	Type
And that might seem a bit surprising, because my full-time work at the foundation is mostly about vaccines and seeds, about the things that we need to invent and deliver to help the poorest two billion live better lives.	Et cela peut sembler un peu surprenant parce que mon travail à temps plein à la Fondation concerne plutôt les vaccins et les semences, les choses que nous devons inventer et distribuer pour aider les deux milliards des plus pauvres à vivre mieux.	226	256	1.13274	Not Isometric
The climate getting worse means that many years, their crops won't grow: there will be too much rain, not enough rain; things will change in ways their fragile environment simply can't support.	Le climat se détériore, ce qui signifie qu'il y aura de nombreuses années où leurs cultures ne pousseront pas. Il y aura trop de pluie, ou pas assez de pluie.	199	162	0.8140	Not Isometric
So, the climate changes will be terrible for them.	Les changements climatiques seront terribles pour eux.	50	54	1.08	Isometric

Table 1: Examples from MUST-C dataset. Here SL is source length, TL is target length and LR is length ratio that is calculated by TL/SL. Isometric sentences are those, whose LR ratio lies withing 0.95-1.10.

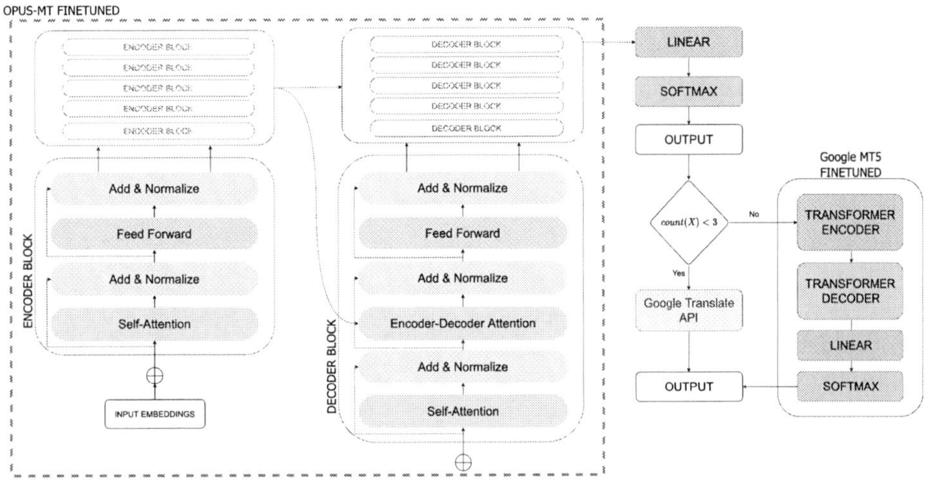

Figure 1: Architectural representation of the flow of our pipeline. The first block in the figure represents the OPUS-MT model that we use for EN-FR translation. The right part in the diagram showcase the 2 paraphrasing models used: Google MT5 fine tuned and Google Translation API. Based on the condition we decide which model to use after translation.

translation, we use the previously mentioned verbosity control prompt engineering method. The table 1 examples of how these prompts are used during translation.

4.2 Paraphrasing & Length Correction

According to Zhao et al. (21) the main goal of sentence paraphrasing is to improve the clarity of a sentence by using different wording that conveys the same meaning. For this task, we are fine-tuning Google's MT5 model (18) on PAWS-X French dataset (19) to leverage the functionality of Text paraphrasing. We have fabricated the use of the prompt engineering approach (7) (12) to enable the model to recognize the paraphrasing task as well as modify its parameter based on the argument to generate isometric text. We append Manually engineered prompts during training for both of the models, as mentioned earlier, based on the source and target text. However, during testing, the prompt for each input sentence is modified based on the conditional task of isometric text generation (see Figure 2)

5 Experimental Setup

During the experimentation, we used three datasets: 1) WMT, 2) MUST-C 3) PAWS-X. Table 3 shows the exact train/test/dev split of all the three datasets. Also, the task provides us with a blind dataset for each language pair. Particularly En-Fr pairs in the blind consisted of very few characters per sentence. After experimentation, we found that our model was not performing well for sentences with less than five words. To solve this issue, we used Google Translator API, which improved the length ratio and length constraint significantly.

Model	MUST-C Fr					Blind En-Fr				
	BERT Score			Length Compliance		BERT Score			Length Compliance	
	P	R	F1	Length Ratio	Length Range	P	R	F1	Length Ratio	Length Range
System 1	0.87	0.86	0.86	1.11	46.4	0.62	0.63	0.62	1.64	40.5
System 2	**0.87**	**0.86**	**0.87**	**1.08**	49.6	**0.79**	**0.80**	**0.80**	**1.10**	**47.5**
System 3	0.86	0.85	0.85	1.08	**51.3**	0.79	0.80	0.79	1.11	46.8

Table 2: prediction on MUST-C v1.2 En-Fr and blind dataset.

We experimented with various approaches that involved multi-task training and hierarchical architectures. Initially, we experimented with a multi-task training approach. For this, we used Google's MT5 transformer-based architecture, which we implement using a simple transformer library[1]. We fine-tuned this architecture for two distinct tasks 1) Text Paraphrasing & 2) Machine Translation as described here (3). The model supports improvising the generated text based on the desired task. Prompt engineering was a key aspect of this multi-task training approach. Details of how prompts are generated for different task and length is explained in previous sections. Next, we experimented with the Helsinki OPUS-MT pre-trained model for machine translation, which uses a modified version of transformer-based architecture. This system was build using hugging transformers library (17)[2] For fine-tuning the same we use the standard cross-entropy loss objective on target sequence along with label smoothing (9). We use beam search with a beam size of 10 and select the best of the top 5 hypotheses for the En-Fr track. We initialize the model with a learning rate of $2^{-}5$ with a "cosine schedule with warmup" (8).

We also train a separate system constituting Google's MT5 pre-trained model for text paraphrasing. For this we're using an Ada-Factor optimizer (13), with a cross-entropy loss as objective. Also, we use a beam size of 5 and select the top 3 hypotheses accordingly. The model is initialized with pre-trained weights from the transformers library. We use the base version with a total of 580M parameters. We use a batch size of 32 and epochs equal to 1. Each model is trained on a cluster of 4 Tesla V100-PCIE GPU with a memory size of 32510MiB each.

[1] https://simpletransformers.ai/

[2] https://github.com/huggingface/transformers

Dataset	MUST-C	PAWS-X
Langauge	en-fr	fr-fr
Train	275086	49401
Validation	1413	2000
Test	2633	2000

Table 3: description of various datasets used during the experimentation.

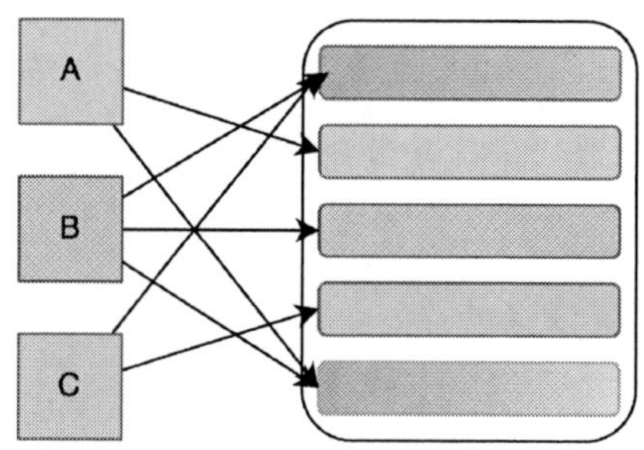

Figure 2: Multi task model architecture of updating parameters according to the prompts supplied

5.1 Evaluation Measures

This task is evaluated on two parameters. The first is the quality of translation, and the second is the length constraint. We use BERTscore (20) and BLEUscore (10) for qualitative analysis of the translated sentences and Length Compliance matrix for the isometric constraint. Table 1 in appendix 7 shows a detailed overview of how Length Compliance matrix works. We can see that the optimal predictions lie within the LR range of 0.95 and 1.10.

6 Result and Analysis

As shown in Table 2, system three has gained a substantial increase in overall Length compliance metrics. However, the BERT Score has depleted by 0.5. The Length Ratio for the OPUS-MT system is 1.085, close to the ideal value in isometric

Algorithm 1 Algorithm for our pipeline

1. Variables
   - S Source text [train]
   - T Target text [train]
   - S_t Source text [test]
2. Pre-Processing
   - **procedure** GENERATE-LENGTH-PROMPT(S, T)
   - **for** $i \leftarrow 1$ to S **do**:
   - $prompt \leftarrow f(S, T)$ ▷ Eq. 1
   - $S_i^{'} \leftarrow prompt + S_i$
   - **end for**
   - **end procedure**
   - $S_t^{'} \leftarrow$ normal + S_t ▷ process test-data
3. Neural Machine Translation
   - **procedure** TRAIN-MT-MODEL($S^{'}, T$)
   - input-ids, attention-mask, labels $\leftarrow$ Tokenizer
   - translation-model $\leftarrow$ Model("OPUS-MT-en-fr")
   - loss-function $\leftarrow$ criterion() ▷ cross entropy loss
   - translation-model.train(input-ids, attention-mask, labels, loss-function)
   - **end procedure**
   - $T_p \leftarrow$ translation-model.predict($S_t^{'}$)
4. Text Paraphrasing
   - Train MT5 model on PAWS-X dataset ▷ follow step 3
   - **procedure** GENERATE-TASK-PROMPT
   - **for** $i \leftarrow 1$ to $S_t^{'}$ **do**
   - $prompt \leftarrow f(S_{t_i}^{'}, T_{p_i})$ ▷ Eq. 1
   - **if** $prompt \neq$ normal **then**
   - $para\_prompt \leftarrow f^{'}(S_{t_i}^{'}, T_{p_i})$ ▷ Eq. 2
   - $T_{p_i}^{'} \leftarrow para\_prompt + T_{p_i}$
   - **else** continue
   - **end if**
   - **end for**
   - **end procedure**
   - $O \leftarrow$ paraphrase-model.predict($T_p^{'}$) ▷ final output

translation. As stated earlier, the task of isometric translation aims to generate the translations with the target to source length ratio between 0.90 and 1.10, after considering the $\pm 10\%$ shift in the characters. We achieve this through two of our systems, with system-1 achieving a length ratio of 0.85 and system-2 achieving 0.87.

Secondly, the Length Range matrix represents the percentage of total translated sentences falling under the ideal length ratios range. Two of our suggested models are close to 50%, suggesting that almost half of the predictions are isometric with high BLEUscore and BERTscore. The reason of decrease in the BERTscore of system 3 is that the model loses essential information while predicting the output. Our analysis shows that verbosity control can sometimes lead to abrupt shortening of results, where the model skips words after a specific limit.

Along with Length Compliance(LC) metrix, outputs are evaluated for their adequacy and quality of translation. This task emphasizes more towards BERTscore rather than BLEUscore. When the length of source and target varies, BLEUscore does not adapt well; however, BERTscore can evaluate based on semantics. The challenge is to translate the source text to the target language with ideal length compliance while also maintaining the semantic meaning of the output.

While our suggested models are also performing equally well on the blind dataset provided by the organizer, however, a significant dip can be seen with the Length ratio & BERT score for the predicted outputs. The reason being is that the blind data covers a versatile range of source input with a word count ranging from 1 to 44. The PAWS-X dataset has an average length of 10-15 words and cannot provide a variety of training examples with a much lower token count. Thus, while predicting, the model performs rather poorly for short-length examples. To solve this we have employed Google Translate API. However, for some instances within the 5-8 word count, the model can still not convert the input sequence to its target language ("French") counterpart.

Our experiments with the Google MT5 model, which is fine-tuned for machine translation and text paraphrasing, have shown considerable promise. However, it still needs rigorous experimentation and hyper-parameter tuning. In addition to quantitative, we vouch for qualitative analysis of our results in Table 4. Which describes the correct output corresponding to isometric source-target text. As shown in the fourth row of the Table, our system can precisely shorten the length of translated text while retaining semantical similarity. Secondly, as set out in the second and third row of the Table, few phrases in the English & French vocabulary do not align lexically together; thus, the model partitions the source text and translates each word separately.

7 Conclusion & Future Work

In this work, we propose a hierarchical MT approach, using prompt engineering to attribute the OPUS-MT and MT5 paraphrasing model. We evaluate the proposed approach in the Isometric machine translation case, where translated text is expected to match the source length to synchronize the source and target text. Our finding shows that though the model has been trained precisely for generating constrained output, However, a lot of improvements can be employed to produce more optimal results. Firstly, the paraphrasing model could not generalize for short sentences (i.e., LR < 0.95). Secondly, the MUST-C dataset has an unequal distribution of instances for all three categories of length ranges, which imposes an uncertain suspicion over the model predictions. Moreover, our finding shows that the proposed approach can perform better than Lakew et al. (6), length aware positional encoding based NMT approach.

References

[1] Ondřej Bojar, Christian Federmann, Mark Fishel, Yvette Graham, Barry Haddow, Philipp Koehn, and Christof Monz. 2018. Findings of the 2018 conference on machine translation (WMT18). In *Proceedings of the Third Conference on Machine Translation: Shared Task Papers*, pages 272–303, Belgium, Brussels. Association for Computational Linguistics.

[2] Tom B. Brown, Benjamin Mann, Nick Ryder, Melanie Subbiah, Jared Kaplan, Prafulla Dhariwal, Arvind Neelakantan, Pranav Shyam, Girish Sastry, Amanda Askell, Sandhini Agarwal, Ariel Herbert-Voss, Gretchen Krueger, Tom Henighan, Rewon Child, Aditya Ramesh, Daniel M. Ziegler, Jeffrey Wu, Clemens Winter, Christopher Hesse, Mark Chen, Eric Sigler, Mateusz Litwin, Scott Gray, Benjamin Chess, Jack Clark, Christopher Berner, Sam McCandlish, Alec Radford, Ilya Sutskever, and Dario Amodei. 2020. Language models are few-shot learners. *CoRR*, abs/2005.14165.

[3] Rakesh Chada. 2020. Simultaneous paraphrasing and translation by fine-tuning transformer models. In *Proceedings of the Fourth Workshop on Neural Generation and Translation*, pages 198–203, Online. Association for Computational Linguistics.

[4] Mattia A. Di Gangi, Roldano Cattoni, Luisa Bentivogli, Matteo Negri, and Marco Turchi. 2019. MuST-C: a Multilingual Speech Translation Corpus. In *Proceedings of the 2019 Conference of the North American Chapter of the Association for Computational Linguistics: Human Language Technologies, Volume 1 (Long and Short Papers)*, pages 2012–2017, Minneapolis, Minnesota. Association for Computational Linguistics.

[5] Marcin Junczys-Dowmunt, Roman Grundkiewicz, Tomasz Dwojak, Hieu Hoang, Kenneth Heafield, Tom Neckermann, Frank Seide, Ulrich Germann, Alham Fikri Aji, Nikolay Bogoychev, André F. T. Martins, and Alexandra Birch. 2018. Marian: Fast neural machine translation in C++. *CoRR*, abs/1804.00344.

[6] Surafel Melaku Lakew, Mattia Antonino Di Gangi, and Marcello Federico. 2019. Controlling the output length of neural machine translation. *CoRR*, abs/1910.10408.

[7] Pengfei Liu, Weizhe Yuan, Jinlan Fu, Zhengbao Jiang, Hiroaki Hayashi, and Graham Neubig. 2021. Pre-train, prompt, and predict: A systematic survey of prompting methods in natural language processing. *CoRR*, abs/2107.13586.

Source Text (EN)	Target Text (FR)	Translated Text (FR)	SL	TL	PL	LR	Type
I just came back from a community that holds the secret to human survival.	Je viens de revenir d'une communauté qui détient le secret de la survie de l'humanité	Je reviens d'une communauté qui garde le secret de la survie humaine.	74	86	69	0.932	Not Isometric
The act of kindness she noted above all others: someone had even gotten her a pair of shoes.	Le gentil geste qu'elle a remarqué parmi tous les autres : quelqu'un lui avait même amené une paire de chaussures	L'acte de gentillesse qu'elle a remarqué par dessus tout : quelqu'un lui avait même offert une paire de chaussures.	92	115	115	1.25	Not Isometric
If you have something to give, give it now.	Si vous avez quelque chose à donner, donnez-le maintenant.	Si vous avez quelque chose à donner, donnez-le maintenant.	43	58	58	1.34	Not Isometric
Serve food at a soup kitchen. Clean up a neighborhood park. Be a mentor.	Servez de la nourriture dans une soupe populaire, nettoyez un parc dans votre quartier, soyez un mentor.	Servez de la nourriture dans une soupe. Nettoyez un parc. Soyez un mentor.	72	104	74	1.027	Isometric
This is the world of wild bonobos in the jungles of Congo.	Voici le monde des bonobos sauvages dans les jungles du Congo.	C'est le monde des bonobos sauvages dans la jungle du Congo.	58	62	60	1.034	Isometric

Table 4: Predicted Results from MUST-C dataset. Here SL is source length, TL is target length, PL is predicted length and LR is length ratio that is calculated by PL/SL. Isometric sentences are those, whose LR ratio lies withing 0.95-1.10

[8] Ilya Loshchilov and Frank Hutter. 2016. SGDR: stochastic gradient descent with restarts. *CoRR*, abs/1608.03983.

[9] Rafael Müller, Simon Kornblith, and Geoffrey E. Hinton. 2019. When does label smoothing help? *CoRR*, abs/1906.02629.

[10] Kishore Papineni, Salim Roukos, Todd Ward, and Wei-Jing Zhu. 2002. Bleu: a method for automatic evaluation of machine translation. In *Proceedings of the 40th Annual Meeting of the Association for Computational Linguistics*, pages 311–318, Philadelphia, Pennsylvania, USA. Association for Computational Linguistics.

[11] Colin Raffel, Noam Shazeer, Adam Roberts, Katherine Lee, Sharan Narang, Michael Matena, Yanqi Zhou, Wei Li, and Peter J. Liu. 2019. Exploring the limits of transfer learning with a unified text-to-text transformer. *CoRR*, abs/1910.10683.

[12] Laria Reynolds and Kyle McDonell. 2021. Prompt programming for large language models: Beyond the few-shot paradigm. *CoRR*, abs/2102.07350.

[13] Noam Shazeer and Mitchell Stern. 2018. Adafactor: Adaptive learning rates with sublinear memory cost. *CoRR*, abs/1804.04235.

[14] Jörg Tiedemann. 2012. Parallel data, tools and interfaces in OPUS. In *Proceedings of the Eighth International Conference on Language Resources and Evaluation (LREC'12)*, pages 2214–2218, Istanbul, Turkey. European Language Resources Association (ELRA).

[15] Jörg Tiedemann and Santhosh Thottingal. 2020. OPUS-MT – building open translation services for the world. In *Proceedings of the 22nd Annual Conference of the European Association for Machine Translation*, pages 479–480, Lisboa, Portugal. European Association for Machine Translation.

[16] Ashish Vaswani, Noam Shazeer, Niki Parmar, Jakob Uszkoreit, Llion Jones, Aidan N. Gomez, Lukasz Kaiser, and Illia Polosukhin. 2017. Attention is all you need. *CoRR*, abs/1706.03762.

[17] Thomas Wolf, Lysandre Debut, Victor Sanh, Julien Chaumond, Clement Delangue, Anthony Moi, Pierric Cistac, Tim Rault, Rémi Louf, Morgan Funtowicz, and Jamie Brew. 2019. Huggingface's transformers: State-of-the-art natural language processing. *CoRR*, abs/1910.03771.

[18] Linting Xue, Noah Constant, Adam Roberts, Mihir Kale, Rami Al-Rfou, Aditya Siddhant, Aditya Barua, and Colin Raffel. 2020. mt5: A massively multilingual pre-trained text-to-text transformer. *CoRR*, abs/2010.11934.

[19] Yinfei Yang, Yuan Zhang, Chris Tar, and Jason Baldridge. 2019. PAWS-X: A cross-lingual adversarial dataset for paraphrase identification. *CoRR*, abs/1908.11828.

[20] Tianyi Zhang, Varsha Kishore, Felix Wu, Kilian Q. Weinberger, and Yoav Artzi. 2019. Bertscore: Evaluating text generation with BERT. *CoRR*, abs/1904.09675.

[21] Sanqiang Zhao, Rui Meng, Daqing He, Andi Saptono, and Bambang Parmanto. 2018. Integrating transformer and paraphrase rules for sentence simplification. In *Proceedings of the 2018 Conference on Empirical Methods in Natural Language Processing*, pages 3164–3173, Brussels, Belgium. Association for Computational Linguistics.

Author Index